P9-CJV-602

Determinants of Substance Abuse

Biological, Psychological, and Environmental Factors

PERSPECTIVES ON INDIVIDUAL DIFFERENCES

CECIL R. REYNOLDS, *Texas A&M University, College Station*
ROBERT T. BROWN, *University of North Carolina, Wilmington*

PERSPECTIVES ON BIAS IN MENTAL TESTING
Edited by Cecil R. Reynolds and Robert T. Brown

PERSONALITY AND INDIVIDUAL DIFFERENCES
A Natural Science Approach
Hans J. Eysenck and Michael W. Eysenck

DETERMINANTS OF SUBSTANCE ABUSE
Biological, Psychological, and Environmental Factors
Edited by Mark Galizio and Stephen A. Maisto

THE NEUROPSYCHOLOGY OF INDIVIDUAL DIFFERENCES
A Developmental Perspective
Edited by Cathy F. Telzrow and Lawrence C. Hartlage

A Continuation Order Plan is available for this series. A continuation order will bring delivery of each new volume immediately upon publication. Volumes are billed only upon actual shipment. For further information please contact the publisher.

Determinants of Substance Abuse
Biological, Psychological, and Environmental Factors

Edited by

MARK GALIZIO
University of North Carolina
Wilmington, North Carolina

and

STEPHEN A. MAISTO
Vanderbilt University
Nashville, Tennessee

PLENUM PRESS • NEW YORK AND LONDON

Library of Congress Cataloging in Publication Data

Main entry under title:

Determinants of substance abuse.

(Perspectives on individual differences)
Includes bibliographies.
1. Substance abuse. 2. Substance abuse—Social aspects. I. Galizio, Mark. II. Maisto,
Stephen A. III. Series.
RC564.D47 1985   616.86   85-3405
ISBN 0-306-41873-8

©1985 Plenum Press, New York
A Division of Plenum Publishing Corporation
233 Spring Street, New York, N.Y. 10013

Printed in the United States of America

Contributors

VINCENT J. ADESSO • Department of Psychology, University of Wisconsin at Milwaukee, Milwaukee, Wisconsin

MICHAEL T. BARDO • Department of Psychology, University of Kentucky, Lexington, Kentucky

ROBERT J. BARRETT • Veterans Administration Medical Center and Departments of Psychology and Pharmacology, Vanderbilt University, Nashville, Tennessee

JOHN K. BELKNAP • Department of Pharmacology, School of Medicine, University of North Dakota, Grand Forks, North Dakota

TRUDY BLOCK • Clinical Psychology Institute, Ft. Lauderdale, Florida

GLENN R. CADDY • Department of Psychology, Nova University, Ft. Lauderdale, Florida

KATE B. CAREY • Department of Psychology, Vanderbilt University, Nashville, Tennessee

GERARD J. CONNORS • Department of Psychiatry and Behavioral Sciences, University of Texas Medical School at Houston, Houston, Texas

W. MILES COX • Psychology Service (116B), Richard L. Roudebush Veterans Administration Medical Center, and Department of Psychiatry, Indiana University School of Medicine, Indianapolis, Indiana

JOHN C. CRABBE • Research Service, VA Medical Center, and Departments of Medical Psychology and Pharmacology, Oregon Health Sciences University, Portland, Oregon

MARK GALIZIO • Department of Psychology, University of North Carolina at Wilmington, Wilmington, North Carolina

CAROLE V. HARRIS • Department of Psychiatry and Center for Alcohol Research, University of Florida, Gainesville, Florida

RILEY E. HINSON • Department of Psychology, University of Western Ontario, London, Ontario, Canada

STEPHEN A. MAISTO • Department of Psychology, Vanderbilt University, Nashville, Tennessee

DENNIS MCCARTY • Alcohol and Health Research Services, Inc., 134 Main Street, Stoneham, Massachusetts

JOHN D. MCSWIGAN • Research Service, VA Medical Center, and Department of Medical Psychology, Oregon Health Sciences University, Portland, Oregon

ALAN C. OGBORNE • Addiction Research Foundation and University of Western Ontario, London, Ontario, Canada

MARCUS E. RISNER • National Institute on Drug Abuse, Addiction Research Center, P.O. Box 5180, Baltimore, Maryland

LINDA C. SOBELL • Addiction Research Foundation and University of Toronto, Toronto, Ontario, Canada

MARK B. SOBELL • Addiction Research Foundation and University of Toronto, Toronto, Ontario, Canada

ARTHUR R. TARBOX • Department of Psychiatry and Behavioral Sciences, University of Texas Medical School at Houston, Houston, Texas

JALIE A. TUCKER • Department of Psychiatry and Center for Alcohol Research, University of Florida, Gainesville, Florida

RUDY E. VUCHINICH • Department of Psychiatry and Center for Alcohol Research, University of Florida, Gainesville, Florida

Preface

With the recent increase in the scope of drug and alcohol problems has come an awareness of the need for solutions. In this context, federal support for research on drug problems increased tremendously during the last 10 to 15 years with the establishment of the National Institute on Drug Abuse (NIDA) and the National Institute on Alcohol Abuse and Alcoholism (NIAAA). Funding from these and other sources has led to a substantial increase in the quantity and quality of published work related to substance abuse. As data accumulate, it is becoming more apparent that substance abuse problems are extremely complex and are influenced by a variety of biological psychological, and environmental variables. Unfortunately it has proved difficult to go beyond this conclusion to a description of how these multiple factors work together to influence the development of, and recovery from, drug and alcohol dependence.

The purpose of this book is to try to meet that objective by including, in one volume, literature reviews and theoretical analyses from a wide variety of drug researchers. We chose the authors in an attempt to assure that each of the various levels of analysis appropriate to the substance abuse problems would be included. In each case, the author was asked to consider how the variables in is or her particular domain might contribute to the appearance of individual differences in both alcohol and drug problems. The resulting volume should be a valuable source for seminars at the advanced undergraduate or graduate levels or as a reference volume for the substance abuse researcher or clinician who wishes to take a more interdisciplinary approach to the problems.

We wish to acknowledge the contributions of Series Editors Robert T. Brown and Cecil Reynolds, who encouraged us to consider developing this volume and helped us to shape its tone. We also thank Plenum Editor Eliot Werner whose support and patience helped keep the project together. Part of our work on this volume was supported by Grant #AA00100 from the National Institute on Alcohol Abuse and Alcoholism (Maisto), Grant #8330 from the North Carolina Alcoholism Research Authority, and

Grant #RII-8308469 from the National Science Foundation. We would also like to express our unwavering appreciation to our wives for their tolerance during this project.

MARK GALIZIO
SEPHEN A. MAISTO

Contents

PART I

Introduction

CHAPTER 1

Individual Differences in Substance Abuse

An Introduction

STEPHEN A. MAISTO, MARK GALIZIO, and KATE B. CAREY

Virtually every adolescent and adult in the United States today is exposed each day to the opportunity to use alcohol and tobacco. A smaller, but still significant, percentage of the population is exposed to the opportunity to use a range of illicit drugs from marijuana to heroin. Most of the members of our society have or will have some experience with a variety of psychoactive drugs. Some—but by no means all or most—will become casualties: they will become dependent on one or more drugs. A fundamental question that must be addressed in any serious theory of substance abuse is the problem of individual differences. One way of trying to understand why some individuals become dependent on or abuse drugs, whereas others do not, is to describe characteristics that are discriminative. Some of these factors have been highlighted in recent national surveys.

RECENT DEMOGRAPHIC DATA

In 1979, 10% of adult male household residents aged 21 to 25 years reported to interviewers that they abstained from alcohol, but 36% of the

STEPHEN A. MAISTO • Department of Psychology, Vanderbilt University, Nashville, Tennessee 37240.   MARK GALIZIO • Department of Psychology, University of North Carolina at Wilmington, Wilmington, North Carolina 28406.   KATE B. CAREY • Department of Psychology, Vanderbilt University, Nashville, Tennessee 37240.

same sample said that they drank an average of more than 60 drinks a month. In contrast, 38% of the men who were 61 to 70 years old said that they were abstainers, but only 8% reported that they drank more than 60 alcoholic drinks a month. Women also were surveyed about their drinking patterns, and 15% of those who were 21 to 25 years old reported that they abstained from alcohol, whereas 6% of them said that they typically consumed more than 60 drinks a month. Age and sex also differentiated frequency of alcohol-related negative social consequences. In this regard, 15% of the men aged 18 to 20 years reported such consequences, whereas the comparable figure for men 61 to 70 years old was 5%. Women apparently experienced a much more lower rate of alcohol-related social consequences. The figures ranged from 6% for 21–25-year-olds to 0 for women 61 years or older.

The survey data also revealed distinctions in drinking patterns and problems as a function of region of the country where the respondent lived as well as marital status. As had been the case with previous national probability household surveys of American drinking practices, the results of the 1979 survey reported by Clark and Midanik (1982) showed that there are differences in frequencies of various patterns of alcohol use and alcohol abuse (as defined by alcohol-related negative consequences) that one correlated with characteristics of the individual usually called *sociodemographic*.

The national survey data on the use of prescription and nonprescription drugs other than alcohol similarly show that sociodemographic markers discriminate among individuals. For example, Fishburne, Abelson, and Cisin (1979) presented descriptive data collected from interviews of a national probability household sample of youth, younger adults, and older adults during 1979. The most extensive data were reported for marijuana use. Among the younger adults (ages 18 to 25), reports of ever having used marijuana differed most as a function of sex (men = 75%; women = 61%), region of residence (the South was associated with the lowest percentages, and the Northeast, Northcentral region, and West were comparable), and population of area of residence (the highest percentage of reported use was among respondents who lived in large metropolitan regions). In response to the question of use during the past month, differences in percentages were correlated with age, sex, education, region of residence, and population of area of residence. More pronounced differences in marijuana use (both lifetime and current) were even more striking among the older adults. Age of respondents produced the sharpest distinction, as 48% of the 26–34-year-olds said that they had ever used the drug, compared to only 10% of respondents who were 35 years or older. The comparable data for use during the past month were 17% and 2%, respectively.

This Fishburne and Cisin (1980) report is a virtual catalog of differences in use of many drugs other than marijuana as a function of different demographic factors. This finding of the importance of demographic variables in classifying individuals' drug use is, of course, consistent with the data from the available excellent surveys of American drinking practices and problems.

UTILITY OF DEMOGRAPHIC DATA

Demographic data describing differences in substance use and abuse* are of interest in their own right. For example, such data directly address the questions that a concerned society asks about patterns of substance use among its citizens and become the bases of policy decisions regarding regulation of drugs and alcohol. In a related way, a society may use sociodemographic information as a means to identify segments of the population at high risk for abuse; these groups would be the primary targets for possible government-supported prevention and treatment interventions. Finally, demographic data are of inherent interest in the study of substance use as a function of the "macroenvironment." The importance of this level of analysis of substance abuse is recognized in this book by devoting a full chapter to it (see Chapter 9).

Another use of demographic data relates to the basis for compiling this book and, indeed, is the reason why such data were briefly described in this introductory chapter. Sociodemographic differences in substance

---

* There has long been controversy about definitions of substance (in this context, alcohol and other drugs) use and abuse. In this book we will try to maintain consistency in definitions across the various chapters and will use the third edition of the *Diagnostic and Statistical Manual of Mental Disorders* (DSM-III) (American Psychiatric Association, 1980) as the standard. In this manual, distinction is made among substance use, substance abuse, and substance dependence. *Substance abuse* is characterized by a pattern of "pathological" use, impairment in social or occupational functioning that is related to use of the substance, and with such disturbance lasting at least 1 month. For all drugs besides alcohol and marijuana, *substance dependence* is defined by the presence of tolerance to the drug or evidence of withdrawal symptoms. However, alcohol and marijuana dependence diagnoses also require evidence of a pattern of pathological use or impairment in social or occupational functioning that is related to the use of the respective drugs. Finally, *substance use* is defined by a pattern of consumption of a substance that does not meet the criteria for abuse or dependence.

Although there are some problems with these definitions, such as determining "pathological" use and degree of tolerance to a substance, they are consistent with current research and not specific to any single theoretical approach. Furthermore, the DSM-III is widely disseminated and accessible. Therefore the DSM-III definitions will be used in this book rather than other definitions that have been proposed.

use and abuse are an initial alert that there is sometimes a high degree of variance among individuals in the use of drugs and alcohol. These demographic differences may be further analyzed on a "finer" level because there are individual differences within any sociodemographic classification. The reliable finding of individual differences must be explained before it can be claimed that the development and maintenance of substance abuse is understood. Such understanding is, at least implicitly, the ultimate goal of all the drug and alcohol research that has filled library shelves throughout the world.

RECENT ESTIMATES OF THE ECONOMIC COST OF DRUG AND ALCOHOL ABUSE

Understanding substance abuse is not merely of academic interest. In 1980 the Institute of Medicine published a report on opportunities for research on alcoholism (alcohol dependence in DSM-III terminology; American Psychiatric Association, 1980), alcohol abuse, and related problems. One of the chapters in that report concerned justifying increased federal support for alcohol-related research because of the great *economic* cost of abusive drinking to American society. The cost estimates cited were taken from a study done for the National Institute on Alcohol Abuse and Alcoholism and were based on 1975 data (Berry, Boland, Smart, & Kanak, 1977). Cost was briefly analyzed in six areas, including lost production, health care costs, motor vehicle accidents, fire losses, crime, and social responses. The analyses of the effects of alcohol abuse and alcoholism on these areas showed an estimated social economic cost of $42.9 billion to $60 billion (The $42.9 billion estimate is $1 billion less than the *combined* cost estimates for cancer, respiratory disease, and endocrine, nutritional, and metabolic diseases.)

A more recent study produced results consistent with those of Berry *et al.* (1977). The later study, conducted by the Research Triangle Institute (*The Alcoholism Report*, 1982) was concerned with the use of a common methodology for estimating the social economic cost of alcohol abuse, drug abuse, and mental illness. The estimates were based on the year 1977 and covered direct (treatment, support) and indirect (mortality and morbidity) "core costs" and direct (motor vehicle crashes) "other related costs." The final estimates derived, which were considered conservative, were $49.4 billion for alcohol abuse, $16.4 billion for drug abuse, and $40.3 billion for mental illness. Therefore, alcohol abuse was estimated to cost American society more than either of the other two problem areas in 1977, and the cost of all areas was substantial. Of course, social economic cost estimates do not include an index for the human suffering that is associated with drug and alcohol abuse.

TOWARD AN UNDERSTANDING OF DRUG AND ALCOHOL ABUSE

It is clear, therefore, that the U.S. and other societies have much to be gained by a better understanding of the development and maintenance of substance abuse. Although MD and PhD clinicians appear to shy away from treating substance abusers, there does not seem to be a shortage of substance abuse researchers, especially those who are inclined to publish theories about their subject matter. A casual look at the scientific literature on substance abuse would lead the novice reader to believe that this is the most overexplained set of problems known to the health professions. For example, Lettieri, Sayers, and Pearson (1980) edited a National Institute on Drug Abuse monograph on *selected* contemporary theories of drug abuse. The book is remarkable because it covers descriptions of 43 theories by over 50 different theorists. Furthermore, the theories span the disciplines and subdisciplines of the social/ behavioral/biological sciences. A look at the literature on alcohol abuse would reveal a similar quantity and diversity in theory (Maisto & Caddy, 1981; Roebuck & Kessler, 1972).

This smorgasbord of theory can be viewed both positively and negatively. On the negative side is the sheer volume of information that has to be pored over, assimilated, and discriminated by anyone who is serious about studying substance abuse. Unfortunately, this formidable task is made impossible by the absence of data systematically testing most of the current theories.

The positive side, however, is that the array of theories provides encouragement that the field can progress. First, because the many theories of substance abuse are from multiple disciplines, there seems to be formal recognition that substance abuse is a complex phenomenon. In this regard, current knowledge suggests that the many facets of substance abuse have to be accounted for and that it is premature to discount any one theoretical approach (Galizio, 1982). Indeed, this is the reason for our decision to construe individual differences in substance abuse as defined by multidimensional—biological, psychological, and environmental—factors. Accordingly, we make the assumption that such individual differences will eventually be explained by critical analysis of data from all three of these domains. Furthermore, systematic pursuit of this approach should lead to a refinement of theory by "survival-of-the-fittest," or most powerful, constructs to explain substance abuse. The next chapters in this book are a significant step in that direction by their provision of a critical review of the available biological, psychological, and environmental data on substance abuse.

OVERVIEW OF THE BOOK

The chapters in the second part of the book concern a review of biological factors in substance abuse. The first chapter by Crabbe, McSwigan, and Belknap covers genetic contributions to substance abuse, which are receiving an ever-increasing amount of attention from researchers. Crabbe *et al.* consider human studies on alcohol abuse and, more extensively, animal studies of ethanol, opiate, and barbiturate use. Bardo and Risner follow with a thorough consideration of basic principles of pharmacology and neurochemistry and how these are applied to discover the determinants of, and responses to, drugs. The implications of the findings of biochemical researchers for treatment of drug abuse are also explored. The chapter by Hinson centers on a review of research and theory on the influences of conditioning on drug tolerance. Hinson also discusses what the available data may mean for withdrawal and for relapse following a period of abstinence. Chapter 5 is by Barrett, who provides an extensive, empirically oriented review of behavioral approaches to drug use and abuse. Barrett covers some essentials of behavioral approaches and animal models and then reviews the recent research, much of which was completed in his laboratory, on reinforcing properties of drugs, opponent process theory and drug use, and opponent process explanation of relapse to drug abuse.

Part III of the book covers psychological and environmental variables in substance abuse and begins with Adesso's chapter on cognitive factors. This chapter concentrates on the construct of *expectancy* as a determinant of substance use and abuse and of responses to drugs. Adesso focuses primarily on research involving human use of alcohol because the vast majority of experiments have involved that drug; however, the conclusions that he draws likely have some relevance for other drugs as well. The chapter by Cox provides an overview of the extensive literature on personality correlates of substance abuse. Chapter 8 is by McCarty and is concerned with the "microsetting" as a complex of factors in substance abuse. McCarty reviews the available research on the effects of the immediate setting on the use of alcohol and, to a lesser extent, on other drug use and their consequences. The implications of the empirical literature on microsetting effects for drug and alcohol abuse treatment and prevention are also discussed. Connors and Tarbox conclude this section with their chapter on the "macrosetting." This chapter complements McCarty's by reviewing aspects of the environment that affect whole populations of individuals. Such environmental influences include cultural factors, geographic location, population of place of residence, and general availability of alcohol and drugs.

The last part of the book concerns individual difference factors and treatment of substance abuse. Caddy and Block begin this part with a review of the large literature on factors that discriminate among individuals in their response to the treatment of alcoholism. This is followed by two chapters that address the critical question of relapse, which was discussed by several of the previous authors. Ogborne, Sobell, and Sobell address relapse from a different point of view. These authors review the empirical evidence on environmental factors as determinants of functioning after treatment for alcohol abuse and apply these findings to the design and evaluation of alcoholism treatment programs. Tucker, Vuchinich, and Harris provide an extensive review of the literature on relapse to tobacco, narcotic, and alcohol use. These authors pay most attention to the research that provides information on processes of relapse and present an initial theoretical integration of this diverse literature.

Galizio and Maisto conclude the book with an integrative statement regarding individual differences in substance abuse. By the time they wrote their chapter they had had the advantage of the data and wisdom provided in the previous chapters. This granted them, and we hope will give you, a broader perspective from which to examine why people differ in their use of and reactions to drugs.

REFERENCES

American Psychiatric Association. *Diagnostic and statistical manual of mental disorders* (3rd ed.). Washington, D.C.: American Psychiatric Association, 1980.

Berry, R. E., Boland, J. P., Smart, C. N., & Kanak, J. R. *The economic cost of alcohol abuse—1975*. Final report, Contract No. ADM 281-76-0016. Prepared for the National Institute on Alcohol Abuse and Alcoholism, 1977.

Clark, W., & Midanik, L. Alcohol use and alcohol problems among U. S. adults. In Alcohol consumption and related problems. *Alcohol and Health Monograph* 1. Rockville, Md.: National Institute on Alcohol Abuse and Alcoholism, 1982.

Fishburne, P. M., Abelson, H. I., & Cisin, I. H. *The national survey on drug abuse: 1979*. Washington, D.C.: National Institute on Drug Abuse, 1979.

Galizio, M. In defense of reductionism. *Bulletin of the Society of Psychologists in Substance Abuse*, 1982, *1*, 98–99.

Lettieri, D. J., Sayers, M., & Pearson, H. W. (Eds.), *Theories on drug abuse*. Rockville, Md.: National Institute on Drug Abuse, 1980.

Maisto, S. A., & Caddy, G. R. Self-control and addictive behavior: Present status and prospects. *International Journal of the Addictions*, 1981, *16*, 109–133.

Roebuck, J., & Kessler, R. *The etiology of alcoholism*. Springfield, Il.: Charles C. Thomas, 1972.

The Alcoholism Report, 1982, *X*, 3–4.

PART II

Biological Factors

CHAPTER 2

The Role of Genetics in Substance Abuse

JOHN C. CRABBE, JOHN D. McSWIGAN, and J. K. BELKNAP

OVERVIEW

Many factors clearly influence substance abuse. Our goal in this chapter is to acquaint the reader with a literature devoted to the hypothesis that an individual's unique genetic constitution is one important factor. We believe that the studies performed during the last 20 years strongly imply that some humans suffer from a genetic predisposition to develop alcoholism. Extensive animal experiments corroborate this hypothesis and have begun to offer clues as to what, exactly, may be inherited. There are virtually no experiments demonstrating familial patterns of abuse for substances other than ethanol. Nonetheless, a growing animal literature demonstrates that responsiveness to opiates and barbiturates is also influenced markedly by inheritance. A few studies suggest that responsiveness to all psychoactive substances tends to be inherited to some degree.

We will first define our terms because *substance abuse* must be conceptualized somewhat differently in humans and in laboratory ani-

JOHN C. CRABBE • Research Service, VA Medical Center, and Departments of Medical Psychology and Pharmacology, Oregon Health Sciences University, Portland, Oregon 97201.   *JOHN D. McSWIGAN* • Research Service, VA Medical Center, and Department of Medical Psychology, Oregon Health Sciences University, Portland, Oregon 97201.   *J. K. BELKNAP* • Department of Pharmacology, School of Medicine, University of North Dakota, Grand Forks, North Dakota 58202. Preparation of this review was supported by NIDA Grants DA 02799 to John C. Crabbe and DA 02723 to J. K. Belknap, and by a grant from the Veterans Administration to John C. Crabbe.

mals. We then discuss the goals of experimental pharmacogenetic work with substances of abuse. Again, the goals differ somewhat between humans and laboratory animals. We then briefly describe the experimental methods available to analyze the possible genetic susceptibility for development of drug abuse in humans. This section is followed by a review of the human pharmacogenetic data on alcoholism. Following this, we briefly describe methods employed with laboratory animals to assess genetic versus environmental contributions to drug responses. The next section reviews the problems in alcohol pharmacogenetic research and considers their implications. Two shorter sections review the smaller animal literatures on opiate and barbiturate pharmacogenetics. In the final section, we attempt to evaluate the success of the pharmacogenetic enterprise *in toto*. Particularly because the level of genetic analysis with experimental animals is more complex than that with humans, we try to identify those animal models and experimental approaches we feel to be most likely to produce meaningful data relevant to the human condition.

DRUG DEPENDENCE

INTRODUCTION

The nature and causes of drug dependence are complex and differ among agents. It is useful to define drug dependence operationally as consisting of two components. First, *physical dependence* can be inferred from the emergence of physiological withdrawal symptoms that are alleviated by administration of the drug. Second, *psychological dependence* can be deduced from verbal self-reports of need for the drug as well as drug-seeking behavior. Because much of the literature we will review is concerned with work with animals, psychological dependence can only be implied by experiments designed to elicit drug-seeking behavior. Subsequent application of findings with these studies to humans should be undertaken with caution as the underlying motivational state of an animal is often not clear. Thus, for the purpose of organizing our discussion, we will identify two categories of drug effects, keeping in mind that the distinction between them is not intended to support particular conceptual descriptions of their nature. First, we will consider the effects of the drug on the organism. Second, we will examine the drug-seeking behavior engaged in by the organism, which may or may not imply a psychological need state.

DRUG EFFECTS

For a given dependence-inducing drug and organism, a complete understanding of the drug requires analysis of three aspects of drug effects. First, the initial sensitivity of the naive organism to the effects of the drug upon first exposure should be identified. Second, tolerance may develop if the drug is repeatedly administered at a given dose. Tolerance may be defined as the necessity to increase the dose to maintain the same level of effect (alternatively, the effect will diminish for reasons other than organ toxicity when a constant dosage is repeated). Third, the nature of the syndrome when the drug is withdrawn after the induction of physical dependence must be understood. This is necessary because physical dependence on a drug cannot be directly assessed. Rather, the degree of physical dependence must be inferred from the severity and duration of the withdrawal syndrome (Kalant, LeBlanc, & Gibbins, 1971).

A complicating factor in assessing these three aspects is that no drug exerts a single effect. Furthermore, both initial sensitivity and tolerance to different effects of the same drug may vary in magnitude, across individuals and certainly among species, and the rate of development of tolerance to different effects may also differ (Kalant *et al.*, 1971). However, for many drugs, the general response topography is similar across a range of organisms, including man. Thus, studying animals seems in many cases to be a reasonable model for understanding drug effects in humans. As we shall see, the use of animal models has greatly facilitated the progress of experiments designed to assess the role of genetic constitution in drug sensitivity, tolerance, and dependence/withdrawal.

DRUG-SEEKING BEHAVIOR

The second component of drug dependence, drug-seeking behavior, is somewhat more problematic in the generalization of results with animals to humans. Although drug-seeking behavior can be reliably and validly measured in both animals and man, only humans can verbalize their reasons for seeking and using the drug. Their opinions may or may not have validity, but insofar as they do, there is a gap in what can be assessed with animals and the nature of the psychological need state in humans. The reasons for voluntarily administering a drug will likely be different for humans than for other animals; so we must interpret all studies of drug-seeking behavior using animal models with care. This is especially critical when animal models of drug self-administration are employed to assess the role of genetic factors predisposing to dependence liability.

GOALS OF GENETIC STUDIES OF SUBSTANCE ABUSE

A proportion of individuals in our society abstain totally from all drugs of abuse. The predominant proportion employ substances of abuse, particularly alcohol, without developing abusive patterns of self-administration. A third group abuses one or more drugs to the point of physical and/or psychological dependence. Thus, drug use is characterized by large individual differences. This argues that mere experience with drugs themselves is not capable of inducing and maintaining drug dependence in general; rather, individual difference factors intrinsic to drug users must contribute to whether a particular drug is self-administered to the point of abuse. Such individual difference factors include the person's unique genetic constitution.

The ultimate goal of pharmacogenetic studies of substance abuse is to identify the genetic factors predisposing certain humans to develop abusive patterns of drug self-administration. For example, those predisposed to develop alcoholism may inherit a hypersensitivity to the hedonic properties of the drug. On the other hand, they might equally well be found to inherit a lack of sensitivity to the dysphoric effects that follow excessive drinking. As will be seen when human genetic studies are reviewed, we have as yet relatively little information about what exactly might be inherited, and it will obviously be a complex undertaking to identify the predisposing factors.

Because we do not understand the basis for abuse *per se*, it is unreasonable to expect genetic analyses to achieve this long-term goal directly. Rather, the approach taken by pharmacogenetic experiments has been to address two more modest goals. Initially, experiments with animal models and human studies demonstrated the presence of significant genetic influence on drug sensitivity, tolerance, dependence/withdrawal, and drug-seeking behavior. Subsequently, studies with animals attempted to identify and characterize animal models (e.g., particular inbred strains or selected lines) that would be suitable for more mechanism-oriented work. Studies using a variety of genetic techniques have been quite successful in achieving these more modest goals for a number of substances. These experiments have been reviewed (Belknap, 1980a; Crabbe & Belknap, 1980; Horowitz & Dudek, 1983). We will not recapitulate earlier reviews in this chapter but will instead highlight some of the earlier findings and review subsequent work. Readers are referred to an earlier paper (Crabbe & Belknap, 1980) for a systematic consideration of pharmacogenetic techniques and their success in identifying genetic influences on sensitivity, tolerance, dependence/withdrawal, and drug-seeking behavior.

The rapid growth of pharmacogenetic work in the study of alcohol's effects has allowed progress to the point where the next step in the pharmacogenetic analysis of drug abuse may be taken. Specifically, we can now begin to make cautious predictions about what exactly might be inherited that predisposes animals to sensitivity to several effects of alcohol and even to physical dependence liability. Although the human literature is meager in this regard, some studies in progress may allow such predictions, and they will be reviewed. The animal research includes a growing number of experiments designed to assess genetic relationships among different responses to ethanol, including self-administration to the point of physical dependence and withdrawal. Because the ability to predict genetic sensitivity to one effect of ethanol from genetic sensitivity to another must be based on studies of genetic correlation (that is, influence of the same genes on both traits), it is on these approaches that we will concentrate the present chapter.

The purpose of this chapter is to review the existing evidence for the role inheritance plays in determining the response to drugs of abuse. Pharmacogenetic information regarding ethanol is rather extensive in comparison with other drugs of abuse. Because the amount of information available allows some rather clear conclusions to be drawn, we will concentrate this review on ethanol and devote the initial sections to it. Recent reviews of the genetic basis for rate of metabolism and the development of metabolic tolerance to ethanol have been published (Broadhurst, 1978; Collins, 1979; Deitrich & Collins, 1977; Erwin, Heston, McClearn, & Deitrich, 1976; Horowitz & Dudek, 1983; Reed, 1978). Generally speaking, it would appear that the issue of ethanol metabolism may be dissociated from the other pharmacological effects described without critically damaging our analysis of these effects. Specifically, genetically determined differences in metabolism do not seem to be firmly linked to differences in susceptibility to alcoholism in humans (for example see, Schwitters, Johnson, McClearn, & Wilson, 1982) or to physical dependence in animals. Consequently, we will not consider metabolic tolerance development but refer the interested reader to the previously mentioned reviews.

There is a small but steadily growing literature on the pharmacogenetics of opiates. This literature and the yet smaller number of studies on barbiturates consists almost entirely of differences among inbred strains. We will devote later sections to opiates and barbiturates, respectively. Finally, both stimulants and benzodiazepines are known to be at least prone to abuse if not capable of inducing physical dependence. However, the pharmacogenetic literature on these classes of drugs is still very small. Rather than simply listing the existing genetic studies regarding these drug classes, we feel it more appropriate to forestall their review until there is sufficient data to allow some general conclusions.

HUMAN PHARMACOGENETICS OF ETHANOL

INTRODUCTION

In pharmacogenetic research, the initial goal is to determine the presence and extent of hereditary influence on the trait of interest, especially in regard to individual or population differences in drug response. Subsequent investigation of the mechanisms mediating these genetic differences have the goal of increasing understanding of the target trait. We will present a very brief review of the more widely used pharmacogenetic methods for human research in this section, referring to the more detailed and technical publications available in the literature as appropriate.

HUMAN METHODS

Twin Studies

Monozygotic twins share all nuclear genes by common inheritance whereas dizygotic twins share 50% of their genes, on the average, the same proportion as full siblings. When an individual is identified as having the trait under examination (i.e., is a *proband*), that individuals's co-twin may then be examined to see if he or she also is, for example, alcoholic and is thus concordant for the trait. If within-family environmental factors are similar, a higher rate of concordance for monozygotic twins than for dizygotic twins is evidence of genetic influence on the trait. Twin studies are sometimes criticized because of alleged more similar treatment of monozygotic than dizygotic twins by their parents. However, the more similar treatment of monozygotics must be relevant to the target trait, in this case the development of substance abuse. In addition to giving evidence for genetic involvement in a trait, twin studies can demonstrate the involvement of environmental factors because monozygotic concordance of less than 100% necessarily implies that something in the environment affects expression of the trait.

Adoption Studies

A related strategy for assessing the influence of genetic factors on traits in humans is to examine concordance as a function of degree of genetic relatedness in individuals that have been adopted. If subjects are chosen who have been adopted before the age of 3 to 6 months old, it is generally assumed that the influences of genetic predisposition and those of environmental influence on the trait studied may be differentiated. An additional advantage of this method over twin-based methods is the larger pool of subjects that can be studied.

Discriminant Analysis and at Risk Studies

An important step in research on any human biochemical/genetic disorder is the development of reliable diagnostic criteria for the correct classification of diagnostic groups. Ideally, the criteria should be objective and have the capacity to detect individuals premorbidly. Initially a discriminant function is developed (for example, using a group of laboratory tests) by examining reliably diagnosed individuals versus controls. The discriminant function is formed from that combination of tests giving the clearest separation of the two groups. Once a set of tests can be shown to be successful in separating, for example, alcoholics from nonalcoholics, it must be validated on a new sample to assess generalizability. A discriminant test battery that has been demonstrated as reliable and valid could subsequently be used with premorbid at risk groups to evaluate its predictive power. Although at risk studies would benefit by the use of the discriminant function approach, they have more typically reported using clinical diagnostic criteria. Subjects are chosen on the basis of the presence or absence of alcoholism in their first-degree relatives and matched on their own drinking history and other relevant variables. The individuals are followed prospectively, and parameters thought to be relevant to the development of alcoholism are assessed. If groups are initially formed on the basis of degrees of biological relationship to an alcoholic proband, discriminant factors are presumptively genetically mediated.

HUMAN STUDIES OF ETHANOL ABUSE

Twin and Adoption Studies

Before reviewing human studies, we must say a word about the definition of alcoholism. To define alcoholism and rediscuss the various conflicting opinions about the definition is beyond the scope of this chapter. We will accept the definition used by the authors cited, and only if we strongly disagree with the use in the particular study under discussion will we address the effect of the definition on the results obtained. The work in the area of human genetics of alcoholism has, to a large extent, focused on classical techniques for human genetic analysis, namely twin and adoption studies. Work reported prior to 1977 was critically reviewed by Shields (1977). Our review of the human literature will concentrate on work done since that time. The foundation for this work resides in the well-established fact that alcoholism runs in families. This evidence has been recently reviewed (Goodwin, 1980). Twin studies have demonstrated an increased concordance for monozygotic versus dizygotic twins for problem drinking (Jonsson & Nilsson, 1968; Kaprio, Sarna, Koskenvuo, & Rontasalo, 1978; Loehlin, 1972; Partanen, Bruun, & Markkanen, 1966) and for alcoholism itself (Kaij, 1960). Partenen *et al.* (1966) examined 839 Finnish twin pairs, 198 monozygotic and 641 dizygotic. They assessed concordance for scores on three factors (Density, Amount, and Lack of Control) based on a factor analysis of drinking behavior. The authors estimated heritabilities (that proportion of the variance of an observable character that is attributable to genetic causes) and arrived at values of $H = .39$, $.36$, and $.14$ for Density, Amount, and Lack of Control, respectively. A linear combination of the three factors had a higher genetic heritability than any did individually, suggesting that they were somewhat independent. When twin pairs were grouped by age, the H values increased significantly for Density and Lack of Control, but not for Amount, due to a decrease in the monozygotic within-pair variance. This could result from younger monozygotic pairs having spent less time apart than older pairs, tending to make them more similar. These authors interpreted their results as indicative of a genetic component for alcoholism but not for the social consequences of drinking. Gottesman and Carey (1983) reanalyzed Kaij's (1960) data and demonstrated that the population prevalence and the inclusion of problem drinking in addition to more restrictively defined alcoholism had large effects on the estimate of heritability derived from twin data. Specifically, they estimated higher heritability in more strictly defined cases (although the number of cases was lower) than in more broadly defined cases. The other twin studies cited previously are in general agreement with a role for genetics in alcohol abuse.

An interesting approach to the genetic relationships among different ethanol effects was recently provided by Hrubec and Omenn (1981). They examined the twin registry of the National Academy of Sciences National Research Council. Almost 16,000 male twin pairs were classified for prevalence and concordance for alcoholism, alcoholic psychosis, liver cirrhosis and pancreatitis. Monozygotic twins had at least twice the concordance rates of dizygotic twins for all but the last disorder. Higher monozygotic concordance for alcoholic psychosis and liver cirrhosis could not be explained by the higher alcoholism concordance. The authors suggested that these data support different genetic predispositions for specific biomedical consequences of alcoholism. In our view, they also provide *ipso facto* evidence for genetic heterogeneity in control of alcohol-related effects in man. That is, different alcohol-related effects appear to be affected by different groups of genes. As with all twin analysis, there is the possibility that the increased concordance of monozygotic twins is a result of more similar "treatment" of monozygotic than dizygotic twins. In addition, there is no separation of genetic and environmental effects in twins raised with their families. Such separation of genetic and environmental effects can only be approached by the analysis of adopted individuals.

An early adoption study by Roe and Burks (1945) reported no significant increase in alcoholism in the adopted-away first-degree relatives of alcoholics. However, this study has been criticized for small sample size and the fact that the adoptees were not into the age of risk for alcoholism (Oakeshott & Gibson, 1981). More recent adoption studies (Cadoret & Gath, 1978; Goodwin, Schulsinger, Hermansen, Guze, & Winokur, 1973; Schuckit, Goodwin, & Winokur, 1972) find that in males there is an approximately fourfold excess of alcoholism in the adopted-away offspring of alcoholics versus control adoptees, but there appears to be no appreciable difference in females.

In a recent Swedish adoption study (Bohman, Sigvardsson, & Cloninger, 1981; Cloninger, Bohman, & Sigvardsson, 1981) with a large sample size (862 male and 913 female adoptees), evidence for the existence of genetic predisposition for two types of alcoholism was reported. For males, the two types were characterized as follows. Type I (milieu type) is characterized by mild alcohol abuse, minimal criminality, and no history of treatment for alcoholism for biological mothers and fathers; postnatal environment is important for frequency and severity of alcoholism in adopted sons; and alcoholism is usually mild. Type II (male limited) is characterized by severe alcohol abuse, severe criminality, history of frequent treatment for alcoholism in biological fathers but normal alcohol use in mothers; postnatal environment does not affect frequency of alcoholism in adoptees; and adoptees' alcoholism is usually recurrent or moderate and may be severe. In female adoptees, alcoholism was found to be more often inherited through the mother but could be through the father and was Type I as outlined before. The more common type was associated with more extended exposure of adopted offspring to their biological parents, whereas the less common type was more highly heritable in males (Bohman *et al.*, 1981; Cloninger *et al.*, 1981).

To establish this typology, the authors initially classified all illegitimate adopted-out children born between 1930–1949 as either nonalcoholic, mild, moderate, or severe alcohol abusers. They then performed a discriminant analysis on socioeconomic, drinking, and criminality-related variables in the biological parents of these children (Cloninger *et al.*, 1981). The discriminant analysis resulted in three significant functions for the biological parents of male adoptees; however, the data provided seem to indicate that the biological parents of moderate alcohol abusers were the only group that was clearly different from the other three, in our view. The biological parents of mild and severe abuse adoptees were very similar and more like the parents of nonalcoholics. This outcome is difficult to put in a theoretical context. The authors conclude that genetic predisposition to develop moderate abuse is genetically distinct and that rearing environment has little input into expression of this trait. For both mild and severe abuse, separate genetic factors were identified, and the influence of environment had about equal weight. This study may provide the basis for the identification of multiple, genetically distinct forms of alcoholism that could, if replicated, improve the chances for finding biological/biochemical variables important in the pathogenesis of alcoholism. However, a subsequent study with females (Bohman *et al.*, 1981) yielded different discriminant factors, adding complexity to an already complex picture.

In all the studies mentioned before, an important consideration is the effect of assortative mating (in this context, nonrandom choice of mate based on perceived similarities or differences from self) on the estimated contribution of genetics to the development of alcoholism. A recent study examined the degree of resemblance of alcoholics and their parents (Hall, Hasselbrock, & Stebenaw, 1983a). The authors found that when the alcoholic proband's mother's drinking was compared to father's drinking style, there was concordance for abstinence and social drinking but not for problem drinking. In contrast, when fathers were examined based on mother's drinking style, there was increasing concordance across severity from abstinence (21%) to problem drinking (70%). In the second study (Hall, Hasselbrock, & Stebenaw, 1983b), the drinking style of the spouses of alcoholics was examined and compared to probands and their parents. A major finding was that 31.1% of husbands of female alcoholics were diagnosed alcoholic themselves. There was no strong relationship between problem drinking in the spouses of female alcoholics and the alcoholic's father's drinking behavior, a finding that is unexpected *a priori*. It is salient that in individuals who become alcoholic there may well have been assortative mating by their parents for alcoholism, increasing both the genetic and environmental loading. This report bears replicating and points to the need to consider assortative mating when doing genetic studies.

Discriminant Analysis and at Risk Studies

The previously mentioned experiments seem to offer clear evidence for genetic involvement in alcoholism. The adoption studies in particular eliminate the possibility that alcoholism is simply imitative. A logical next step is to assess possible factors of either a biochemical or psychological nature that may contribute to the expression of alcoholism in genetically predisposed individuals. Several recent studies by Schuckit and his colleagues have reported preliminary results from a prospective study of San Diego college students who have been classified *family history positive* or *family history negative* on the basis of self-report of their own and family members' drinking patterns. In one report, family-history-positive individuals were found to have significantly higher acetaldehyde levels after an acute dose of ethanol compared to family-history-negative controls (Schuckit & Rayses, 1979). However, considerable controversy attends the determination of blood acetaldehyde concentration, and these results may be artifactual (see C. J. P. Eriksson, 1983). Although there was no difference in blood ethanol levels between the two groups after administration of a fixed dose of ethanol (Schuckit, 1980, 1981), the family-history-positive subjects reported feeling less intoxicated than family-history-negative subjects (Schuckit, 1980). Behar *et al.* (1983) investigated the effects of a single dose (.5 ml/kg) of ethanol on children 8 to 15 years old with and without a family history of alcoholism. They confirmed the lack of a significant difference between the two groups in blood alcohol levels but also found no difference in acetaldehyde levels. In addition, the groups did not differ in plasma cortisol, epinephrine, norepinephrine or beta-endorphin levels. Finally, the groups were not differentiated on several behavioral or cognitive measures.

In two subsequent articles, Schuckit *et al.* examined two enzymes as possible correlates of family-history-positive or family-history-negative status. They reported no difference between family-history-positive versus family-history-negative individuals for either baseline activity or activity after an ethanol challenge for either dopamine-β-hydroxylase or monoamine oxidase (Schuckit, O'Connor, Duby, Vega, & Moss, 1981; Schuckit, Shaskan, Duby, Vega, & Moss, 1982). In a study of active and resting muscle tension before and after ethanol ingestion, family-history-positive subjects showed more relaxation than family-history-negative subjects in the resting (but not the active) condition (Schuckit, Engstrom, Alpert, & Duby, 1981). A self-report study of family-history-positive and family-history-negative individuals revealed more alcohol, drug abuse, and psychiatric problems in the family-history-positive subjects (Schuckit, 1982). A final study from this group (Elmasian, Neville, Woods, Schuckit, & Bloom, 1982) will be discussed with EEG studies shortly.

In summary, Schuckit and his colleagues have been conducting a long-term prospective study of individuals with and without a family history of alcohol abuse. To date, preliminary experiments have failed to reveal striking differences between family-history-positive and family-history-negative individuals. Because these individuals were raised by their biological parents, this design does not allow separation of genetic from environmental factors, a shortcoming shared with twin studies. However, as family-history-positive and family-history-negative subjects enter demographically higher risk age groups over the course of the study, there should be interesting findings with respect to factors that can precipitate alcoholism in predisposed individuals.

Finding biochemical variables that can reliably and validly differentiate alcoholics from nonalcoholics would be of great value for any subsequent psychiatric genetic study of alcoholism. Eckardt and his co-workers (Eckardt, Ryback, Rawlings, & Graubard, 1981) have evaluated previous reports of the ability of gamma-glutamyltranspeptidase and mean corpuscular volume to differentiate alcoholics from nonalcoholics in a new population. They report that by themselves gamma-glutamyltranspeptidase and mean corpuscular volume were poor discriminators (94% of nonalcoholics were classified correctly, but only 34% of alcoholics were classified correctly). However, if a discriminant analysis (with 24 different clinical tests) was used, including or excluding gamma-glutamyltranspeptidase and mean corpuscular volume, the correct classification went up to 100% for nonalcoholics and 98% for alcoholics. This is an impressive degree of differentiation and certainly deserves further exploration. The number of tests and associated costs may make the procedure expensive for routine use, but for research the costs could be justified. In addition, with further work, this type of analysis may be possible with a much smaller set of tests. In fact, the authors report that by limiting the analysis to the 12 best discriminating variables, correct classification was 98% for alcoholics and 95% for nonalcoholics (Eckardt et al., 1981). We believe that this analysis would be very useful in a population such as the one that Schuckit et al. are studying and would allow testing of predictive validity as the group enters the age of higher risk.

Possible markers for genetic influences of alcohol's effects on the central nervous system are differences between alcoholics and nonalcoholics in electroencephalograms (EEG) after ethanol challenge. Recent studies have examined the effect of alcohol on genetic variants of the normal EEG in alcoholics and their relatives (Propping, Kruger, & Janah, 1980; Propping, Kruger, & Mark, 1981). In individuals with "borderline alpha EEG," alcohol had a greater synchronizing effect than on individuals with other characteristic wave forms. The authors interpret this to mean that alcohol can exert differential effects on individuals with different genetically based EEGs (Propping *et al.*, 1980). In the second study (Propping *et al.*, 1981), male alcoholics did not differ from their controls in alpha or theta waves, whereas female alcoholics had a shift from alpha and theta to beta wave forms. The authors argue that in females, a poorly synchronized EEG pattern is a possible indicator for a predisposition to alcoholism. However, this is not a specific indicator because similar findings have been reported for schizophrenic individuals. These experiments have been reviewed (Propping, 1983).

In a third study, Elmasian *et al.* (1982) examined the event-related evoked potential of individuals at high and low familial risk for developing alcoholism. Family-history-positive subjects, whether under the influence of alcohol or not, had significantly smaller amplitude P_3 components to the event-related evoked potential than family-history-negative subjects. Family-history-positive subjects also exhibited an increase in latency of P_3 during drinking conditions compared to baseline and had increased mean reaction time to the test stimulus. These results are consistent with a higher level of distractibility in family-history-positive subjects. The authors suggest that event-related evoked potentials may be useful in the identification of individuals at risk for developing alcoholism. Finally, a recent paper (Pollock, Valakava, Goodwin, Mednick, Gabrielli, Knop, & Schulsinger, 1983) reports that the 19–21-year-old sons of alcoholics show greater sensitivity to the effect of alcohol on alpha frequency EEG than control subjects. Blood alcohol concentrations did not differ. These results were taken to indicate a greater physiological sensitivity to alcohol in sons of alcoholics. However, the sons of alcoholics self-reported requiring more drinks to "feel tipsy" than controls. Although the self-reported estimates of alcohol intake was the same in the two groups, it is possible that the groups could differ in drinking history and, therefore, tolerance to alcohol.

Another approach to identifying the nature of genetic determination of alcohol effects is to screen individuals on multiple responses to ethanol. If related individuals are tested, the resulting phenotypic correlations can be partitioned into genetic and environmental components (Falconer, 1960). Wilson and his colleagues have approached this goal by developing a large battery of behavioral tests to examine initial sensitivity and acute behavioral tolerance to ethanol in different populations (Wilson, Erwin, & McClearn, 1984). In a preliminary study with this method, 29 pairs of brothers were examined before and after ethanol ingestion using this battery (5 pairs served as controls). The authors reported moderate intraclass correlations for initial sensitivity to ethanol, although a number of the correlations were negative, which makes interpretation difficult. For acute tolerance, the intraclass correlations were mostly nonsignificant. As pointed out by the authors, the fact that difference scores were used increases variability, making significance difficult to achieve. Also, the study was fairly ambitious, using 13 behavioral tests, each with a duration of approximately 5 minutes. Subsequent studies using a subset of tests most sensitive to the effects of alcohol will allow these investigators to achieve finer discrimination (Wilson, Erwin, McClearn, Plomin, Johnson, Ahern, & Cole, 1984).

In summary, studies with human subjects indicate that there is a genetic component to alcoholism. Clearly, alcoholism is not absolutely determined by genetic factors because monozygotic twins are not 100% concordant. It is likely that the genetic influence is one of predisposition to the development of alcoholism. We have yet virtually no clues as to *what* exactly might be inherited. It would be valuable to know the number of genes involved; if a limited number of genes are important, further biochemical studies will be more likely to be successful. Some studies indicated that there may be multiple, genetically distinct subtypes of alcoholism. Work has begun to shift to a search for genetic and/or biochemical markers of alcoholism with the ultimate goal being premorbid identification of predisposed individuals. If such markers are found to be reliable predictors, they could then be used in at risk individuals to aid in the prevention of alcoholism.

We turn our attention now to the much more extensive animal literature in the field of genetics of substance abuse. For the purpose of genetic studies, animal models are more tractable than human studies. Control over breeding pairs based on a selection criterion is one obvious example of the type of experiment that can only be done in animals. In addition, treatments can be assigned with precision, and trait-relevant features can be explored to any level desired.

ANIMAL PHARMACOGENETICS OF ETHANOL

ANIMAL METHODS

Inbred Strains

An inbred strain is the product of at least 20 generations of (usually) brother-by-sister matings. All members of such a strain can be considered to be genetically identical to one another for all practical purposes. It is safe to assume that any two or more inbred strains will differ genetically from one another because the particular genes found in any one inbred strain are largely due to chance. If rearing, environment, and experimental treatment conditions are the same for all strains, any differences found between strains on a particular trait of interest can be assumed to be genetically based. Many inbred strains of mice and rats are available for scientific research. The principal usage of inbred strains in pharmaco-genetic research is to examine the presence of genetic influence on the trait in question. Although we will note exceptions later, the questions of relationship between genetics and drug effects are generally pursued using more powerful genetic techniques. The advantages and disadvantages of inbred strains as well as extensive descriptions of their nature have been discussed (Altman & Katz, 1979; Crispens, 1975; Falconer, 1960; Green, 1966, 1968; Hay, 1980; Ingram & Corfman, 1980; McClearn, 1967, 1972).

Single Gene and Quantitative Genetic Techniques

If there is a significant genetic contribution to a character, subsequent genetic analyses may be undertaken to detect the influence of single genes on the trait in question and thereafter to map those genes to a particular chromosome (linkage group). If a single gene has a relatively large influence on the trait of interest so that its influence can be distinguished from background "noise" due to environmental effects, measurement error, and the effects of other trait-relevant genes of small effect, mapping may be possible. That is, the specific location of the gene on a particular chromosome may be identified. A recently established method is the use of recombinant inbred (RI) strains such as those developed by Bailey (1971). Discussions of the RI technique have been published (Bailey, 1971; Klein, 1978), and Eleftheriou and Elias (1975) give a useful introduction. Where parental inbred strains differ markedly in the trait of interest, the RI technique can offer a rapid and efficient means of identifying and mapping single genes with major influence on the trait.

Many lines of mice or rats, like humans, are genetically variable (e.g. "Swiss" mice, "Sprague-Dawley" rats). When the resemblance between relatives in such a genetically heterogeneous (noninbred) nonselected population is determined, it is possible to make quantitative assessments of the degree and mode of genetic determination (Falconer, 1960). Perhaps the most common method is to index the resemblance between the mean of the parents and the mean of their respective offspring by computing the parent–offspring regression. Quantitative methods are relatively infrequently used, mostly due to the large numbers of animals that must be studied. However, these methods offer the most information for studying the genetic architecture, or nature of the influence of gene interactions on the trait.

Selective Breeding

Selective breeding (or selection) refers to the systematic intermating of chosen individuals for the purpose of changing the genetic and phenotypic (observable) characteristics of a population with respect to a particular trait. In pharmacogenetic research, the usual practice is to change the population mean in two opposite directions (high and low values of a trait), that is, for both extremes concurrently (bidirectional selection).

A successful selection project is useful for three reasons: first, information can be gained concerning the existence and degree of genetic control of the trait in question; second, organisms tailormade for a specific purpose can be developed; and third, the selection lines become potentially valuable research material in testing mechanisms hypothesized to be associated with the selected trait. Because the latter will be a primary focus of the present review, a brief discussion is appropriate here. From a genetic standpoint, selective breeding should result in changes in gene frequencies for only those genes that have impact on the trait under selection. Gene frequencies for genes not affecting the selected trait should be unchanged within the limits of sampling error. This stands in contrast to the fixation of gene frequencies in an inbred strain. During generations of inbreeding, some genes are lost, and others are permanently fixed in the inbred strain, but *which* genes are retained is entirely due to chance. In addition, under constant environmental conditions, the differences between two selection lines are entirely due to these differences in gene frequency, that is, they are entirely due to genetic causes. Thus, the fact that bidirectional selection of mice for duration of sleep time following a dose of ethanol has resulted in selection line differences on other variables (e.g., membrane fluidity, liability to physical dependence development, etc.) means that the latter (known as correlated responses) are very likely due to other effects of some of the same genes that influence duration of sleep time. This is known as pleiotropy, or the effect of a single gene on more than one system, and it implies that common mechanisms by common gene action are involved. Conversely, if the two selection lines do not differ on a particular variable, then this variable and sleep time are genetically independent and thus do not share common genetic mechanisms.

Selectively bred lines have been the most productive genetic tool applied to questions of whether all different aspects of drug responses, from sensitivity to drug-seeking behavior, are influenced by the same genes or by independently acting genes. As we shall see, the existence of three separately selected lines of mice and rats for traits related to ethanol dependence severity offers hope that the genetic determination of dependence will be linked genetically to some other trait (correlated responses) in these lines, or to more easily analyzed responses to ethanol, such as sensitivity or tolerance.

The logic for utilizing selected lines and drawing conclusions about genetic influences holds only to the extent that the differences between the bidirectionally selected lines are due to selective breeding and are not due to other events that can occur. For example, a gene or block of genes could be retained in one line and not in the other (as occurs during inbreeding) due to chance factors alone (sampling error) and not because of selection (DeFries, 1981). This possibility can be greatly minimized by: (a) maintaining adequate sample sizes in each generation; (b) adopting measures to minimize inbreeding; (c) employing replicate lines (e.g., two independent sets of bidirectionally selected lines, or a total of four selected lines); and (d) using nonselected control groups.

ANIMAL STUDIES OF ETHANOL

Studies with Inbred Strains

Regardless of which effect of alcohol is considered, inbred strains of rats and mice have been found to differ markedly in response to alcohol (Belknap, 1980a; Horowitz & Dudek, 1983). Since many studies have examined several strains under controlled environmental conditions, such differences are taken as evidence for a genetic contribution to ethanol sensitivity. Three inbred strains of mice have been extensively studied, allowing rather firm conclusions to be drawn. An earlier review (Belknap, 1980a) identified two patterns in the available strain difference data. First, mice from the BALB/c inbred strain were consistently reported to be more sensitive to ethanol's effects than were the other two strains. Their susceptibility to ethanol was documented in several laboratories with several different tasks and doses of alcohol. Since the particular genetic constitution of BALB/c mice was a chance event, we conclude with some confidence that certain random constellations of genes may generally predispose mice to ethanol responsiveness.

The second general conclusion that could be drawn was that the relative sensitivity of the other two frequently studied strains, C57BL/6 and DBA/2, was highly response dependent. C57BL/6 mice were more sensitive to ethanol than DBA/2 mice in some responses but were less sensitive in others. This suggests that diverse physiological systems that underlie different responses to ethanol are responsible for the differential strain sensitivity to various effects of alcohol that characterizes C57 and DBA mice.

More recent studies with inbred strains have generally supported these conclusions. In a study of sensitivity to several effects of ethanol in 20 inbred strains of mice, it was reported that strains differed markedly in all tasks (Crabbe, 1983). Although some (for example, DBA/1J and BALB/cAnN) were generally sensitive or insensitive to ethanol across most tasks, most strains showed response-dependent sensitivity in that they were relatively sensitive on some measures and insensitive on others.

The extent of inbred strain differences in response to ethanol can be extreme in both the magnitude and the direction of response to ethanol treatment. BALB/c (Lapin & Nazarenko, 1978; Randall, Carpenter, Lester, & Friedman, 1975) and DBA/2 (Crabbe, Janowsky, Young, & Rigter, 1980b) mice respond to intraperitoneal ethanol with enhanced activity when tested in an open field whereas C57BL/6 mice show reduced activity (Crabbe *et al.*, 1980b; Lapin & Nazarenko, 1978; Randall, Carpenter, Lester, & Friedman, 1975). The C57 versus DBA/2 comparison is apparent across a range of ethanol doses (Crabbe, Johnson, Gray, Kosobud, and Young, 1982). There is a transient increase in activity in C57 mice before the onset of activity reduction; however, DBA/2 mice show no signs of decreased activity for up to $2\frac{1}{2}$ hours after injection with alcohol. The differences in open-field activity cannot be attributed to either dose of ethanol (Crabbe, Johnson, Gray, Kosobud, & Young, 1982) or its metabolic product, acetaldehyde (Fioriglio, Wood, Hartline, & Schneider, 1980). Thus, these two strains show both quantitative and qualitative differences in response to ethanol treatment. A subsequent experiment with C57, DBA, and BALB mice also replicated the strain-specific nature of open-field response to ethanol (Kiianmaa, Hoffman, & Tabakoff, 1983). They found that naltrexone could antagonize both activating and depressant responses to ethanol in the strains. However, the strains differed in sensitivity to both effects of naltrexone, and their sensitivities to antagonism were not parallel.

Recent experiments have sought to identify the pharmacologic basis for such strain-specific and task-specific sensitivity to ethanol. Kiianmaa and Tabakoff (1983) pursued the strain difference in ethanol's effects on activity by monitoring dopamine metabolism. Ethanol had a biphasic effect on dopamine release in all strains. Stimulated strains (BALB/c and DBA/2) had larger suppressions of dopamine release after low doses of ethanol and smaller increases in dopamine release after high doses than did the depressed strain (C57BL/6). Ethanol also stimulated synthesis of dopamine in monophasic, dose-dependent fashion: C57BL/6 mice were less sensitive to this effect. Tolerance developed to the high-dose but not the low-dose effects of ethanol on dopamine metabolism in all three strains. Thus, the strain-specific and task-specific behavioral responses to ethanol in the open field were paralleled by responses in dopamine metabolism.

As pointed out by Horowitz and Dudek (1983), although it is often assumed that strain differences in response to a drug indicate differential target tissue (e.g., central nervous system) sensitivity, this is usually not demonstrated. Strains may differ in drug absorption, distribution, or other peripheral effects of the drug. Within the central nervous system, the drug may affect membrane channels, receptors, or enzymatic function (Horowitz & Dudek, 1983). The well-known difference in preference for ethanol shown by C57 mice versus DBA mice is probably due, at least in part, to taste (a preabsorptive effect) rather than any postabsorptive phar-macologic effects of the drug (Belknap, Belknap, Berg, & Coleman, 1977; Belknap, Coleman, & Foster, 1978). A recent drug study suggests that ethanol may penetrate the placenta of DBA mice more easily than the placenta of CD-1 or C57 mice to produce embryotoxic and teratogenic effects (Giknis, Damjanov, & Rubin, 1980).

Response-specific sensitivity may indeed not be limited to ethanol but may for some strains extend to other alcohols or sedative-hypnotic compounds. Belknap and Deutsch (1982) studied DBA/2 and C57BL/6 mice for their sensitivity to different alcohols. phenobarbital, and acet-aldehyde by studying stumbling (ambulatory ataxia). They found C57 mice to be more sensitive to all agents than DBA mice. One interpretation of this result is that the genetic difference underlying alcohol sensitivity between these two strains may generalize across compounds in much the same way that certain strains seem to be generally responsive to the effects of a single agent, ethanol, on different tasks.

Two generalizations were offered at the beginning of this section: (1) some constellations of genes, represented by inbred strains, predispose mice for ethanol responsiveness; and (2) relative strain sensitivity to eth-anol is response dependent, which implies that different physiological mechanisms underlie different responses to ethanol. These generaliza-tions apply not only to studies of ethanol sensitivity but also to the development of tolerance, physical dependence (i.e., withdrawal severity), and preference for, or acceptance of, ethanol solutions. Although reports of strain differences in rate and degree of tolerance development are not numerous, they are consistent in reporting large strain differences in mice (Crabbe, Janowsky, Young, Kosobud, Stack, & Rigter, 1982; Crabbe, Johnson, Gray, Kosobud, & Young, 1982; Crabbe, Rigter, & Kerbusch, 1980;

Grieve, Griffiths, & Littleton, 1979; Littleton, Grieve, Griffiths, & John, 1978; Moore & Kakihana, 1978; Tabakoff & Ritzmann, 1979). Studies on inbred strains are thus far in agreement in showing that C57BL/6 mice readily develop both acute and chronic functional tolerance, whereas DBA/2 mice do not (Crabbe, Janowsky, Young, Kosobud, Stack, & Rigter, 1982; Crabbe, Johnson, Gray, Kosobud, & Young, 1982; Grieve et al., 1979; Littleton et al., 1978; Moore & Kakihana, 1978; Tabakoff & Ritzmann, 1979). However, DBA/2 mice develop tolerance at least under some conditions (Parsons, Gallaher, & Goldstein, 1982). It appears that tolerance development as well as initial sensitivity to ethanol is task specific. Masur and Boerngen (1980) noted that genetically heterogeneous (i.e., not inbred, not selected) mice did not develop tolerance to the locomotor-activating effects of ethanol. Subsequent investigations with C57 and DBA (Crabbe, Johnson, Gray, Kosobud, & Young, 1982) and BALB/c inbred mice have confirmed that this failure is to some degree general across strains (Tabakoff & Kiianmaa, 1981).

There are only a few reports of inbred strain differences in withdrawal reactions following chronic alcohol intoxication. After chronic exposure to ethanol vapor inhalation, DBA/2 (Crabbe, Young, & Kosobud, 1983; Goldstein & Kakihana, 1974; Grieve et al., 1979; Griffiths & Littleton, 1977) and BALB/c (Crabbe, Young, & Kosobud, 1983; Goldstein & Kakihana, 1974) mice were much more susceptible to withdrawal reactions than C57BL/6 mice. When dependence was induced with a liquid diet technique (Kakihana, 1979), similar results were observed. One of these studies examined 20 inbred strains of mice (Crabbe, Young, & Kosobud, 1983) and found, in agreement with earlier studies, that corrections for strain differences in blood alcohol concentrations attained did not affect the pattern of results observed. It is worth repeating that in all such experiments the degree of ethanol dependence must be inferred from the degree of withdrawal severity. Thus, strain differences in the sign used to assess dependence on ethanol, rather than any effect of ethanol withdrawal per se, may contribute to apparent withdrawal-severity differences (Horowitz & Dudek, 1983). Although inbred strains are known to differ in the handling-induced convulsion sign typically employed to measure withdrawal severity (Crabbe, Janowsky, Young, & Rigter, 1980a), these differences were also unable to account for the large strain differences in ethanol withdrawal severity (Crabbe, Young, & Kosobud, 1983).

The earliest pharmacogenetic information on ethanol was the observation of McClearn and Rodgers (1959) that inbred strains of mice differed widely in their preference for drinking weak ethanol solutions versus water. There are now many genetic studies of preference drinking and the closely related trait, acceptance, which is defined as the amount of alcohol accepted by animals when it is offered as the only source of fluid. Readers are referred to reviews for discussions of the role of genes in the control of preference and acceptance (Collins, 1979; Drewek, 1980; Kakihana & Butte, 1980). We will summarize here only briefly the findings of preference studies.

Some inbred strains of mice or rats prefer alcohol over a wide range of concentrations and experimental conditions (e.g., C57BL/6), whereas other strains may be characterized as alcohol avoiders (e.g., DBA/2). Most inbred strains, however, display intermediate preference or acceptance. Within most inbred strains, preference is intermediate in two senses. First, average values for these strains fall between those of extreme alcohol-avoiding and alcohol-preferring strains, suggesting determination of preference drinking by multiple genes. Such polygenic determination has also been demonstrated directly (Fuller, 1964; Whitney, McClearn, & DeFries, 1970). Second, within many inbred strains, there is large interanimal variability in preference for and in acceptance of ethanol. Because all mice in an inbred strain are genetically virtually identical, this suggests the importance of environmental factors in addition to, or interacting with, genotypic differences. This can hardly be considered surprising, for taste and smell thresholds and aversions, novelty, osmoregulation, as well as circadian variations, postabsorptive differences, and a number of experimental variables all participate in the differences among inbred strains (Belknap et al., 1977, 1978).

Single-Gene and Quantitative Genetic Techniques

What, then, have more complex genetic analyses been able to tell us about these various ethanol-related traits? A few studies employing single-gene or quantitative analyses have been reported, and we will now turn our attention to these.

The Bailey recombinant inbred strains have been used to study the reduction in ambulatory activity in a toggle box induced by ethanol (Oliverio & Eleftheriou, 1976). Some of the lines, including the C57BL/6 parent strain, showed a marked decline in activity; other lines resembled the BALB/c progenitor strain, with a relatively small decrease in activity following alcohol administration. Because all recombinant inbred strains resembled either one or the other parent inbred strain, it was possible to construct a strain distribution pattern by classifying each recombinant inbred strain as C57-like or BALB-like. The strain distribution suggested the influence of a single gene, designated as *eam* (ethanol activity modifier), which appears to be on Chromosome No. 4. A subsequent experiment tested the Bailey recombinant inbred strains for their sensitivity to the hypothermic effects of intraperitoneal ethanol (Crabbe, Rigter, & Kerbusch, 1980). Large strain differences in sensitivity to ethanol were apparent. No strain distribution suggestive of single-gene control of this response was detected. Studies with this battery of recombinant inbred strains are somewhat limited in statistical power due to the small number (seven) of recombinant inbred lines from this cross.

Another battery of 24 recombinant inbred strains has been developed from the C57BL/6 and DBA/2 strains. One of us has tested the response of 16 of these recombinant inbred strains to several effects of ethanol (Crabbe, Kosobud, Young, & Janowsky, 1983). The CXD recombinant inbred mice were tested for effects of ethanol on loss of righting reflex, locomotor ataxia, open-field activity, hypothermic sensitivity, acceptance of ethanol, and severity of ethanol withdrawal after forced inhalation. The parent strains differed markedly in the effects of ethanol on all measures. The potential influence of a single gene on ethanol acceptance and on ethanol withdrawal severity was detected. However, it was not possible to map either of these putative genes to a specific chromosomal location because their strain distributions did not match those for any mapped gene. Pittman, Rogers, and Bloom (1982) studied tolerance development to ethanol hypothermia in Brattleboro rats. Normal rats exposed to ethanol vapor for 21 days showed tolerance when subsequently challenged with i.p. ethanol. Brattleboro rats, homozygous or heterozygous for diabetes insipidus (due to lacking both, or a single allele of the gene for vasopressin, respectively), did not develop tolerance. This suggests the important influence of the vasopressin gene on alcohol tolerance development.

MacPhail and Elsmore (1980) and Crabbe, Rigter, & Kerbusch (1980) employed ethanol as an agent to induce conditioned taste aversions in C57 and BALB mice and their reciprocal hybrid crosses. The F_1 mice, like the C57 parent, showed the development of aversion, a result consistent with dominant inheritance.

Quantitative studies of alcohol preference have been reviewed by others (Drewek, 1980; Whitney *et al.*, 1970). These studies generally indicate a low heritability (about .10 ± 0.15) of alcohol preference and acceptance. This suggests that only about 10% of the total variability in ethanol-drinking behavior was due to genetic influences. Genetically segregating HS mice were tested for ethanol preference and, subsequently, for the development of physical dependence induced by forced ethanol drinking (Allen, Fantom, & Wilson, 1982). Correlations between preference, withdrawal severity, and the amount of liquid diet consumed were not significant. The authors concluded that these variables were not genetically related. Such a phenotypic correlation has both genetic and nongenetic components. It is possible that the environmental and genetic components of the phenotypic correlation might be operating in different directions, with the result that an actual genetic correlation was masked. Drewek and Broadhurst (1981, 1983) employed a complex quantitative genetic technique (triple test cross) to analyze the genetic architecture of ethanol preference drinking. They reported dominance for low ethanol preference in rats.

Reed (1977) studied approximately 1,500 mice of a genetically heterogeneous stock and calculated genetic correlations between a number of measures of neurosensitivity to ethanol using regression-based methods. His results indicated that the effects of ethanol on body temperature, open-field activity, and heart rate were essentially not genetically correlated. This would argue that genes influencing one of these responses had no influence on the others. Activity may be an exceptional measure of ethanol's effects (e.g., tolerance may not develop to this effect of ethanol) and appears on the basis of several different genetic methodologies to be distinct from measures of ataxia, hypnosis, and hypothermia (Crabbe, 1983; Crabbe & Belknap, 1980). Thus, Reed's finding of genetic independence of these effects of ethanol may not necessarily generalize to other effects of ethanol.

One aspect of the genetic determination of drug response that can be elucidated by quantitative genetic techniques is the functional dependence or independence of different responses for a given drug. For example, the relationship between functional tolerance and dependence is of great interest, largely because most theoretical models presume that development of tolerance necessarily precedes dependence (Kalant *et al.*, 1971). Such a relationship would predict that rate or degree of development of functional tolerance should be positively correlated with the intensity of the withdrawal syndrome when drug administration ceases. If a number of inbred strains are tested for both tolerance and physical dependence, the mean values of the strains on each response may be correlated. This correlation coefficient provides an estimate of the genetic codetermination (genetic correlation) of these variables (Hegmann & Possidente, 1981). Examination of the currently available information for the two most often studied inbred strains suggests that the exact opposite outcome seems to be the case. Although C57BL/6 mice exhibit more functional tolerance development, they show a less severe withdrawal syndrome than do DBA/2 mice. A possible explanation for this is that a strain that rapidly adapts to the presence of alcohol (C57BL/6) may rapidly adapt to its absence and therefore exhibit minimal withdrawal symptoms (Littleton, 1980).

On the other hand, comparison of only two inbred strains is insufficient for determining a correlation because two points determine a straight line. Therefore, one of us (J.C.C.) investigated this relationship in 20 inbred strains of mice. Neurosensitivity to several effects of ethanol (Crabbe, 1983), tolerance to the hypothermic effect of ethanol (Crabbe, Janowsky, Young, Kosobud, Stack, & Rigter, 1982), and ethanol withdrawal severity (Crabbe, Young, & Kosobud, 1983) varied widely in the 20 inbred strains. The correlations between strain mean values suggest that some of the same genes affected several responses to ethanol (Hegmann & Possidente, 1981). Three clusters of variables related to neurosensitivity were detectable: basal activity (in the absence of ethanol), ethanol-induced increases and decreases in activity, and variables related to body temperature and the hypothermic effect of ethanol. These three groups of variables were largely uncorrelated, suggesting that three largely independent constellations of genes underlie the ethanol sensitivity measures studied.

One of the strongest relationships to emerge from these studies was a high genetic correlation ($r = .65$) between initial hypothermic sensitivity and tolerance to the hypothermic effect of ethanol (Crabbe, Janowsky, Young, Kosobud, Stack, & Rigter, 1982). One goal of these experiments was to identify some measure of neurosensitivity that correlated with tolerance and/or physical dependence development. The hypothermic effect of ethanol and tolerance to ethanol hypothermia correlated negatively with ethanol withdrawal severity, suggesting that the hypothermic sensitivity and tolerance in a mouse might serve to predict genetic susceptibility to ethanol withdrawal severity (Crabbe, Young, & Kosobud, 1983).

Analysis of Selected Lines

Introduction. A number of lines of rats or mice have been selected for sensitivity or resistance to different effects of ethanol. To the extent that these studies have been successful in avoiding the pitfalls outlined in the section entitled, "Selective Breeding," these lines should differ principally in genes exerting substantial influence on the trait for which they were selected. As such, any other differences between selected lines probably represent other (pleiotropic) effects of the selected genes. Thus, correlated response changes offer strong inference of common genetic determination of the responses. It must be emphasized that selection studies must be managed with care if results are to be free of confounding with nongenetic factors. Furthermore, if at all possible, selected lines should be replicated during selection so that fortuitous correlations of responses may be detected. To date, only the newest of the selected lines available have been produced under conditions even approximating ideal.

Even with the limitations inherent in their development, much interesting information has been derived from them.

One such set of lines, the Long-sleep and Short-sleep mouse lines, have been rather extensively characterized. We will focus our discussion on research that attempts to identify correlated responses to selection, particularly those correlated with ethanol withdrawal severity and ethanol drug-seeking behavior.

Long-Sleep and Short-Sleep Lines. Beginning with a genetically heterogeneous stock of mice, McClearn and Kakihana (1973) selected for short and long duration of loss of righting reflex after giving a standard i.p. dose of alcohol. A description of the selection study has been given (McClearn & Kakihana, 1981). Long-sleep mice now sleep about 15 times as long as Short-sleep mice after a fixed dose of ethanol, and there is now virtually no overlap between the two selection lines. The realized heritability, or proportion of total variability due to genetic differences, was estimated to be .18 after five generations of selection (McClearn & Kakihana, 1981). For earlier reviews of research with these lines of mice, the reader is referred to reviews by Belknap (1980a), Collins (1979, 1981), Deitrich and Collins (1977), and McClearn and Anderson (1979).

Differences between the Long-sleep and Short-sleep lines in duration of loss of righting reflex are almost entirely due to differences in neurosensitivity. Although metabolic rate is known to be a major determinant of duration of loss of righting reflex after ethanol (Damjanovich & MacInnes, 1973), the rates of alcohol elimination, alcohol dehydrogenase activity, and aldehyde dehydrogenase activity did not differ between Long-sleep and Short-sleep mice from the 12th selected generation (Heston, Erwin, Anderson, & Robbins, 1974; Kakihana, 1977).

Recently, it has been reported that the Short-sleep line achieves lower blood ethanol concentrations than the Long-sleep line and metabolizes ethanol somewhat more rapidly. These relatively small differences were found in mice from the 20th and 21st selected generations and are thought to have been introduced by the necessity for increasing the doses of ethanol given Short-sleep mice and decreasing that given Long-sleep mice as response to selection progressed. Specifically, adjustments made in the 16th selected generation possibly were responsible (Gilliam & Collins, 1982b). Before the differences in metabolism arose, Short-sleep mice regained the righting reflex at blood alcohol concentrations that are 65% higher than those in Long-sleep mice, and the ED_{50} for alcohol-induced loss of righting reflex in Short-sleep mice was about twice that for Long-sleep mice (Erwin *et al.*, 1976; Heston *et al.*, 1974; Tabakoff & Ritzmann, 1979). The selection response was earlier reported to generalize to some of the general depressants, especially the alcohols, but not to all of them;

in particular, the lines did not differ in hypnotic sensitivity to pentobarbital (Erwin *et al.*, 1976; Sanders, Sharpless, Collins, McClearn, & Flanagan, 1978). This implied that the genetic basis for response to depressants is not unitary. A recent investigation of mice from the 28th to 31st selected generations reported that Short-sleep mice were more susceptible to pentobarbital than Long-sleep mice, both in duration of loss of righting reflex and in hypothermic response. These differences were not, however, in central nervous system sensitivity to pentobarbital but rather to a faster rate of barbiturate elimination. This probably represents another change in response characteristics due to changing doses during continued generations of selection (O'Connor, Howerton, & Collins, 1982). The lines do, however, differ in sensitivity to other alcohols, with Long-sleep mice being more sensitive (Howerton, O'Connor, & Collins, 1983).

Short-sleep and Long-sleep mice differ in a number of characteristics besides alcohol sensitivity (Baker, Melchior, & Deitrich, 1980; Church, Fuller, & Dudek, 1976; Dudek & Fanelli, 1980; Kakihana, 1977; Kakihana, 1976; Sanders, 1976; Siemans & Chan, 1976). The Long-sleep and Short-sleep selected mouse lines differ systematically in their response to a number of effects of ethanol. With a few exceptions, the Short-sleep mice appear to be generally insensitive to ethanol, whereas the Long-sleep mice are generally sensitive (Belknap, 1980a; Brick & Horowitz, 1982; Erwin & Towell, 1983; Gilliam & Collins, 1982a, 1982b, 1983; Moore & Kakihana, 1978; Sanders & Sharpless, 1978).

Electrophysiological changes induced by a hypnotic dose of ethanol parallel the behavioral changes (Ryan, Barr, Sanders, & Sharpless, 1979; Sorensen, Dunwiddie, McClearn, Freedman, & Hoffer, 1981; Sorensen, Palmer, Dunwiddie, & Hoffer, 1980; Spuhler, Hoffer, Weiner, & Palmer, 1982). These studies have been reviewed (Seiger, Sorensen, & Palmer, 1983). In an elegant series of experiments, it has been demonstrated that the sensitivity of cerebellar Purkinje neurons to depression of firing by locally applied ethanol is much more marked in Long-sleep than in Short-sleep mice. No differences were seen in other brain areas or when halothane was applied (Sorensen *et al.*, 1980, 1981). When fetal cerebellar grafts from Long-sleep or Short-sleep mice were explanted to the anterior chamber of the eye in a within-line and between-line design, sensitivity of the transplanted tissue was found to resemble exactly that of the donor rather than the recipient (Palmer, Sorensen, Freedman, Olson, Hoffer, & Seiger, 1982). That the sensitivity of Purkinje neurons to ethanol depression is a correlated response to selection and not a fortuitous line difference was verified in an experiment by Spuhler *et al.* (1982). They tested mice from the eight inbred strains from which the Long-sleep/Short-sleep foundation population was derived for sensitivity to ethanol's effect on the loss of the righting reflex and on Purkinje cell firing. Analysis of covariance yielded estimates of heritability of sleep time and sensitivity to firing inhibition of .54 and .77, respectively. When mean values for the two parameters in the eight inbred strains were correlated to estimate the genetic correlation between these parameters, the correlation coefficient was .997. These results strongly imply that the same genes mediate the effects of ethanol on both a behavioral response (sleep time) and on the firing rate of a particular type of nerve cell (Purkinje cells).

Several recent papers have documented neurochemical differences between the lines both before and after ethanol administration (Dibner, Zahniser, Wolfe, Rabin, & Molinoff, 1980; Erwin & Towell, 1983; Horowitz, Dendel, Allan, & Major, 1982; Masserano & Weiner, 1982). Finally, Horowitz and his colleagues (Brick & Horowitz, 1982; Horowitz & Allan, 1982) found that Short-sleep mice suffered more morphine withdrawal than Long-sleep mice and that Short-sleep mice were more sensitive to morphine hypothermia. These findings indicate some degree of common genetic determination of sensitivity to ethanol and morphine, an intriguing suggestion of a common mechanism between these two drugs.

Because Long-sleep and Short-sleep mice were selected strictly on the basis of their acute sensitivity to ethanol, it is of interest to see whether they differ with regard to tolerance and/or physical dependence on ethanol. Results again suggest task-specific differences between the lines. Long-sleep and Short-sleep mice regain their righting reflex at the same blood alcohol concentration at which they lost it; in other words, neither strain displayed acute tolerance to this effect of ethanol. Although Short-sleep mice developed chronic tolerance to the loss of righting reflex faster than did the Long-sleep mice, there was no marked difference between the lines in the development of tolerance to the hypothermic effect of ethanol over 5 days of twice-daily administration of ethanol (Tabakoff, Ritzmann, Raju, & Deitrich, 1980).

Goldstein and Kakihana (1975) exposed mice of both lines to ethanol vapor for 3 days to induce physical dependence. The lines had the same blood alcohol concentrations during intoxication. Short-sleep mice had three to seven times more severe withdrawal convulsions on handling; thus Short-sleep mice were more sensitive to dependence development even though they are less sensitive to the acute hypnotic effects of alcohol. It was suggested that the line differences in withdrawal reactions may have arisen fortuitously during the course of selection because no significant correlation between sleep times and withdrawal reactions was found in the genetically heterogeneous outbred stock from which the

Long-sleep and Short-sleep lines were selected. Alternatively, as mentioned earlier, such a phenotypic correlation may not necessarily reveal the presence of an underlying genetic correlation (Falconer, 1960). Thus, withdrawal intensity and sleep time may indeed be genetically correlated because of the pleiotropism (common gene action).

Most Affected and Least Affected Lines.   Rat lines have been selectively bred for sensitivity and resistance to alcohol-induced reduction in motor activity in a stabilimeter following a 1.5 g/kg i.p. dose of ethanol. Since the 13th generation, there has been no overlap between the two lines. This difference has been thought to result from differential neurosensitivity because the lines had virtually identical rates of alcohol elimination in early selected generations (Lester, Lin, Anandam, Riley, Worsham, & Freed, 1977; Riley, Freed, & Lester, 1976; Riley, Worsham, Lester, & Freed, 1977). Most Affected rats are also more sensitive to pentobarbital, and their alcohol sensitivity extends over a wide dose range, but activity after saline injections is the same in the two lines (Riley, Lochry, & Freed, 1978; Worsham & Freed, 1977; Worsham, Riley, Anandam, Lister, Freed, & Lester, 1977). A recent experiment (Mayer, Khanna, Kalant, & Chau, 1982) has reported that Most Affected male rats metabolize ethanol more slowly than Least Affected male rats, but no differences were found between females or in the rate of metabolism of pentobarbital. These investigators failed to find sensitivity differences between the lines to pentobarbital. Shapiro and Riley (1980) demonstrated that Most Affected rats were more impaired in one-way and two-way shuttle avoidance tasks than Least Affected rats, whereas Least Affected rats had higher levels of wheel-turning activity. Bass and Lester (1981a) found greater impairment after ethanol in an escape jumping task in Most Affected rats.

Thus, Most Affected rats are generally more sensitive to ethanol than their Least Affected counterparts. However, Least Affected rats were more impaired by alcohol in a swim escape task (Bass & Lester, 1979). Bass and Lester (1983) demonstrated that the implied negative genetic correlation between swim impairment and activity impairment in the lines did not result in a negative phenotypic correlation on these variables in animals from the segregating F_2 population derived from the cross of the lines. Although this is not conclusive evidence for a lack of genetic correlation, as we have noted, Bass and Lester also demonstrated that the two responses loaded on different factors derived from principal component analysis, strengthening the interpretation of fortuitous association. As we discussed earlier, such an "accidental" line difference could have occurred when a set of relevant genes was not transmitted to any offspring in one line because the only rats possessing those genes were not chosen to mate. Also, Most Affected and Least Affected animals do not differ when tested on the moving belt test (Lester *et al.*, 1977), a measure that emphasizes alcohol-induced motor incoordination (ataxia) rather than activity (Gibbins, Kalant, & LeBlanc, 1968). ethanol administered every other day by intubation for 19 days induced tolerance to its hypoactivating effect in the Most Affected line but not in the Least Affected line (Riley & Lochry, 1977). However, the lines developed about the same degree of tolerance to the hypnotic effect of ethanol assessed with the sleep time test. Most aspects of sensitivity differences between the lines have been reviewed (Bass and Lester, 1981b).

Alcohol Nontolerant and Alcohol Tolerant Lines. Rat lines are currently being selected at the Alko Laboratories in Finland for sensitivity (Alcohol Nontolerant) and resistance (Alcohol Tolerant) to alcohol-induced (2 g/kg) impairment on a tilting plane test (ability to remain on a board that is gradually tilted away from the horizontal) and rotarod performance (ability to maintain balance on a rotating dowel). After several generations, there is more than a twofold difference between the lines bred for sensitivity (Alcohol Nontolerant: ANT) and insensitivity (Alcohol Tolerant: AT) to alcohol, respectively, on both measures (Ericksson & Rusi, 1981). The Alcohol Tolerant rats have been tested for voluntary ethanol consumption and were found to drink twice the amount of 10% ethanol solution versus water as the Alcohol Nontolerant rats. During forced ethanol consumption, this difference was not evident, and differences in preference between the lines were no longer apparent in a posttest period. Volumes of ethanol consumed were well within the metabolic capacity of rats (Ericksson & Rusi, 1981).

ALKO Alcohol, Alcohol (AA), and ALKO Nonalcohol (ANA) Rats. Eriksson has also selectively bred rats for high (Alko Alcohol) and low (Alko Nonalcohol) preference (K. Eriksson, 1968, 1975). These animals have been most intensively studied for biochemical and metabolic variables related to ethanol drinking (Inoue, Rusi, & Lindros, 1980; Rusi, Eriksson, & Maki, 1977; York, 1981). An extensive review of the experiments with these lines has appeared (C. J. P. Eriksson, 1981) that concludes that at least three factors regulate drinking in these lines, namely caloric need, acetaldehyde avoidance, and intoxication avoidance.

P and NP Rats. Lumeng, Li, and their colleagues are conducting a selection study in rats who prefer (Preferring) and who do not prefer (Nonpreferring) alcohol solutions (Lumeng, Hawkins, & Li, 1977). Early results with these lines were recently reviewed (Li, Lumeng, McBride, & Waller, 1981). Preferring rats drink 10 to 12 g/kg ethanol per day, an amount in excess of their metabolic capacity. There is no difference in ethanol metabolism between the lines. Nonpreferrring rats were found to be more sensitive to ethanol hypothermia and loss of righting reflex. Recent reports from this group have shown that Preferring rats are less sensitive to ethanol impairment on an escape jumping task (Lumeng, Waller, McBride, & Li, 1982). Also, Preferring rats have generally lower serotonin and serotonin metabolite levels in several brain areas than Nonpreferring rats, whereas the lines do not differ markedly in catecholamine concentrations (Murphy, McBride, Lumeng, & Li, 1982). Most importantly, Preferring rats will voluntarily drink sufficient ethanol to exhibit signs of withdrawal after 15 to 20 weeks (Waller, McBride, Lumeng, & Li, 1982a). Finally, infusions of ethanol or treatment with ethanol metabolism inhibitors were both effective in reducing consumption in Preferring rats (Waller, McBride, Lumeng, & Li, 1982b). They interpreted this to indicate that the pharmacologic effects of ethanol rather than taste or smell factors were the more important regulators of ethanol drinking. These lines of rats should prove to be valuable models for studies designed to uncover genetic correlates of dependence susceptibility.

Lines Selected for Ethanol Withdrawal Intensity. D. B. Goldstein (1973) first demonstrated that lines could be selectively bred for ethanol withdrawal severity, but her mouse lines were not maintained. Two groups are currently developing lines of mice that differ in ethanol withdrawal severity. Investigators at the Institute for Behavioral Genetics are conducting a within-family selection for severity of withdrawal after chronic treatment with a liquid diet containing ethanol (Allen, Petersen, Wilson, McClearn, & Nishimoto, 1983). These lines are derived from the HS (heterogeneous Stock) that served as the parent population for the Long-sleep and Short-sleep mouse lines. Mice are selected for severe ethanol withdrawal or mild ethanol withdrawal on the basis of an index derived from seven withdrawal signs. The lines are replicated, so that two Severe Ethanol Withdrawal and two Mild Ethanol Withdrawal lines are being selected; two unselected control lines are also maintained. After five generations of selection, the lines differ in withdrawal severity. There is asymmetry in response to selection; Severe Ethanol Withdrawal lines are diverging more rapidly than Mild Ethanol Withdrawal lines. Realized heritability after five generations is approximately .15. The seven variables comprising the selection index were approximately equally weighted at the start of selection (McClearn, Wilson, Peterson, & Allen, 1982). The same factor structure was apparent after five generations of selection, suggesting that the same character was still being selected (Allen *et al.,* 1983). These lines await testing for correlated responses to selection.

The other ongoing selection also is derived from the HS mouse stock (Crabbe, Kosobud, & Young, 1983). Mice rendered physically dependent on ethanol by ethanol vapor inhalation are scored for withdrawal severity using the handling-induced convulsion. Within-family selection is employed. One male and one female mouse from each of the nine original families (litters) were chosen at random to constitute a control (Withdrawal Seizure Control) line. The Withdrawal Seizure Control lines thus serve as controls for the small but unavoidable degree of inbreeding. From the remaining mice, the highest male and female from each family were chosen for the Withdrawal Seizure Prone line and the lowest scoring male and female from each family were chosen for the Withdrawal Seizure Resistant line. The experiment is replicated; thus, there are two Withdrawal Seizure Prone, two Withdrawal Seizure Resistant, and two Withdrawal Seizure Control lines that are maintained and selected completely independently. Thus, this selection differs from the Colorado selection in the method of ethanol administration and in the index of withdrawal. In most other respects (foundation stock, use of replicated within-family selection, approximate breeding population size), the studies are quite similar.

Selection has progressed to Generation S_{11} and is continuing. Withdrawal Seizure Prone mice were reported to have significantly higher seizure scores than Withdrawal Seizure Control mice after five selected generations, (Crabbe, Kosobud, & Young, 1983). Response to selection in the direction of resistance to ethanol dependence is less marked, but the difference between Withdrawal Seizure Resistant and Withdrawal Seizure Control mice is statistically significant. Factors other than sensitivity differences in ethanol withdrawal severity could not account for the line differences. Blood ethanol concentrations at the time of withdrawal did not differ significantly within either sex for either replication. Therefore, the line differences in withdrawal severity are probably due to functional (central nervous system) rather than dispositional mechanisms such as rates of metabolism, absorption, or distribution. There were only small differences among the lines in either baseline handling-induced convulsions or in the very slight effect of pyrazole on handling-induced convulsions (Crabbe, Kosobud, & Young, 1983).

Mice from the Withdrawal Seizure Prone and Withdrawal Seizure Resistant lines were rendered physically dependent and compared systematically for a number of withdrawal signs other than handling convulsions. Withdrawal Seizure Prone mice displayed more severe tremor than did Withdrawal Seizure Resistant mice during withdrawal. In addition, Withdrawal Seizure Resistant mice showed a high incidence of backward walking. Nonsignificant differences between the lines were found for changes in open-field activity, hyperreactivity, and the rate of metabolism of ethanol after withdrawal (Kosobud, Crabbe, & Tam, 1984). The LD_{50} to pentylenetetrazole-, picrotoxin-, bicuculline-, strychnine-, and electroconvulsive shock-induced seizures in the lines was determined to see if Withdrawal Seizure Prone mice had simply developed excitable nervous systems during selection. The LD$_{50}$'s did not differ significantly (McSwigan, Crabbe, & Young, 1984). Belknap, Crabbe, Danielson, & Lamé (1984b) rendered Withdrawal Seizure Prone and Withdrawal Seizure Resistant mice physically dependent on phenobarbital by feeding them a drug admixed chow. Withdrawal Seizure Prone mice achieved significantly greater withdrawal scores than did Withdrawal Seizure Resistant mice at identical brain phenobarbital concentrations. In other work (Harris, Crabbe, & McSwigan, 1984) rigidity of brain synaptosomal membranes was found not to differ between Withdrawal Seizure Prone and Withdrawal Seizure Resistant mice. Induction of physical dependence on ethanol increased membrane rigidity in both lines to the same extent. Thus, early studies with these mice suggest that (1) the Withdrawal Seizure Prone and Withdrawal Seizure Resistant lines differ principally in their severity of withdrawal from ethanol; (2) other withdrawal signs than convulsions have been affected by the selective breeding; (3) differences in metabolism of ethanol, administered dose of ethanol, or in the general excitability of the central nervous system between the lines cannot account for the ethanol withdrawal differences; (4) there is genetic cross-dependence between ethanol and phenobarbital; and (5) a parameter of brain synaptosomal membrane order appears not to be related to the genetic predisposition to develop ethanol physical dependence.

Other Selected Lines. Anderson and McClearn (1981) have selected mice for acceptance (High Ethanol Acceptance) or rejection (Low Ethanol Acceptance) of alcohol solutions offered without alternatives. The successful selection for this character provides *ipso facto* evidence for genetic control, but no other studies have as yet been reported with these lines. The classic selection study involving alcohol preference in rats is that of Mardones and co-workers. A recent review (Mardones & Segovia-Riquelme, 1983) summarizes 32 years of work with these lines (UChA, Nondrinkers; UChB, Drinkers). The development of tolerance to the effect of ethanol on loss of righting reflex was reported in lines of rats bred for high (UChB) and low (UChA) consumption. Only the UChA rats developed tolerance under the conditions tested (Tampier, Quintanilla, & Mardones, 1981).

ANIMAL PHARMACOGENETIC STUDIES WITH OPIATES

STUDIES WITH INBRED STRAINS

Over the past few years a rather impressive amount of research has been conducted with opiate compounds using various inbred strains, most commonly the BALB/c, C57BL/6, and DBA/2 mouse strains. Much of this work has been recently reviewed by Oliverio and Castellano (1981), Horowitz (1981), Horowitz and Dudek (1983), Shuster (1984), and Crabbe and Belknap (1980), so only some of the highlights will be noted here with regard to the more commonly studied strains. The previously mentioned reviews should be consulted for a more complete picture of this area of research.

DBA/2 mice have frequently been reported to exhibit a greater opiate-induced analgesic response to i.p. or i.c.v. morphine, butorphanol, buprenorphine, d-amino acids, met-enkephalin and enkephalin analogs than do mice of the C57BL/6 strain on the hot plate test (Alleva, Castellano, & Oliverio, 1980; Eidelberg, Erspamer, Kreinick, & Harris, 1975; Filibeck, Castellano, & Oliverio, 1981a, 1981b; Frigeni, Bruno, Carenzi, Racagni, Santini, 1978; Oliverio & Castellano, 1974; Racagni, Bruno, Iuliano, Longiave, Mandelli, and Berti, 1978; Racagni, Bruno, Iulinao, & Paoletti, 1979). To some extent these marked strain differences may be due to experimental (learning?) effects because all of the previously mentioned authors used repeated hot plate tests following, and sometimes before, the injection of the narcotic analgesic (Collins & Whitney, 1978; Horowitz, 1981). However, when experiential effects were eliminated by using a single exposure to the hot plate, Belknap, Oordewier, Lamé, and Danielson (1984) still found DBA/2 mice to exhibit greater analgesia then C57BL/6 mice based on latencies to paw lick. The C3H/He and BALB/c strains appear to more closely resemble the DBA/2 strain rather than the C57BL/6 strain on this measure of analgesia (Belknap et al., 1984; Eidelberg et al., 1975; Oliverio & Castellano, 1974). In contrast, when the tail-flick test of analgesia is used, the C57BL/6 strain shows a greater response than the BALB/c strain (Baran, Shuster, Eleftheriou, & Bailey, 1975; Shuster, Webster, Yu, & Eleftheriou, 1975). With the writhing test of analgesia, the C57BL/6 and DBA/2 strains show roughly equal analgesic responses (Brase, Loh, & Way, 1977). Overall, these results suggest a high degree of genetic independence among these three measures of analgesia, implying that rather different traits are being assessed. This conclusion is in accord with most of the evidence from nongenetic sources (Tyers, 1980).

Substantial doses of morphine and similar drugs have long been known to produce a marked increase in activity ("running fit") in Swiss-Webster mice (Goldstein & Sheehan, 1969), but among inbred strains, this effect is highly strain dependent. The C57BL/6 strain exhibits marked increases in open-field or "toggle box" activity in response to a wide range of morphine doses, whereas the DBA/2 strain does not (Brase et al., 1977; Collins & Whitney, 1978; Filibeck et al., 1981b; Frigeni et al., 1978; Hynes & Berkowitz, 1982; Muraki, Uzumaki, & Kato, 1982; Oliverio & Castellano, 1974; Racagni et al., 1979; Sansone & Oliverio, 1980). The C3H/He and

BALB/c strains are also "runners," although to a lesser extent than C57BL6 mice, whereas the A and AKR strains are essentially "nonrunners" (Belknap et al., 1984a; Brase et al., 1977; Horowitz, 1981; Hynes & Berkowitz, 1982; Muraki et al., 1982; Oliverio & Castellano, 1974; Sansone & Oliverio, 1980; Shuster et al., 1975).

The recent lively interest in opiate receptors has led to a number of studies using inbred strains. Shuster (1984) found the Jackson (J) subline of the C57BL/6 strain to exhibit only half of the apparent number of ^{3}H-dihydromorphine binding sites as the Bailey (By) subline, whereas no difference was seen with ^{3}H-naloxone. Baran et al. (1975) and Eidelberg et al. (1975) found no difference in ^{3}H-naloxone binding in the whole brain between C57BL/6 and BALB/c mice, but a markedly lower apparent number of receptors were found in the CXBK strain, one of the seven recombinant inbred strains developed by Bailey (1971) from a BALB/c × C57BL/6 cross (Baran et al., 1975). These mice also have been reported to show poor development of electropuncture analgesia, a response attributed to endogenous opiate activity (Peets & Pomeranz, 1978). Reggiani, Battaini, Kobayashi, Spano, and Trabucchi (1980) found no differences between DBA/2 and C57BL/6 mice in ^{3}H-naloxone or ^{3}H-dihydromorphine binding in any part of the brain that was examined. However, the apparent number of ^{3}H-Leu-enkephalin binding sites was considerably higher in C57BL/6 relative to DBA/2 mice in the striatum but not in the other brain areas studied. In contrast, based on a Scatchard analysis of ^{3}H-naloxone binding in whole brain P_2 preparation, Belknap et al. (1984) found a significantly higher apparent number (B_{max}) of receptor sites in DBA/2 and C3H/He mice relative to C57BL/6 mice (about 30% more), whereas the C3H/He strain exhibited a lower binding affinity (40% higher K_D) than the other two strains, which were approximately equal in this respect. Thus, these in vitro receptor characteristics of the DBA/2 strain suggest a greater opiate sensitivity relative to those of the C57BL/6 strain and perhaps also the C3H/He strain. Of course, many factors determine in vivo opiate sensitivity in addition to whole brain receptor binding. For example, Brase et al. (1977) found that a half hour after a fixed i.p. dose of morphine, the brain concentrations of the drug were about 50% higher in the C57BL/6 and C3H/He strains compared to the DBA/2 strain, which suggests considerable dispositional differences (metabolism, absorption, distribution) among these strains. Several of us (Belknap et al., 1984) have recently replicated these findings. Recently, Barbaccia, Reggiana, Spano, and Trabucchi (1981) reported a much higher septal met-enkephalin concentration in DBA/2 mice versus C57BL/6, which is of interest partly because some of the actions of morphine may be mediated by met-enkephalin release (e.g., Basbaum & Fields, 1978). Second messenger involvement (cAMP, cGMP) may also play a role vis-à-vis strain differences in opiate sensitivity (Racagni *et al.*, 1978, 1979).

With regard to tolerance acquisition as assessed by daily repetitions of the hot plate and the running response, the C57BL/6 strain exhibited greater tolerance on both measures than the BALB/c strain, whereas the DBA/2 strain showed the least tolerance of all for activity and greatest degree of tolerance on the hot plate (Eidelberg *et al.*, 1975; Oliverio & Castellano, 1974). Thus, the strain exhibiting the greatest initial response also developed the greatest degree of tolerance on both measures.

A recent experiment suggests that opioid tolerance may be genetically determined even insofar as its presence or absence (Ternes, Ehrman, & O'Brien, 1983). Although rhesus monkeys were found to acquire tolerance to the sedative effects of hydromorphine infusions on food-reinforced lever pressing, cynomolgus monkeys showed no tolerance after more than 100 exposures. Rhesus monkeys also showed naloxone precipitated withdrawal whereas cynomolgus did not. Such a species difference is consistent with genetic mediation of opioid tolerance and physical dependence. To study physical dependence, almost all of the reported experiments have used the jumping response in rodents following serial opiate injections or morphine pellet implantation, and large inbred strain differences appear to be the norm (Brase *et al.*, 1977; Eidelberg *et al.*, 1975; Ho, Loh, & Way, 1977; Huang, 1980; Reinhard, Kosersky, & Peterson, 1976). Among the more commonly used inbred strains, the C57BL/6J strain seems to exhibit a greater sensitivity to naloxone-induced jumping than the BALB/c strain (Eidelberg *et al.*, 1975; Reinhard *et al.*, 1976). It is highly probable that the brain morphine concentrations were not equivalent across strains in spite of the administration of equal drug doses. Brase *et al.* (1977) reported widely differing brain concentrations of morphine among six mouse strains implanted with equivalent morphine pellets.

Drug-seeking behavior has been relatively infrequently studied. Horowitz and his colleagues (Horowitz, 1981; Horowitz, Whitney, Smith, & Stephan, 1977) found C57BL/6 mice to exhibit a marked preference for a morphine–saccharine solution over water when presented with a two-bottle choice situation, whereas most of the other six strains studied showed an avoidance. In C57BL/6 mice, the intake of morphine can be quite substantial, reaching 500 mg/kg per day in some experiments (Belknap *et al.* 1984a) and resulting in a marked degree of physical dependence as evidenced by a number of withdrawal signs, both with and without naloxone challenge (Belknap, 1980b).

One can summarize this section concerning inbred strains by noting how often in the preceding review the C57BL/6 strain has been reported to be unique in its response to opiate drugs. This strain is also singular in many responses to ethanol. Following opiate administration, the C57BL/6 strain has distinguished itself as a marked "runner" (hyperactive) in the open field, low on hot-plate-assessed analgesia, very sensitive to naloxone-induced jumping after chronic morphine exposure, and a very high intake of morphine–saccharin solutions when given a choice with water. In contrast, the DBA/2 strain is frequently reported to be opposite on all of these opiate-sensitive measures. No doubt, the frequent choice of these two strains by most investigators is a reflection of their contrasting pattern of opiate responses.

Selective Breeding Studies

Nichols and Hsiao (1967) selectively bred rats for high and low consumption of (and preference for) morphine solutions after the rats had previously been chronically exposed to several cycles of serial i.p. morphine injections and subsequent withdrawal. A large divergence between the two bidirectionally selected lines (about fourfold) was apparent in voluntary morphine consumption after three generations of selection. A parallel difference was also seen in voluntary alcohol consumption following the same chronic i.p. morphine treatment, suggesting a genetic commonality between morphine and alcohol on this measure of preference. These lines no longer exist.

Beginning with a Swiss Webster foundation population, Judson and Goldstein (1978) bidirectionally selected for high and low levorphanol-induced locomotor activity ("running fit") in mice. After three generations of selection, a 3.5-fold difference between the high ("runner") and low ("nonrunner") selection lines was evident. Selection progress was unusually rapid in the low activity line, suggesting that there may be one or two single genes accounting for much of this rapid response (Falconer, 1960). The low activity line, which was the least sensitive to the activity-increasing effects of levorphanol, was found to be the most sensitive to the antinociceptive effects of this drug on the hot plate. This suggests an inverse relationship (negative genetic correlation) between activity and hot-plate-assessed analgesia, which is supported by most of the inbred strain data reviewed before and the nociceptive response selection project described later. The selection for "running fits" has been allowed to lapse.

The most recent selection project involving opiates is that of Belknap, Haltli, Goebel, and Lamé (1982, 1983) based on hot-plate-assessed analgesia in response to i.p. levorphanol, a morphinelike narcotic analgesic. After 10 generations of selective breeding, the Low Antinociceptive Response line had a fivefold higher effective dose of levorphanol than the High Antinociceptive Response line to achieve a doubling of hot plate reaction latency scores relative to those seen with saline injections. Similar selection line differences were also seen with morphine. Throughout this project, each mouse was exposed to the hot plate only once to eliminate possible conditioning effects. Brain concentrations of levorphanol (and morphine) were found to be closely similar in the two selected lines (and in the control line), so the High Antinociceptive Response/Low Antinociceptive Response line differences in analgesic response are due to differential central nervous system sensitivity rather than dispositional factors such as differences in rates of drug metabolism, absorption, or permeability of the blood–brain barrier. The tail-flick and writhing tests of analgesia yielded no significant differences between the High Antinociceptive Response and Low Antinociceptive Response lines in the seventh selected generation, indicating a high degree of genetic independence among these measures, as was the case among the inbred strain studies reviewed previously. On other measures sensitive to opiates, the High Antinociceptive Response line was found to be less active in the open field and more sensitive to hypothermia and Straub tail after levorphanol compared to the Low Antinociceptive Response line across a wide range of i.p. doses. No selection line differences were seen in naloxone-induced jumping or "wet dog" shakes in mice chronically implanted with a morphine pellet. No significant differences in ^{3}H-naloxone binding in the whole brain or in spinal cord P_2 preparations were evident in terms of opiate receptor density (B_{max}) or affinity (K_D) derived from Scatchard plots (fourth and fifth selected generations), but the trends were in the expected direction. Binding studies on more localized anatomical areas and with different ligands are needed here.

ANIMAL PHARMACOGENETIC STUDIES WITH BARBITURATES

STUDIES WITH INBRED STRAINS

With regard to short-acting barbiturates, by far the most common measure of *in vivo* sensitivity has been duration of loss of the righting reflex ("sleep time"). Although rather large inbred strain differences have frequently been reported, these appear to be largely due to dispositional factors (especially differential rates of metabolism), which is beyond the scope of this review (Jay, 1955; Lush & Lovell, 1978; Vesell, 1968). Our present knowledge concerning functional (central-nervous-system-mediated) factors can be rather briefly summarized because the number of published studies is rather small.

Vesell (1968) found no significant differences in brain hexobarbital concentrations at the time of regaining the righting reflex among 15 mouse strains, including the C57BL/6, DBA/2, and BALB/c strains. In contrast, more recent studies using pentobarbital found the C57BL/6 strain to be more sensitive than either the BALB/c or DBA/2 strain based on brain concentrations of the drug at time of regaining the righting reflex (Chan & Siemens, 1979; Randall & Lester, 1974; Siemens & Chan, 1976). These findings do not parallel those regarding ethanol reviewed previously, suggesting that different mechanisms are operating for ethanol versus pentobarbital on this measure of sensitivity.

TOLERANCE AND PHYSICAL DEPENDENCE

Chan and Siemens (1979) measured blood and brain pentobarbital concentrations at the time of the loss of the righting reflex and again when the righting reflex was regained. DBA/2 mice showed clear evidence of acute tolerance development, whereas C57BL/6 mice showed none at all. This is the reverse of findings with ethanol reviewed before in this chapter. With regard to chronic tolerance and physical dependence, Yamamoto and Ho (1978) reported strain differences among five mouse strains in righting reflex loss, tolerance, and cumulative mortality following 48 hours of pentobarbital pellet implantation. These differences may be due to dispositional factors rather than functional ones. Belknap and his co-workers reported that the DBA/2 strain exhibits a greater withdrawal syndrome intensity than does the C57BL/6 strain following chronic exposure to a phenobarbital-admixed powdered diet (Belknap, Ondrusek, Berg, & Waddingham, 1977; Belknap, Waddingham, & Ondrusek, 1973). The DBA/2 strain was found to exhibit much higher brain phenobarbital concentrations under these conditions than the C57BL/6 strain in spite of equivalent intakes of the drug. This indicates that the strain differences in withdrawal severity are largely due to differential rates of drug metabolism. However, the pattern of withdrawal signs is quite different between these two strains; the C57BL/6 strain is more susceptible to tremor and tonic-clonic seizures and much less susceptible to wild running and hyperactivity than the DBA/2 strain (Belknap & Mitchell, 1981; Ondrusek, Belknap, & Leslie, 1979).

CONCLUSIONS

As we have discussed earlier, human and animal pharmacogenetic investigations share the common goal of ascertaining the presence (and degree) of genetic influence on drug-related traits. Human experiments further attempt to identify what the inherited factors are that lead to an individual's genetic susceptibility or resistance to drug abuse. Because they are one step removed from the ultimate problem of human abuse, animal experiments generally address the complementary goals of identifying suitable animal models for drug effects and then systematically exploring more fundamental questions with those animal models (e.g., the relevant mechanism of action or relationships among drug sensitivity and tolerance). This divergence in the goals of human and animal studies requires that their success be assessed somewhat differently, and we will undertake this in this section.

Human studies have, in our opinion, established clearly that an increased risk to develop alcoholism may be inherited. Studies employing different methods agree that a close biological relationship to an alcoholic predisposes individuals *on the average* to develop drinking problems. The biological mechanism mediating this increased genetic susceptibility is as yet uncertain. For example, few studies have clearly distinguished altered sensitivity to particular drug effects or specific differences in drug-directed behavior in genetically predisposed individuals as compared to those not genetically at risk. Ongoing research is tending more frequently to focus on these critical distinctions, and solid results seem likely to emerge before too long. There is, at this point, a vanishingly small human literature addressing genetic predisposition to other substances of abuse.

Animal studies have demonstrated unequivocally that virtually all responses to alcohol are influenced to some extent by hereditary factors. Because myriad effects of the drug have been explored in a variety of genotypes and environmental conditions, it seems unlikely that any important aspect of alcohol's pharmacology will turn out to be free of genetic influence. The smaller literature with opiates and barbiturates is not as extensive in any regard (genotypes, response systems, specific agents studied), but all the existing evidence suggests that genotypic influences will emerge as being similarly important for these and all other classes of psychoactive agents. Thus, animal as well as human experiments have successfully attained or are well underway toward attainment of their first goal, that of demonstrating and quantifying the importance of genetic influence in understanding drug responses.

The research reviewed in this chapter has led to the identification of some very interesting and potentially important animal models for drug effects. For example, the widely available and relatively inexpensive BALB/c inbred mouse strain seems to be a good basic preparation for studying the sensitivity of the nervous system to ethanol. A number of behavioral and more obviously physiological responses to ethanol seem to be pronounced in this strain. Conversely, the C57BL/6 inbred mouse strain seems to be idiosyncratic in its sensitivity not only to alcohol but also to opiates and barbiturates. This suggests that it is perhaps not the best strain for studies that one hopes to generalize to the entire species, but it can be an excellent choice for studying phenomena known to be clearly exhibited by this strain (e.g., morphine or alcohol preference).

The animal models thus identified are already being exploited for more in depth studies directed toward drug mechanisms. For a number of reasons discussed throughout this review, those lines of mice and rats genetically selected for a particular response to a drug offer extremely valuable models for subsequent mechanism-oriented experiments. An important objective in this review has been to summarize studies aimed at characterizing potentially useful animal models, so as to encourage more work to exploit their usefulness especially at a more molecular level. For example, the Long-sleep and Short-sleep selected mouse lines have profited from the advantage of seniority with its resultant thorough characterization. The recent experiments on Purkinje cell sensitivity in these lines should greatly further understanding of the mechanism of ethanol's hypnotic effects. Lines selected for ethanol withdrawal and self-administration phenotypes seem to us to offer hope of similar advances in understanding the critical mechanisms underlying these central characteristics of drug abuse. Lines selected for sensitivity to opiate analgesia should also be of great help, for example, in sorting out the role of multiple opiate receptors and the drugs that interact with them to produce analgesia.

Finally, we would like to offer a number of general observations that we believe have emerged from the pharmacogenetic literature on drugs of abuse. Some of these are not particularly novel, but they are clearly exemplified from the genetic approaches undertaken. Thus, they are in a sense epiphenomena of the commitment shared by researchers in this area to develop and explore good animal models. In modern times, few investigators would deny genetic influence on any measurable drug-related trait. We submit, however, that many investigators tend to conceive of drug responses somewhat monolithically. For example, the general tendency is to speak of "ethanol tolerance" when one is actually studying only tolerance to a single effect of the drug, such as hypothermia. A clear conclusion from the pharmacogenetic literature is that genetic control, although omnipresent, is response specific. Inbred strains sensitive to ethanol's hypothermic effect may be highly insensitive to ethanol's effect to reduce activity. Although this lack of generality of genetic control may seem at first to be an obstacle, it also represents the specificity that will allow animal models to achieve their ultimate goal of predicting individual differences in susceptibility to develop physical dependence.

A related manifestation of this principle is that drug responses, particularly behavioral responses, are quite specific. For example, "analgesia" assessed by one technique may be determined by very different mechanisms from "analgesia" assessed by another technique. Lines selected for opiate-induced analgesia (High Antinociceptive Response, Low Antinociceptive Response line) measured on a hot plate may not differ in sensitivity to analgesia measured by the tail-flick test or writhing test. Thus, particulars of the task studied are an important component of the behavioral pharmacogenetic paradigm. This issue seems especially important when the phenotype investigated is withdrawal from physical dependence. Withdrawal is clearly a multifaceted phenomenon, and genetic control of withdrawal may not extend equally to all components. Additionally, some genes may influence some components of withdrawal whereas others influence different components. A lucid discussion of this point is found in Horowitz and Dudek (1983). It is interesting that some biomedical consequences of alcoholism may be independently influenced by heredity (Hrubeck & Omenn, 1981), suggesting that this caveat applies directly to human studies.

Studies with inbred strains and selected lines suggest that those genotypes highly sensitive to a given effect of a drug may indeed have a greater tendency to develop tolerance to that effect with extended drug exposure. Thus, animal models may lead to greater conceptual clarity regarding the pharmacological relationships among sensitivity, tolerance, dependence, withdrawal, and drug-seeking activity.

Finally, genetic studies have clearly illustrated that some responses to a particular drug may be pharmacologically idiosyncratic. Tolerance does not seem to develop to the activity-stimulating properties of ethanol in mice, although this effect may be antagonized differentially with opiate antagonists in different strains. How the repeated administration of a compound can lead to tolerance to some effects and not tolerance to other effects (see Okamoto, Boisse, Rosenbert, & Rosen, 1978) may fruitfully be analyzed in genetically appropriate subject populations.

In summary, individual differences in the susceptibility of humans to abuse drugs have a demonstrable genetic component. The increasing availability and intensity of study of animal models for highly articulated pharmacogenetic responses is leading to a growing ability to control and study critical responses in the laboratory. Together, the human and animal genetic experiments are progressing toward the common goal of furthering our understanding of what factors genetically predispose some individuals to drug abuse.

ACKNOWLEDGMENTS

We thank Helen Hall for her painstaking help with the manuscript.

REFERENCES

Allen, D. L., Fantom, H. J., & Wilson, J. R. Lack of association between preference for and dependence on ethanol. *Drug and Alcohol Dependence*, 1982, *9*, 119–125.

Allen, D. L., Petersen, D. R., Wilson, J. R., McClearn, G. E., & Nishimoto, T. K. Selective breeding for a multivariate index of ethanol dependence in mice: Results from the first five generations. *Alcoholism: Clinical & Experimental Research*, 1983, *7*, 443–447.

Alleva, E., Castellano, C., & Oliverio, A. Effects of L- and D-amino acids on analgesia and locomotor activity of mice: Their interaction with morphine. *Brain Research*, 1980, *198*, 249–252.

Altman, P. L., & Katz, D. D. *Inbred and genetically defined strains of laboratory animals*. Bethesda, M.D.: F.A.S.E.B., 1979.

Anderson, S. M., & McClearn, G. E. Ethanol consumption: Selective breeding in mice. *Behavior Genetics*, 1981, *11*, 291–301.

Bailey, D. W. Recombinant-inbred strains: An aid to finding identity, linkage and function of histocompatibility and other genes. *Transplantation*, 1971, *11*, 325–327.

Baker, R., Melchior, C., & Deitrich, R. The effect of halothane on mice selectively bred for differential sensitivity to alcohol. *Pharmacology Biochemistry and Behavior*, 1980, *12*, 691–695.

Baran, A., Shuster, L., Eleftheriou, B. E., & Bailey, D. W. Opiate receptors in mice: Genetic differences. *Life Sciences*, 1975, *17*, 633–640.

Barbaccia, M. L., Reggiani, A., Spano, P., & Trabucchi, M. Ethanol-induced changes in dopaminergic function in three strains of mice characterized by a different population of opiate receptors. *Psychopharmacology*, 1981, *74*, 260–262.

Basbaum, A. I., & Fields, H. Endogenous pain control mechanisms: Review and hypothesis. *Annals of Neurology*, 1978, *4*, 451–462.

Bass, M. B., & Lester, D. Rats bred for ethanol sensitivity: Impairment of swimming by ethanol and pentobarbital. *Psychopharmacology*, 1979, *63*, 161–167.

Bass, M. B., & Lester, D. Task-dependent ethanol effects on escape in rats bred for ethanol sensitivity. *Pharmacology Biochemistry and Behavior*, 1981, *15*. 33–36. (a)

Bass, M. B., & Lester, D. Selective breeding for ethanol sensitivity: least affected and most affected rats, In G. E. McClearn, R. A. Deitrich, & V. G. Erwin (Eds.), *Development of animal models as pharmacogenetic tools* (USDHHS-NIAA, Research Monograph No. 6). Washington D.C.: U.S. Government Printing Office, 1981. (b)

Bass, M. B., & Lester, D. Genetic analysis of sensitivity to ethanol-induced depression of motor activity and impairment of swimming in rats. *Behavior Genetics*, 1983, *13*, 77–89.

Behar, D., Berg, C. J., Rapoport, J. L., Nelson, W., Linnoila, M., Cohen, M., Bozevich, D., & Marshall T. Behavioral and physiological effects of ethanol in high-risk and control children: A pilot study. *Alcoholism: Clinical and Experimental Research*, 1983, *7*, 404–410.

Belknap, J. K. Genetic factors in the effects of alcohol: Neurosensitivity, functional tolerance, and physical dependence. In H. Rigter & J. Crabbe (Eds.), *Alcohol tolerance and dependence*. Amsterdam: Elsevier/North Holland Biomedical Press, 1980. (a)

Belknap, J. K. Morphine physical dependence and thermoregulatory dysfunction in mice. *Federation Proceedings*, 1980, *39*, 763. (b)

Belknap, J. K., & Deutsch, C. K. Differential neurosensitivity to three alcohols, acetaldehyde and phenobarbital in C57BL/6J and DBA/2J mice. *Behavior Genetics*, 1982, *12*, 309–318.

Belknap, J. K., & Mitchell, M. A. Barbiturate physical dependence in mice; Effects on body temperature regulation. *Journal of Pharmacology and Experimental Therapeutics*, 1981, *218*, 647–652.

Belknap, J. K., Waddingham, S., & Ondrusek, G. Barbiturate dependence in mice induced by a short-term oral procedure. *Physiological Psychology*, 1973, *l*, 394–396.

Belknap, J. K., Ondrusek, G., Berg, J., & Waddingham, S. Barbiturate dependence in mice. Effects of continuous vs. discontinuous drug administration. *Psychopharmacology*, 1977, *51*, 195–198.

Belknap, J. K., Belknap, N. D., Berg, J., & Coleman, R. R. Preabsorptive vs. postabsorptive control of ethanol intake in C57BL/6J and DBA/2J mice. *Behavior Genetics* 1977, *7*, 414–425.

Belknap, J. K., Coleman, R. R., & Foster, K. Alcohol consumption and sensory threshold differences between C57BL/6J and DBA/2J mice. *Physiological Psychology*, 1978, *6*, 71–74.

Belknap, J. K., Haltli, N., Goebel, D., & Lamé M. Intercorrelations between levorphanol-induced antinociception, hypothermia, activity and constipation in a genetically heterogeneous mouse population, and the results of selective breeding for antinociception. *Proceedings of the Western Pharmacology Society*, 1982, *25*, 299–302.

Belknap, J. K., Haltli, N., Goebel, D., & Lamé, M. Selective breeding for high and low levels of opiate-induced analgesia in mice. *Behavior Genetics*, 1983, *13*, 383–396.

Belknap, J. K., Oordewier, B. Lamé, M., & Danielson, P. W. Genetic dissociation of opiate effects: Screening several opiate-sensitive measures among three inbred mouse strains. Unpublished manuscript, 1984. (a)

Belknap, J. K., Crabbe, J. C., Danielson, P. W., and Lamé, M. Genetic sensitivity to the ethanol withdrawal syndrome: Genetic cross-sensitivity to a barbituate and a benzodiazepine in mice. *Society for Neuroscience Abstracts*, 1984, *10*, 571. (b)

Bohman, M., Sigvardsson, S., & Cloninger, C. R. Maternal inheritance of alcohol abuse. *Archives of General Psychiatry*, 1981, *38*, 965–969.

Brase, D. A., Loh, H. H., & Way, E. L. Comparison of the effects of morphine on locomotor activity, analgesia and primary and protracted physical dependence in six mouse strains. *Journal of Pharmacology and Experimental Therapeutics*, 1977, *201*, 368–374.

Brick, J., & Horowitz, G. P. Alcohol and morphine induced hypothermia in mice selected for sensitivty to ethanol. *Pharmacology Biochemistry and Behavior*, 1982, *16*, 473–479.

Broadhurst, P. L. *Drugs and the inheritance of behavior.* New York: Plenum Press, 1978.

Cadoret, R. J., & Gath, A. Inheritance of alcoholism in adoptees. *British Journal of Psychiatry*, 1978, *132* 252–258.

Chan, A. W. K., & Siemens, A. J. Development of acute tolerance to pentobarbital: Differential effects in mice. *Biochemical Pharmacology*, 1979, *28*, 549–552.

Church, A. C., Fuller, J. L., & Dudek, B. C. Salsolinol differentially affects mice selected for sensitivity to alcohol. *Psychopharmacology*, 1976, *47*, 49–52.

Cloninger, C. R., Bohman, M, & Sigvardsson, S. Inheritance of alcohol abuse. *Archives of General Psychiatry*, 1981, *38*, 861–868.

Collins, A. C. Genetics of ethanol preference: Role of neurotransmitters. In E. Majchrowicz & E. Noble (Eds.), *Biochemistry and pharmacology of ethanol* (Vol. 2.), New York: Plenum Press, 1979.

Collins, A. C. A review of research using the short-sleep and the long-sleep mice. In G. E. McClearn, R. A. Deitrich, & V. G. Erwin (Eds.), *Development of animal models as pharmacogenetic tools* (USDHHS-NIAAA Research Monograph No 6). Washington D.C.: U.S. Government Printing Office, 1981.

Collins, R. L., & Whitney, G. Genotype and test experience determine responsiveness to morphine. *Psychopharmacology*, 1978, *56*, 57–60.

Crabbe, J. C. Sensitivity to ethanol in inbred mice: Genotypic correlations among several behavioral responses. *Behavioral Neuroscience*, 1983, *97*, 280–289.

Crabbe, J. C., & Belknap, J. K. Pharmacogenetic tools in the study of drug tolerance and dependence. *Substance and Alcohol Actions/Misuse*, 1980, *1*, 385–413.

Crabbe, J. C., Janowsky, J. S., Young, E. R., & Rigter, H. Handling induced convulsions in twenty inbred strains of mice. *Substance and Alcohol Actions/Misuse*, 1980, *1*, 149–153. (a)

Crabbe, J. C., Janowsky, J. S., Young, E. R., & Rigter, H. Strain-specific effects of ethanol on open field activity in inbred mice. *Substance and Alcohol Actions/Misuse*, 1980, *1*, 537–543. (b)

Crabbe, J. C., Rigter, H., & Kerbusch, Sj. Genetic analysis of tolerance to ethanol hypothermia in recombinant inbred mice: Effect of desglycinamide-(9)-arginine-(8)-vasopressin. *Behavior Genetics*, 1980, *10*, 139–153.

Crabbe, J. C., Janowsky, J. S., Young, E. R., Kosobud, A., Stack, J., & Rigter, H. Tolerance to ethanol hypothermia in inbred mice: Genotypic correlations with behavioral responses. *Alcoholism: Clinical and Experimental Research*, 1982, *6*, 446–458.

Crabbe, J. C., Johnson, N. A., Gray, D. K., Kosobud, A., & Young, E. R. Biphasic effects of ethanol on open-field activity: Sensitivity and tolerance in C57BL/6N and DBA/2N mice. *Journal of Comparative and Physiological Psychology*, 1982, *96*, 440–451.

Crabbe, J. C., Kosobud, A., & Young, E. R. Genetic selection for ethanol withdrawal severity: Differences in replicate mouse lines. *Life Sciences*, 1983, *33*, 955–962.

Crabbe, J. C., Kosobud, A., Young, E. R., & Janowsky, J. S. Polygenic and single-gene determination of responses to ethanol BXD/Ty recombinant inbred mouse strains. *Neurobehavioral Toxicology and Teratology*, 1983, *5*, 181–187.

Crabbe, J. C., Young, E. R., & Kosobud, A. Genetic correlations with ethanol withdrawal severity. *Pharmacology Biochemistry and Behavior*, 1983, *18*, 541–547.

Crispens, C. G., *Handbook on the laboratory mouse*. Springfield, Ill.: Charles C. Thomas, 1975.

Damjanovich, R. P., & MacInnes, J. W. Factors involved in ethanol narcosis: Analysis in mice of three inbred strains. *Life Sciences*, 1973, *13*, 55–65.

DeFries, J. C. Current perspectives on selective breeding: Example and theory. In G. E. McClearn, R. A. Deitrich & V. G. Erwin (Eds.) *Development of animal models as pharmacogenetic tools* (USDHHS-NIAAA Research Monograph No. 6). Washington D.C.: U.S. Government Printing Office, 1981.

Deitrich, R. A., & Collins A. C. Pharmacogenetics of alcoholism. In K. Blum (Ed.), *Alcohol and opiates: Neurochemical and behavioral mechanisms*. New York: Academic Press, 1977.

Dibner, M. D., Zahniser, N. R., Wolfe, B. B., Rabin, R. A., & Molinoff, P. B. Brain neurotransmitter receptor systems in mice genetically selected for differences in sensitivity to ethanol. *Pharmacology Biochemistry and Behavior*, 1980, *12*, 509–513.

Drewek, K. J. Inherited drinking and its behavioural correlates. In K. Eriksson, J. D. Sinclair, & K. Kiianmaa (Eds.), *Animal models in alcohol research*. London: Academic Press, 1980.

Drewek, K. J., & Broadhurst, P. L. A simplified triple test-cross analysis of alcohol preference in the rat. *Behavior Genetics*, 1981, *11*, 517–531.

Drewek, K. J., & Broadhurst, P. L. The genetics of alcohol preference in the female rat confirmed by a full triple-test cross. *Behavior Genetics*, 1983, *13*, 107–116.

Dudek, B. C., & Fanelli, R. J. Effects of gamma-butyrolactone, amphetamine, and haloperidol in mice differing in sensitivity to alcohol. *Psychopharmacology*, 1980, *68*, 89–97.

Eckardt, M. J., Ryback, R. S., Rawlings, R. R., & Graubard, B. I. Biochemical diagnosis of alcoholism. A test of the discriminating capabilities of gamma-glutamyl transpeptidase and mean corpuscular volume. *Journal of the American Medical Association*, 1981, *246*, 2707–2710.

Eidelberg, E., Erspamer, R., Kreinick, C. J., & Harris, J. Genetically determined differences in the effects of morphine on mice. *European Journal of Pharmacology*, 1975, *32*, 329–336.

Eleftheriou, B. E., & Elias, P. K. Recombinant inbred strains: A novel genetic approach for psychopharmacogenetics. In B. E. Eleftheriou (Ed.), *Psychopharmacogenetics*. New York: Plenum, 1975.

Elmasian, R., Neville, H., Woods, D., Schuckit, M., & Bloom, F. Event-related brain potentials are different in individuals at high and low risk for developing alcoholism. *Proceedings of the National Academy of Science U.S.A.*, 1982, *79*, 7900–7903.

Eriksson, C. J. P. Finnish selection studies on alcohol-related behaviors: Factors regulating voluntary alcohol consumption. In G. E. McClearn, R. A. Deitrich, & V. G. Erwin (Eds.) *Development of animal models as pharmacogenetic tools*. Washington: USDHHS-NIAAA Research Monograph No. 6, 1981.

Eriksson, C. J. P. Human blood acetaldehyde concentration during ethanol oxidation (Update, 1982). *Pharmacology Biochemistry and Behavior*, 1983, *18*(Supplement 1), 141–150.

Eriksson, K. Genetic selection for voluntary alcohol consumption in the albino rat. *Science*, 1968, *159*, 739–741.

Eriksson, K. Alcohol imbibition and behavior: A comparative genetic approach. In B. Eleftheriou (Ed.), *Psychopharmacogenetics*. New York: Plenum, 1975.

Eriksson, K., & Rusi, M. Finnish selection studies on alcohol-related behaviors: General outline. In G. E. McClearn, R. A. Deitrich & V. G. Erwin (Eds.) *Development of animal models as pharmacogenetic tools* (Research Monograph No. 6). Washington: USDHHS-NIAAA, 1981.

Erwin, V. G., Heston, W. D., McClearn, G. E., & Deitrich, R. A. Effect of hypnotics on mice genetically selected for sensitivity to ethanol. *Pharmacology Biochemistry and Behavior*, 1976, *4*, 679–683.

Erwin, V. G., & Towell, J. F. Ethanol-induced hyperglycemia mediated by the central nervous system. *Pharmacology Biochemistry and Behavior*, 1983, *18*(Supplement 1), 559–563.

Falconer, D. S. *Introduction to quantitative genetics*. New York: Ronald Press, 1960.

Filibeck, U., Castellano, C., & Oliverio, A. Cross tolerance between D-amino acids and morphine in mice. *Brain Research*, 1981, *212*, 227–229. (a)

Filibeck, U., Castellano C., & Oliverio, A. Differential effects of opiate agonists-antagonist on morphine-induced hyperexcitability and analgesia in mice. *Psychopharmacology*, 1981, *73*, 134–136. (b)

Fioriglio, C., Wood, J., Hartline, R. A., & Schneider, C. W. A quantitative analysis of ethanol and acetaldehyde expired by inbred mouse strains. *Pharmacology Biochemistry and Behavior*, 1980, *12*, 467–469.

Frigeni, V., Bruno, F., Carenzi, A., Racagni, G., & Santini, V. Analgesia and motor activity elicited by morphine and enkephalins in two inbred strains of mice. *Journal of Pharmacy and Pharmacology*, 1978, *30*, 310–311.

Fuller, J. L. Measurement of alcohol preference in genetic experiments. *Journal of Comparative and Physiological Psychology*, 1964, *57*, 85–88.

Gibbins, R. J., Kalant, H., & LeBlanc, A. E. A technique for accurate measurement of moderate degrees of alcohol intoxication in small animals. *Journal of Pharmacology and Experimental Therapeutics*, 1968, *159*, 236–242.

Giknis, M. L. A., Damjanov, I., & Rubin, E. The differential transplacental effects of ethanol in four mouse strains. *Neurobehavioral Toxicology*, 1980, *2*, 235–237.

Gilliam, D. M., & Collins, A. C. Acute ethanol effects on blood pH, PCO_2, and PO_2 in LS and SS mice. *Physiology and Behavior*, 1982, *28*, 879–883. (a)

Gilliam, D. M., & Collins, A. C. Circadian and genetic effects on ethanol elimination in LS and SS mice. *Alcoholism: Clinical and Experimental Research*, 1982, *6*, 344–349. (b)

Gilliam, D. M., & Collins, A. C. Differential effects of ethanol concentrations on blood pH, PCO_2 and PO_2 in LS and SS mice. *Physiology and Behavior*, 1983, *30*, 295–300.

Goldstein, A., & Sheehan, P. Tolerance to opioid narcotics. I. Tolerance to the "running fit" caused by levorphanol in the mouse. *Journal of Pharmacology and Experimental Therapeutics*, 1969, *169*, 175–184.

Goldstein, D. B. Inherited differences in intensity of alcohol withdrawal reactions in mice. *Nature*, 1973, *245*, 154–156.

Goldstein, D. B. & Kakihana, R. Alcohol withdrawal reactions and reserpine effects in inbred strains of mice. *Life Sciences*, 1974, *15*, 415–425.

Goldstein, D. B., & Kakihana, R. Alcohol withdrawal reactions in mouse strains selectively bred for long or short sleep times. *Life Sciences*, 1975, *17*, 981–986.

Goodwin, D. W. The genetics of alcoholism. *Substance and Alcohol Actions/Misuse*, 1980, *1*, 101–117.

Goodwin, D. W., Schulsinger, F., Hermansen, L., Guze, S. B., & Winokur, G. Alcohol problems in adoptees raised apart from alcoholic parents. *Archives of General Psychiatry*, 1973, *28*, 238–243.

Gottesman, I. I., & Carey, G. Extracting meaning and direction from twin data. *Psychiatric Developments*, 1983, *1*, 35–50.

Green, E. L. *Biology of the laboratory mouse.* New York: McGraw-Hill, 1966.

Green, E. L. *Handbook on genetically standardized mice* (2nd ed.). Bar Harbor, Maine: Jackson Laboratory, 1968.

Grieve, S. J., Griffiths, P. J., & Littleton, J. M. Genetic influences on the rate of development of ethanol tolerance and the ethanol physical withdrawal syndrome in mice. *Drug and Alcohol Dependence*, 1979, *4*, 77–86.

Griffiths, P. J., & Littleton, J. M. Concentrations of free amino acids in brains of mice of different strains during the physical syndrome of withdrawal from alcohol. *British Journal of Experimental Pathology*, 1977, *58*, 391–399.

Hall, R. L., Hesselbrock, V. M., & Stabenaw, J. R. Familial distribution of alcohol use: I. Assortative mating in the parents of alcoholics. *Behavior Genetics*, 1983, *13*, 361–372. (a)

Hall, R. L., Hesselbrock, V. M., & Stabenaw, J. R. Familial distribution of alcohol use: II. Assortative mating of alcoholic probands. *Behavior Genetics*, 1983, *13*, 373–382 (b)

Harris, R. A., Crabbe, J. C., & McSwigan, J. D. Relationship of membrane physical properties to alcohol dependence in mice selected for genetic differences in alcohol withdrawal. *Life Sciences*, 1984, *35*, 2601–2608.

Hay, D. A. Genetics in the analysis of behavior. *Neuroscience and Biobehavioral Reviews*, 1980, *4*, 489–508.

Hegmann, J., & Possidente, B. Estimating genetic correlations from inbred strains. *Behavior Genetics*, 1981, *11*, 103–114.

Heston, W. D., Erwin, V. G., Anderson, S. M., & Robbins, H. A comparison of the effects of alcohol on mice selectively bred for differences in ethanol sleep-time. *Life Sciences*, 1974, *14*, 365–370.

Ho, I. K., Loh, H. H., & Way, E. L. Morphine analgesia, tolerance and dependence in mice from different strains and vendors. *Journal of Pharmacy and Pharmacology*, 1977, *29*, 583–584.

Horowitz, G. P. Pharmacogenetic models and behavioral responses to opiates. In G. E.

McClearn, R. A. Deitrich, & V. G. Erwin (Eds.) *Development of animal models as pharmacogenetic tools* (USDHHS-NIAAA Research Monograph No. 6). Washington D.C.: U.S. Government Printing Office, 1981.

Horowitz, G. P., & Allan, A. M. Morphine withdrawal in mice selectively bred for differential sensitivity to ethanol. *Pharmacology Biochemistry and Behavior*, 1982, *16*, 35–39.

Horowitz, G. P., Whitney, G., Smith, J. C., & Stephan, F. K. Morphine ingestion: Genetic control in mice. *Psychopharmacology*, 1977, *52*, 119–122.

Horowitz, G. P., Dendel, P. S., Allan, A. M., & Major L. F. Dopamine-beta-hydroxylase activity and ethanol-induced sleep time in selectively bred and heterogeneous stock mice. *Behavior Genetics*, 1982, *12*, 549–561.

Horowitz, G. P., & Dudek, B. C. Behavioral pharmacogenetics. In J. L. Fuller & E. C. Simmel (Eds.), *Behavior genetics: Principles and applications*. Hillsdale, N.J.: Erlbaum, 1983.

Howerton, T. C., O'Connor, M. F., & Collins, A. C. Differential effects of long-chain alcohols in long- and short-sleep mice. *Psychopharmacology*, 1983, *79*, 313–317.

Hrubec, Z., & Omenn, G. S. Evidence of genetic predisposition to alcoholic cirrhosis and psychosis: Twin concordances for alcoholism and its biological end points by zygosity among male veterans. *Alcoholism: Clinical and Experimental Research*, 1981, *5*, 207–215.

Huang, J. T. Morphine pellet implanted in mouse brain: Observation of behavioral change and physical dependence. *Research Communications in Substance Abuse*, 1980, *1*, 29–37.

Hynes, M. D., & Berkowitz, B. A. Lack of an opiate response to nitrous oxide in mice resistant to the activity-stimulating effects of morphine. *Journal of Pharmacology and Experimental Therapeutics*, 1982, *220*, 499–503.

Ingram, D. K., & Corfman, T. P. An overview of neurobiological comparisons in mouse strains. *Neuroscience and Biobehaviorial Reviews*, 1980, *4*, 421–435.

Inoue, K., Rusi, M., & Lindros, K. O. Brain aldehyde dehydrogenase activity in rat strains with high and low ethanol preferences. *Pharmacology Biochemistry and Behavior*, 1981, *14*, 107–111.

Jay, G. E. Variation in response to various mouse strains to hexobarbital. *Proceedings of the Society for Experimental Biology*, 1955, *90*, 378–380.

Jonsson, F., & Nilsson, T. Alkoholkonsumption hos monozygota och dizygota tvillingar. *Nord Hyg Tidskr*, 1968, *49*, 21–25.

Judson, B. A., & Goldstein, A. Genetic control of opiate-induced locomotor activity in mice. *Journal of Pharmacology and Experimental Therapeutics*, 1978, *206*, 56–60.

Kaij, L. *Alcoholism in twins*. Stockholm: Almqvest and Wilsell, 1960.

Kakihana, R. Adrenocortical function in mice selectively bred for different sensitivity to ethanol. *Life Sciences*, 1976, *18*, 1131–1138.

Kakihana, R. Alcohol intoxication and withdrawal in inbred strains of mice: Behavioral and endocrine studies. *Behavioral and Neural Biology*, 1979, *26*, 97–105.

Kakihana, R. Endocrine and autonomic studies in mice selectively bred for different sensitivity to ethanol. In M. M. Gross (Ed.), *Alcohol intoxication and withdrawal* (Vol 3a). New York: Plenum Press, 1977.

Kakihana, R., & Butte, J. C. Biochemical correlates of inherited drinking in laboratory animals. In K. Eriksson, J. D. Sinclair, & K. Kiianmaa (Eds.), *Animal models in alcohol research*. London: Academic Press, 1980.

Kalant, H., LeBlanc, A. E., & Gibbins, R. J. Tolerance to, and dependence on, some non-opiate psychotropic drugs. *Pharmacological Reviews*, 1971, *23*, 135–191.

Kaprio, J., Sarna, S., Koskenvuo M., & Rantasalo, I. The Finnish twin registry, baseline characteristics. Section II: History of symptoms and illness use of drugs, physical characteristics, smoking, alcohol and physical activity. *Kansanterveystieteen Julkaisuja M*, 1978, *37*, Helsinki.

Kiianmaa, K., & Tabakoff, B. Neurochemical correlates of tolerance and strain differences in the neurochemical effects of ethanol. *Pharmacology Biochemistry and Behavior*, 1983, *18*(Supplement 1,) 383–388.

Kiianmaa, K., Hoffman, P. L., & Tabakoff, B. Antagonism of the behavioral effects of ethanol by naltrexone in BALB/c, C57BL/6, and DBA/2 mice. *Psychopharmacology*, 1983, *79*, 291–294.

Klein, T. W. Analysis of major gene effects using recombinant inbred strains and related congenic lines. *Behavior Genetics*, 1978, *8*, 261–268.

Kosobud, A., Crabbe, J. C., & Tam, B. R. Alcohol withdrawal in mice bred for resistance and susceptibility to alcohol withdrawal seizures. *Alcoholism: Clinical and experimental research*, 1984, *8*, 101 (Abstract).

Lapin, I. P., & Nazarenko, S. E. Comparison of the excitatory and anesthetic effects of ethanol in C57BL/6 and BALB/c mice: Relation to blood ethanol concentration. *Medical Biology*, 1978, *56*, 281–285.

Lester, D., Lin, G., Anandam, N., Riley, E. P., Worsham, E. D., & Freed, E. X. Selective breeding of rats for differences in reactivity to alcohol: An approach to an animal model of alcoholism. IV. Some behavioral and chemical measures. In R. G. Thurman, H. William-son, H. Drott, & B. Chance (Eds.), *Alcohol and aldehyde metabolizing systems*. New York: Academic Press, 1977.

Li, T.-K., Lumeng, L., McBride, W. J., & Waller, M. B. Indiana selection studies on alcohol-related behaviors. In G. E. McClearn, R. A. Deitrich, & V. G. Erwin (Eds.), *Development of animal models as pharmacogenetic tools* (Research Monograph No 6). Washington: USDHHS-NIAAA, 1981.

Littleton, J. M. The assessment of rapid tolerance to ethanol. In H. Rigter & J. Crabbe (Eds.), *Alcohol tolerance and dependence*. Amsterdam: Elsevier/North Holland Biomedical Press, 1980.

Littleton, J. M., Grieve, S. J., Griffiths, P. J., & John, G. R. Ethanol-induced alteration in membrane phospholipid composition: Possible relationship to development of cellular tolerance to ethanol. In H. Begleiter (Ed.), *Biological effects of alcohol*. New York: Plenum Press, 1978.

Loehlin, J. C. An analysis of alcohol related questionnaire items from the national merit twin study. *Annals of the New York Academy of Science*, 1972, *197*, 117–120.

Lumeng, L., Hawkins, T. D., & Li, T.-K. New strains of rats with alcohol preference and nonpreference. In R. G. Thurman, J. R. Williamson, H. R. Drott, & B. Chance (Eds.), *Alcohol and aldehyde metabolizing systems* (Vol. III). New York: Academic Press, 1977.

Lumeng, L., Waller, M. B., McBride, W. J., & Li, T.-K. Different sensitivities to ethanol in alcohol-preferring and -nonpreferring rats. *Pharmacology Biochemistry and Behavior*, 1982, *16*, 125–130.

Lush, I. E., & Lovell, D. A correlation between hexobarbitone and pentobarbitone sleeping times in fifteen different inbred strains of mice. *General Pharmacology*, 1978, *9*, 167–170.

MacPhail, R. C. & Elsmore, T. F. Ethanol-induced flavor aversions in mice: A behavior genetic analysis. *Neurotoxicology*, 1980, *1*, 625–634.

Mardones, J., & Segozia-Riquelme, N. Thirty-two years of selection of rats by ethanol pref-erence: UChA and UChB strains. *Neurobehavioral Toxicology and Teratology*, 1983, *5*, 171–178.

Masserano, J. M., & Weiner, N. Investigations into the neurochemical mechanisms mediating differences in ethanol sensitivity in two lines of mice. *Journal of Pharmacology and Experimental Therapeutics*, 1982, *221*, 404–409.

Masur, J., & Boerngen R. The excitatory component of ethanol in mice: A chronic study. *Pharmacology Biochemistry and Behavior*, 1980, *13*, 777–780.

Mayer, J. M., Khanna, J. M., Kalant, H., & Chau, A. Factors involved in the differential response to ethanol, barbital and pentobarbital in rats selectively bred for ethanol sensitivity. *Psychopharmacology*, 1982, *78*, 33–37.

McClearn, G. E. Genes, generality and behavioral reserach. In J. Hirsch (Ed.), *Behavior-genetic analysis*. New York: McGraw-Hill, 1967.

McClearn, G. E. Genetics as a tool in alcohol research. *Annals of the New York Academy of Sciences*, 1972, *197*, 26–31.

McClearn, G. E., & Anderson, S. M. Genetics and ethanol tolerance. *Drug and Alcohol Dependence*, 1979, *4*, 61–76.

McClearn, G. E., & Kakihana, R. Selective breeding for ethanol sensitivity in mice. *Behavior Genetics*, 1973, *3*, 409–410. (Abstract)

McClearn, G. E., & Kakihana, R. Selective breeding for ethanol sensitivity: Short-sleep and long-sleep mice. In G. E. McClearn, R. A. Dietrich, & V. G. Erwin (Eds.), *Development of animal models as pharmacogenetic tools* (Research Monograph No. 6). Washington: USDHHS-NIAAA, 1981.

McClearn, G. E., & Rodgers, D. A. Differences in alcohol preference among inbred strains of mice. *Quarterly Journal of Studies on Alcohol*, 1959, *20*, 691–695.

McClearn, G. E., Wilson, J. R., Petersen, D. R., & Allen, D. L. Selective breeding in mice for severity of the ethanol withdrawal syndrome. *Substance and Alcohol Actions/Misuse*, 1982, *3*, 135–143.

McSwigan, J. D., Crabbe, J. C., & Young, E. R. Specific ethanol withdrawal seizures in genetically selected mice. *Life Sciences*, 1984, *35*, 2119–2126.

Moore, J. A., & Kakihana, R. Ethanol-induced hypothermia in mice: Influence of genotype on development of tolerance. *Life Sciences*, 1978, *23*, 2332–2338.

Muraki, T., Uzumaki, H., & Kato, R. Strain differences in morphine-induced increase in plasma cyclic AMP and GMP levels in relation to locomotor activity in male mice. *Psychopharmacology*, 1982, *76*, 316–319.

Murphy, J. M., McBride, W. J., Lumeng, L., & Li, T.-K. Regional brain levels of monoamines in alcohol-preferring and -nonpreferring lines of rats. *Pharmacology Biochemistry and Behavior*, 1982, *16*, 145–149.

Nichols, J. R., & Hsiao, S. Addiction liability of albino rats: Breeding for quantitative differences in morphine drinking. *Science*, 1967, *157*, 561–563.

O'Connor, M. F., Howerton, T. C., & Collins, A. C. Effects of pentobarbital in mice selected for differential sensitivity to ethanol. *Pharmacology Biochemistry and Behavior*, 1982, *17*, 245–248.

Oakeshott, J. G., & Gibson, J. B. The genetics of human alcoholism: A review. *Australia and New Zealand Journal of Medicine*, 1981, *11*, 123–128.

Okamoto, M., Boisse, M. R., Rosenberg, H. C. & Rosen, R. Characteristics of functional tolerance during barbiturate physical dependence production. *Journal of Pharmacology and Experimental Therapeutics*, 1978, *207*, 906–915.

Oliverio, A., & Castellano, C. Genotype-dependent sensitivity and tolerance to morphine and heroin: Dissociation between opiate-induced running and analgesia in the mouse. *Psychopharmacology*, 1974, *39*, 13–22.

Oliverio, A., & Castellano, C. Behavioral effects of opiates: A pharmacogenetic analysis. In W. B. Essman & L. Valzelli (Eds.), *Current developments in psychopharmacology* (Vol. 6). New York: Spectrum, 1981.

Oliverio, A., & Eleftheriou, B. E. Motor activity and alcohol: Genetic analysis in the mouse. *Physiology and Behavior*, 1976, *16*, 577–581.

Ondrusek, M. G., Belknap, J. K., & Leslie, S. W. Effects of acute and chronic barbiturate administration on synaptosomal calcium accumulation. *Molecular Pharmacology*, 1979, *15*, 386–395.

Palmer, M. R., Sorensen, S., Freedman, R., Olson, L., Hoffer, B. J., & Seiger, O. Differential ethanol sensitivity of intraocular cerebellar grafts in long-sleep and short-sleep mice. *Journal of Pharmacology and Experimental Therapeutics*, 1982, *222*, 480–487.

Parsons, L. M., Gallaher, E. J., & Goldstein, D. B. Rapidly developing functional tolerance to ethanol is accompanied by increased erythrocyte cholesterol in mice. *Journal of Pharmacology and Experimental Therapeutics*, 1982, *223*, 472–476.

Partanen, J. K., Bruun, K., & Markkanen, T. *Inheritance of drinking behavior*. Helsinki: Finnish Foundation of Alcohol Studies, 1966.

Peets, J. M., & Pomeranz, B. CXBK mice deficient in opiate receptors show poor electroacupuncture analgesia. *Nature*, 1978, *273*, 675–676.

Pittman, Q. J., Rogers, J., & Bloom, F. E. Arginine vasopressin deficient Brattelboro rats fail to develop tolerance to the hypothermia effects of ethanol. *Regulatory Peptides*, 1982, *4*, 33–41.

Pollock, V. E., Volavka, J., Goodwin, D. W., Mednick, S. A., Gabrielli, W. F., Knop, J., & Schulsinger, F. The EEG after alcohol administration in men at risk for alcoholism, *Archives of General Psychiatry*, 1983, *40*, 857–861.

Propping, P. Pharmacogenetics of alcohol's CNS effect: Implications for the etiology of alcoholism. *Pharmacology Biochemistry and Behavior*, 1983, *18*,(Supplement 1), 549–553.

Propping, P., Kruger, J., & Janah, A. Effect of alcohol on genetically determined variants of the normal electroencephalogram. *Psychiatry Research*, 1980, *2*, 85–98.

Propping, P., Kruger, J., & Mark, N. Genetic disposition to alcoholism. An EEG study in alcoholics and their relatives. *Human Genetics*, 1981, *59*, 51–59.

Racagni, G., Bruno F., Iuliano, E., Longiave, D., Mandelli, V., & Berti, F. Comparative *in vitro* and *in vivo* studies between morphine and methionine-enkephalin: Genotype dependent response in two different strains of mice. *Advances in Biochemical Psychopharmacology*, 1978, *18*, 289–297.

Racagni, G., Bruno F., Iuliano, E., & Paoletti, R. Differential sensitivity to morphine-induced analgesia and motor acvtivity in two inbred strains of mice: Behavioral and biochemical correlations. *Journal of Pharmacology and Experimental Therapeutics*, 1979, *209*, 111–116.

Randall, C. L., & Lester D. Differential effects of ethanol and pentobarbital on sleep times in C57BL and BALB mice. *Journal of Pharmacology and Experimental Therapeutics*, 1974, *188*, 27–33.

Randall, C. L., Carpenter, J. A., Lester, D., & Friedman, H. J. Ethanol-induced mouse strain differences in locomotor activity. *Pharmacology Biochemistry and Behavior*, 1975, *3*, 533–535.

Reed, T. E. Three heritable responses to alcohol in a heterogeneous randomly mated mouse strain. Inferences for humans. *Journal of Studies on Alcohol*, 1977, *38*, 618–632.

Reed, T. E. Racial comparisons of alcohol metabolism: Background, problems and results. *Alcoholism: Clinical and Experimental Research*, 1978, *2*, 83–87.

Reggiani, A., Battaini, F., Kobayashi, H., Spano, P., & Trabucchi, M. Genotype-dependent sensitivity to morphine: Role of different opiate receptor populations. *Brain Research*, 1980, *189*, 289–294.

Reinhard, J. F., Koserksy, D. S., & Peterson, G. R. Strain-dependent differences in responses to chronic administration of morphine: Lack of relationship to brain catecholamine levels in mice. *Life Sciences*, 1976, *19*, 1413–1420.

Riley, E. P., & Lochry, E. A. Effects of initial tolerance on acquired tolerance to alcohol in two selectively bred rat strains. *Drug and Alcohol Dependence*, 1977, *28*, 485–494.

Riley, E. P., Freed, E. X., & Lester, D. Selective breeding of rats for differences in reactivity to alcohol. An approach to an animal model of alcoholism. I. General procedure. *Journal of Studies on Alcohol*, 1976, *37*, 1535–1547.

Riley, E. P., Worsham. E. D., Lester, D., & Freed, E. X. Selective breeding of rats for differences in reactivity to alcohol. An approach to an animal model of alcoholism. II. Behavioral measures. *Journal of Studies on Alcohol*, 1977, *39*, 1705–1717.

Riley, E. P., Lochry, E. A., and Freed, E. X. Differential tolerance to pentobarbital in rats bred for differences in alcohol sensitivity. *Psychopharmacology*, 1978, *58*, 167–170.

Roe, A., & Burks, B. Adult adjustment of foster children of alcoholic and psychotic parentage and influence of the former home (Memoirs of the section on alcohol studies, Yale University). *Quarterly Journal of Studies on Alcohol*, No. 3, 1945.

Rusi, M., Eriksson, K., & Maki, J. Genetic differences in the susceptibility to acute ethanol intoxication in selected rat strains. In M. M. Gross (Ed.), *Alcohol intoxication and withdrawal* (Vol 3a). New York: Plenum Press, 1977.

Ryan, L. J., Barr, J. E., Sanders, B., & Sharpless, S. K. Electrophysiological responses to ethanol, pentobarbital, and nicotine in mice genetically selected for differential sensitivity to ethanol. *Journal of Comparative and Physiological Psychology*, 1979, 93, 1035–1052.

Sanders, B. Sensitivity to low doses of ethanol and pentobarbital in mice selected for sensitivity to hypnotic doses of ethanol. *Journal of Comparative and Physiological Psychology*, 1976, 90, 394–398.

Sanders, B., & Sharpless, S. K. Dissociation between the anticonvulsant action of alcohol and its depressant action in mice of different genotypes. *Life Sciences*, 1978, 23, 2593–2600.

Sanders, B., Sharpless, S. K., Collins, A. C., McClearn, G. E., & Flanagan, C. Activating and anesthetic effects of general depressants. *Psychopharmacology*, 1978, 56, 185–189.

Sansone, M., & Oliverio, A. Effects of chlordiazepoxide-morphine combinations on spontaneous locomotor activity in three inbred strains of mice. *Archives Internationales de Pharmacologie et Therapie*, 1980, 247, 71–75.

Schuckit, M. A. Self-rating of alcohol intoxication by young men with and without family histories of alcoholism. *Journal of Studies on Alcohol*, 1980, 41, 242–249.

Schuckit, M. A. Peak blood alcohol levels in men at high risk for the future development of alcoholism. *Alcoholism: Clinical and Experimental Research*, 1981, 5, 64–66.

Schuckit, M. A. A study of young men with alcoholic close relatives. *American Journal of Psychiatry*, 1982, 139, 791–794.

Schuckit, M. A., & Rayses, I. Ethanol ingestion: Differences in blood acetaldeyhde concentrations in relatives of alcoholics and controls. *Science*, 1979, 203, 54–55.

Schuckit, M. A., Goodwin, D. W., & Winokur, G. A half-sibling study of alcoholism. *American Journal of Psychiatry*, 1972, 128, 1132–1136.

Schuckit, M. A., Engstrom, D., Alpert, R., & Duby, J. Differences in muscle-tension in response to ethanol in young men with and without family histories of alcoholism. *Journal of Studies on Alcohol*, 1981, 42, 918–924.

Schuckit, M. A., O'Connor, D. T., Duby, J., Vega, R., & Moss, M. Dopamine-beta-hydroxylase activity levels in men at high risk for alcoholism and controls. *Biological Psychiatry*, 1981, 16, 1067–1075.

Schuckit, M. A., Shaskan, E., Duby, J., Vega, R., & Moss, M. Platelet monoamine oxidase activity in relatives of alcoholics. Preliminary study with matched control subjects. *Archives of General Psychiatry*, 1982, 39, 137–140.

Schwitters, S. Y., Johnson, R. C., McClearn, G. E., & Wilson, J. R. Alcohol use and the flushing response in different racial-ethnic groups. *Journal of Studies on Alcohol*, 1982, 43, 1259–1262.

Seiger, A., Sorensen, S. M., & Palmer, M. R. Cerebellar role in the differential ethanol sensitivity of long sleep and short sleep mice. *Pharmacology Biochemistry and Behavior*, 1983, 18(Supplement 1), 495–499.

Shapiro, N. R., & Riley, E. P. Avoidance behavior in rats selectively bred for differential alcohol sensitivity. *Psychopharmacology*, 1980, 72, 79–83.

Shields, J. Genetics and alcoholism. In G. Edwards & M. Grant (Eds.), *Alcoholism: New knowledge new responses*. London: Croom Helm, 1977.

Shuster, L., Pharmacogenetics of drugs of abuse. In M. Braude (Ed.), *Substance abuse: Genetic, perinatal and development aspects*. New York: Raven Press, 1984.

Shuster, L., Webster, G. W., Yu, G., & Eleftheriou, B. E. A genetic analysis of the response to morphine in mice: Analgesia and running. *Psychopharmacology*, 1975, 42, 249–254.

Siemens, A. J. & Chan, A. W. K. Differential effects of pentobarbital and ethanol in mice. *Life Sciences*, 1976, *19*, 581–590.

Sorenson, S., Palmer, M. Dunwiddie, T., & Hoffer, B. Electrophysiological correlates of ethanol-induced sedation in differentially sensitive lines of mice. *Science*, 1980, *210*, 1143–1145.

Sorenson, S., Dunwiddie, T., McClearn, G., Freedman, R., & Hoffer, B. Ethanol-induced depressions in cerebellar and hippocampal neurons of mice selectively bred for differences in ethanol sensitivity: An electrophysiological study. *Pharmacology Biochemistry and Behavior*, 1981, *14*, 227–234.

Spuhler, K., Hoffer, B., Weiner, N., & Palmer M. Evidence for genetic correlation of hypnotic effects and cerebellar Purkinje neuron depression in response to ethanol in mice. *Pharmacology Biochemistry and Behavior*, 1982, *17*, 569–578.

Tabakoff, B., & Kiianmaa, K. Does tolerance develop to the activating, as well as the depressant, effects of ethanol? *Pharmacology Biochemistry and Behavior*, 1982, *17*, 1073–1076.

Tabakoff, B., & Ritzmann, R. F. Acute tolerance in inbred and selected lines of mice. *Drug and Alcohol Dependence*, 1979, *4*, 87–90.

Tabakoff, B., Ritzman, R. F., Raju, T. S., & Deitrich, R. A. Characterization of acute and chronic tolerance in mice selected for inherent differences in sensitivity to ethanol. *Alcoholism: Clinical and Experimental Research*, 1980, *4*, 70–73.

Tampier, L., Quintanilla, M. E., & Mardones, J. Genetic differences in tolerance to ethanol: A study in UChA and UChB rats. *Pharmacology Biochemistry and Behavior*, 1981, *14*, 165–168.

Ternes, J. W., Ehrman, R., & O'Brien, C. Cynomolgus monkeys do not develop tolerance to opioids. *Behavioral Neuroscience*, 1983, *97*, 327–330.

Tyers, M. B. A classification of opiate receptors that mediate antinociception in animals. *British Journal of Pharmacology*, 1980, *69*, 503–512.

Vesell, E. S. Factors altering the responsiveness of mice to hexobarbital. *Pharmacology*, 1968, *1*, 81–97.

Waller, M. B., McBride, W. J., Lumeng, L, & Li, T.-K. Induction of dependence on ethanol by free-choice drinking in alcohol-preferring rats. *Pharmacology Biochemistry and Behavior*, 1982, *16*, 501–507. (a)

Waller, M. B., McBride, W. J., Lumeng, L., & Li, T.-K. Effects of intravenous ethanol and of 4-methylpyrazole on alcohol drinking in alcohol-preferring rats. *Pharmacology Biochemistry and Behavior*, 1982, *17*, 763–768. (b)

Whitney, G., McClearn, G. E., & DeFries, J. C. Heritability of alcohol preference in laboratory mice and rats. *Journal of Heredity*, 1970, *61*, 165–169.

Wilson, J. R., Erwin, V. B., & McClearn, G. E. Effects of ethanol: I. Acute metabolic tolerance and ethnic differences. *Alcoholism: Clinical and Experimental Research*, 1984, *8*, 226–232.

Wilson, J. R., Erwin, V. G., McClearn, G. E., Plomin, R., Johnson, R. C., Ahern, F. M., & Cole, R. E. Effects of ethanol: II. Behavioral sensitivity and acute behavioral tolerance. *Alcoholism: Clinical and Experimental Research*, 1984, *8*, 366–374.

Worsham, E. D., & Freed, E. X. Generality of differential sensitivity to alcohol in selectively bred rats. *Physiological Psychology*, 1977, *5*, 429–432.

Worsham, E. D., Riley, E. P., Anandam, N., Lister, P., Freed, E. X., & Lester, D. Selective breeding of rats for differences in reactivity to alcohol: An approach to an animal model of alcoholism. III. Some physical and behavioral measures In M. M. Gross (Ed.), *Alcohol intoxication and withdrawal* (Vol 3a). New York: Plenum Press, 1977.

Yamamoto, I., & Ho, I. K. Sensitivity to continuous administration of pentobarbital in different strains of mice. *Research Communications in Chemical Phathology and Pharmacology*, 1978, *19*, 381–388.

York, J. L. Consumption of intoxicating beverages by rats and mice exhibiting high and low preferences for ethanol. *Pharmacology Biochemistry and Behavior*, 1981, *15*, 207–214.

CHAPTER 3

Biochemical Substrates
of Drug Abuse

MICHAEL T. BARDO and MARCUS E. RISNER

INTRODUCTION

A variety of psychosocial factors are thought to predispose an individual to initiate the abuse of illicit drugs (Gorsuch & Butler, 1976). Once initiated, a number of psychopharmacological factors also come to play a role in the continuance of self-administration behavior. One important factor is the ability of the drug to produce a positive affective state or reinforcement upon its initial administration. For example. Haertzen, Kocher, & Miyasato (1983) found that the degree of reinforcement derived from the first drug experience was related directly to the magnitude of the subsequent drug habit. The relationship was true for several drugs including alcohol, barbiturates, minor tranquilizers, cocaine, stimulants, marijuana, solvents, hallucinogens, and opiates but was not true for caffeine (coffee) or nicotine (cigarettes). Thus, an understanding of the abuse potential of many psychoactive drugs requires an appreciation of the reinforcing value of the initial drug experience.

It is now clear that the reinforcing properties of psychoactive drugs also involve an assortment of biochemical mechanisms. This chapter will review some recent research that has attempted to elucidate the biochemical substrates of drug reinforcement and abuse. First, some basic

MICHAEL T. BARDO • Department of Psychology, University of Kentucky, Lexington, Kentucky 40506.   *MARCUS E. RISNER* • National Institute on Drug Abuse, Addiction Research Center, P.O. Box 5180, Baltimore, Maryland 21224.

biochemical principles of drug action in the central nervous system (CNS) and periphery will be covered. Next, various factors that may alter an individual's biochemical response to psychoactive drugs will be discussed. Finally, we will mention some of the exciting new research developments that suggest that effective treatment of drug abuse in humans may include a biochemical mode of therapy in conjunction with psychotherapy.

BASIC PRINCIPLES

All psychoactive drugs that are abused produce some alteration in the chemical message sent from one neuron to the next within the synapses of the central nervous system. As we will see, this alteration in synaptic neurotransmission occurs because each psychoactive drug has a unique chemical structure that causes it to attach to different portions of a neuron or to enzymes located outside of the neuron. Once these attachment sites or receptors are occupied by the drug molecules, the normal chemical message between two neurons becomes either inhibited or enhanced. The alteration in chemical neurotransmission produces a concomitant alteration in electrical neurotransmission within the central nervous system, and this may be expressed ultimately as an alteration in mood or behavior.

Before altering chemical neurotransmission within the central nervous system, however, a psychoactive drug must enter the bloodstream and cross into the brain from capillaries that offer a structural resistance known as the blood–brain barrier. Once absorbed into the brain, a drug will continue to produce its psychoactive effect until it diffuses back into the bloodstream, where it can be carried to the liver and be metabolized to an inactive compound that is excreted readily. The following sections outline briefly these basic pharmacological principles.

PHARMACOLOGICAL PRINCIPLES

Routes of Drug Administration

Drugs of abuse are typically self-administered either orally, by injection, or by inhalation. The oral route is the most commonly used method of drug self-administration among the general population. Unlike the injection and inhalation routes, there is little social stigma associated with taking drugs orally, either in the form of pills containing prescription and nonprescription remedies or in the form of beverages containing alcohol or caffeine. The primary advantage of the oral route is that the drug effect is prolonged because the cells lining the gastrointestinal tract provide a structural barrier that slows absorption of the drug into the bloodstream. However, some drugs are deactivated by acids or enzymes within the gastrointestinal tract, and thus they produce weak effects by the oral route. In addition, drugs administered orally must first pass through the liver, where they may be metabolized to inactive compounds before reaching the brain. Contrary to the popular lore of drug users on the street, the problems of oral absorption are not obviated completely by "snorting" drugs like cocaine through the nose, as cocaine administered intranasally is partially passed through the nasopharynx and swallowed into the gastrointestinal tract before it is absorbed (Van Dyke, Jatlow, Ungerer, Barash, & Byck, 1978).

The injection route involves administering a soluble drug either intravenously (IV), intramuscularly (IM), or subcutaneously (SC). In medical practice, the injection route offers several advantages over the oral route. First, the concentration of the drug within the bloodstream is easier to control because individual differences in the rate of absorption are minimized. Second, the injection route can be used when the patient is unconscious. Third, the onset of the drug effect is rapid, especially when administered intravenously. The rapid onset of the drug effect is a major reason why drugs of abuse are often self-administered by injection. In addition, some drugs of abuse, such as heroin, may be injected because they are poorly absorbed via the oral route. A major problem with injecting drugs of abuse involves the use of nonsterile syringes that may transmit various infectious diseases, including hepatitis and perhaps Acquired Immune Deficiency Syndrome (AIDS).

The inhalation route is also used to self-administer a variety of drugs of abuse, including anesthetic gases such as nitrous oxide, volatile hydrocarbons such as those found in some glues, and small particles such as nicotine and tetrahydrocannabinol (THC) that are found in cigarette and marijuana smoke, respectively. These drugs cross the cells that line the lungs and rapidly enter the blood stream to penetrate the brain. Unfortunately, inhalation of drugs may irritate the lung tissue, and chronic use may produce permanent tissue damage. Moreover, anesthetic gases may induce oxygen deprivation or hypoxia, and prolonged use of volatile hydrocarbons has been linked to irreversible brain damage.

Blood–Brain Barrier

Once absorbed into the blood, most drugs diffuse readily into various body tissues and internal organs. However, not all drugs will penetrate the brain, as the blood capillaries within the brain provide a protective barrier that is not found in peripheral circulation. In peripheral capillaries, the endothelial cells that make up the capillary wall are separated by pores that allow most drugs to pass readily between cells. In contrast, the endothelial cells of capillaries within the brain are packed closely, leaving tight junctions that allow only small drug molecules, but not plasma proteins, to pass between cells (see Figure 1). This so-called blood–brain barrier may be reinforced further by the end-foot processes of the nonneural astrocytes which surround the brain capillaries. Another distinction between capillaries in the periphery and the brain is that the endothelial cells of brain capillaries have many more mitochondria, the intracellular organelles that convert glucose and oxygen into energy utilized by the cell. The large number of mitochondria present in brain capillaries provide the energy required to remove various molecules from the brain via active transport systems (see Katzman, 1981).

While the tight junctions of the blood–brain barrier inhibit the passage of many drugs, most psychoactive drugs penetrate the brain readily by passing directly across the membrane surface of the capillary endothelial cell. The outer membrane of the endothelial cell as well as most other cells throughout the body consists of a bilayer of phospholids (fats) that has many proteins embedded within its surface. This membrane has a fluidlike quality that makes it permeable to drugs that are soluble in fat and relatively impermeable to drugs that are soluble in water. In

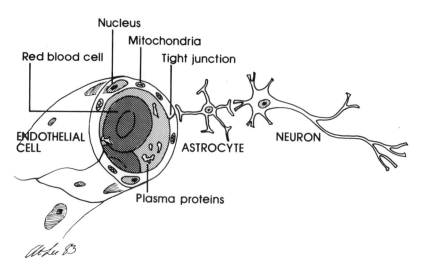

Figure 1. The blood–brain barrier in a capillary within the brain. Drugs that have a large molecular size or that are bound to plasma proteins are unable to pass from the blood through the tight junction between endothelial cells.

addition, drugs that are not bound to plasma proteins and that have a neutral ionic charge rather than an ionized charge are most likely to cross the membrane of the endothelial cell. In general, drugs of abuse tend to be lipid soluble, nonionized small molecules that penetrate the brain by crossing directly across the endothelial cells of the capillaries.

Metabolism and Excretion of Drugs

The major organ responsible for deactivating psychoactive drugs circulating within the blood is the liver. Cells within the liver contain numerous microsomes, which are intracellular organelles specialized in synthesizing enzymes that can metabolize psychoactive drugs. Drugs can be metabolized by either microsomal or nonmicrosomal liver enzymes by the process of either *oxidation, reduction, hydrolysis,* or *conjugation* (see Mayer, Melmon, & Gilman, 1980). In general, oxidation involves the addition of an oxygen atom to the drug molecule, whereas reduction involves the removal of an oxygen atom, or the addition of an hydrogen atom, to the drug molecule. In contrast, hydrolysis involves the splitting of a drug molecule into two inactive fragments by incorporating a molecule of water (H_2O); one fragment incorporates the hydroxyl group (OH^-), and the other fragment incorporates the hydrogen ion ($H+$). Finally, conjugation involves deactivating a drug by coupling it with some substance within the body, usually a protein or carbohydrate. In general, these four different metabolic reactions convert the drug to a water-soluble product that is readily excreted from the body. However, in some cases, a drug is excreted in an unchanged form.

The major organ responsible for excreting drug metabolites from the body is the kidney, which is made up of a large number of functional units called *nephrons* (see Figure 2). Each nephron consists of a tight knot of capillaries known as the glomerulus through which arterial blood flows under high pressure. The high pressure and porous nature of the glomerulus capillary causes much of the plasma fluid to exit, including water, glucose, electrolytes (such as sodium and chloride), active drug molecules, and inactive drug metabolites. Surrounding the glomerulus capillaries is a portion of the nephron known as Bowman's capsule, which absorbs the fluid exiting the glomerulus and channels it down a series of nephron tubules that dump eventually into the urinary bladder. Before leaving the kidney, however, most of the fluid constituents are reabsorbed into the venous blood supply within the nephron, including most of the water, glucose, electrolytes, the unmetabolized drug molecules. However, the drug metabolites that are ionized and fat insoluble are not reabsorbed across the venous capillary wall, and thus they end up in the urine.

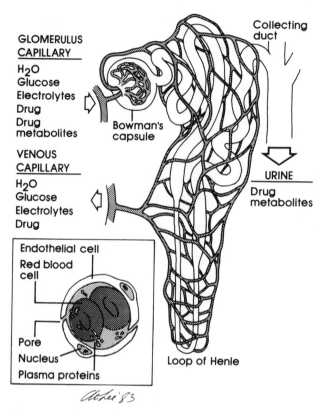

GLOMERULUS
CAPILLARY
H$_2$O
Glucose
Electrolytes
Drug
Drug
metabolites

Bowman's
capsule

VENOUS
CAPILLARY
H$_2$O
Glucose
Electrolytes
Drug

Collecting
duct

URINE
Drug
metabolites

Endothelial cell
Red blood
cell

Pore
Nucleus
Plasma proteins

Loop of Henle

Figure 2. The excretion of drug metabolites from a kidney nephron. Constituents of the blood enter Bowman's capsule and then are reabsorbed into the blood by venous capillaries. However, drug metabolites are not reabsorbed but are excreted in the urine.

NEUROCHEMICAL PRINCIPLES

Neurotransmitters

The CNS of mammals contains many different chemical messengers or neurotransmitters. Each individual neuron usually has the capacity to synthesize and release only one particular neurotransmitter, although recent evidence indicates clearly that two or more different neurotransmitters may coexist within the same neuron (Hokfelt, Johansson, Ljungdahl, Lundberg, & Schultzberg, 1980). The synthesis of a neurotransmitter occurs in the cell body of a neuron, where the nucleus containing the genetic program required to construct neurotransmitter molecules is located (see Figure 3). Also, located within the neuronal cell body are numerous ribosomes and the Golgi apparatus. The ribosomes, which

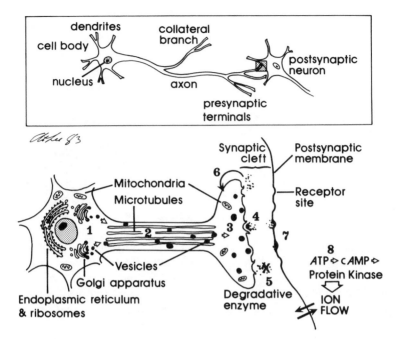

Figure 3. The various neurochemical mechanisms that may be altered by psychoactive drugs. The numbers 1 to 8 illustrate that drugs may produce an effect by altering one or more of the following neurotransmitter mechanisms: (1) synthesis; (2) transport; (3) storage; (4) release; (5) degradation; (6) reuptake; (7) receptor activation; and (8) second messenger activation.

may be either free floating or attached to folded membranes known as *endoplasmic reticula,* are the sites at which proteins required by the neuron are synthesized. The Golgi apparatus is a membranous organelle that may package newly synthesized neurotransmitter molecules into small spherical storage compartments called *vesicles.* A photograph from an electron microscope would reveal that the Golgi apparatus is surrounded by a multitude of vesicles budding out from its surface. As long as a neurotransmitter is packaged within a vesicle, it is protected from degradative enzymes that inhabit the intraneuronal fluid. Each of these vesicles contains a fixed amount or quantum of neurotransmitter substance.

Although a neurotransmitter substance is synthesized and packaged into vesicles within the neuronal cell body, it is not used as a chemical messenger until it is transported to a portion of the neuron known as the *presynaptic terminal.* The presynaptic terminal is an enlarged knob, found at the end of each axon that is specialized for releasing the neurotransmitter into the synapse. Neurons that have branching axonal projections that contact many other neurons have a multitude of presynaptic terminals. To get from the cell body to a presynaptic terminal, a neurotransmitter vesicle must travel down the length of the axon, which may cover a distance of 1 m or more in some neurons within the human body. The transport down the axon, which is called axoplasmic flow, appears to be guided along microtubules that run the length of the axon.

Once deposited into the presynaptic terminal, the vesicle awaits its turn to release its neurotransmitter content into the synapse by a process called *exocytosis*. Exocytosis involves the rupturing of a vesicle such that its content is released into the synapse and the vesicular membrane becomes fused with the outer membrane of the presynaptic terminal. The process of exocytosis is not a random occurrence but instead is linked directly to the arrival of an electrical signal or action potential at the presynaptic terminal. (For a review of the electrical properties of neurons, see Carlson, 1980). The exact mechanism involved in the conversion of an electrical signal into a chemical release is not known presently, although it is clear that entry of calcium into the presynaptic terminal is a necessary condition for exocytosis to occur (Carpenter & Reese, 1981). However, the process of exocytosis remains hypothetical, as there is some evidence to suggest that neurotransmitters may be leaked slowly from vesicles rather than discharged rapidly in quanta as expected from exocytosis (Tauc, 1982.)

Nonetheless, once a neurotransmitter is released into the synapse, it is subject to one of three different fates. First, the neurotransmitter may attach itself to a receptor located on the membrane surface of the next neuron, the postsynaptic neuron. As will be discussed in the next section, this receptor occupation by the neurotransmitter can produce a functional alteration in the firing rate of the postsynaptic neuron. Second, the neurotransmitter may be deactivated by local enzymes present in the extracellular fluid. These metabolic enzymes are relatively specific for which neurotransmitters they will deactivate. Once deactivated, some extracellular metabolites, or by-products, are transported into the blood and excreted through the kidneys. Thus, by measuring the levels of neurotransmitter metabolites in the blood or urine, one can derive an estimate of the functional activity of neurons in the central nervous system. Finally, if a neurotransmitter is not deactivited, it may be taken back into the presynaptic terminal, where it is repackaged into a vesicle and used again in exocytosis. This reuptake mechanism is evident with many, but not all, neurotransmitter systems. It is an active transport process, and mitochondria are located in the presynaptic terminal to supply the energy required for reuptake.

The mechanisms of the neurotransmitter function that have been described thus far may be altered by a variety of psychoactive drugs (see Figure 3). Some drugs block the biosynthesis of neurotransmitters within the neuronal cell body, whereas others block the transport of the neurotransmitter from the cell body to the presynaptic terminal. By blocking either the normal synthetic or transport processes, the stores of neurotransmitter substance being released from the presynaptic terminal eventually become depleted, as the reuptake process does not recover all of the neurotransmitter within the synapse. In addition, some psychoactive drugs alter normal neurotransmitter function by disrupting the storage, release, or reuptake processes at the presynaptic terminal. Amphetamine, for example, stimulates the release of the neurotransmitter dopamine, whereas cocaine blocks the reuptake of dopamine into the presynaptic terminal. Thus, both amphetamine and cocaine increase the availability of dopamine within the synapse, albeit by different mechanisms of action. An increase in dopamine within the synapse is also obtained following the administration of a drug that inhibits the degradative enzyme, monoamine oxidase (MAO), which normally inactivates dopamine within the synapse. Finally, many psychoactive drugs of abuse alter the normal function of neurotransmitters by acting directly upon the receptor sites for neurotransmitters located on the postsynaptic neuron. A summary of the different neuronal mechanisms of action of psychoactive drugs is presented in Figure 3.

In order to understand the biochemical substrates of drug abuse, a few of the specific neurotransmitters that have been identified within the brain are discussed here. In particular, various drugs of abuse involve the neurotransmitters dopamine, norepinephrine, serotonin, and gamma-aminobutyric acid (GABA). The biosynthetic pathways for each of these different neurotransmitters share several common features (see Figure 4). First, each of these neurotransmitters is synthesized from an amino acid precursor (tyrosine, tryptophan, or glutamate) that is either found in our diet or that is synthesized readily from an essential amino acid found in our diet. Second, the synthesis and metabolism of each neurotransmitter is controlled by the availability of different endogenous enzymes that are required to perform the different biochemical reactions. The enzymes involved in synthesizing the neurotransmitter are found generally within the neuron, whereas the enzymes involved in metabolizing the neurotransmitter after it is released from the presynaptic terminal are found generally outside the neuron, within the synapse. The names of these enzymes usually have suffixes ending in -ase, which means to decompose chemically. Finally, the decomposition or metabolism of each of these neurotransmitters ends in a product that can be

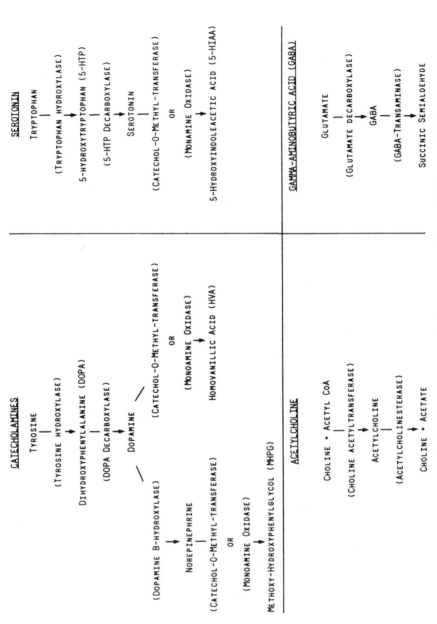

Figure 4. Biosynthetic pathways for catecholamines, serotonin, acetylcholine, and GABA.

removed from the brain and excreted. Detailed reviews of the biosynthetic pathways for these and other neurotransmitters can be found in Cooper, Bloom, and Roth (1982) and Siegel, Albers, Agranoff, and Katzman (1981).

Recent evidence indicates that peptides, which are chains of amino acids, may also function as neurotransmitters in the brain (Guillemin, 1978; Snyder, 1980). In particular, the endorphin and enkephalin opioid peptides may be involved in the action of drugs of abuse. The endorphins are large molecules, consisting of a sequence of 16 or more amino acids, which are cleaved off of an even larger precursor molecule called *pro-opiomelanocortin*. In contrast, the enkephalins are smaller molecules, consisting of a sequence of only 5 amino acids, which are cleaved off of a different precursor molecule called *proenkephalin*. Both the endorphins and enkephalins can produce a number of behavioral effects that are similar to those produced by morphine. Recent reviews of the psychopharmacological aspects of opioid peptides can be found in Frederickson and Geary (1982) and Olson, Olson, Kastin, and Coy (1984).

Receptors

Embedded within the outer membrane surface of each neuron are numerous receptors, which are protein structures specialized in recognizing specific neurotransmitter substances at the synapse. Although each neuron typically synthesizes and releases only one neurotransmitter, there may be a variety of different receptor types on the surface of a single neuron, depending upon how many different neurons synapse upon it. In general, each receptor is capable of recognizing only one particular type of neurotransmitter, thus preventing "cross-talk" between two synapses that reside close together but that utilize different neurotransmitters. To date, receptors have been isolated for each one of the neurotransmitters found within the brain.

When a receptor is occupied by a neurotransmitter that alters neurotransmission, the receptor is said to be *activated.* Receptor activation involves some change within the postsynaptic neuron that leads ultimately to an increase or decrease in the permeability of the postsynaptic membrane to ions involved in electrical neurotransmission. Excitatory neurotransmitters are those that increase the firing rate of postsynaptic neurons by increasing membrane permeability to ions, whereas inhibitory neurotransmitters decrease the firing rate of postsynaptic neurons by decreasing membrane permeability to ions. The exact nature of the intraneuronal events responsible for transforming a chemical message at the receptor into an electrical message at the postsynaptic membrane is not known presently. However, in some cases, receptor activation is known to stimulate the synthesis of cyclic AMP (adenosine monophosphate) from ATP (adenosine triphosphate) within the postsynaptic neuron. The stimulation of cyclic AMP subsequently activates intraneuronal protein kinases, which in turn alters the conformation of membrane proteins involved in maintaining the ionic charge across the membrane. This cyclic AMP-dependent mechanism within the postsynaptic neuron is called the *second messenger* to the neurotransmitter.

Many drugs of abuse produce their effect on the brain by occupying receptors utilized normally by neurotransmitters or by altering the second messenger system. In general, for a drug to occupy a receptor site, it must have a strong chemical attraction or affinity for the receptor, such that it can displace the natural neurotransmitter from its own receptor. Many drugs found in plant extracts or synthesized in the laboratory have greater affinity for the receptor than the endogenous neurotransmitter. Perhaps it seems surprising that the endogenous neurotransmitter may not have maximal affinity for its own receptor site. However, it should be realized that an essential property of neurotransmitter–receptor interactions is that they are reversible (Burt, 1985). The most efficient chemical message sent across the synapse is by a neurotransmitter that attaches to and detaches from the receptor optimally. This contrasts with a number of psychoactive drugs that *attach* readily to the receptor but do not *detach* readily. In some cases, drugs may even attach or bind to receptors irreversibly.

When a drug attaches to postsynaptic receptors to alter synaptic neurotransmission, then the drug is said to have a *direct action*. This contrasts with the *indirect action* of some drugs, in which an alteration in synaptic neurotransmission is obtained even though the drug does not attach to postsynaptic receptors. Drugs that have a direct action on receptors are classified as either *agonists* or *antagonists*, and they often have chemical structures similar to that of the natural neurotransmitter. Agonist drugs activate the receptors in a manner that mimics the action of the natural neurotransmitter. In contrast, antagonist drugs occupy the receptors but do not activate them, thus producing a functional blockade of the postsynaptic neuron. One cannot determine *a priori* whether an agonist or antagonist drug will increase or decrease the firing rate of the postsynaptic neuron. If the natural neurotransmitter is excitatory on the firing rate of a postsynaptic neuron, then an agonist drug will increase the firing rate, and an antagonist will decrease it. However, if the neurotransmitter is inhibitory on the firing rate of a postsynaptic neuron, then an agonist drug will decrease the firing rate, and an antagonist will increase it. Both agonist and antagonist drugs are used extensively by psychopharmacologists to investigate the neurochemical processes that mediate various behaviors. In addition, as will be discussed later, antagonist drugs offer a potentially useful pharmacologic tool to treat some cases of drug abuse.

Brain Mechanisms of Drug Reinforcement

Perhaps the most important psychopharmacologic factor involved in the self-administration of drugs of abuse involves a drug's capacity to produce a positive affective state or reinforcement. Until recently, very little was known about the brain mechanisms involved in drug reinforcement. However, as is discussed later, the demonstration that laboratory animals will self-administer a variety of drugs of abuse has provided an important model by which the brain mechanisms of drug reinforcement have been investigated. The significant advances in our understanding of the brain mechanisms of drug reinforcement have been reviewed recently (Fibiger, 1978; Wise, 1980, 1982, 1983).

Strong evidence now indicates that the *mesolimbic system* of the brain is involved in drug reinforcement. The mesolimbic system consists of dopamine-containing neurons that have their cell bodies in the midbrain ventral tegmental area (see Figure 5). These cell bodies project long axons forward via the medial forebrain bundle to innervate the nucleus accumbens and other diffuse structures of the limbic system, including the septum, amygdala, and olfactory tubercle (Issacson, 1974). Electrical stimulation of the mesolimbic pathway along the medial forebrain bundle is reinforcing, and this reinforcing effect is thought to be produced by the release of dopamine from the presynaptic terminals that innervate the target limbic structures (Ewing, Bigelow, & Wrightman, 1983). Although it is not known presently how the release of dopamine from the mesolimbic system is controlled normally, it has been speculated that axonal inputs from the locus coeruleus and lateral hypothalamus may modulate the activity of the mesolimbic system (Wise, 1980).

The dopamine mesolimbic system appears to play an essential role in mediating the reinforcing effect of stimulant drugs such as amphetamine and cocaine. As mentioned previously, both amphetamine and cocaine activate dopamine systems by increasing the availability of dopamine within the synapse. Dopamine antagonists such as pimozide, which are effective in blocking the reinforcing effect of electrical stimulation of the medial forebrain bundle (Wauquier & Niemegeers, 1972), are also effective in reducing the reinforcing effect of stimulant drugs (Risner & Jones, 1976; Yokel & Wise, 1976). Moreover, a lesion in the nucleus accumbens, a major target structure for the dopamine mesolimbic system, produces a decrease in the reinforcing effect of stimulant drugs

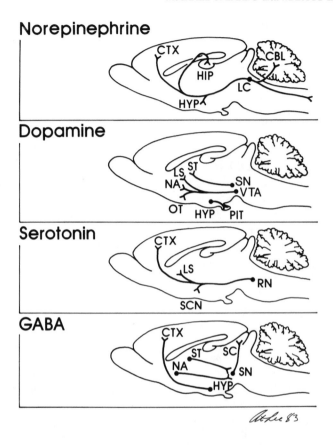

Figure 5. A sagittal side view of the rat brain showing cell bodies (●) and axonal projections for some major neurotransmitter pathways. Abbreviations: cerebellum (CBL); cortex (CTX); hippocampus (HIP); hypothalamus (HYP); locus coeruleus (LC); limbic system (LS); nucleus accumbens (NA); olfactory tubercle (OT); pituitary (PIT); raphe nucleus (RN); striatum (ST); substantia nigra (SN); superior colliculus (SC); suprachiasmatic nucleus (SCN); ventral tegmental area (VTA).

(Roberts, Corcoran, & Fibiger, 1977). It is not clear presently, however, whether other dopamine systems, such as the nigrostriatal and tuberohypophyseal systems, are also involved in the maintenance of self-administration of stimulant drugs.

In addition to mediating the reinforcing effect of stimulant drugs, recent evidence indicates that the dopamine mesolimbic system may mediate, at least in part, the reinforcing effect of opiate drugs such as heroin and morphine (see Bozarth, 1983). Opiate receptors have been localized on dopamine-containing neurons in the mesolimbic system (Pollard, Llorens, Bonnet, Costentin, & Schwartz, 1977). In general, the administration of morphine produces an excitatory effect on the firing rate of neurons within the major dopaminergic pathways of the brain (Klemm, 1981), and this excitatory effect is accompanied by an increase in the synthesis and release of dopamine (Iwamoto & Way, 1979). Most important, however, morphine is reinforcing when microinjected directly into the ventral tegmental area of the mesolimbic system but not when microinjected into a brain region just outside the ventral tegmental area (Phillips & LePiane, 1980). Also, the reinforcing effect of morphine in the ventral tegmental area is blocked by the administration of the opiate antagonist naloxone, suggesting that opiate receptors in this brain region are involved in drug reinforcement.

In contrast to stimulant and opiate drugs, the brain mechanisms involved in the reinforcing effects of other drugs of abuse are less well understood. The most widely abused class of drugs today are the sedative hyponotics, which includes alcohol, methaqualone (Quaalude), the barbiturates (e.g., Seconal, Nembutal, and Amytal), and the benzodiazepines (e.g., Librium, Valium, and Dalmane). Despite their wide abuse, little is known about the neuroanatomical pathways involved in the action of sedative hypnotics. However, it is thought that alcohol and barbiturates have a general depressant action on neuronal membranes, whereas the benzodiazepines have a more selective action at inhibitory GABA synapses (Harvey, 1980). Although the benzodiazepines are sometimes classified as GABA antagonists, this classification is probably inaccurate. Rather than attaching directly to the GABA receptor, it appears that benzodiazepines potentiate GABA neurotransmission either by coupling with the GABA receptor to enhance receptor affinity for GABA or by displacing an endogenous inhibitor of GABA (Costa, 1979). In any case, the sedative effect of the benzodiazepines is derived from their inhibition of the midbrain reticular formation.

Finally, the brain mechanisms involved in the reinforcing effects of the hallucinogens and THC are poorly understood, in large part because laboratory animals will not readily self-administer these drugs. However, it is known that lysergic acid diethylamide (LSD) is an agonist drug at serotonin receptors located on cell bodies of serotonin-containing neurons in the raphe nucleus (Cooper et al., 1982). In addition, recent evidence indicates that acetylcholine pathways within the limbic system mediate, at least in part, some of the behavioral effects of THC (Miller & Branconnier, 1983). It remains to be determined whether hallucinogenic drugs influence the mesolimbic system or some other reward system within the mammalian brain.

BIOCHEMICAL DETERMINANTS OF INDIVIDUAL DIFFERENCES IN DRUG RESPONSE

Two people who are administered identical doses of a psychoactive drug may display quite different reactions. Also, one person who is administered identical doses of some psychoactive drug on two different occasions may display different reactions. The between-individual and within-individual differences in reactivity to psychoactive drugs reflect, at least in part, a difference in biochemical factors. Various biochemical differences exist between and within individuals, including differences in drug absorption, metabolism, blood–brain barrier permeability, neurotransmitter turnover, and receptor availability. This section will discuss briefly several of the major factors that influence the biochemical mechanisms involved in drug action.

Period of Development

Drugs of abuse tend to produce their most potent and long-lasting effect when administered during either early development or old age. During fetal and neonatal development, the immature liver is deficient in enzymes required to metabolize drugs (Morselli, 1976), and the blood–brain barrier is incompletely formed (Kupferberg & Way, 1963). During old age, there is a decline in the drug-metabolizing capacity of the liver (Schmucker, 1979) and a decline in blood flow to the kidney (Richey & Bender, 1977). In addition, the aging process may compromise the blood–brain barrier, as recent evidence indicates that endothelial cells from brain capillaries in aged monkeys are thinner and have fewer mitochondria than capillaries from young monkeys (Burns, Kruckeberg, Comerford, & Buschmann, 1979). Thus, as a consequence of these various factors, there is an increased concentration of drug that reaches the brain during both early development and old age (Truex & Schmidt, 1980).

In addition to peripheral factors, various neurochemical factors within the CNS change with age. In the developing rat, the brainstem locus coeruleus begins synthesizing norepinephrine at about 14 days into gestation and midbrain dopaminergic nuclei begin synthesizing dopamine at about 18 days into gestation (Loizou, 1972). After 21 days, when the rat is born, the level of catecholamines in the whole brain is only about one-third the level found in adults (Coyle & Henry, 1973). From birth to adulthood, there is a progressive increase in catecholamine levels due to collateral branching of axons and to an increase in the number of presynaptic terminals that become functional. Similarly, the levels of other neurotransmitter substances increase during postnatal development, including levels of acetylcholine (Coyle & Yamamura, 1976), serotonin (Loizou and Salt, 1970), GABA (Coyle and Enna, 1976), and opioid peptides (Bayon, Shoemaker, Bloom, Mauss, & Guillemin, 1979). With each neurotransmitter system, there tends to be a caudal-to-rostral pattern of maturation as adult levels of neurotransmitter are reached in hindbrain regions prior to forebrain regions.

Synchronized with the ontogenesis of presynaptic neurotransmitter substances is the ontogenesis of postsynaptic receptor sites. In general, the development of postsynaptic receptors precedes the development of presynaptic neurotransmitter input (Coyle & Campochiaro, 1976; Haynes & Zakarian, 1981), indicating that these two developmental events may involve at least partially independent processes. Nonetheless, like the ontogenesis of neurotransmitter substances, the ontogenesis of receptor systems generally follows a caudal-to-rostral pattern of maturation (Bardo, Bhatnagar, & Gebhart, 1981). Thus, psychoactive drugs that affect hindbrain mechanisms may be more efficacious earlier in development than drugs that affect forebrain mechanisms.

Various neurochemical changes also occur during old age. Perhaps most important, there is a progressive decline in the number of neurons within the brain and a concomitant increase in astrocytes (Lansfield, Rose, Sandles, Wohlstadter, & Lynch, 1977). Correlated with the degeneration of neurons, there is a diminution in content of various neurotransmitters and receptors in different brain regions. Recent evidence suggests that degeneration of cholinergic neurotransmission occurs during aging and that this neurochemical change may play a major role in the memory dysfunction that sometimes accompanies old age (Bartus, Dean, Beer, & Lippa, 1982). Dopaminergic neurotransmission also appears to degenerate with age as there is a decrease in both dopamine synthesis (Reis, Ross, & Joh, 1977) and the number of dopamine receptors (Memo, Lucchi, Spano, & Trabucchi, 1980). Further, there is a decline with age in levels of beta-endorphin in the hypothalamus and striatum (Gambert, Garthwaite, Pontzer, & Hagen, 1980) and a decline in the number of opiate receptors in the striatum and hippocampus (Hess, Joseph, & Roth, 1981). However, the age-dependent diminution in neurochemical systems is not found universally through the CNS. For example, GABAergic systems appear to remain relatively unchanged during the aging process (Lippa, Critchett, Ehlert, Yanamura, Enna, & Bartus, 1981), and the concentration of met-enkephalin in the hypothalamus actually increases with age (Steger, Sonntag, Van Vugt, Forman, & Meites, 1980).

Given the extensive biochemical changes that occur across the entire life span, it is not surprising that a myriad of studies have shown that psychoactive drugs produce different effects when administered at different ages. Within the field of developmental psychopharmacology, extensive research with animals has been done with stimulants, sedative hypnotics, and opiates. Only a few selected studies will be mentioned here, but a more detailed account of this rapidly expanding research field can be found in Mabry and Campbell (1977).

Although stimulants such as amphetamine or methylphenidate (Ritalin) produce a hyperactive effect in adults, they may produce a paradoxical calming effect when administered to hyperactive children. Evidence from animals suggests that, under certain conditions, the response to stimulants is qualitatively different between infants and adults. For example, Campbell and Randall (1977) found that preweanling rats administered amphetamine became hyperactive when tested alone in an isolated chamber but became *hypo*active when tested in the presence of an adult rat. In contrast, older rats administered amphetamine became hyperactive regardless of whether they were tested in an isolated chamber or in the presence of an adult. These results suggest that amphetamine may produce a calming effect in infants only when appropriate, biologically relevant stimuli are available.

Infants also display an altered response to opiates relative to adults. Auguy-Valette, Cros, Gouarderes, Gout, and Pontonnier (1978) tested rats at different ages between 5 and 120 days of age and observed an age-related biphasic change in the analgesic effect of morphine. The first phase (5 to 15 days) was characterized by an incremental sensitivity to morphine-induced analgesia that was paralleled by an increase in the number of opiate receptors in the whole brain. The second phase (15 to 30 days) was characterized by a decremental sensitivity to morphine-induced analgesia that was paralleled by a decrease in brain permeability to the drug. These observations indicate that both the number of opiate receptors and the permeability of the blood–brain barrier influence the analgesic efficacy of morphine, although their influence is evident at different stages of infancy. Similarly, ontogenetic differences in the effect of morphine are evident with other behaviors in the rat, including locomotor activity, catalepsy, and stereotyped gnawing (Caza & Spear, 1980).

Finally, the behavioral effects of many psychoactive drugs are altered during old age. For example, administration of alcohol produces greater intoxication, more severe withdrawal symptoms, and a larger risk of lethal overdose in aged mice as compared to younger mice (Wiberg, Trenholm, & Coldwell, 1970; Wood, Armbrecht, & Wise, 1982). This change reflects, at least in part, a reduced rate of alcohol metabolism by the aged liver (Collins, Yeager, Lebsack, & Panter, 1975). In addition, the anorexic effect of amphetamine is increased in aged animals (Richey & Bender, 1977).

However, it should be noted that not all drug effects are enhanced during old age, as amphetamine is less effective in increasing spontaneous locomotor activity in older animals (Richey & Bender, 1977). Unfortunately, it is unclear presently what neurochemical factors are critical in determining whether older individuals will display an enhanced response to psychoactive drugs.

CIRCADIAN RHYTHMS

The potency and duration of action for many drugs vary with the time of day they are administered because many biochemical parameters fluctuate on diurnal or circadian rhythms. Rodents maintained on normal light/dark cycles are most active during the dark phase. It is during the active dark phase that sedative hypnotic and opiate drugs are most rapidly metabolized in the rodent liver (Holcslaw, Miya, & Bousquet, 1975). This metabolic circadian rhythm is abolished by continuous lighting, indicating that the rhythm is stimulus bound rather than determined by an internal clock. Within the brain, there is also a circadian rhythm evident with various neurotransmitter–receptor systems, including those systems involving acetylcholine (Saito, Yamashita, Yamazaki, Okada, Satomi, & Fujieda, 1975), dopamine (Bruinink, Lichtensteiger, & Schlumpf, 1983; Lemmer & Berger, 1978), serotonin (Scheving, Harrison, Gordon, & Pauly, 1968), and opioid peptides (Naber, Wirz-Justice, & Kafka, 1981; Wesche & Frederickson, 1979). In some cases, these circadian rhythms are maintained under continuous lighting, indicating that they are synchronized to an internal clock.

The efficacy of various drugs also follows a circadian rhythm. For example, the analgesic effect of morphine in mice varies with the time of day (Oliverio, Castellano, & Puglisi-Allegra, 1982), which perhaps reflects a circadian variation in levels of endogenous opioid peptides in the brain. Similarly, the lethal effect of morphine follows a circadian rhythm (Campos, Lujan, Lopez, Figuerohernandez, & Rodriquez, 1983). Moreover, drug-dependent laboratory animals will adjust the intake of some drugs according to the time of day. Mice given unrestricted access to alcohol under a normal light/dark cycle will drink most during the earliest and latest portions of the active dark phase (Millard & Dole, 1983). When maintained under constant darkness, mice will subsequently increase their alcohol intake. The increased intake during the active dark phase presumably reflects a circadian increase in the level of the hormone melatonin secreted from the pineal gland and hypothalamus (Geller, 1971).

GENDER

The efficacy of psychoactive drugs may also differ between males and females, in part because there are sex differences in drug metabolism (O'Malley, Crooks, Duke, & Stevenson, 1971) and various neurohormonal factors (Greenough, Carter, Steerman, & DeVoogd, 1977; Pfaff & McEwen, 1983). Sex differences in drug response have been observed with morphine self-administration behavior (Alexander, Coambs, & Hadaway, 1978) and with amphetamine-induced rotational behavior in rats (Robinson, Becker, & Presty, 1982). In female rats, amphetamine-induced release of dopamine from the striatum also varies with the stage of the estrous cycle (Becker & Ramirez, 1981). Further, Middaugh, Zemp, and Boggan (1983) have demonstrated that pregnant mice are more sensitive to the behavioral effects of phenobarbital as compared to nonpregnant female mice. These findings suggest clearly that drug effects are at least partially dependent upon the neurohormonal status of the organism.

STRESS

Evidence indicates that profound and long-lasting biochemical changes may occur when an organism is exposed to acute or chronic stress. Within the brain, acute stress produces an increase in the release of various neurotransmitters, including norepinephrine (Tanaka, Kohno, Nakagawa, Ida, Takeda, & Nagasaki, 1982), dopamine (Herman, Guillonneau, Dantzer, Scatton, Semerdjian-Rouquier, & Le Moal, 1982), serotonin (Palkovits, Brownstein, Kizer, Saavedra, & Kopin, 1976), GABA (Manev & Pericic, 1983), and opioid peptides (Amir, Brown, & Amit, 1980). In general, repeated exposure to stress induces an adaptation of these neurochemical effects (Stone & McCarty, 1983), although the magnitude and duration of change in each neurotransmitter system varies considerably from one brain region to another. In addition, the neurochemical change depends upon the age of the individual, as stress-induced depletions of norepinephrine in the hypothalamus and forebrain have been shown to be more severe in older rats than in younger rats (Ritter & Pelzer, 1978).

In conjunction with neurochemical changes, stress may enhance the efficacy of various psychoactive drugs. However, recent evidence indicates that the effects of stress are evident only when the stress is inescapable. To demonstrate this, MacLennan and Maier (1983) exposed two groups of rats to similar stressful foot shock, except that one group was allowed to escape the foot shock, whereas the other group had no escape route. When challenged subsequently with either amphetamine or cocaine, only those rats given inescapable foot shock exhibited an enhanced stimulatory response as measured by stereotyped behaviors. In contrast, animals that were given escapable foot shock displayed a response to the stimulants that was similar to that shown by nonstressed control animals. In further studies, inescapable stress, but not escapable stress, has been shown to potentiate amphetamine-induced startle behavior (Kokkinidis & MacNeill, 1982) and morphine-induced analgesia (Hyson, Ashcraft, Drugan, Grau, & Maier, 1982). These recent findings demonstrate that stress *per se* is not the critical factor in altering the drug effect, but the inability to escape from stress is paramount.

Although inescapable stress clearly influences the neurochemical mechanisms of drug action, there is surprisingly little evidence to support the popular assumption that stressful situations lead to an increase in drug abuse. For example, in a recent review of the research on the interaction of stress and alcohol intake, Pohorecky (1981) concluded that attempts to elevate alcohol intake in animals by using physical stressors has been disappointing. Despite some reports to the contrary (e.g., Derr & Lindblad, 1980), it appears that stressful treatment actually suppresses the intake of alcohol in laboratory animals (Ng Cheong Ton, Brown, Michalakeas, & Amit, 1983). However, it should be noted that the physical stress used in studies with laboratory animals may be an inadequate model of the interaction between psychological stress and drug abuse in humans.

IMPLICATIONS FOR TREATMENT OF DRUG ABUSE

Regardless of the specific clinical strategy used to treat drug abuse in humans, there are two main therapeutic goals: (1) physiological withdrawal from the drug (or, at least, regulated use of the drug); and (2) psychological rehabilitation of the client (e.g., through career counseling and job skills training). These two goals are generally part of any treatment program, whether its emphasis is psychotherapeutic (such as psychodynamic, cognitive, or behavioral), pharmacotherapeutic (such as methadone maintenance or antagonist administration), or something between these two extremes (Bennett, Vourakis, & Woolf, 1983; Lettieri, Sayers, & Pearson, 1980). Although some health-care professionals believe in the predominant use of psychotherapy instead of pharmacotherapy, or vice versa, most prefer a combination of features from both positions. It may be valuable, for example, to give the client some therapeutic drugs to provide short-term relief of withdrawal symptoms before intense psychotherapy is initiated. In the case of opiates, the centrally acting adrenergic agonist, clonidine, has been shown to reduce the sympathetic overactivity that occurs during withdrawal (Gold, Redmon, & Kleber, 1979). There are several programs that utilize pharmacological tools in their treatment approach. Some of the experimental evidence that underlies pharmacotherapies for opiate and stimulant abuse is discussed in the remainder of this section. (For a discussion of pharmacotherapies for the abuse of sedative hypnotics and other drugs, see Jaffe, 1980.)

Before discussing the recent research developments in the pharmacologic treatment of drug abuse, it should be mentioned that there are many different theories of drug abuse, each emphasizing a different facet of the problem. Some theories tend to focus on the factors that are responsible for the initiation of drug-taking behavior; others emphasize factors that support the continuation of drug-taking; whereas yet a third group is especially concerned with termination of the behavior. Regardless of the emphasis, however, a common thread runs through all theories and definitions of drug abuse: *excessive drug taking behavior.* Indeed, a pathological pattern of excessive drug taking is generally considered to be the primary criterion for distinguishing drug *abuse* from nonpathological drug *use* (American Psychiatric Association, 1980). Examples of pathological drug use by humans include an inability to stop or reduce use, intoxication through the day, continued drug taking in the face of undeniable physical harm, and the perceived need to use the drug before "normal" functioning can occur. Evidence for these examples may be difficult to obtain because of the inability of people to accurately remember details of their drug-taking experiences. The influence of personality and/or social factors may also cloud the reliability of the observations. Several nationally based surveys (such as the Drug Abuse Warning Network, or DAWN), attempt to systematically monitor the degree of illicit drug use. Epidemiological data from these surveys provide information about the extent of drug abuse among the population. Other sources of information about the extent of drug abuse in humans is discussed by Griffiths, Bigelow, and Henningfield (1980).

ANIMAL MODEL OF DRUG REINFORCEMENT

It has not always been accepted that animals could be used to study drug self-administration or even be made physically dependent on a drug. For example, Light and his associate (Light, 1929; Light & Torrance, 1929) claimed that withholding heroin from a dependent person produced minimal physiological changes that they felt could not completely account for the total array of signs and symptoms demonstrated by the addict. It was concluded that the narcotic abstinence syndrome was deliberately feigned by the addict to receive sympathy and more heroin. Because the syndrome was viewed as a form of malingering with no apparent biochemical substrate, narcotic dependence was viewed as a sociopersonality disturbance with a limited biochemical basis.

The report of Tatum, Seevers, and Collins (1929) offered convincing proof that dependence and subsequent withdrawal signs could, indeed, be demonstrated in the laboratory using both monkeys and dogs. Shortly after this initial report, Kolb and Dumez (1931) and Seevers (1936) replicated these findings, and Himmelsbach, Gerlach, and Stanton (1935) extended this work by producing narcotic dependence in rats. Thus, it was firmly established that laboratory animals could be used to study some of the biochemical parameters of drug abuse and dependence.

An early experiment by Spragg (1940) set the stage for studying the behavioral aspects of drug taking in laboratory animals. Chimpanzees were made physically dependent on morphine by giving them morphine injections twice daily for several months. When given a choice between a box containing a banana and a box containing a morphine-filled syringe, the chimpanzees would choose the food when their physical dependence was well maintained but would choose the drug when their morphine had been withheld from them. Spragg's results clearly suggested that drugs could serve as reinforcers in animals and would maintain behavior that led to their delivery. Subsequent methodological and conceptual developments by Nichols and associates (Headlee, Coppock, & Nichols, 1955; Nichols, Headlee, & Coppock, 1956), Weeks (1962; Weeks & Collins, 1964), Thompson and Schuster (1964), and Seevers and associates (Deneau, Yanagita, & Seevers, 1969) firmly established the use of laboratory animals to study drugs as reinforcers using operant conditioning procedures. These procedures have been successfully applied to a variety of species (e.g., baboon, monkey, dog, cat, and rat), using several routes of administration (e.g., intravenous, oral, intraperitoneal, and intramuscular) across many pharmacological categories (e.g., opiates, stimulants, and sedative hypnotics). In general, there is good concordance between drugs that are self-administered in the laboratory and those that are abused by man (Griffiths et al., 1980; Johanson & Schuster, 1981; Thompson & Unna, 1977). The drug self-administration model has proven to be a powerful method for studying drug-taking behavior by animals under controlled laboratory conditions. Moreover, this animal model has been used extensively by investigators who seek to understand the biochemical causes and treatments of drug abuse.

OPIATE ABUSE

The search for a pharmacological agent that could be used to "cure" opiate dependence has been conducted for a long time with varying degrees of success. For example, Sigmund Freud successfully used cocaine to wean a patient from morphine, but in the process he created a cocaine abuser (Gay, Inaba, Sheppard, Newmeyer, & Rappolt, 1975). Even heroin, when it was first introduced, was thought to have some utility for the treatment of morphine addiction. Over the years several other drugs have been proposed as aids in the treatment of narcotic dependence, including other opiate agonists such as methadone, opiate antagonists such as cyclazocine and naltrexone, and nonopiate drugs such as the phenothiazines and clonidine. These, and other treatments, are briefly summarized next.

Methadone is an orally effective, synthetic compound that has a pharmacological profile much like that of morphine. It has a relatively long duration of action and can substitute for other opiates in suppressing the abstinence syndromes that follow their withdrawal (Jaffe & Martin, 1980). Methadone substitution is the "treatment of choice" for the detoxification of opiate addicts (see Wikler, 1980), and methadone maintenance is the most widely used treatment for narcotic dependence (Lowinson & Milman, 1979). The success of methadone maintenance is usually attributed to the development of cross-tolerance to other opiates following chronic administration. Presumably, this state of "narcotic blockade" is sufficient to prevent the euphorigenic effect of narcotics if they are self-administered (Dole, Nyswander, & Kreek, 1966; Kreek, 1979). The success of methadone maintenance may be due in part to the reinforcing properties of methadone *per se*. Indeed, the subjective effects of methadone are qualitatively similar to those of morphine (Martin, Jasinski, Haertzen, Kay, Jones, Mansky, & Carpenter, 1973); both drugs produce euphoria, as measured by the Addiction Research Center Inventory. That methadone has reinforcing properties in its own right is also supported by the results of studies using laboratory animals. For example, Harrigan and Downs (1978) reported that methadone would maintain self-administration behavior when tested in rhesus monkeys.

The value of using opiate antagonists as a treatment for opiate dependence has been recognized for some time. Approximately 30 years ago, Wikler (reviewed in Wikler, 1980) theorized that many aspects of the opiate withdrawal syndrome could become conditioned to environmental stimuli and that these conditioned stimuli played an important role in relapse to drug use long after withdrawal from the drug was completed. It was hypothesized that if a postaddict client reverted to narcotic self-administration while being treated with an antagonist, no euphoric effects of the narcotic would be felt by the client, and the conditioned relapse would eventually extinguish. Martin and his co-workers (Martin, Fraser, Gorodetzky, & Rosenberg, 1965; Martin, Gorodetzky, & McClane, 1966) reported that cyclazocine, a long-acting, orally effective opiate antagonist, blocked the effects of morphine. Moreover, tolerance did not develop to these effects, and the subjective effects were unlike those of morphine. However, when tested in the clinic using heroin addicts who volunteered for treatment with cyclazocine, it was quickly apparent that patient compliance was low, presumably due to the adverse side effects produced by cyclazocine (see Jaffe, 1980). The development of naltrexone, an orally effective, long-acting opiate antagonist with relatively few side effects, has produced encouraging results (see reviews by Julius & Renault, 1976; O'Brien, Greenstein, Evans, Woody, & Arndt, 1983). Although naltrexone appears to hold promise as an efficacious treatment, its actual utility may be limited unless "extinction trials" (i.e., opiate self-administration in the presence of naltrexone) occur frequently enough to extinguish drug-taking behavior. That repeated treatment with opiate antagonists will reduce the reinforcing efficacy of opiates has also been demonstrated in laboratory animals. Killian, Bonese, and Schuster (1978) found that high doses of naloxone decreased the rate of responding maintained by heroin in a way like that seen when saline was substituted for heroin.

Although several nonopiates have been used for the opiate withdrawal syndrome, few have proven valuable as a method of relieving the symptoms or helping maintain a drug-free individual. An early study by Fraser and Isbell (1956), for example, concluded that major tranquilizers such as chlorpromazine and reserpine were ineffective in treating acute morphine abstinence; in fact, reserpine tended to exacerbate the intensity of the symptoms. Sedative hypnotics such as the barbiturates are also not practical aids in suppressing withdrawal symptoms because relief is evident only when the client is administered anesthetic doses (Jaffe, 1980). Recent clinical studies with the nonopiate antihypertensive clonidine suggest that this drug may be effective in suppressing and/or reducing the signs and symptoms of opiate withdrawal (see review by Washton & Resnick, 1981). The emergence of untoward side effects and the development of tolerance to the actions of clonidine may limit its clinical usefulness, however. Furthermore, studies in rhesus monkeys demonstrate the ability of clonidine to maintain intravenous self-administration behavior (Woolverton, Wessinger, Balster, & Harris, 1981). Thus clonidine, like methadone, has reinforcing properties in its own right, and this factor must be considered when the effectiveness of clonidine as a treatment for narcotic abuse is measured.

Finally, the possibility of blocking the reinforcing properties of opiates through immunization has also been tested. Schuster and colleagues (summarized in Schuster, 1981) actively immunized monkeys by treating them with a morphine–protein conjugate that produced morphine and heroin antibodies. Subsequent self-administration of heroin in the same monkeys was considerably lower than that seen before immunization. Although there are numerous practical problems that would be associated with immunization as a treatment for human addicts, the demonstration of its effectiveness in animals has great theoretical value.

STIMULANT ABUSE

The nonmedical use of stimulants has fluctuated widely over years, and many drugs from this pharmacological category continue to be abused despite the psychiatric and physical problems they can cause (see Ellinwood, 1979). For example, the chronic, high-dose use of amphetamine is known to produce excessive motor and verbal behavior, along with frenetic, compulsive, and even bizarre actions (Post, 1981). Additionally, the apparent similarity between many of the signs and symptoms associated with psychomotor stimulant overdose and paranoid schizophrenia has been demonstrated in humans under controlled laboratory conditions (Griffith, Cavanaugh, Held, & Oates, 1970). Although the intravenous abuse of amphetamine has declined somewhat in recent years, the abuse of another stimulant, cocaine, has increased appreciably and is currently a major drug of abuse in the United States. Like amphetamine, the ability of cocaine to produce paranoid and schizophreniform psychoses is well documented (Post, 1975), but cocaine is the unanimous "recreational drug of choice" among experienced abusers (Siegel, 1977). It is interesting to note that, among the many stimulants self-administered by laboratory animals, cocaine appears to be the most reinforcing drug in this category (Griffiths, Brady, & Snell, 1978; Risner & Silcox, 1981).

In contrast to the many treatment programs that are available for use with opiate addicts, there are only a few options for treating compulsive users of stimulants. Maintenance approaches, analogous to the methadone programs for opiate abusers, have not been used extensively for stimulants (Jaffe, 1980). No demonstrated physical withdrawal syndrome occurs following abrupt discontinuation of stimulant use, but psychological symptoms such as apathy, depression, irritability, and disorientation may occur for several months. Although some clinicians have had moderate success using sedative pharmacologic agents such as haloperidol (Haldol) or diazepam (Valium) to attenuate the minor discomfort following termination of stimulant use (Angrist, Less, & Gershon, 1974), most attempt to achieve total, drug-free withdrawal. Recently, the tricyclic antidepressant, desipramine, was successfully used as a therapeutic tool to treat amphetamine and cocaine-dependent persons (Tennant & Rawson, 1983). The ability of desipramine to selectively enhance catecholamine activity (through blockade of reuptake) was the basis for selecting this treatment because chronic amphetamine use depletes catecholamines from the CNS.

As discussed previously, a number of drugs have been developed to specifically antagonize the effects of opiates. Unfortunately, there are no specific antagonists that can be used to block the effects of stimulants. Ellinwood (1979) commented that a major obstacle that has beset the search for a stimulant antagonist drug is the fact that stimulants have several modes of action, and these different modes are not clearly defined. The possibility of using specific dopamine antagonists exists, especially because there is considerable evidence that many effects of amphetamine and other stimulants can be blocked or attenuated following treatment with these drugs. For example, several dopamine antagonists have been shown to alter the reinforcing properties of several stimulants (see review by Wise, 1982). Risner and colleagues (Risner & Jones, 1976, 1980, unpublished data) trained dogs to self-administer several stimulants (including d-amphetamine, methamphetamine, cocaine, and mazindol) during short, daily sessions. Following stabilization of drug-taking behavior, the dogs were treated with the dopaminergic antagonist, pimozide, immediately before the next drug session. Responding was altered in a way suggesting that the reinforcing effects of the stimulant agonists maintaining behavior had been attenuated. Attempts to treat human amphetamine abusers with chronic pimozide have met with only partial success (Gunne, Anggard, & Jonsson, 1972), perhaps because of the undesirable side effects that accompany administration of neuroleptics (Ellinwood, 1979). Nonetheless, the use of these drugs to treat stimulant abuse may have clinical value, especially when used in combination with psychotherapy, which tries to help the patient deal with personality problems that may be responsible for stimulant abuse (Post, 1981).

CONCLUSION

As we have seen in this chapter, the effects of a drug depend not only on biochemical factors such as its chemical structure, route of administration, and rate of metabolism, but also on individual biochemical differences among the organisms receiving the drug. The species of the organism, its age, gender, and health status are all known to alter the effect of a drug, some more markedly than others. Analogously, the selection and outcome of treatment for drug abuse in humans will also be determined in part by the individual characteristics of the client. As Jaffe (1975, 1980) has discussed, drug abusers are a heterogeneous group of people, and many aspects of their backgrounds may influence responsivity to treatment. The mix of biochemical, behavioral, situational, and physiological factors is clearly not the same for every person. Consequently, we should not expect to reliably use the same therapeutic approach across the entire spectrum of individuals who need help in their efforts to overcome drug abuse. As clinicians become increasingly aware of the need for greater individualization in their practice, specific subpopulations such as youth, women, the elderly, and minorities are all having treatment programs tailored uniquely for them (DuPont, Goldstein, O'Donnell, & Brown, 1979; Krasnegor, 1979). These specific treatment programs reflect the importance of individual differences in the biochemical substrates of drug abuse.

ACKNOWLEDGMENTS

We greatly appreciate the assistance of Ms. Wanda Roberts in preparing this manuscript.

REFERENCES

Alexander, B. K., Coambs, R. B., & Hadaway, P. F. The effect of housing and gender on morphine self-administration in rats. *Psychopharmacology*, 1978, *58*, 175–179.

American Psychiatric Association. *Diagnostic and statistical manual of mental disorders* (3rd ed.). Washington, D.C.: American Psychiatric Association, 1980.

Amir, S., Brown, Z. W., & Amit, Z. The role of endorphins in stress: Evidence and speculations. *Neuroscience & Biobehavioral Reviews*, 1980, *4*, 77–86.

Angrist, M. D., Less, H. K., & Gershon, S. The antagonism of amphetamine-induced symptomatology by a neuroleptic. *American Journal of Psychiatry*, 1974, *131*, 817–819.

Auguy-Valette, A., Cros,. J., Gouarderes, C., Gout, A., & Pontonnier, G. Morphine analgesia and cerebral opiate receptors: A developmental study. *British Journal of Pharmacology*, 1978, *63*, 303–308.

Bardo, M. T., Bhatnagar, R. K., & Gebhart, G. F. Opiate receptor ontogeny and morphine-induced effects: Influence of chronic footshock stress in preweanling rats. *Developmental Brain Research*, 1981, *1*, 487–495.

Bartus, R. T., Dean, R. L., Beer, B., & Lippa, A. S. The cholinergic hypothesis of geriatric memory dysfunction. *Science*, 1982, *217*, 408–417.

Bayon, A., Shoemaker, W. J., Bloom, F. E., Mauss, A., & Guillemin, R. Perinatal development of the endorphin- and enkephalin-containing systems in the rat brain. *Brain Research*, 1979, *179*, 93–101.

Becker, J. B., & Ramirez, V. D. Sex differences in the amphetamine stimulated release of catecholamines from rat striatal tissue *in vitro*. *Brain Research*, 1981, *204*, 361–372.

Bennett, G., Vourakis, C., & Woolf, D. S. (Eds.). *Substance abuse, pharmacologic, developmental, and clinical perspectives.* New York: Wiley, 1983.

Bozarth, M. A. Opiate reward mechanisms mapped by intracranial self-administration. In J. E. Smith & J. D. Lane (Eds.), *The neurobiology of opiate reward processes.* Amsterdam: Elsevier, 1983.

Bruinink, A., Lichtensteiger, W., & Schlumpf, M. Ontogeny of diurnal rhythms of central dopamine, serotonin and spirodecanone binding sites and of motor activity in the rat. *Life Sciences*, 1983, *33*, 31–38.

Burns, E. M., Kruckeberg, T. W., Comerford, L. E., & Buschmann, M. T. Thinning of capillary walls and declining numbers of endothelial mitochondria in the cerebral cortex of aging primate, *Macaca nemestrina. Journal of Gerontology*, 1979, *34*, 642–650.

Burt, D. R. Criteria for receptor identification. In H. I. Yamamura, S. J. Enna, & M. J. Kuhar (Eds.), *Neurotransmitter receptor binding.* New York: Raven Press, 1985.

Campbell, B. A., & Randall, P. J. Paradoxical effects of amphetamine on preweanling and postweanling rats. *Science*, 1977, *195*, 888–891.

Campos, A. E., Lujan, M., Lopez, E., Figueroahernandez, J., & Rodrigues, R. Circadian variation in the lethal effect of morphine in the mouse. *Proceedings of the Western Pharmacology Society*, 1983, *26*, 101–104.

Carlson, N. R. *Physiology of behavior.* Boston: Allyn & Bacon, 1980.

Carpenter, D. O., & Reese, T. S. Chemistry and physiology of synaptic transmission. In G. J. Siegel, R. W. Albers, B. W. Albers, B. W. Agranoff, & R. Katzman (Eds.), *Basic neurochemistry.* Boston: Little, Brown, 1981.

Caza, P. A., & Spear, L. P. Ontogenesis of morphine-induced behavior in the rat. *Pharmacology, Biochemistry, & Behavior*, 1980, *13*, 45–50.

Collins, A. C., Yeager, T. N., Lebsack, M. E., & Panter, S. S. Variations in alcohol metabolism: Influence of sex and age. *Pharmacology, Biochemistry, & Behavior*, 1975, *3*, 973–978.

Cooper, J. R., Bloom, F. E., & Roth, R. H. *The biochemical basis of neuropharmacology.* New York: Oxford University Press, 1982.

Costa, E. The role of gamma-aminobutyric acid in the action of 1,4-benzodiazepines. *Trends in Pharmacological Science*, 1979, *1*, 41.

Coyle, J. T. & Campochiaro, P. Ontogenesis of dopamine-cholinergic interactions in the rat striatum: A neurochemical study. *Journal of Neurochemistry*, 1976,*27*, 673–678.

Coyle, J. T. & Enna, S. J. Neurochemical aspects of the ontogenesis of GABAergic neurons in the rat brain. *Brain Research* 1976, *111*, 119–133.

Coyle, J. T., & Henry D. Catecholamines in fetal and newborn rat brain. *Journal of Neurochemistry*, 1973, *21*, 61–67.

Coyle, J. T., & Yamamura, H. I. Neurochemical aspects of the ontogenesis of cholinergic neurones in the rat brain. *Brain Research* 1976, *118*, 429–440.

Deneau, G. E., Yanagita, T., & Seevers, M. H. Self-administration of psychoactive substances by the monkey—A measure of psychological dependence. *Psychopharmacologia*, 1969, *16*, 30–48.

Derr, R., & Lindblad, S. Stress-induced consumption of ethanol by rats. *Life Sciences*, 1980, *27*, 2183–2186.

Dole, V. P., Nyswander, M. E., & Kreek, M. J. Narcotic blockade. *Archives of Internal Medicine*, 1966, *118*, 304–309.

DuPont, R. L., Goldstein, A., O'Donnell, J., & Brown, B. (Eds.), *Handbook on drug abuse.* Rockville, Md.: National Institute on Drug Abuse, 1979.

Ellinwood, E. Amphetamines/anorectics. In R. L. DuPont, A. Goldstein, J. O'Donnell, & B. Brown (Eds.), *Handbook on drug abuse*. Rockville, Md.: National Institute on Drug Abuse, 1979.

Ewing, A. G., Bigelow, J. C., & Wrightman, R. M. Direct *in vivo* monitoring of dopamine released from two striatal compartments in the rat. *Science*, 1983, *221*, 169–171.

Fibiger, H. C. Drugs and reinforcement mechanisms: A critical review of the catecholamine theory. *Annual Review of Pharmacology and Toxicology*, 1978, *18*, 37–56.

Fraser, H. F., & Isbell, H. Chlorpromazine and reserpine: (A) Effects of each and of combinations of each with morphine, (B) failure of each in treatment of abstinence from morphine. *Archives of Neurology and Psychiatry*, 1956, *76*, 257–262.

Frederickson, R. C. A., & Geary, L. E. Endogenous opioid peptides: Review of physiological, pharmacological, and clinical aspects. *Progress in Neurobiology*, 1982, *19*, 19–69.

Gambert, S. R., Garthwaite, R. L., Pontzer, C. H., & Hagen, T. C. Age-related changes in central nervous system beta-endorphin and ACTH. *Neuroendocrinology*, 1980, *31*, 252–255.

Gay, G. R., Inaba, D. S., Sheppard, C. W., Newmeyer, J. A., & Rappolt, R. S. Cocaine: History, epidemiology, human pharmacology, and treatment. A perspective on a debut for an old girl. *Clinical Toxicology*, 1975, *8*, 149–178.

Geller, I. Ethanol preference in the rat as a function of photoperiod. *Science*, 1971, *173*, 456–459.

Gold, M. S., Redmon, D. E., & Kleber, H. D. Noradrenergic hyperactivity in opiate withdrawal supported by clonidine reversal of opiate withdrawal. *American Journal of Psychiatry*, 1979, *136*, 100–102.

Gorsuch, R. L., & Butler, M. C. Initial drug abuse: A review of predisposing social psychological factors. *Psychological Bulletin*, 1976, *83*, 120–137.

Greenough, W. T., Carter, C. S., Steerman, C., & DeVoogd, T. J. Sex differences in dendritic patterns in hamster preoptic area. *Brain Research* 1977, *126*, 63–72.

Griffith, J. D., Cavanaugh, J. H., Held, J., & Oates, J. A. Experimental psychosis induced by the administration of *d*-amphetamine. In E. Costa & S. Garattini (Eds.), *Amphetamines and related compounds*. New York: Raven Press, 1970.

Griffiths, R. R., Bigelow, G. E., & Henningfield, J. E. Similarities in animal and human drug-taking behavior. In N. K. Mello (Ed.), *Advances in substance abuse* (Vol. 1). Greenwich: JAI Press, 1980.

Griffiths, R. R., Brady, J. V., & Snell, J. D. Progressive-ratio performance maintained by drug infusions: Comparison of cocaine, diethylproprion, chlorphentermine, and fenfluramine. *Psychopharmacology*, 1978, *56*, 5–13.

Guillemin, R. Peptides in the brain: The new endocrinology of the neuron. *Science*, 1978, *202*, 390–402.

Gunne, L. M., Anggard, E., & Jonsson, L. E. Clinical trials with amphetamine-blocking drugs. *Psychiatria Neurologia Neurochirgia*, 1972, *75*, 225–226.

Haertzen, C. A., Kocher, T. R., & Miyasato, K. Reinforcements from the first drug experience can predict later drug habits and/or addiction: Results with coffee, cigarettes, alcohol, barbiturates, minor and major tranquilizers, stimulants, marijuana, hallucinogens, heroin, opiates and cocaine. *Drug and Alcohol Dependence*, 1983, *11*, 147–165.

Harrigan, S. E., & Downs, D. A. Self-administration of heroin, acetyl-methadol morphine, and methadone in rhesus monkeys. *Life Sciences*, 1978, *22*, 619–624.

Harvey, S. C. Hypnotics and sedatives. In A. G. Gilman, L. S. Goodman, & A. Gilman (Eds.), *The pharmacological basis of therapeutics* (6th ed.). New York: Macmillan, 1980.

Haynes, L. W., & Zakarian, S. Microanatomy of enkephalin-containing neurones in the developing rat spinal cord *in vitro*. *Neuroscience*, 1981, *6*, 1899–1916.

Headlee, C. P., Coppock, H. W., & Nichols, J. R. Apparatus and technique involved in a laboratory method of testing the addictiveness of drugs. *Journal of American Pharmaceutical Association*, 1955, *44*, 229–231.

Herman, J. P., Guillonneau, D., Dantzer, R., Scatton, B., Semerdjian-Roquier, L., & Le Moal, M. Differential effects of inescapable footshocks and of stimuli previously paired with inescapable footshocks on dopamine turnover in cortical and limbic areas of the rat. *Life Sciences*, 1982, *30*, 2207–2214.

Hess, G. D., Joseph, J. A., & Roth, G. S. Effect of age on sensitivity to pain and brain opiate receptors. *Neurobiology of Aging*, 1981, *2*, 49–55.

Himmelsbach, C. K., Gerlach, G. H., Stanton, E. J. A method for testing addiction, tolerance and abstinence in the rat. Results of its application to several morphine alkaloids. *Journal of Pharmacology and Experimental Therapeutics*, 1935, *53*, 179–187.

Hokfelt, T., Johansson, O., Ljungdahl, A., Lundberg, J. M., & Schultzberg, M. Peptidergic neurones. *Nature*, 1980, *284*, 515–521.

Holcslaw, T. L., Miya, T. S., & Bousquet, W. S. Circadian rhythms in drug action and drug metabolism in the mouse. *Journal of Pharmacology and Experimental Therapeutics*, 1975, *195*, 320–332.

Hyson, R. L., Ashcraft, L. F., Drugan, R. C., Grau, J. W., & Maier, S. F. Extent and control of shock affects naltrexone sensitivity of stress-induced analgesia and reactivity to morphine. *Pharmacology, Biochemistry, & Behavior*, 1982, *17*, 1019–1025.

Issacson, R. L. *The limbic system.* New York: Plenum Press, 1974.

Iwamoto, E. T., & Way, E. L. Opiate actions and catecholamines. In H. H. Loh & D. H. Ross (Eds.), *Neurochemical mechanisms of opiates and endorphins (Advances in biochemical psychopharmacology)* (Vol. 30). New York: Raven Press, 1979.

Jaffe, J. H. Drug addiction and drug abuse. In L. S. Goodman & A. Gilman (Eds.), *The pharmacological basis of therapeutics* (5th ed.). New York: Macmillan, 1975.

Jaffe, J. H. Drug addiction and drug abuse. In A. G. Gilman, L. S. Goodman, & A. Gilman (Eds.), *The pharmacological basis of therapeutics* (6th ed.). New York: Macmillan, 1980.

Jaffe, J. H., & Martin, W. R. Opioid analgesics and antagonists. In A. G. Gilman L. S. Goodman, & A. Gilman (Eds.), *The pharmacological basis of therapeutics* (6th ed.). New York: Macmillan, 1980.

Johanson, C. E., & Schuster, C. R. Animal models of drug self-administration. In N. K. Mello (Ed.), *Advances in substance abuse* (Vol. II). Greenwich: JAI Press, 1981.

Julius, D., & Renault, P. (Eds.) *Narcotic antagonists: Naltrexone, progress report.* Rockville, Md.: National Institute on Drug Abuse, 1976.

Katzman, R. Blood–brain–CSF barriers. In G. J. Siegel, R. W. Albers, B. W. Agranoff, & R. Katzman (Eds.), *Basic neurochemistry.* Boston: Little, Brown, 1981.

Killian, A. K., Bonese, K., & Schuster, C. R. The effects of naloxone on behavior maintained by cocaine and heroin injections in the rhesus monkey. *Drug and Alcohol Dependence*, 1978, *3*, 245–251.

Klemm, W. R. Opiate mechanisms: Evaluation of research involving neuronal action potentials. *Progress in Neuro-Psychopharmacology*, 1981, *5*, 1–33.

Kokkinidis, L., & MacNeill, E. P. Stress-induced facilitation of acoustic startle after *d*-amphetamine administration. *Pharmacology, Biochemistry, & Behavior*, 1982, *17*, 413–417.

Kolb, L., & Dumez, A. G. Experimental addiction of animals to opiates. *United States Public Health Service Reports*, 1931, *46*, 698–713.

Krasnegor, N. A. (Ed.). *Behavioral analysis and treatment of substance abuse.* Rockville, Md.: National Institute on Drug Abuse, 1979.

Kreek, M. J. Methadone in treatment: Physiological and pharmocological issues. In R. L. DuPont, A Goldstein, J. O'Donnell, & B. Brown (Eds.), *Handbook on drug abuse*. Rockville, Md.: National Institute on Drug Abuse, 1979.

Kupferberg, H. J., & Way, E. L. Pharmacologic basis for the increased sensitivity of the newborn rat to morphine. *Journal of Pharmacology and Experimental Therapeutics*, 1963, *141*, 105–112.

Lansfield, P. W., Rose, G., Sandles, L., Wohlstadter, T. C., & Lynch, G. Patterns of astroglial hypertrophy and neuronal degeneration in the hippocampus of aged memory-deficient rats. *Journal of Gerontology*, 1977, *32*, 3–12.

Lemmer, B., & Berger, T. Diurnal rhythm in the central dopamine turn-over in the rat. *Archives of Pharmacology* 1978, *303*, 257–261.

Lettieri, D., Sayers, M., & Pearson, H. W. (Eds.). *Theories on drug abuse, selected contemporary perspectives*. Rockville, Md.: National Institute on Drug Abuse, 1980.

Light, A. B. Opium addiction; XI. General summary. *Archives of Internal Medicine*, 1929, *44*, 870–876.

Light, A. B., & Torrance, E. G. Opium addiction; I. The conduct of the addict in relation to investigative study. *Archives of Internal Medicine*, 1929, *44*, 206–211.

Lippa, A. S., Critchett, D. J., Ehlert, F., Yamamura, H. I., Enna, S. J., & Bartus, R. T. Age-related alterations in neurotransmitter receptors: An electrophysiological and biochemical analysis. *Neurobiology of Aging*, 1981, 2, 3–8.

Loizou, L. A. The postnatal ontogeny of monoamine-containing neurons in the central nervous sytem of the albino rat. *Brain Research*, 1972, *40*, 395–418.

Loizou, L. A., & Salt, P. Regional changes in monoamines of the rat brain during postnatal development. *Brain Research* 1970, *20*, 476–470.

Lowinson, J. A., & Milman, R. B. Clinical aspects of methadone maintenance treatment. In R. L. DuPont, A. Goldstein, J. O'Donnell, & B. Brown (Eds.), *Handbook on drug abuse*. Rockville, Md.: National Insitute on Drug Abuse, 1979.

Mabry, P. D., & Campbell, B. A. Developmental psychopharmacology. In L. L. Iversen, S. D. Iversen, & S. H. Snyder (Eds.), *Handbook of psychopharmacology: Principles of behavioral pharmacology*. (Vol. 7). New York: Plenum, 1977.

MacLennan, A. J., & Maier, S. F. Coping and the stress-induced potentiation of stimulant stereotypy in the rat. *Science*, 1983, *219*, 1091–1093.

Manev, H., & Pericic, D., Hypothalamic GABA system and plasma corticosterone in ether stressed rats. *Pharmacology, Biochemistry, & Behavior*, 1983, *18*, 847–850.

Martin, W. R., Fraser, H. F., Gorodetzky, C. W., & Rosenberg, O. E. Studies on the dependence-producing potential of the narcotic antagonist 2-cyclo-proplymethyl-2'-hydroxy-5,9-dimethyl-6,7 benzomorphan (cyclazocine, WIN-20,740, ARC II-C-3). *Journal of Pharmacology and Experimental Therapeutics*, 1965, *150*, 426–436.

Martin, W. R., Gorodetzky, C. W., & McClane, T. K. An experimental study in the treatment of narcotic addicts with cyclazocine. *Clinical Pharmacology and Therapeutics*, 1966, 7, 455–465.

Martin, W. R., Jasinski, D. R., Haertzen, C. W., Kay, D. C., Jones, B. E., Mansky, P. A., & Carpenter, R. W. Methadone—A reevaluation. *Archives of General Psychiatry*, 1973, *28*, 286–295.

Mayer, S. E., Melmon, K. L., & Gilman, A. G. The dynamics of drug absorption, distribution, and elimination. In A. G. Gilman, L. S. Goodman, & A. Gilman (Eds.), *The pharmacological basis of therapeutics*. New York: Macmillan, 1980.

Memo, M., Lucchi, L., Spano, P. F., & Trabucchi, M. Aging process affects a single class of dopamine receptors. *Brain Research* 1980, *202*, 488–492.

Middaugh, L. D., Zemp, J. W., & Boggan, W. O. Pregnancy increases reactivity of mice to phenobarbital. *Science*, 1983, *220*, 534–536.

Millard, W. J., & Dole, V. P. Intake of water and ethanol by C57BL mice: Effect of an altered light-dark schedule. *Pharmacology, Biochemistry, & Behavior*, 1983, *18*, 281–284.

Miller, L. L., & Branconnier, R. J. Cannabis: Effects on memory and the cholinergic limbic system. *Psychological Bulletin*, 1983, *93*, 441–456.

Morselli, P. L. Clincial pharmacokinetics in neonates. *Clinical Pharmacokinetics*, 1976, *1*, 81–98.

Naber, D., Wirz-Justice, A., & Kafka, M. S. Circadian rhythm in rat brain opiate receptor. *Neuroscience Letters*, 1981, *21*, 45–50.

Nichols, J. R., Headlee, C. P., & Coppock, H. W. Drug addiction; I. Addiction by escape training. *Journal of the American Pharmaceutical Association*, 1956, *45*, 788–791.

Ng Cheong Ton, M. J., Brown, Z., Michalakeas, A., & Amit, Z. Stress induced suppression of maintenance but not of acquisition of ethanol consumption in rats. *Pharmacology, Biochemistry, & Behavior*, 1983, *18*, 141–144.

O'Brien, C. P., Greenstein, R. A., Evans, B., Woody, G. E., & Arndt, R. Opioid antagonists: Do they have a role in treatment programs? In L. S. Harris (Ed.), *Problems of drug dependence, 1982*. Rockville, Md.: National Institute on Drug Abuse, 1983.

Oliverio, A., Castellano, C., & Puglisi-Allegra, S. Opiate analgesia: Evidence for circadian rhythms in mice. *Brain Research* 1982, *249*, 265–270.

Olson, G. A., Olson, R. D., Kastin, A. J., & Coy, D. H. Endogenous opiates: 1983. *Peptides*, 1984, *5*, 975–992.

O'Malley, K., Crooks, J., Duke, E., & Stevenson, I. H. Effect of age and sex on human drug metabolism. *British Medical Journal*, 1971, *3*, 607–609.

Palkovits, M., Brownstein, J., Kizer, J. S. Saavedra, J., & Kopin, I. J. Effect of stress on serotonin concentration and tryptophan hydroxylase activity of brain nuclei. *Neuroendocrinology*, 1976, *22*, 298–304.

Pfaff, D. W., & McEwen, B. S. Actions of estrogens and progestins on nerve cells. *Science*, 1983, *219*, 808–814.

Phillips, A. G., & LePiane, F. G. Reinforcing effects of morphine microinjection into the ventral tegmental area. *Pharmacology, Biochemistry, & Behavior*, 1980, *12*, 965–968.

Pohorecky, L. A. The interaction of alcohol and stress: A review. *Neuroscience & Biobehavioral Reviews*, 1981, *5*, 209–229.

Pollard, H., Llorens, D., Bonnet, J. J., Costentin, J., & Schwartz, J. C. Opiate receptors on mesolimbic dopaminergic neurons. *Neuroscience Letters*, 1977, *7*, 295–299.

Post, R. M. Cocaine psychosis: A continuum model. *American Journal of Psychiatry*, 1975, *132*, 225–231.

Post, R. M. Psychomotor stimulants as activators of normal and pathological behavior: Implications for the excesses in mania. In S. J. Mule' (Ed.), *Behavior in excess, an examination of the volitional disorders*. New York: Free Press, 1981.

Reis, D. J., Ross, R. A., & Joh, T. H. Changes in the activity and amounts of enzymes synthesizing catecholamines and acetylcholine in brain, adrenal medulla, and sympathetic ganglia of aged rat and mouse. *Brain Research*, 1977, *136*, 465–474.

Richey, D. P., & Bender, A. D. Pharmacokinetic consequences of age. *Annual Review of Pharmacology and Toxicology*, 1977, *17*, 49–65.

Risner, M. E., & Jones, B. E. Role of noradrenergic and dopaminergic processes in amphetamine self-administration. *Pharmacology, Biochemistry, & Behavior*, 1976, *5*, 447–482.

Risner, M. E., & Jones, B. E. Intravenous self-administration of cocaine and norcocaine by dogs. *Psychopharmacology*, 1980, *71*, 83–89.

Risner, M. E. & Silcox, D. L. Psychostimulant self-administration by beagle dogs in a progressive-ratio paradigm. *Psychopharmacology*, 1981, *75*, 25–30.

Ritter, S., & Pelzer, N. L. Magnitude of stress-induced brain norepinephrine depletion varies with age. *Brain Research*, 1978, *152*, 170–175.

Roberts, D. C. S., Corcoran, M. E., & Fibiger, H. C. On the role of ascending catecholaminergic systems in intravenous self-administration of cocaine. *Pharmacology, Biochemistry, & Behavior*, 1977, *6*, 615–620.

Robinson, T. E., Becker, J. B., & Presty, S. K. Long-term facilitation of amphetamine-induced rotational behavior and striatal dopamine release produced by a single exposure to amphetamine: Sex differences. *Brain Research*, 1982, *253*, 231–241.

Saito, Y., Yamashita, I., Yamazaki, K., Okada, F., Satomi, R., & Fujieda, T. Circadian fluctuation of brain acetylcholine in rats. *Life Science*, 1975, *16*, 281–288.

Scheving, L. E., Harrison, W. H., Gordon, P., & Pauly, J. E. Daily fluctuations in biogenic amines of the rat brain. *American Journal of Psyiology*, 1968, *214*, 166–173.

Schmucker, D. L. Age-related changes in drug disposition. *Pharmacological Reviews*, 1979, *30*, 445–456.

Schuster, C. R. Opiates, In S. J. Mule' (Ed.), *Behavior in excess, an examination of the volitional disorders*. New York: Free Press, 1981.

Seevers, M. H. Opiate addiction in the monkey; I. Methods of study. *Journal of Pharmacology and Experimental Therapeutics*, 1936, *56*, 147–161.

Siegel, G. J., Albers, R. W., Agranoff, B. W., & Katzman, R. (Eds.). *Basic neurochemistry*. Boston: Little, Brown, 1981.

Siegel, R. K. Cocaine: Recreational use and intoxication. In R. C. Petersen & R. C. Stillman (Eds.), *Cocaine: 1977*. Rockville, Md.: National Institute on Drug Abuse, 1977.

Snyder, S. H. Brain peptides as neurotransmitters. *Science*, 1980, *209*, 976–983.

Spragg, S. D. S. Morphine addiction in chimpanzees. *Comparative Psychology Monographs*, 1940, *15*, 1–132.

Steger, R. W., Sonntag, W. E., Van Vugt, D. A., Forman, L. J., & Meites, J. Reduced ability of naloxone to stimulate leutenizing hormone and testosterone release in aging male rats: Possible relation to increase in hypothalamic met^5-enkephalin. *Life Sciences*, 1980, *27*, 747–753.

Stone, E. A., & McCarty, R. Adaptation to stress: Tyrosine hydroxylase activity and catecholamine release. *Neuroscience & Biobehavioral Reviews*, 1983, *7*, 29–34.

Tanaka, M., Kohno, Y., Nakagawa, R., Ida, Y., Takeda, S., & Nagasaki, N. Time-related differences in noradrenaline turnover in rat brain regions by stress. *Pharmacology, Biochemistry, & Behavior*, 1982, *16*, 315–319.

Tatum, A. L., Seevers, M. H., & Collins, K. H. Morphine addiction and its physiological interpretation based on experimental evidences. *Journal of Pharmacology and Experimental Therapeutics*, 1929, *36*, 447–475.

Tauc, L. Nonvesicular release of neurotransmitter. *Physiological Reviews*, 1982, *62*, 857–893.

Tennant, F. S., & Rawson, R. A. Cocaine and amphetamine dependence treated with desipramine. In L. S. Harris (Ed.), *Problems of drug dependence, 1982*. Rockville, Md.: National Institute on Drug Abuse, 1983.

Thompson, T., & Schuster, C. R. Morphine self-administration and food-reinforced and avoidance behavior in rhesus monkeys. *Psychopharmacologia*, 1964, *5*, 87–94.

Thompson, T., & Unna, K. (Eds.) *Predicting dependence liability of stimulant and depressant drugs*. Baltimore: University Park Press, 1977.

Truex, L. L., & Schmidt, M. J. ^{3}H-amphetamine concentrations in the brains of young and aged rats: Implications for assessment of drug effects in aged animals. *Neurobiology of Aging*, 1980, *1*, 93–95.

Van Dyke, C., Jatlow, P., Ungerer, J., Barash, P. G., & Byck, R. Oral cocaine: Plasma concentrations and central effects. *Science*, 1978, *200*, 211–213.

Washton, A. M., & Resnick, R. B. Clonidine vs. methadone for opiate detoxification: Double-blind outpatient trials. In L. S. Harris (Ed.), *Problems of drug dependence, 1980*. Rockville, Md.: National Institute on Drug Abuse, 1981.

Wauquier, A., & Niemegeers, C. J. E. Intracranial self-stimulation in rats as a function of various stimulus parameters. II. Influence of haloperidol, pimozide and pipamperone on medial forebrain bundle stimulation with monopolar electrodes. *Psychopharmacologia*, 1972, *27*, 191–202.

Weeks, J. R. Experimental morphine addiction: Method for automatic intravenous injections in unrestrained rats. *Science*, 1962, *138*, 143–144.

Weeks, J. R., & Collins, R. J. Factors affecting voluntary morphine intake in self-maintained addicted rats. *Psychopharmacologia*, 1964, *6*, 267–279.

Wesche, D. L., & Frederickson, R. C. A. Diurnal differences in opioid peptide levels correlated with nociceptive sensitivity. *Life Sciences*, 1979, *24*, 1861–1868.

Wiberg, G. S., Trenholm, H., & Coldwell, B. B. Increased ethanol toxicity in old rats: Changes in LD_{50}, *in vivo* and *in vitro* metabolism and liver alcohol dehydrogenase activity. *Toxicology and Applied Pharmacology*, 1970, *16*, 718–727.

Wikler, A. *Opioid dependence, mechanisms and treatments*. New York: Plenum Press, 1980.

Wise, R. A. Action of drugs of abuse on brain reward systems. *Pharmacology, Biochemistry, & Behavior*, 1980, *13*(Suppl. 1), 213–223.

Wise, R. A. Neuroleptics and operant behavior: The anhedonia hypothesis. *Behavioral and Brain Sciences*, 1982, *5*, 39–87.

Wise, R. A. Brain neuronal systems mediating reward processes. In J. E. Smith & J. D. Lane (Eds.), *The neurobiology of opiate reward processes*. Amsterdam: Elsevier, 1983.

Wood, W. G., Armbrecht, H. J., & Wise, R. W. Ethanol intoxication and withdrawal among three age groups of C57BL/6NNIA mice. *Pharmacology, Biochemistry, & Behavior*, 1982, *17*, 1037–1041.

Woolverton, W. L., Wessinger, W. D., Balster, R. L., & Harris, L. S. Intravenous clonidine self-administration by rhesus monkeys. In L. S. Harris (Ed.), *Problems of drug dependence, 1980*. Rockville, Md.: National Institute on Drug Abuse, 1981.

Yokel, R. A., & Wise, R. A. Attenuation of intravenous amphetamine reinforcement by central dopamine blockade in rats. *Psychopharmacology*, 1976, *48*, 311–318.

CHAPTER 4

Individual Differences in Tolerance and Relapse

A Pavlovian Conditioning Perspective

RILEY E. HINSON

Environmental stimuli and events are known to affect the occurrence of relapse in detoxified addicts (cf. Hinson & Siegel, 1982). For example, the likelihood of the detoxified addict's relapsing may be lessened if he or she does not return to the prior drug-taking environment following treatment (Robins, Helzer, &. Davis, 1975). One way in which environmental stimuli may affect relapse is suggested by an analysis of the role of environmental stimuli in tolerance. *Tolerance* refers to a decrease in the magnitude of a drug effect that occurs with repeated administrations of the same dose of the drug. A substantial amount of research demonstrates that environmental stimuli affect the display of tolerance. For example, Mitchell and co-workers (Ferguson & Mitchel, 1969; Adams, Yeh, Woods, & Mitchell, 1969) reported that the expected tolerant response was displayed to the last of a series of morphine injections only if the final injection was administered in the same environmental context as all the prior injections. Siegel and his co-workers (Siegel, 1975a, 1977; Krank, Hinson, & Siegel, 1981; Siegel, Hinson, &. Krank, 1978) have proposed an analysis of the role of environmental stimuli in tolerance based on the

RILEY E. HINSON • Department of Psychology, University of Western Ontario, London, Ontario N6A 5C2, Canada. Preparation of this chapter was supported in part by a grant from the Natural Sciences and Engineering Research Council of Canada.

suggestion by Pavlov (1927) that the administration of a drug constitutes a classical conditioning trial. According to this analysis, the environmental stimuli accompanying drug administration serve as the conditional stimulus (CS) for the drug effect that constitutes the unconditional stimulus (UCS). Repeated administrations of the drug to the organism in the context of the same cues lead to the development of an association between the environmental CS and pharmacological UCS.

The Pavlovian conditioning analysis of tolerance has been extended to partially account for the role of environmental stimuli in relapse. This chapter begins by reviewing recent experimental evidence demonstrating that Pavlovian conditioning contributes to tolerance (reviews of earlier research can be found in Hinson & Siegel, 1980, 1982; Siegel, 1979). Briefly, this evidence demonstrates that tolerance is more pronounced if the drug injection is "expected" (i.e., occurs with drug-associated stimuli); that tolerance may be attenuated by placebo injections; and that tolerance development may actually be slowed by drug administrations. Research suggesting a role for Pavlovian conditioned environmental stimuli on postdetoxification withdrawal and relapse is then presented. The treatment implications of the role of Pavlovian conditioning in relapse are also described.

A considerable amount of research demonstrates that individuals differ in the rate and degree to which they develop tolerance (see Chapter 2 in this volume). Most of this research has examined such individual differences in tolerance from a neurochemical or neuroanatomical perspective. The emphasis on the neurochemical bases of individual differences in tolerance reflects the fact that, until recently, most theorizing on the mechanisms of tolerance also emphasized neurochemistry. However, nonpharmacological factors affect the development of tolerance, and thus individual differences in tolerance may also reflect these factors. The present chapter will also discuss how individual differences in tolerance and relapse may be viewed from the perspective of the role of Pavlovian conditioning.

PAVLOVIAN CONDITIONING AND TOLERANCE

Tolerance as Adaptation

Tolerance has long been viewed as a form of adaptive response (e.g., Himmelsbach, 1943). The administration of a drug to the organism disrupts the normal level of functioning in a variety of physiological systems—for example, the administration of insulin causes hypoglycemia

(Siegel, 1975b), and the administration of ethanol disrupts temperature regulation (Crowell, Hinson, & Siegel, 1981). Homeostatic disruption in a physiological system elicits reflexivelike counterreactions or compensatory responses to offset the magnitude and duration of the disruption (Himmelsbach, 1943). It has also been suggested (Solomon, 1977) that affective responses are homeostatically regulated. Thus, events that cause extreme affective responses (whether euphoria or dysphoria) elicit opponent processes to restabilize the affective system.

The phenomenon of *acute tolerance* may result from such reflexively elicited compensatory responses (cf. Hinson & Siegel, 1980). Acute tolerance refers to the demonstration of a smaller drug effect on the descending, than ascending, portion of the drug–blood concentration curve at the same concentration level (Kalant, LeBlanc, & Gibbins, 1971, p. 243).

TOLERANCE AND ANTICIPATORY ADAPTATION

Counterreactions or compensatory responses elicited in response to homeostatic disruption are of obvious adaptive significance (cf. Hecht, Baumann, & Hecht, 1967; Obal, 1966). However, adaptive responses do not occur only in response to homeostatically disrupting stimuli; they may also occur in anticipation of such stimuli. The capacity of the organism to respond in anticipation of a stimulus is the basis of Pavlovian conditioning. A substantial body of research demonstrates that Pavlovian conditioning does, in fact, occur with drugs (for reviews, see Bykov, 1959; Siegel, 1983; Wikler, 1973). In a pharmacological conditioning experiment, the drug may produce a homeostatic disturbance that results in the elicitation of reflexive counterreactions. In such cases, the homeostatic disturbance produced by the drug may be conceptualized as the UCS and the reflexive compensatory response it elicits as the unconditional response (UCR). If the drug is repeatedly administered in the context of the same set of cues, the organism may come to anticipate the homeostatic disturbance produced by the drug whenever these cues are presented. In such cases, through Pavlovian conditioning, a conditional response (CR) would result that would resemble the reflexive compensatory response.*

The development of an association between an environmental CS

---

* There may be cases where the consequences of drug administration do not correspond to this description. The contribution of Pavlovian conditioning to such cases is outside the scope of this chapter. For some discussion, see Eikelboom and Stewart (1982), Hinson and Poulos (1981), and Siegel (1983).

and pharmacological UCS may be revealed by presenting the usual pre-drug cues without the drug—rather, for such a conditional response test, a placebo is administered. There are, in fact, several demonstrations of the conditioning of drug-compensatory responses. In one such experiment (Crowell et al., 1981), rats were given a total of 20 injections of ethanol, one injection every 4 days. Ethanol was injected each time in the context of a distinctive set of environmental stimuli (a room in which white noise was constantly present). Initially, the injection of ethanol resulted in a decrease in body temperature (hypothermia). During a CR test session, all rats were administered a placebo (physiological saline). Some rats were given the placebo in the context of the distinctive environmental stimuli (i.e., with the usual predrug cues), whereas other rats were given the placebo in the animal colony room, an environment not associated with prior drug injections. The results were that animals administered the placebo in the animal colony room evidenced little thermic change, whereas animals given the placebo with the usual predrug cues exhibited an *increase* in body temperature. The authors suggested that this hyperthermia represented a compensatory CR. Similarly, Krank *et al.* (1981) reported a conditional hyperalgesic response in rats who were administered a placebo with environmental stimuli previously associated with morphine-induced analgesia. Many other examples of such drug-compensatory CRs have been summarized by Siegel (1979, 1983) and Wikler (1973).

Siegel (1975a) suggested that drug-compensatory responses elicited by the usual predrug cues contribute to tolerance. Drug-compensatory CRs would be expected to partially cancel the actual drug effect. As the drug is repeatedly administered in the context of the same cues, the conditional compensatory responses would be expected to become stronger, thereby more completely canceling the drug effect during subsequent drug administrations. Just as acute tolerance may in part result from the antagonistic action of counterreactions reflexively elicited by drug-induced upset (cf. Hinson & Siegel, 1980), the tolerance that occurs when the drug is repeatedly administered may result in part from counterreactions elicited in anticipation of drug-induced upset.

EVIDENCE FOR A ROLE OF PAVLOVIAN CONDITIONING IN TOLERANCE

The results of a substantial amount of research demonstrate that Pavlovian conditioning does, in fact, contribute to tolerance. Some of this evidence has been reviewed elsewhere (Hinson & Siegel, 1980; Poulos, Hinson, & Siegel, 1981; Siegel, 1978a, 1979, 1983). A review of recent evidence will be provided here.

The Situation Specificity of Tolerance

According to a Pavlovian conditioning analysis, tolerance results in part because the usual predrug cues elicit drug-compensatory responses that partially cancel the drug effect. Based on this analysis, it would be expected that tolerance would be more pronounced when the drug is administered with the usual predrug cues than when the drug is administered in the absence of these cues. This is because only the usual predrug cues elicit the drug-compensatory CR that cancels the drug effect. The results of many experiments confirm this prediction. The design of these experiments differed in some details (see Siegel, 1979, for a discussion of experimental designs in studies of tolerance situation specificity), but their essential features can be appreciated by reference to a recent study demonstrating the role of Pavlovian conditioning in tolerance to the lethal effects of intravenous heroin (Siegel, Hinson, Krank, & McCully, 1982). In the experiment, rats were administered several sublethal doses of heroin via chronically implanted intravenous catheters. Each infusion of heroin was given in the context of a distinctive set of environmental stimuli. Finally, these drug-experienced animals were administered a dose of heroin (15 mg/kg) that was lethal to over 90% of a group of drug-naive animals. However, it would be expected that the drug-experienced organism would be able to survive a dose that would be lethal to the drug-naive organism (Hug, 1972). The normally lethal dose of heroin was administered to some of the drug-experienced rats in the context of the environmental stimuli associated with all previous infusions of heroin (Same tested). The other drug-experienced rats received the high dose of heroin in the context of stimuli not previously associated with heroin (Different tested). The results of this experiment are shown in Table 1 (also included in Table 1 is the death frequency for a group

Table 1. Rat Mortality after the Injection of Heroin at 15 mg/kg[a]

Group	Number of rats	Mortality (%)
Same tested	37	32.4
Different tested	42	64.3
Control	28	96.4

[a] From "Heroin 'Overdose' Death: Contribution of Drug-Associated Environmental Cues" by S. Siegel, R. E. Hinson, M. D. Krank, and J. McCully, *Science*, 1982, *216*, 436–437. Copyright 1982 by The American Association for the Advancement of Science. Reprinted by permission.

of previously drug-naive rats administered 15 mg/kg of heroin intravenously; they are referred to as the *control*). It is clear that Same-tested
animals tolerated the high dose of heroin better than Different-tested
animals, despite the fact that both groups of animals had the identical
pharmacological history.

The results of many similar experiments replicate the finding that
Same-tested animals are more tolerant than Different-tested animals. The
situation specificity of tolerance has been demonstrated with a wide
variety of drugs (morphine [e.g., Siegel, 1975a]; ethanol [e.g., Lê, Poulos,
& Cappell, 1979]; pentobarbital [e.g., Cappell, Roach, & Poulos, 1981];
amphetamine [e.g., Poulos, Wilkinson, & Cappell, 1981]; haloperidol [e.g.,
Poulos & Hinson, 1982], scopolamine [e.g., Poulos & Hinson, 1984]; and
chlordiazepoxide [e.g., Greely & Cappell, 1982]); a variety of response
systems (analgesia [e.g., Siegel, 1976]; hyperthermia [e.g., Siegel, 1978b];
hypothermia [e.g., Mansfield & Cunningham, 1980]; lethality [e.g., Siegel
et al., 1982]; behavioral sedation [e.g., Hinson, Poulos, & Cappell, 1982];
anorexia [e.g., Poulos *et al.*, 1981]; adipsia [e.g., Poulos & Hinson, 1984];
catalepsy [e.g., Hinson, Poulos, & Thomas, 1982]); and a wide range of
drug doses.

Extinguishability of Tolerance

Established CRs are well retained (Mackintosh, 1974, pp. 412–413). If
tolerance results in part from conditioning, it would be expected that
tolerance would also be well retained. In many cases, tolerance is well
retained (Andrews, 1943; Cochin & Kornetsky, 1964; Gitlow, Dziedzic, &
Dziedzic, 1977), although under some conditions of tolerance development, tolerance is not well retained (cf. Hinson & Siegel, 1980).

Established CRs may be attenuated if the CS is repeatedly presented
without the UCS; the procedure is *extinction*. To the extent that Pavlovian
conditioning contributes to tolerance, it would be expected that tolerance
would also be extinguishable.

In a prototypical experiment (Siegel, 1975a, Experiment 3), rats were
given daily injections of morphine, each injection in a distinctive context.
Initially, the morphine produced analgesia as assessed with the hot-plate
technique (cf. Fennessy & Lee, 1975); however, with repeated administrations of the same dose of morphine, the analgesia was attenuated (i.e.,
tolerance developed). Following the development of tolerance, animals
were not given morphine for 2 weeks after which time they were again
injected with morphine and assessed for analgesia on the hot-plate. During the 2-week morphine-free period some rats were simply left undis-

turbed. Other rats, by contrast, were given daily placebo injections during this time—that is, these rats were presented with the usual predrug cues, but a placebo (physiogical saline) was injected instead of the drug. According to the Pavlovian conditioning analysis, these repeated placebo sessions should serve as extinction trials, and consequently the animal should show a greater loss of tolerance than animals that were simply undisturbed during the 2 weeks. The results confirmed the predictions of the Pavlovian analysis—animals given repeated placebo sessions lost a significant degree of tolerance, whereas animals simply left undisturbed did not show a loss of tolerance. Results of other experiments demonstrate that tolerance to ethanol hypothermia (Crowell *et al.*, 1981) and the lethal effects of morphine (Siegel, Hinson, & Krank, 1979) are also attenuated by repeated presentations of the usual predrug cues without the drug.

Inhibition of Tolerance

In the typical Pavlovian conditioning procedure, the CS is explicitly paired with the UCS; the result is the development of CRs. If prior to presenting the CS and UCS in the explicitly paired manner, the two stimuli are presented explicitly unpaired, subsequent CR formation is retarded (cf. Rescorla, 1969); the procedure is called *inhibitory conditioning*. If Pavlovian conditioning is a general characteristic of tolerance, then tolerance should be subject to inhibitory conditioning. With respect to tolerance, inhibitory conditioning would be expected to result in retardation of the development of the compensatory CR that would have, as a consequence, the slowing of the development of tolerance. The occurrence of inhibitory conditioning has been recently demonstrated with respect to morphine analgesic tolerance (Siegel, Hinson, & Krank, 1981). In the Siegel *et al.* (1981) study, different groups of rats received differing experiences with an environmental CS and morphine prior to receiving explicitly paired presentations of the CS and morphine. An inhibitory conditioning group received the environmental CS and morphine in an explicitly unpaired manner (morphine was injected 4 hours after the CS), whereas different control groups received either explicit pairings of the CS and morphine, presentations of the CS only, injections of morphine only, or no experience with either stimulus. Subsequently, rats in all groups received explicit pairings of the environmental CS and morphine, and the rate of tolerance development was assessed using the hot-plate procedure (cf. Siegel *et al.*, 1981). The results of this experiment are shown in Figure 1. The important aspect of these data for the present discussion is that

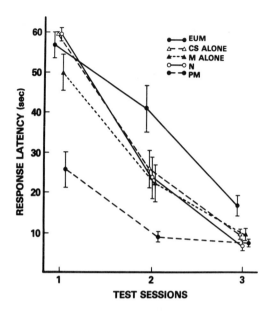

Figure 1.   Mean paw lick latencies (± 1 standard error of the mean) for each of the three tolerance test days in the inhibitory conditioning experiment. (Group designations: EUM, explicitly unpaired morphine; CS alone, presentations of the CS only; M alone, injections of morphine only; N, no experience with either stimulus; PM, explicitly paired morphine.) See text for details. (From "Morphine-Induced Attenuation of Morphine Tolerance" by S. Siegel, R. E. Hinson, and M. D. Krank, *Science*, 1981, *212*, 1533–1534. Copyright 1982 by The American Association for the Advancement of Science. Reprinted by permission.)

tolerance development was slowest in rats that had prior exposure to explicitly unpaired presentations of the CS and morphine despite the fact that these rats had the same pharmacological history as rats in the explicitly paired morphine group and the morphine-alone group, and they had *more* experience with morphine than rats in the saline and no-experience groups. Thus, prior experience with morphine retarded tolerance development. According to the conditioning analysis of tolerance, this is expected because the prior experience with morphine and the CS in an explicitly unpaired manner should have retarded the development of the drug-compensatory CR. The retardation of tolerance acquisition by Pavlovian conditional inhibitory procedures has been recently replicated by Fanselow and German (1982) for morphine analgesia and by Hinson and Siegel (1983b) for pentobarbital hypothermia.

ASSOCIATIVE AND NONASSOCIATIVE ASPECTS OF TOLERANCE

Research summarized in the preceding sections provides evidence for a role of Pavlovian conditioning in tolerance. However, in some of this research there is also evidence of tolerance not attributable to Pavlovian conditioning. Thus, in some studies of tolerance situation specificity (e.g., Hinson & Siegel, 1983a; Siegel *et al.*, 1982; Tiffany & Baker, 1981), drug-experienced animals tested without the usual predrug cues displayed more tolerance than control, drug-naive animals. The absence of the predrug cues in the Different-tested condition should preclude the elicitation of the conditional drug-compensatory response, and thus tolerance observed in the Different-tested condition cannot be attributable to Pavlovian conditioning.

Although the administration of a drug usually conforms to the procedures of a Pavlovian conditioning trial (Pavlov, 1927), there are some methods of drug administration that do not favor the occurrence of Pavlovian conditioning. The inhalation procedure, in which an animal continuously inhales ethanol vapor for several days (for a review, see Goldstein, 1980), does not conform to the procedures of Pavlovian conditioning. However, rapid and pronounced tolerance occurs with the inhalation procedure. Similarly, ethanol tolerance has been induced by gastric intubation, a procedure that may not involve optimal conditions for Pavlovian conditioning (cf. Melchior & Tabokoff, 1981). Additionally, morphine tolerance has been induced by implantation of a morphine-containing pellet that slowly dissolves, releasing the opiate (e.g., Advokat, 1981). The continuous presence of the drug under diverse environmental conditions is not optimal for Pavlovian conditioning. Tolerance induced by these continuous delivery procedures is, unlike tolerance resulting from discrete, signaled drug administrations, not well retained (cf. Hinson & Siegel, 1980). This finding suggests that tolerance induced by inhalation, intubation, and pellet implantation is nonassociative in nature. Kesner and Baker (1981) have discussed other methods of drug administration that may affect the extent to which Pavlovian conditioning contributes to tolerance.

A final point concerns the relationship between neurochemical and learning factors in tolerance. At several points in this chapter, a distinction has been made between these two factors. Although these two types of factors may be distinguished for purposes of exposition, it is obvious that in the organism neurochemistry and learning interact. Indeed, recent research has examined some ways in which neurochemistry and learning may interact to produce tolerance (Hinson *et al.*, 1982; Poulos & Hinson, 1982). Thus, it should be understood that by emphasizing the role of

Pavlovian conditioning in tolerance, the intent is not to suggest that neurochemical (or for that matter sociological, personality, etc.) factors are unimportant.

TOLERANCE AND INDIVIDUAL DIFFERENCES IN DRUG-COMPENSATORY RESPONDING

Among a group of animals, individuals will display differing levels of tolerance following the same amount of drug exposure. A considerable amount of research (see Chapter 2, this volume) has been devoted to identifying factors involved in such individual differences in tolerance acquisition. Research summarized in the preceding sections of this chapter indicates that Pavlovian conditioning contributes to tolerance. Thus, it is likely that individual differences in tolerance may reflect differences in the conditioning of drug-compensatory CRs.

The results of a recent experiment (Hinson & Siegel, 1983a) demonstrate that individual differences in tolerance are indeed related to individual differences in conditioning of drug responses. The experiment involved the assessment of tolerance to the behavioral sedative effects of morphine in rats using the Same-tested and Different-tested design described previously. As expected on the basis of the conditioning analysis, the results of the experiment demonstrated that Same-tested animals displayed more tolerance than Different-tested animals. Evidence of the drug-compensatory response was also obtained: tolerant, Same-tested animals exhibited behavioral hyperexcitability (circling, jumping, hopping) that has been suggested to be a compensatory response to behavioral sedation (cf. Hinson *et al.*, 1982). Conversely, Different-tested animals, which were not tolerant, did not exhibit such behavioral hyperexcitability. Most relevant to the present discussion, however, was the finding that the different levels of tolerance exhibited among Same-tested animals were significantly positively correlated with the frequency of hyperexcitable behavior exhibited by individual animals. Thus, individual differences in the strength of the hypothesized compensatory CR were associated with individual differences in tolerance.

FACTORS AFFECTING CONDITIONING OF DRUG-COMPENSATORY RESPONSES

The results of the Hinson and Siegel study (1983a) suggest that factors contributing to individual differences in the acquisition of drug-compensatory CRs may be important to individual differences in tolerance. Unfortunately, at this time there is no research directly addressed to identifying factors influencing individual differences in the rate of acquisition of drug-compensatory responses. It is possible, however, to suggest some factors that might be involved. Additionally, the results of some psychopharmacogenetic research provide preliminary evidence for assessing the potential contribution of some of these suggested factors. However, this evidence must be interpreted with caution because the research was not specifically designed to examine learning factors in tolerance.

Perhaps the most obvious potential source of individual differences in the acquisition of drug-compensatory responses relates to differences in conditionability. Thus, animals that condition rapidly might be expected to acquire the compensatory CR rapidly and thereby display rapid acquisition of tolerance. There is a long history of research on individual and strain differences in apparent learning ability (see review by Broadhurst, 1978; see also the discussion by Wahlsten, 1972, of the difficulties in interpretation of this research). However, none of this research has attempted to examine whether animals selected for differences in conditionability also differ in tolerance acquisition. The relationship between conditionability and tolerance acquisition is an area deserving of future psychopharmacogenetic research.

A second potential source of variability in the conditioning of drug-opposite responses relates to the phenomenon of acute tolerance. *Acute tolerance* refers to less of a drug effect on the descending, compared to ascending, portion of the blood–drug concentration curve at the same drug concentration (cf. Kalant *et al.*, 1971). It has been suggested (Hinson & Siegel, 1980) that acute tolerance may result from the counterreactions or drug-compensatory responses reflexively elicited by the actual drug effect (cf. Hecht *et al.*, 1967; Himmelsbach, 1943; Obal, 1966; Solomon, 1977). The conditioning analysis of tolerance suggests that these reflexively elicited counterreactions come, through a process of Pavlovian conditioning, to occur in anticipation of the actual drug effect. Thus, it might be expected that individual differences in the reflexive response would affect the course of acquisition of the conditional response. Because acute tolerance may result in part from the reflexive drug-compensatory response, individual differences in acute tolerance may be relevant to individual differences in the conditioning of drug-compensatory responses. The relationship between acute tolerance and the tolerance that occurs over the course of repeated drug administrations is unclear (Littleton, 1980; Tabakoff, Melchior, & Hoffman, 1982). With respect to psychopharmacogenetic research, there have been no studies involving selective breeding for differences in acute tolerance with subsequent examination of the development of tolerance with repeated drug administrations. There are, however, studies that have identified differences in tolerance in selectively bred lines and different strains of animals and that have also examined acute tolerance.

The results of a study by Tabakoff and Ritzmann (1979) suggest that individual differences in acute tolerance may be related to individual differences in tolerance that occur over the course of repeated drug administrations. Studies of inbred strains of mice have consistently demonstrated that C57BL/6 mice readily develop tolerance to the loss of the righting reflex and hypothermia produced by ethanol, whereas DBA/2 mice do not (see Chapter 2, this volume; also Belknap, 1980). Ritzmann and Tabakoff (1980) have reported that C57BL/6 mice show greater acute tolerance than do DBA/2 mice. Thus, although these inbred strains were not selectively bred for differences in either chronic or acute tolerance, there is a relationship between the degree to which a strain evidences acute adaptation to drug-induced homeostatic imbalance and chronic adaptation to such imbalance. In important research, Melchior and Tabakoff (1981) have reported evidence that Pavlovian conditioning contributes to tolerance to the hypnotic and hypothermic effects of ethanol in C57BL/6 mice. Similarly, Quintanilla and Tampier (1982) have reported a relationship between acute and chronic tolerance in UChA rats (genetically low ethanol consumers) and UChB rats (genetically high ethanol consumers). UChA rats exhibit acute tolerance to ethanol-induced narcosis and also give evidence of tolerance to ethanol-induced narcosis with chronic administration. By contrast, UChB rats do not give evidence of acute tolerance to ethanol-induced narcosis and do not develop tolerance over the course of chronic ethanol administration.

Evidence for a relationship between acute tolerance and the tolerance that develops with repeated drug administrations has also been found for the impairing effects of ethanol on a pursuit-tracking task in humans (Beirness & Vogel-Sprott, 1983). The task required the subject to use a "steering wheel" to move a pointer to targets that were illuminated at random. After nonintoxicated performance on the task had stablized, each subject (male social drinkers) performed the task following consumption of .84 ml/kg absolute alcohol. Acute tolerance was determined for each subject by taking the difference in performance on the task at equivalent blood alcohol concentrations (assessed with a "breathalyzer") occurring when blood alcohol concentration was rising compared to after it had peaked and was falling (cf. Kalant et al., 1971). All subjects then received three additional sessions, one a week, involving the consumption of ethanol and performance of the task. Chronic tolerance was determined for each subject by taking the difference in the degree of impairment during the first drinking session (the one in which acute tolerance was determined) and the degree of impairment during the final drinking session. Analyses indicated a significant relationship between acute tolerance and chronic tolerance, with the degree of acute tolerance exhibited during the first alcohol session accounting for approximately 70% of the variance in the rate of chronic tolerance development. These results indicate that individual differences in the degree of acute adaptation to ethanol may be related to individual differences in the development of tolerance in humans.

PAVLOVIAN CONDITIONING AND WITHDRAWAL AND RELAPSE

ANTICIPATORY ADAPTATION AND POSTDETOXIFICATION WITHDRAWAL SYMPTOMS

Treatment for alcohol and opiate addiction has been characterized as a "revolving door" scenario in which the addict is detoxified and reports feeling cured, but upon release, the addict experiences withdrawallike symptoms and relapses to drug taking (cf. Hinson & Siegel, 1980; Hunt, Barnett, & Branch, 1971). Wikler (1977) has described an example.

> After being detoxified . . . , the postaddict felt fine and had no craving for heroin or morphine but just before his release, or on his way home, or after arriving in his drug-ridden environment, he felt sick, craved a fix, and then hustled to obtain it. Some postaddicts described the sickness in more detail: running nose, watery eyes, sweating, chills, nausea and vomiting . . . . One postaddict remarked that the sickness resembled heroin abstinence phenomena. (Wikler, 1977, p. 35)

Many detoxified addicts report that the occurrence of withdrawallike symptoms provides strong motivation for the resumption of drug taking (cf. Wikler, 1977). Wikler (1977) suggested that postdetoxification withdrawal symptoms may result in part from conditioning. Consider the situation in which the addict is in an environment where he or she has frequently used drugs in the past, or it is the time of day when the drug is typically administered, or any of a variety of drug-associated stimuli occur (see Hinson & Siegel, 1980, and Poulos et al., 1981, for a discussion of the nature of drug-associated stimuli). According to the conditioning model, in these situations the usual predrug stimuli elicit drug-compensatory CRs. If the drug is administered, the drug-compensatory CRs partially cancel the actual drug effect, producing tolerance. However, if the drug is not administered in these situations, the drug-compensatory CRs may achieve expression. The results of a number of studies (Crowell et al., 1981; Krank et al., 1981; see reviews by Hinson & Siegel, 1980; Poulos *et al.*, 1981; Siegel, 1979, 1983), in fact, demonstrate the occurrence of drug responses when the usual predrug cues are presented not followed by the drug. It has been suggested (e.g., Siegel, 1979) that the drug-compensatory CRs elicited by the usual predrug cues when the drug is not administered may provide a basis for some aspects of postdetoxification withdrawal symptoms and thus may contribute to relapse.

An animal experiment by Ternes (1977) demonstrates the occurrence of withdrawallike reactions elicited by the usual predrug stimuli. In the experiment, rhesus monkeys were injected on a number of occasions with morphine or methadone; each injection of the drug was paired with a distinctive set of environmental stimuli that consisted of, among other things, tape-recorded music. Ternes (1977) described one detoxified monkey's reaction upon hearing the tape-recorded music.

> After the animal had been weaned from the drug and maintained drug-free for several months, the experimenter played the tape-recorded music and the animal showed the following signs: he became restless, had piloerection, yawned, became diuretic, showed rhinorrhea, and again sought out the drug injection. (pp. 167–168)

Restlessness, rhinorrhea, yawning, and piloerection are known as withdrawal signs in monkeys (Ternes, 1977).

It is relevant at this point to make a distinction between withdrawal responses that occur soon after the start of abstinence (e.g., Friedman, 1980) and withdrawallike symptoms that occur in the postaddict long after detoxification (e.g., Ternes, 1977; Wikler, 1977). Withdrawal responses that occur soon after the start of abstinence and that also disappear within a few days or at most weeks after the start of abstinence most likely are a direct result of the long-standing physiological disruption induced by chronic drug exposure. It is unlikely that drug-compensatory CRs contribute to these acute withdrawal responses. However, it is also unlikely that these acute withdrawal responses contribute to the resumption of drug taking following a long drug-free period. The withdrawallike responses that occur in the postaddict long after detoxification (e.g., Flaherty, McGuire, & Gatski, 1955; Kissin, Shenker, & Shenker, 1959; Ternes, 1977; Wagman & Allen, 1975; Wikler, 1977) may, by contrast, result from "anticipatory adaptation"—that is, when the postaddict encounters stimuli previously associated with drug administration, the body reacts with adaptive counterreactions in anticipation of the drug effect that has previously occurred in these situations. Because the drug is not now administered, the anticipatory adaptive responses achieve expression.

EVIDENCE FOR A ROLE OF ENVIRONMENTAL STIMULI IN POSTDETOXIFICATION WITHDRAWAL AND RELAPSE

There are several lines of evidence that are consistent with the suggestion that withdrawallike responses in postaddicts result in part from anticipatory adaptation based on Pavlovian conditioning. First, there is much evidence that postaddicts are most likely to experience withdrawallike symptoms when confronted with cues previously associated with drug administration: (1) self-reports by addicts indicate that cues (places, smells, drinking buddies, tastes, etc.) that have in the past been regularly associated with drug taking elicit withdrawal sickness and craving (Blakey & Baker, 1980; Ludwig & Stark, 1974; Mathew, Claghorn, & Largen, 1979; Meyer, Kaplan, & Stroebel, 1981; Pomerleau, Fertig, Baker, & Cooney, 1983); (2) heroin addicts presented slides or videotapes of drug-associated stimuli report experiencing "withdrawal sickness" and give evidence of physiological responses (heart rate and respiration changes, sniffing, yawning) similar to those classically associated with opiate withdrawal (O'Brien, 1976; Sideroff & Jarvik, 1980; Teasdale, 1973); (3) alcoholics placed in a mock barroom setting report subjective feelings of withdrawal, exhibit overt physiological withdrawal symptoms, and engage in alcohol-acquisitive behavior (Ludwig, Cain, Wikler, Taylor, & Bendfeldt, 1977); (4) alcoholics told that a beverage contained alcohol, when in fact it did not (an "expectancy" manipulation in the completely balanced placebo design), exhibited physiological responses possibly reflecting withdrawal (Berg, LaBerg, Skutle, & Ohman, 1981); and (5) alcoholics allowed to "sniff" their favorite alcoholic beverage exhibited increased swallowing, heart rate, and galvanic skin response (GSR) (Pomerleau *et al.*, 1983).

Another line of evidence consistent with an anticipatory adaptation analysis of postdetoxification withdrawal symptoms involves the influence of environmental stimuli on relapse. Addicts report that the occurrence of postdetoxification withdrawal symptoms increases the likelihood of resumption of drug use (e.g., Wikler, 1977). If drug-compensatory CRs contribute to postdetoxification symptoms, then it would be expected that relapse should be most likely in situations where drug-associated stimuli prevail. The experiment by Ternes (1977) in which a detoxified monkey "relapsed" to drug seeking when presented with the usual predrug cues provides evidence for this. An animal experiment by Thompson and Ostlund (1965) also demonstrates this: rats were first orally addicted to a morphine solution in a distinctive environmental context, and then they underwent a period of abstinence in which water replaced the morphine solution. Finally, all rats were again given access to the morphine solution; for some rats access was given in the original addiction environment, and for other rats access was given in an environment not previously associated with the drug. The results showed that rats initiated consumption sooner and consumed larger quantities in the original addiction environment than in the nondrug environment.

Epidemiological data are consistent with the results of the Ternes (1977) and Thompson and Ostlund (1965) studies in demonstrating that relapse to drug use in human addicts is strongly influenced by the context into which the detoxified addict is released (Robins *et al.*, 1975; Saunders & Kershaw, 1979).

Another line of evidence consistent with a Pavlovian analysis of post-detoxification withdrawal involves procedures that attenuate the symptoms. As described previously, drug-compensatory CRs are well retained over long drug-free periods. The fact that postdetoxification withdrawal symptoms occur following a long drug-free period is consistent with the suggestion that drug-compensatory CRs may underlie these symptoms. In order to attenuate drug-compensatory CRs, it is necessary to repeatedly present the usual predrug cues without the drug—that is, to employ extinction procedures. If postdetoxification withdrawal symptoms are partially based on drug-compensatory CRs, it should be necessary to use extinction to attenuate these symptoms. A study by Blakey and Baker (1980) demonstrates the extinguishability of withdrawal sickness and craving in alcoholics. Each alcoholic in this study first identified the events or stimuli that elicited withdrawal sickness, craving, and bouts of drinking. These stimuli included, among other things, the smell of alcohol, traveling home by a particular pub, being with a particular group of drinking buddies, and so forth. Then, each alcoholic was systematically exposed to the cues that elicited withdrawal symptoms while drinking was not allowed (i.e., extinction). Self-ratings of withdrawal sickness and craving elicited by the drug-associated stimuli progressively diminished over the course of repeated sessions of exposure without drink. Analogous results have also been reported in a single-case study by Hodgson and Rankin (1976) involving exposure to alcohol-related stimuli. The demonstration that repeated presentations of drug-associated cues without the drug are effective in attenuating postdetoxification withdrawal symptoms suggests that extinction therapy may be useful in treatment programs for drug addiction (cf. Hinson & Siegel, 1980; Pomerleau *et al.*, 1983; Poulos *et al.*, 1981; Siegel, 1983).

STRESS AND RELAPSE: AN ANALYSIS BASED ON DRUG-COMPENSATORY CRs

Stress, anxiety, and depression are commonly associated with the occurrence of relapse in detoxified heroin addicts (e.g., Fulmar & Lapidus,

1980) and alcoholics (e.g., Ludwig & Stark, 1974). There are many ways in which stress and other emotional states may contribute to the occurrence of relapse. For example, many hypotheses have been offered relating the psychodynamics of stress to drug use (e.g., Barry, 1974). Additionally, stress may act as a cue for the elicitation of drug-compensatory CRs if drug administration has previously been reliably associated with stress (cf. Poulos et al., 1981). The results of a recent animal experiment (Hinson et al., 1982) indicate another way in which stress may contribute to relapse based on the Pavlovian conditioning analysis of postdetoxification symptoms. As described previously, the results of many experiments (see Siegel, 1983, for a review) demonstrate that presentation of the usual predrug cues without the drug often results in the occurrence of drug-compensatory responses. Some experiments (e.g., LaHoste, Olson, Olson, & Kastin, 1980) have, however, failed to demonstrate the occurrence of drug-compensatory responding following the presentation of the usual predrug cues. This suggests that under some conditions the postaddict may not experience withdrawal sickness in the presence of drug-associated stimuli. The results of a study by Hinson et al. (1982) demonstrate that drug-compensatory CRs, which may not be elicited if only the predrug cues are presented, can gain expression if some type of stressor occurs in conjunction with the usual predrug cues. In the experiment, rats tolerant to the sedative-hypnotic effect of pentobarbital did not exhibit a drug-compensatory CR during a placebo test. Although there was no overt drug-compensatory CR during placebo testing, it was still possible that the usual predrug cues elicited a "latent" state of anticipatory adaptation. This reasoning was based on the fact that withdrawal hyperexcitability in animals addicted to sedative hypnotics is often not observable unless some type of challenge stimulation is presented (cf. Kalant et al., 1971). In order to test for a latent state of anticipatory adaptation, a central nervous system (CNS) stimulant (cocaine) was administered either in the presence of the usual pentobarbital injection cues or in the presence of cues not previously associated with pentobarbital. The results showed an *enhanced* effect of cocaine (measured by the number of animals exhibiting convulsions) in the presence of the usual pentobarbital cues compared to the cues not previously associated with the drug. These results suggest that predrug cues may elicit a "latent" state of anticipatory adaptation. In some situations, this latent state may not gain expression unless some type of "stressor" occurs. The demonstration that a stressor may unmask latent drug-compensatory CRs suggests a way in which stress may contribute to relapse: if the postaddict experiences stress in conjunction with drug-associated stimuli, there may be an increased likelihood of postdetoxification withdrawal symptoms and craving.

Although the foregoing analysis of the role of stress in relapse is admittedly speculative, it does have some potentially important clinical implications. If stress increases the likelihood that drug-compensatory CRs will occur when the postaddict encounters drug-associated cues, then stress management should be an important component of treatment for drug addiction. The suggestion that stress management be included in treatment for drug addiction is not unique to the conditioning analysis of relapse. However, stress management in combination with extinction of drug-associated cues may be particularly effective in reducing the likelihood that the postaddict will experience postdetoxification withdrawal symptoms and resume drug taking.

INDIVIDUAL DIFFERENCES IN RESPONSIVENESS TO DRUG CUES AND RELAPSE

The study by Hinson and Siegel (1983a) described previously demonstrates that individual differences in drug-compensatory CRs are correlated with individual differences in tolerance. Similarly, based on the conditioning analysis of postdetoxification withdrawal discussed previously, it would be expected that individual differences in conditional responding to drug-related stimuli might be related to the likelihood of relapse. There is, in fact, evidence for this. In one study, Kennedy (1971; cited in Pomerleau *et al.*, 1983) found that alcoholics who continued to exhibit a pupil dilatory response to the smell of their favorite alcoholic beverage at the end of treatment were more likely to relapse within 3 months than were patients who did not exhibit this response. Meyer, Kaplan, Stroebel, O'Brien, and Virgolio (1981) found that alcoholics who showed greater psychogalvanic reactivity to the sight of a can of beer chose beer over a lottery ticket as reinforcement for an operant task significantly more often than alcoholics who showed little reactivity to the drug cues. Kaplan, Meyer, and Stroebel (1982) also reported that increased desire to drink and increased heart rate in response to alcohol-associated stimuli were significantly correlated with the probability that alcoholic subjects would select and consume an optional drink. These results demonstrate that differences in reactivity to drug-related stimuli are related to relapse and drug-acquisitive behavior. Consequently, Pomerleau *et al.* (1983) have suggested that testing an addict's reactivity to drug-related stimuli at the end of treatment may provide a useful technique for assessing the likelihood of relapse.

SUMMARY AND CONCLUSIONS

This chapter has reviewed recent research relating to the role of Pavlovian conditioning in tolerance, postdetoxification withdrawal, and relapse to drug use. A primary interest has been to examine how Pavlovian conditioning may relate to individual differences in these phenomena.

The Pavlovian analysis suggests that the elicitation of drug-compensatory CRs by the usual predrug cues contributes to both tolerance and postdetoxification withdrawal. Obviously, individuals differ in the variety of cues that have been associated with drug administration in the past. Based on the Pavlovian conditioning analysis, individuals with equivalent drug exposure would then be expected to differ in their level of tolerance depending on what environmental cues are present at a given time. The research summarized in this chapter on the situation specificity of tolerance demonstrates just this type of result. Additionally, the Pavlovian analysis indicates that the same individual may be tolerant in a situation where predrug cues occur but would not be tolerant in another situation where predrug cues do not occur. Such results have been demonstrated in some studies of the situation specificity of tolerance (Crowell *et al.*, 1981). Thus, the Pavlovian analysis indicates that the source of some individual differences in tolerance is not attributable to neurochemical or neuroanatomical differences in organisms but rather to the associative history of environmental cues present at the time of drug administration.

The importance of individual differences attributable to the associative history of environmental cues is further demonstrated by research summarized in this chapter on postdetoxification relapse. The occurrence of postdetoxification withdrawal symptoms, "craving," and relapse are very much influenced by individual reactivity to drug-associated stimuli (cf. Pomerleau *et al.*, 1983). This suggests the need for some degree of "individualization" in treatment of drug addicts (cf. Poulos *et al.*, 1981). The call for individualization in treatment is not unique to a Pavlovian analysis of relapse. However, the Pavlovian analysis does provide an explicit indication of some aspects of treatment that may be profitably tailored to the individual patient. The study by Blaky and Baker (1980) discussed in this chapter provides an example of how individualized extinction therapy is effective in treatment.

Individual differences in tolerance have been researched in terms of genetically based differences in neurochemical or neuroanatomical substrates of drug action (see Chapter 2, this volume). This research has greatly advanced the understanding of individual differences in drug responsiveness. In this chapter, individual differences in tolerance were discussed within the framework of the Pavlovian conditioning analysis of tolerance. It was suggested that individual differences in conditionability would be expected to contribute to individual differences in tolerance from the perspective of the Pavlovian conditioning analysis. However, no research was available to assess this suggestion. Additionally, it was suggested how individual differences in acute adaptation to drug effects (as possibly reflected in the phenomenon of acute tolerance) may be important to tolerance from a Pavlovian conditioning analysis. The Pavlovian conditioning analysis of the role of acute adaptation in tolerance suggests that the more acutely adaptive an individual is to a drug effect the more rapidly that individual may become tolerant. The studies by Ritzman and Tabakoff (1980), Tabakoff and Ritzman (1979), Quintanilla and Tampier (1982), and Bierness and Vogel-Sprott (1983) provide preliminary support for this analysis.

ACKNOWLEDGMENTS

C. X. Poulos and S. Siegel provided many helpful comments during the preparation of this chapter.

REFERENCES

Adams, W. H., Yeh, S. Y., Woods, L. A., & Mitchell, C. L. Drug-test interaction as a factor in the development of tolerance to the analgesic effect of morphine. *Journal of Pharmacology and Experimental Therapeutics*, 1969, *168*, 251–257.

Advokat, C. Analgesic tolerance produced by morphine pellets is facilitated by analgesic testing. *Pharmacology, Biochemistry and Behavior*, 1981, *14*, 133–137.

Andrews, H. L. The effect of opiates on the pain threshold in post-addicts. *Journal of Clinical Investigation*, 1943, *22*, 511–516.

Barry, H. Psychological factors in alcoholism. In B. Kissin & H. Begleiter (Eds.), *The biology of alcoholism* (Vol. 3). *Clinical pathology*. New York: Plenum Press, 1974.

Beirness, D., & Vogel-Sprott, M. *The development of alcohol tolerance: Acute recovery as a predictor*. Paper presented at meetings of the Canadian Psychological Association, 1983.

Belknap, J. K. Genetic factors in the effects of alcohol: Neurosensivity, functional tolerance and physical dependence. In H. Rigter & J. C. Crabbe, Jr. (Eds.), *Alcohol tolerance and dependence*. Amsterdam: Elsevier/North Holland, 1980.

Berg, G., LaBerg, J. C., Skutle, A., & Ohman, A. Instructed versus pharmacological effects of alcohol in alcoholics and social drinkers. *Behaviour Research and Therapy*, 1981, *19*, 55–66.

Blakey, R., & Baker, R. An exposure approach to alcohol abuse. *Behaviour Research and Therapy*, 1980, *18*, 319–325.

Broadhurst, P. L. *Drugs and the inheritance of behavior*. New York: Plenum Press, 1978.

Bykov, K. M., *The cerebral cortex and the internal organs*. Moscow: Foreign Languages Publishing House, 1959.

Cappell, H., Roach, C., & Poulos, C. X. Pavlovian control of cross-tolerance between pentobarbital and ethanol. *Psychopharmacology*, 1981, *74*, 54–57.

Cochin, J., & Kornetsky, C. Development and loss of tolerance to morphine in the rat after single and multiple injections. *Journal of Pharmacology and Experimental Therapeutics*, 1964, *145*, 1–10.

Crowell, C. R., Hinson, R. E., & Siegel, S. The role of conditional drug responses in tolerance to the hypothermic effects of ethanol. *Psychopharmacology*, 1981, *73*, 51–54.

Eikelboom, R., & Stewart, J. Conditioning of drug-induced physiological responses. *Psychological Review*, 1982, *89*, 507–528.

Fanselow, M. S., & German, C. Explicitly unpaired delivery of morphine and the test situation: Extinction and retardation of tolerance to the suppressing effects of morphine on locomotor activity. *Behavioral and Neural Biology*, 1982, *35*, 231–241.

Fennessy, M. R., & Lee, J. R. The assessment of and the problems involved in the experimental evaluation of narcotic analgesics. In S. Ehrenpreis & A. Neidle (Eds.), *Methods in narcotics research*. New York: Marcel Dekker, 1975.

Ferguson, R. K., & Mitchell, C. L. Pain as a factor in the development of tolerance to morphine analgesia in man. *Clinical Pharmacology and Therapeutics*, 1969, *10*, 372–383.

Flaherty, J. A., McGuire, H. T., & Gatski, R. L. The psychodynamics of the "dry drunk." *American Journal of Psychiatry*, 1955, *112*, 460–464.

Friedman, H. J. Assessment of physical dependence on and withdrawal from ethanol in animals. In H. Rigter & J. C. Crabbe, Jr. (Eds.), *Alcohol tolerance and dependence*. Amsterdam: Elsevier/North Holland, 1980.

Fulmar, R. H., & Lapidus, L. B. A study of professed reasons for beginning and continuing heroin use. *International Journal of the Addictions*, 1980, *15*, 631–645.

Gitlow, S. E., Dziedzic, S. W., & Dziedzic, L. M. Tolerance to ethanol after prolonged abstinence. In M. M. Gross (Ed.), *Alcohol intoxication and withdrawal* (Vol. IIIa). *Biological aspects of ethanol*. New York: Plenum Press, 1977.

Goldstein, D. B. Inhalation of ethanol vapor. In H. Rigter & J. C. Crabbe, Jr. (Eds.), *Alcohol tolerance and dependence*. Amsterdam: Elsevier/North Holland, 1980.

Greely, J., & Cappell, H. *Tolerance to chlordiazepoxide sedation*. Paper presented at meetings of the Canadian Psychological Association, 1982.

Hecht, T., Baumann, R., & Hecht, K. The somatic and vegetative-regulatory behavior of the healthy organism during conditioning of the insulin effect. *Conditional Reflex*, 1967, *2*, 96–112.

Himmelsbach, C. K. Can the euphoric, analgetic and physical dependence effects of drugs be separated? IV. With reference to physical dependence. *Federation Proceedings*, 1943, *2*, 201–203.

Hinson, R. E., & Poulos, C. X. Sensitization to the behavioral effects of cocaine: Modulation by Pavlovian conditioning. *Pharmacology, Biochemistry and Behavior*, 1981, *15*, 559–562.

Hinson, R. E., & Siegel, S. The contribution of Pavlovian conditioning to ethanol tolerance and dependence. In H. Rigter & J. C. Crabbe, Jr. (Eds.), *Alcohol tolerance and dependence*. Amsterdam: Elsevier/North Holland, 1980.

Hinson, R. E., & Siegel, S. Nonpharmacological bases of drug tolerance and dependence. *Journal of Psychosomatic Research*, 1982, *26*, 495–503.

Hinson, R. E., & Siegel, S. Anticipatory hyperexcitability and tolerance to the narcotizing effect of morphine in the rat. *Behavioral Neuroscience*, 1983, *97*, 759–767. (a)

Hinson, R. E., & Siegel, S. *Pavlovian inhibitory conditioning in tolerance to pentobarbital-induced hypothermia*. Paper presented at meetings of the Canadian Psychological Association, 1983. (b)

Hinson, R. E., Poulos, C. X., & Cappell, H. Effects of pentobarbital and cocaine in rats expecting pentobarbital. *Pharmacology, Biochemistry and Behavior*, 1982, *16*, 661–666.

Hinson, R. E., Poulos, C. X., & Thomas, W. L. Learning in tolerance to haloperidol-induced catalepsy. *Progress in Neuro-Psychopharmacology and Biological Psychiatry*, 1982, *6*, 395–398.

Hodgson, R. J., & Rankin, H. J. Modification of excessive drinking by cue exposure. *Behavior Research and Therapy*, 1976, *14*, 305–307.

Hunt, W. A., Barnett, L. W., & Branch, L. G. Relapse rates in addiction programs. *Journal of Clinical Psychology*, 1971, *27*, 455–456.

Kalant, H., LeBlanc, A. E., & Gibbins, R. J. Tolerance to, and dependence on, some nonopiate psychotropic drugs. *Pharmacological Reviews*, 1971, *23*, 135–191.

Kaplan, R. F., Meyer, R. E., & Stroebel, C. F. The symptoms of alcohol withdrawal as predictors of behavioral and physiological responses to an ethanol stimulus. *Proceedings of the 44th Annual Scientific Meeting of the Committee on Problems of Drug Dependence,* 1982.

Kennedy, D. A. *Pupilometrics as an aid in the assessment of motivation, impact of treatment, and prognosis of chronic alcoholics.* Unpublished doctoral dissertation, University of Utah, 1971.

Kesner, R. P., & Baker, T. G. A two-process model of opiate tolerance. In J. Martinez, G. L. Jensen, R. R. Messing, H. E. Rigter, and J. L. McGaugh (Eds.), *Endogenous peptides and learning and memory processes.* New York: Academic Press, 1981.

Kissin, B., Shenker, V., & Shenker, A. The acute effects of ethyl alcohol and chlorpromazine on certain physiological functions in alcoholics. *Quarterly Journal of Studies on Alcohol,* 1959, *20,* 480–492.

Krank, M. D., Hinson, R. E., & Siegel, S. Conditional hyperalgesia is elicited by environmental signals of morphine. *Behavioral and Neural Biology,* 1981, *32,* 148–157.

LaHoste, G. J., Olson, R. D., Olson, G. A., & Kastin, A. J. Effects of Pavlovian conditioning and MIF-1 on the development of morphine tolerance in rats. *Pharmacology, Biochemistry and Behavior,* 1980, *13,* 799–804.

Lê, A. D., Poulos, C. X., & Cappell, H. Conditioned tolerance to the hypothermic effect of ethyl alcohol. *Science,* 1979, *206,* 1109–1110.

Littleton, J. M. The assessment of rapid tolerance to ethanol. In H. Rigter & J. C. Crabbe (Eds.), *Alcohol tolerance and dependence.* Amsterdam: Elsevier/North Holland, 1980.

Ludwig, A. M., Cain, R. B., Wikler, A., Taylor, R. M., & Bendfeldt, F. Physiological and situational determinants of drinking behavior. In M. M. Gross (Ed.), *Alcohol intoxication and withdrawal* (Vol. IIIb). *Studies in alcohol dependence.* New York: Plenum Press, 1977.

Ludwig, A. M., & Stark, L. H. Alcohol craving: Subjective and situational aspects. *Quarterly Journal of Studies on Alcohol,* 1974, *35,* 108–130.

Mackintosh, N. J. *The psychology of animal learning.* New York: Academic Press, 1974.

Mansfield, J. G., & Cunningham, C. L. Conditioning and extinction of tolerance to the hypothermic effect of ethanol in rats. *Journal of Comparative and Physiological Psychology,* 1980, *94,* 962–969.

Mathew, R. J., Claghorn, J. L., & Largen, J. Craving for alcohol in sober alcoholics. *American Journal of Psychiatry,* 1979, *136,* 603–606.

Melchior, C. L., & Tabokoff, B. Modification of environmentally cued tolerance to ethanol in mice. *Journal of Pharmacology and Experimental Therapeutics,* 1981, *219,* 175–180.

Meyer, R. E., Kaplan, R. F., & Stroebel, C. F. Factors affecting the stimulus-control of craving in hospitalized alcoholics. *Journal of Psychiatric Research,* 1981, *16,* 137.

Meyer, R. E., Kaplan, R., Stroebel, C. F., O'Brien, J. E., & Virgilio, L. *Conditioning factors in alcoholism.* Paper presented at the annual meeting of the American Psychiatric Association, New Orleans, May 1981.

Obal, F. The fundamentals of the central nervous control of vegetative homeostasis. *Acta Physiology Academy of Science, Hungry,* 1966, *30,* 15–29.

O'Brien, C. P. Experimental analysis of conditioning factors in human narcotic addiction. *Pharmacological Reviews,* 1976, *27,* 533–543.

Pavlov, I. P. *Conditioned Reflexes* (G. V. Anrep, trans.). London: Oxford University Press, 1927.

Pomerleau, O. F., Fertig, J., Baker, L., & Cooney, N. Reactivity to alcohol cues in alcoholics and non-alocholics: Implications for a stimulus control analysis of drinking. *Addictive Behaviors,* 1983, *8,* 1–10.

Poulos, C. X., & Hinson, R. E. Pavlovian conditional tolerance to haloperidol catalepsy: Evidence of dynamic adaptations in dopaminergic systems. *Science,* 1982, *218,* 491–492.

Poulos, C. X., & Hinson, R. E. A homeostatic model of Pavlovian conditioning: Tolerance to scopolamine-induced adipsia. *Behavioral Neuroscience,* 1984, *10,* 75–89.

Poulos, C. X., Hinson, R. E., & Siegel, S. The role of Pavlovian processes in drug tolerance and dependence: Implications for treatment. *Addictive Behaviors,* 1981, *6,* 205–211.

Poulos, C. X., Wilkinson, D. A., & Cappell, H. Homeostatic regulation and Pavlovian conditioning in tolerance to amphetamine-induced anorexia. *Journal of Comparative and Physiological Psychology,* 1981, *95,* 735–746.

Quintanilla, M. E., & Tampier, L. UCLB rats do not develop actue tolerance in ethanol narcosis time. *IRCS Medical Science-Biochemistery,* 1982, *10,* 535.

Rescorla, R. A. Pavlovian conditioned inhibition. *Psychological Bulletin,* 1969, *72,* 77–94.

Ritzmann, R. F., & Tabakoff, B. Strain differences in the development of acute tolerance to ethanol. In H. Begleiter (Ed.), *Biological effects of alcohol.* New York: Plenum Press, 1980.

Robins, L. N., Helzer, J. E., & Davis, P. H. Narcotic use in Southeast Asia and afterwards. *Archives of General Psychiatry,* 1975, *32,* 955–961.

Saunders, W. M., & Kershaw, P. W. Spontaneous remission from alcoholism—A community study. *British Journal of Addiction,* 1979, *74,* 251–265.

Sideroff, S. I., & Jarvik, M. E. Conditional responses to a videotape showing heroin related stimuli. *International Journal of the Addictions,* 1980, *15,* 529–536.

Siegel, S. Evidence from rats that morphine tolerance is a learned response. *Journal of Comparative and Physiological Psychology,* 1975, *89,* 498–506. (a)

Siegel, S. Conditioning insulin effects. *Journal of Comparative and Physiological Psychology,* 1975, *89,* 189–199. (b)

Siegel, S. Morphine analgesic tolerance: Its situation specificity supports a Pavlovian conditioning model. *Science,* 1976, *193,* 323–325.

Siegel, S. Morphine tolerance acquisition as an associative process. *Journal of Experimental Psychology: Animal Behavior Processes,* 1977, *3,* 1–13.

Siegel, S. A Pavlovian conditioning analysis of morphine tolerance. In N. A. Krasnegor (Ed.), *Behavioral tolerance: Research and treatment implications.* Washington, D.C.: U.S. Government Printing Office, 1978. (a)

Siegel, S. Tolerance to the hyperthermic effect of morphine in the rat is a learned response. *Journal of Comparative and Physiological Psychology,* 1978, *92,* 1137–1149. (b)

Siegel, S. The role of conditioning in drug tolerance and addiction. In J. D. Keehn (Ed.), *Psychopathology in animals: Research and treatment implications.* New York: Academic Press, 1979.

Siegel, S. Classical conditioning, drug tolerance, and drug dependence. In Y. Israel, F. B. Glaser, H. Kalant, R. E. Popham, W. Schmidt, and R. G. Smart (Eds.), *Research advances in alcohol and drug problems* (Vol. 7). New York: Plenum Press, 1983.

Siegel, S., Hinson, R. E. & Krank, M. D. The role of predrug signals in morphine analgesic tolerance: Support for a Pavlovian conditioning model of tolerance. *Journal of Experimental Psychology: Animal Behavior Processes,* 1978, *4,* 188–196.

Siegel, S., Hinson, R. E., & Krank, M. D. Modulation of tolerance to the lethal effect of morphine by extinction. *Behavioral and Neural Biology,* 1979, *25,* 257–262.

Siegel, S., Hinson, R. E., & Krank, M. D. Morphine-induced attenuation of morphine tolerance. *Science,* 1981, *212,* 1533–1534.

Siegel, S., Hinson, R. E., Krank, M. D., & McCully, J. Heroin "overdose" death: Contribution of drug-associated environmental cues. *Science,* 1982, *216,* 436–437.

Solomon, R. L. An opponent-process theory of acquired motivation: The affective dynamics of addiction. In J. D. Mazer & M. E. P. Seligman (Eds.), *Psychopathology: Experimental models.* San Francisco: Freeman, 1977.

Tabakoff, B., & Ritzman, R. F. Acute tolerance in inbred and selected lines of mice. *Drug and Alcohol Dependence,* 1979, *4,* 87–90.

Tabakoff, B., Melchior, C. L., & Hoffman, P. L. Commentary on ethanol tolerance. *Alcoholism—Clinical and Experimental Research,* 1982, *6,* 252–259.

Teasdale, J. D. Conditioned abstinence in narcotic addicts. *International Journal of the Addictions,* 1973, *8,* 273–292.

Ternes, J. W. An opponent process theory of habitual behavior with special reference to smoking. In M. E. Jarvik, J. W. Cullen, E. R. Gritz, T. M. Vogt, and L. J. West (Eds.), *Research on smoking behavior.* Washington, D.C.: U.S. Government Printing Office, 1977.

Thompson, T., & Ostlund, W., Jr. Susceptibility to readdiction as a function of the addiction and withdrawal environments. *Journal of Comparative and Physiological Psychology,* 1965, *60,* 388–392.

Tiffany, S. T., & Baker, T. B. Morphine tolerance in the rat: Congruence with a Pavlovian paradigm. *Journal of Comparative and Physiological Psychology,* 1981, *95,* 747–762.

Wahlsten, D. Genetic experiments with animal learning: A critical review. *Behavioral Biology,* 1972, *7,* 143–182.

Wagman, A., & Allen, R. Effects of alcohol ingestion and abstinence on slow wave sleep of alcoholics. In M. M. Gross (Ed.), *Alcohol intoxication and withdrawal: Experimental studies.* New York: Plenum Press, 1975.

Wikler, A. Conditioning of successive adaptive responses to the initial effects of drugs. *Conditional Reflex,* 1973, *8,* 193–210.

Wikler, A. The search for the psyche in drug dependence: A 35-year retrospective survey. *Journal of Nervous and Mental Disease,* 1977, *165,* 29–40.

CHAPTER 5

Behavioral Approaches to Individual Differences in Substance Abuse

Drug-taking Behavior

ROBERT J. BARRETT

The plethora of theories that attempt to account for substance abuse include a bewildering assortment drawn from a broad cross-section of the life sciences. Recently, the National Institute on Drug Abuse (Lettieri, Sayers, & Pearson, 1980) reviewed 43 contemporary theories of drug abuse, representing nine different disciplines, including psychiatry, sociology, criminology, anthropology, biology, genetics, biomedical sciences, and psychology. Within psychology alone the theories were further subdivided into general, learning, social, and developmental psychology. Abbreviated titles such as life theme, family, neuropharmacological, bioanthropological, self-derogation, incomplete mourning, existential, biological rhythm, ego/self, conditioning, and interactive framework theory were described as *representative* selections from contemporary perspectives. Although some of the theories involved concepts from more than one discipline, few of them would qualify as truly multidisciplinary in approach.

It is difficult to defend a single-discipline approach to understanding a problem as clearly multidimensional as drug abuse. However, inter-

ROBERT J. BARRETT • Veterans Administration Medical Center and Departments of Psychology and Pharmacology, Vanderbilt University, Nashville, Tennessee 37240. This work was supported by the Veterans Administration.

disciplinary research on behavior-related problems in general has often been difficult to establish. An encouraging development in this respect is the emergence of behavioral medicine as a discipline (Schwartz, 1980; Weiss & Schwartz, 1982). Behavioral medicine is concerned with *integrating* information from multiple levels of investigation, with emphasis on identifying junctures at which vertical synthesis between disciplines can occur.

Historical traditions explain, in part, why research on behavioral-biomedical problems such as drug abuse have generally not been inter-disciplinary. In particular, more radical behaviorists, trained in the Skin-nerian operant conditioning tradition, have been discouraged from seek-ing biological explanations for behavior. The fervor of this conviction is illustrated by the following quotation from Skinner (1938):

> I venture to assert that no fact of the nervous system has as yet ever told anyone anything new about behavior, and from the point of view of a de-scriptive science that is the only criterion to be taken into account.... The current fashion in proceeding from a behavioral fact to its neural correlate instead of validating the fact as such and then proceeding to deal with other problems in behavior, seriously hampers the development of a science of behavior. (pp. 425, 428)

That the general skepticism concerning the value of interdisciplinary research has not been limited to behaviorists is illustrated in the following quote by the philosopher and physicist Ernst Mach (cited from Skinner, 1938):

> It often happens that the development of two different fields of science goes on side by side for long periods without either of them exercising an influence on the other. On occasion, again they may come into closer contact, when it is noticed that unexpected light is thrown on the doctrines of the one by the doctrines of the other.... But the period of buoyant hope, the period of over-estimation of this relation which is supposedly to explain everything, is quickly followed by a period of disillusionment, when the two fields in question are once more separated, and each pursues its own aims putting its own special questions and applying its own methods. But on both of them the temporary contact leaves abiding traces behind. Apart from the positive addition to knowledge, which is not to be despised, the temporary relation between them brings about a transformation of our conceptions, clarifying them and per-mitting of their application over a wider field than that for which they were originally formed. (p. 432)

Both statements emphasize the need to develop knowledge within a discipline before attempting to integrate knowledge across disciplines. They also suggest that the latter can detract from the former. This was a concern for Skinner in 1938 because the experimental analysis of be-havior was not yet an established discipline. However, as Mach noted, an important by-product of interdisciplinary research is that it promotes conceptual growth. The disciplines have developed. Now conceptual growth is needed before significant advances are likely to occur in understanding drug abuse behavior.

CONCEPTUAL CONSIDERATIONS

The way in which a research problem and the goals of the work are initially conceptualized determines the direction of the actual research. With respect to substance abuse, a theory is useful to the extent that it can explain drug-taking *behavior*. A behavioral analysis of substance abuse begins with the assumption that drug-taking behavior follows the same fundamental laws that explain the acquisition and maintenance of more conventional forms of operant behavior. It emphasizes that drug-taking behavior is not reflexive. Rather, it is a goal-directed, purposeful, operant response. This conceptual premise in no way diminishes the importance of physiological, genetic, sociological, or other determinants of drug abuse. It merely establishes a necessary requirement for a theory of drug abuse: namely that the theory must demonstrate how proposed causal variables translate into *drug-taking behavior*. This does not always occur. For example, many biochemical studies designed to identify determinants of alcohol abuse have looked for differences in alcohol metabolism between alcohol abusers and nonabusers. The reports of these studies often fail to include a discussion about how such metabolic differences might be causally related to alcohol abuse. Would alcoholics be expected to metabolize alcohol more or less rapidly than nonalcoholics? In general, would one expect alcohol metabolism of abusers or nonabusers to deviate most from the norm? The answers to these and similar questions involve development of a sound conceptualization of drinking as an operant behavior. Viewing alcohol abuse as operant behavior leads one to ask what it is about alcohol that some people find more reinforcing than others. Only after the behavioral principles controlling the use of alcohol (or any other psychoactive drug) are known is it possible to construct meaningful theories about how a biochemical characteristic might alter drug-taking behavior.

The theory presented later integrates behavioral and physiological principles to explain drug use and abuse. More specifically, the theory addresses the following questions: (1) Why do people initially use psychoactive drugs? (2) Why do some people continue to use a particular drug, whereas others do not after initial experimentation? (3) What factors account for the escalation of drug use to drug abuse? and (4) What accounts for the high incidence of relapse among drug abusers after periods of abstinence?

The theory is presented first, in its entirety, followed in the later sections by empirical support for its various components. The opponent-process theory of motivation developed by Solomon (Solomon, 1977, 1980; Solomon & Corbit, 1973, 1974) contributed substantially to the direction of our drug abuse research. The opponent-process theory provides an important conceptual framework to acccount for the interaction between associative processes and direct biological effects of psychoactive drugs. The work of Wikler (1980) was also important in demonstrating the value of an interdisciplinary approach to understanding drug-taking behavior.

A BIOBEHAVIORAL THEORY OF DRUG USE AND ABUSE

The present theory emphasizes that no single factor is sufficient to produce drug abuse. Rather this behavior is causally related to multiple organismic and environmental determinants.

Initial Drug Use

Research on initial drug use indicates that drug availability, peer-group influence, and moral and legal considerations are important (Jessor & Jessor, 1977). It is recognized that the influence of these variables can change over time. Nevertheless, the role of these variables in determining the probability that a person will abuse drugs should not be underestimated. For example, a strongly held religious conviction that precludes the use of any psychoactive drug will be sufficient to prevent drug use and abuse independent of other predictive factors. In this regard, there are any number of factors that would be sufficient to preclude a person from abusing drugs. It is more difficult to identify the various conditions that are necessary and sufficient to predict drug abuse.

Repeated Drug Use

People use psychoactive drugs because they prefer the hedonic state that immediately follows drug administration to the state that immediately preceded use of the drug. The characteristics (both qualitative and quantitative) of the relative hedonic states vary as a function of drug, dose, present environment, and past drug-taking history, as well as individual differences related to the drug's pharmacodynamic and pharmacokinetic properties. Thus, this theory requires no assumptions about exactly how the person "feels" either before or after drug use. It maintains only that the latter is preferred.

Drug Abuse

Following use of a psychoactive drug two events occur in temporal sequence. One is a primary effect, which is hedonically positive, which is followed by a compensatory, hedonically negative effect (Solomon, 1977, 1980; Solomon & Corbit, 1973, 1974). The compensatory, or "opponent," hedonic state reflects the operation of normal homeostatic, regulatory mechanisms in reaction to the drug's disruption of steady-state equilibrium. The intensity and duration of the compensatory response is determined by the interaction of both pharmacodynamic and pharmacokinetic drug characteristics with individual pharmacogenetic factors.

The primary and compensatory physiological processes caused by drug administration are temporally distinct. Therefore, abrupt termination of drug use results in a period of time during which the opponent-processes are dominant. This is followed by a gradual return to predrug, steady-state levels. If use of the drug is repeated before the system has returned to steady-state levels, there is a decrease in the drug's primary hedonic effect and an increase in the intensity of the opponent hedonic effect. Thus, after chronic use of a drug the hedonic state initially experienced will be diminished by an amount equal to the altered hedonic baseline. This diminished drug effect is an example of pharmacodynamic tolerance. Thus, for an individual who has used a drug chronically, the dose that initially produced a change in hedonic state from "normal" to "euphoric" might produce a change of similar magnitude, but from "dysphoric" to "normal."

The underlying physiological processes that oppose the primary drug effect, producing tolerance, are also responsible for the behavioral signs of withdrawal that develop when drug use is suddenly terminated. Drug dependence thus refers to the *dependence* of a system on an amount of drug sufficient to balance the compensatory processes and prevent withdrawal.

This understanding of *pharmacodynamic tolerance, drug dependence,* and *drug withdrawal* proposes that all three constructs refer to the same compensatory physiological processes induced by chronic drug use. Because abrupt termination after chronic use of a psychoactive drug produces hedonic changes opposite to those for which the drug was originally used, it is not difficult to understand the motivation for continued drug use. Furthermore, if the chronic user seeks to experience the original drug effect, he or she must increase both its dose and/or the frequency of use. These changes in drug-taking behavior, although initially effective in overcoming tolerance, eventually induce equivalent increases in the strength of the opponent hedonic state, making the negative consequences of discontinuing drug use even greater.

Distinctions between *physiological* and *psychological* dependence have often been the source of misleading inferences about underlying mechanisms. For example, it is not always clear what is implied by the common observation that chronic use of drugs such as alcohol and morphine produces both physiological and psychological dependence, whereas amphetamine and cocaine are said to produce *only* psychological dependence. The distinction is meaningful only to the extent that it differentiates between dependence on a drug's psychoactive and nonpsychoactive effects. The underlying mechanisms, however, are always physiological.

Relapse

Even though drug abuse leads to a variety of personal, social, and physical problems, the incidence of relapse following successful detoxification is generally high for most psychoactive drugs. Two factors are important in understanding relapse: (1) if the predrug hedonic state was undesirable (depression, anxiety, etc.) then the original motivation for drug self-medication will likely continue to be a factor; and (2) during periods of extended drug use, withdrawal symptoms can become classically conditioned to cues present in the individual's drug-taking environment. Therefore, even after long periods of abstinence, reexposure to these environmental stimuli can elicit conditioned withdrawal-like symptoms. These conditioned responses can reinstate the motivation to use the drug because the individual has learned that the drug will produce immediate (although temporary) relief from the negative hedonic states associated with withdrawal.

EMPIRICAL SUPPORT

Empirical justification for the theory outlined above comes from a review of both the human and animal literature as well as from the results of studies specifically designed to test the theory.

REINFORCING PROPERTIES OF PSYCHOACTIVE DRUGS

Human Studies

The literature addressing the question of why people use psychoactive drugs is remarkably confusing. A number of investigators have proposed that people take drugs for their euphoric effects (Isbell, 1958; Jasinski, 1977; Martin, Haertzen, & Hewett, 1978). Euphoria is generally, operationally defined on the basis of inventories or checklists such as the Profile of Mood States (POM) developed by McNair, Lorr, and Droppleman (1971) or the Morphine–Benzedrine Group Scale (MBG) of the Addiction Research Center Inventory (ARCI) (Hill, Haertzen, Wolback, & Miner, 1963). Euphoria, as measured by these tests, is produced by virtually all drugs with high abuse potential including morphine (Jasinski, Martin, & Hoeldtke, 1971); methadone, methamphetamine, methylphenidate, phenmetrazine (Martin, Sloan, Sapira, & Jasinski, 1971); cocaine, d-amphetamine (Fischmann, Schuster, Resnekov, Fennel, Schick, & Krasnegor, 1976); heroin (Jasinski & Nutt; 1972), codeine, etorphine, propoxyphene (Jasinski, Nutt, & Griffith, 1974); and pentobarbital (McClane & Martin, 1976). Not surprising, drugs that produce dysphoria such as naloxone (Jasinski, 1972), nalorphine (Jasinski, 1973a), and fenfluramine (Griffith, Nutt, & Jasinski, 1975) are also drugs that are not abused.

Another way in which subjective drug effects have been categorized involved asking drug users why they habitually used various psychoactive drugs. A NIDA-sponsored study conducted by O'Donnell, Voss, Clayton, Slatin, and Room (1976) reported a wide variety of reasons given by 20–30-year-old men who were questioned about their use of alcohol, marijuana, psychedelics, stimulants, sedatives, heroin, opiates, and cocaine. Of the reasons given, "to get high or stoned," was the most often cited. In fact, depending on the drug, this was given as a reason by 65 to 99% of the respondents. Other reasons were "to heighten your senses—like taste, touch, or hearing," "to help you forget your worries," "to help you get to sleep or relax," and "because you were bored."

Clinical data, however, emphasize that with continued use of psychoactive drugs, including alcohol, opiates, stimulants, and antianxiety agents, there is an increase in dysphoria, anxiety, irritability, and aggressiveness (Mello, 1972; Watson, Hartmann & Schildkraut, 1972; Wikler, 1980). These data have been used to question the notion that people use drugs for their mood elevating, positive hedonic effects. In particular, a frequently cited study by Wikler (1952) monitored changes in hedonic state of a "postaddict during self-regulated" but supervised access to morphine over a $3\frac{1}{2}$-month period. Wikler reported that the subject gradually increased the amount and frequency of morphine use, attaining an average of about 1,100 mg/day in 12 divided doses. More importantly, it was observed that after the first few days of morphine use the euphoric effects gradually disappeared except for a brief period immediately following each injection. Furthermore, the patient's prevailing mood eventually became one of dysphoria. When asked why he continued to take the drug the subject explained that he experienced some, "gratification through the suppression, by each dose of morphine, of the mild abstinence changes (perceived by the patient as a "need" or "craving") that ensued a few hours after the previous dose" (Wikler, 1980, p. 169). On the basis of similar clinical data, Mello (1972), Alexander and Hadaway (1982), and others (Dews, 1973; Wikler, 1980) have labeled what they refer to as the positive reinforcement explanation of chronic drug use as *simplistic* and *most doubtful*. Alexander and Hadaway (1982) claim that proponents of a hedonic explanation of drug use revert to the more descriptive but circular meaning of reinforcement when confronted with evidence that euphoria is no longer experienced after chronic use of a psychoactive drug. Wikler (1980) is also opposed to a hedonic (reward, pleasure, positive reinforcement, or euphoria-based) explanation of psychoactive drug use, as evident from the following statement:

> The pleasure–pain principle, is an empty tautology since it is incapable of refutation by any conceivable objective data that might seem contradictory, inasmuch as it can be "saved" by invocation of untestable, unconscious, intervening variables. (p. vii)

It is misleading, however, to suggest that these clinical observations are evidence against a hedonic explanation of drug use and abuse. The relevant issue is not whether drugs continue to produce some rather arbitrarily defined affective state called *euphoria*. The critical consideration is that the drugs continue to have mood-elevating or mood-enhancing properties after chronic use, independent of the absolute level of the resulting hedonic state or what label one might wish to attach to it. For the purpose of illustration, consider a hypothetical experiment in which changes in affect are measured on a 10-point hedonic scale. The first time a drug was used it might enhance mood by 3 hedonic units (e.g., 5.5 to 8.5), corresponding to a change from "normal" to "euphoric." After chronic use of the drug, the same drug dose might produce an equivalent mood elevation (e.g., 2.5 to 5.5), but now it corresponds to a change from "dysphoria" to "normal." This illustration parallels the effects reported by the subject in Wikler's (1952) experiment. Although it is true that morphine no longer produced euphoria after chronic use, the subject nevertheless continued to use the drug because it prevented the negative hedonic state that accompanies morphine withdrawal. What remained constant was a preference for the morphine state.

The present theory proposes that people continue to use psychoactive drugs not because they necessarily "feel good" or "euphoric" but only that they "feel" *better* soon after taking the drug than they did immediately before.

In order to understand why people continue to use drugs that will eventually result in negative hedonic states, it is instructive to consider research on delay of reinforcement that has shown that for both positive (de Villiers, 1977; Rachlin & Green, 1972) and negative (Davitz, Mason, Mowrer, & Virek, 1957) reinforcement there is an inverse relationship between reinforcement value or effectiveness and delay of reinforcement. One of the characteristics that distinguishes drugs of abuse from other types of reinforcers is that their positive hedonic effects occur virtually immediately after administration, whereas the negative hedonic effects are delayed. The importance of delay of reinforcement can be illustrated by comparing the drug-taking behavior characteristic of two classes of drugs known to alter hedonic state or affective behavior: CNS stimulants (amphetamine, methylphenidate, and cocaine), and tricyclic antidepressants (amitriptyline, nortriptyline, imipramine). CNS stimulants initially have immediate mood-enhancing properties, but after the chronic use of increasing doses, dysphoria begins to prevail unless the drug is administered frequently. Nevertheless, concerted legal, social, and medical efforts are necessary to control drug use (Smith, 1969). On the other hand, antidepressants often produce immediate, although mild undesirable effects, but after chronic use of increasing doses, a gradual improvement in mood often develops. Unlike the CNS stimulants, however, concentrated efforts have to be made to encourage people to use these drugs, as is evidenced by the generally low rates of compliance that characterize antidepressant use (Wilcox, Gillan, & Hare, 1965). Thus, an important determinant of drug use is the immediate mood-altering property of the drug, independent of whether the eventual (delayed) effects of continued use are therapeutic or detrimental.

Animal Studies

Animal studies have demonstrated the reinforcing properties of commonly abused psychoactive drugs. In the early 1960s investigators (Thompson & Schuster, 1964; Weeks, 1962) demonstrated that rats and monkeys will learn to press a lever to self-administer morphine through chronic indwelling venous catheters. Subsequent research has established, with few exceptions, that drugs with abuse potential in humans

are self-administered by animals. Such drugs include profadol, methadone, etorphine, butorphanol, and buprenorphine (Woods, 1977); pro-
piran, pentazocine, propoxyphene, and codeine (Hoffmeister & Schlichting, 1972); heroin (Hoffmeister & Wuttke, 1974); d-amphetamine and
methamphetamine (Balster & Schuster, 1973); phenmetrazine and methylphenidate (Wilson, Hitomi, & Schuster, 1971); and ethanol, phenobarbital, and cocaine (Deneau, Yanagita, & Seevers, 1969). Neither humans
nor animals self-administer the opiate antagonists naloxone and nalorphine (Balster, Aigner, Carney, & Harris, 1977; Griffith, Nutt, & Jasinski,
1975; Hoffmeister & Schlichting, 1972; Jasinski, 1972, 1973b; Woods &
Tessel, 1974). Other drugs that are neither self-administered by animals
nor abused by humans include chlorpromazine (Deneau *et al.*, 1969;
Hoffmeister & Goldberg, 1973) fenfluramine; (Gotestan & Anderson, 1975);
imipramine, protriptyline, maprotiline, and iprindole (Yanagita, Takahashi, & Oinuma, 1972); and acetylsalicylic acid and other antipyretic
analgesics (Hoffmeister & Wuttke, 1973, 1975). Furthermore, animals learn
to respond in order to escape or avoid the administration of chlorpromazine, nalorphine, and cyclazocine (Hoffmeister, 1975; Hoffmeister & Wuttke,
1973, 1974, 1975), drugs among those listed before as producing dysphoria
in humans.

Additional animal data show that behavior maintained by psychoactive drugs follows the same principles or laws as behavior maintained by
more conventional reinforcers (Pickens & Thompson, 1968, 1971; Thompson & Pickens, 1972). Cues present during drug administration can function as discriminative stimuli and subsequently influence the probability
of drug taking. For example, after rats were trained to self-administer
ethanol (Meisch & Thompson, 1973), the odor of ethanol or the interoceptive cues associated with noncontingent ethanol injections (Pickens
& Thompson, 1971; Stretch, Gerber, & Wood, 1971) precipitated drug self-
administration. Thus, the interoceptive changes associated with reinforcement acquire discriminative stimulus properties that lead to continued drug self-administration. This is similar to the "priming" effect of
noncontingent stimulation in the intracranial self-stimulation paradigm.
In addition, exteroceptive stimuli that are selectively paired with the
delivery of psychoactive drugs can also take on conditioned reinforcing
properties and will themselves maintain responding. For instance, Schuster and Woods (1968) demonstrated that monkeys previously trained to
press a lever for morphine would respond for a red light if it had previously been paired with morphine administration.

In addition to demonstrating conditioned reinforcement, responding
for psychoactive drugs is responsive to schedules of reinforcement

(Thompson & Pickens, 1972); punishment (Smith & Davis, 1974); and extinction (Grove & Schuster, 1974; Pickens & Thompson, 1968).

PHARMACODYNAMIC REGULATORY PROCESSES AND OPPONENT HEDONIC STATES

The data discussed next represent the results from a comprehensive series of experiments specifically designed to test the opponent-process explanation of tolerance, drug dependence, and withdrawal. In these animal experiments, d-amphetamine (AMPH) was used as the prototype drug of abuse.

Tolerance to the Reinforcing Properties of Amphetamine

In a study by McCown and Barrett (1980) male Sprague-Dawley rats implanted with chronic, indwelling, jugular vein catheters were trained to lever press in an operant chamber for infusions of AMPH on a continuous schedule of reinforcement (CRF). Each lever press resulted in the delivery of 0.125 mg/kg AMPH. Animals were daily given four-hour training sessions until the number of reinforcements per test session became stable. For some animals the AMPH concentration was then doubled to 0.25 mg/kg/reinforcement, whereas the volume remained constant. It was observed that animals compensated for the higher concentration by appropriately decreasing the number of reinforcements obtained. The results agree with previous observations that rats will self-administer AMPH (Pickens & Harris, 1968; Yokel & Pickens, 1973). The next question we asked was whether rats, like humans, would develop tolerance to the reinforcing property of AMPH.

To test for tolerance, four of the subjects were injected with AMPH three times a day for 4 consecutive days. The first dose was 1.0 mg/kg. On each succeeding injection the dose was incremented by 1.0 mg/kg of AMPH such that the final dose on the fourth day was 12 mg/kg. The fifth rat was injected with equal volumes of saline. Thirty-six hours after the final injection, the animals were returned to the operant chamber and tested for tolerance to AMPH. The results are presented in Figure 1, where each animal's number of reinforcements are shown prior to and following the chronic regimen. As can be seen, all animals who received chronic AMPH developed tolerance as evidenced by the increased amount of drug that they self-administered.

Tolerance can be defined in one of two ways: (1) reduced effect of a given drug dose after repeated administration; and/or (2) a need to increase drug dose in order to reinstate the original drug response. The

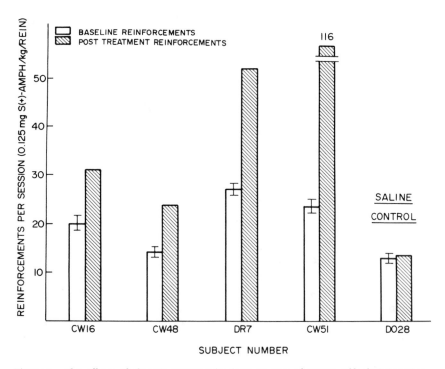

Figure 1. The effects of chronic AMPH injections on rate of AMPH self-administration. Each subject showed at least a 50% increase in the amount of AMPH self-administered after chronic treatment. A saline control subject shows no change from baseline. (From "The Development of Tolerance to the Rewarding Effects of Self-Administered S (+) – Amphetamine" by T. J. McCown and R. J. Barrett, *Pharmacology, Biochemistry & Behavior,* 1980, *12,* 137–141. Copyright 1980 by *Pharmacology, Biochemistry & Behavior.* Reprinted by permission.)

development of tolerance is generally attributed to one or more of the following three mechanisms: (1) dispositional; (2) pharmacodynamic; and (3) behavioral. The first two are relevant to the experiment under discussion. *Dispositional tolerance* refers to decreased drug effects that result from reductions in the concentration of drug reaching the target site. This can occur following chronic use of drugs (e.g., barbiturates, alcohol) that induce liver enzymes involved in their metabolism. Dispositional tolerance generally does not alter peak drug effects and usually results in not more than a twofold shift in the dose-response function (Kalant, Leblanc, & Gibbins, 1971). *Pharmacodynamic tolerance* refers to adaptive changes (cellular adaptation) that occur within the physiological systems directly affected by the drug. These adaptive processes oppose the primary (homeostatically disrupting) effects of the drug. Pharmaco-dynamic tolerance can account for a tenfold change or greater in drug potency (Kalant et al., 1971).

In order to determine the extent to which tolerance to the reinforcing properties of AMPH was the result of dispositional and/or pharmaco-dynamic tolerance, groups of rats were injected with either chronic AMPH or saline according to the regimen described previously. Thirty-six hours after the final injection, all animals received 10 mg/kg AMPH i.v. and were sacrificed 15, 30, 60, or 120 minutes later (n = 4–6 per group). In order to determine whether chronic AMPH alters the rate of drug disappear-ance, whole brain AMPH levels were determined at each of the afore-mentioned time intervals using the methyl orange assay (Axelrod, 1954). Figure 2 shows that the rate of AMPH disappearance for the chronic AMPH and chronic saline groups did not differ. The half-lives were 53.5 and 58.5 minutes, respectively. These data indicate that dispositional tolerance is not responsible for the diminished reinforcement properties of AMPH after chronic administration.

The results, rather, suggest that tolerance is due to pharmacody-namic processes. AMPH appears to induce compensatory, physiological processes that oppose its primary action. Tolerance then is observed when the drug is administered prior to the complete dissipation of the opponent processes resultant from previous use of the drug. According to this model, abrupt abstinence after a period of chronic AMPH admin-istration should be followed by a rebound hedonic state opposite to the drug's primary mood-enhancing property. This prediction agrees with the observation that depression is often associated with termination of amphetamine use by humans (Watson et al., 1972). This adaptive shift presumably is itself followed by a gradual return to the steady-state base-line if abstinence is maintained. The drug self-administration paradigm, however, does not provide a way to directly assess such changes. There-fore, we adopted a behavioral measure where it was possible to observe changes in baseline behavior following chronic AMPH.

Intracranial Self-Stimulation (ICSS)

The discovery (Olds & Milner, 1954) that rats will work for electrical stimulation of certain brain regions, but not others, has been used as an animal model for anatomical and neurochemical mapping of the "reward system." It has been assumed that the resulting system mediates natural reinforcements or rewards as well as the reinforcing properties of elec-trical stimulation studied in the laboratory. Recently, Wise and Bozarth (1981, 1982) reviewed evidence suggesting that drugs of abuse act directly

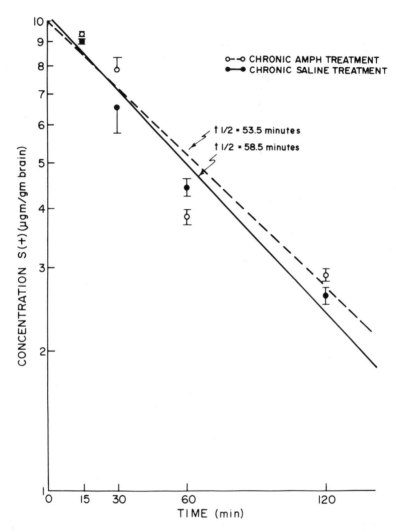

Figure 2. The effect of chronic AMPH or chronic saline on brain disappearance rates of AMPH following administration of a 10 mg/kg IV dose of AMPH. No significant difference in AMPH half-line was observed as a function of whether the animals were pretreated with chronic AMPH or chronic saline. (From "The Development of Tolerance to the Rewarding Effects of Self-Administered S (+)− Amphetamine" by T. J. McCown and R. J. Barrett, *Pharmacology, Biochemistry & Behavior*, 1980, *12*, 137–141. Copyright 1980 by *Pharmacology, Biochemistry & Behavior*. Reprinted by permission.)

on the neurochemical substrates of reward. They postulate that the ascending and descending dopaminergic systems, linked in the medial forebrain bundle (MFB), are the neurotransmitter systems that mediate the reinforcing effects of both AMPH and electrical stimulation of the MFB. In agreement with this view, previous studies (Stein, 1964; Stein & Ray, 1960; C. D. Wise & Stein, 1970) have reported facilitation of ICSS responding following administration of dopamine (DA) agonists and disruption following DA antagonists (Fouriezos & Wise, 1976; Franklin, 1978; Schaefer & Michael, 1980). It is also well known from independent biochemical studies that AMPH enhances DA function through several mechanisms including DA-enhanced release (Von Voigtlander & Moore, 1973). Thus, if the reinforcing properties of MFB self-stimulation and AMPH self-administration are mediated by a common endogenous substrate, ICSS responding should provide a sensitive measure of changes in "reward system" function following chronic AMPH.

The procedure used in our experiments (Anderson, Leith, & Barrett, 1978; Barrett & White, 1981) involved a variation of the descending method of limits used in psychophysics. Sprague-Dawley rats implanted with electrodes in the MFB were trained to lever press for 0.2-second pulses of electrical stimulation. The current intensity was reduced by 5% of the starting intensity every 5 sec until 15 descending current intensities had been presented. At the end of the 15th step, the current was automatically reset to the highest intensity. Reset was signaled to the animal by means of a cue light. The first lever press following reset restarted the step-down timer, and the cue light was turned off 5 sec later.

Two measures of ICSS behavior were obtained for each animal: (1) a profile of changes in rate (responses/min) as a function of current intensity; and (2) a measure of the "reward threshold" current, that is, the average intensity at which an animal stopped responding during each series of 15 descending currents. Figure 3 shows data on the two measures from a typical animal tested following an acute injection of AMPH (0.50 mg/kg) or saline. As can be seen, AMPH produces both a shift to the right in the rate X current intensity profile (Figure 3, upper panel) and also a decrease in the reward threshold (Figure 3, lower panel).

To study the adaptive processes that account for tolerance to AMPH's reinforcing properties, two groups of animals ($n = 6$), matched on the basis of their rate X current intensity profiles and reward thresholds, were given daily injections of either saline or AMPH (10 mg/kg) for 16 consecutive days. Thirty-six hours after the final injection all animals were tested for ICSS responding during a standard 30-minute test session. On the following day both groups were injected with AMPH (0.50 mg/kg) 15 minutes prior to the 30-minute test session.

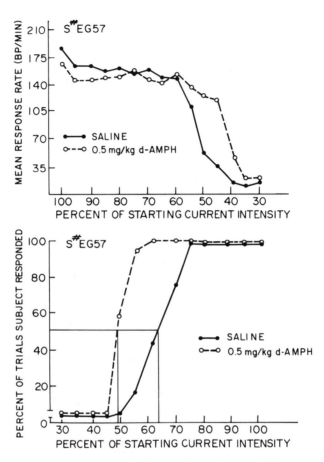

Figure 3. The top panel shows the facilitating effect of acute AMPH on rate of ICSS responding during the step-down procedure. In the lower panel it can be seen that acute AMPH lowers the reward threshold current intensity.

The results of this experiment are presented in Figure 4. The top panel shows the rate X current intensity profiles for the two groups prior to the chronic injections. The middle panel shows the effects chronic AMPH had on the ICSS baseline. As can be seen, there was a marked shift to the left in the rate X current intensity function. More detailed evidence, presented later, confirms that this behavioral change reflects adaptive changes specific to the neurochemical substrates mediating reinforcement. In the lower panel of Figure 4, it can be seen that the animals administered chronic AMPH made significantly fewer responses when

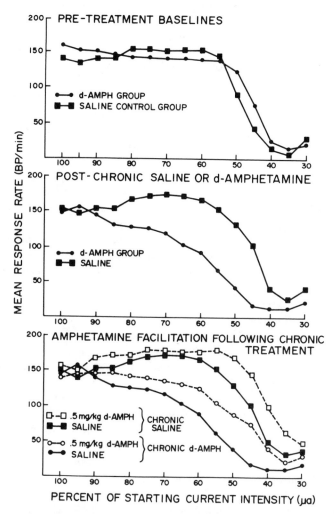

Figure 4. Rate of responding for ICCS on the current intensity step-down procedure prior to (top panel) and following either chronic saline or chronic AMPH injections (middle panel). The bottom panel shows that tolerance (the difference between the two broken lines) to the acute effects of AMPH is due to the shift in baseline produced by chronic AMPH. (From "Increased Reward Thresholds in Rats Following Chronic Amphetamine" by R. J. Barrett and D. K. White, *Federation Proceedings*, 1981, *40*, 277. Copyright 1981 by *Federation Proceedings*. Reprinted by permission.)

injected with 0.50 mg/kg AMPH 30 minutes before testing than did the chronic saline animals (compare the two dashed lines). This difference operationally defines tolerance. What was especially instructive in this study was the finding that tolerance reflected the shift in the baseline induced by chronic AMPH. For comparison purposes, the postchronic injection baselines are replotted for the two groups. It can be seen that the *change* from baseline seen after the 0.50 mg/kg injection of AMPH does not differ as a function of chronic treatment. In subsequent studies with AMPH and other drugs of abuse, we have found a shift in baseline to be the rule rather than the exception after chronic drug administration. The finding later proved to be critical in understanding the relationship between tolerance, "psychic" withdrawal, and drug dependence.

One problem with interpreting decrements in response rate is that such changes could result from physical debilitation accompanying the administration of chronic AMPH rather than to effects on mechanisms mediating reward. However, the rate-independent reward threshold data support the latter interpretation. The reward threshold data from this experiment, shown in Figure 5, reveal that chronic AMPH (lower panel) produced a significant increase in the reward threshold (baseline shift). An acute dose of AMPH prior to the test session effectively lowered the reward threshold for both groups (chronic saline in upper panel). Again, this acute AMPH effect was of similar magnitude for both groups but was superimposed upon different baselines. When no further AMPH was administered to these animals, the rate X current intensity profiles and reward thresholds returned to predrug values over a period of 7 to 10 days.

The results from this experiment indicate that pharmacodynamic mechanisms account for the tolerance that develops to AMPH's enhancement of reward system function. Although acute AMPH lowers the reward threshold, there is an increase in reward threshold following chronic AMPH. However, even after chronic AMPH, additional doses of the drug still effectively lower reward threshold although from a different baseline. These results agree with the findings, discussed previously, that chronic AMPH does not change the metabolic half-life of AMPH. Thus, the shift in ICSS baseline following termination of chronic AMPH administration provides a measure of the adaptive changes (rebound) that occur in the neurotransmitter systems mediating reward.

These findings have important implications for understanding AMPH abuse. They indicate that acute AMPH enhances the functioning of the reward system. In addition, however, they demonstrate that chronic AMPH administration induces adaptive, homeostatic mechanisms that oppose the primary effects of AMPH. These pharmacodynamic processes are not

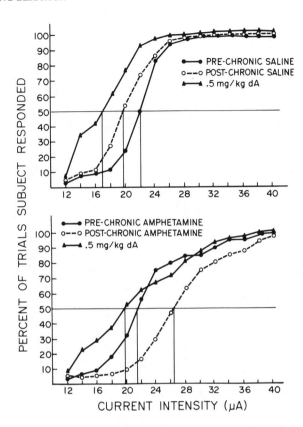

Figure 5. Changes in reward thresholds as a function of chronic saline (top panel) or chronic AMPH (lower panel) injections and a subsequent acute AMPH injection. Note that chronic AMPH produced a marked increase in reward threshold, whereas a moderate decrease was observed in the saline controls. This shift in reward threshold baseline accounts for the tolerance observed following acute AMPH. Although acute AMPH effectively lowered the threshold for both groups, the threshold was significantly lower for the chronic saline (17 μA) than for the chronic AMPH (20 μA) groups satisfying the operational definition of tolerance. (From "Increased Reward Thresholds in Rats Following Chronic Amphetamine" by R. J. Barrett and D. K. White, *Federation Proceedings*, 1981, 40, 277. Copyright 1981 by *Federation Proceedings.* Reprinted by permission.)

only responsible for drug tolerance; they also account for drug dependence and drug withdrawal. Thus, *drug dependence* refers to the situation where chronic use of AMPH has altered the homeostatic "set point" such that some minimum amount of AMPH is now necessary to "feel" normal. Attempts to terminate further AMPH use result in the appearance of withdrawal symptoms (depression) because the opponent physiological processes are unopposed by the primary drug effect. The withdrawal symptoms are hedonically opposite to the drug's primary mood-enhancing properties. Furthermore, as tolerance develops to the mood-enhancing effects of AMPH, an individual would be expected to increase the drug dose in order to reinstate the intensity of the original experience. Although temporarily effective, higher doses would in turn induce a stronger opponent process, completing the "vicious cycle" characteristic of drug abuse.

The ICSS data presented here demonstrate the effects that chronic AMPH use can have on the neurochemical processes likely to be involved in mediating hedonic states in humans. Although there are no obvious physical symptoms of withdrawal following termination of chronic AMPH use, the negative hedonic state (depression, dysphoria) (Watson *et al.*, 1972) that accompanies AMPH abstinence would provide a strong incentive to continue using this drug.

As noted earlier, each of the two measures that we used to assess ICSS responding provided independent evidence that chronic AMPH modifies substrates specifically involved in mediating reward. They did not support the possibility that the chronic drug treatment produced some "nonspecific" disruption of performance. An additional study was conducted to further test this interpretation. The objective of this experiment was to compare the effect on the ICSS rate X current intensity profile of intentionally diminishing the reinforcing value of the stimulating current with the change produced when chronic AMPH is administered.

Six Sprague-Dawley rats were implanted with MFB electrodes and trained to respond for electrical stimulation according to the procedures previously described. Training continued on the step-down procedure until the response profiles and reward thresholds showed little day-to-day variation. The reinforcing value of the stimulating current was then diminished in one of two ways. Either the starting current intensity was lowered or the duration of each electrical pulse was shortened, whereas the initial starting current intensity remained unchanged. The upper and middle panels of Figure 6 show the results from a typical animal when the starting current intensity was lowered (from 30 μA to 25 and 20 μA) or when the duration of each stimulation was shortened (from 200 msc to 150 and 100 msc). As can be seen, in both cases reducing the reinforcement value resulted in the response rate X current intensity profile being shifted to the left. There is also a tendency for the animals to increase their maximal rate of responding as a way of compensating for the diminished reinforcement. In the lower panel it can be seen that a

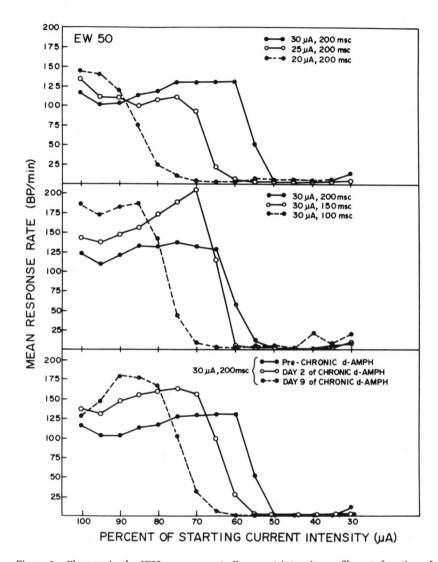

Figure 6. Changes in the ICSS response rate X current intensity profile as a function of changes in starting current intensity (top panel), duration of each stimulus pulse (middle panel), and chronic AMPH administration (lower panel). (From "Increased Reward Thresholds in Rats Following Chronic Amphetamine" by R. J. Barrett and D. K. White, *Federation Proceedings,* 1981, *40,* 277. Copyright 1981 by *Federation Proceedings.* Reprinted by permission.)

similar profile develops when rather than altering the stimulation parameters, the subject is administered 10 mg/kg AMPH immediately after
each 30-minute test session. The data shown in addition to the baseline
are from tests given 24 hours after the second and ninth injections. These
data further support the hypothesis that chronic AMPH administration
induces homeostatic, adaptive processes specific to the systems that
mediate the reinforcing properties of electrical stimulation. To the extent
that homologous substrates control human affect, the present results are
relevant to understanding the depression or dysphoria observed in humans following chronic AMPH use.

Mechanisms Mediating Opponent Processes

Throughout this chapter I have referred to "opponent processes" or
"adaptive regulatory mechanisms" that oppose the primary action of a
drug but have not speculated on the specific nature of the processes
involved. These will depend on the drug's primary mechanism of action.
As previously discussed, DA has been shown to play an important role
in the reinforcing properties of AMPH in animals and humans.

In a recent study, Barrett and White (1980) tested whether the opponent process observed following chronic AMPH required stimulation
of dopaminergic receptors or was a result of AMPH's direct action on
other neurotransmitter systems. To answer this question rats were trained
on the ICSS step-down procedure and assigned to one of four treatment
groups. Two of these groups were injected with chronic AMPH (10 mg/kg
each day for 7 consecutive days), but first they received an additional
injection of either saline (Sal-AMPH) or 1.0 mg/kg of haloperidol, a DA
receptor antagonist (Hal-AMPH) 30 minutes prior to the daily AMPH injection. The two remaining groups received either haloperidol followed
by saline (Hal-Sal) or two saline injections (Sal-Sal) on each of the 7
treatment days. Forty hours after the final injection, the subjects were
tested for self-stimulation. Figure 7 shows the threshold current intensity,
for the four treatment groups, expressed as a percentage of the starting
current intensity. As expected, animals injected with saline followed by
AMPH (Sal-AMPH) showed an increase in reward threshold as previously
described. Prior to chronic AMPH, this group responded on the step-
down procedure until the current intensity was reduced to about 50%
of the starting intensity. Following chronic AMPH the same subjects would
not respond once the current was lower than 70% of its initial intensity.

In the group that had received a haloperidol injection prior to each
AMPH injection (Hal-AMPH), however, the reward threshold did not change.
These data therefore suggest that DA receptor stimulation is a necessary

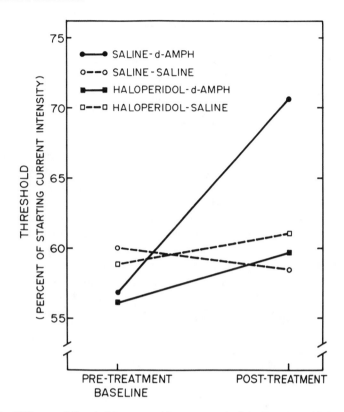

Figure 7. ICSS reward thresholds expressed as a percent of starting current intensity pre- and posttreatment with chronic injections. Note that injections of haloperidol prior to d-AMPH blocked the increase in reward threshold produced by chronic d-AMPH (saline-d-AMPH group). (From "Reward System Depression Following Chronic Amphetamine: Antagonism by Haloperidol" by R. J. Barrett and D. K. White, *Pharmacology, Biochemistry and Behavior,* 1980, *13,* 555–559. Copyright 1980 by *Pharmacology, Biochemistry and Behavior.* Reprinted by permission.)

condition for the induction of the adaptive processes that oppose AMPH's primary effect.

A further implication of the opponent-process or rebound explanation of the shift in baseline following chronic AMPH is that a baseline shift in the opposite direction should occur following chronic administration of a drug that disrupts reward function when administered acutely. Previous studies have shown that acute administration of halperidol disrupts ICSS responding and increases reward thresholds (Schaefer & Holtzman, 1979; Schaefer & Michael, 1980). To test for the predicted bidirectionality of the opponent process (White & Barrett, 1984), animals were trained on the ICSS step-down procedure and then injected with haloperidol for 16 consecutive days (0.50 mg/kg for the first 9 days and 1.0 mg/kg over the final 7 days). Twenty-four hours after the final haloperidol injection and once daily thereafter, the animals were tested for self-stimulation. Figure 8 shows the rate X current intensity profiles from tests administered prior to, and 24 to 72 hours subsequent to, the final haloperidol injection. At 24 hours the balance is still slightly in the direction of reduced reward system function (suggesting residual haloperidol), but by the 72-hour test an opponent facilitory effect is apparent. This facilitation of ICSS responding gradually diminished over approximately the next 7 days, by which time predrug baseline levels of responding had been recovered. Other investigators using similar procedures have also reported facilitation of ICSS behavior following chronic treatment with DA receptor blockers (Ettenberg & Milner, 1977; Ettenberg & Wise, 1976; Seeger & Gardner, 1979).

The mechanisms responsible for the adaptive increase in reward system functioning following chronic haloperidol treatment likely involve changes in DA receptor sensitivity. It has previously been demonstrated that following chronic neuroleptic treatment, compensatory increases

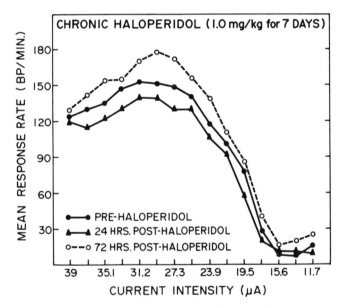

Figure 8. Rate of responding for ICSS as a function of current intensity and time since termination of chronic haloperidol injections. Response rates for the intermediate intensities were increased significantly at the 72-hour retest interval. (From White & Barret, 1984.)

occur in DA receptor responsivity (Friedhoff & Alpert, 1978). This dener-vation or "disuse" supersensitivity (Cannon & Rosenbleuth, 1949) may be produced by several different mechanisms such as changes in the re-ceptor's affinity for the agonist, increased receptor density, alterations in receptor coupling to adenylate cyclase, and/or alteration in postreceptor-coupled phenomena (Friedhoff & Alpert, 1978). In addition, haloperidol has been shown to initially accelerate DA synthesis that Carlsson and Lindquist (1963) suggest is due to receptor feedback activation of DA neurons. To the extent that haloperidol-induced DA receptor supersen-sitivity and enhancd DA synthesis persist following termination of halo-peridol administration, DA-mediated behavior such as ICSS should be enhanced.

Drug Discrimination: A Converging Measure

All animal models of human behavior involve assumptions regarding their appropriateness. Because any one paradigm has limitations, an efficient research strategy is to adopt more than one animal paradigm to model the human behavior of interest. This approach allows one to converge on a generic explanation rather than depending on the strengths and weaknesses of a single paradigm.

In order to converge on the opponent-process explanation of drug abuse, we employed the two-choice drug-discrimination paradigm as an additional animal model for assessing changes in the physiological sub-strates thought to control hedonic or affected-related states in humans. The drug-discrimination paradigm involves training animals to discrim-inate between interoceptive cues associated with the presence and ab-sence of a drug in order to learn which of two responses will be followed by reinforcement.

With psychoactive drugs, the cues that animals use to learn such discriminations seem to closely parallel subjective drug effects described by humans. This can be inferred from the results of generalization studies in which animals are trained to discriminate the cue properties of a particular drug and then are tested on a variety of other drugs to deter-mine which ones will substitute for the training drug. Using such pro-cedures with animals, psychoactive drugs fall into categories nearly iden-tical to those based on human verbal descriptions of the mood-altering properties of the same drugs. For example, at appropriate doses, humans cannot readily discriminate among the subjective effects of AMPH, co-caine, and methylphenidate (Fischmann, 1977). This agrees with the find-ing that these three drugs have equivalent and interchangeable cue prop-erties in rats at selected doses (Silverman & Ho, 1977). Both humans and animals can, however, distinguish these drugs from opiates, benzodiazepines, and barbiturates as well as from other drugs with psychoactive characteristics different from those of CNS stimulants. Thus, the drug-discrimination paradigm provides an animal behavior that can be used to study the hedonic or mood-altering properties of psychoactive drugs and has the specific advantage that the datum of interest (choice behavior) is not directly affected by rate of responding.

If, as suggested, the properties of a drug that are used by animals to learn a discrimination also reflect the actions of the drug that are responsible for its mood-enhancing effects in humans, then tolerance should develop to the cue properties of AMPH in rats as it does to its mood-elevating properties in humans. Previous drug-discrimination research has produced contradictory conclusions regarding the development of tolerance to the cue properties of drugs. Shannon and Holtzman (1976) have demonstrated tolerance to the discriminative stimulus properties of opiates, but Colpaert and co-workers (Colpaert, 1978; Colpaert, Kuyps, Niemegeers, & Janssen, 1976; Colpaert, Niemegeers, & Janssen, 1978) have concluded that tolerance does not occur. Our work (Barrett & Leith, 1981) has confirmed the development of tolerance and in addition has provided an explanation for Colpaert's failure to do so (Barrett & Steranka, 1983).

The Barrett and Leith (1981) and Barrett and Steranka (1983) drug-discrimination studies involved depriving rats to 80% of their free-feeding weight and training them to lever press for milk reinforcement in a standard two-lever operant chamber on a variable-interval 20 seconds (VI-20") schedule of reinforcement. The animals received an injection of saline or AMPH 15 minutes prior to the start of each 20-minute training session depending on whether the right or left lever was designated correct. Responses on the correct lever were reinforced, whereas incorrect responses initiated a 15- to 30-second delay period during which no reinforcements were available. Animals received an equal number of AMPH and saline training sessions. Periodically, in order to assess the acquisition of the discrimination, no reinforcements were administered during the first 2.5 minutes of a training session, and the percentage of the total number of responses made on the correct lever was determined. Training continued until animals averaged at least 80% correct discrimination following both AMPH and saline injections.

In the first experiment (Barrett & Leith, 1981) independent groups ($n = 6$) of rats were trained to discriminate one of three doses of AMPH (0.50, 1.00, and 1.50 mg/kg) from saline in the two-lever discrimination task. Following acquisition of the discrimination, dose-response functions were determined for each group during 5-minute extinction sessions (see Figure 9). All groups were then injected with chronic AMPH

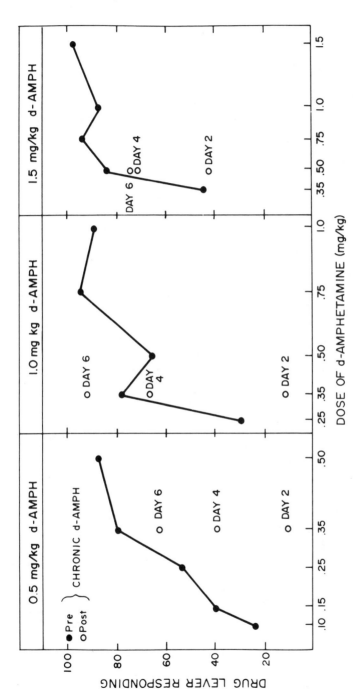

Figure 9. Percentage of responding on the AMPH lever as a function of five test doses of AMPH for each of three training-dose groups. Data points labeled Day 2, Day 4, and Day 6 represent the results of the three tests for tolerance following chronic administration of AMPH. (From "Tolerance to the Discriminative Stimulus Properties of Amphetamines" by R. J. Barrett and N. J. Leith, *Neuropharmacology*, 1981, *20*, 251–255. Copyright 1981 by *Neuropharmacology*. Reprinted by permission.)

three times a day for 4 days according to the dosage regimen (1–12 mg/kg per injection) described previously for McCown and Barrett (1980). The animals received no training during the 4-day injection period. Two, 4, and 6 days following the final AMPH injection, animals from each group were injected with an intermediate dose of AMPH and were tested for tolerance during a 5-minute extinction period. To maximize detecting changes in cue saliency, doses were chosen from the middle range of the dose-response function.

Figure 9 shows the dose-response functions and postchronic AMPH test data for the three groups. On Day 2 animals in the 0.50 mg/kg and 1.00 mg/kg AMPH training-dose groups showed complete tolerance to the AMPH cue, responding as though they had been injected with saline. The 1.50 mg/kg group also showed tolerance when tested on 0.35 mg/kg of AMPH. By Day 6 after the chronic AMPH regimen, discrimination had recovered to prechronic AMPH levels. These results clearly indicate that tolerance develops to the cue properties of AMPH. Although choice behavior is not directly affected by response rate, it was interesting to observe that total number of responses did not differ on the pre- and postchronic AMPH tests, indicating that the chronic AMPH regimen did not disrupt performance.

One of the limitations of the drug-discrimination paradigm in studying mechanisms responsible for tolerance is that similar to the drug self-administration paradigm, it does not provide a way of characterizing the drug-free baseline following chronic AMPH. Although we can infer that the rat does not "feel" like it received AMPH, we cannot infer that it "feels" normal simply because it responds on the saline lever because any cue that is distinctly different from the training drug cue will generally result in saline lever responding (Colpaert, 1978). However, if animals trained to discriminate AMPH from saline were chronically administered a drug with cues *opposite* to those of AMPH, then the opponent-process theory predicts a postdrug AMPH-like state. In order to test this prediction, animals were trained to discriminate either 0.50 mg/kg or 1.50 mg/kg AMPH from saline and then were injected for 10 consecutive days with 1.0 mg/kg of the DA receptor antagonist haloperidol. In terms of its action on DA, haloperidol can be considered to have effects opposite to those of AMPH.

Figure 10 shows that subjects tested following chronic haloperidol exhibited a marked facilitation of the AMPH cue. This suggests that as predicted, chronic haloperidol induced an opponent increase in DA activity. This increase appeared to be additive with that associated with the test dose of AMPH. Thus, after the chronic haloperidol regimen, animals in the 0.50 mg/kg training-dose group made 93% of their re-

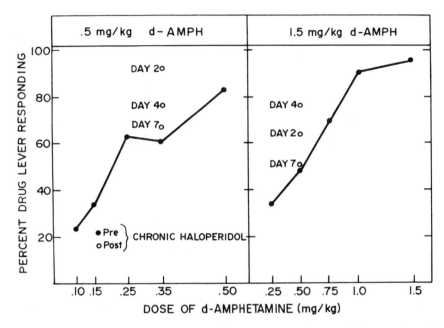

Figure 10. Percentage of responding on the AMPH lever as a function of five test doses of AMPH for each of two training-dose groups. Data points labeled Day 2, Day 4, and Day 7 are the results of the three postchronic haloperidol test sessions and can be compared to the results of testing with the same doses (0.25 and 0.35 mg/kg for the 0.50 and 1.50 mg/kg training-dose groups, respectively) prior to treatment with chronic haloperidol. (From "Drug-Discrimination in Rats: Evidence for Amphetamine-like Cue State Following Chronic Haloperidol" by R. J. Barrett and L. R. Steranka, *Pharmacology, Biochemistry and Behavior,* 1983, 18, 611–617. Copyright 1983 by *Pharmacology, Biochemistry and Behavior.* Reprinted by permission.)

sponses on the AMPH lever when tested on 0.35 mg/kg AMPH. Prior to the chronic injections, this group had selected the drug lever 60% of the time when tested with the same AMPH dose (0.35 mg/kg). By Day 7 responding on the AMPH lever returned to predrug percentages.

A saline test was also conducted on Day 1 following chronic haloperidol. The 0.50 mg/kg training-dose group made 44% of its responses on the AMPH lever; the 1.50 mg/kg group made 23%. This compared to 8% and 6%, respectively, for the two groups on the last prehaloperidol saline test. Thus, following chronic haloperidol, the subjects, when tested without drug (saline), responded as though they had received AMPH in agreement with predictions from the opponent-process theory. Less apparent was why the 0.50 mg/kg training-dose group chose the AMPH lever nearly twice as often as did the 1.50 mg/kg group because all animals had received identical chronic haloperidol regimens. In understanding this result, it was important to consider the effect of training dose on dose-response function. Linear regression lines shown in Figure 11 were plotted for the dose-response functions of the training-dose groups. By substituting for Y (44 or 23%) in the appropriate linear regression equation and solving for X (dose of AMPH), it was calculated that the predicted dose of AMPH corresponding to 44% and 23% AMPH lever responding was 0.186 mg/kg and 0.188 mg/kg AMPH for the 0.50 mg/kg and 1.50 mg/kg training-dose groups, respectively. In other words, after chronic haloperidol injections both groups responded on the saline test as though they had been injected with 0.18 mg/kg AMPH. These data thus provide

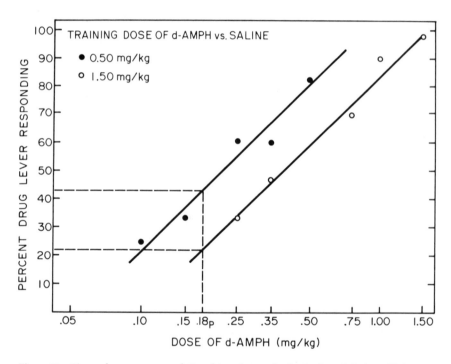

Figure 11.   Linear dose-response relationships observed prior to chronic haloperidol treatment for animals trained on either 0.50 mg/kg or 1.50 mg/kg of AMPH. Also shown is that when these animals were tested on saline following chronic haloperidol they responded as though injected with doses of AMPH (predicted *p* from the linear regression equations) equivalent to 0.183 and 0.188 mg/kg of AMPH for the low- and high-dose training groups, respectively. (From "Drug-Discrimination in Rats: Evidence for Amphetamine-like Cue State Following Chronic Haloperidol" by R. J. Barrett and L. R. Steranka, *Pharmacology, Biochemistry and Behavior,* 1983, *18,* 611–617. Copyright 1983 by *Pharmacology, Biochemistry and Behavior.* Reprinted by permission.)

a direct quantitative as well as qualitative behavioral measure of the opponent process induced by haloperidol. They are also consistent with the data that showed facilitation of ICSS responding after chronic halo-peridol. Although haloperidol itself produces symptoms of depression in some humans (Forrest, 1969), it is not known whether an opponent change in affect is experienced when chronic haloperidol use is abruptly terminated.

The results from these drug-discrimination studies suggested that an AMPH-induced opponent process might be directly measurable by training animals to discriminate haloperidol from saline and then testing them on saline following a chronic AMPH regimen. If AMPH induces homeostatic processes opposite to its primary DA-activating effects, then animals should respond as though administered haloperidol when tested on saline after chronic AMPH. An even more appealing procedure, how-ever, involved training animals to discriminate between amphetamine and haloperidol (White & Barrett, 1984). Presumably, this would be equiv-alent to discriminating between a positive hedonic state associated with increased DA activation (AMPH) and a negative hedonic state associated with decreased DA activation (haloperidol).

Preliminary data revealed that animals trained to discriminate be-tween 0.50 mg/kg AMPH and 0.03 mg/kg haloperidol responded with about equal frequency on the two levers when they were tested in the drug-free state following injections with water. After criterion discrimi-nation of at least 80% correct lever choice was observed in both states, a dose-response function was determined by testing the animals on lower doses of the two training drugs as well as in the drug-free state. Three groups ($n = 10$) matched on the basis of their lever choice percentages in the drug-free state were then injected daily for 10 consecutive days with either AMPH (10 mg/kg), haloperidol (1.0 mg/kg), or equal volumes of distilled water. All subjects were then given 5-minute extinction tests in the drug-free state 24, 48, 72, and 96 hours after the last chronic injection.

As Figure 12 shows, after the chronic AMPH regimen, animals re-sponded as though they had received haloperidol. Animals that had been injected with chronic haloperidol responded as though injected with AMPH. These effects were most pronounced on the 24- and 48-hour tests. Choice behavior then gradually returned to predrug baseline levels. An-imals injected chronically with water showed no significant change in discrimination due to the 10 days without training.

The ordinate on the right side of Figure 12 shows the doses of the two drugs normally required to produce comparable choice behavior when given acutely. Thus, 24 hours after chronic haloperidol, animals

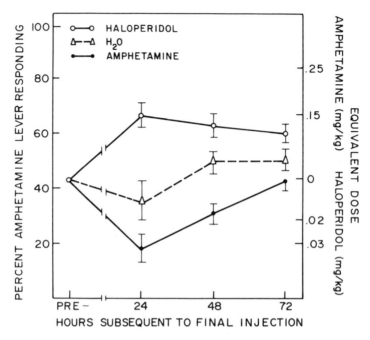

Figure 12. Percentage responding on the AMPH lever for animals trained to discriminate haloperidol from AMPH, prior to or 24, 48, and 72 hours following chronic injections of AMPH, haloperidol, or distilled water. The ordinate on the right shows the doses of AMPH and haloperidol that produced comparable AMPH lever responding prior to the chronic injection regimens. Note that 24 hours following chronic AMPH injections the animals responded as though injected with 0.03 mg/kg haloperidol, whereas following chronic haloperidol injections they responded as though injected with about 0.15 mg/kg AMPH. The animals were injected with distilled water prior to all test sessions. (From White & Barrett, 1984.)

responded on the AMPH lever with the same relative frequency as when they had received approximately 0.15 mg/kg AMPH. Chronic AMPH animals tested in the drug-free state at the 24-hour interval responded on the haloperidol lever as though they had been injected with 0.03 mg/kg haloperidol prior to testing.

In addition to confirming that tolerance develops to the cue properties of psychoactive drugs, the studies presented here suggest an explanation for why Colpaert *et al.* (1976, 1978) did not observe tolerance to the discriminative stimulus properties of drugs. The distinction between the Colpaert studies and other studies that have reported tolerance (Barrett & Leith, 1981; Miksic & Lal, 1977; Shannon & Holtzman, 1976) is that Colpaert continued training during the period of chronic drug administration, whereas the other investigators suspended training during the chronic regimens. This procedural difference is important because as demonstrated before, chronic drug administration does not diminish the *difference* between the drug and drug-free cue states. Instead, the chronic drug gradually shifts the baseline upon which the acute drug effect is superimposed. Training throughout chronic drug administration results in the gradual transfer of discrimination to the changing properties of the respective drug and no-drug cue states. The result of this gradual retraining is that tolerance, as defined by a diminished ability to discriminate between drug and no drug, is never observed. Likewise, chronic administration of the cue drug prior to the start of discrimination training (Colpaert *et al.*, 1978) fails to disrupt acquisition because the only condition necessary for discrimination learning to occur is that the drug and the no-drug cue states be discriminable.

Opposite Changes in Behavior Following Acute and Chronic Administration of an Antianxiety Agent

In addition to the drug self-administration, ICSS, and drug-discrimination paradigms, the conflict procedure developed by Geller and Seifter (1960) has proven to be a valuable animal model of subjective mood states in humans. This paradigm has been shown to be selectively sensitive to drugs that have anxiolytic action in humans. Sepinwall and Cook (1978) reported a nearly perfect correlation ($r = +.97$) between the average clinically effective antianxiety dose in humans and the minimum dose required to produce "antianxiety" effects using the conflict paradigm with animals. It therefore provided an attractive animal paradigm to test the possibility that opponent increases in conflict or "anxiety" develop during chronic administration of a clinically efficacious antianxiety agent.

Using Pollard and Howard's (1979) modification of the original conflict procedure, Barrett (1984) trained rats to respond for food reinforcement on a VI-2' schedule during 30-minute test sessions. After the animals showed stable VI responding, the conflict component was added to the schedule. This component consisted of 2-minute periods, signaled by a tone, during which every response produced food reinforcement. In addition, after the first two responses, each subsequent response during this period also produced an electric shock delivered through the grid floor. The intensity of the first shock was .05 mA (0.5 sec duration for all shocks). Shock intensity was incremented by .05 mA on every other response that was made during the tone. In each daily 30-minute test session, three conflict periods were scheduled. The two measures of interest were the number of responses made during the baseline VI period and the mean number of responses during the conflict periods. Two groups matched on these measures were injected with saline 30 minutes prior to testing on Days 1 and 2. On Day 3 the groups were injected with either 2.5 mg/kg of diazepam or an equal volume of saline 30 minutes prior to testing. This procedure was repeated on Days 4 to 7 and Days 10 to 11. The animals were neither tested nor injected on Days 8 and 9. On Day 12, all animals were tested without any prior injection, and on Day 13 animals in both groups received 2.5 mg/kg diazepam prior to the session.

The results presented in Figure 13 show the effects of the treatments on the mean number of responses made during the conflict period. The first dose of diazepam (Day 3) significantly increased responding in the conflict period. This facilitation of responding typifies the effects of antianxiety drugs when tested in this paradigm. By Day 10, some tolerance

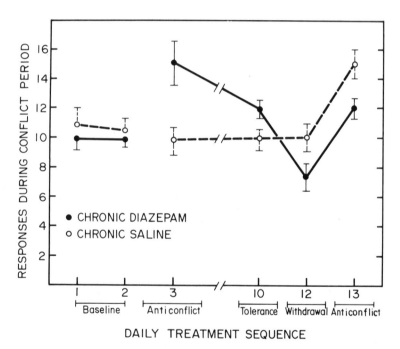

Figure 13. Number of responses made during a tone-signaled conflict period as a function of repeated injections of saline or diazepam. On Day 12 when animals in the chronic diazepam group were tested without drug an opponent decrease in conflict (decreased responding) was observed. Note that the difference between the two groups on Day 13 (tolerance) is accounted for by this compensatory baseline shift induced by chronic diazepam. (From Barrett, 1984.)

had developed to the "antianxiety" effect as evidenced by the diminished facilitation of responding during the tone compared to Day 3. Furthermore, on Day 12, when the animals were tested without diazepam for the first time since the start of the experiment, evidence of an opponent process emerged. The chronic diazepam group made fewer responses in the conflict period compared both to the saline controls on Day 12 and also to their own predrug baseline rates on Days 1 and 2. Thus, these data demonstrated that a postdrug rebound increase in conflict or "anxiety" occurred following chronic administration of diazepam. The groups did not differ on response rate during the VI component.

As with chronic AMPH in the ICSS studies, the shift that occurred in the drug-free baseline following chronic drug treatment completely accounted for the apparently diminished drug effect (tolerance) observed on Day 10. This is also apparent from a comparison of the data on Day 13 when the control group was first injected with diazepam. The difference between the two groups in number of responses made during the tone is entirely accounted for by the lower baseline of the chronic diazepam group. The absolute magnitude of *change* from the respective predrug baseline is virtually identical for the two groups.

These data illustrate the abuse potential of diazepam. To the extent that acute diazepam has antianxiety properties, it appears that chronic use can induce an opponent increase in anxiety that would become evident upon abrupt termination of drug use. Furthermore, it is likely that an individual would increase the drug dose in an attempt to maintain the original antianxiety effect. As with AMPH, the diazepam data thus suggest that tolerance, drug dependence, and withdrawal are all manifestations of homeostatic regulatory processes that are unmasked following abrupt termination of drug use and that gradually dissipate over time if abstinence is continued.

Additional Data from the Animal Literature

In addition to the studies that we specifically designed to investigate the role of opponent processes in mediating tolerance, drug dependence, and drug withdrawal following chronic administration of psychoactive drugs, data from several previous animal experiments are relevant to this question. Although most of the previous research on tolerance did not include tests to assess changes in baseline behavior; when such tests were made, predrug floor effects often precluded them from demonstrating opponent processes. Nevertheless, in several of these experiments an opponent process is evident. Three of these experiments demonstrated hyperalgesia in animals tested without the drug following chronic administration of the opioid analgesic morphine (Krank, Hinson, & Siegel, 1981; Siegel, 1975) or fentanyl (Colpaert *et al.*, 1978). The work of Siegel and co-workers is discussed in greater detail in the chapter by Hinson (Chapter 4) in this volume.

Majchrowicz (1981) reviewed a considerable amount of animal and human data and documented the opponent-process phenomena associated with the chronic use of ethanol. He concluded that the literature indicates a general reversal in central nervous system functioning during ethanol withdrawal. He describes the general CNS depressant effects of ethanol when initially administered and then describes the tolerance that develops with continued ethanol use. Upon termination of ethanol administration, there is a relatively rapid transition in general CNS function from depression to hyperexcitability. These withdrawal signs in animals include

> Tremors of . . . limbs, body, tail or head, body rigidity, spontaneous and induced convulsive seizures, hyperreflexia, muscle fasciculation, chattering of teeth, wet shakes, hyperactivity, stereotyped body movement and induced running episodes. (p. 2067)

Majchrowicz interpreted these withdrawal symptoms as reflecting the influence of adaptive homeostatic mechanisms that are unmasked by the abrupt termination of ethanol administration.

Human Literature on Opponent Processes

The data presented here suggest that normal homeostatic physiological processes can account for the development of tolerance, drug dependence, and drug withdrawal observed with chronic administration of psychoactive drugs. It is important to recognize that these adaptive mechanisms are not unique to psychoactive drugs or to the physiological processes controlling hedonic states but, rather, are commonly observed in other biological systems in reaction to a sustained period of drug-induced disequilibrium. Table 1 presents a list of drugs that, when administered chronically, induce compensatory opponent processes manifested when their use is abruptly terminated. Included are drugs that are not known for their psychoactive effects (atropine, clonidine, adrenocorticosteroids), drugs that have prominent psychoactive effects as well as effects on other systems (alcohol, morphine, midazolam, diazepam), and drugs that are used primarily for their psychoactive properties (AMPH and cocaine). This list is not exhaustive, but it serves to emphasize that drug-induced adaptive processes are not limited to psychoactive drugs.

Opponent processes do have a special significance in the case of psychoactive substances because they involve changes in the organism's

Table 1. Similar Homeostatic Processes Characterize Physiological and Psychological Dependence

Drug	Acute effect	Opponent effect	Reference[a]
Physiological Dependence			
Atropine	Antisialosis	Hypersalviation	1
Clonidine	Antihypertensive	Hypertensive crisis	2
Adrenocorticosteroids	Increased steroids	Adrenal insufficiency	3
Physiological and Psychological Dependence			
Alcohol	Anticonvulsant	Convulsions	4
	Tension reduction	Increased tension	4
Diazepam	Antianxiety	Increased anxiety	5
Midazolam	Sleep induction	Insomnia	6
Morphine	Hypotension	Hypertension	7
	Pupil constriction	Pupil dilation	7
	Constipation	Diarrhea	7
	Analgesia	Hyperalgesia	8
	Euphoria	Dysphoria	7
Psychological Dependence			
Amphetamine	Enhanced mood	Depression	9
Cocaine	Enhanced mood	Depression	10

[a] (1) Finch (1938); (2) Webster, Moeberg, and Rincon (1974); (3) Haynes and Murad (1980); (4) Majchrowicz (1981); (5) Pertusson and Lader (1981); (6) Kales, Soldatos, Bixler, and Kales (1983); (7) Wikler (1980, Chapter 3); (8) Krank, Hinson, and Siegel (1981); (9) Watson, Hartman and Schildkraut (1972); (10) Van Dyke and Byck (1982).

hedonic state and consequently all motivated, goal-directed operant behavior. This can be illustrated by a comparison of the adaptive processes that occur following chronic use of two different drugs, the antihypertensive drug clonidine and the psychoactive drug AMPH. (Clonidine does have some psychoactive properties and AMPH can alter blood pressure, but these effects are not important to the present discussion.) Abrupt termination of either clonidine or of AMPH results in the appearance of a response opposite to the one for which the drug was initially used. Thus, rebound hypertension can occur following chronic clonidine, just as dysphoria occurs following repeated doses of AMPH. In fact, hyertensive patients are warned that abrupt termination of clonidine use can incur a severe hypertensive crisis (Connolly, Briant, George, & Dollery, 1972; Webster, Moeberg, & Rincon, 1974). In this regard, patients on clonidine medication become "dependent" on some minimal dose of this drug to maintain their blood pressure within the predrug range. The hypertensive rebound observed in the event of abrupt termination is a symptom of "withdrawal." Tolerance to the antihypertensive effects of clonidine is recognized clinically, and consequently the dose is adjusted until a satisfactory steady-state level is achieved. Thus, although clonidine is used to alter physiological processes that control cardiovascular function and AMPH is used to alter physiological processes that control hedonic function, the adaptive processes induced by the chronic use of the two drugs have similar characteristics.

Few human experiments have been specifically designed to identify opponent processes related to changes in hedonic state following the repeated use of psychoactive drugs. Nevertheless, evidence exists in support of the hypothesis that opponent processes are an important factor in understanding substance abuse. For example, the absence of a linear relationship between hedonic effects and plasma concentrations of psychoactive drugs is consistent with the theory that adaptive pharmacodynamic processes are induced that directly oppose the primary action of the drug. A study of the effects of cocaine on humans found that, after subjects smoked cocaine paste, they reported a feeling of euphoria that peaked at 20 minutes and was no longer noticeable at 40 minutes (Van Dyke & Byck, 1982). A period of dysphoria followed that was greatest at 55 minutes and dissipated by 75 minutes after drug use. Plasma concentrations of cocaine did not correlate with the overall time course of the mood-altering effects of the drug, although the time of the peak effects was similar. Although the euphoria effect had completely disappeared 40 minutes after drug use, blood plasma concentrations of cocaine at that time were only slightly lower than their peak levels. The plasma concentrations were still about 50% of the peak concentrations at 55 minutes after the cocaine was smoked, at which time the rebound dysphoria was most pronounced.

A similar lack of correlation has been reported between blood ethanol concentrations (BEC) and mood states (Majchrowicz, 1981). In fact, after chronic use of ethanol, BECs as high as 100 to 200 mg/dl were associated with a short-lived period of normalcy. This was followed by the onset of withdrawal symptoms if BECs were allowed to fall much lower.

There also are data indicating that there is no direct correlation between blood plasma concentrations of benzodiazepines and their psychoactive effects in humans (Gottschalk, Noble, Stolzoff, Bates, Cable, Uliana, Birch, & Fleming, 1973). As with cocaine and alcohol, these findings suggest the presence of phamacodynamic processes that oppose the drugs' primary action and predict opponent withdrawal responses upon termination of drug use. Rebound insomnia has been reported following abrupt withdrawal of fosazepam (Allen & Oswald, 1976); temazepam (Bixler, Kales, Soldatos, Scharf, & Kales, 1978); lorazepam (Globus,

Phoebus, Humphries, Boyd, Gaffney, & Gaffney, 1974); nitrazepam (Adam, Adamson, Brezinova, Hunter, & Oswald, 1976); and flunitrazepam (Bixler, Kales, Soldatos, & Kales, 1977).

A recent report by Kales, Soldatos, Bixler, and Kales (1983) observed that after 1 or 2 weeks of nightly administration of the short-acting benzodiazepine hypnotics midazolam and triazolam, early morning insomnia developed. Midazolam initially decreased wake time to 37.5% below baseline for the first 6 hours of the night and 7.4% for the last 2 hours. After the drug had been taken for approximately 1 week, midazolam continued to reduce waking time during the first 6 hours by 32.8%, but it now *increased* wake time by 103% during the last 2 hours. In addition, a rebound increase in tension or anxiety during the daytime was observed among the subjects who received midazolam or triazolam each night. These data agree with previous reports of rebound increases in anxiety when short- or intermediate-acting benzodiazepines were taken during the day (Kales, Scharf, Kales, & Soldatos, 1979). One problem in identifying rebound anxiety during treatment with anxiolytic agents is that these withdrawal symptoms are often mistaken for the original clinical complaint (J. D. Kales, 1981; Petursson & Lader, 1981). For this reason, data from animal models of anxiety such as those reported following chronic diazepam (Barrett, 1984) are especially useful.

A Note on Physiological versus Psychological Dependence

Tolerance, dependence, and withdrawal will occur following chronic administration of the drugs listed in Table 1, but only those drugs that are used for their psychoactive effects are abused. However, the psychoactive property of these drugs is not their only effect. For example, a single dose of morphine typically produces pupillary constriction, respiratory depression, hypothermia, analgesia, hypotension, delayed peristalsis (constipation), and variable changes in hedonic state (Wikler, 1980, pp. 38–39). All of these effects except the mood enhancement and analgesia are considered undesirable side effects by the morphine addict. Following chronic use of morphine, tolerance develops to all of these effects, and termination of drug use is accompanied by the predicted opponent withdrawal symptoms: pupillary dilation, increased respiratory rate, hyperthermia, hypertension, diarrhea (Wikler, 1980, pp. 46–47) as well as hyperalgesia and dysphoria (Haertzen & Hooks, 1969). Although it is often stated that tolerance does not develop to pupillary constriction and constipation in morphine addicts, this is likely due to differences in morphine's potency in producing these responses compared to its mood-altering potency. The fact that pupil dilation and diarrhea are observed following morphine abstinence is evidence for a baseline shift that would assure the observation of tolerance if doses on the sensitive portion of the respective dose-response functions were tested.

It is interesting that dysphoria and perhaps the related hyperalgesia are generally regarded as evidence of "psychological" dependence, whereas the remaining symptoms are interpreted as signs of "physical" dependence. According to such logic the list of drugs shown in Table 1 includes substances that produce primarily physical dependence (atropine, clonidine, adrenocorticosteroids); others that produce both psychological and physical dependence (alcohol, morphine, midazolam, diazepam); and a third category that is generally considered to produce psychological but not physical dependence (AMPH and cocaine). As previously mentioned, the psychological-physiological distinction has created much confusion in the drug-abuse literature with respect to its theoretical implications. The data that have been presented in this chapter indicate that the term *psychological dependence* should not be interpreted as inferring a form of drug dependence that occurs as the result of some unique process. Rather, *psychological* used as an adjective is valid to describe dependence only insofar as it identifies a specific *response* system in the same way that one might refer to cardiovascular, renal, pulmonary, or gastrointestinal dependence. Generally, these would all be subsumed under the category of *physical dependence*. The psychological-physiological distinction should not be used to imply that the mechanisms that mediate postmorphine dysphoria, for example, are less dependent on physiological processes than are pupillary constriction, diarrhea, or hypertension.

It has been more difficult to measure changes accurately in hedonic state (psychological) following chronic drug use than it has been to record changes in temperature, heart rate, tremors, and blood pressure (physiological). This is especially true in animal research and may be one reason why theories about the motivation for drug abuse have often ignored withdrawal symptoms related to hedonic state and have emphasized avoidance of the aversive physical withdrawal symptoms to explain continued drug use. This explanation fails to account for the fact that all drugs of abuse cause psychological dependence whether or not, in addition, they produce physical dependence. Although avoidance of the physical symptoms of withdrawal no doubt contributes to the motivation for continued drug use, researchers have begun to question the extent to which this is important. For instance, Alexander and Hadaway (1982) have written that

> it is by now an undisputed fact that withdrawal symptoms are typically, far milder than the blood-curdling media discriptions (Jones & Jones, 1977; Le Dain, 1973, p. 318; Zinberg, Harding, & Apsler, 1978) and that even if addicts

were especially sensitive to discomfort, they could effectively relieve withdrawal distress with other chemicals, particularly tranquilizers. (p. 372)

These authors are probably correct insofar as they are referring to physical withdrawal symptoms. However, they fail to distinguish between physical symptoms of withdrawal and withdrawal related to a drug's mood-altering or hedonic properties. It is the latter that are critical to understanding the motivation for continued use of psychoactive drugs.

The identification and characterization of drug-induced opponent processes appear to be vital for understanding both the behavioral and the physiological determinants of substance abuse. The fact that many drugs induce counteradaptive processes has important implications for conceptualizing substance abuse. The data presented here illustrate that the fundamental physiological actions of, or reactions to, psychoactive drugs are not unique. Rather, what distinguishes these drugs from other drugs is that some of their effects are on biological systems that control how a person "feels."

CLASSICAL CONDITIONING OF THE OPPONENT PROCESS: A MECHANISM CONTRIBUTING TO RELAPSE

The explanation of drug-taking behavior presented so far accounts for the initial use and subsequent abuse of psychoactive drugs. In addition to those two phenomena, a comprehensive explanation of drug abuse must address the high rates of recidivism characteristic of drug abusers. It might seem reasonable to expect that once an individual had successfully terminated drug use and had remained abstinent through the postdrug withdrawal period, he or she would be unlikely to ever again become drug dependent. The negative consequences of the behavior leading to drug dependence theoretically should provide a powerful incentive to avoid subsequent abuse of psychoactive drugs. However, the evidence (Schachter, 1982) indicates that recidivism is the rule rather than the exception, irrespective of the particular substance involved. In fact, an individual with a history of drug abuse appears to have an increased rather than decreased probability of future addiction (Young, Herling, & Woods, 1981). This indicates that detoxification is only the first step in treating drug-abuse behavior.

Recently, data have shown that a classical conditioning process may in part mediate the relapse often seen even after extended periods of complete abstinence. This suggestion was first made by Wikler (1948). He accounted for the high incidence of opiate readdiction by proposing that environmental cues associated with recurrent episodes of drug withdrawal could come to function as conditioned stimuli (CSs). In the Pavlovian model, termination of drug use would be thought of as an unconditional stimulus (UCS), eliciting the withdrawal syndrome, which would constitute an unconditioned response (UCR). After repeated CS–UCS pairings, the laws of conditioning predict that environmental cues would acquire the ability to elicit the withdrawal syndrome as a conditioned response (CR). The role of classical conditioning in understanding drug abuse is the topic of another chapter in this volume (Chapter 4) and will not be discussed here. However, it should be apparent that long after complete abstinence from drug use environmental cues could reinstate conditioned aversive withdrawal symptoms that would provide strong motivation to again use drugs that had previously been effective in relieving these symptoms.

INDIVIDUAL DIFFERENCES

The explanation of drug abuse proposed stresses the conceptual importance of recognizing that drug abuse involves voluntary, goal-directed, operant behavior that like other complex behaviors is multi-determined. A much debated issue concerns the role of genetic factors in determining drug-abuse liability. Because this topic is dealt with in another chapter in this volume (Chapter 2) only a brief discussion will be presented here. A behavioral explanation of drug abuse provides a theoretical framework from which to evaluate the potential influence of inherited characteristics. The field of psychopharmacogenetics is concerned with studying inherited differences that can alter both the pharmacokinetic and pharmacodynamic properties of specific psychoactive drugs (Omenn, 1978; Omenn & Motulsky, 1975; Vessel, 1973).

Much of the research on genetic contributions to drug abuse has involved studies on alcohol. Often, these studies have tested for differences in alcohol metabolism between alcohol abusers and nonabusers. However, the conceptual link between the putative metabolic anomaly and its implication for predicting alcohol abuse is seldom elaborated. The behavioral approach to understanding drug abuse predicts that metabolic differences are important to the extent that they might alter alcohol's reinforcing properties. Thus, individual differences in how alcohol is metabolized can be a factor in determining the relative incidence of toxic side effects to desired psychoactive effects. At greater "risk" for alcohol abuse would be individuals who experienced the fewest aversive side effects, thereby allowing them to consume large quantities of alcohol. Although alcohol's acute effects would be highly reinforcing for these individuals, they would experience equally intense opponent responses.

Recent studies on alcohol metabolism among Orientals illustrates how genetically determined differences can influence drug abuse liability (Ewing, Rouse, & Aderhold, 1979; Fukui & Wakasugo, 1972; Stamatoyannopoulas, Chen, & Fukui, 1975). These studies observed that a large percentage of Orientals have an "atypical alcohol dehydrogenase" that is thought to result in the more rapid formation but slower clearance of the toxic metabolite acetaldehyde. Because acetaldehyde is thought to be responsible for producing unpleasant side effects such as flushing and vomiting, Orientals are in effect genetically "protected" from consuming large quantities of alcohol (Schaefer, 1979). Thus, it is not surprising that the incidence of alcohol abuse is very low among Orientals (Barnett, 1955; Wang, 1968). One report (Deitrich & McClearn, 1981) describes these toxic side effects as analogous to having a built-in "antiabuse reaction" because similar toxic symptoms occur when alcohol is consumed following pretreatment with the drug disulfiram that blocks the normal metabolism of acetaldehyde. There are other reports of metabolic differences between alcohol abusers and nonabusers, but it is often difficult to distinguish between cause and effect in these studies (Behar & Winokur, 1979) because chronic alcohol itself can alter normal liver function.

An inherited predisposition for affective disorders is another way heredity might influence the probability of drug abuse because such individuals would presumably be more likely to use psychoactive drugs for the purpose of self-medication. Thus, many drugs of abuse no doubt provide effective, although temporary, symptomatic relief. Although there are many reports, for example, that drug abusers have a higher incidence of depression than normals (Behar & Winokur, 1979), it is difficult to determine whether the psychiatric problems cause, or are themselves caused by, excessive drug use. Nevertheless, the point is that in assessing the role of genetic contribution to drug abuse it is important to consider how heredity might influence a drug's acute reinforcing properties. This behavioral approach emphasizes that a person does not inherit alcoholism *per se* but might inherit an affective disorder for which alcohol initially provided temporary relief.

CONCLUDING REMARKS

Throughout this chapter I have emphasized the importance of correctly conceptualizing the nature of the drug-abuse problem. Contemporary theories continue to be divided on the issue of whether drug abuse should be considered a "disease" (Jellinek, 1960) or a "behavioral disorder" (Bandura, 1969; Narrol, 1967; Pomerleau, Pertschuk, & Stinnett,

1976). Historically, complex sociopolitical rather than empirical factors have often been the motivational considerations that led to this distinction. Failure to resolve this conceptual disharmony has greatly impeded the development of productive interdisciplinary research programs.

The biobehavioral explanation of drug abuse outlined in this chapter illustrates the interpretive value of integrating information from both the behavioral and biomedical sciences where the primary concern is to account for relevant data irrespective of their disciplinary origin. Often, if conceptual barriers can be avoided, data from different disciplines can be shown to converge on a common interpretation. Conceptually, the present explanation requires recognition of the fact that drug abuse involves goal-directed, motivated behavior that conforms to fundamental principles of behavior. Within this framework, biochemical, physiological, pharmacological, genetic, and environmental factors can be shown to interact in a behaviorally lawful manner to account for the behavior that defines drug abuse.

ACKNOWLEDGMENTS

I am indebted to Janis Anderson for her critical reading of the manuscript and for many helpful stylistic and content-related suggestions. Also, throughout the preparation of the manuscript Helen Barrett offered many important insights that helped clarify key points.

REFERENCES

Adam, K., Adamson, L., Brezinova, V., Hunter, W. M., & Oswald, I. Nitrazepam: Lastingly effective but trouble on withdrawal. British Medical Journal, 1976, 1, 1558–1560.
Alexander, B. K., & Hadaway, P. F. Opiate addiction: The case for an adaptive orientation. Psychological Bulletin, 1982, 92, 367–381.
Allen, S., & Oswald, I. Anxiety and sleep after fosazepam. British Journal of Clinical Pharmacology, 1976, 3, 165–168.
Anderson, J. L., Leith, N. J., & Barrett, R. J. Tolerance to amphetamine's facilitation of self-stimulation responding: Anatomical specificity. Brain Research, 1978, 145, 37–48.
Axelrod, J. Studies on sympathomimetic amines. II. The biotransformation and physiological disposition of d-amphetamine. Journal of Pharmacology and Experimental Therapeutics, 1954, 110, 315.
Balster, R. L., & Schuster, C. R. A comparison of d-amphetamine, 1-amphetamine, and methamphetamine self-administration in rhesus monkeys. Pharmacology, Biochemistry and Behavior, 1973, 1, 67–71.
Balster, R. L., Aigner, T. G., Carney, J. M., & Harris, L. S. Intravenous self-administration procedures as part of a preclinical abuse liability evaluation program for analgesic drugs. Problems of drug dependence. Proceedings of the Thirty-Ninth Annual Scientific Meeting, Committee on Problems of Drug Dependence, 1977, 394–411.

Bandura, A. *Principles of behavior modification*. New York: Holt, Rinehart & Winston, 1969.

Barnett, M. L. Alcoholism in the Cantonese of New York City: An anthropological study. In O. Diethelm (Ed.), *Etiology of chronic alcoholism*. Springville, Ill.: Charles C Thomas, 1955.

Barrett, R. J. Manuscript in preparation, 1984.

Barrett, R. J., & Leith, N. J. Tolerance to the discriminative stimulus properties of amphetamine. *Neuropharmacology*, 1981, *20*, 251–255.

Barrett, R. J., & Steranka, L. R. Drug-discrimination in rats: Evidence for amphetamine-like cue state following chronic haloperidol. *Pharmacology, Biochemistry and Behavior*, 1983, *18*, 611–617.

Barrett, R. J., & White, D. K. Reward system depression following chronic amphetamine: Antagonism by haloperidol. *Pharmacology, Biochemistry and Behavior*, 1980, *13*, 555–559.

Barrett, R. J., & White, D. K. Increased reward thresholds in rats following chronic amphetamine. *Federation Proceedings*, 1981, *40*, 277 (abstract).

Behar, D., & Winokur, G. Research in alcoholism and depression. A two-way street under construction. In R. W. Pickens & L. L. Heston (Eds.), *Psychiatric factors in drug abuse*, New York: Grune & Stratton, 1979.

Bixler, E. O., Kales, A., Soldatos, C. R., & Kales, J. D. Flunitrazepam, an investigational hypnotic drug: Sleep laboratory evaluations. *Journal of Clinical Pharmacology*, 1977, *17*, 569–578.

Bixler, E. O., Kales, A., Soldatos, C. R., Scharf, M. B., & Kales, J. D. Effectiveness of temazepam with short-, intermediate-, and long-term use: Sleep laboratory evaluation. *Journal of Clinical Pharmacology*, 1978, *18*, 110–118.

Cannon, W. B., & Rosenbleuth, A. (Eds.), *The supersensitivity of denervated structures*. New York: Macmillan, 1949.

Carlsson, A., & Lindquist, M. Effect of chlorpromazine or haloperidol on formation of 3-methoxytyramine and normetanephrine in mouse brain. *Acta Pharmacologica et Toxicologia*, 1963, *20*, 140–144.

Colpaert, F. C. Discriminative stimulus properties of narcotic analgesic drugs. *Pharmacology, Biochemistry and Behavior*, 1978, *9*, 863–887.

Colpaert, F. C., Kuyps, J. M. D., Niemegeers, C. J. E., & Janssen, P. A. J. Discriminative stimulus properties of fentanyl and morphine: Tolerance and dependence. *Pharmacology, Biochemistry and Behavior*, 1976, *5*, 401–408.

Colpaert, F. C., Niemegeers, C. J. E., & Janssen, P. A. J. Studies on the regulation of sensitivity to the narcotic cue. *Psychopharmacology*, 1978, *17*, 705–713.

Connolly, M. E., Briant, R. H., George, C. F., & Dollery, C. T. A crossover comparison of clonidine and methyldopa in hypertension. *European Journal of Clinical Pharmacology*, 1972, *4*, 222–227.

Davitz, J. R., Mason, D. J., Mowrer, O. H., & Virek, P. Conditioning of fear: A function of delay of reinforcement. *American Journal of Psychology*, 1957, *70*, 69–74.

Deitrich, R. A., & McClearn, G. E. Neurobiological and genetic aspects of the etiology of alcoholism. *Federation Proceedings*, 1981, *40*, 2051–2055.

Deneau, G. A., Yanagita, T., & Seevers, M. H. Self-administration of psychoactive substances by the monkey. A measure of psychological dependence. *Psychopharmacologia*, 1969, *16*, 30–48.

de Villiers, P. Choice in concurrent schedules and a quantitative formulation of the law of effect. In W. K. Honig & J. E. R. Staddon (Eds.), *Handbook of operant behavior*. Englewood Cliffs, N.J.: Prentice-Hall, 1977.

Dews, P. B. The behavioral context of addiction. In L. Goldberg & F. Hoffmeister (Eds.), *Psychic dependence*. Berlin: Springer-Verlag, 1973.

Ettenberg, A., & Milner, P. J. Effects of dopamine supersensitivity on lateral hypothalmic self-stimulation in rats. *Pharmacology, Biochemistry and Behavior*, 1977, *7*, 507–514.

Ettenberg, A., & Wise, R. A. Non-selective enhancement of locus coeruleus and substantia nigra self-stimulation after termination of chronic dopaminergic receptor blockade with pimozide in rats. *Psychopharmacology Communication,* 1976, *7,* 117–124.

Ewing, J. A., Rouse, B. A., & Aderhold, R. M. Studies of the mechanism of Oriental hypersensitivity to alcohol. In M. Galanter (Ed.), *Currents in alcoholism: Biomedical issues and clinical effects of alcoholism* (Vol. 5). New York: Grune & Stratton, 1979.

Finch, G. Salivary conditioning in atropinized dogs. *American Journal of Physiology,* 1938, *124,* 136–141.

Fischmann, M. W. Evaluating the abuse potential of psychotropic drugs in man. In T. Thompson and K. R. Una (Eds.), *Predicting dependence liability of stimulant and depressant drugs.* Baltimore: University Park Press, 1977.

Fischmann, M. W., Schuster, C. R., Resnekov, L., Fennel, W., Shick, J. F. E., & Krasnegor, N. A. Cardiovascular and subjective effects of intravenous cocaine in man. *Archives of General Psychiatry,* 1976, *33,* 983–989.

Forrest, A. D. Depressive changes after fluphenazine treatment. *British Medical Journal,* 1969, *4,* 169.

Fouriezos, G., & Wise, R. A. Pimozide-induced extinction of intracranial self-stimulation: Response patterns rule out motor or performance defects. *Brain Research,* 1976, *103,* 377–380.

Franklin, K. B. J. Catecholamines and self-stimulation: Reward and performance deficits dissociated. *Pharmacology, Biochemistry & Behavior,* 1978, *9,* 813–820.

Friedhoff, A. J., & Alpert, M. Receptor sensitivity modification as a potential treatment. In M. A. Lipton, A. DiMascio, & K. F. Killam (Eds.), *Psychopharmacology: A generation of progress.* New York: Raven Press, 1978.

Fukui, M., & Wakasugo, L. Liver alcohol dehydrogenase in a Japanese population. *Japanese Journal of Legal Medicine,* 1972, *26,* 46–51.

Geller, I., & Seifter, J. The effects of meprobamate, barbiturates, d-amphetamine and promazine on experimentally induced conflict in the rat. *Psychopharmacologia,* 1960, *1,* 482–492.

Globus, G., Phoebus, M. A., Humphries, J., Boyd, R., Gaffney, D., & Gaffney, S. The effect of lorazepam on anxious insomniacs' sleep as recorded in the home environment. *Journal of Clinical Pharmacology,* 1974, *14,* 192–201.

Gotestam, K. G., & Anderson, B. E. Self-administration of amphetamine analogues in rats. *Pharmacology, Biochemistry & Behavior,* 1975, *3,* 229–233.

Gottschalk, L. A., Noble, E. P., Stolzoff, G. E., Bates, O. E., Cable, C. G., Uliana, R. L., Birch, H., & Fleming, E. W. Relationships of chlordiazepoxide blood levels to psychological and biochemical responses. In S. Garattini & E. Mussini (Eds.), *The benzodiazepines,* New York: Raven Press, 1973.

Griffith, J. D., Nutt, J. G., & Jasinski, D. R. A comparison of fenfluramine and amphetamine in man. *Clinical Pharmacology & Therapeutics,* 1975, *18,* 563–570.

Grove, R. N., & Schuster, C. R. Suppression of cocaine self-administration by extinction and punishment. *Pharmacology, Biochemistry & Behavior,* 1974, *2,* 199–208.

Haertzen, C. A., & Hooks, N. T. Changes in personality and subjective experience associated with the chronic administration and withdrawal of opiates. *Journal of Nervous and Mental Disorders,* 1969, *148,* 606–614.

Haynes, R. C., & Murad, F. Adrenocorticotropic hormone: Adrenocortical steroids and their synthetic analogs; Inhibitors of adrenocortical steroid biosynthesis. In A. G. Gilman, L. S. Goodman, & A. Gilman (Eds.), *The pharmacological basis of therapeutics* (6th ed.). New York: Macmillan, 1980.

Hill, H. E., Haertzen, C. A., Wolback, A. B., & Miner, E. J. The Addiction Research Center Inventory: Standardization of scales which evaluate subjective effects of morphine, amphetamine, pentobarbital, alcohol, LSD-25, parahexyl and chlorpromazine. *Psychopharmacologia*, 1963, *4*, 167–183.

Hoffmeister, F. Negative reinforcing properties of some psychotropic drugs in drug-naive rhesus monkeys. *Journal of Pharmacology and Experimental Therapeutics*, 1975, *192*, 468–477.

Hoffmeister, F., & Goldberg, S. R. A comparison of chlorpromazine, imipramine, morphine and d-amphetamine self-administration in cocaine-dependent rhesus monkeys. *Journal of Pharmacology and Experimental Therapeutics*, 1973, *187*, 8–14.

Hoffmeister, F., & Schlichting, U. U. Reinforcing properties of some opiates and opioids in rhesus monkeys with histories of cocaine and codeine self-administration. *Psychopharmacologia*, 1972, *23*, 55–74.

Hoffmeister, F., & Wuttke, W. Self-administration of acetylsalicylic acid and combinations with codeine and caffeine in rhesus monkeys. *Journal of Pharmacology and Experimental Therapeutics*, 1973, *186*, 266–275.

Hoffmeister, F., & Wuttke, W. Self-administration: Positive and negative reinforcing properties of morphine antagonists in rhesus monkeys. In M. C. Braude, L. S. Harris, E. L. May, J. P. Smith, & J. E. Villarreal (Eds.), *Narcotic antagonists: Advances in biochemical psychopharmacology.* New York: Raven Press, 1974.

Hoffmeister, F., & Wuttke, W. Further studies on self-administration of antipyretic analgesics and combinations of antipyretic analgesics with codeine in rhesus monkeys. *Journal of Pharmacology and Experimental Therapeutics*, 1975, *193*, 870–875.

Isbell, H. Human pharmacology and addiction liability of normorphine. *Journal of Pharmacology and Experimental Therapeutics*, 1958, *122*, 359–369.

Jasinski, D. R. Studies on the subjective effects of narcotic antagonists. In W. Keup (Ed.), *Drug abuse: Current concepts and research.* Springfield, IL: Charles C Thomas, 1972.

Jasinski, D. R. Narcotic antagonists of low dependence liability—Theoretical and practical implications of recent studies. In L. Brills & E. Hainns (Eds.), *The yearbook of drug abuse.* New York: Behavioral Publications, 1973. (a)

Jasinski, D. R. Assessment of the dependence liability of opiates and sedative hypnotics. In L. Goldberg & F. Hoffmeister (Eds.), *Psychic dependence* (Bayer-Symposium IV). Berlin: Springer-Verlag, 1973. (b)

Jasinski, D. R. Clinical evaluation of sedative-hypnotics for abuse potential. In T. Thompson & K. R. Unna (Eds.), *Predicting dependence liability of stimulant and depressant drugs.* Baltimore: University Park Press, 1977.

Jasinski, D. R., & Nutt, J. G. Progress Report of the Assessment Program of the NIMH Addiction Research Center. *Proceedings of the Committee on Problems of Drug Abuse*, 1972.

Jasinski, D. R., Martin, W. R., & Hoeldtke, R. Studies of the dependence-producing properties of GPA-1657, profadol and propiram in man. *Clinical Pharmacology and Therapeutics*, 1971, *12*, 613–649.

Jasinski, D. R., Nutt, J. G., & Griffith, J. D. Effects of diethylpropion and d-amphetamine after subcutaneous and oral administration. *Clinical Pharmacology and Therapeutics*, 1974, *16*, 645–652.

Jellinek, E. M. *The disease concept of alcoholism.* New Haven: Hillhouse Press, 1960.

Jessor, R., & Jessor, S. L. *Problem behavior and psychosocial development: A longitudinal study of youth.* New York: Academic Press, 1977.

Jones, H., & Jones, H. *Sensual drugs.* Cambridge, England: Cambridge University Press, 1977.

Kalant, H., Leblanc, A. E., & Gibbins, R. J. Tolerance to and dependence on some non-opiate psychotropic drugs. *Pharmacology Review*, 1971, *23*, 135–191.

Kales, A., Scharf, M. B., Kales, J. D., & Soldatos, C. R. Rebound insomnia: A potential hazard following withdrawal of certain benzodiazepine drugs. *Journal of the American Medical Association*, 1979, *241*, 1692–1695.

Kales, A., Soldatos, C. R., Bixler, E. O., & Kales, J. D. Early morning insomnia with rapidly eliminated benzodiazepines. *Science*, 1983, *220*, 95–97.

Kales, J. D. Benzodiazepine hypnotics: Carryover effectiveness, rebound insomnia, and performance effects. In S. I. Szara & J. P. Ludford (Eds.), *Benzodiazepines: A review of research results 1980* (NIDA Research Monograph No. 33, U.S. Public Health Services Publication No. 81-1052). Washington, D.C.: U.S. Government Printing Office, 1981.

Krank, M. D., Hinson, R. E., & Siegel, S. Conditioned hyperalgesia is elicited by environmental signals of morphine. *Behavioral and Neural Biology*, 1981, *32*, 147–148.

Le Dain, G. *Final report of the commission of inquiry into the non-medical use of drugs*. Ottawa, Ontario: Information Canada (Catalogue No. H21-5370/2), 1973.

Leith, N. J., & Barrett, R. J. Self-stimulation and amphetamine: Tolerance to d- and 1-isomers and cross tolerance to cocaine and methylphenidate. *Psychopharmacology*, 1981, *74*, 23–28.

Lettieri, D. J., Sayers, M., & Pearson, H. W. *Theories on drug abuse* (NIDA Research Monograph No. *30*, U.S. Public Health Services Publication No. 80-967). Washington, D.C.: U.S. Government Printing Office, 1980.

Majchrowicz, E. Reversal in central nervous system function during ethanol withdrawal in humans and experimental animals. *Federation Proceedings*, 1981, *40*, 2065–2072.

Martin, W. R., Haertzen, C. A., & Hewett, B. B. Psychopathology and pathophysiology of narcotic addicts, alcoholics, and drug abusers. In M. A. Lipton, A. DiMascio, & K. F. Killam (Eds.), *Psychopharmacology: A generation of progress*. New York: Raven Press, 1978.

Martin, W. R., Sloan, J. W., Sapira, J. D., & Jasinski, D. R. Physiologic, subjective and behavioral effects of amphetamine, methamphetamine, ephedrine, phenmetrazine, and methylphenidate in man. *Clinical Pharmacology and Therapeutics*, 1971, *12*, 245–258.

McClane, T. K., & Martin, W. R. Subjective and physiologic effects of morphine, pentobarbital and meprobamate. *Clinical Pharmacology and Therapeutics*, 1976, *20*, 192–198.

McCown, T. J., & Barrett, R. J. The development of tolerance to the rewarding effects of self-administered S (+) – amphetamine, *Pharmacology, Biochemistry & Behavior*, 1980, *12*, 137–141.

McNair, D. M., Lorr, M., & Droppleman, L. F. *Profile of mood states*. San Diego: Educational and Industrial Testing Service, 1971.

Meisch, R. A., & Thompson, T. Ethanol as a reinforcer: Effects of fixed-ratio size and food deprivation. *Psychopharmacologia*, 1973, *28*, 171–183.

Mello, N. K. Behavioral studies of alcoholism. In B. Kissin & H. Begleiter (Eds.), *The biology of alcoholism* (Vol. 2). *Physiology and behavior*. New York: Plenum Press, 1972.

Miksic, S., & Lal, H. Tolerance to morphine-produced discriminative stimuli and analgesia. *Psychopharmacology*, 1977, *54*, 217–221.

Narrol, H. G. Experimental application of reinforcement principles to the analysis and treatment of hospitalized alcoholics. *Quarterly Journal of Studies on Alcohol*, 1967, *28*, 105–115.

O'Donnell, J. S., Voss, H. L., Clayton, R. R., Slatin, G. T., & Room, R. G. W. *Young men and drugs—A national survey* (NIDA Research Monograph No. 5, U.S. Public Health Services Publication No. 76-311). Washington, D.C.: U.S. Government Printing Office, 1976.

Olds, J., & Milner, P. Positive reinforcement produced by electrical stimulation of septal area and other regions of rat brain. *Journal of Comparative and Physiological Psychology*, 195, 47, 419–427.

Omenn, G. S. Pharmacogenetics: An overview and new approaches. *Human Genetics*, 1978, Supplement 1, 83–90.

Omenn, G. S., & Motulsky, A. G. Pharmacogenetics: Clinical and experimental studies in man. In B. F. Eleftheriou (Ed.), *Psychopharmacogenetics*. New York: Plenum Press, 1975.

Petursson, H., & Lader, M. H. Benzodiazepine dependence. *British Journal of Addiction*, 1981, 76, 133–145.

Pickens, R., & Harris, W. C. Self-administration of d-amphetamine by rats. *Psychopharmacologia*, 1968, 12, 158–163.

Pickens, R., & Thompson, T. Cocaine-reinforced behavior in rats: Effects of reinforcement magnitude and fixed-ratio size. *Journal of Pharmacology and Experimental Therapeutics*, 1968, 161, 122–129.

Pickens, R., & Thompson, T. Cocaine-reinforced behavior in rats: Effects of reinforcement magnitude and fixed-ratio size. *Journal of Pharmacology and Experimental Therapeutics*, 1968, 161, 122–129.

Pickens, R., & Thompson, T. Characteristics of stimulant drug reinforcement. In T. Thompson & R. Pickens (Eds.), *Stimulus properties of drugs*. New York: Plenum, 1971.

Pollard, G. T., & Howard, J. L. The Geller-Seifter conflict paradigm with incremental shock. *Psychopharmacology*, 1979, 62, 117–121.

Pomerleau, O., Pertschuk, M., & Stinnett, J. A critical examination of some current assumptions in the treatment of alcohol. *Journal of Studies on Alcohol*, 1976, 37, 849–867.

Rachlin, H., & Green, L. Commitment, choice and self-control. *Journal of the Experimental Analysis of Behavior*, 1972, 17, 15–22.

Schachter, S. Recidivism and self-cure of smoking and obesity. *American Psychologist*, 1982, 37, 436–444.

Schaefer, G. J., & Holtzman, S. G. Free operant and autotitration brain self-stimulation procedures in the rat: A comparison of drug effects. *Pharmacology, Biochemistry & Behavior*, 1979, 10, 127–135.

Schaefer, G. J., & Michael, R. P. Acute effects of neuroleptics on brain self-stimulation thresholds in rats. *Psychopharmacology*, 1980, 67, 9–15.

Schaefer, J. M. Ethnic differences in response to alcohol. In R. Pickens & L. Heston (Eds.), *Psychiatric factors in drug abuse*. New York: Grune & Stratton, 1979.

Schuster, C. R., & Woods, J. H. The conditiond reinforcing effects of stimuli associated with morphine reinforcement. *International Journal of Addiction*, 1968, 3, 223–230.

Schwartz, G. E. Behavioral medicine and systems theory: A new synthesis. *National Forum*, 1980, 4, 25–30.

Seeger, T. F., & Gardner, E. L. Enhancement of self-stimulation behavior in rats and monkeys after chronic neuroleptic treatment: Evidence for mesolimbic supersensitivity. *Brain Research*, 1979, 175, 49–57.

Sepinwall, J., & Cook, L. Behavioral pharmacology of antianxiety drugs. In L. L. Iversen, S. D. Iversen, & S. S. Snyder (Eds.), *Handbook of psychopharmacology* (Vol. 13). New York: Plenum Press, 1978.

Shannon, H. E., & Holtzman, S. G. Evaluation of the discriminative effects of morphine in the rat. *Journal of Pharmacology and Experimental Therapeutics*, 1976, 198, 54–65.

Siegel, S. Evidence from rats that morphine tolerance is a learned response. *Journal of Comparative and Physiological Psychology*, 1975, 89, 498–506.

Siegel, S., Hinson, R. E., Krank, M. D., & McCully, J. Heroin "overdose" death: Contribution of drug-associated environmental cues. *Science*, 1982, *216*, 436–437.

Silverman, P. B., & Ho, B. T. Characterization of discriminative response control by psychomotor stimulants. In H. Lal (Ed.), *Discriminative stimulus properties of drugs*. New York: Plenum Press, 1977.

Skinner, B. F. *The behavior of organisms, An experimental analysis*. New York: Appleton-Century-Crofts, 1938.

Smith, R. C. Traffic in amphetamines. *Journal of Psychedelic Drugs*, 1969, *2*, 20–24.

Smith, S. G., & Davis, W. M. Punishment of amphetamine and morphine self-administration behavior. *Psychological Record*, 1974, *24*, 432–435.

Solomon, R. L. An opponent-process theory of motivation: IV. The affective dynamics of addiction. In J. D. Maser & M. E. P. Seligman (Eds.), *Psychopathology: Experimental models*. San Francisco: Freeman, 1977.

Solomon, R. L. The opponent-process theory of acquired motivation: The cost of pleasure and the benefits of pain. *American Psychologist*, 1980, *35*, 691–712.

Solomon, R. L., & Corbit, J. D. An opponent-process theory of motivation: II. Cigarette addiction. *Journal of Abnormal Psychology*, 1973, *81*, 158–171.

Solomon, R. L., & Corbit, J. D. An opponent-process theory of motivation: I. Temporal dynamics of affect. *Psychological Review*, 1974, *81*, 119–146.

Stamatoyannopoulas, G., Chen, S. H., & Fukui, M. Liver alcohol dehydrogenase in Japanese: High population frequency of atypical form and its possible role in alcohol sensitivity. *American Journal of Human Genetics*, 1975, *27*, 789–796.

Stein, L. Self-stimulation of the brain and central stimulant action of amphetamine. *Federation Proceedings*, 1964, *23*, 836–850.

Stein, L., & Ray, O. S. Brain stimulation reward "thresholds" self-determined in rats. *Psychopharmacologia*, 1960, *1*, 251–256.

Stretch, R., Gerber, G. J., & Wood, S. M. Factors affecting behavior maintained by response-contingent intravenous infusion of amphetamine in squirrel monkeys. *Canadian Journal of Physiology and Pharmacology*, 1971, *49*, 581–589.

Thompson, T., & Pickens, R. Drugs as reinforcers: Schedule considerations. In R. Gilbert & J. D. Keehn (Eds.), *Schedule effects: Drugs, drinking and aggression*. Toronto: University of Toronto Press, 1972.

Thompson, T., & Schuster, C. R. Morphine self-administration and food-reinforced and avoidance behaviors in rhesus monkeys. *Psychopharmacologia*, 1964, *5*, 87–84.

Van Dyke, C., & Byck, R. Cocaine. *Scientific American*, 1982, *246*(3), 128–146.

Vessell, E. S. Advances in pharmacogenetics. In A. G. Steinberg & A. G. Bearn (Eds.), *Progress in medical genetics*. New York: Grune & Stratton, 1973.

Von Voigtlander, P. F., & Moore, K. E. Involvement of nigrostriatal neurons in the *in vivo* release of dopamine by amphetamine, amantadine and tyramine. *Journal of Pharmacology and Experimental Therapeutics*, 1973, *184*, 542.

Wang, R. P. A study of alcoholism in Chinatown. *International Journal of Social Psychiatry*, 1968, *14*, 260–267.

Watson, R., Hartmann, E., & Schildkraut, J. J. Amphetamine withdrawal: Affective state, sleep patterns, and MHPG excretion. *American Journal of Psychiatry*, 1972, *129*, 263–269.

Webster, J. S., Moeberg, C., & Rincon, G. National history of severe proximal coronary artery disease as documented by coronary cineangiography. *American Journal of Cardiology*, 1974, *33*, 195–200.

Weeks, J. R. Experimental morphine addiction: Method for automatic intravenous injection in unrestrained rats. *Science*, 1962, *138*, 143–144.

Weiss, S. M., & Schwartz, G. E. Behavioral medicine: The biobehavioral perspective. In R. Williams & R. Sururt (Eds.), *Proceedings of NATO Symposium on Behavioral Medicine.* New York: Plenum Press, 1982.

White, D. K., & Barrett, R. J. Manuscript in preparation, 1985.

Wikler, A. Recent progress in research on the neurophysiologic basis of morphine addiction. *American Journal of Psychiatry,* 1948, *105,* 329–338.

Wikler, A. A psychodynamic study of a patient during self-regulated readdiction to morphine. *Psychiatric Quarterly,* 1952, *260,* 270–293.

Wikler, A. *Opioid dependence.* New York: Plenum Press, 1980.

Wilcox, P. R. C., Gillan, R., & Hare, E. H. Do psychiatric patients take their drugs? *British Medical Journal,* 1965, *2,* 790.

Wilson, M. C., Hitomi, M., & Schuster, C. R. Psychomotor stimulant self-administration as a function of dosage per injection in the rhesus monkey. *Psychopharmacologia,* 1971, *22,* 271–281.

Wise, C. D., & Stein, L. Amphetamine facilitation of behavior by augmented release of norepinephrine from the medial forebrain bundle. In E. Costa & S. Garrattini (Eds.), *Amphetamines and related compounds.* New York: Raven Press, 1970.

Wise, R. A., & Bozarth, M. A. Brain substrates for reinforcement and drug self-administration. *Progress in Neuro-Psychopharmacology,* 1981, *5,* 467–474.

Wise, R. A., & Bozarth, M. A. Action of drugs of abuse on brain reward systems: An update with specific attention to opiates. *Pharmacology, Biochemistry & Behavior,* 1982, *17,* 29–243.

Woods, J. H. Narcotic reinforced responding—A rapid screening procedure. *Proceedings of the Committee on Problems of Drug Dependence,* 1977, 420–437.

Woods, J. H., & Tessel, R. E. Fenfluramine: Amphetamine congener that fails to maintain drug-taking behavior in the rhesus monkey. *Science,* 1974, *185,* 1067–1069.

Yanagita, T., Takahashi, S., & Oinuma, N. Drug dependence liability of tricyclic antidepressants evaluated in monkeys. *Japanese Journal of Clinical Pharmacology,* 1972, *3,* 289–294.

Yokel, R. A., & Pickens, R. Self-administration of optical isomers of amphetamine and methamphetamine by rats. *Journal of Pharmacology and Experimental Therapeutics,* 1973, *187,* 27–33.

Young, A. M., Herling, S., & Woods, J. H. History of drug exposure as a determinant of drug self-administration. In T. Thompson & G. E. Johanson (Eds.), *Behavioral pharmacology of human drug dependence* (NIDA Research Monograph No. 37, U.S. Public Health Services Publication No. 81-1137). Washington, D.C.: U.S. Government Printing Office, 1981.

Zinberg, N. E., Harding, W. M., & Apsler, R. What is abuse? *Journal of Drug Issues,* 1978, *8,* 9–35.

PART III

Psychosocial Factors

CHAPTER 6

Cognitive Factors in Alcohol and Drug Use

VINCENT J. ADESSO

INTRODUCTION

Drug use is currently thought to be determined by the interaction of a host of biological, behavioral, and cognitive factors. This chapter will attempt to explicate the role of cognitive factors in drug use. Special emphasis will be placed on alcohol use as it is assumed that findings with alcohol are generally applicable to other drug use.

For the most part, research on cognitive factors in drug use has been guided by cognitive social learning theories of behavior (Bandura, 1977a, 1977b; Phares, 1976, Rotter, 1954, 1966, 1975; Rotter, Chance, & Phares, 1972). Social learning theory, as originally described by Rotter and elaborated by Phares and others, states that the probability of a particular behavior is a function of three variables: (1) the individual's cognitive expectancy that a particular outcome or reinforcement will follow a particular behavior; (2) the individual's perception of the value of the outcome or reinforcement; and (3) the nature of the psychological situation in which the behavior is to occur. Rotter (1954, p. 107) has defined expectancy as the subjective probability "that a particular reinforcement will

---

VINCENT J. ADESSO • Department of Psychology, University of Wisconsin at Milwaukee, Milwaukee, Wisconsin 53201.

occur as a function of a specific behavior...in a specific situation or situations." Expectancies about behavior-reinforcement sequences may be generalized or specific. *Generalized expectancies* are elicited by situations that the individual perceives as having similar stimulus properties. *Specific expectancies* are based on prior experience with a particular situation. As an individual acquires more experience in a given situation, generalized expectancies decrease in predictive power relative to specific expectancies.

Expectancies are learned, and their magnitude depends upon past experience with given behavior-reinforcement contingencies. Social learning theorists regard expectancies as prime determinants of behavior and see reinforcement alone as inadequate to explain behavior. Thus, "behavior is determined by the degree to which people *expect* that their behavior will lead to goals, as well as by reinforcement through goal achievement" (Phares, 1976, p. 13). *Reinforcement value* may be defined as "the degree of preference for any reinforcement to occur if the possibilities of their occurring were all equal" (Rotter, 1954, p. 107). Reinforcement value is subjective and relative. The probability of a particular behavior's occurring is, therefore, a function of the three classes of variables described before, interacting with each other in complex ways.

Bandura (1977a, 1977b) has indicated that the expectancies described by Rotter and his associates are action-outcome expectancies, defining the individual's belief that a given behavior will lead to a given outcome. Bandura has distinguished these from expectancies of personal efficacy, which he views as the belief that one is capable of successfully executing the behavior required in a given situation to produce a desired outcome. Unless the individual believes that he or she can perform the necessary actions to attain a desired outcome, his or her behavior is not likely to be affected by the belief that a certain course of action will produce that outcome. Thus, action-outcome and efficacy expectancies interact in the determination of behavior. This model clearly gives a central role to expectancies and other cognitions in behavior control. Antecedent and consequent events influence behavior to the extent that they are incorporated into the individual's cognitive-symbolic system. The impact of antecedent and consequent events is mediated by cognitions through the process of reciprocal determinism. Reinforcement influences behavior primarily through its incentive and informational functions. Much human learning takes place through the observation of others. In summary, from a cognitive social learning point of view, behavior is acquired and maintained through differential reinforcement, modeling experiences, and cognitive self-regulatory mechanisms. These interact reciprocally with situational events and their perception by the individual.

This chapter will begin with a brief discussion on contemporary approaches to studying placebo effects in drug research, with emphasis on the balanced placebo design. This will be followed by a consideration of the manner in which expectancies are developed and a review of some of the research on expectancy effects and drinking. A brief overview of the nature and importance of a variety of set (expectancy) and setting factors in controlling responses to alcohol will be presented next. The chapter will be concluded with an examination of some theoretical hypothesis about the mechanisms underlying expectancies.

PLACEBOS AND THE BALANCED PLACEBO DESIGN

Drugs are believed to have specific (pharmacological) and nonspecific (psychological) effects (Shapiro & Morris, 1978). However, the failure of researchers to use adequate placebo controls to separate the pharmacological and psychological effects of drugs has obscured the magnitude of the psychological effects, thereby lending credence to theories of drug use that did not include cognitive mediating mechanisms and other psychological factors. Marlatt and Rohsenow (1980) have exhaustively reviewed the role of placebos in alcohol research and detailed the development of the balanced placebo design. They noted that traditionally alcohol researchers have relied on either a double-blind procedure to assess alcohol's effects between subjects or a crossover Latin square design for studying these effects within subjects. Both of these designs are problematic in that they do not allow an adequate separation of pharmacological from expectancy effects of alcohol. Furthermore, because of informed consent considerations, subjects must be told that they may receive a drug or a placebo, leaving them to guess which they have received. This approach undoubtedly leads to variation in the expectancies that are generated in subjects and confusion in the obtained results.

Carpenter (1968) suggested the use of an "antiplacebo" design. In contrast to the standard placebo design in which subjects are led to believe that they are receiving the drug whether they receive it or a placebo, in the antiplacebo design subjects are led to believe that they are receiving the placebo regardless of whether they receive the drug or a placebo. Carpenter felt that the antiplacebo design could serve as a control for the standard placebo design and would allow separation of expectancy and pharmacological effects of the drug.

Ross and his colleagues (Lyerly, Ross, Krugman, & Clyde, 1964; Ross, Krugman, Lyerly, & Clyde, 1962) had earlier combined the placebo and antiplacebo designs to form the balanced placebo design. This four-group design completely crosses the drug that subjects expect to receive with the drug that they actually receive (expect drug/receive drug, expect drug/receive placebo, expect placebo/receive placebo, expect placebo/receive drug). Thus, by providing controls for both drug and placebo conditions within a 2 × 2 factorial design, the cognitive or expectancy effects of a drug may be separated from its pharmacological effects. If the effects of the drug were due to its pharmacological properties alone, then subjects who received the drug, whether or not they expected it, would behave differently than subjects who received the placebo. If the drug's effects were due to cognitive factors, then subjects who believed they had received the drug, whether or not they actually had, would behave differently than subjects who believed they had not received the drug.

The work of Ross and his co-workers investigating placebo effects for stimulants and tranquilizers found that expectancy was a primary determinant of the effects of these drugs. However, the balanced placebo design was not employed again until the early 1970s when two groups of researchers simultaneously employed it to study the phenomenon of "loss of control" among alcoholics and social drinkers. These studies, which produced very similar results, suggested that loss of control is mediated by expectancies of drinkers about the effects of alcohol on subsequent drinking behavior. This early work opened the door for other researchers interested in examining the role of cognitive factors in alcohol use.

DEVELOPMENT AND RANGE OF EXPECTANCIES

A cognitive social learning model posits that cognitions are central to an understanding of alcohol use. Expectancies about the effects of alcohol are developed through exposure to parental, peer and other drinking models, the media, and cultural rituals as well as through one's own experience. Before an individual has gained much direct experience with a drug, he or she has only generalized expectancies from which to derive predictions about the effects of the drug. As the individual accrues experience with the drug, his or her expectancies become more specific, based upon these experiences.

Two studies have attempted to trace the development of expectancies about the effects of alcohol. In the first of these studies, Christiansen, Goldman, and Inn (1982) administered a questionnaire to 1,580 12- to 19-year-old adolescents to determine the expectancies of these individuals about the effects of alcohol. To analyze the data, the subjects were divided into three age groups: 12- to 14-year-olds, 15- to 16-year-olds, and 17- to 19-year-olds. Factor analyses of the subjects' responses yielded six factors across the three age groups: physical tension reduction, diversion from worry, increased interpersonal power, magical transformation of experiences, enhanced pleasure, and modification of social-emotional behavior. The number and structure of the factors obtained was not identical across groups but showed considerable similarity. The two younger groups had a separate factor for the expectation that alcohol produces functional impairment, and the older group had a separate factor for sexual enhancement. The authors interpreted these findings to mean that two processes are responsbile for producing alcohol-related expectancies: social learning and experience with alcohol. It was clear from their findings that well-developed expectancies existed prior to the time that these adolescents began to drink. It was equally clear that increasing age and drinking experience resulted in more crystallized expectancy factors. These authors also compared low- and high-frequency drinkers across age groups. They found that the factors obtained for low-frequency drinkers included items that reflected enhancement of pleasure and interpersonal functioning, whereas those for the high-frequency drinkers emphasized increased expectations of power, sexuality, and tension reduction. That is, the high-frequency drinkers had more specific expectations about the effects of alcohol and the low-frequency drinkers had more global expectations.

In a similar study with 1,660 adolescents, Christiansen and Goldman (1983) found that social drinking among adolescents was related to expectations of positive social effects. Problem drinking was associated with expectations of improvements in cognitive and motor abilities.

It does seem, then, that the two processes of social learning and experience with a drug contribute to the development of expectancies about the effects of a drug. This is precisely what social learning theory would predict: with increased experience one develops more specific expectancies from the generalized expectancies acquired through social learning processes.

SUMMARY OF RESEARCH ON EXPECTANCY EFFECTS

The conventional explanation of alcohol's effects on behavior is known as the *disinhibition hypothesis*, which posits an indirect effect of alcohol on behavior. According to this position, certain behaviors, which are usually held under inhibitory control through fear and anxiety, are released from this control through alcohol's depressant effect on the cortex. As a result of this disinhibiting effect, the consumption of alcohol would be expected to result in a pharmacologically mediated release of such behaviors as control over drinking, sex, and aggression. However, reviews of the tension reduction literature (Adesso, 1980; Cappell, 1975; Cappell & Herman, 1972), showing that the effects of alcohol on mood and behavior are inconsistent, do not lend much support to such a disinhibiting function for alcohol. Using the balanced placebo design, a number of specific expectancies about the effects of alcohol on particular classes of behavior have been investigated. These studies have attempted to determine whether or not behavior becomes disinhibited after drinking and whether behavior changes after drinking are due to the pharmacological actions of alcohol or to expectancy sets of drinkers about the behavioral effects of alcohol.

From their review of the cross-cultural evidence on drunken comportment, MacAndrew and Edgerton (1969) concluded that the presence of alcohol in the body does not inevitably lead to, nor produce, disinhibition. They contended that one's drunken comportment is a function of what behavioral effects of alcohol one learns to expect as a member of a given society. In those societies that view drunkenness as a time-out from the usual social sanctions, the behavior of intoxicated persons will give the impression of disinhibition. However, even in such societies, the behavior changes that occur with drinking are maintained within certain socially sanctioned limits, which are also learned.

In a cognitive social learning approach, the role of expectancies in mediating alcohol's effect is central, though the exact manner in which expectancies produce their effects is not known. Expectancy set may affect behavior after drinking through learned associations between drinking and certain responses and through use of drinking as an acceptable excuse for engaging in otherwise unacceptable or antisocial behaviors. This has been referred to as the *discriminative disengagement of self-evaluative reactions* (Wilson, 1981). From this perspective, if drinking is followed by increases in certain classes of behaviors, it is because people have learned to expect these changes during intoxication and not because of the physical effects of alcohol. Thus, drinking sets the occasion for a change in behavior.

The research that has examined the expectancies of drinkers (e.g., Brown, Goldman, Inn, & Anderson, 1980; Rohsenow, 1983; Southwick, Steele, Marlatt, & Lindell, 1981) has found a consistent pattern of expected changes in sexual and aggressive behaviors among social drinkers. Another widely held expectancy, at least among alcoholics, is that they are unable to control their responses to alcohol. This lack of control is central to the conceptualization of alcoholism as a disease, the involuntary nature of which has been epitomized in the constructs of craving and loss of control. Although self-report studies (e.g., Clark, 1976; Orford, 1973) indicate that these phenomena are experienced some of the time by some individuals, loss of control and craving have been observed so rarely in experimental drinking studies (Adesso, 1980) that some investigators (e.g., Mello, 1975) have suggested that the constructs be discarded altogether.

In order to separate cognitive and pharmacological components of these constructs, Marlatt, Demming, and Reid (1973) studied both nonabstinent alcoholics and social drinkers within a balanced placebo design. After receiving a priming dose of alcohol or placebo, subjects participated in a taste-rating task. The results indicated that only subjects' expectancies affected their drinking. Those subjects who believed they were consuming alcohol drank more than those who believed they were consuming a nonalcoholic beverage, regardless of the actual content of the drinks. Similar results have been reported by Asp (1977), Berg, Laberg, Skutle, and Ohman (1981), and Engle and Williams (1972). Maisto, Lauerman, and Adesso (1977) have suggested that these results indicate that craving and loss of control are determined by cognitive factors rather than physical response to alcohol. Marlatt (1978) has proposed a cognitive social learning interpretation of craving and loss of control based on the alcoholic's lack of adequate coping skills and resultant low expectations of self-efficacy for dealing with stressful situations.

A second commonly held expectancy is that consumption of alcohol may result in an increase in aggressive and violent acts. Research that has relied on self-reports of drinkers has not produced a consistent pattern of results (Adesso, 1980). Laboratory-based research, with the exception of the work of Bennett, Buss, and Carpenter (1969), has tended to find that alcohol consumption is associated with increased aggression (Pihl, Zeichner, Niaura, Nagy, & Zacchai, 1981; Shuntich & Taylor, 1972; Taylor & Gammon, 1975, 1976; Taylor, Gammon, & Capasso, 1976; Taylor, Vardaris, Rawtich, Gammon, Cranston, & Lubetkin, 1976; Taylor, Schmutte, & Leonard, 1977; Zeichner & Pihl, 1979, 1980). In these studies, the relation between alcohol and aggression was clearly mediated by a number of setting factors such as the presence of a threat of retaliation and social pressure. Furthermore, the preceding studies have used only the traditional placebo and sober controls. This is important, as placebo subjects often seemed aware that they were not receiving alcohol. Lang, Goeckner, Adesso, and Marlatt (1975) controlled for expectancy effects with a balanced placebo design. They found that the belief that one has consumed alcohol, and not alcohol itself, was the primary determinant of aggressive responding. However, as Lang and his associates used male, heavy social drinkers, whereas other studies did not select for heavy drinking, the generality of these results may be limited to heavy-drinking males.

At least at the moderate doses used in these studies, it is not simply the pharmacological effects of alcohol that induced aggression. A combination of expectancies, situational factors, and individual differences contributed to the appearance of aggression after drinking. The disinhibition theory seems inadequate to explain the observed results. It seems, instead, that individuals learn associations between alcohol consumption and a variety of behaviors. The appearance of these behaviors is mediated by differential reinforcement, the models to which an individual is exposed, and the cognitive expectancies held by an individual within a given situation. A cognitive social learning analysis of the effects of alcohol on aggression seems better suited to the data than one based on the disinhibition hypothesis.

As with aggression, the effects of alcohol on sexual behavior are purportedly well understood. The conventional wisdom holds that alcohol disinhibits sexual desire and behavior, although at higher levels of intoxication sexual performance may be impeded. This view has been nicely summarized by Shakespeare, who held that alcohol "provokes the desire, but it takes away the performance" (Shakespeare, 1915, p. 149). Early explorations of this relation (Carpenter & Armenti, 1972; Kalin, 1972) suggested the importance of setting factors in determining alcohol's effects on sexual fantasies. Experimental drinking studies with alcoholics (e.g., Tamerin & Mendelson, 1969; Tamerin, Weiner, & Mendelson, 1970) found increases in self-reported sexual feelings and observed sexual behavior during drinking.

Subsequent research has investigated the effects of exposure to sexually stimulating materials while drinking on sexual arousal. For male alcoholics (Wilson, Lawson, & Abrams, 1978) and for male (Briddell, Rimm, Caddy, Krawitz, Sholis, & Wunderlin, 1978; Briddell & Wilson, 1976; Farkas & Rosen, 1976; Malatesta, Pollack, Wilbanks, & Adams, 1979; Rubin & Henson, 1976; Wilson & Lawson, 1976b) and female (Malatesta, Pollack, Crotty & Peacock, 1982; Wilson & Lawson, 1976a, 1978) nonalcoholics, moderate doses of alcohol have been found to be negatively and linearly related to physiologically monitored sexual arousal. However, the correlation between subjective and physiological indexes of arousal has tended to be positive for males (Briddel et al., 1978; Briddell & Wilson, 1976; Malatesta et al., 1979; Wilson & Lawson, 1976b) and negative for females (Malatesta et al., 1982; Wilson & Lawson, 1976a, 1978).

Several studies have examined the role of expectancy in the effects of alcohol on sexual arousal. Attempts to manipulate expectancies about the effects of alcohol on arousal have failed to yield significant expectancy effects (Briddell & Wilson, 1976; Wilson & Lawson, 1976a). Studies that manipulated expectancies about drug conditions using the balanced placebo design have found significant expectancy effects with males (Abrams & Wilson, 1983; Briddell et al., 1978; Wilson & Lawson, 1976b) but not with females (Wilson & Lawson, 1978).

Finally, Lang, Searles, Lauerman, and Adesso (1980) with male non-alcoholics and Lauerman, Adesso, and Lang (1982) with nonalcoholic females studied sex guilt as a mediating factor in the relation of expectancy to alcohol's effect on sexual arousal. As predicted, high-sex-guilt males who expected alcohol looked at erotic slides longer than their counterparts in the expected placebo conditions. For females there was no interaction between sex guilt and expectancy for the viewing time measure. Lansky and Wilson (1981) extended this research and found that among male nonalcoholics who believed that they had consumed alcohol, only those who were higher in sex guilt became more sexually aroused.

These studies have consistently found a dose-related linear decrease in sexual arousal following alcohol. Although only low to moderate doses have been used in these studies, it is probably the case that at high doses sexual performance would be impaired. As only sexual imagery and sexual arousal have been investigated experimentally, it is difficult to speculate about the effects on other aspects of sexuality. The results of Viamontes (1975) indicate that alcohol impairs alcoholics' sexual performance and the work of Malatesta and his associates (1979, 1982) suggests decreased ability to attain orgasm.

The decrease in sexual arousal at moderate doses of alcohol appears attributable to social and psychological variables. The role of expectancy in mediating this effect is clear for males. For females, the controlling variables are more difficult to pinpoint. Wilson and Lawson (1978) attempted to explain this failure to find an expectancy effect with females by hypothesizing that men may have stronger expectancies or greater cognitive control over sexual arousal than women, as women may have more difficulty linking genital sensations with cognitive events. Women may also be socialized to be more sensitive to social inhibitions, and they seem to expect increased anxiety after drinking (e.g., Abrams & Wilson, 1979).

At any rate, the disinhibition hypothesis seems inadequate to account for these data. Although people may expect to feel more aroused after drinking, their physiological responses indicate the reverse, with the possible exception of a mild arousal effect at very low doses. It seems that drinking may serve other functions for them than direct physiological disinhibition of sexual responses. Sobell and Sobell (1973) proposed that the apparent disinhibition occurring after drinking may serve as a powerful reinforcer for drinking. Lang *et al.* (1975) suggested that drinking permits a misattribution of responsibility for deviant acts performed while intoxicated. The drinker can blame his or her intoxicated state rather than himself or herself for antisocial behavior in which he or she engages while drunk. Wilson (1977, 1981) has tied much of the research evidence together into a cognitive social learning analysis of the alcohol–sex relationship. Given the evidence to date, such a model is better supported than one based on physiological disinhibition.

However, the effects of drinkers' expectancies on their behaviors after consuming alcohol are not limitless. Using the balanced placebo design, studies examining the effects of alcohol and expectancy on cognitive performance (Miller, Adesso, Fleming, Gino, & Lauerman, 1978), motor skills (Connors & Maisto, 1980; Rimm, Sininger, Faherty, Whitley, & Perl, 1982; Vuchinich & Sobell, 1978; Williams, Goldman, & Williams, 1981), and mood (Connors & Maisto, 1979; McCollam, Burish, Maisto, & Sobell, 1980) have not found a main effect for expectancy but a main effect for alcohol consumption or an interaction. To understand boundaries of expectancy effects better, the next section will present an overview of some of the factors that mediate expectancy.

SET AND SETTING EFFECTS

Expectancy sets are mediated by a variety of setting factors, which may help to determine which expectancy is activated in a specific situation and the nature of the individual's response to that situation. The influence of three types of setting factors—individual, interpersonal, and environmental—on expectancies will be discussed here. The factors interact with an individual's beliefs to determine response to drugs.

INDIVIDUAL DIFFERENCE VARIABLES

It has been assumed traditionally that the only variable of importance between individuals who use drugs was whether or not the individual was classified as an abuser. However, recent research has indicated that several factors differentiate among drug users.

Drug History

The amount of experience an individual has with a drug is likely to affect both that individual's drug-using behavior and his or her expectations about the effects to be obtained from the drug. Several studies have shown that social drinkers and alcoholics differ both in the ways in which they drink and in the expectations that they hold about the effects of alcohol.

Using the taste-rating task, the drinking behaviors of alcoholics and social drinkers has been compared (Marlatt *et al.*, 1973; Miller & Hersen, 1972). In this unobtrusive method for observing drinking, the subject is presented with a variety of beverages to be rated on a number of taste dimensions during periods ranging from 10 to 30 minutes while measures of amount consumed, number of sips taken, and sip rate are obtained. Male alcoholics consistently consume more at a faster rate than male nonalcoholics in this task.

Another methodological approach to comparing the drinking of alcoholics and nonalcoholics involves using a simulated bar setting. Two studies using prolonged drinking periods (Shaefer, Sobell, & Mills, 1971; Sobell, Schaefer, & Mills, 1972) found that male alcoholics drank more, took larger sips, and drank faster than their social drinking counterparts. Alcoholics also preferred straight drinks, whereas social drinkers preferred mixed drinks. These results were replicated by Williams and Brown (1974) with New Zealand alcoholic and social drinking males, except that the New Zealand groups preferred weaker drinks than the American subjects.

With the possible exception of the study by Saunders and Richard (1978), the ecological validity of these laboratory measures of drinking behavior has generally been supported by naturalistic studies of the drinking behavior of bar patrons (Babor & Mendelson, 1979; Cutler & Storm, 1975; Hunter, Hannon, & Marchi, 1979; Kessler & Gomberg, 1974; Plant, Kreitman, Miller, & Duffy, 1977; Reid, 1978; Rosenbluth, Nathan, & Lawson, 1978; Sommer, 1965). There is, however, some indication that barroom patrons take less time and fewer sips per drink than social drinkers in laboratory settings (Billings, Weiner, Kessler, & Gomberg, 1976).

With regard to marijuana, Cappell & Pliner (1974) found that drug history interacts with subjective level of intoxication, with more experienced smokers reporting higher levels of intoxication. Babor (1978) summarized research showing differences in the effects of marijuana on social interactions among moderate and heavy smokers, with moderate smokers decreasing social interaction more than heavy users.

These results indicate that drug history interacts with drug behavior. However, the question remains as to whether or not drinking history also interacts with expectations about the effects of drinking. A number of reports have shown that reported motivations for drinking are a function of drinking history. These researches have generally shown that drinking motivations can be divided into those relating to positive reinforcement (social drinking) and those relating to negative reinforcement (escape or personal) drinking. For example, Farber, Khavari, and Douglass (1980) found that escape drinkers scored higher on indexes of alcohol consumption and that alcoholics tended to be escape drinkers. Similarly, Mulford and Miller (1960, 1963) showed that those who drank for alcohol's personal effects tended to be heavy alcohol consumers.

Some recent studies have focused more directly on the expected consequences of alcohol consumption in social drinkers with varying amounts of drinking experience. Brown *et al.* (1980) studied the reinforcing consequences that might be expected after a moderate amount of alcohol. They found that among college students, those with a history of light alcohol consumption were more likely to expect more globally positive effects, whereas heavier drinkers were more likely to have specific expectations about the enhancement of sexual and aggressive behaviors. Christiansen and Goldman (1983) reported that adolescents who drink in a social manner expected alcohol to enhance social behavior, whereas adolescents who reported alcohol-related problems expected improvements in their cognitive and motor functioning. Southwick *et al.* (1981) studied positive and negative expectancies associated with both moderate and excessive alcohol consumption. All drinkers expected behavioral impairment, though greater impairment was expected with excessive than with moderate consumption. After moderate consumption, heavier drinkers expected increased pleasure and stimulation, whereas abstainers did not. Compared to all other drinkers, abstainers expected significantly more negative effects after excessive drinking. These results suggested that heavier drinkers tend to expect greater positive effects and the same negative effects from drinking as other drinkers. Rohsenow (1983) also found that drinking history was not related to expectations of negative consequences, such as impairment from drinking. She did find, however, that moderate and heavy drinkers tended to expect alcohol to enhance social and sexual pleasure and to reduce tension more than light drinkers did. Rohsenow also found that light drinkers expected less pleasure from drinking than did moderate and heavy drinkers and that light drinkers expected others to derive more pleasure from drinking than they would. She conjectured that this may explain their light-drinking status.

Thus, a fairly clear pattern of results emerges from these studies indicating an interaction between drinking history and expectations about the effects of consumption. All drinkers seem to expect a degree of impairment with consumption, but heavier drinkers also expect more positive effects than do light drinkers. With increased drinking experience, it appears that positive expectations about the effects of consumption may become more specific and crystallized; that is, the expectancies move from generalized to specific.

Predrinking Emotional State

From the preceding studies, it seems that drinking is associated with the expectation of escape from, or avoidance of, negative emotional states, including tension among both social and problem drinkers. Wilson and Abrams (1977) reported that 88% of social drinkers expected alcohol to reduce anxiety level; the remaining respondents expected no effect on anxiety from alcohol. Deardorff, Melges, Hout, and Savage (1975) found that the reduction of psychological and physical discomfort was a motive for drinking among both problem and nonproblem drinkers. Vargas and Adesso (1979) reported that social drinkers who scored high on measures of negative emotional state drank more than subjects who scored lower. Russell and Mehrabian (1975) have developed a theory that suggests that predrinking emotional state affects the emotional outcome derived from drinking. McClelland, Davis, Kalin, and Wanner (1972) believe that individuals who feel a strong need for personal power will drink heavily. Tamerin (1975) found that among both men and women alcoholics the probability of the desire to drink and actual drinking were enhanced by feelings of anxiety, depression and anger. Several studies have also suggested that a high percentage of relapses among recovering alcoholics may be attributable to negative emotional states (e.g., Marlatt & Gordon, 1979).

Not surprisingly, the most favored traditional explanation of drinking is the tension-reduction theory, which hypothesizes that alcohol reduces tension (and presumably other negative emotional states) and that it is consumed because of its tension-reducing properties (Conger, 1956). However, research that has attempted to evaluate both the tension-reducing properties of alcohol and the tendency of drinkers to consume alcohol for its tension-reducing effects has produced an inconsistent and methodologically flawed set of results (Adesso, 1980; Cappell, 1975; Cappell & Herman, 1972). Thus, although alcoholics have consistently reported that they expect positive emotional changes from drinking, most studies have observed increases in negative emotional states during prolonged drinking (Davis, 1971; McGuire, Stein, & Mendelson, 1966; Mc Namee, Mello, & Mendelson, 1968; Nathan & O'Brien, 1971; Nathan, Titler, Lowenstein, Solomon, & Rossi, 1970; Tamerin & Mendelson, 1969; Tamerin et al., 1970), though some studies have reported brief periods of euphoria at the beginning of drinking (Nathan & O'Brien, 1971; Nathan et al., 1970; Tamerin & Mendelson, 1969) or immediately following a drink

(Davis, 1971; Menaker, 1967). Results with nonalcoholics (McGuire *et al.*, 1966; Nathan & O'Brien, 1971) and female alcoholics (Tracey & Nathan, 1976) have not produced consistent emotional responses during periods of prolonged drinking.

There appears to be a discrepancy between the expectancies that drinkers hold about the effects of alcohol on their emotional states and the actual effects of alcohol on these states. Marlatt (1976), among others, has suggested that this discrepancy may be explained by a biphasic response to alcohol. At low doses, alcohol may be associated with increased physiological arousal, which the drinker may interpret as feelings of excitement, energy, and power. As the dose of alcohol increases and time passes, the depressant effects of alcohol come to predominate, and the feelings of euphoria change to dysphoria. These feelings of dysphoria, probably due to their delayed onset, may increase rather than decrease the probability of further consumption as the drinker attempts to regain the previously experienced euphoria. The biphasic pattern of response to alcohol seems to be an example of the basic "opponent process" that underlies reactions to many drugs and emotional states in general (Solomon, 1977; Solomon & Corbit, 1974). The pleasurable effects of low doses of alcohol may form the basis for the expectancy that alcohol will reduce unpleasant emotional states, including tension. It is this expectancy of tension reduction rather than the actual effects of alcohol that seems to provide its reinforcing function. There is some evidence that alcoholics expect drinking to produce stronger positive effects than do social drinkers (Senter, Heintzelman, Dorfmueller, & Hinkle, 1979), suggesting their greater motivation to drink may be related to this expectancy. As Bandura (1977a) has indicated, it is expected consequences rather than actual ones that govern behavior.

It is also possible to determine the relative importance of subjects' expectancies in determining their response to a drug by using the balanced placebo design. With the exception of the study by Levenson, Sher, Grossman, Newman, and Newlin (1980), the nine studies of tension reduction that have used this design to date suggest that, for both alcoholics (Kola, 1970) and nonalcoholics (Abrams & Wilson, 1979; Connors & Maisto, 1979; McCollam, Burish, Maisto, & Sobell, 1980; Polivy, Schueneman, & Carlson, 1976; Sutker, Allain, Brantley, & Randall, 1982, Vuchinich, Tucker, & Sobell, 1979; Wilson & Abrams, 1977), alcohol's effects are determined in large part by the cognitive expectancies of the drinker, though males and females may have different expectancies. (Abrams & Wilson, 1979; Myrsten, Hollstedt, & Holmberg, 1975; Sutker *et al.*, 1982; Wilson & Abrams, 1977). Male subjects tend to expect decreased anxiety after drinking, whereas female subjects seem to expect increases. Thus, it is the expectancy held by a subject and not the pharmacological properties of alcohol that seems primarily responsible for the mood-altering effects of alcohol.

Sex

Early studies of drinking tended to lump male and female subjects together or to generalize conclusions from male to female subjects. The inappropriateness of these strategies has become increasingly clear as the differences in the behaviors and expectancies of male and female drinkers become better understood.

The amount of research comparing the drinking behavior of males and females is relatively small. Male alcoholics have been observed to have a biphasic drinking pattern in laboratory studies in which alcohol must be earned through work (e.g., Mello & Mendelson, 1970; Nathan & O'Brien, 1971). Male alcoholics tended to drink for long periods, then tapered their drinking or abstained completely for a period. Female alcoholics (Tracey & Nathan, 1976) and male nonalcoholics (Nathan & O'Brien, 1971) seemed to be maintenance drinkers. The female alcoholics of Tracey and Nathan (1976) were more like the male social drinkers of Schaefer et al. (1971) and Sobell et al. (1972) in terms of ordering mixed drinks, taking smaller sips, drinking more slowly and drinking less than alcoholic males. A partial explanation for the lower consumption levels of females may be that, for a given dose of alcohol, women are reported to reach a higher blood alcohol level than men (e.g., Jones & Jones, 1976), possibly because women retain more fluids than men (Wallgren & Barry, 1970).

With respect to alcohol's ability to alleviate tension, males and females may have different expectancies (Abrams & Wilson, 1979; Myrsten et al., 1975; Wilson & Abrams, 1977). Males tended to expect decreased anxiety after drinking; females seemed to expect increases. Brown et al. (1980) found that their female subjects expected generally positive social experiences when drinking, whereas males expected arousal and aggressive behavior. They reported that these differences were not attributable to differences in drinking history but may have been related to the tendency of males to consume greater amounts of alcohol than females. Southwick et al. (1981) found no sex differences in expectancies associated with drinking. Rohsenow (1983) speculated that differences in drinking habits between men and women may have affected the results of Brown et al. (1980). Therefore, she statistically controlled for the effects of drinking habits and found that women expected less global positive effects, social and physical pleasure and relaxation, and more cognitive/motor impairment than men after a few drinks but did not differ in expectations of sexual enhancement, aggression, expressiveness, or irresponsibility. She conjectured that the differences between her results and those of Brown *et al.* (1980) may have been due to the confound either of sex and drinking habits or of personal and general expectancies in the Brown *et al.* study . At any rate, the findings from the few studies do not provide a clear picture of the different expectancies held by men and women but do suggest that such differences exist.

Personality Characteristics

One might expect that there exists a sizable body of literature exploring the ways in which expectations about the effects of alcohol are moderated by various personality characteristics. However, there is a dearth of research in this area. In fact, only three studies exploring this type of relationship were found. Lang *et al.* (1980) examined the relations between expectancies about the effects of alcohol on sexual arousal and an individual's level of sex guilt. For male social drinkers, they found that the higher the sex guilt the greater the tendency to expect that sexual inhibitions would be lowered by low-to-moderate doses of alcohol. Lauerman *et al.* (1982) found the same personality expectancy interaction for female social drinkers for both low-to-moderate and high doses of alcohol. Lansky and Wilson (1981) found that higher sex guilt, nonalcoholic male subjects experienced greater arousal to sexual stimuli when they believed they had consumed alcohol. Thus, the ways in which personality variables interact with expectancies about the effects of alcohol are in serious need of further investigation. The available research does suggest that the probability that an expectancy set will affect behavior depends on the utility or reinforcement value of that expectancy for a given individual in a specific situation.

INTERPERSONAL FACTORS

The interpersonal nature of the situation in which most drinking occurs might be expected to play a role in the effect of alcohol on mood and behavior and on the expectancies drinkers hold about these effects. Except for the study by Warren and Raynes (1972), it has been generally found that nonalcoholic subjects drinking in isolation and in laboratory settings report negative emotional changes, whereas those drinking in groups and in comfortable settings tend to report positive mood changes (Ekman, Frankenhaeuser, Goldberg, Hagdahl, & Myrsten, 1964; Frankenhaeuser, Myrsten, & Jarpe, 1962; Kalin, 1972, Kalin, McClelland, & Kahn, 1965; Persson, Sjoberg, & Svensson, 1978; Pliner & Cappell, 1974; Smith

& Smith & Carpenter, in Freed, 1970; Smith, Parker, & Noble, 1975; Williams, 1966). Observations of drinkers in the natural environment have shown that most bar patrons tend to drink in groups (e.g., Cutler & Storm, 1975).

Marlatt and Gordon (1979) reported that interpersonal factors are important in relapses among alcoholics, smokers, and heroin addicts. Interpersonal stresses have also been found to increase drinking among alcoholics (e.g., Miller, Hersen, Eisler, & Hillman, 1974). Thus, alcoholics seem to expect that alcohol will help to facilitate socializing and to reduce interpersonal stress responses. With few exceptions (Goldman, Taylor, Carruth, & Nathan, 1973; Martorano, 1974; Nathan, Goldman, Lisman, & Taylor, 1972; Nathan & O'Brien, 1971), studies of male alcoholics that assessed the effects of alcohol on their social interactions, using either acute (Diethelm & Barr, 1962) or chronic administration (Docter & Bernal, 1964; Griffiths, Bigelow, & Liebson, 1974, 1975; McGuire et al., 1966; McNamee et al., 1968; Mendelson, LaDou, & Solomon, 1964; Tamerin & Mendelson, 1969; Tamerin et al., 1970; Thornton, Alternman, Skoloda, & Gottheil, 1976), have uniformly observed increases in the rate (if not always the quality) of social interactions except when subjects were highly intoxicated. Alcohol has been observed to facilitate social interactions among nonalcoholics (Babor, 1978; McGuire et al., 1966; Nathan & O'Brien, 1971) and female alcoholics (Tracey & Nathan, 1976). Thus, for both alcoholic and nonalcoholic populations it seems that drinking leads to a facilitation of social interaction. In contrast, Babor (1978) concluded that marijuana and heroin produce a general suppression of social interaction.

As noted before, three studies have assessed the expectancies that nonalcoholics hold about the effects of drinking (Brown et al., 1980; Rohsenow, 1983; Southwick et al., 1981). All three studies found that subjects held expectancies regarding the enhancement of socializing through drinking. Heavier drinkers seem to expect greater effects from drinking on socializing (Rohsenow, 1983; Southwick et al., 1981). Although Brown et al. (1980) found that females expected generally positive social experiences when drinking, whereas males expected arousal and aggressive behavior, Rohsenow (1983) did not find this difference. In fact, she found that women expected less social pleasure than men.

People in general seem to expect that alcohol will facilitate socializing and enhance social pleasure, and it does seem to do so. To determine whether this effect is due to some direct effect of alcohol or to the expectations that people hold it is necessary to look at research using the balanced placebo design wherein the expectancy and pharmacological effects of alcohol may be separated. Studies using this design (e.g., Abrams & Wilson, 1979; Wilson & Abrams, 1977) suggest that it is expectancy and not alcohol that determines subjects' reactions to social interactions, though males and females may hold opposite expectancies. Wilson, Perold, and Abrams (1981) have recently illustrated that, when expectations are disconfirmed, they can produce reverse effects. Subjects who were led to believe they had consumed alcohol showed a reduction in anxiety compared to those who believed they had not. However, when faced with an imminent social interaction, the subjects who believed they had consumed alcohol became more anxious than those who believed they had not. This study also showed that male subjects who believed that a female drinking companion was intoxicated showed less anxiety than males who did not have this belief. So the pharmacological properties of alcohol seem less important than the expectancies that people hold about the effects of alcohol in determining social facilitation and stress reduction while drinking.

ENVIRONMENTAL FACTORS

Although the traditional models of drinking have viewed it as a response to internal, usually aversive drive states, it is also possible to construe drinking as a response to external, environmental events and the individual's perception of those events. A host of environmental factors has been shown to affect drinking. In the previous section on interpersonal factors, it was stated that research has generally found that nonalcoholic subjects drinking in laboratory settings report negative emotional changes, whereas those drinking in comfortable and more naturalistic settings tend to report positive mood changes. There is even some suggestive evidence that the pleasantness of the environment may affect both the desire to drink and actual drinking (Russell & Mehrabian, 1975). Several studies also indicate that alcoholics will control their drinking to remain in an enriched environment (e.g., Bigelow, Cohen, Liebson, & Faillance, 1972; Cohen, Liebson, & Faillance, 1973).

Another tactic to study the effects of environmental factors on drinking has been to examine the influence of alcohol-related cues on consumption. Ludwig, Wikler, and Stark (1974) found that alcoholics' alcohol-acquisition behavior increased in a cues-present over a cues-absent condition. Miller, Hersen, Eisler, Epstein, and Wooten (1974) replicated this result with social drinkers but not with alcoholics. Further research is needed to reconcile these opposing results.

Both positive and negative reinforcement contingencies have been shown to affect drinking rates and patterns. Mello (1972) summarized much of the work that she did with Mendelson, indicating the operant nature of drinking as a response that can be influenced by its consequences. These early findings have been replicated and extended with both alcoholics (e.g., Bigelow *et al.*, 1972; Bigelow & Liebson, 1972; Cohen *et al.*, 1973) and nonalcoholics (Babor, Mendelson, Greenberg, & Kuehnle, 1978). Others (e.g., Miller, Hersen, Eisler, & Hemphill, 1973; Sobell & Sobell, 1973; Wilson, Leaf, & Nathan, 1975) have shown that drinking may be controlled by aversive consequences as well.

It is apparent that drinking may be controlled by its environmental consequences. However, in a cognitive social learning theory approach, reinforcement does not directly influence behavior, but rather it serves incentive and informational functions that are cognitively mediated. Most learning in humans occurs through observation and symbolic coding of the behavior of others. With regard to alcoholism and drinking, it is widely believed that the cultural and familial drinking practices to which one is exposed serve as models for one's own drinking behavior. To date, eight studies have attempted to elucidate the effects of models on drinking behavior (Caudill & Marlatt, 1975; Cooper, Waterhouse, & Sobell, 1979; Dericco & Garlington, 1977; Garlington & Dericco, 1977; Hendricks, Sobell, & Cooper, 1978; Leid & Marlatt, 1979; Reid, 1978; Watson & Sobell, 1982). Using nonalcoholics, these studies have shown that drinkers may be affected by both the consumption rate (high versus low) and social demeanor (warm versus cold) of the model. However, females and light-drinking males may not be as susceptible to the modeling effect.

It is unfortunate that drinkers' expectancies about the effects of different environmental factors on their drinking have not been directly studied. However, inferences about drinkers' expectancies can be drawn from research that has looked at the situations in which alcoholics expect to relapse. Representative of this approach is the work of Marlatt (1973) and Marlatt and Gordon (1979), which suggests that most relapses can be accounted for by four situational categories. Two of the categories are interpersonal and consist of situations in which (1) the individual becomes frustrated and angry without being able to express these feelings, and (2) the individual feels an inability to resist social pressure exerted by others to drink. The remaining two categories are intrapersonal and consist of situations in which (3) the individual experiences negative emotional states such as depression, anxiety, and boredom, and (4) the individual experiences intrapersonal temptations analogous to craving. These data have led Marlatt and Gordon (1979) to propose a cognitive-behavioral model of relapse, in which a person's expectations of self-efficacy interact with the availability and effectiveness of coping strategies to determine response to situations in which drinking might occur.

Although it is clear that environmental factors, including positive and negative reinforcement contingencies (which are probably cognitively mediated) and the behavior of others, are important determinants of drinking behavior, it is apparent that we know relatively little about the expectancies that drinkers hold regarding the effects of various environmental factors on drinking. Additional research is needed to demonstrate the effects of models in the natural environment and the expectations of drinkers about environmental factors.

THEORETICAL MODELS OF EXPECTANCY EFFECTS

The research reviewed in this chapter has shown that people have a variety of generalized and specific expectations about the effects of alcohol on their behavior and that these expectancies may often exert a more powerful influence over behavior than the pharmacological actions of alcohol. These findings are supportive of a cognitive social learning theory of alcohol's effects. However, two problems remain. First, not all classes of behavior have shown the prepotency of expectancy over pharmacological effects; second, the processes underlying expectancy effects are unknown. To deal with these problems, one must examine the theoretical models that have been advanced to explain expectancy effects.

Shapiro and Morris (1978) have identified a number of possible mechanisms to explain placebo effects. However, two models have been formulated to explain the processes underlying the effects of expectancy on response to alcohol, and these will be reviewed here. The first is based on attribution theory. This model, initially proposed by Kola (1970) and Wilson (1977) and elaborated by Marlatt and Rohsenow (1980), is derived from Schachter's (1964) interactionist theory of emotion and Valins's (1966) extension of it. Schachter proposed that behavioral and affective responses to a drug are not a simple function of its pharmacological properties or the state of the physiological arousal it produces. Rather, response to a drug depends on both physiological arousal and the individual's cognitive evaluation of this state of arousal. Given a state of diffuse emotional arousal, similar to that produced by alcohol, for which the individual has no immediately available explanation, Schachter proposed that the person will experience a need to understand and label the feelings experienced. Cognitive interpretations of diffuse states of arousal depend on cues from the environment, past learning, or prior experience with the drug.

Marlatt and Rohsenow (1980) have indicated that most of the research on expectancy effects using the balanced placebo design fails to conform to the predictions of Schachter's interactionist theory because expectancy alone was typically found to be the only significant determinant of behavior rather than an interaction between the pharmacological effects of alcohol and expectancy. Therefore, Marlatt and Rohsenow proposed that the Valins extension of Schachter's theory better fits the data. Valins's misattribution hypothesis suggests that cognitive labeling (induced by instructions) can significantly influence emotional responding even in the absence of a pharmacologically induced state of arousal. Marlatt and Rohsenow suggest that people are motivated to attribute arousal and associated behaviors to the consumption of alcohol (or the belief that alcohol has been consumed). The motivation may come from the use of drinking as an excuse for engaging in culturally proscribed behaviors such as sex and aggression, as this excuse is socially sanctioned. This temporary immunity from responsibility for one's behavior while drinking serves as a differential reinforcement for disinhibited behavior while drinking. Marlatt and Rohsenow speculate that this may explain why interpersonal behaviors have shown expectancy effects, but cognitive and motor behaviors have not. They also conjectured that expectancies may influence behavior less when they are weak or vague or when they involve undesirable consequences. None of these explanations seems able to handle the failure of research to show expectancy effects on mood states.

Two possible mechanisms underlying the effectiveness of the instructional (expectancy) manipulation in balanced placebo studies have been proposed by Marlatt and Rohsenow. Both rely on the assumption that internal states of arousal, similar, perhaps, to those produced by consumption of a moderate amount of alcohol, may be elicited by external stimuli. The task in which the subject is involved may be associated with strong external sources of arousal such as sexual stimuli or social interactions. In addition, subjects who are led to believe that they are consuming alcohol may experience a classically conditioned arousal response to the cues associated with drinking such as the sight of a bottle of liquor. In both instances, the externally elicited arousal may be attributed to alcohol consumption.

Maisto, Connors, and Sachs (1981) have criticized explanations of expectancy effects based on attribution theory. They have offered a reference-level model to explain the initiation and continuation of drinking as well as the behavioral and psychological effects derived from drinking. In this dynamic model, the anticipated and desired effects of drinking a given amount of alcohol combine with environmental and perceptual factors to determine what behavioral and psychological effects are produced when drinking. Some behaviors are under greater volitional control than others. The degree to which a behavior is under volitional control determines the degree to which it is subject to influence by nonpharmacological factors. The failure to find expectancy effects on tasks involving cognitive and motor skills may be attributable to the low level of control individuals may exercise over these behaviors. Social behaviors seem more susceptible to voluntary control and would, therefore, be expected to give evidence of expectancy effects. The failure to find an expectancy effect on mood states is not clearly explained by this model.

Although there is not sufficient evidence available to evaluate these models, it is clear that both would fit nicely within a cognitive social learning theory of alcohol use and its effects. These models do help to understand the role of expectancy in influencing behavior, and they support the importance of cognitive, situational, and physiological factors in a comprehensive theory of drug use. Finally, these models help point the way for future research by suggesting variables of importance that need further specification.

CONCLUSIONS

Cognitive social learning theory seems to hold considerable promise for aiding in the understanding of drug use. Drinkers have well-defined expectancies about the effects of alcohol on a variety of behaviors. These expectancies begin as generalized expectancies that are developed by observation of models, indirect experience, and exposure to the media. As the individual gains direct experience with alcohol, these expectancies become more specific. A number of setting factors interact with expectancy set to determine the use and effects of alcohol.

Research investigating the effects of drug-related expectancies on behavior has been greatly aided by the introduction of the balanced placebo design. Work with this design has effectively demonstrated that expectancies may have a variety of effects on behavior. Future research would do well to separate individuals with different expectancies to control for variance on this factor. Nevertheless, we now know that drug effects are frequently not solely the products of their pharmacological properties, and this is an important step in understanding drug actions and people's motivations for using drugs.

Although research has established the importance of cognitive factors in drug use, questions still remain about the range of behaviors that are subject to these influences and the processes underlying them. Some promising models have been developed, but little research is currently available to evaluate them. These models will undoubtedly serve a heuristic function for the field.

REFERENCES

Abrams, D. B., & Wilson, G. T. Effects of alcohol on social anxiety in women: Cognitive versus physiological processes. *Journal of Abnormal Psychology*, 1979, *88*, 161–173.

Abrams, D. B., & Wilson, G. T. Alcohol, sexual arousal and self-control. *Journal of Personality and Social Psychology*, 1983, *45*, 188–198.

Adesso, V. J. Experimental studies of human drinking behavior. In H. Rigter & J. C. Crabbe, Jr. (Eds.), *Alcohol tolerance and dependence*, Amsterdam: Elsevier, 1980.

Asp, D. R. Effects of alcoholics' expectation of a drink. *Journal of Studies on Alcohol*, 1977, *38*, 1790–1795.

Babor, T. F. Studying social reactions to drug self-administration. In N. Krasnegor (Ed.), *Human substance abuse: Methods for studying self-administration*. (Research Monograph Series 20), Washington, D.C.: NIDA, 1978.

Babor, T. F., & Mendelson, J. H., Greenberg, I., & Kuehnle, J. Experimental analysis of the "Happy Hour": Effects of purchase price on alcohol consumption. *Psychopharmacology*, 1978, *58*, 35–41.

Babor, T. F., & Mendelson, J. H. *Empirical correlates of self-report drinking measures*. Paper presented at the 10th Annual Medical-Scientific Conference, National Council on Alcoholism, Washington, D.C., 1979.

Bandura, A. Self-efficacy: Toward a unifying theory of behavioral change. *Psychological Review*, 1977, *84*, 191–215. (a)

Bandura, A. *Social learning theory*. Englewood Cliffs, N.J.: Prentice-Hall, 1977. (b)

Bennett, R. M., Buss, A. H., & Carpenter, J. A. Alcohol and human physical aggression. *Quarterly Journal of Studies on Alcohol*, 1969, *30*, 870–876.

Berg, G., Laberg, J. C., Skutle, A., & Ohman, A. Instructed versus pharmacological effects of alcohol in alcoholics and social drinkers. *Behaviour Research and Therapy*, 1981, *19*, 55–66.

Bigelow, G., Cohen, M., Liebson, I., & Faillance, L. A. Abstinence or moderation? Choice by alcoholics. *Behaviour Research and Therapy*, 1972, *10*, 209–214.

Bigelow, G., & Liebson, I. Cost factors controlling alcoholic drinking. *Psychological Record*, 1972, *22*, 305–314.

Billings, A. G., Weiner, S., Kessler, M., & Gomberg, C. A. Drinking behavior in laboratory and barroom settings. *Journal of Studies on Alcohol*, 1976, *37*, 85–89.

Briddell, D. W., & Wilson, G. T. The effects of alcohol and expectancy set on male sexual arousal. *Journal of Abnormal Psychology*, 1976, *85*, 225–234.

Briddell, D. W., Rimm, D. C., Caddy, G. R., Krawitz, G., Sholis, D., & Wunderlin, R. G. Effects of alcohol and cognitive set on sexual arousal to deviant stimuli. *Journal of Abnormal Psychology*, 1978, *87*, 418–430.

Brown, S. A., Goldman, M. S., Inn, A., & Anderson, L. R. Expectations of reinforcement from alcohol: Their domain and relation to drinking patterns. *Journal of Consulting and Clinical Psychology*, 1980, *48*, 419–426.

Cappell, H. An evaluation of tension models of alcohol consumption. In R. J. Gibbins, Y. Israel, H. Kalant, R. E. Popham, W. Schmidt, & R. G. Smart (Eds.), *Research advances in alcohol and drug problems* (Vol. 2). New York: Wiley, 1975.

Cappell, H., & Herman, C. P. Alcohol and tension reduction: A review. *Quarterly Journal of Studies on Alcohol*, 1972, *33*, 33–64.

Cappell, H. D., & Pliner, P. Regulation of the self-administration of marihuana by psychological and pharmacological variables. *Psychopharmacologia*, 1974, *40*, 65–76.

Carpenter, J. A. Contributions from psychology to the study of drinking and driving. *Quarterly Journal of Studies on Alcohol*, 1968 (Supplement No. 4), 234–251.

Carpenter, J. A., & Armenti, N. P. Some effects of ethanol on human sexual and aggressive behavior. In B. Kissin & H. Begleiter (Eds.), *The biology of alcoholism* (Vol. 2). New York: Plenum Press, 1972.

Caudill, B. D., & Marlatt, G. A. Modeling influences in social drinking: An experimental analogue. *Journal of Consulting and Clinical Psychology*, 1975, *43*, 405–415.

Christiansen, B. A, & Goldman, M. S. Alcohol-related expectancies versus demographic/background variables in the prediction of adolescent drinking. *Journal of Consulting and Clinical Psychology*, 1983, *51*, 249–257.

Christiansen, B. A., Goldman, M. S., & Inn, A. Development of alcohol-related expectancies in adolescents: Separating pharmacological from social-learning influences. *Journal of Consulting and Clinical Psychology*, 1982, *50*, 336–344.

Clark, W. B. Loss of control, heavy drinking and drinking problems in a longitudinal study. *Quarterly Journal of Studies on Alcohol*, 1976, *37*, 1256–1290.

Cohen, M., Liebson, I., & Faillance, L. Controlled drinking by chronic alcoholics over extended periods of free access. *Psychological Reports*, 1973, *32*, 1107–1110.

Conger, J. J. Reinforcement theory and the dynamics of alcoholism. *Quarterly Journal of Studies on Alcohol*, 1956, *17*, 296–305.

Connors, G. J., & Maisto, S. A. Effects of alcohol, instructions, and consumption rate on affect and physiological sensations. *Psychopharmacology*, 1979, *62*, 261–266.

Connors, G. J., & Maisto, S. A. Effects of alcohol, instructions, and consumption rate on motor performance. *Journal of Studies on Alcohol*, 1980, *41*, 509–517.

Cooper, A. M., Waterhouse, G. J., & Sobell, M. B. Influence of gender on alcohol consumption in a modeling situation. *Journal of Studies on Alcohol*, 1979, *40*, 562–570.

Cutler, R. E., & Storm, T. Observational study of alcohol consumption in natural settings: The Vancouver beer parlor. *Journal of Studies on Alcohol*, 1975, *36*, 1173–1183.

Davis, D. Mood changes in alcoholic subjects with programmed and free-choice experimental drinking. In N. K. Mello & J. H. Mendelson (Eds.), *Recent advances in studies of alcoholism: An interdisciplinary symposium*. Washington, D.C.: U.S. Government Printing Office, 1971.

Deardorff, C. M., Melges, F. T., Hout, C. N., & Savage, D. J. Situations related to drinking alcohol: A factor analysis of questionnaire responses. *Journal of Studies on Alcohol*, 1975, *36*, 1184–1195.

Dericco, D. A., & Garlington, W. K. The effect of modeling and disclosure of experimenter's intent on drinking rate of college students. *Addictive Behaviors*, 1977, *2*, 135–139.

Diethelm, O., & Barr, R. M. Psychotherapeutic interviews and alcohol intoxication. *Quarterly Journal of Studies on Alcohol*, 1962, *23*, 243–251.

Docter, R. F., & Bernal, M. E. Immediate and prolonged psychophysiological effects of sustained alcohol intake in alcoholics. *Quarterly Journal of Studies on Alcohol*, 1964, *25*, 438–450.

Ekman, G., Frankenhaeuser, M., Goldberg, L., Hagdahl, R., & Myrsten, A.-L., Subjective and objective effects of alcohol as functions of dosage and time. *Psychopharmacologia*, 1964, *6*, 399–409.

Engle, K. B., & Williams, T. K. Effect of an ounce of vodka on alcoholics' desire for alcohol. *Quarterly Journal of Studies on Alcohol*, 1972, *33*, 1099–1105.

Farkas, G. M., & Rosen, R. C. The effect of alcohol on elicited male sexual response. *Journal of Studies on Alcohol*, 1976, *37*, 265–272.

Farber, P. D., Khavari, K. A., & Douglass, F. M., IV. A factor analytic study of reasons for drinking: Empirical validation of positive and negative reinforcement dimensions. *Journal of Consulting and Clinical Psychology*, 1980, *48*, 780–781.

Frankenhaeuser, M. S., Myrsten, A.-L., & Jarpe, G. Effect of moderate doses of alcohol on intellectual functioning. *Psychophamacologia*, 1962, *3*, 344–351.

Freed, E. X. Alcoholism and manic-depressive disorders. Some perspectives. *Quarterly Journal of Studies on Alcohol,* 1970, *31,* 62–89.

Garlington, W. K., & Dericco, D. A. The effect of modeling on drinking rate. *Journal of Applied Behavior Analysis,* 1977, *10,* 207–211.

Goldman, M. S., Taylor, H. A., Carruth, M. L., & Nathan, P. E. Effects of group decision-making on group drinking by alcoholics. *Quarterly Journal of Studies on Alcohol,* 1973, *34,* 807–822.

Griffiths, R. R., Bigelow, G., & Liebson, I. Assessment of effects of social interactions in alcoholics. *Psychopharmacologia,* 1974, **38,** 105–110.

Griffiths, R. R., Bigelow, G., & Liebson, I. Effect of ethanol self-administration on choice behavior: Money vs. socializing. *Pharmacology, Biochemistry and Behavior,* 1975, *3,* 443–446.

Hendricks, R. D., Sobell, M. B., & Cooper, A. M. Social influences on human ethanol consumption in an analogue situation. *Addictive Behaviors,* 1978, *3,* 253–259.

Hunter, P. A., Hannon, R., & Marchi, D. *Alcohol consumption in natural settings as a function of sex, age and income level.* Paper presented at the Association for the Advancement of Behavior Therapy Convention, 1979.

Jones, B. M., & Jones, M. K. Women and alcohol: Intoxication, metabolism, and the menstrual cycle. In M. Greenblatt & M. A. Schuckit (Eds.) *Alcoholism problems in women and children.* New York: Grune & Stratton, 1976.

Kalin, R. Social drinking in different settings. In D. C. McClelland, W. N. Davis, R. Kalin, & E. Wanner (Eds.), *The drinking man.* New York: Free Press, 1972.

Kalin, R., McClelland, D. C., & Kahn, M. The effects of male social drinking upon fantasy. *Journal of Personality and Social Psychology,* 1965, *1,* 441–452.

Kessler, M., & Gomberg, C. Observations of barroom drinking: Methodology and preliminary results. *Quarterly Journal of Studies on Alcohol,* 1974, *35,* 1392–1396.

Kola, L. A. *Alcohol instructional set, subjective expectations and tension reduction in alcoholics.* Unpublished doctoral dissertation, Boston University Graduate School, 1970.

Lang, A. R., Goeckner, D. J., Adesso, V. J., & Marlatt, G. A. Effects of alcohol on aggression in male social drinkers. *Journal of Abnormal Psychology,* 1975, *84,* 508–518.

Lang, A. R., Searles, J., Lauerman, R., & Adesso, V. Expectancy, alcohol, and sex guilt as determinants of interest in and reaction to sexual stimuli. *Journal of Abnormal Psychology,* 1980, *89,* 644–653.

Lansky, D., & Wilson, G. T. Alcohol, expectations, and sexual arousal in males: An information processing analysis. *Journal of Abnormal Psychology,* 1981, *90,* 35–45.

Lauerman, R. J., Adesso, V. J., & Lang, A. R. *The influence of sex guilt, expectancy, and alcohol on female college students' reactions to sexual stimuli.* Unpublished manuscript, 1982.

Leid, E. R., & Marlatt, G. A. Modeling as a determinant of alcohol consumption: Effect of subject sex and prior drinking history. *Addictive Behaviors,* 1979, *4,* 47–54.

Levenson, R. W., Sher, K. J., Grossman, L. M., Newman, J., & Newlin, D. B. Alcohol and stress response dampening: Pharmacological effects, expectancy, and tension reduction. *Journal of Abnormal Psychology,* 1980, *89,* 528–538.

Ludwig, A. M., Wikler, A., & Stark, L. H. The first drink: Psychobiological aspects of craving. *Archives of General Psychiatry,* 1974, *30,* 439–547.

Lyerly, S. B., Ross, S., Krugman, A. D., & Clyde, D. J. Drugs and placebos: The effects of instructions upon performance and mood under amphetamine sulfate and chloral hydrate. *Journal of Abnormal and Social Psychology,* 1964, *68,* 321–327.

MacAndrew, C., & Edgerton, R. B. *Drunken comportment.* Chicago: Aldine, 1969.

Maisto, S. A., Connors, G. J. & Sachs, P. R. Expectation as a mediator in alcohol intoxication: A reference level model. *Cognitive Therapy and Research,* 1981, *5,* 1–18.

Maisto, S. A., Lauerman, R., & Adesso, V. J. A comparison of two experimental studies of the role of cognitive factors in alcoholics' drinking. *Quarterly Journal of Studies on Alcohol*, 1977, *38*, 145–149.

Malatesta, V., Pollack, R., Crotty, T., & Peacock, L. Acute alcohol intoxication and female orgasmic response. *Journal of Sex Research*, 1982, *18*, 1–17.

Malatesta, V., Pollack, R., Wilbanks, W., & Adams, H. Alcohol effects on the orgasmic-ejaculatory response in human males. *Journal of Sex Research*, 1979, *15*, 101–107.

Marlatt, G. A. Alcohol, stress and cognitive control. In I. G. Sarason & C. D. Spielberger (Eds.), *Stress and anxiety* (Vol. 3) Washington, D.C.: Hemisphere, 1976.

Marlatt, G. A. Craving for alcohol, loss of control, and relapse: A cognitive-behavioral analysis. In P. E. Nathan, G. A. Marlatt, & T. Løberg (Eds.) *Alcoholism: New directions in behavioral research and treatment*. New York: Plenum Press, 1978.

Marlatt, G. A. *A comparison of aversive conditioning procedures in the treatment of alcoholism*. Paper presented at a meeting of the Western Psychological Association, 1973.

Marlatt, G. A., & Rohsenow, D. Cognitive processes in alcohol use: Expectancy and the balanced placebo design. In N. Mello (Ed.), *Advances in substance abuse: Behavioral and biological research*. Greenwich: JAI Press, 1980.

Marlatt, G. A., Demming, B., & Reid, J. B. Loss of control drinking in alcoholics: An experimental analogue. *Journal of Abnormal Psychology*, 1973, *81*, 233–241.

Marlatt, G. A., & Gordon, J. R. Determinants of relapse: Implications for the maintenance of behavior change. In P. Davidson (Ed.), *Behavioral medicine: Changing health lifestyles* (Vol. 10). New York: Brunner/Mazel, 1979.

Martorano, R. D. Mood and social perception in four alcoholics: Effects of drinking and assertion training. *Quarterly Journal of Studies on Alcohol*, 1974, *35*, 445–457.

McClelland, D. C., Davis, W. N., Kalin, R. & Wanner, W. *The drinking man*. New York: The Free Press, 1972.

McCollam, J., Burish, T., Maisto, S. A., & Sobell, M. B. Alcohol's effects on physiological arousal and self-reported affect and sensations. *Journal of Abnormal Psychology*, 1980, *89*, 224–233.

McGuire, M. T., Stein, S., & Mendelson, J. H. Comparative psychosocial studies of alcoholic and nonalcoholic subjects undergoing experimentally induced ethanol intoxication. *Psychosomatic Medicine*, 1966, *28*, 13–26.

McNamee, H. B., Mello, N. K., & Mendelson, J. H. Experimental analysis of drinking patterns of alcoholics: Concurrent psychiatric observations. *American Journal of Psychiatry*, 1968, *124*, 1063–1069.

Mello, N. K. Behavioral studies of alcoholism. In B. Kissin & H. Begleiter (Eds.), *The biology of alcoholism* (Vol. 2). New York: Plenum Press, 1972.

Mello, N. K. A semantic aspect of alcoholism. In H. D. Cappell & A. E. LeBlanc (Eds.), *Biological and behavioral approaches to drug dependence*. Toronto: Addiction Research Foundation, 1975.

Mello, N. K., & Mendelson, J. H. The effects of prolonged alcohol ingestion on the eating, drinking, and smoking patterns of chronic alcoholics. In W. A. Hunt (Ed.), *Learning mechanisms in smoking*. Chicago: Aldine, 1970.

Menaker, T. Anxiety about drinking in alcoholics. *Journal of Abnormal Psychology*, 1967, *72*, 43–49.

Mendelson, J. H., LaDou, H., & Solomon, P. Experimentally induced chronic intoxication and withdrawal in alcoholics. Part 3: Psychiatric findings. *Quarterly Journal of Studies on Alcohol*, Supplement No. 2, 1964.

Miller, M. E., Adesso, V. J., Fleming, J. P., Gino, A., & Lauerman, R. Effects of alcohol on the storage and retrieval processes of heavy social drinkers. *Journal of Experimental Psychology: Human Learning and Memory*, 1978, *4*, 246–255.

Miller, P. M., & Hersen, M. Quantitative changes in alcohol consumption as a function of electrical aversion conditions. *Journal of Clinical Psychology*, 1972, *28*, 590–593.

Miller, P. M., Hersen, M., Eisler, R. M., & Hemphill, D. P. Electrical aversion therapy with alcoholics: An analogue study. *Behaviour Research and Therapy*, 1973, *11*, 491–498.

Miller, P. M., Hersen, M., Eisler, R. M., Epstein, L. H., & Wooten, L. S. Relationship of alcohol cues to the drinking behavior of alcoholics and social drinkers: An analogue study. *Psychological Record*, 1974, *24*, 61–66.

Miller, P. M., Hersen, M., Eisler, R. M., & Hilsman, G. Effects of social stress on operant drinking of alcoholics and social drinkers. *Behaviour Research and Therapy*, 1974, *12*, 261–263.

Mulford, H. A., & Miller, D. E. Drinking in Iowa: III. A scale of definitions of alcohol related to drinking behavior. *Quarterly Journal of Studies on Alcohol*, 1960, *21*, 267–278.

Mulford, H. A., & Miller, D. E. Preoccupation with alcohol and definitions of alcohol: A replication of two cumulative scales. *Quarterly Journal of Studies on Alcohol*, 1963, *24*, 682–696.

Myrsten, A.-L., Hollstedt, C., & Holmberg, L. Alcohol-induced changes in mood and activation in males and females as related to catecholamine excretion and blood-alcohol level. *Scandinavian Journal of Psychology*, 1975, *16*, 303–310.

Nathan, P.E., & O'Brien, J. S. An experimental analysis of the behavior of alcoholics and nonalcoholics during prolonged experimental drinking: A necessary precursor to behavior therapy? *Behavior Therapy*, 1971, *2*, 455–475.

Nathan, P. E., Goldman, M. S., Lisman, S. A., & Taylor, M. A. Alcohol and alcoholics: A behavioral approach. *Transactions of the New York Academy of Sciences*, 1972, *34*, 602–627.

Nathan, P. E., Titler, N. A., Lowenstein, L. M., Solomon, P., & Rossi, A. M. Behavioral analysis of chronic alcoholism. *Archives of General Psychiatry*, 1970, *22*, 419–430.

Orford, J. A comparison of alcoholics whose drinking is totally uncontrolled and those whose drinking is mainly controlled. *Behaviour Research and Therapy*, 1973, *11*, 565–576.

Persson, L.-O., Sjoberg, L., & Svensson, E. Mood effects of alcohol. *Goteborg Psychological Reports*, 1978, *8*, 1–21.

Phares, E. J. *Locus of control in personality*. Morristown, N.J.: General Learning Press, 1976.

Pihl, R. O., Zeichner, A., Niaura, R., Nagy, K., & Zacchia, C. Attribution and alcohol-mediated aggression. *Journal of Abnormal Psychology*, 1981, *90*, 468–475.

Plant, M. A. Kreitman, N., Miller, T.-I., & Duffy, J. Observing public drinking. *Journal of Studies on Alcohol*, 1977, *38*, 867–880.

Pliner, P., & Cappell, H. Modification of the affective consequences of alcohol: A comparison of social and solitary drinking. *Journal of Abnormal Psychology*, 1974, *83*, 418–425.

Polivy, J., Schueneman, A. L., & Carlson, K. Alcohol and tension reduction: Cognitive and physiological effects. *Journal of Abnormal Psychology*, 1976, *85*, 595–600.

Reid, J. B. Study of drinking in natural settings. In G. A. Marlatt & P. E. Nathan (Eds.), *Behavioral approaches to alcoholism*. New Brunswick, N.J.: Rutgers Center of Alcohol Studies, 1978.

Rimm, D. C., Sininger, R. A., Faherty, J. D., Whitely, M. D., & Perl, M. B. A balanced placebo investigation of the effects of alcohol vs. expectancy on simulated driving behavior. *Addictive Behaviors*, 1982, *7*, 27–32.

Rohsenow, D. J. Drinking habits and expectancies about alcohol's effects for self versus others. *Journal of Consulting and Clinical Psychology*, 1983, *51*, 752–756.

Rosenbluth, J., Nathan, P. E., & Lawson, D. M. Environmental influences on drinking by college students in a college pub: Behavioral observation in the natural environment. *Addictive Behaviors*, 1978, *3*, 117–121.

Ross, S., Krugman, A. D., Lyerly, S. B., & Clyde, D. J. Drugs and placebos: A model design. *Psychological Reports*, 1962, *10*, 383–392.

Rotter, J. B. *Social learning and clinical psychology*. Englewood Cliffs, N.J.: Prentice-Hall, 1954.

Rotter, J. B. Generalized expectancies for internal versus external control of reinforcement. *Psychological Monographs*, 1966, *80*, 1–28.

Rotter, J. B. Some problems and misconceptions related to the construct of internal versus external control of reinforcement. *Journal of Consulting and Clinical Psychology*, 1975, *43*, 56–67.

Rotter, J. B., Chance, J., & Phares, E. J. (Eds.), *Applications of a social learning theory of personality*. New York: Holt, Rinehart & Winston, 1972.

Rubin, H., & Henson, D. Effects of alcohol on male sexual responding. *Psychopharmacology*, 1976, *47*, 123–134.

Russell, J. A., & Mehrabian, A. The mediating role of emotions in alcohol use. *Quarterly Journal of Studies in Alcohol*, 1975, *36*, 1508–1536.

Saunders, B., & Richard, G. "In vino veritas": An observational study of alcoholics' and normal drinkers' patterns of consumption. *British Journal of Addiction*, 1978, *73*, 375–380.

Schachter, S. The interaction of cognitive and physiological determinants of emotional state. In L. Berkowitz (Ed.), *Advances in Experimental Social Psychology*. New York: Academic Press, 1964.

Schaefer, H. H., Sobell, M. B., & Mills, K. C. Baseline drinking behavior in alcoholics and social drinkers: Kinds of drinks and sip magnitude. *Behaviour Research and Therapy*, 1971, *9*, 23–27.

Shakespeare, W. *Macbeth*. A new Variorum Edition (5th Edition) H. H. Furness, Jr. (Ed.) Philadelphia: Lippincot, 1915, p. 149.

Senter, R. J., Heintzelman, M., Dorfmueller, M., & Hinkle, H. A. A comparative look at ratings of the subjective effects of beverage alcohol. *Psychological Record*, 1979, *29*, 49–56.

Shapiro, A. K., & Morris, L. A. Placebo effects in medical and psychological therapies. In S. L. Garfield & A. E. Bergin (Eds.) *Handbook of psychotherapy and behavior change* (2nd ed.). New York: Wiley, 1978.

Shuntich, R. J., & Taylor, S. P. The effects of alcohol on human physical aggression. *Journal of Experimental Research in Personality*, 1972, *6*, 34–38.

Smith, R. C., Parker, E. S., & Noble, E. P. Alcohol and affect in dyadic social interaction. *Psychosomatic Medicine*, 1975, *37*, 25–40.

Sobell, M. B. & Sobell, L. C. Individualized behavior therapy for alcoholics. *Behavior Therapy*, 1973, *4*, 49–72.

Sobell, M. B., Schaefer, H. H., & Mills, K. C. Differences in baseline drinking behavior between alcoholics and normal drinkers. *Behavior Research and Therapy*, 1972, *10*, 257–267.

Solomon, R. L. An opponent-process theory of acquired motivation: The affective dynamics of addiction. In J. Maser & M. E. P. Seligman (Eds.), *Psychopathology: Experimental models*. San Francisco: Freeman, 1977.

Solomon, R. L., & Corbit, J. D. An opponent-process theory of motivation. I. Temporal dynamics of affect. *Psychological Review*, 1974, *81*, 119–145.

Sommer, R. The isolated drinker in the Edmonton beer parlor. *Quarterly Journal of Studies on Alcohol*, 1965, *26*, 95–110.

Southwick, L., Steele, C., Marlatt, A., Lindell, M. Alcohol-related expectancies: Defined by phase of intoxication and drinking experience. *Journal of Consulting and Clinical Psychology*, 1981, *49*, 713–721.

Sutker, P. B., Allain, A. N., Brantley, P. J., & Randall, C. L. Acute alcohol intoxication, negative affect and automatic arousal in women and men. *Addictive Behaviors*, 1982, *7*, 17–25.

Tamerin, J. S. The importance of psychosocial factors on drinking in alcoholics; relevance for traffic safety. In S. Israelstam & S. Lambert (Eds.), *Alcohol, drugs, and traffic safety.* Toronto: Addiction Research Foundation, 1975.

Tamerin, J. S., & Mendelson, J. H. The psychodynamics of chronic inebriation: Observation of alcoholics during the process of drinking in an experimental group setting. *American Journal of Psychiatry,* 1969, *125,* 886–899.

Tamerin, J. S., Weiner, S., & Mendelson, J. H. Alcoholics' expectancies and recall of experiences during drinking. *American Journal of Psychiatry,* 1970, *126,* 1697–1704.

Taylor, S. P., & Gammon, C. B. Effects of type and dose of alcohol on human physical aggression. *Journal of Personality and Social Psychology,* 1975, *32,* 169–175.

Taylor, S. P., & Gammon, C. B. Aggressive behavior of intoxicated subjects: The effect of third-party intervention. *Quarterly Journal of Studies on Alcohol,* 1976, *37,* 917–930.

Taylor, S. P., Gammon, C. B., & Capasso, D. R. Aggression as a function of the interaction of alcohol and threat. *Journal of Personality and Social Psychology,* 1976, *34,* 938–941.

Taylor, S. P., Vardaris, R. M., Rawtich, A. B., Cranston, J. W., & Lubetkin, R. The effects of alcohol and delta-9-tetrahydrocannabinol on human physical aggression. *Aggressive Behavior,* 1976, *2,* 153–161.

Taylor, S. P., Schmutte, G. T., & Leonard, K. E., Jr. Physical aggression as a function of alcohol and frustration. *Bulletin of the Psychonomic Society,* 1977, *9,* 217–218.

Thornton, C. C., Alterman, A. I., Skoloda, T. E., & Gottheil, E. Drinking and socializing in "introverted" and "extroverted" alcoholics. *Annals of the New York Academy of Sciences,* 1976, *273,* 481–487.

Tracey, D. A., & Nathan, P. E. Behavioral analysis of chronic alcoholism in four women. *Journal of Consulting and Clinical Psychology,* 1976, *44,* 832–842.

Valins, S. Cognitive effects of false heart-rate feedback. *Journal of Personality and Social Psychology,* 1966, *4,* 400–408.

Vargas, J. M., & Adesso, V. J. *The effects of setting, emotional status, and drinker experience upon the drinking behavior and post-consumption emotional status of social drinkers.* Unpublished manuscript, University of Wisconsin at Milwaukee, 1979.

Viamontes, J. A. Sexual depressant effect of alcohol. *Medical Aspects of Human Sexuality,* 1975, *9,* 31.

Vuchinich, R. E., & Sobell, M. B. Empirical separation of physiological and expected effects of alcohol on complex perceptual motor performance. *Psychopharmacology,* 1978, *60,* 81–85.

Vuchinich, R. E., Tucker, J. A., & Sobell, M. B. Alcohol, expectancy, cognitive labeling and mirth. *Journal of Abnormal Psychology,* 1979, *88,* 641–651.

Wallgren, H., & Barry, H. *Actions of alcohol.* Amsterdam: Elsevier, 1970.

Warren, G. H., & Raynes, A. E. Mood changes during three conditions of alcohol intake. *Quarterly Journal of Studies on Alcohol,* 1972, *33,* 979–989.

Watson, D. W., & Sobell, M. B. Social influences on alcohol consumption by black and white males. *Addictive Behaviors,* 1982, *7,* 87–91.

Williams, A. F. Social drinking, anxiety, and depression. *Journal of Personality and Social Psychology,* 1966, *3,* 689–693.

Williams, R. J., & Brown, R. A. Differences in baseline drinking behavior between New Zealand alcoholics and normal drinkers. *Behaviour Research and Therapy,* 1974, *12,* 287–294.

Williams, R. M., Goldman, M. S., & Williams, D. L. Expectancy and pharmacological effects of alcohol on human cognitive and motor performance: The compensation for alcohol effect. *Journal of Abnormal Psychology,* 1981, *90,* 267–270.

Wilson, G. T. Alcohol and human sexual behavior. *Behaviour Research and Therapy,* 1977, *15,* 239–252.

Wilson, G. T. The effects of alcohol on human sexual behavior. In N. K. Mello (Ed.), *Advances in substance abuse: Behavioral and biological research* (Vol. 2). Greenwich: JAI Press, 1981.

Wilson, G. T., & Abrams, D. B. Effects of alcohol and social anxiety and physiological arousal: Cognitive versus pharmacological processes. *Cognitive Therapy and Research,* 1977, *1,* 195–210.

Wilson, G. T., & Lawson, D. M. Expectancies, alcohol and sexual arousal in male social drinkers. *Journal of Abnormal Psychology,* 1976, *85,* 587–594. (a)

Wilson, G. T., & Lawson, D. M. The effects of alcohol on sexual arousal in women. *Journal of Abnormal Psychology,* 1976, *85,* 489–497. (b)

Wilson, G. T., & Lawson, D. M. Expectancies, alcohol, and sexual arousal in women. *Journal of Abnormal Psychology,* 1978, *87,* 358–367.

Wilson, G. T., Leaf, R., and Nathan, P. E., The aversive control of excessive drinking by chronic alcoholics in the laboratory setting. *Journal of Applied Behavior Analysis,* 1975, *8,* 13–26.

Wilson, G. T., Lawson, D. M., & Abrams, D. B. Effects of alcohol on sexual arousal in male alcoholics. *Journal of Abnormal Psychology,* 1978, *87,* 609–616.

Wilson, G. T., Perold, E. A., & Abrams, D. B. The effects of expectations of self-intoxication and partner's drinking on anxiety in dyadic social interaction. *Cognitive Therapy and Research,* 1981, *5,* 251–264.

Zeichner, A., & Pihl, R. E. Effects of alcohol and behavior contingencies on human aggression. *Journal of Abnormal Psychology,* 1979, *88,* 153–160.

Zeichner, A., & Pihl, R. O. Effects of alcohol and instigator intent on human aggression. *Journal of Studies on Alcohol,* 1980, *41,* 265–276.

CHAPTER 7

Personality Correlates of Substance Abuse

W. MILES COX

INTRODUCTION

Substance abuse, as the title of this volume indicates, has multiple causes, including biological, psychological, and environmental variables that interact with one another to determine whether a given individual will actually come to abuse an addictive substance. However, as the title of this chapter suggests, the personality characteristics that covary with substance abuse may or may not act as causative factors. Furthermore, personality characteristics may be antecedents, concomitants, or consequences of substance abuse.

Personality was not always accorded its present role in the etiology of substance abuse. In fact, the "addictive personality" at one time was regarded as the primary, if not exclusive, cause of substance abuse. The exact origin of this concept is uncertain, but its impetus appears to have come from two sources: (1) psychoanalysis, which sought to find the cause of substance abuse within the intrapsychic forces of addicted individuals; and (2) the disease concept of substance abuse, which sought to identify some inadequacy in the addicted individual that would account for the disease with which he or she was afflicted. Regardless of its source, however, the addictive personality is a univariate explanation of substance abuse, and in that sense it resembles earlier attempts to

W. MILES COX • Psychology Service (116B), Richard L. Roudebush Veterans Administration Medical Center, and Department of Psychiatry, Indiana University School of Medicine, Indianapolis, Indiana 46202.

attribute the cause of substance abuse to the "demonic" properties of abused substances themselves.

Recent scientific research has made it clear that personality is, in fact, a significant correlate of substance abuse. As one group of researchers has concluded, the empirical findings now offer a "challenge to any attempt to minimize the relevance of personality concepts or to relegate them to a minor role" (Jessor & Jessor, 1977, p. 133). However, instead of being an exclusive cause of substance abuse, personality variables have been shown to interact with a variety of biological, psychological, and environmental variables to determine whether or not a given individual will come to use and abuse addictive substances. Our concerns in this chapter are to identify the personality characteristics that covary with substance abuse and to understand how they are related to its development.

SOME PRELIMINARY CONSIDERATIONS

In order to understand the subject matter of this chapter better and to put it into proper perspective, we need to answer the following preliminary questions.

What Is Personality?

There are two traditions for defining personality: the intrapsychic view and the differential view. According to the intrapsychic view, "personality is the dynamic organization within the individual of those psychophysical systems that determine his characteristic behavior and thought" (Allport, 1937, p. 28). Personality, according to the differential view, is represented by Henry Murray's term *personology*:

> [It is] the branch of psychology which principally concerns itself with the study of human lives and the factors that influence their course, which investigates individual differences and types of personality. (Murray, 1938, p. 4)

Although the two traditions are not mutually exclusive, they do represent quite different research approaches. Historically, the intrapsychic approach has sought to describe the unconscious needs and conflicts of addicted individuals, whereas the differential approach has sought psychometrically to distinguish addicted from nonaddicted individuals. More recently, situationist (Mischel, 1968) and interactionist (Endler & Magnusson, 1976) approaches have emphasized, respectively, the influence of the situation in which behavior occurs and the interaction between traits and situations.

A new formulation of the intrapsychic approach has been offered by Klinger (1977, 1983) who views personality as the branch of psychology that accounts for "how the parts [subsystems] of a person come together to produce total behavioral outcomes" (1983, p. 30). Because current research emphasizes interactions among the biological, psychological, and environmental determinants of substance abuse, Klinger's (1977, 1983) approach seems especially fruitful for understanding how these subsystems come together to determine how a given individual comes to use and abuse addictive substances.

What Is Substance Abuse?

The excessive use of a variety of substances—including alcohol, caffeine, tobacco, illegal psychoactive drugs, and even food—is subsumed under the term *substance abuse*. Common processes, including physical and/or psychological dependence, are thought to underlie these as well as other excessive activities such as compulsive gambling, watching television, work, and exercise (Levison, Gerstein, & Maloff, 1983).

In this chapter, we attempt to integrate the research findings on the personality correlates of the various forms of substance abuse. In doing so, we also discuss the research on substance use when it helps to elucidate the personality correlates of substance abuse. Throughout the chapter, however, we emphasize alcohol and other psychoactive drugs simply because it is in these areas that the research on the personality correlates of substance abuse has been focused.

How Do We Identify the Personality Correlates of Substance Abuse?

The procedure of much of the research on the personality correlates of substance abuse has been simply to administer a standardized personality test to institutionalized substance abusers and to compare the results with those from a sample of nonsubstance abusers. The difficulties with this procedure have been discussed in detail by previous writers (Cox, 1983; Lang, 1983; Nathan & Lansky, 1978; Pihl & Spiers, 1978), and only the three major criticisms will be discussed here.

First, there are problems with the subjects who have been tested. Institutionalized patients are not representative of all persons who abuse substances, and it may be inaccurate to generalize beyond these samples. Testing patients in treatment, moreover, does not allow us to separate the personality antecedents, concomitants, and consequences of substance abuse. However, despite these shortcomings, we should recognize that substance-abusing patients are important to know about in their own right; alternative possibilities for testing substance abusers are quite limited; and testing patients generates hypotheses that can be explored with more rigorous methodology.

Second, there are difficulties with the measurements that have been taken. For example, the personality tests themselves often appear to have been chosen not for their psychometric properties nor their relevance to theories about substance abuse but rather because they were readily available, easily administered and scored, and perhaps already were routinely administered in a treatment program. In addition, no assessments have generally been made of patients' substance abuse. All patients have been assumed to be a homogeneous group of "substance abusers" merely because they were enrolled in a treatment program. Undoubtedly, patients in treatment represent a variety of patterns of substance abuse with a corresponding variety of personality characteristics.

Third, there are difficulties with the procedures for data analysis. That is, personality measures from an entire sample of substance abusers have been averaged together under the assumption that the average scores represent the entire group. The inaccuracies that inhere in this procedure have been graphically illustrated in recent studies using multivariate statistical techniques to establish personality typologies among substance abusers. These studies are discussed later in the chapter.

Findings from studies of institutionalized patients using the procedure described before naturally must be accepted cautiously. Nevertheless, our caveats are not intended to imply that all the research has been of this caliber. On the contrary, there are now many well-controlled experimental studies (using both patients in treatment and analog subjects) and well-designed longitudinal investigations that greatly enhance our understanding of the personality correlates of substance abuse.

We turn now to the research findings to see what has been discovered about the personality correlates of substance abuse from these various research procedures.

RESEARCH FINDINGS

The published literature on the personality correlates of substance abuse is voluminous. The magnitude of the literature is illustrated by the fact that in the PsyINFO data base alone, there are currently more than 1,500 entries related to personality and alcoholism, drug addiction, or other addictive behaviors. Approximately 70% of these entries deal with alcoholism, 20% with drug addiction, and 10% with other addictive behaviors. Even the review articles and chapters of this body of literature have become numerous.

In the present chapter, we organize the literature around three major topics: (1) personality precursors of substance abuse; (2) personality characteristics of substance abusers; and (3) effects of addictive substances on personality. When appropriate, we draw on the conclusions reached by earlier reviewers.

PERSONALITY PRECURSORS OF SUBSTANCE ABUSE

Studies investigating the personality precursors of substance abuse have sought to identify substance abusers' distinguishing personality characteristics before the onset of substance abuse. These research endeavors are particularly helpful in clarifying the etiology of substance abuse and identifying appropriate measures for its prevention.

Cox, Lun, and Loper (1983) recently reviewed the literature on the personality precursors of alcohol abuse and described three basic procedures that have been used to identify prealcoholic personality characteristics: archival, archival longitudinal, and retrospective. Because investigators of prealcoholic personality characteristics have had to rely on whatever data were available to them, all three procedures have methodological limitations. Nevertheless, there is a remarkable consistency in their findings. Across studies that included a variety of subjects and testing procedures, prealcoholics have been consistently described as nonconforming, independent, undercontrolled, and impulsive individuals.

We need to call attention to one of the archival investigations of prealcoholics (Hoffmann, Loper, & Kammeier, 1974; Kammeier, Hoffmann, & Loper, 1973; Loper, Kammeier, & Hoffmann, 1973) because of its relevance to findings that we will discuss later in the chapter. These investigators compared Minnesota Multiphasic Personality Inventory (MMPI) protocols from alcoholics undergoing treatment with protocols that had been taken from (1) the same individuals when they had been college freshmen and (2) the prealcoholics' college classmates. Results indicated that the prealcoholics were significantly higher than their classmates on one validity scale (the Frequency scale), two clinical scales— Scale 4 (Psychopathic Deviate) and Scale 9 (Hypomania)—and on derived scales designed specifically to detect alcoholism. These differences suggested that the prealcoholics were more impulsive, nonconforming, and gregarious than their classmates but not more maladjusted. The treatment protocols, on the other hand, did indicate significant maladjust-

ment and psychological distress. In a similar study, Goldstein and Sappington (1977) compared the MMPI protocols of college freshmen who
later in college became heavy drug users with the freshmen protocols of
a matched control sample. The preusers were significantly higher than
their classmates on Scale 3 (Hysteria), Scale 4 (Psychopathic Deviate), and
Scale 9 (Hypomania) but were significantly lower on the Barron Ego Strength
Scale. From these differences, the authors inferred that the preusers were
more socially skillful, adventurous, impulsive, and less compliant than
the control subjects.

In contrast to the studies reviewed by Cox, Lun, and Loper (1983), a
number of recent studies have used prospective longitudinal designs.
These studies are prospective in the sense that their design was decided
upon in advance of actual data collection, and they are longitudinal
because they have obtained personality assessments on more than one
occasion. However, because subjects were followed for relatively brief
periods, these studies have identified personality precursors of substance
use rather than substance abuse.

Studies by Jessor and Jessor (1977, 1978) found that adolescents were
distinguished before they began to use addictive substances by their
independence, failure to value conventional institutions, critical view of
society, and tolerance for transgression. There is considerable convergence between Jessor and Jessor's findings and those of other investigators who have found that future drug users are independent, rebellious,
and do not value academic accomplishment (Kandel, 1978, 1980; Wingard,
Huba, & Bentler, 1980). On the other hand, although adolescent substance
use has also been associated with low self-esteem and psychological
distress (Pandina & Schuele, 1983), it is unclear whether these difficulties
actually preceded substance use. Some investigators have reported that
anxiety, depression, low self-esteem, and other indications of psychopathology predict future drug use, but others have failed to confirm these
relationships (Jessor, 1979; Orive & Gerard, 1980; Sieber, 1981; Sutker,
1982). The discrepancies might be explained by the finding that negative
personality precursors are associated with users of "hard," illegal drugs
but not users of alcohol (Huba & Bentler, 1982; Wingard, Huba, & Bentler,
1980). In addition, because the extent of adolescent drug use increases
linearly with an increase in the number of risk factors (Bry, McKeon, &
Pandina, 1982), negative personality characteristics might be viewed as
one of many possible precursors.

In summary, many studies have found that persons who in the future
will use and develop difficulties with alcohol and other drugs have personality characteristics that distinguish them from other persons. Future
substance users and abusers show independence, nonconformity, and

impulsivity. On the other hand, there is no uniform evidence that substance users and abusers were maladjusted or psychologically distressed prior to their substance use.

PERSONALITY CHARACTERISTICS OF SUBSTANCE ABUSERS

A variety of unidimensional and multidimensional personality tests have been administered to substance abusers in order to identify their distinctive personality characteristics. Unidimensional tests have identified substance abusers' salient personality characteristics, whereas multidimensional tests have provided comprehensive descriptions of their personalities.

Unidimensional Measures

Affect. The tests that have been used to evaluate the affect of substance abusers include anxiety, depression, and other mood scales and inventories; adjective checklists; and affective scales from multidimensional personality inventories (Freed, 1978).

Results of studies using these tests provide substantial evidence that alcoholics entering treatment have strong feelings of anxiety and depression (Barnes, 1983; Cox, 1979; Lang, 1983). In fact, the degree of self-reported anxiety and depression has been found to be directly related to the degree of alcohol dependence (Skinner & Allen, 1982). Moreover, alcoholics are fairly commonly diagnosed as having anxiety disorders and affective disorders (Bowen, Cipywnyk, D'Arcy, & Keegan, 1984; Powell, Penick, Othmer, Bingham, & Rice, 1982; Schuckit & Morrissey, 1979). Typically, however, alcoholics' anxiety and depression subside considerably as they proceed through treatment and remain abstinent from alcohol.

Findings of studies testing the affect of nonalcoholic problem drinkers, on the other hand, are less clear-cut than those testing alcoholics. Although some investigators have identified negative affect among problem drinkers (Sutker, Brantley, & Allain, 1980), others have been unable to do so (Donovan & Jessor, 1978; MacAndrew, 1982) or have found only weak relationships between negative affect and alcohol problems (Midanik, 1983). It appears, therefore, that the intense negative affect observed among alcoholics is largely a consequence of long-term alcohol abuse.

Negative affect also characterizes drug abusers besides alcohol abusers. For example, both heroin addicts and multiple-drug abusers entering treatment have been commonly described as anxious and/or depressed (Craig, 1979a, 1979b, 1982; Dorus & Senay, 1980; Platt & Labate, 1976), and drug abusers are sometimes diagnosed as having affective disorders

(Rounsaville, Weissman, Kleber, & Wilber, 1982; Steer & Schut, 1979). Nevertheless, like alcoholics, drug abusers show significant improvement in their affect with treatment and abstinence from drugs (Dorus & Senay, 1980).

Negative affect is associated with the abuse of another psychoactive drug—caffeine. Heavy caffeine consumers have been found to be both anxious and depressed (Gilbert, 1976; Gilliland & Bullock, 1984; Greden, 1981; James & Stirling, 1983; Sawyer, Julia, & Turin, 1982). In severe cases, a syndrome termed *caffeinism* that is marked primarily by affective and psychosomatic disturbances (but which sometimes includes more serious psychological disturbances) is often indistinguishable from anxiety neurosis. Nevertheless, these symptoms abate with abstinence from caffeine.

In summary, alcoholics, heroin addicts, multiple-drug abusers, and heavy users of caffeine are all characterized by anxiety and depression. In each case, however, the drug abusers's negative affect diminishes with abstinence from the drug.

Self-Esteem. Instruments that have been used to test the self-esteem of substance abusers include adjective checklists, Q-sorts, and self-concept scales and inventories. One commonly used instrument is the Tennessee Self-Concept Scale, which yields scores on five subscales: Physical Self, Moral-Ethical Self, Personal Self, Family Self, and Social Self.

Feelings of low self-esteem have been very consistently reported among alcoholics (Cox, 1979). Alcoholics evaluate themselves unfavorably and often show wide discrepancies between their perceived self and ideal self. One study found, paradoxically, that although alcoholics describe themselves as having less subjective distress when intoxicated than when sober, they perceive themselves to be more resentful, selfish, irresponsible, and to have more negative self-regard while intoxicated (Mac-Andrew, 1979a). Because the later characteristics are inconsistent with alcoholics' ideal self, it appears that drinking might provide "time-out" for the expression of alcoholics' negative personality characteristics that they do not value (MacAndrew & Edgerton, 1969). The feelings of low self-esteem among alcoholics are often recalcitrant (Cooper, 1983; O'-Leary, Chaney, & Hudgins, 1978), sometimes persisting even when alcoholics maintain sobriety (Wiseman, 1981). Nevertheless, promising, new techniques have been developed for helping alcoholics to achieve feelings of self-confidence and self-efficacy (Goldstein & Marlatt, in press).

Attention has been given to gender differences in self-esteem among alcoholics as well as to relationships among self-esteem and various sexual problems. Although both male and female alcoholics suffer from low self-esteem, these feelings are especially pronounced among female alcoholics (Benson & Wilsnack, 1983). A possible explanation for this gender difference is that the defensive style of male alcoholics enables them to neutralize their underlying feelings of low self-esteem (Heilbrun & Schwartz, 1980; Tarbox, 1979). Nevertheless, among both male and female alcoholics, various sexual problems (including those related to sexual roles, sexual identity, and sexual orientation) are prevalent, and it seems likely that reciprocal interactions occur among alcohol, self-esteem, and sexual problems, such that each type of problem exacerbates the other (Benson & Wilsnack, 1983; Gomberg, in press; Wilsnack, 1984).

Although feelings of low self-esteem have also been reported among heroin addicts and other drug abusers, these feelings appear to be less pronounced and less prevalent among these substance abusers than among alcoholics. In fact, addicts characteristically respond in a defensive rather than a self-effacing manner (Craig, 1982; Pihl & Spiers, 1978; Platt & Labate, 1976). However, one study that directly compared the self-concept of alcoholics and heroin addicts (Carroll, Klein, & Santo, 1978) found that alcoholics were more passive and compliant and had greater emotional distress than addicts, but otherwise the self-concepts of alcoholics and addicts were similar.

Finally, as we saw in the section on personality precursors, low self-esteem does not necessarily occur prior to substance abuse. Nevertheless, among adolescents, low self-esteem has been associated with the heavy use of both alcohol and other drugs (Beckman & Bardsley, 1981; Pandina & Schuele, 1983), suggesting that low self-esteem is an early consequence of substance abuse.

To recapitulate, feelings of low self-esteem are common among substance abusers generally, but they are especially prevalent among alcoholics and especially acute among female alcoholics. Although low self-esteem appears in large measure to be a consequence of the substance abuser's involvement with drugs, these feelings often become ingrained and do not readily subside when substance use is discontinued.

Field Dependence/Independence.   Witkin and his associates (Witkin, Lewis, Hertzman, Machover, Meissner, & Wapner, 1954) proposed that people's perceptual style reflects their core personality structure. To study perception–personality relationships, this research group used three laboratory tests (the Body-Adjustment Test, Embedded-Figures Test, and Rod-and-Frame Test) from which they identified field dependence/independence as a basic perceptual dimension. Although field-dependent persons do not evince a pervasive dependence in their psychological functioning as was originally believed, field-dependent and field-independent people do function differently in their interpersonal behaviors (Witkin & Goodenough, 1977).

Witkin, Karp, and Goodenough (1959) found that alcoholics were more field dependent than matched controls, and they suggested that field dependence/independence is a stable individual difference and that people who are field dependent are predisposed to become alcoholic or to develop some other disorder related to overdependence. Subsequent research has clearly demonstrated that alcoholics are, in fact, field dependent and often extremely so (Goldstein, 1976; Sugerman & Schneider, 1976); however, it is unclear whether field dependence is an antecedent, concomitant, or consequence of alcoholism. If field dependence were affected by the ingestion of alcohol or related to the length of the alcoholic's drinking history or sobriety, this evidence would suggest that field dependence among alcoholics is a consequence of alcoholism. However, such tests of the stability of field dependence have yielded conflicting results (Danahy & Kahn, 1981; Goldstein, 1976; Sugerman & Schneider, 1976). Because field dependence is associated with brain-damaged patients as well as alcoholics, it is possible that alcoholics' field dependence merely reflects brain damage caused by alcohol. However, neuropsychological testing of alcoholics has shown that they do not show global deficits in mental functioning like those of brain-damaged individuals. Instead, they show very specific cognitive deficits that appear to be related to their lack of foresight and inability to realize the consequences of their actions (Goldstein, 1976).

Substance abusers other than alcoholics have also been found to be field dependent. They include obese persons (McArthur & Burstein, 1975) and heroin abusers (Arnon, Kleinman, & Kissin, 1974; Ross, 1979). On the other hand, sedative-hypnotic abusers have not differed from matched control subjects (Holm, Bergman, & Borg, 1980), and heavy marijuana smokers have shown greater field independence and a generally higher level of cognitive functioning than matched controls (Weckowicz, Collier, & Spreng, 1977; Weckowicz & Janssen, 1973).

In conclusion, it has become clearly established that alcoholics are field dependent. Although exceptions occur, there are indications that other substance abusers are field dependent as well. Although the meaning of substance abusers' field dependence is at present equivocal, it undoubtedly will become clear in the context of recent neuropsychological theory that attempts to integrate cognitive and personality variables related to substance abuse (Tarter & Alterman, in press).

Locus of Control.   It seems intuitive that substance abusers would perceive themselves as being out of control, not only regarding their substance use but in other aspects of their lives as well. Hence, the locus of control (LOC) of substance abusers has been a popular topic to study. Six different LOC scales have been used in this research (see Rohsenow,

1983a), but Rotter's Internal-External (I-E) Scale has been used most frequently. Despite its widespread use, however, the construct validity of the I-E Scale has been questioned (de Blij & Hinrichsen, 1980). On the I-E Scale, persons scoring in the external direction perceive that events happening to them result from forces external to themselves, such as fate, chance, or powerful others, whereas persons scoring in the internal direction perceive themselves to be in control of events in their lives.

Studies of the LOC of alcoholics have given inconsistent results, with alcoholics sometimes described as more internally controlled than nonalcoholics and sometimes more externally controlled. However, these inconsistencies can be accounted for by the methodological difficulties that abound in these studies. Virtually all studies that have utilized appropriate comparison groups have found, as originally expected, that alcoholics are more external in their perception of control than are nonalcoholics (Rohsenow, 1983a). Moreover, among nonalcoholics, degree of external control has been found to be directly related to the quantity and frequency of alcohol consumption (Barnes, 1983; Naditch, 1975a; Rohsenow, 1983a). However, despite the consistent tendency for increased drinking to be associated with increased external control, both alcoholics and social drinkers vary systematically in their perception of control as a function of a variety of demographic variables (Cox & Baker, 1982a, 1982b; Rose, Powell, & Penick, 1978).

More important than knowing whether the average alcoholic is internally or externally controlled is to consider how alcoholics' LOC is related to their psychological adjustment and their treatment for alcohol problems. With regard to psychological adjustment, alcoholics who are more externally controlled have been found to have more psychological distress and psychopathology and more severe drinking problems than alcoholics who are more internally controlled (Rohsenow & O'Leary, 1978; Rohsenow, 1983a). Similar relationships between maladjustment and externality have also been found for nonalcoholics (Lefcourt, 1982). With regard to treatment, although internally controlled alcoholics are more successfully treated for their alcohol problems, they show greater recidivism from treatment and are responded to less favorably by treatment personnel than externally controlled alcoholics (Rohsenow, 1983a). These differences between internally controlled and externally controlled alcoholics have important implications for matching alcoholics with the most appropriate treatment modalities (Abbott, 1984; Rohsenow, 1983a).

The LOC studies with heroin addicts have shown results contrary to prediction. In fact, some studies suggest that heroin addicts actually become more internally controlled as their length of involvement with heroin increases, and explanations have been offered to account for this paradoxical outcome (Craig, 1982; Platt & Labate, 1976; Plumb, D'Amanda, & Taintor, 1975). Nevertheless, results have varied markedly, depending on the demographic characteristics of the sample of heroin addicts studied and those of the nonaddicted comparison groups (Craig, 1979a), indicating that heroin addicts, like alcoholics, actually represent a variety of LOC orientations.

Users of other psychoactive drugs (amphetamines, multiple drugs) have sometimes shown an external LOC (Makedonsky, 1977; Pearlstein, 1980) but sometimes have not differed from comparison groups (Hall, 1978; Krakowiak & Cross, 1979). Cigarette smokers (Schwebel & Kaemmerer, 1977), gamblers (Devinney, 1978; Lester, 1980; Zenker & Wolfgang, 1982), and adults with eating disorders (Allerdissen, Florin, & Rost, 1981; Dunn & Ondercin, 1981) appear to be externally controlled, although obese and nonobese children appear not to differ (Geller, Keane, & Scheirer, 1981). Finally, among drug abusers (Snowden, 1978), cigarette smokers (Mlott & Mlott, 1975; Rosenbaum & Argon, 1979), and obese persons (Chavez & Michaels, 1980; Kincey, 1981; Paine, O'Neil, Malcolm, Sexauer, & Currey, 1980; Schreiber, Schauble, Epting, & Skovholt, 1979), internally controlled substance abusers generally respond better to treatment than externally controlled substance abusers.

In summary, the literature on the LOC of substance abusers has not given a consistent pattern of results. The inconsistencies are due both to methodological considerations and to the fact that the LOC of substance abusers differs according to their demographic characteristics and the substance that they abuse. Despite these variations, substance abusers on the whole appear to be more external than internal in their LOC.

Stimulus Intensity Modulation. In her theory about peoples' responses to pain and other stimulation, Petrie (1967) described three types of persons who differ according to how they modulate the intensity of the stimulus. *Augmenters* are highly sensitive to stimulation; *reducers* are low in sensitivity; and *moderates* are intermediate. The three types can be identified with the Kinesthetic Aftereffect Task, in which blindfolded subjects estimate the size of stimulus blocks that they have examined with their fingers. At the extremes, augmenters overestimate size, whereas reducers underestimate size. Physiological and paper-and-pencil measures for identifying augmenters, reducers, and moderates have been developed as well (Barnes, 1976).

The possible relevance of stimulus intensity modulation for alcoholism became apparent when Petrie (1967) discovered that alcohol affects augmenters and reducers differently. Because augmenters become less sensitive after they have ingested alcohol and reducers are unaffected by alcohol, Petrie (1967) reasoned that alcoholics might be augmenters who drink alcohol for its stimulus-modulating effect. In fact, alcoholics have been found to be augmenters (Barnes, 1983; Petrie, 1967), and they also tend to use sensitizing defenses more than nonalcoholics (Donovan, Rohsenow, Schau, & O'Leary, 1977). Moreover, laboratory studies have found that alcohol acts as an analgesic for alcoholics but not nonalcoholics and that college students who receive a stimulus-modulating effect from alcohol customarily drink alcohol for its medicating effect (Brown & Cutter, 1977). Thus, the evidence consistently suggests that augmenters experience a different effect from alcohol and are more likely to encounter difficulties with their alcohol consumption than other individuals.

Little information is available on the stimulus intensity modulation of substance abusers other than alcoholics. However, there is some evidence (Barnes & Fishlinsky, 1976; Petrie, 1967) that cigarette smokers are reducers and nonsmokers are augmenters (perhaps because augmenters find the stimulation from cigarette smoking aversive). One study (Kohn, Barnes, Fishlinsky, Segal, & Hoffmann, 1979) found that heroin addicts did not differ from matched controls.

In conclusion, the finding that augmenters derive a different reinforcing effect from alcohol and develop greater problems with their alcohol consumption than reducers is an intriguing discovery, and it is surprising that the stimulus intensity modulation of substance abusers has not been studied more thoroughly. However, recent research is again investigating the different physiological responses to alcohol of persons who are and are not prone to develop alcohol problems (Sher & Levenson, 1982).

Sensation Seeking. Sensation seeking is defined as "the need for varied, novel, and complex sensations and experiences and the willingness to take physical and social risks for the sake of such experience" (Zuckerman, 1979, p. 10). This need has usually been measured with Zuckerman's Sensation Seeking Scale, the latest revision of which (SSS V, Zuckerman, 1979) is a 40-item, forced-choice questionnaire that yields a score for Total Sensation Seeking as well as scores on four subscales: Thrill and Adventure Seeking, Experience Seeking, Disinhibition, and Boredom Susceptibility.

Zuckerman originally proposed that persons high in sensation seeking feel and function best at a high level of cortical arousal and that they therefore are motivated to engage in activities that increase their arousal. Taking stimulant drugs is one arousing activity in which high sensation seekers were expected to engage. However, contrary to expectation, minimal evidence has accrued to indicate that high-sensation seekers have a predilection for stimulant drugs (Zuckerman, 1979), or that stimulant drugs have different effects on persons high and low in sensation seeking (Carrol, Zuckerman, & Vogel, 1982).

Even though sensation seeking does not influence one's choice of psychoactive drugs (stimulants, depressants, or hallucinogens), persons high in sensation seeking do engage in more frequent and more varied drug use than persons low in sensation seeking. That sensation seeking is related to the amount and variety of drug use has been demonstrated among both young drug users (Carrol, Zuckerman, & Vogel, 1982; Galizio, Rosenthal, & Stein 1983; Kohn, Barnes, & Hoffman, 1979; Segal, Huba, & Singer, 1980) and drug abusers in treatment (Galizio & Stein, 1983; Kilpatrick, Sutker, Roitzsch, & Miller, 1976; Sutker, Archer, & Allain, 1978). Moreover, sensation seeking is directly related to cigarette smoking, preference for stimulating foods, and the amount of alcohol consumed in experimental drinking situations (Schwarz, Burkhart, & Green, 1982; Sutker, Malatesta, Allain, & Randall, 1981; Zuckerman, 1979).

In view of the preceding findings, Zuckerman has rejected the optimal level of arousal view of sensation seeking. He has relegated arousal to a secondary role and now views sensation seeking as the organism's general sensitivity to reinforcement that can be accounted for by the catecholamines and their enzymes (Zuckerman, 1983; Zuckerman, Buchsbaum, & Murphy, 1980).

Multidimensional Measures

Fantasy Processes.   Historically, the fantasies of substance abusers have been studied in order to evaluate their unconscious motivations for abusing addictive substances. A variety of projective tests have been used for this purpose (Cox, 1979; Hartung & Skorka, 1980; Neuringer & Clopton, 1976; Ondercin, 1984; Pihl & Spiers, 1978), but the most commonly used tests have been the Rorschach Inkblot Test and the Thematic Apperception Test (TAT).

At one time, the Rorschach Inkblot Test was widely employed by psychoanalytic therapists to diagnose alcoholics and other substance abusers and to compare them with nonsubstance abusers. Various Rorschach signs were used to evaluate the basic psychoanalytic assumptions that substance abusers are characterized by oral fixation, "latent homosexuality," dependency conflicts, and self-destructive tendencies (Barnes, 1983; Cox, 1979; Lang, 1983). Although distinctive Rorschach responses by abusers of a variety of different substances have been reported (Craig, 1979a, 1982; Gordon, 1980; Pihl & Spiers, 1978; Strober & Goldenberg, 1981), the evidence as a whole is equivocal and cannot be regarded as supporting psychoanalytic assumptions (Freed, 1976). Moreover, Rorschach studies of substance abusers have been criticized methodologi-cally because blind procedures have not been used for administering and scoring the test and comparison groups have often been inappro-priate or have not been used at all. Although the reliability and validity of the Rorschach itself have been questioned by some writers (Phares, 1979), others view it as having respectable reliability and validity (Exner, 1974).

The reliability and validity of the TAT have also been questioned (Phares, 1979). Nevertheless, research with the TAT has led to important insights regarding men's (McClelland, Davis, Kalin, & Wanner, 1972) and women's (Wilsnack, 1976) motivations for using and abusing alcohol and other substances, and conclusions from the TAT research have been substantiated with other personality tests (Carney, 1981; Nell & Strümpfer 1978; Scoufis & Walker, 1982). This research indicates that when men drink heavily they entertain fantasies about gaining power over other people. Hence, men who have strong, unmet needs to be powerful are more likely than others to drink heavily and develop problems with al-cohol. On the other hand, when women drink, they entertain fantasies about caring for and nurturing other people, and women who have strong, unmet needs to feel womanly are more likely than others to drink heavily and develop problems with alcohol. In short, both men and women who feel inadequate about their sex roles are likely to use alcohol in order to acquire the feelings that are consistent with society's traditional sex-role expectations (Benson & Wilsnack, 1983).

Research using projective tests with substance abusers has waned considerably in recent years. However, alternative procedures for as-sessing the fantasy processes of substance users and abusers are being explored. For example, using the Thought Sampling Questionnaire with college students, Klinger and Cox (1984a) studied relationships among impulses to drink alcohol, frustration of goals, and affective variables but found that, on the whole, formal properties of thought flow did not vary with impulses to drink, feelings of progress toward goals, anxiety, or depression. From their use of the Imaginal Processes Inventory with college students, Segal, Huba, and Singer (1980) concluded that the best single predictor of the initiation of drug use is the tendency to seek varied and unusual experiences.

Eysenck and Eysenck's Personality Inventories. According to Eysenck and Eysenck (1976; Eysenck, 1981), personality can be depicted along three dimensions: extraversion/introversion (E), neuroticism/stability (N), and psychoticism (P). Examples of the personality characteristics that the three respective dimensions reflect are sociability, impulsiveness, carefreeness, and activity (E); worry, tenseness, anxiety, and emotionality

(N); and emotional coldness, hostility, egocentricity, and lack of superego control (P). These personality characteristics are thought to be biologically mediated (Eysenck, 1981; Zuckerman, 1983).

Several personality inventories have been developed by Eysenck and Eysenck to measure E, N, and P. They include the Eysenck Personality Inventory (EPI) that yields scores on E and N and the Eysenck Personality Questionnaire (EPQ) that yields scores on E, N, and P. The E scale from the EPI appears to have both impulsivity and sociability components, whereas the E Scale from the EPQ appears to be a pure measure of sociability (Rocklin & Revelle, 1981).

Research with alcoholics using the EPI has consistently found them to score higher than nonalcoholics on N, but they usually have not differed on E (Barnes, 1983; Cox, 1979; Eysenck & Eysenck, 1976; Lang, 1983). Similar results have been obtained with the EPQ, and, in addition, alcoholics have shown elevations on P (Rankin, Stockwell, & Hodgson, 1982). Likewise, drug abusers (narcotic and multiple-drug abusers) have consistently shown elevations on both N and P but have shown levels comparable to or lower than control groups on E (Eysenck & Eysenck, 1976; Gossop, 1978; Kilpatrick, Sutker, Roitzsch, & Miller, 1976). Even young drug users have scored higher than nonusers on N and P (Wells & Stacey, 1976). It appears that abusers' neuroticism (their emotional instability) is a consequence of their heavy alcohol consumption, whereas their psychoticism (lack of impulse control) reflects enduring personality characteristics (Rankin, Stockwell, & Hodgson, 1982).

Studies using the EPI to compare cigarette smokers and nonsmokers have frequently found that smokers are more extraverted than nonsmokers and are sometimes more neurotic (Eysenck, 1980, 1982). The relationship betweeen smoking and extraversion has been found among adolescents (Jamison, 1979), and a longitudinal study (Cherry & Kiernan, 1978) found that adolescents who in the future will smoke are more extraverted and neurotic than those who will not. On the other hand, several recent studies using the EPQ and other instruments suggest that cigarette smoking may be more closely associated with P than with E (McManus & Weeks, 1982; Spielberger & Jacobs, 1982; Stanaway & Watson, 1981).

In summary, both alcoholics and other drug abusers have shown elevations on the N and P Scales of Eysenck and Eysenck's personality inventories, whereas smokers have shown elevations on the E and P Scales. Whereas the elevations on E and P appear to reflect enduring personality characteristics, the elevation on N appears to reflect emotionality that is a consequence of substance abuse.

Minnesota Multiphasic Personality Inventory.   The Minesota Multi-phasic Personality Inventory (MMPI) is the multidimensional personality inventory that has been used most frequently to identify the personality correlates of substance abuse. In fact, a substantial portion of all research studies utilizing the MMPI has dealt with substance abuse (Butcher & Tellegen, 1978). In these studies, researchers have observed substance abusers' scores on the MMPI standard scales and various derived scales, especially those derived scales designed specifically to identify alcoholics and other drug abusers. In addition, the MMPI has been used to develop typologies of substance abusers' personalities.

CLINICAL SCALES AND PROFILES.   Among alcoholics, a variety of MMPI profile configurations has been observed. In spite of the variety, however, it is quite common for alcoholics to be elevated on Scale 4 (Psychopathic Deviate) and to show secondary elevations on Scale 2 (Depression) and Scale 7 (Psychasthenia) (Clopton, 1978; Cox, 1979; Owen & Butcher, 1979). The elevation on Scale 4 is generally taken to indicate disregard for social customs, impulsivity and low tolerance for frustration, inability to profit from experience, and failure to form meaningful personal relationships (Dahlstrom, Welsh, & Dahlstrom, 1972). The elevations on both Scales 2 and 7, on the other hand, indicate subjective distress. In particular, Scale 2 reflects pessimism and dispair, lack of psychic energy, and inability to enjoy life, whereas Scale 7 reflects worry, indecisiveness, and obsessive ruminations (Dahlstrom *et al.*, 1972). The 4-2-7 profile has been observed among alcoholics who differ widely in demographic characteristics (Owen & Butcher, 1979; Patterson, Charles, Woodward, Roberts, & Penk, 1981; Uecker, Boutilier, & Richardson, 1980).

Alcoholics' elevations on Scales 2 and 7 seem to result from their abuse of alcohol. That is, elevations on these scales have not been observed among prealcoholics (Loper, Kammeier, & Hoffmann, 1973), and they often are significantly reduced when alcoholics become abstinent during treatment (Edwards, Bucky, & Schuckit, 1977; Ornstein, 1981; Pettinati, Sugerman, & Maurer, 1982; Sutker & Archer, 1979). On the other hand, the elevation on Scale 4 is apparent among prealcoholics (Loper *et al.*, 1973) and does not attenuate as a result of treatment (Cox, 1979). Despite the frequency and magnitude of alcoholics' elevation on Scale 4, MacAndrew (1983) has found that elimination of the three items from this scale that pertain directly to alcohol abuse eliminates the statistically significant difference between alcoholics and nonalcoholics. MacAndrew (1983), therefore, has expressed pessimism about the use of the MMPI standard scales to distinguish alcoholics from nonalcoholics.

The MMPI profiles of narcotic addicts are similar to those of alcoholics (Craig, 1979b, 1982; Craig & Baker, 1982; Holland, 1977; Sutker & Archer, 1979; Sutker, Archer, Brantley, & Kilpatrick, 1979). That is, although a variety of profile configurations has been observed among heroin addicts, the most prominent feature of their profiles, like that of alcoholics, is elevation on Scale 4. Moreover, heroin addicts often show a secondary elevation on Scale 2, although this elevation is not so pronounced as it is among alcoholics. On the other hand, unlike alcoholics, heroin addicts typically are elevated on Scale 9; in fact, the 4-9 profile is the most common profile among heroin addicts. Scale 9 reflects overactivity, emotional excitement, and sociability (Dahlstrom et al., 1972). Addicts' elevation on neither Scale 4 nor Scale 9 changes as a consequence of treatment, but their elevation on Scale 2 does subside considerably.

Considerable attention has been given to identifying MMPI differences among heroin addicts from various ethnic goups and between those who volunteer and do not volunteer for treatment. Regarding ethnicity, white heroin addicts have consistently shown greater psychopathology on the MMPI than have black or Hispanic addicts (Penk, Robinowitz, Kidd, & Nisle, 1979; Penk, Robinowitz, Roberts, Dolan, & Atkins, 1981; Penk, Robinowitz, Woodward, & Hess, 1980; Sutker, Archer, & Allain, 1980). Regarding volunteerism, various claims and counterclaims have been made concerning the possiblity that MMPI differences between addicts and nonaddicts are magnified when addicts volunteering for treatment are tested (Penk & Robinowitz, 1981; Sutker & Allain, 1981).

We can compare the MMPI profiles of alcoholics and narcotic addicts with those of a variety of other substance abusers. They include marijuana smokers (Bachman & Jones, 1979), gamblers (Graham, 1978; Lowenfeld, 1979), and persons with eating disorders (Hutzler, Keen, Molinari, & Carey, 1981; Leon, Carroll, Chernyk, & Finn, in press; Leon, Eckert, Teed, & Buchwald, 1979; Wampler, Lauer, Lantz, Wampler, Evens, & Madura, 1980). Each of these categories of substance abusers (like alcoholics and heroin addicts) shows a primary elevation on Scale 4 (which is not amenable to treatment) and often shows a secondary elevation on Scale 2 (which does attenuate considerably during the course of treatment). Contrariwise, abusers of amphetamines, barbiturates, LSD, nonopiate sedative hypnotics, and multiple-drug abusers typically have markedly disturbed MMPI profiles (Lachar, Gdowski, & Keegan, 1979; Penk, Fudge, Robinowitz, & Neman, 1979; Penk, Woodward, Robinowitz, & Parr, 1980; Wesson, Carlin, Adams, & Beschner, 1978). Although they are elevated on Scales 4 and 2, like other substance abusers, these drug abusers also frequently have a pronounced elevation on Scale 8 (Schizophrenia), reflecting their disordered thought processes and unusual perceptions (Dahlstrom et al., 1972).

There is some indication that the severe psychopathology is drug induced (McLellan, Woody, & O'Brien, 1979), and it is often highly recalcitrant (Sutker & Archer, 1979).

To summarize, a wide variety of substance abusers show a primary elevation of Scale 4 of the MMPI. The elevation on Scale 4 seems to reflect the core of substance abusers' personality, having been observed before the onset of substance abuse and not changing with treatment. A variety of substance abusers also show secondary elevations on Scales 2 and 7, but the elevations on these scales do fluctuate, suggesting that they represent personality reactions to substance abuse. Finally, the elevations on Scales 8 and 9 shown by abusers of some substances change little with treatment.

ADDICTION SCALES. Because none of the MMPI standard scales was developed with the intention of measuring the personality characteristics of substance abusers, MMPI-derived scales have been constructed for that specific purpose (Apfeldorf, 1978; Cox, 1979; Craig, 1982; Miller, 1976; Schmolck, 1983). In fact, at least 20 addiction scales have been derived by selecting those items from the full MMPI to which substance abusers and nonsubstance abusers respond differently.

By far, the MacAndrew Alcoholism Scale (MAC, MacAndrew, 1983) is the most thoroughly researched addiction scale, and it is the scale that is now widely used in clinical settings. The MAC Scale consists of 49 MMPI items that originally were found to discriminate male alcoholic outpatients from male nonalcoholic psychiatric outpatients. However, the scale has been cross-validated many times on diverse samples of alcoholics and consistently identifies alcoholics approximatley 85% of the time (MacAndrew, 1981a). Factor analyses suggest that alcoholics who score high on the scale are bold, aggressive, and pleasure-seeking individuals (MacAndrew, 1981a).

Recently, MacAndrew (1979b, 1980) has identified a set of 18 MMPI items that differentiates "true positive" alcoholics who score high on the MAC Scale from "false negative" alcoholics who score low on the MAC Scale. Inspection of these items suggests that the latter alcoholics are fearful, reticient individuals who are constricted in their interests. In light of this finding, MacAndrew (1983) has proposed that there are two fundamentally different personality types among alcoholics. Primary alcoholics who score high on the MAC Scale are reward seekers who seem to drink actively and impulsively; secondary alcoholics who score low on the MAC scale are punishment avoiders who seem to drink alcohol in an attempt to cope with their emotional discomfort. Both types experience considerable emotionality and depression (MacAndrew, 1981b), and MacAndrew (1979b, 1980) likens the two respective types to unstable extraverts and unstable introverts as identified by Eysenck and Eysenck's typology.

That the MAC Scale measures enduring personality characteristics that probably predate alcoholism is suggested by elevations on the scale among prealcoholics (Hoffmann et al., 1974), persons at risk for developing alcohol problems (Saunders & Schuckit, 1981), and young alcohol abusers (MacAndrew, 1979c). Furthermore, a variety of other substance abusers— including heroin addicts and multiple-drug abusers (Lachar, Berman, Grisell, & Schooff, 1976) and male smokers (Leon, Kolotkin, & Korgeski, 1979; Willis, Wehler, & Rush, 1979)—have scores on the MAC Scale similar to those of alcoholics, suggesting that the scale measures a general proneness for addictive behaviors. In fact, the MAC Scale has been found to identify heroin addicts even more accurately than the Heroin Addiction Scale (Cavior, Kurtzberg, & Lipton, 1967) that was designed specifically to do so (Lachar, Berman, Grisell, & Schooff, 1979).

Finally, despite the success and widespread use of the MAC Scale, reservations about its use have been expressed (Graham & Schwartz, 1981; Merenda & Sparadeo, 1981; Schmolck, 1983), and sporadic use of other addiction scales continues (Hays & Stacy, 1983; Holmes, Dungan, & McLaughlin, 1982; Zager & Megargee, 1981).

PERSONALITY SUBTYPES. Recognizing the drawbacks of depicting the personality characteristics of the average substance abuser, researchers have used the MMPI and multivariate classification techniques to identify constellations of personality characteristics among substance abusers (Cox, 1979; Jackson, 1983; Morey & Blashfield, 1981; Nerviano & Gross, 1983; Skinner, 1982).

Alcoholic personality subtypes identified with the MMPI were recently summarized by Nerviano and Gross (1983) who gave the subtypes the following descriptive labels: chronic severe distress, passive-aggressive sociopath, antisocial sociopath, reactive-acute depression, severely neurotic psychophysiological, mixed character-dysphoria, and paranoid alienated. The variety of these subtypes illustrates the heterogeneity of personality characteristics among alcoholics. Nevertheless, two of the seven subtypes have been repeatedly replicated (Morey & Blashfield, 1981; Skinner, 1982): (1) alcoholics with a 2-7-8 profile who show chronic severe distress and (2) alcoholics with a 4-2-3 profile who are described as passive-aggressive sociopaths. The two subtypes exhibit distinctly different drinking styles as well as different problems associated with their drinking (Morey & Blashfield, 1981; Skinner, 1982). Distressed, neurotic alcoholics are heavier drinkers and show greater drinking-related impairment; their excessive drinking appears to be their attempt to cope with distress. Sociopathic alcoholics display longer term—yet more moderate—drinking and have fewer detrimental consequences; their excessive drinking appears primarily to reflect their lack of impulsive control.

There have been few studies using the MMPI to identify personality subtypes among substance abusers other than alcoholics (Skinner, 1982). Nevertheless, the subtypes that have been identified closely resemble those found among alcoholics. For example, Berzins, Ross, English, and Haley (1974) identified two subtypes of heroin addicts. The first subtype had a 2-4-8 profile and was characterized by high levels of subjective distress, nonconformity, and confused thinking. Patients of this subtype were thought to use heroin to control their distressed feelings. The second subtype had a single peak on Scale 4 and was thought to use heroin for hedonistic pursuits and to reduce feelings of hostility and resentment. Carlin and Strauss (1977) have identified similar personality subtypes among multiple-drug abusers.

The mere identification of personality subtypes among substance abusers has little immediate significance. Instead, the ultimate fruitfulness of this research will come from efforts to match personality subtypes with the most appropriate treatment and prevention strategies. Preliminary attempts to accomplish this end have already been undertaken (Conley, 1981; Conley & Prioleau, 1983; Finney & Moos, 1979; O'Leary, Donovan, Chaney, & O'Leary, 1980).

Other Personality Inventories. Several additional personality inventories have been used to study the personality characteristics of various substance abusers. For example, the California Psychological Inventory has been administered to drug abusers (Laufer, Johnson, & Hogan, 1981), persons with eating disorders (Strober, 1980), and alcoholics (Kurtines, Ball, & Wood, 1978). The Sixteen Personality-Factor Questionnaire has been used to study cigarette smokers (Malcolm & Shephard, 1978) and alcoholics (Hart, 1979) and to compare alcohol and other drug abusers (Ciotola & Peterson, 1976). The Personality Research Form has also been used to compare alcohol and other drug users and abusers (Carroll, Malloy, Roscioli, & Godard, 1981; Huba, Segal, & Singer, 1977). Finally, the Edwards Personal Preference Schedule has been used to study cigarette smokers (Simon & Primavera, 1976) and caffeine users (Primavera, Simon, & Camisa, 1975). Studies using these personality inventories have, in general, presented isolated findings, or their findings have served to amplify those obtained with other personality tests. For this reason, we are unable to draw salient conclusions about substance abusers' personality characteristics from studies using these inventories.

On the other hand, substantial progress has been made in the identification of personality subtypes among substance abusers with the use of the Differential Personality Inventory, Personality Research Form, and Sixteen Personality-Factor Questionnaire (Jackson, 1983; Nerviano & Gross, 1983; Skinner, 1982). The subtypes identified with these personality inventories have been related to substance abusers' demographic characteristics, cognitive functioning, drinking practices, and responsiveness to treatment (Jackson, 1983; Zivich, 1981). Some of the subtypes closely resemble those found with the MMPI. Nevertheless, the research identifying substance abusers' personality subtypes with these personality inventories as well as with the MMPI is still largely in a descriptive stage (Skinner, 1982).

EFFECTS OF ADDICTIVE SUBSTANCES ON PERSONALITY CHARACTERISTICS

In order to understand why people use and abuse addictive substances, it is important to know the immediate and long-range effects of these substances on personality characteristics, and much attention has recently been given to identifying these effects. However, the research has focused almost entirely on alcohol and caffeine, with only sporadic studies with other psychoactive drugs having appeared (see Pliner & Cappell, 1974).

In the experimental research on alcohol, alcohol has been administered to both alcoholics and social drinkers—both ad libitum and in predetermined dosages—during single experimental sessions (acute administration) and for prolonged drinking periods that last as long as several weeks (chronic administration). In these studies, changes in subjects' affect resulting from their consumption of alcohol have often been the focus of attention. Although the research has shown that drinkers commonly expect that alcohol will change their affect in positive ways (Beckman, 1980; Brown, Goldman, Inn, & Anderson, 1980; Christiansen, Goldman, & Inn, 1982; Rohsenow, 1983b; Southwick, Steele, & Marlatt, 1981), the actual consequences of drinking can be quite different. Thus, in acute administration studies, alcohol has been found to enhance positive affect as well as to palliate or intensify negative affect (Adesso, 1980; Keane & Lisman, 1980; Langenbucher & Nathan, 1983; Pihl & Smith, 1983; Sutker, Tabakoff, Goist, & Randall, 1983). Whether the effects are positive or negative, however, varies systematically with such factors as the dosage of alcohol and the setting in which it is consumed, whether the alcohol is drunk by a male or a female, and whether the blood–alcohol level is ascending or descending when affect is measured (Adesso, 1980; Gaines, 1979; Vuchinich & Tucker, 1980). In chronic administration studies, although alcohol may produce a brief, initial period of euphoria, negative affect commonly mounts as drinking continues, especially among alcoholics (Adesso, 1980).

Of paramount importance for the present discussion is the relationship between drinkers' affective responses to alcohol and their enduring personality characteristics. In this regard, one of the most intriguing findings has been that social drinkers who score high on the MAC Alcoholism Scale (and who thus presumably are at risk for developing problems with alcohol) experience greater stress reduction from consuming alcohol than do subjects who score low on the MAC Scale (Sher & Levenson, 1982). Moreover, persons already classed as problem drinkers show greater subjective anxiety reduction from drinking alcohol than nonproblem drinkers (Eddy, 1979). These persons for whom the tension-reduction consequence of alcohol consumption is salient also appear to differ from others in their actual drinking practices. Thus, college males with traditional masculine interests, nonconformist tendencies, and low social anxiety (i.e., those resembling high scorers on the MAC Scale) have been found to drink at significantly higher rates than college males not exhibiting these characteristics (Rohsenow, 1982a). The evidence is mixed, however, with regard to whether fluctuations in drinkers' dysphoric moods are accompanied by fluctuations in their drinking rates (Aneshensel & Huba, 1983; Rohsenow, 1982a). Likewise, although some laboratory studies have found that when drinkers are placed in stressful situations they increase their alcohol consumption, other studies have not observed this relationship (Gabel, Noel, Keane, & Lisman, 1980; Noel & Lisman, 1980; Pihl & Smith, 1983; Steele, Southwick, & Critchlow, 1981; Sutker, Libet, Allain, & Randall, 1983). In contrast to the variety of immediate effects that alcohol can have on drinkers' affect, there are clear indications that the consistent long-term consequences of alcohol consumption are to intensify drinkers' chronic feelings of dysphoria (Aneshensel & Huba, 1983; Rohsenow, 1982b). Furthermore, when drinkers reduce their alcohol intake, their affect shows significant improvement (Birnbaum, Taylor, & Parker, 1983).

In addition to affect, laboratory studies have investigated the effect that alcohol has on self-awareness and self-esteem. It has been found that alcohol serves to decrease drinkers' self-awareness and that it does so by interfering with the encoding of self-relevant information, particularly among subjects who are high in self-consciousness (Hull, Levenson, Young, & Sher, 1983). In addition, both experimentally induced and real-life failure experiences have been associated with increased alcohol consumption among persons who are high in self-consciousness (Hull & Young, 1983, 1984). These results suggest that alcohol would serve to enhance drinkers' self-esteem, but in point of fact, some studies have found increases, whereas others have found decreases in self-esteem following subjects' consumption of alcohol (Langenbucher & Nathan, 1983). One variable that seems to determine which of these effects alcohol has on self-esteem is the gender of the drinker. Thus, in a social drinking situation involving married couples, Konovsky and Wilsnack (1982) found that the women's self-esteem significantly decreased, whereas the men's self-esteem showed a near-significant increase.

The experimental research investigating the effects of caffeine on personality has found that the immediate effects of caffeine on affect, like those of alcohol, can be either positive or negative (Chait & Griffiths, 1983; Gilbert, 1976). However, as we saw in the section on affect, the long-range affective consequences of heavy caffeine consumption are consistently negative. Much of the laboratory research on caffeine and personality evolves from Eysenck and Eysenck's (1976; Eysenck, 1981) theory that introverts and extraverts differ in their chronic level of cortical arousal. According to this view, stimulant drugs such as caffeine that alter cortical arousal should affect introverts and extraverts differently, and the research has borne out this expectation. However, the differential effects that caffeine has on introverts and extraverts appears to be more closely related to the impulsivity rather than the sociability component of extraversion, and the effects are mediated by additional variables such as the time of day when caffeine is ingested (Humphreys & Revelle, 1984). Moreover, the differential effects that occur vary with the particular dependent variable that is measured (Blount & Cox, 1982).

In summary, the immediate effects of consuming either alcohol or caffeine can be quite variable and can be experienced by the user of these drugs as either positive or negative. Nevertheless, a person's decision to use an addictive substance appears to depend in large measure on the anticipated positive effects that the substance will have on his or her personality. We should emphasize, nonetheless, that the decision also appears to depend critically on the nondrug incentives that are available to the person to pursue and enjoy (Klinger, 1977; Klinger & Cox, 1984b).

CONCLUSIONS

What final conclusions can we draw about the personality correlates of substance abuse, and how can we account for the personality correlates of substance abuse in terms of the coming together of substance abusers' biological, psychological, and environmental subsystems (Klinger 1977, 1983)?

We saw considerable converging evidence that future substance abusers exhibit personality characteristics that distinguish them from persons who will not come to abuse addictive substances. Specifically, future substance abusers are characterized by disregard for social mores, independence, impulsivity, and affinity for adventure. These are enduring personality characteristics that appear to be biologically mediated (Eysenck, 1981; Zuckerman, 1983). Persons exhibiting these personality characteristics are able to satisfy their psychological needs through substance use, and they appear to be especially susceptible to environmental influences promoting substance use.

We observed similar personality characteristics among actual substance abusers that we saw among future substance abusers. That is, substance abusers are characterized by disregard for established social customs, lack of control and foresight, inability to maintain lasting personal commitments, and the need for unusual and varied experiences. On the other hand, unlike future substance abusers, actual substance abusers experience considerable psychological distress that usualy manifests itself as anxiety, depression, and obsessive worry. Whereas substance abusers' psychological discomfort readily responds to treatment and attenuates considerably when abstinence is maintained, the personality characteristics that are shared by future and actual substance abusers are generally quite resistent to change.

We saw that abused substances can have a variety of effects on personality. Whereas taking addictive substances can have the immediate consequence of enhancing positive personality characteristics or either increasing or decreasing negative characteristics, the consistent, long-range consequences are to intensify negative personality characteristics. Nevertheless, the immediate, positive effects are especially strong for persons exhibiting the personality characteristics of the typical substance abuser, and for these persons the reinforcement that comes from substance use appears to occur for reasons that are biologically mediated (Petrie, 1967; Sher & Levenson, 1982).

For a variety of reasons, therefore, persons who display the impulsive and unconventional pleasure seeking that characterizes substance abusers seem to be strongly motivated to use substances and often learn to do so habitually. Because, moreover, the reinforcement that such persons derive from substance use occurs intermittently, the habit is likely to become firmly ingrained. As the substance use accelerates and biochemical changes in the substance user ensue (Nestoros, 1980), a vicious cycle is likely to develop such that the substance user becomes increasingly motivated to experience the reinforcing effects of substance use that are increasingly difficult to attain. Finally, as the long-range negative consequences of substance use take their toll, the substance user turns increasingly to addictive substances for their medicating effects. It is at this point that adverse reactions are likely to occur (Naditch, 1975b), like those that we observed among substance abusers entering treatment.

Our summary depiction of the personality correlates of substance abuse is, of course, highly generalized. Significant deviations from the general description occur among individual substance abusers as well as among the various substances that are abused. Researchers have begun to investigate these variations through the identification of personality subtypes among substance abusers, and future researchers should delve further into the implications that personality subtypes have for the treatment and prevention of substance abuse.

There are two additional pressing needs for future research as well. First, prospective longitudinal research would be of considerable value in separating the personality characteristics that are antecedents, concomitants, and consequences of substance abuse and in identifying appropriate strategies for the primary prevention of substance abuse. Second, identifying the personality correlates of substance abuse would be advanced considerably by the use of instruments designed especially for substance users and abusers (Wanberg & Horn, 1983, in press). Finally, the theoretical implications of the empirical findings discussed in this chapter need to be carefully explored, and these explorations are being made in companion chapters (Cox, in press-a, in press-b).

REFERENCES

Abbott, M. W. Locus of control and treatment outcome in alcoholics. *Journal of Studies on Alcohol*, 1984, *45*, 46–52.

Adesso, V. J. Experimental studies of human drinking behavior. In H. Rigter & J. C. Crabbe, Jr. (Eds.), *Alcohol tolerance and dependence* Amsterdam: Elsevier, 1980.

Allerdissen, R., Florin, I., & Rost, W. Psychological characteristics of women with bulimia nervosa (bulimarexia). *Behavioural Analysis and Modifications*, 1981, *4*, 314–317.

Allport, G. W. *Pattern and growth in personality*. New York: Holt, Rinehart & Winston, 1937.

Aneshensel, C. S., & Huba, G. J. Depression, alcohol use, and smoking over one year: A four-wave longitudinal causal model. *Journal of Abnormal Psychology*, 1983, *92*, 134–150.

Apfeldorf, M. Alcoholism scales of the MMPI: Contributions and future directions. *International Journal of the Addictions*, 1978, *13*, 17–53.

Arnon, D., Kleinman, M., & Kissin, B. Psychological differentiation in heroin addicts. *International Journal of the Addictions*, 1974, *9*, 151–159.

Bachman, J., & Jones, R. T. Personality correlates of cannabis dependence. *Addictive Behaviors*, 1979, *4*, 361–371.

Barnes, G. E. Individual differences in perceptual reactance: A review of the stimulus intensity modulation individual difference dimension. *Canadian Psychological Review*, 1976, *17*, 29–52.

Barnes, G. E. Clinical and prealcoholic personality characteristics. In B. Kissin & H. Begleiter (Eds.), *The biology of alcoholism* (Vol.6) *The pathogenesis of alcoholism: Psychosocial factors.* New York: Plenum Press, 1983.

Barnes, G. E. & Fishlinsky, M. Stimulus intensity modulation, smoking, and craving for cigarettes. *Addictive Diseases: An International Journal,* 1976, 2, 479–484.

Beckman, L. J. Perceived antecedents and effects of alcohol consumption in women. *Journal of Studies on Alcohol,* 1980, 41, 518–530.

Beckman, L. J., & Bardsley, P. E. The perceived determinants and consequences of alcohol consumption among young women heavy drinkers. *International Journal of the Addictions,* 1981, 16, 75–88.

Benson, C. S., & Wilsnack, S. C. Gender differences in alcoholic personality characteristics and life experiences. In W. M. Cox (Ed.), *Identifying and measuring alcoholic personality characteristics* San Francisco: Jossey-Bass, 1983.

Berzins, J. I., Ross, W. F., English, G. E., & Haley, F. V. Subgroups among opiate addicts: A typological investigation. *Journal of Abnormal Psychology,* 1974, 83, 65–73.

Birnbaum, I. M., Taylor, T. H., & Parker, E. S. Alcohol and sober mood state in female social drinkers. *Alcohol: Clinical and Experimental Research,* 1983, 7, 362–368.

Blij, K. de, & Hinrichsen, J. J. Construct validity of Rotter's locus of control scale in men alcoholics. *Journal of Studies on Alcohol,* 1980, 41, 463–475.

Blount, J. P., & Cox, W. M. *State-dependent learning with caffeine in a college classroom setting.* Paper presented at the 90th Annual Convention of the American Psychological Association, Washington, D.C., August 1982.

Bowen, R. C., Cipywnyk, D., D'Arcy, C., & Keegan, D. Alcoholism, anxiety disorders, and agoraphobia. *Alcoholism: Clinical and Experimental Research,* 1984, 8, 48–50.

Brown, R. A., & Cutter, H. S. G. Alcohol, customary drinking behavior, and pain. *Journal of Abnormal Psychology,* 1977, 86, 179–188.

Brown, S. A., Goldman, M. S., Inn A., & Anderson, L. R. Expectations of reinforcement from alcohol: Their domain and relation to drinking patterns. *Journal of Consulting and Clinical Psychology,* 1980, 48, 419–426.

Bry, B. H., McKeon, P., & Pandina, R. J. Extent of drug use as a function of number of risk factors. *Journal of Abnormal Psychology,* 1982, 91, 273–279.

Butcher, J. N., & Tellegen, A. Common methodological problems in MMPI research. *Journal of Consulting and Clinical Psychology,* 1978, 46, 620–628.

Carlin, A. S., & Strauss, F. F. Descriptive and functional classifications of drug abusers. *Journal of Consulting and Clinical Psychology,* 1977, 45, 222–227.

Carney, M. E. Heroin addiction: A quest for power or pleasure? *International Journal of the Addictions,* 1981, 16, 69–74.

Carrol, E. N., Zuckerman, M., & Vogel, W. H. A test of the optimal level of arousal theory of sensation seeking. *Journal of Personality and Social Psychology,* 1982, 42, 572–575.

Carroll, J. F. X., Klein, M. I., & Santo, Y. Comparison of the similarities and differences in the self-concepts of male alcoholics and addicts. *Journal of Consulting and Clinical Psychology,* 1978, 46, 575–576.

Carroll, J. F. X., Malloy, T. E., Roscioli, D. L., & Godard, D. R. Personality similarities and differences in four diagnostic groups of women alcoholics and drug addicts. *Journal of Studies on Alcohol,* 1981, 42, 432–440.

Cavior, N., Kurtzberg, R. L., & Lipton, D. S. The development and validation of a heroin addiction scale with the MMPI. *International Journal of the Addictions,* 1967, 2, 129–137.

Chait, L. D., & Griffiths, R. R. Effects of caffeine on cigarette smoking and subjective response. *Clinical Pharmacology and Therapeutics,* 1983, 34, 612–622.

Chavez, E. L., & Michaels, A. C. Evaluation of the health locus of control for obesity treatment. *Psychological Reports,* 1980, 47, 709–710.

Cherry, N., & Kiernan, K. E. A longitudinal study of smoking and personality. In R. E. Thorton (Ed.), *Smoking behaviour*. London: Churchill Livingstone, 1978.

Christiansen, B. A., Goldman, M. S., & Inn, A. Development of alcohol-related expectancies in adolescents: Separating pharmacological from social-learning influences. *Journal of Consulting and Clinical Psychology*, 1982, *50*, 336–344.

Ciotola, P. V., & Peterson, J. F. Personality characteristics of alcoholics and drug addicts in a merged treatment program. *Journal of Studies on Alcohol*, 1976, *37*, 1229–1235.

Clopton, J. Alcoholism and the MMPI. *Journal of Studies on Alcohol*, 1978, *39*, 1540–1558.

Conley, J. J. An MMPI typology of male alcoholics: Admission, discharge, and outcome comparisons. *Journal of Personality Assessment*, 1981, *45*, 33–39.

Conley, J. J., & Prioleau, L. A. Personality typology of men and women alcoholics in relation to etiology and prognosis. *Journal of Studies on Alcohol*, 1983, *44*, 996–1010.

Cooper, S. E. The influence of self-concept outcomes of intensive alcoholism treatment. *Journal of Studies on Alcohol*, 1983, *44*, 1087–1092.

Cox, W. M. The alcoholic personality: A review of the evidence. In B. A. Maher (Ed.), *Progress in experimental personality research* (Vol. 9) New York: Academic Press, 1979.

Cox, W. M. (Ed.). *Identifying and measuring alcoholic personality characteristics*. San Francisco: Jossey-Bass, 1983.

Cox, W. M. Personality theory. In C. D. Chaudron & D. A. Wilkinson (Eds.), *Theories of alcoholism*. Toronto: Addiction Research Foundation, in press. (a)

Cox, W. M. Personality factors. In H. T. Blane & K. E. Leonard (Eds.), *Psychological theories of drinking and alcoholism*. New York: Guilford, in press. (b)

Cox, W. M., & Baker, E. Sex differences in locus of control and problem drinking among college students. *Bulletin of the Society of Psychologists in Substance Abuse*, 1982, *1*, 104–106. (a)

Cox, W. M., & Baker, E. Are male, heavy wine drinkers more internally controlled than others? *Bulletin of the Society of Psychologists in Substance Abuse*, 1982, *1*, 165– 168. (b)

Cox, W. M., Lun, K., & Loper, R. G. Identifying prealcoholic personality characteristics. In W. M. Cox (Ed.), *Identifying and measuring alcoholic personality characteristics*. San Francisco: Jossey-Bass, 1983.

Craig, R. J. Personality characteristics of heroin addicts: A review of the empirical literature with critique—Part I. *International Journal of the Addictions*, 1979, *14*, 513–532. (a)

Craig, R. J. Personality characteristics of heroin addicts: A review of the empirical literature with critique—Part II. *International Journal of the Addictions*, 1979, *14*, 607–626. (b)

Craig, R. J. Personality characteristics of heroin addicts: Review of empirical research 1976–1979. *International Journal of the Addictions*, 1982, *17*, 227–248.

Craig, R. J., & Baker, S. L. (Eds.). *Drug dependent patients: Treatment and research*. Springfield, Il.: Charles C Thomas, 1982.

Dahlstrom, W. G., Welsh, G. S., & Dahlstrom, L. E. *An MMPI handbook* (Vol. 1). Minneapolis: University of Minnesota Press, 1972.

Danahy, S., & Kahn, M. W. Consistency of field dependence in treated alcoholics. *International Journal of the Addictions*, 1981, *16*, 1271–1275.

Devinney, R. B. Gamblers: A personality study. *Dissertation Abstracts International*, 1978, *40*, 429–430B.

Donovan, D. M., Rohsenow, D. J., Schau, E. J., & O'Leary, M. R. Defensive style in alcoholics and nonalcoholics. *Journal of Studies on Alcohol*, 1977, *38*, 265–470.

Donovan, J. E., & Jessor, R. Adolescent problem drinking: Psychosocial correlates in a national sample study. *Journal of Studies on Alcohol*, 1978, *39*, 1506–1524.

Dorus, W., & Senay, E. C. Depression, demographic dimensions, and drug abuse. *American Journal of Psychiatry*, 1980, *137*, 699–704.

Dunn, P. K., & Ondercin, P. Personality variables related to compulsive eating in college women. *Journal of Clinical Psychology*, 1981, 37, 43–49.

Eddy, C. C. Effects of alcohol on anxiety in problem- and nonproblem-drinking women. *Alcoholism: Clinical and Experimental Research*, 1979, 3, 107–114.

Edwards, E., Bucky, S. F., & Schuckit, M. Personality and attitudinal change for alcoholics treated at the navy's alcohol rehabilitation center. *Journal of Community Psychology*, 1977, 5, 180–185.

Endler, N. S., & Magnussen, D. *Interactional psychology and personality*. Washington, D.C.: Hemisphere, 1976.

Eysenck, H. J. *The causes and effects of smoking*. Beverly Hills, Calif.: Sage, 1980.

Eysenck, H. J. (Ed.). *A model for personality*. Berlin: Springer-Verlag, 1981.

Eysenck, H. J. Schenck and the personality of smokers. *Personality and Individual Differences*, 1982, 3, 217–218.

Eysenck, H. J., & Eysenck, S. B. G. *Psychoticism as a dimension of personality*. London: Hodder & Stoughton, 1976.

Exner, J. E. *The Rorschach: A comprehensive system*. New York: Wiley, 1974.

Finney, J. W., & Moos, R. H. Treatment and outcome for empirical subtypes of alcoholic patients. *Journal of Consulting Clinical Psychology*, 1979, 47, 25–38.

Freed, E. X. Alcoholism and the Rorschach Test: A review. *Journal of Studies on Alcohol*, 1976, 37, 1633–1654.

Freed, E. X. Alcohol and mood: An updated review. *International Journal of the Addictions*, 1978, 13, 173–200.

Gabel, P. C., Noel, N. E., Keane, T. M., & Lisman, S. A. Effects of sexual versus fear arousal on alcohol consumption in college males. *Behaviour Research and Therapy*, 1980, 18, 519–526.

Gaines, L. S. Cognition and the environment: Implications for a self-awareness theory of drinking. In T. C. Harford & L. S. Gaines (Eds.), *Research Monograph No. 7: Social drinking contexts*. Washington, D.C.: National Institute on Alcohol Abuse and Alcoholism, 1979.

Galizio, M., Rosenthal, D., & Stein, F. A. Sensation seeking, reinforcement, and student drug use. *Addictive Behaviors*, 1983, 8, 243–252.

Galizio, M., & Stein, F. S. Sensation seeking and drug choice, *International Journal of the Addictions*, 1983, 18, 1039–1048.

Geller, S. E., Keane, T. M., & Scheirer, C. J. Delay of gratification, locus of control, and eating patterns in obese and nonobese children. *Addictive Behaviors*, 1981, 6, 9–14.

Gilbert, R. M. Caffeine as a drug of abuse. In R. G. Gibbon, Y. Israel, H. Kalant, R. E. Popham, W. Schmidt, & R. G. Smart (Eds.), *Research advances in alcohol and drug problems* (Vol. 3). New York: Wiley, 1976.

Gilliland, K., & Bullock, W. Caffeine: A potential drug of abuse. In H. Shaffer & B. Stimmel (Eds.), *The addictive behaviors*. New York: Haworth Press, 1984.

Goldstein, G. Perceptual and cognitive deficit in alcoholics. In G. Goldstein & C. Neuringer (Eds.), *Empirical studies of alcoholism* Cambridge, Mass.: Ballinger, 1976.

Goldstein, J. W., & Sappington, J. T. Personality characteristics of students who became heavy drug users: An MMPI study of an *avant-garde. American Journal of Drug and Alcohol Abuse*, 1977, 4, 401–412.

Goldstein, S., & Marlatt, G. A. Building self-confidence, self-efficacy, and self-control. In W. M. Cox (Ed.), *Treatment and prevention of alcohol problems: A resource manual*. New York: Academic Press, in press.

Gomberg, E. L. Alcohol, gender, and sexual problems: An interface. In W. M. Cox (Ed.), *Treatment and prevention of alcohol problems: A resource manual*. New York: Academic Press, in press.

Gordon, L. B. Preferential drug abuse: Defenses and behavioral correlates. *Journal of Personality Assessment*, 1980, *44*, 345–350.

Gossop, M. R. A comparative study of oral and intravenous drug-dependent patients on three dimensions of personality. *International Journal of the Addictions*, 1978, *13*, 135–142.

Graham, J. R. *MMPI characteristics of alcoholics, drug abusers, and pathological gamblers.* Paper presented at the 13th annual MMPI Symposium, University of the Americas, Cholula, Puebla, Mexico, March 1978.

Graham, J. R., & Schwartz, M. F. Methodological issues and the construct validity of the MacAndrew alcoholism scale: A response to the rebuttal and contructive comments of Merenda and Sparadeo. *Journal of Consulting and Clinical Psychology*, 1981, *49*, 971–973.

Greden, J. F. Caffeine. In S. J. Mule (Ed.), *Behavior in excess: An examination of the volitional disorders.* New York: Free Press, 1981.

Hall, J. N. Relationship between locus of control and drug effects in users of narcotics, stimulants, hypnotic-sedatives, and hallucinogens. *International Journal of the Addictions*, 1978, *13*, 143–147.

Hart, L. S. A 16PF study of men and women alcoholics. *Journal of Studies on Alcohol*, 1979, *40*, 1082–1084.

Hartung, J., & Skorka, D. The HIT clinical profile of psychedelic drug users. *Journal of Personality Assessment*, 1980, *44*, 237–245.

Hays, R., & Stacy A. A study of the reliability and validity of the Holmes Alcoholism Scale. *Journal of Clinical Psychology*, 1983, *39*, 284–286.

Heilbrun, A. B., Jr., & Schwartz, H. L. Self-esteem and self-reinforcement in men alcoholics: An explanation of a paradox. *Journal of Studies on Alcohol*, 1980, *41*, 1134–1142.

Hoffmann, H., Loper, R. G., & Kammeier, M. L. Identifying future alcoholics with MMPI alcoholism scales. *Quarterly Journal of Studies on Alcohol*, 1974, *35*, 490–498.

Holland, T. R. Multivariate analysis of personality correlates of alcohol and drug abuse in a prison population. *Journal of Abnormal Psychology*, 1977, *36*, 644–650.

Holm, L., Bergman, H., & Borg, S. Field dependence in patients with exclusive abuse of hypnotics or sedatives. *Perceptual and Motor Skills*, 1980, *50*, 987–992.

Holmes, C. B., Dungan, D. S., & McLaughlin, T. P. Validity of five MMPI alcoholism scales. *Journal of Clinical Psychology*, 1982, *38*, 661–664.

Huba, G. J., & Bentler, P. M. A developmental theory of drug use: Derivation and assessment of a causal modeling approach. In P. B. Baltes & O. G. Brim (Eds.), *Life-span development and behavior* (Vol. 4). New York: Academic Press, 1982.

Huba, G. J., Segal, B., & Singer, J. L. Organization of needs in male and female drug and alcohol users. *Journal of Consulting and Clinical Psychology*, 1977, *45*, 34–44.

Hull, J. G., & Young, R. D. Self-consciousness, self-esteem, and success-failure as determinants of alcohol consumption in male social drinkers. *Journal of Personality and Social Psychology*, 1983, *44*, 1097–1109.

Hull, J. G., & Young, R. D. The self-awareness reducing effects of alcohol consumption: Evidence and implications. In J. Suls & A. G. Greenwald (Eds.), *Psychological perspectives on the self* (Vol. 2). Hillsdale, N.J.: Erlbaum, 1984.

Hull, J. G., Levenson, R. W., Young, R. D., & Sher, K. J. Self-awareness-reducing effects of alcohol consumption. *Journal of Personality and Social Psychology*, 1983, *44*, 461–473.

Humphreys, M. S., & Revelle, W. Personality, motivation, and performance: A theory of the relationship between individual differences and information processing. *Psychological Review*, 1984, *91*, 153–184.

Hutzler, J. C., Keen, J., Molinari, V., & Carey, L. Super-obesity: A psychiatric profile of patients electing gastric stapling for the treatment of morbid obesity. *Journal of Clinical Psychology*, 1981, *42*, 458–462.

Jackson, D. N. Differential Personality Inventory types among alcoholics. In W. M. Cox (Ed.), *Identifying and measuring alcoholic personality characteristics.* San Francisco: Jossey-Bass, 1983.

James, J. E., & Stirling, D. P. Caffeine: A survey of some of the known and suspected deleterious effects of habitual use. *British Journal of Addiction,* 1983, *78,* 251–258.

Jamison, R. N. Cigarette smoking and personality in male and female adolescents. *Psychological Reports,* 1979, *44,* 842.

Jessor, R. Marijuana: A review of recent psychosocial research. In R. L. Dupont, A. Goldstein, & J. Donnell (Eds.), *Handbook on drug abuse.* Washington, D.C.: U. S. Government Printing Office, 1979.

Jessor, R., & Jessor S. *Problem behavior and psychosocial development: A longitudinal study.* New York: Academic Press, 1977.

Jessor R., & Jessor, S. Theory testing in longitudinal research on marijuana use. In D. Kandel (Ed.), *Longitudinal research on drug use.* Washington, D.C.: Hemisphere, 1978.

Kammeier, M. L., Hoffmann, H., & Loper, R. G. Personality characteristics of alcoholics as college freshmen and at time of treatment. *Quarterly Journal of Studies on Alcohol,* 1973, *34,* 390–399.

Kandel, D. B. *Longitudinal research on drug use: Empirical findings and methodological issues.* Washington, D. C.: Hemisphere, 1978.

Kandel, D. B. Drug and drinking behavior among youth. In A. Inkeles, N. J. Smelser, & R. H. Turner (Eds.), *Annual review of sociology* (Vol. 6). Palo Alto, Calif.: Annual Reviews, 1980.

Keane, T. M., & Lisman, S. A. Alcohol and social anxiety in males: Behavioral, cognitive, and physiological effects. *Journal of Abnormal Psychology,* 1980, *89,* 213–223.

Kilpatrick, D. G., Sutker, P. B., Roitzsch, J. C., & Miller, W. C. Personality correlates of polydrug abuse. *Psychological Reports,* 1976, *38,* 311–317.

Kincey, J. Internal-external control and weight loss in the obese: Predictive and discriminant validity and some possible clinical implications. *Journal of Clinical Psychology,* 1981, *37,* 100–103.

Klinger, E. *Meaning and void: Inner experience and the incentives in people's lives.* Minneapolis: University of Minnesota Press, 1977.

Klinger, E. Course syllabus for Psychology 3400, University of Minnesota, Morris, 1983.

Klinger, E., & Cox, W. M. *Dimensions of thought flow in everyday life.* Unpublished manuscript, University of Minnesota, Morris, 1984. (a)

Klinger, E., & Cox, W. M. *Motivational predictors of alcoholics' responses to inpatient treatment.* Unpublished manuscript, University of Minnesota, Morris, 1984. (b)

Kohn, P. M., Barnes, G. E., Fishlinsky, M., Segal, R., & Hoffman, F. M. Experience-seeking characteristics of methadone clients. *Journal of Consulting and Clinical Psychology,* 1979, *47,* 980–981.

Kohn, P. M., Barnes, G. E., & Hoffman, F. M. Drug-use history and experience seeking among adult male correctional inmates. *Journal of Consulting and Clinical Psychology,* 1979, *47,* 708–715.

Konovsky, M., & Wilsnack, S. C. Social drinking and self-esteem in married couples. *Journal of Studies on Alcohol,* 1982, *43,* 319–333.

Krakowiak, P. A., & Cross, H. J. A social-learning approach to student marijuana use. *International Journal of the Addictions,* 1979, *14,* 789–796.

Kurtines, W. M., Ball, L. R., & Wood, G. H. Personality characteristics of long-term recovered alcoholics: A comparative analysis. *Journal of Consulting and Clinical Psychology,* 1978, *46,* 971–977.

Lachar, D., Berman, W., Grisell, J. L., & Schooff, K. The MacAndrew Alcoholism Scale as a general measure of substance misuse. *Journal of Studies on Alcohol,* 1976, *37,* 1609–1615.

Lachar, D., Berman, W., Grisell, J. L., & Schooff, K. A heroin addiction scale for the MMPI: Effectiveness in differential diagnosis in a psychiatric setting. *International Journal of the Addictions,* 1979, *14,* 135–142.

Lachar, D., Gdowski, C. L., Keegan, J. F. MMPI profiles of men alcoholics, drug addicts, and psychiatric patients. *Journal of Studies on Alcohol,* 1979, *40,* 45–56.

Lang, A. R. Addictive personality: A viable construct? In P. K. Levison, D. R. Gerstein, & D. R. Maloff (Eds.), *Commonalities in substance abuse and habitual behavior.* Lexington, Mass.: Lexington Books, 1983.

Langenbucher, J., & Nathan, P. E. The "wet" alcoholic: One drink . . . then what? In W. M. Cox (Ed.), *Identifying and measuring alcoholic personality characteristics.* San Francisco: Jossey-Bass, 1983.

Laufer, W. S., Johnson, J. A., & Hogan, R. Ego control and criminal behavior. *Journal of Personality and Social Psychology,* 1981, *41,* 179–184.

Lefcourt, H. M. *Locus of control: Current trends in theory and research* (2nd ed.). Hillsdale, N.J.: Erlbaum, 1982.

Leon, G. R., Carroll, K., Chernyk, B., & Finn, S. Binge eating and associated habit patterns within college student and clinically identified populations. *International Journal of Eating Disorders,* in press.

Leon, G. R., Eckert, E. K., Teed, D., & Buchwald, H. Changes in body image and other psychological factors after intestinal bypass surgery for massive obesity. *Journal of Behavioral Medicine,* 1979, *2,* 39–55.

Leon, G. R., Kolotkin, R., & Korgeski, G. MacAndrew Addiction Scale and other MMPI characteristics associated with obesity, anorexia and smoking behavior. *Addictive Behaviors,* 1979, *4,* 401–407.

Lester, D. Choice of gambling activity and belief in locus of control. *Psychological Reports,* 1980, *47,* 22.

Levison, P. K., Gerstein, D. R., & Maloff, D. R. *Commonalities in substance abuse and habitual behavior.* Lexington, Mass.: Lexington Books, 1983.

Loper, R. G., Kammeier, M. L., & Hoffmann, H. MMPI characteristics of college freshmen males who later become alcoholics. *Journal of Abnormal Psychology,* 1973, *82,* 159–162.

Lowenfeld, B. H. Personality dimensions of the pathological gambler. *Dissertation Abstracts International,* 1979, *40,* 456B.

MacAndrew, C. A retrospective study of drunkenness-associated changes in the self-depictions of a large sample of male outpatient alcoholics. *Addictive Behaviors,* 1979, *4,* 373–381. (a)

MacAndrew, C. Evidence for the presence of two fundamentally different, age-independent characterological types within unselected runs of male alcohol and drug abusers. *American Journal of Drug and Alcohol Abuse,* 1979, *6,* 207–221. (b)

MacAndrew, C. On the possibility of the psychometric detection of persons who are prone to the abuse of alcohol and other substances. *Addictive Behaviors,* 1979, *4,* 11–20. (c)

MacAndrew, C. Male alcoholics, secondary psychopathy and Eysenck's theory of personality. *Personality and Individual Differences,* 1980, *1,* 151–160.

MacAndrew, C. What the MAC scale tells us about men alcoholics. *Journal of Studies on Alcohol,* 1981, *42,* 604–625. (a)

MacAndrew, C. Similarities in the self-depictions of men alcoholics and psychiatric outpatients. *Journal of Studies on Alcohol,* 1981, *42,* 421–431. (b)

MacAndrew, C. An examination of the relevance of the individual differences (A-Trait) formulation of the tension reduction theory to the etiology of alcohol abuse in young males. *Addictive Behaviors,* 1982, *7,* 39–45.

MacAndrew, C. Alcoholic personality or personalities: Scale and profile data from the MMPI. In W. M. Cox (Ed.), *Identifying and measuring alcoholic personality characteristics.* San Francisco: Jossey-Bass, 1983.

MacAndrew, C., & Edgerton, R. B. *Drunken comportment.* Chicago: Aldine, 1969.

Makedonsky, M. M. Locus of control, learned helplessness, and abstainers: A study of the psychological characteristics of young male drug and alcohol abstainers. *Dissertation Abstracts International,* 1977, *38,* 1891B.

Malcolm, S., & Shephard, R. J. Personality and sexual behavior of the adolescent smoker. *American Journal of Drug and Alcohol Abuse,* 1978, *5,* 87–96.

McArthur, L. Z., & Burstein, B. Field dependent eating and perception as a function of weight and sex. *Journal of Personality,* 1975, *43,* 402–420.

McClelland, D. C., Davis, W. N., Kalin, R., & Wanner, E. *The drinking man.* New York: Free Press, 1972.

McLellan, A. T., Woody, G. E., & O'Brien, C. P. Development of psychiatric illness in drug abusers. *New England Journal of Medicine,* 1979, *301,* 1310–1314.

McManus, I. C., & Weeks, S. J. Smoking, personality, and reasons for smoking. *Psychological Medicine,* 1982, *12,* 349–356.

Merenda, P. F., & Sparadeo, F. Rebuttal to and constructive comments on "Construct Validity of the MacAndrew Alcoholism Scale." *Journal of Consulting and Clinical Psychology,* 1981, *49,* 968–970.

Midanik, L. Alcohol problems and depressive symptoms in a national survey. In B. Stimmel (Ed.), *Psychological constructs of alcoholism and substance abuse.* New York: Haworth Press, 1983.

Miller, W. R. Alcoholism scales and objective assessment methods: A review. *Psychological Bulletin,* 1976, *83,* 649–674.

Mischel, W. *Personality and assessment.* New York: Wiley, 1968.

Mlott, S. R., & Mlott, Y. D. Dogmatism and locus of control in individuals who smoke, stopped smoking, and never smoked. *Journal of Community Psychology,* 1975, *3,* 53–57.

Morey, L. C., & Blashfield, R. K. Empirical classifications of alcoholism: A review. *Journal of Studies on Alcohol,* 1981, *42,* 925–937.

Murray, H. A. *Explorations in personality.* New York: Oxford University Press, 1938.

Naditch, M. P. Locus of control and drinking behavior in a smaple of men in army basic training. *Journal of Consulting and Clinical Psychology,* 1975, *43,* 96. (a)

Naditch, M. P. Relations of motives for drug use and psychopathology in the development of acute adverse reactions to psychoactive drugs. *Journal of Abnormal Psychology,* 1975, *84,* 374–385. (b)

Nathan, P. E., & Lansky, D. Common methodological problems in research on the addictions. *Journal of Consulting and Clinical Psychology,* 1978, *46,* 713–726.

Nell, V., & Strümpfer, D. J. W. The power motive, *n* power, and fear of weakness. *Journal of Personality Assessment,* 1978, *42,* 56–62.

Nerviano, V. J., & Gross, H. W. Personality types of alcoholics on objective inventories. *Journal of Studies on Alcohol,* 1983, *44,* 837–851.

Nestoros, J. N. Ethanol specifically potentiates GABA-mediated neurotransmission in feline cerebral cortex. *Science,* 1980, *209,* 708–710.

Neuringer, C., & Clopton, J. R. The use of psychological tests for the study of the identification, prediction, and treatment of alcoholism. In G. Goldstein & C. Neuringer (Eds.), *Empirical studies of alcoholism.* Cambridge, Mass.: Ballinger, 1976.

Noel, N. E., & Lisman, S. A. Alcohol consumption by college women following exposure to unsolvable problems: Learned helplessness or stress induced drinking? *Behaviour Research and Therapy,* 1980, *18,* 429–440.

O'Leary, M. R., Chaney, E. J., & Hudgins, W. Self-concept: Effects of alcoholism, hospitalization, and treatment. *Psychological Reports*, 1978, *42*, 655–661.

O'Leary, M. R., Donovan, D. M., Chaney, E. F., & O'Leary, D. E. Relationship of alcoholic personality subtypes to treatment follow-up measures. *Journal of Nervous and Mental Disease*, 1980, *168*, 475–480.

Ondercin, P. A. Organization of needs in anorectic, bulimic and obese college women. *Journal of Personality Assessment*, 1984, *48*, 162–167.

Orive, R., & Gerard, H. B. Personality, attitudinal, and social correlates of drug use. *International Journal of the Addictions*, 1980, *15*, 869–881.

Ornstein, P. Psychometric test changes following alcohol inpatient treatment and their relationships to posttreatment drinking behaviors. *International Journal of the Addictions*, 1981, *16*, 263–271.

Owen, P., & Butcher, J. Personality factors in problem drinking: A review of the evidence and some suggested directions. In R. Pickens & L. Heston (Eds.), *Psychiatric factors in drug abuse*. New York: Grune & Stratton, 1979.

Paine, P. M., O'Neil, P. M., Malcolm, R., Sexauer, J. D., & Currey, H. S. Experienced control and participation in treatment of obesity. *Psychological Reports*, 1980, *47*, 1127–1134.

Pandina, R. J., & Schuele, J. A. Psychosocial correlates of alcohol and drug use of adolescent students and adolescents in treatment. *Journal of Studies on Alcohol*, 1983, *44*, 950–973.

Patterson, E. T., Charles, H. L., Woodward, W. A., Roberts, W. R., & Penk, W. E. Differences in measures of personality and family environment among black and white alcoholics. *Journal of Consulting and Clinical Psychology*, 1981, *49*, 1–9.

Pearlstein, R. C. Comparison of perceived locus of control among heroin addicts, alcoholics, and amphetamine abusers. *International Journal of the Addictions*, 1980, *15*, 277–282.

Penk, W. E., & Robinowitz, R. We agree: A rejoinder from Penk and Robinowitz to Sutker and Allain. *Journal of Abnormal Psychology*, 1981, *90*, 177–178.

Penk, W. E., Fudge, J. W., Robinowitz, R., & Neman, R. S. Personality characteristics of compulsive heroin, amphetamine, and barbiturate users. *Journal of Consulting and Clinical Psychology*, 1979, *47*, 583–585.

Penk, W. E., Robinowitz, R., Kidd, R., & Nisle, A. Perceived family environments among ethnic groups of compulsive heroin users. *Addictive Behaviors*, 1979, *4*, 297–309.

Penk, W. E., Robinowitz, R., Woodward, W. A., & Hess, J. L. MMPI factor scale differences among heroin addicts differing in race and admission status. *International Journal of the Addictions*, 1980, *15*, 329–337.

Penk, W. E., Woodward, W. A., Robinowitz, R., & Parr, W. C. An MMPI comparison of polydrug and heroin abusers. *Journal of Abnormal Psychology*, 1980, *89*, 299–302.

Penk, W. E., Robinowitz, R., Roberts, W. R., Dolan, M. P., & Atkins, H. G. MMPI differences of male Hispanic-American, black, and white heroin addicts. *Journal of Consulting and Clinical Psychology*, 1981, *49*, 488–490.

Petrie, A. *Individuality in pain and suffering*. Chicago: University of Chicago Press, 1967.

Pettinati, H. M., Sugerman, A. A., & Maurer, H. S. Four year MMPI changes in abstinent and drinking alcoholics. *Alcoholism: Clinical and Experimental Research*, 1982, *6*, 487–494.

Phares, E. J. *Clinical psychology*. Homewood, Il.: Dorsey, 1979.

Pihl, R., & Spiers, P. The etiology of drug abuse. In B. A. Maher (Ed.), *Progress in experimental personality research* (Vol. 8). New York: Academic Press, 1978.

Pihl, R. O., & Smith, S. Of affect and alcohol. In L. A. Pohorecky & J. Brick (Eds.), *Stress and alcohol use*. Amsterdam: Elsevier, 1983.

Platt, J. J., & Labate, C. *Heroin addiction: Theory, research, and treatment*. New York: Wiley, 1976.

Pliner, P., & Cappell, H. Modification of affective consequences of alcohol: A comparison of social and solitary drinking. *Journal of Abnormal Psychology*, 1974, *83*, 418–425.

Plumb, M. M., D'Amanda, C., & Taintor, Z. Chemical substance abuse and perceived locus of control. In D. J. Lettieri (Ed.), *Predicting adolescent drug abuse: A review of issues, methods and correlates.* Rockville, Md.: National Institute on Drug Abuse, 1975.

Powell, B. J., Penick, E. C., Othmer, E., Bingham, S. F., & Rice, A. S. Prevalence of additional psychiatric syndromes among male alcoholics. *Journal of Clinical Psychiatry,* 1982, *43,* 404–407.

Primavera, L. H., Simon, W. E., & Camisa, J. M. An investigation of personality and caffeine use. *British Journal of Addiction,* 1975, *70,* 213–215.

Rankin, H., Stockwell, T., & Hodgson, R. Personality and alcohol dependence. *Personality and Individual Differences,* 1982, *3,* 145–151.

Rocklin, T., & Revelle, W. The measurement of extraversion: A comparison of the Eysenck Personality Inventory and the Eysenck Personality Questionnaire. *British Journal of Social Psychology,* 1981, *20,* 279–284.

Rohsenow, D. J. Social anxiety, daily moods, and alcohol use over time among heavy social drinking men. *Addictive Behaviors,* 1982, *7,* 311–315. (a)

Rohsenow, D. J. The Alcohol Use Inventory as predictor of drinking by male heavy social drinkers. *Addictive Behaviors,* 1982, *7,* 387–395. (b)

Rohsenow, D. J. Alcoholics' perceptions of control. In W. M. Cox (Ed.), *Identifying and measuring alcoholic personality characteristics.* San Francisco: Jossey-Bass, 1983. (a)

Rohsenow, D. J. Drinking habits and expectancies about alcohol's effects for self versus others. *Journal of Consulting and Clinical Psychology,* 1983, *51,* 752–756. (b)

Rohsenow, D. J., & O'Leary, M. R. Locus of control research on alcoholic populations: A review. II. Relationship to other measures. *International Journal of the Addictions,* 1978, *13,* 213–226.

Rose, G. S., Powell, B. J., & Penick, E. C. Determinants of locus of control orientation in male alcoholics. *Journal of Clinical Psychology,* 1978, *34,* 250–251.

Rosenbaum, M., & Argon, S. Locus of control and success in self-initiated attempts to stop smoking. *Journal of Clinical Psychology,* 1979, *35,* 870–872.

Ross, L. Heroin addiction and cognitive style: Disembedding performance in the male heroin addict. *British Journal of Addiction,* 1979, *74,* 51–56.

Rounsaville, B. J., Weissman, M. M., Kleber, H., & Wilber, C. Heterogeneity of psychiatric diagnosis in treated opiate addicts. *Archives of General Psychiatry,* 1982, *39,* 161–166.

Saunders, G. R., & Schuckit, M. A. MMPI scores in young men with alcoholic relatives and controls. *Journal of Nervous and Mental Disease,* 1981, *169,* 456–458.

Sawyer, D. A., Julia, H. L., & Turin, A. C. Caffeine and human behavior: Arousal, anxiety, and performance effects. *Journal of Behavioral Medicine,* 1982, *5,* 415–439.

Schmolck, P. *On construct validation of empirical scales: The case of MacAndrew's "Alcoholism Scales".* Paper presented at the Eighth International Conference on Personality assessment, Copenhagen, Denmark, August 1983.

Schreiber, F. M., Schauble, P. G., Epting, F. R., & Skovholt, T. M. Predicting successful weight loss after treatment. *Journal of Clinical Psychology,* 1979, *35,* 851–854.

Schuckit, M. A., & Morrissey, E. R. Psychiatric problems in women admitted to an alcoholic detoxification center. *American Journal of Psychiatry,* 1979, *136,* 611–617.

Schwarz, R. M., Burkhart, B. R., & Green, S. B. Sensation-seeking and anxiety as factors in social drinking by men. *Journal of Studies on Alcohol,* 1982, *43,* 1108–1114.

Schwebel, A. I., & Kaemmerer, W. F. Smoking, alienation, and locus of control factors. *Omega,* 1977, *8,* 239–246.

Scoufis, P., & Walker, M. Heavy drinking and the need for power. *Journal of Studies on Alcohol,* 1982, *43,* 1010–1019.

Segal, B., Huba, G. J., & Singer, J. L. *Drugs, daydreaming, and personality: A study of college youth.* Hillsdale, N.J.: Erlbaum, 1980.

Sher, K. J., & Levenson, R. W. Risk for alcoholism and individual differences in the stress-response-dampening effect of alcohol. *Journal of Abnormal Psychology*, 1982, *91*, 350–367.

Sieber, M. F. Personality scores and licit and illicit substance use. *Personality and Individual Differences*, 1981, *2*, 235–241.

Simon, W. E., & Primavera, L. H. The personality of the cigarette smoker: Some empirical data. *International Journal of the Addictions*, 1976, *11*, 81–94.

Skinner, H. A. Statistical approaches to the classification of alcohol and drug addiction. *British Journal of Addiction*, 1982, *77*, 259–273.

Skinner, H. A., & Allen, B. A. Alcohol dependence syndrome: Measurement and validation. *Journal of Abnormal Psychology*, 1982, *91*, 199–209.

Snowden, L. R. Personality tailored covert sensitization of heroin abuse. *Addictive Behaviors*, 1978, *3*, 43–49.

Southwick, L., Steele, C., & Marlatt, G. A. Alcohol-related expectancies: Defined by phase of intoxication and drinking experience. *Journal of Consulting and Clinical Psychology*, 1981, *49*, 713–721.

Spielberger, C. D., & Jacobs, G. A. Personality and smoking behavior. *Journal of Personality Assessment*, 1982, *46*, 396–403.

Stanaway, R. G., & Watson, D. W. Smoking and personality: A factorial study. *Journal of Clinical Psychology*, 1981, *20*, 213–214.

Steele, C. M., Southwick, L. L., & Critchlow, B. Dissonance and alcohol: Drinking your troubles away. *Journal of Personality and Social Psychology*, 1981, *41*, 831–846.

Steer, R. A., & Schut, J. Types of psychopathology displayed by heroin addicts. *American Journal of Psychiatry*, 1979, *136*, 1463–1465.

Strober, M. Personality and symptomatological features in young, nonchronic anorexia nervosa patients. *Journal of Psychosomatic Research*, 1980, *24*, 353–359.

Strober, M., & Goldenberg, I. Ego boundary disturbance in juvenile anorexia nervosa. *Journal of Clinical Psychology*, 1981, *37*, 433–438.

Sugerman, A. A., & Schneider, D. U. Cognitive styles in alcoholism. In R. E. Tarter & A. A. Sugerman (Eds.), *Alcoholism: Interdisciplinary approaches to an enduring problem*. Reading, Mass.: Addison-Wesley, 1976.

Sutker, P. B. Adolescent drug and alcohol behaviors. In T. Field, A. Huston, H. Quay, L. Troll, & G. Finley (Eds), *Review of human development*. New York: Wiley, 1982.

Sutker, P. B., & Allain, A. N. Comments on voluntarism: Reply to Penk and Robinowitz. *Journal of Abnormal Psychology*, 1981, *90*, 175–176.

Sutker, P. B., & Archer, R. P. MMPI characteristics of opiate addicts, alcoholics, and other drug abusers. In C. S. Newmark (Ed.), *MMPI: Current clinical and research trends*. New York: Praeger, 1979.

Sutker, P. B., Archer, R. P., & Allain, A. N. Drug abuse patterns, personality characteristics, and relationships with sex, race, and sensation seeking. *Journal of Consulting and Clinical Psychology*, 1978, *46*, 1374–1378.

Sutker, P. B., Archer, R. P., Brantley, P. J., & Kilpatrick, D. G. Alcoholics and opiate addicts: Comparison of personality characteristics. *Journal of Studies on Alcohol*, 1979, *40*, 635–644.

Sutker, P. B., Archer, R. P., & Allain, A. N. Psychopathology of drug abusers: Sex and ethnic considerations. *International Journal of the Addictions*, 1980, *15*, 605–613.

Sutker, P. B., Brantley, P. J., & Allain, A. N. MMPI response patterns and alcohol consumption in DUI offenders. *Journal of Consulting and Clinical Psychology*, 1980, *48*, 350–355.

Sutker, P. B., Malatesta, V. J., Allain, A. N., & Randall, C. L. Analogue drinking assessment: Sensation seeking and gender. *Journal of Behavioral Assessment*, 1981, *3*, 167–177.

Sutker, P. B., Libet, J. M., Allain, A. N., & Randall, C. L. Alcohol use, negative mood states, and menstrual cycle phases. *Alcoholism: Clinical and Experimental Research*, 1983, *7*, 327–331.

Sutker, P. B., Tabakoff, B., Goist, Jr., K. C., & Randall, C. L. Acute alcohol intoxication, mood states, and alcohol metabolism in women and men. *Pharmacology Biochemistry & Behavior*, 1983, *18*, 349–354.

Tarbox, A. R. Self-regulation and sense of competence in men alcoholics. *Journal of Studies on Alcohol*, 1979, *40*, 860–867.

Tarter, R. E., & Alterman, A. I. Neurobehavioral theory of alcoholism etiology. In C. D. Chaudron & D. A. Wilkinson (Eds.), *Theories of alcoholism*. Toronto: Addiction Research Foundation, in press.

Uecker, A. E., Boutilier, L. R., & Richardson, E. "Indianism" and MMPI scores on men alcoholics. *Journal of Studies on Alcohol*, 1980, *41*, 357–362.

Vuchinich, R. E., & Tucker, J. A. A critique of cognitive labeling explanations of the emotional and behavioral effects of alcohol. *Addictive Behaviors*, 1980, *5*, 179–188.

Wampler, R. S., Lauer, J. B., Lantz, J. B., Wampler, K. S., Evens, M. G., & Madura, J. A. Psychological effects of intestinal bypass surgery. *Journal of Counseling Psychology*, 1980, *27*, 492–499.

Wanberg, K. W., & Horn, J. L. Assessment of alcohol use with multidimensional concepts and measures. *American Psychologist*, 1983, *38*, 1055–1069.

Wanberg, K. W., & Horn, J. L. The assessment of persons with problems associated with alcohol use: A multiple-condition approach. In W. M. Cox (Ed.), *Treatment and prevention of alcohol problems: A resource manual*. San Diego: Academic Press, in press.

Weckowicz, T. E., & Janssen, D. Cognitive functions, personality traits, and social values in heavy marijuana smokers and nonsmoker controls. *Journal of Abnormal Psychology*, 1973, *81*, 264–269.

Weckowicz, T. E., Collier, G., & Spreng, L. Field dependence, cognitive functions, personality traits, and social values in heavy cannabis users and nonuser controls. *Psychological Reports*, 1977, *41*, 291–302.

Wells, B. W., & Stacey, B. G. Social and psychological features of young drug misusers. *British Journal of Addiction*, 1976, *71*, 243–251.

Wesson, D. R., Carlin, A. S., Adams, K. M., & Beschner, G. *Polydrug abuse: The results of a national collaborative study*. New York: Academic Press, 1978.

Willis, K. A., Wehler, R., & Rush, W. A. MacAndrew scale scores of smoking and nonsmoking alcoholics. *Journal of Studies on Alcohol*, 1979, *40*, 906–907.

Wilsnack, S. C. The impact of sex roles on women's alcohol use and abuse. In M. Greeblatt & M. A. Schuckit (Eds.), *Alcoholism problems in women and children*. New York: Grune & Stratton, 1976.

Wilsnack, S. C. Drinking, sexuality, and sexual dysfunction in women. In S. C. Wilsnack & L. J. Beckman (Eds.), *Alcohol problems in women*. New York: Guilford, 1984.

Wingard, J. A., Huba, G. J., & Bentler, P. M. A longitudinal analysis of personality structure and adolescent substance use. *Personality and Individual Differences*, 1980, *1*, 259–272.

Wiseman, J. P. Sober comportment: Patterns and perspectives on alcohol addiction. *Journal of Studies on Alcohol*, 1981, *42*, 106–126.

Witkin, H. A., & Goodenough, D. R. Field dependence and interpersonal behavior. *Psychological Bulletin*, 1977, *84*, 661–689.

Witkin, H. A., Lewis, H. B., Hertzman, M., Machover, K., Meissner, P. B., & Wapner, S. *Personality through perception*. New York: Harper, 1954.

Witkin, H. A., Karp, S. A., & Goodenough, D. R. Dependence in alcoholics. *Quarterly Journal of Studies on Alcohol*, 1959, *20*, 493–504.

Zager, L. D., & Megargee, E. I. Seven MMPI alcohol and drug abuse scales: An empirical investigation of their interrelationships, convergent and discriminant validity, and degree of racial bias. *Journal of Personality and Social Psychology*, 1981, *40*, 532–544.

Zenker, S. I., & Wolfgang, A. K. Relationship of Machiavellianism and locus of control to preferences for leisure activity by college men and women. *Psychological Reports*, 1982, *50*, 583–586.

Zivich, J. M. Alcoholic subtypes and treatment effectiveness. *Journal of Consulting and Clinical Psychology*, 1981, *49*, 72–80.

Zuckerman, M. *Sensation seeking: Beyond the optimal level of arousal.* New York: Wiley, 1979.

Zuckerman, M. (Ed.). *Biological bases of sensation seeking, impulsivity, and anxiety.* Hillsdale, N.J.: Erlbaum, 1983.

Zuckerman, M., Buchsbaum, M. S., & Murphy, D. L. Sensation seeking and its biological correlates. *Psychological Bulletin*, 1980, *88*, 189–214.

CHAPTER 8

Environmental Factors in Substance Abuse

The Microsetting

DENNIS McCARTY

Writers who experimented with psychoactive drugs recognized that their responses to drugs were influenced by their expectations and apprehensions, their companions, and the time and place. Baudelaire, for example, used the sedate prose of the 19th century to caution against taking hashish while depressed, sorrowful, or worried and to suggest that a favorable surrounding with music is the best setting.

> Any grief or spiritual unrest . . . will toll like a bell amidst your intoxication and poison your pleasure. . . . If your surroundings are favorable—a picturesque landscape, for example, or a poetically decorated apartment; and if, in addition, you can look forward to hearing a little music; why, then, all is for the best. (Ebin, 1961, p. 21)

Contemporary journalist Hunter Thompson (1979) prescribed a similar setting in less delicate phrases.

> I like to load up on mescaline and turn my amplifier up to 110 decibels for a taste of "White Rabbit" while the sun comes up on the snow peaks along the Continental Divide. (p. 155)

Surroundings and their impact on drug effects and drug use are the focus of this chapter. Attention is restricted to the immediate drug use environment. This environment is the *microsetting* and is differentiated from the larger and more distal legal, cultural, and economic environ-

DENNIS McCARTY • Alcohol and Health Research Services, Inc., 134 Main Street, Stoneham, Massachusetts 02180.

ments discussed as the *macrosetting* in the next chapter. The microsetting is the physical and social context of drug use and includes (a) the physical setting (e.g., room, location, or space); (b) the setting's attributes (e.g., light, temperature, furniture, and paraphernalia); (c) companions and coparticipants; (d) the user's characteristics, attitudes, and expectations; and (e) the interactions of these elements. The discussion begins with an overview of microsetting influences on the acute drug experience (specifically, marijuana and alcohol intoxication). Next, the contributions of the microsetting to the development of opiate and alcohol dependence are examined briefly. Most attention is directed toward the effects of setting on drug and alcohol use. The factors that encourage or discourage drinking in specific microsettings are discussed in detail. Contributions from each facet of the drinking setting are outlined. In addition to the drinker and his or her attributes (age, sex, type of drinker, and attitudes), the drinking setting usually includes companions and overt (toasts and buying rounds) and subtle (norms and modeling) social influences that can encourage more rapid drinking and lengthen the time spent drinking. The physical environment also contributes to the drinking setting. Thus, bar and tavern attributes (physical design, cost of drinks, entertainment, and bartenders) that influence alcohol use are examined. Finally, some of the interactions that may occur among drinkers, their companions, and the physical environment are identified and discussed. The last section of the chapter suggests that microsetting factors and their mediating mechanisms may be put to work in efforts to treat and prevent alcohol and drug abuse.

There are two limitations that should be acknowledged in the analyses of drug use settings. First, the analyses are sometimes based on subjective data sources because much drug use is illicit and occurs in settings not conducive to observation or manipulation. As a result, objective data are frequently limited to studies of alcohol. Alcohol use is legal and can be studied systematically. The second limitation is that generalization from alcohol use settings to the clandestine world of illegal substances is not always warranted. When drug use occurs in a social context, however, the results from investigations of drinking behavior may be applicable. Nonetheless, generalizations must be made cautiously.

MICROSETTING INFLUENCES ON DRUGS AND ALCOHOL

DRUG EFFECTS

Reviews of psychoactive drugs and their use usually recognize that set and setting have a strong impact on a drug's effect on users. A Canadian government report on the nonmedical use of drugs notes that "the general effect of most drugs is greatly influenced by a variety of psychological and environmental factors" (LeDain, 1970, p. 36). Pharmacology alone cannot explain the variation in response to a similar dose of the same substance taken at different times and places (Goode, 1973; Weil, 1972b). Weil (1972a, 1972b) asserts that the most important discovery about psychoactive drugs is that the effects depend on the user's set and setting as much as the drug's pharmacological actions. Similarly, Goode (1973) and Leventhal (1980) advise that the consequences of a drug depend on the interactions among the dose, where the drug is taken, and the interpretation of drug effects. Hostile settings are conducive to interpreting the sometimes ambiguous effects of drugs as discomfort, distress, and, potentially, terror. On the other hand, a comfortable setting may induce interpretations of pleasure and enjoyment (Goode, 1973). Setting is believed to have especially strong influences on marijuana intoxication and experience with hallucinogenics (Goode, 1973; LeDain, 1970; Weil, 1972a, 1972b).

Setting and Marijuana Intoxication

Objective studies of marijuana intoxication, however, provide only limited evidence of effects due to setting. Carlin, Bakker, Halpern, and Dee Post (1972) attempted to facilitate or inhibit a subject's marijuana intoxication. An experimental confederate smoked placebo marijuana cigarettes and acted intoxicated or unaffected. The manipulation of social setting did not affect the subjects' ratings of marijuana potency or self-reported intoxication. When the subject smoked low-dose marijuana, however, performance on hidden figures, digit symbol, and association tests was affected by the setting manipulation. Test scores were better when the confederate acted as though the marijuana had no effect. Carlin et al. (1972) concluded that social setting could affect marijuana behavior at low doses.

Cappell and Pliner (1973) also found support for situational influences on the behavior of those intoxicated from marijuana. Subjects who were instructed to be as accurate as possible reduced errors on a time estimation task. Similarly, Pihl and Sigal (1978) examined the effect of different levels of motivation on the performance of a variety of tasks. Marijuana significantly impaired performance on all tasks, and motivation levels improved nondrugged performance. Motivation had no consistent effect on marijuana performance. Thus, there was little support for situational influences on marijuana's effects. Pihl and Sigal noted, however, that response variation within motivational levels was large and was evidence of interactions between the subject, the setting, and the dose.

In summary, within controlled laboratory settings, manipulations of setting have produced relatively weak evidence of situational influences on the response to marijuana. However, these settings are relatively sterile and are likely to inhibit many marijuana smokers. Thus, the weak situational influences may reflect strong inhibitions induced by the laboratory setting. As a result, phenomenological accounts and interview studies (e.g., Becker, 1963; Thompson, 1972) provide additional data on the effect of the microsetting on drug experiences and effects. Although not an empirical study, Thompson's (1972) fictionalized description of a drug and alcohol spree in Las Vegas is entertaining and includes phenomenological analyses of the interactions among setting, drug effects, and drug use.

Setting and Alcohol Intoxication

The effects of setting on alcohol intoxication are more amenable to objective study. One study demonstrated that the interpretation of intoxication depends on whether the drinker is alone or with others (Pliner & Cappell, 1974). Men and women who drank alcohol in a social setting reported increased friendliness and pleasure—changes in affective dimensions. Conversely, subjects who drank alone reported changes in physical symptomology—clear thinking, sleepiness, and dizziness. Participants who received a placebo drink were not affected by either context. Apparently, alcohol intoxication is interpreted affectively when drinking with others, and solitary drinking fosters attention to physical effects. Other dimensions of the drinking context and their influence on intoxication remain to be investigated (e.g., effects of music, illumination, and temperature).

DEPENDENCE AND TOLERANCE

The microsetting not only influences the interpretation and experience of drug effects, but it can also moderate the development of tolerance and dependence. Tolerance is evident when repeated administrations of a specific dose lead to reduced effects and an increased dose is required to obtain the same effects. Although some of the adaptation is due to physiological and pharmacological factors, nonpharmacological factors can contribute significantly (Krasnegor, 1978).

Opiate Dependence

Siegel (1976), for example, demonstrated that laboratory rats tolerant to a fixed dose of morphine in a labortory setting failed to exhibit tolerance when tested in a different setting. Siegel (1976, 1978) emphasizes the importance of the interaction between drug use and the setting. He asserts that the development of tolerance requires "repeated pairings of environmental cues with the systemic effects of the drug" (1976, p. 325). Moreover, the drug–environment interaction is not limited to narcotics. Studies demonstrate that the setting can contribute to tolerance to alcohol (Cappell, 1981; Poulous, Hinson, & Siegel, 1981); amphetamines (Schuster, 1978); cocaine (Woolverton & Schuster, 1978); and marijuana (Carder, 1978; Ferraro, 1978; Jones, 1978). Hinson (Chapter 4) provides a more detailed discussion of tolerance.

Tolerance is of interest because its development contributes to dependence. The diminished effects, due to tolerance, require more drug to produce the desired effect or to prevent withdrawal discomfort (Krasnegor, 1978). Studies of withdrawal indicate the importance of the setting in drug and alcohol dependence as well. O'Brien, Testa, Ternes, and Greenstein (1978) investigated classical conditioning effects in narcotic users and found that both drug highs and drug withdrawal could be induced through environmental stimuli alone. The drug use ritual was sufficient to elicit withdrawal symptoms in drug-free detoxified addicts. Conversely, self-injected saline produced a drug high if the user believed narcotic was injected.

Another dramatic, although less objective, report of the role of the microsetting on opiate addiction is found in Robins's study of U.S. Army enlistees in Vietnam (cited in McGlothlin, 1975). When surveyed in Vietnam, 20% of the respondents admitted current addiction to opiates. Eight to 12 months after their return, less than 10% reported addiction, and only 5% reported receiving any treatment for addiction. Most of the addicts stopped with little apparent difficulty. The change in macro- and microenvironment from inexpensive, high-quality heroin (macroenvironment factors) and stressful combat conditions (the microenvironment) to expensive, low-grade heroin and a setting of support and opportunity contributed to the termination of dependence (McGlothlin, 1975).

In general, dependence on drugs and alcohol appears to be due to interactions among the user, the drug, and the setting (Falk, Schuster, Bigelow, & Woods, 1982). Falk et al. (1982) propose that the environmental conditions that foster dependence strengthen the reinforcing properties of drugs. Two major situational factors encourage dependence: the age of the user (youths have less experience with other reinforcers; so they are more likely to find drugs attractive) and an absence of viable behavioral alternatives. The weakness of environmental reinforcers is one reason why youths living in inner city ghettos may be especially susceptible to drug dependence (Falk et al., 1982). Thus, special attention is warranted to these two environmental conditions in efforts to prevent drug dependence.

Alcohol Dependence

Alcohol dependence is also associated with environmental stimuli. Just as drug-use rituals induce withdrawal symptoms in narcotic addicts (O'Brien *et al.*, 1978), alcoholics report stronger craving for alcohol when tested in the presence of barroom signs and furniture than when tested in a standard laboratory setting (Ludwig, Cain, Wikler, Taylor, & Bendfeldt, 1977). There is also evidence that emotional states frequently associated with drinking can elicit reports of craving (Ludwig & Stark, 1974). Russell and Mehrabian (1977) also postulate that drugs and alcohol are used to alter specific emotional states. Thus, a variety of internal and external situational cues associated with alcohol use foster withdrawal symptoms and indicate that alcohol dependence is affected by the setting (Poulos *et al.*, 1981).

DRUG USE

Drug effects, tolerance, and dependence are clearly related to variables in the setting. Implicit in these analyses, however, is the effect of the setting on drug use. Addicts and alcoholics in the presence of appropriate internal or external stimuli experience withdrawal symptoms. Consequently, they are likely to seek out and use drugs or alcohol. The microsetting can also moderate drug taking in nondependent individuals and encourage the use of drugs not associated with physical dependence. Most individuals who use popular recreational drugs are not dependent. Thus, the subtle microsetting effects on use probably affect more individuals and more use than the dramatic effects on dependence. The effects on isolated drug use and drinking situations are the focus of this section. Unfortunately, the illicit nature of most drug use means that investigations of the setting's effect on use are difficult.

Survey studies indicate some of the major situational variables that affect usage patterns. The National Survey of Drug Abuse indicates that young adults aged 18 years to 25 years account for most drug use (Rittenhouse, 1979). A national survey of high-school students reported that a perceived social environment of family and peer support for marijuana and alcohol use contribute to higher levels of use (Jessor, Chase, & Donovan, 1980). Peer influence is the strongest predictor of marijuana among high-school students in both the United States and France (Kandel & Adler, 1982). Surveys, however, fail to provide detail on the immediate context of drug and alcohol use.

Research strategies that permit observation of ongoing drug use in its natural context are necessary. Crawford's (1977) use of trained ex-addicts to observe heroin use in the inner city is an innovative strategy. The field workers' notes are the primary data source. Moreover, they provide access to active users and arrange in-depth interviews with trained researchers. For the most part, however, observational and systematic studies of drug use are limited to legal drugs.

Cigarette smoking, for example, can be studied unobtrusively. Glad and Adesso (1976) investigated the contribution of the social setting to smoking. Participants waited for 20 minutes in a tense, hostile environment or a relaxed sociable setting. The subjects' companions in the waiting room either smoked or did not smoke. The incidence of smoking was significantly higher when the confederates smoked. Socially induced smoking was especially noticeable among light smokers. The study demonstrates that the behavior of companions can influence an individual's smoking. Companions are an important influence in the microsetting.

Most studies of situational influences on the use of a drug are investigations of alcohol use. Alcohol's important role in socialization and the system of distribution in controlled settings makes its use especially attractive for study. Because of the large number of studies of alcohol use, the remainder of the discussion focuses on situational variables that influence alcohol use. Drinking situations, particularly in bars and taverns, are examined in the following sections.

SITUATIONAL INFLUENCES ON ALCOHOL USE

A quiet drink alone at home after work, an open bar during a 21st-birthday celebration, and a sip of wine for a religious ceremony are qualitatively and quantitatively different drinking situations. Analyses of diverse settings such as these illustrate the potential contributions of the setting to variations in alcohol use (Harford, 1978). In addition, examinations of drinking situations help identify variables that can either foster or inhibit alcohol use and potential abuse (Harford & Spiegler, 1982). Before specific contexts and influences are examined, however, the general features of where, when, and with whom people drink must be outlined.

COMMON DRINKING SITUATIONS

National surveys consistently find that drinking usually occurs in the home. Cahalan, Cisin, and Crossley (1969) have provided the most extensive data. Most beer and wine drinkers drank in their own home

(87%) and in the homes of friends (68%). Only half (53%) of the respondents who drank beer and wine did so in bars and restaurants. The home was also the most frequent site for drinking liquor. Liquor was drunk more often, however, in bars and restaurants than in friends' homes.

Respondents to the Cahalan *et al.* (1969) survey also indicated that they drank most often with friends. Drinkers were less likely to drink with their family or alone. In addition, men and women stated that they tended to drink more than usual when drinking with close friends. Neighbors, acquaintances from work, and friends from church were associated with less than normal levels of drinking. Apparently, many drinkers moderate their drinking, depending on the situation and their drinking companions.

Finally, Cahalan *et al.* (1969) assessed when drinking usually occurred. More people drink on weekends than on weekdays. About 88% of beer and wine drinkers and 92% of liquor drinkers drank at least once in a while on weekends. In comparison, only 66% of beer and wine drinkers and 57% of liquor drinkers drank on weekdays. Argeriou (1975) and Harford and Gerstel (1981) examined drinking on each day of the week. Friday, Saturday, and Sunday are the days when more people drink, and drink larger amounts. The least drinking occurs on Monday and Tuesday. Both the number who drink and the amount drunk increases each day of the week until peaks are reached on Saturday. Thus, there appears to be a weekly pattern of alcohol consumption.

In summary, drinking at home on weekends with close friends seems to be a modal description of drinking situations. Interesting deviations from the norm emerge, however, when population subgroups are examined. Important differences that illustrate some of the interactions between the drinker and the situation are found among men and women, light, moderate, and heavy drinkers, and younger and older drinkers.

Men and Women

Cahalan *et al.* (1969) reported that both sexes drink most frequently at home but that men were more likely to drink in public settings such as bars and restaurants. More recent analyses (Harford, 1978) agreed in general but suggested that the primary difference between men and women was that men were more likely to drink in bars. Women actually drank in restaurants more frequently than men. Further, women drank more often with their spouse and relatives than men (Cahalan *et al.*, 1969; Harford, 1978). Men, however, were still more likely to drink on each day of the week and in more settings (Harford & Gerstel, 1981). Generally, men integrated drinking into more of their activities than did women (Harford, 1978).

Light, Moderate, and Heavy Drinkers

One basis for the differences between men and women in drinking contexts is that men tend to drink more than women. Studies of drinking contexts consistently demonstrate that heavier drinkers drink in more places and more frequently in public than light and moderate drinkers (Cahalan *et al.*, 1969; Kraft, 1982). As a result, most individuals drinking in bars are heavy drinkers. Heavier drinkers are also more likely to drink alone, although they usually drink with close friends (Cahalan *et al.*, 1969).

Younger and Older Drinkers

The heaviest drinkers tend to be young adults aged 18 to 30 (Clark & Midanik, 1982). Although they may not drink as often as older drinkers, when they drink, young drinkers tend to drink more and in more contexts, primarily on weekends. Older drinkers drink more regularly throughout the week but drink less on each occasion and tend to drink at home (Cahalan *et al.*, 1969; Harford & Gerstel, 1981).

As drinkers age from adolescence and young adulthood into middle age and retirement, the drinking settings change from private to public and finally return to private settings. Surveys of adolescent drinkers tend to report that the home is the context where drinking begins, and it is the one site where drinking occurs most frequently (Blane & Hewitt, 1977). Older teens, however, are more likely to drink in locations not supervised by adults—in parties with peers, secluded spots, and cars (Harford & Spiegler, 1982; Rachal, Maisto, Guess, & Hubbard, 1982). Teens are more likely to drink wth peers than with parents or other adults. The movement away from drinking at home is especially pronounced among teens who drink heavily.

Young adults (18 to 30) are least likely to drink in home settings. They drink with friends in bars and restaurants more frequently than older drinkers (Cahalan *et al.*, 1969). College students are especially likely to drink at large parties or in bars (Kraft, 1982). Kraft, for example, reports that at least once a month 90% of the students of a large university drink at parties and 64% drink in bars. Students who are heavier drinkers drink more frequently in all settings.

Adolescent and young adult drinking situations demonstate substantially more variability than those found among older adults. Older adults drink less in bars, and their weekend drinking patterns are more similar to weekday patterns (Harford & Gerstel, 1981). Harford and Gerstel (1981) suggest that the reduced variability in drinking situations may contribute to the decline in total consumption found in older drinkers.

In summary, people drink throughout the week in a variety of places.

Most drinking occurs in the home. However, individuals who drink heavily drink in many settings in addition to their home. Heavy drinkers are most likely to drink in public settings and account for the majority of public drinking. This means that studies of public drinking contexts will provide data on alcohol use among the drinkers that drink the most and drink most frequently. Consequently, analyses of drinking situations and efforts to indentify contextual variables that inhibit and encourage alcohol use will profit from careful study of drinking in bars and taverns.

VARIABLES THAT FACILITATE OR INHIBIT DRINKING IN BARS

Even though the home is the primary setting for alcohol use, there are few data on drinking practices in the home. Investigators must study more accessible settings where unobtrusive observation and systematic manipulation are feasible. Therefore, situational variables that influence drinking behavior are assessed through studies of drinking in bars, taverns, and cocktail lounges.

Clark (1982) suggests that three sets of situational factors may encourage or discourage drinking in bars: (1) the drinker's characteristics and attitudes; (2) social influence and normative standards; (3) the attributes and characteristics of the setting. Clark also notes that macrosetting influences, specifically legal regulations and policies, have direct effects on drinking in many settings. These influences, however, are outside the realm of the current review. Each of the three microsetting factors is examined in the following sections to assess its influence on alcohol use and its contribution to variations between settings in drinking. It is to be hoped that the findings from bars will help to explain variations in settings, such as the home, that are less accessible to investigation.

DRINKER ATTRIBUTES

Survey data suggest that individuals who use bars and taverns for drinking are primarily young, unmarried, male, heavy drinkers (e.g., Clark, 1966, 1982; Fisher, 1982). These characteristics are also associated with higher levels of drinking in bars. Observational studies reliably demonstrate that men drink more than women and that younger drinkers tend to drink more than older patrons (e.g., Cutler & Storm, 1975; Storm & Cutler, 1981). Assessment of the drinker's usual consumption pattern is difficult because observers know little about the patrons they watch. Babor, Mendelson, Uhly, and Souza (1980), however, observed 16 regular bar patrons (8 women) twice a week for 6 weeks. Michigan Alcoholism

Screening Test (MAST) (Selzer, Vinokur, & Van Rooijen, 1975) scores were obtained after observations were complete. Patrons with higher MAST scores drank more and had more episodes of multiple drinks than individuals with lower scores. Thus, the limited data agree with the expectation that heavier drinkers drink more in the bar setting than lighter drinkers.

Attitudinal factors may also contribute to increased alcohol use in bars. Room (cited in Clark, 1982) notes that a perceived obligation to "pay the rent" may foster drinking. Once an individual enters the tavern, even if for reasons unrelated to drinking, he or she may purchase a drink in order to pay for services being used. Further, the sense of obligation may increase the longer the individual remains in the bar (Clark, 1982). Observational studies consistently find that the longer the patrons are in a bar or lounge, the more they drink (e.g., Cutler & Storm, 1975; Sommer, 1965; Storm & Cutler, 1981).

A different type of cognitive mediation may both encourage and inhibit consumption. Gusfield, Kotarba, and Rasmussen (1982) believe that drinkers want to project an image as competent drinkers. Drinkers try to demonstrate they "can drink in accordance with the standards of the setting and the group of which they are a part; they 'can hold their own'" (p. 160). Competent drinking includes drinking as much as others in the group. However, the ability to recognize intoxication and to stop before the drinker's personal limit is exceeded are also important signs of competent drinking. This facet is similar to Clark's (1982) suggestion that drinkers limit consumption to avoid appearing grossly intoxicated. As a result, maintaining a self-image as a competent drinker not only encourages but also inhibits drinking. Gusfield et al. (1982) suggest that the extent of the inhibition is dependent on external demands, the drinking situation, and drinker characteristics. The need to work or to drive home as well as being female or older permit less drinking without penalty for violating personal or social standards of consumption. Thus, the image of a competent drinker may moderate social expectations of heavy drinking.

SOCIAL INFLUENCES

Few patrons in bars are alone. Cutler and Storm (1975) found only 25% of the men and 5% of the women they observed drinking alone. Most patrons (47%) drank in dyads or triads, and another 25% drank in groups of four. The rest (10%) drank in groups of five or more. Social interaction appears to be a major reason for drinking in bars.

Drinking companions are not only an important element in most drinking situations; they may affect drinking behaviors. Studies of social facilitation (Zajonc, 1965) suggest that the mere presence of companions is a source of arousal and can facilitate well-learned behaviors such as eating and drinking. As a result, effects related to the presence or absence of companions, the number of companions, and modeling are examined to assess the contribution of the social situation to alcohol use in bars. In addition, behavioral standards and norms attributed to important referents may affect consumption levels and are considered part of the social situation.

Drinking Companions

Patrons who drink with friends tend to drink more than individuals who drink alone. Sommer (1965) observed drinking in 32 bars and found that group drinkers drank nearly twice as much as solitary drinkers. Individuals drinking with friends also stayed twice as long. As a result, these data suggest that the rate of consumption is similar for isolated and group drinkers (3.5 glasses of beer per hour) but time in a bar influences the amount drunk.

Cutler and Storm (1975) provided similar data. They observed patrons in "straight," "swinger," "counterculture," and "skid row" beer parlors. Drinkers in each establishment drank about 2.5 beers per hour. They also noted that individuals drinking with friends stayed longer and drank more than solitary drinkers. The rate of drinking, however, was similar for both solitary and group drinkers. The relationships between group size and time in a bar were replicated again in a comparison of drinking patterns in beer parlors and cocktail lounges (Storm & Cutler, 1981).

Finally, Graves, Graves, Semu, and Ah Sam (1982a) investigated the effect of group size among three different ethnic groups. In each culture, time in the bar was primarily determined by the size of the drinking group and was responsible for the amount drunk.

One direct effect of drinking companions, therefore, is to increase the amount of time spent in the bar. Sommer (1965) and Cutler and Storm (1975) imply that companions have a relatively indirect and passive influence on a drinker's alcohol consumption. Storm and Cutler (1981) state directly that individuals in bars enter the setting with strong expectations and that social influence has relatively little impact on drinking behavior.

Sommer's and Cutler and Storm's passive view of group influence contrasts with other analyses. Skog (1982) reexamined the Cutler and Storm (1975) and Sommer (1965) data on the length of time solitary and group drinkers remain in a bar. Solitary drinkers tended to leave at a fairly constant exponential rate. Most isolates (about 60%) left during the first 30 minutes, and about 50% of the remainder left during each successive 30-minute period. Group drinkers, in contrast, were unlikely to leave during the first 30 minutes (only 35% of dyads, 22% of triads, and 15% of larger groups). An exponential departure rate was not apparent until after the second 30-minute period. Skog suggested that individuals in groups drink more because group mechanisms inhibit drinkers from leaving shortly after they arrive. This perspective views drinking companions as contributing actively to differences between solitary and group drinkers.

Rosenbluth, Nathan, and Lawson (1978) also present a more dynamic view of group influences. Men (42) and women (36) in a college pub were observed. During a 1-hour observation period, groups drank more than dyads, and males drinking with males drank the most. The greatest difference between dyad and groups was observed among women. Women in groups drank 50% more than women in dyads. The number of sips per glass was also affected. Men with groups of males or males and females averaged 8.5 to 9.5 sips for each glass. In contrast, a woman drinking with one other woman took nearly twice as many sips (15.5). Rosenbluth *et al.* (1978) concluded that groups facilitate drinking and that the social context is an important element of the alcohol-use microsetting. Moreover, the social context may effect women more strongly than men. Because men tend to drink heavily it is more difficult to increase their consumption levels than those of women.

In short, differences between group drinkers, dyad drinkers, and solitary drinkers are found in a variety of settings. Explanations for the differences, however, are less readily apparent. Skog (1982) notes that the relationship between group size and consumption could be due to many factors. For example, individuals who drink in groups may be different than those who drink alone. Heavy drinkers may prefer group drinking, or younger individuals may be more likely to drink in groups. Reasons for drinking may be a second potential explanation for differences between solitary and group drinkers. Group celebrations may be culturally conducive to greater consumption. Differences in drinking patterns in bars (where sociabilty is emphasized) and lounges (where intimacy is fostered) support this explanation for the effect of group size on drinking (Storm & Cutler, 1981). A final explanation is that the dynamics of social groups may encourage individuals to drink more when in groups than when drinking alone or in dyads. In the analysis of the drinking situation, a hypothesized group dynamic is the most interesting explanation. There are at least three potential mechanisms. Heavy drinkers may influence the quantities their group companions drink because they (a) coerce companions to drink more, using social rituals and direct demands; (b) model high drinking rates that are "contagious"; or (c) establish high normative standards for consumption that companions are expected to match.

Rituals and Demands

Social pressures to drink can be overt. Everyone is expected to drink when a toast is offered. A more subtle ritual that increases consumption is buying drinks in rounds. Skog (1982) suggests that fast drinkers urge slower drinkers to finish so that another round can be ordered. Bruun (1959), for example, observed frequent requests to "drink up" but few to slow down. Clark (1982) speculates that it is inappropriate to suggest that your companions drink more slowly. It implies that their drinking is uncontrolled. The practice of buying drinks for others also exerts subtle pressure to drink more (Clark, 1982). There appears to be a norm of reciprocity. The drinker who receives the drink is obligated to purchase the next drink. As a result of these rituals, patrons who intend to have "just one drink" will have difficulty succeeding when drinking with a group.

Modeling

Modeling is a second form of social influence that increases consumption. Heavy drinkers act as drinking models for other drinkers and help to define a situation as an appropriate setting for increased alcohol use (Caudill & Marlatt, 1975). Heavy drinkers also provide more behavior (sips) to model (Skog, 1982). Caudill and Marlatt (1975) reported the initial demonstration of modeling effects. Male college students participated in a 15-minute wine-tasting study either alone or with an experimental confederate who drank heavily (700 ml of wine) or lightly (100 ml of wine). Models were also warm and friendly or aloof and cold to the subject. Men who participated with the heavy drinker drank significantly more wine ($M = 364.1$ ml) than either men who did not have a model ($M = 180.8$ ml) or men who drank with the light-drinking model ($M = 141.9$ ml). The light-drinking model and no-model conditions did not differ significantly. The attempt to influence the strength of the modeling effect with a warm or cold model had no effect. Caudill and Marlatt concluded that the model provided cues about appropriate behavior. Subsequent studies demonstrated the strength of the modeling effect in a variety of settings and investigated potential parameters.

DeRicco and Garlington (1977; Garlington & DeRicco, 1977) demonstrated that variations in the confederate's rate of drinking during the course of an experimental session were matched by corresponding increases or decreases in the subject's drinking rate. The systematic changes occurred even when the subject was informed that attempts were being made to influence his drinking. Modeling apparently exerts a continuous influence on drinking behavior.

Another study suggests that the modeling effect is strongest when the model drinks at the same time as the subject. Hendricks, Sobell, and Cooper (1978) compared coaction (drinker and model drink at the same time) to imitation (drinker observed model and then drank unwatched) and to facilitation (drinker observed model, then drank while model observed). Individuals exposed to a high-consumption model drank more than those who observed a low-consumption model. The difference, however, was due primarily to the coaction setting. The facilitation and imitation conditions had much weaker influences on the amount drunk. Apparently, the modeling effect is more than facilitation or imitation. Both a social setting and simultaneous drinking are required before a strong modeling effect is observed. Coaction contributes a substantial and unique quality to the effect of the microsetting on alcohol use.

In addition to their physical presence and coaction, the model and drinker bring personal characteristics to the drinking situation. Studies indicate that neither the race (Watson & Sobell, 1982) nor the social status (Collins & Marlatt, 1981) of the model alters the modeling effect. Both the sex and the drinking habits of the drinker, however, appear to interact with model characteristics. Lied and Marlatt (1979) found a strong interaction between the drinker's sex and the drinker's drinking habits. Men and women categorized as heavy drinkers (45 or more drinks per month) were more responsive to differential modeling than light drinkers (17 or less per month). Light and heavy drinkers drank similar amounts if exposed to a high-consumption model. When drinking with a heavy consumption model, however, male and female heavy drinkers drank significantly more than light drinkers. Moreover, male heavy drinkers exposed to a heavy consumption model drank significantly more than female heavy drinkers. Cooper, Waterhouse, and Sobell (1979) reported similar data for the effect of a heavy consumption model on men and women. Wilkins (1980) replicated the differential effect of models on light and heavy drinkers. Lied and Marlatt (1979) speculate that heavy drinkers are more sensitive to variations in drinking norms. A light consumption model promotes restrained drinking. In contrast, a heavy consumption model has a disinhibitory effect on alcohol use among heavy drinkers.

Although the laboratory studies of modeling indicate strong effects, there is only one study that tests modeling influences in real bar settings.

Reid (1978) attempted to replicate the Caudill and Marlatt (1975) study that first reported modeling. Male confederates sat at the bar next to a male patron sitting alone. The model ordered a drink and either was warm and friendly, initiating conversation with the patron, or was aloof and cold, sitting unresponsive, staring into his drink. The model drank at a high (five drinks per hour) or low (one drink per hour) rate. Solitary patrons were also observed as a comparison group. As expected, a strong modeling effect was found. The results, however, differed somewhat from the laboratory results. Caudill and Marlatt (1975) found that only the high-consumption model affected drinking behavior and that the nature of the interaction had no influence on drinking behavior. In the bar, the warm, friendly model significantly increased consumption if heavy drinking was modeled and significantly decreased consumption when light drinking was modeled. The cold, aloof model had no influence on the patron's consumption. Moreover, men sitting next to the cold, low-consumption model condition left the bar significantly sooner than patrons in other conditions.

In summary, the nature of the interaction between drinkers has a substantial impact on whether or not modeling alters drinking behavior. Not only is coaction required, but in bars and taverns a pleasant interaction appears to be necessary. Once a relationship is established, however, the model has a strong bidirectional impact on consumption in the bar.

Consequently, modeling seems to be one mechanism that contributes to increased alcohol consumption among group drinkers. Strength of the influence is a function of the usual drinking level. Heavy drinkers exert more modeling influence and are more easily influenced.

Social Norms and Standards

Two final forms of interpersonal influence that contribute to increased alcohol use are social norms and standards. *Norms* are the behavioral standards and expectations shared by group members and are usually observed as regularities in the behavior of group members (Secord & Backman, 1964).

In a drinking situation, a group expectation that drinking is desirable will tend to exert pressure on its members to drink and to conform to a standard level of consumption. Bruun (1959), for example, concluded that heavy drinking, but not gross intoxication, was valued as a masculine attribute. Thus, drinking less than most was discouraged, although it was permissible to drink more. Skog (1982) suggests that this standard causes individuals who perfer to drink slowly to drink more rapidly and heavily than they would otherwise and does not inhibit the consumption of heavy drinkers. As a result, alcohol use in groups tends to be greater than when individuals are drinking alone.

Norms that encourage increased alcohol use may also foster problems for some group members. Straus (1979) suggests that the social norms often ignore individual variability in response to alcohol. Although many group members may be able to match or exceed the group standard without undesired consequences, some drinkers who are more sensitive to alcohol will drink "too much" trying to meet social expectations. Thus, the failure to recognize individual differences in sensitivity to alcohol is one source of drinking problems. This is especially true in social situations where drinking is expected and important social responsibilities must also be met, for example, a business lunch.

In addition to a differential impact on light and heavy drinkers and individuals who are more sensitive to alcohol, the influence of *normative standards* may vary according to the drinking situation and the demographic characteristics of the drinker. Multiple regression analysis of survey data from high-school students suggests that the students' attitudes are the primary determinant of drinking in pubs and at parties (Schlegel, Crawford, and Sanborn, 1977). Parental norms, however, dictate drinking behavior in the home. The relative influence of norms and attitudes also vary in different adolescent age groups and among adolescents from different socioeconomic backgrounds. Briddle, Bank, and Marlin (1980) report that parental norms and standards determine the attitudes and behaviors of young teens (12 and 13 years of age). Among midteens (14 to 16) and late teens (17 to 19), parental norms had little influence. The major determinant was personal attitude, although peer norms and expectations also contributed. A comparison of working-class adolescents suggests that both parental and peer norms are more influential among working-class youths. Briddle *et al.* also report that an analysis of male and female differences found that parental standards affected the attitudes of teenaged women but had no influence on the attitudes or behaviors of male teenagers. In summary, at least among adolescents, norms exert a variable influence. The influence is dependent on the referent (parent or peer) and the age, sex, and social class of the adolescent (Briddle *et al.*, 1980) as well as the drinking context (Schlegel *et al.*, 1977).

The studies suggest that normative influences may also vary among older, more experienced drinkers. A major constraint on the assumed presence and variability of normative standards among adults, however, is that these influences have not been investigated systematically among them. Thus, it is difficult to identify confidently the contexts in which norms have more or less influence on adult drinking. The assumption in many analyses of public drinking (e.g., Bruun, 1959; Skog, 1982) is that peer standards are influential in taverns. Moreover, the standards are assumed to vary, depending on the drinking occasion and the type of setting (Storm & Cutler, 1981). Nonetheless, the lack of more extensive data means these assumptions must be viewed as only tentative explanations for adult drinking practices and the influence of a group on the amount and rate of consumption.

Social Influences That Discourage Drinking

Most of our discussion has examined social influences that encourage drinking. Nonetheless, social influence may inhibit as well as facilitate consumption. Bruun's (1959) analysis of drinking norms, for example, notes that although norms establish that drinking heavily is desirable, there is also a standard that intoxication is inappropriate. The normative proscription on intoxicated behavior is congruent with the concept of a competent drinker. Gusfield et al. (1982) suggest that individuals wish to be perceived as competent drinkers. Patrons drink heavily but limit consumption so that they do not appear or act intoxicated. Consequently, both attitudinal constraints and normative standards act togther to establish an upper limit on the amount of drinking.

In addition to the normative standard on the most that individuals should drink, modeling may constrict alcohol use in some situations. Reid (1978) demonstrates that a warm, friendly drinking companion who drinks slowly can reduce a bar patron's rate of consumption. Collins and Marlatt (1981) examine the potential application of modeling techniques to the prevention of alcohol abuse. They propose that moderate-drinking models be used to reinforce moderate alcohol use at parties and celebrations. In addition, Collins and Marlatt suggest that individuals modeling appropriate drinking behaviors can be used to teach adolescents responsible drinking habits. In summary, modeling may have a potential to counteract as well as amplify situations and standards that foster abusive levels of alcohol use.

Finally, an additional type of social influence that restricts drinking behavior is similar to the overt influence exerted by rituals like toasts. The rituals are in effect social commands to drink. A social command to limit consumption can be inferred from the response to strangers in neighborhood bars. Cavan (1966) classifies these establishments as *home territory* bars and notes that strangers are treated coldly and rudely. The effect of a shunning treatment is illustrated in Reid's (1978) study. Patrons sitting next to the cold, aloof, noncommunicative, slow-drinking model left more quickly than the other patrons observed. It is likely, then, that hostility toward strangers in neighborhood bars is a noticeable constraint on the amount drunk. The effect, however, may not be as strong in other types of bars.

BAR ATTRIBUTES

The features that make one bar or tavern different from another are its attributes and characteristics. These elements include the interior design, entertainment, cost of drinks, and the bar's management and staff. Generally, the influence of these aspects of the drinking situation on alcohol use and alcohol-related problems have not been systematically investigated. Much of the discussion of bar attributes, therefore, is speculative.

Interior Design

Bars and taverns, no matter where they are located, tend to have a distinctive ambience. Lights are dim, tables small, and a long wooden bar backed by an extensive selection of liquors is the focal point. Prompts for specific brands of beer or types of mixed drinks may be the centerpiece on each table, and clocks, lights, and signs plastered with advertising serve as the principal decor.

Partially a product of tradition and expectation, the contemporary bar also includes elements introduced by market research and Madison Avenue to foster increased sales (i.e., alcohol use). Without access to data on sales, it is difficult to document the specific effects of the elements that contribute to a bar. Nonetheless, it is clear that the setting in its entirety can contribute to increases in consumption. Strickler, Dobbs, and Maxwell (1979) observed men drinking in a sterile laboratory setting and the same subjects drinking in a licensed bar. The men drank significantly more and faster in the bar, even when they were required to pay for their drinks. Although there are more differences between a lab and a bar than just ambience, the bar's decor plus expectations about acceptable behavior (certainly a part of the perceived ambience) influence drinking behavior. The independent contributions of space, density, table prompts, and functional advertisements are more difficult to assess.

A tavern begins as an open, empty space. The size and shape of the space as well as the arrangement of partitions, tables, and booths in the space have strong influences on the behaviors that are likely to occur. A bar with long tables in an open room fosters different behaviors than a bar with private booths or small tables and partitions strategically placed to create an illusion of privacy. Storm and Cutler's (1981) study of beer gardens and cocktail lounges in Edmonton, Alberta, illustrates many of the differences. Legal regulations require beer gardens to be well-lit areas with separate tables. Only beer is served. Cocktail lounges, on the other hand, emphasize small tables and booths with low lighting. Mixed drinks are served in addition to wine and beer. Loud partying and socialization in groups are the principal activities in beer gardens. Conversely, quiet conversation among dating couples seems to be the most common behavior in lounges. Drinking behaviors also differ. Patrons in beer gardens tend to drink more and to drink more rapidly than their counterparts in lounges. Thus, the open interiors of beer gardens foster socialization and heavy drinking, whereas the intimate spaces of cocktail lounges encourage more controlled drinking. In summary, the interior design of bars appears to have a pervasive influence on how the bar, tavern, or lounge is used.

The number of people in the bar may also affect drinking and other activities. The quiet, nearly empty establishment is assumed to be flawed. People apparently perfer, or are more comfortable in, bars and restaurants that are relatively busy. As the number present increases, however, patrons begin to feel crowded. Baum and Valins (1979) suggest that crowding occurs when the ability to regulate the nature and frequency of social interactions is lost. Higher densities can be tolerated in environments that promote the illusion of privacy. Low lighting and booths are two strategies that may facilitate continued control in high-density settings. When control is lost, stress is increased, and interpersonal relationships deteriorate. For example, aggressive incidents in bars become more serious as more people are involved (Graves, Graves, Semu, & Ah Sam, 1982b).

The relationships between high density in bars, alcohol consumption, intoxication, and perceived crowding remain untested. However, theory and observation suggest interesting hypotheses. Zeichner and Pihl (1979) contend that intoxication disrupts the ability to attend to the effects of behavior. As a result, negative contingencies exert less influence on intoxicated individuals, and aggressive incidents are more likely. This reasoning suggests that the negative effects of high density should be amplified among drinkers. Not only would increased density make social interaction more difficult, but intoxication would reduce the sensitivity to norms designed to protect and promote interactions. Anecdotal obvservation, however, suggests a different dynamic. Individuals, at moderate blood–alcohol levels at least, seem to be less sensitive to privacy norms and more open to conversation with strangers and socialization in groups. This analysis suggests that moderate density may promote increased socialization, and crowding is not experienced. Both assessments may be valid, depending on the total density and on how intoxicated the drinkers are. The potential interactions and individual differences remain to be examined systematically.

In addition to the design of the space and the number of individuals present, the decor may influence drinking behavior. Advertising is a prominent feature of the decor in many bars. Lights, mirrors, clocks, and signs may be emblazoned with the trademarks of popular alcoholic beverages. Table prompts, promoting specific brands, decorate every table and booth. According to a beer company executive, point-of-purchase advertising like table prompts is the final step in a promotional plan. Displays and advertisements serve as reminder messages for the consumer when purchases are made. Moreover, studies by the Point-of-Purchase Advertising Institute suggest that 45% of shoppers are influenced by point-of-purchase materials and that 33% buy a specific product because of point-of-purchase advertising ("Reinforcing p-o-p as a sales tool," 1963). In short, although direct data on the impact of barroom advertisements are not available, the presence of the advertising is assumed to influence consumption.

The nature of the influence, however, is unclear. Advertising's effects may be limited to decisions on which brands to purchase (e.g., Heineken versus Miller). More pervasively, advertising may create a setting that suggests that heavier alcohol consumption is permissible. Another possibility is that the influence of the advertising depends on the relative intoxication of the drinker. Distilled beverage advertisements may encourage continued drinking in individuals who are slightly intoxicated (McCarty & Ewing, 1983). Generally, discussion of alcoholic beverage advertising and its impact in bars and taverns is speculative. Objective studies that monitor systematic changes in these advertising elements in real bars are necessary before unbiased analyses of the impact can be made. Only then can interactions and individual differences be anticipated more accurately.

Entertainment

Entertainment and games in the drinking setting may both increase the number of individuals in the bar and affect drinking behavior. Games and entertainment keep patrons in the bar longer, and, as a result, they tend to drink more. Babor, Mendelson, Uhly, and Souza (1980), for example, observed 16 bar regulars on nights with either a televised football game or a piano sing-along as entertainment. The patrons averaged 60% more drinks and stayed twice as long on nights with music. The sing-along also appeared to increase socialization. Individuals were more likely to drink with groups, and fewer individuals drank alone or only with their spouse. Music, therefore, appears to have direct effects on increased socialization and indirectly fosters more time in the tavern and more consumption.

Music may affect drinking behavior directly. Bach and Schaffer (1979) report that the tempo of country music has a significant negative correlation with sip rate. Observers monitored sip rate while records played in the background. Fast music was associated with slower sipping, and, conversely, sipping was faster during slow music. The reasons for the differential impacts, however, are unclear. Speculation suggests that slow music may induce feelings of depression and thus foster more drinking. Alternatively, fast music may be more entertaining. Patrons become more involved in fast music and drink less.

The specific effects on drinking associated with other types of entertainment have not been studied. The general principle appears to be that the longer individuals stay in the bar the more they drink. Though some forms of entertainments may slow the rate of drinking, the increased time results in higher levels of consumption.

Cost of Drinks

Econometric analyses demonstrate that alcoholic beverages are like other commodities in the market: they are sensitive to changes in price and income (Bruun *et al.*, 1975; Cook, 1981). Increases in price lead to decreased consumption and vice versa. As a result, bars attract customers and increase sales by offering reduced price drinks during "happy hour"— late afternoon periods when sales are usually depressed.

The effects of the happy hour on drinking patterns have been examined in two studies. Babor, Greenberg, Mendelson, and Kuehnle (1978) tested the effects of price and price reductions on the drinking habits of men classified as heavy and casual drinkers who were living in an experimental setting. Consumption of alcoholic beverages increased substantially during an afternoon happy hour. The increase was more pronounced among heavy drinkers. Further, happy hour drinking increased total consumption; the increase was in addition to, rather than a substitution for, drinking at other times. A return to the regular price, however, resulted in the termination of most drinking. In other words, drinkers prompted to start during happy hour were not stimulated to continue drinking when happy hour ended. Price exerted an influence even among intoxicated heavy drinkers.

In a second study, Babor *et al.* (1980) assessed the effects of happy hour among 16 regular patrons in a bar. Between three and five o'clock in the afternoon, the price of drinks in a neighborhood tavern was reduced. When happy hour was initiated, 4 of the 16 regulars began to arrive earlier. They averaged 9.6 drinks per visit (4.5 during happy hour; 5.1 afterward). In contrast, nonhappy hour patrons drank an average of 3.7 drinks per visit. Drinkers who started drinking during happy hour usually continued drinking throughout the evening. The abrupt termination of drinking observed in the laboratory study was not noted. However, a switch from mixed drinks to less expensive beer at the end of happy hour demonstrated sensitivity to price.

In both laboratory and real-world settings, therefore, economic contingencies have strong influences on drinking patterns. The effect may be less pronounced in the bar because of differences between the bar patrons and the laboratory subjects. MAST scores, in fact, suggested that several of the happy hour bar patrons might be classified as alcoholics. None of the laboratory subjects was considered alcoholic. Nonetheless, both groups began drinking earlier and altered their consumption when happy hour ended. Thus, light drinkers, heavy drinkers, and alcoholics appear to be responsive to price reduction in bars and taverns. The cost of drinks is an important element in the microsetting that can both encourage and limit consumption.

Bartenders

The final element in the public-drinking setting that may encourage or discourage alcohol consumption is the person who serves the drinks—bartenders, waitresses, and waiters. Gusfield *et al.* (1982) noted that the primary responsibility of bartenders and their staff is to sell alcohol and create an atmosphere conducive to relaxation and enjoyment. They provide drinks as requested and approach customers to encourage additional purchases. Reid (1978) observed that customers were approached with different frequency and might drink faster or slower as a result. Men sitting alone were approached about once every 12 minutes; women sitting alone were approached about once every 21 minutes; and couples were approached only once every 34 minutes. Other demographic and group characteristics might also influence the frequency that waitresses check on a table and consequently influence drinking rates.

In addition to serving drinks, bartenders can also discourage continued drinking. The ability to limit drinking depends, however, on the relationship between the customers and the bartender. The Gusfield *et al.* (1982) ethnographic analysis of driving after drinking in bars identified four general roles for bartenders. In some neighborhood bars, the bartender may be part of the regular gang. Patrons are influenced and controlled through friendship. Bartenders in other neighborhood bars are the center of attention. Their personality and status influence customers. On the other hand, bartenders in singles bars have little interaction with patrons. Their job is to serve drinks as quickly as possible. Bouncers are used to control unruly or unwanted guests. In upper-class bars and restaurants, the bartender also has a subservient role and has little influence on customers. The bartender's relatively high status in neighborhood bars permits limiting as well as serving drinks. Comportment is controlled, and when necessary, the welfare of customers is protected. If a patron drinks too much to drive safely, the bartender may call a taxi or arrange a ride home. There is a distinctly different relationship in singles and upperclass bars. The bartender is simply the person who serves drinks. Customers do not expect intervention, and they view efforts to limit consumption or safeguard their welfare as inappropriate. Thus, the bartender and, by extension, waiters and waitresses influence drinking behavior in some settings.

THE INTERACTIONS OF DRINK, DRINKER, AND SETTING

Within the bar, influences from the drink, the drinker, and the setting interact to create the drinking experience. Some of the readily identified effects for each component have already been discussed. The dynamics and the implications of the interactions among the physiological, cognitive, and environmental variables are less apparent and remain to be examined.

Loud music and dense crowds in a bar may make it difficult to discriminate between internal sources of arousal (e.g., intoxication and emotion) and external stimulation (e.g., loud music and attractive drinking companions). When this happens, arousal due to intoxication may be misattributed to nonalcoholic sources of sensation. Misattribution may increase the perceived intensity of the nonalcoholic stimuli and reduce perceptions of impairment due to alcohol intoxication. Thus, the cognitive interpretation of the physiological and environmental interactions may have important effects on the amount drunk and the behavior engaged in.

Studies on misattribution and the interpretation of intoxication provide evidence of the proposed interactions and their effects on drinking behavior. Schachter (1964) suggests that physiological arousal is often diffuse and nonspecific. Arousal may be interpreted as specific emotions if the behavioral context can be interpreted as emotional. Studies demonstrated that the experience of an emotion, therefore, requires two factors: physiological sensation and an explanation for the sensation (Schachter & Singer, 1962; Schachter & Wheeler, 1962). Moreover, Schachter (1964) speculates that this process may contribute to the emotional and behavioral changes that are observed with drugs. Schachter's analysis suggests that alcohol intoxication can be misattributed to environmental stimuli.

McCarty (1981) gave subjects a placebo medication prior to a moderate (0.48 ml of 95% ethanol per kg body weight) or a low (0.24 ml of 95% ethanol per kg body weight) dose of alcohol. The placebo was purported to produce side effects similar to alcohol, side effects dissimilar to alcohol, or no side effects. Participants rated the source of their physiological sensation 20, 40, and 60 minutes after completing the drink. Incorrect attributions to the medication were greatest at the lower dose and with increasing time. The side-effect instructions did not influence the attribution. Thus, the attribution of sensation to the inert placebo demonstrated that physiological sensations from alcohol intoxication can be incorrectly attributed to nonalcoholic stimuli. The study also showed that misattribution is strongest when alcohol intoxication is less noticeable.

The data suggest, therefore, that misattribution is not only possible but that drinking in bars and taverns may be especially conducive to misattribution. The barroom is filled with strong external stimuli (e.g., noise, companions) that contribute to the drinker's total activation level. As a result, the contribution of alcohol intoxication to total arousal may be difficult to discriminate and a misattribution to an external stimulus likely. Moreover, the strength of the stimulus may be misperceived because alcohol-related sensations are cognitively transferred to the nonalcoholic source.

Zillman (1978) argues that a transfer of excitation can occur when multiple explanations for physiological arousal are plausible. Individuals tend to combine undifferentiated physiological sensations. Consequently, all sensations are attributed to one specific salient stimulus rather than partialed out among the actual sources. The perceived strength of the salient stimulus is enhanced, and emotional behavioral reactions may be amplified as a result of the transfer of excitation.

The transfer of excitation implies that when drinkers are unaware of their intoxication, nonalcoholic stimuli may be evaluated as a stronger influence on emotion and behavior. McCarty, Diamond, and Kaye (1982) report data that support this analysis. Men and women evaluated pictures selected to elicit low or moderate levels of sexual arousal. Before rating pictures, subjects received alcoholic or nonalcoholic drinks. A balanced-placebo design varied drink instruction and drink content independently.

Individuals who did not know they drank alcohol (i.e., subjects who were told that their alcoholic drink did not contain alcohol) reported the strongest levels of arousal. When drinkers did not discriminate their intoxication, the physiological excitation induced by alcohol trnsferred to and intensified the assessment of the nonalcoholic stimuli. The effect was found among both men and women. The transfer of excitation was limited, however, to the more arousing photographic stimuli. Apparently, a transfer of alcoholic excitation requires a moderately strong external stimulus to initiate the misattribution.

In summary, the analysis of misattribution and the transfer of excitation indicates that interactions among cognitions, physiological activation, and environmental stimuli can influence the perceptions of moderately intoxicated drinkers. Misattribution and the transfer of excitation appear to be mechanisms for some of the interaction effects. However, the interactions of drink, drinker, and setting have not been examined systematically. Studies are needed that vary the setting and its characteristics as well as the amount of intoxication. Investigations that assess the effect of misattribution on perceived intoxication and the ability to monitor intoxication levels are also warranted. These investigations will facilitate the development of a more complete understanding of the microsetting and its effect on alcohol and drug abuse.

THE MICROSETTING IN TREATMENT AND PREVENTION

The microsetting's pervasive but sometimes subtle contributions to drug and alcohol effects, dependence, and use are being recognized. Gradually, research is moving beyond a documentation of phenomenological reports toward an identification of the mechanisms that mediate the environmental influences (Chapter 12, this volume). Thus, studies have progressed from the initial attempt to assess marijuana-related impairment (Weil, Zinberg, & Nelson, 1968) to more sophisticated analyses of the environment as a conditioned stimulus in the development of tolerance and dependence (Siegel, 1976) and assessments of the attribution of intoxication and the transfer of excitation to environmental stimuli (McCarty, et al., 1982). The ultimate goals are the indentification of similarities and differences in the use and abuse of different drugs and the development of more effective prevention and treatment strategies that include manipulation of setting variables.

Comparisons between drugs are difficult because of differences in their pharmacological properties and actions. However, an assessment of how drugs are used and the influence of the environment on their use and effects may suggest potential parallels. Both alcohol and marijuana, for example, are frequently used in social settings. Studies indicate that drinking companions may alter the rate and amount of drinking (Rosenbluth *et al.*, 1978) or increase the amount of time in the drinking setting (e.g., Cutler & Storm, 1975; Graves *et al.*, 1982a). If similar unobtrusive investigations can be conducted among marijuana users, the data may indicate that some social situations influence the rate of marijuana smoking or the length of time spent smoking. Other similarities between marijuana and alcohol may be found in the interpretation of intoxication. Just as alcohol's effects are frequently determined by expectancies (Marlatt & Rohsenow, 1980) and can be misattributed (McCarty, 1981), marijuana's effects are also believed to be dependent on the user's expectancies (Weil, 1972a; Weil *et al.*, 1968) and may be susceptible to misattribution and the transfer of excitation.

Similarities between alcohol and drugs other than marijuana may also be found. Opiate use is a qualitatively different experience than most social drinking. Nonetheless, dependence on both drugs seems to have strong classically conditioned components. It appears that the environmental stimuli repeatedly associated with substance use become integral parts of the experience and can elicit much of the observed response.

In short, examination of the microsetting suggests behavioral relationships between substances of abuse. These relationships may provide a basis for a more comprehensive understanding of drug and alcohol abuse and facilitate development of prevention and treatment strategies.

Researchers have already suggested a number of treatment strategies based on the role of the setting in the development of dependence. Poulos *et al.* (1981) suggest that craving is often the result of exposure to environmental stimuli previously associated with use. Consequently, treatment strategies should attempt to extinguish the effects of the environmental cues. Marlatt (1980), for example, uses a relapse prevention strategy that identifies the setting variables associated with abuse and helps patients develop strategies to avoid or circumvent high-risk situations. Analysis of the addict's usual use situation seems to have an important role in the treatment process.

Prevention can also benefit from analysis of the microsetting. Price (1981) identified situational factors associated with increased physical illness. A similar analysis of situations conducive to a high incidence of drug- and/or alcohol-related problems may also be instructive. Jessor's problem behavior theory suggests, for example, that among young adults, settings with low levels of parental or institutional control, high peer support for problem behaviors, and the presence of behavioral models may foster high incidences of marijuana and alcohol abuse (Jessor &

Jessor, 1977). More specifically, Mills, Neal, and Peed-Neal (1983) propose that university-based prevention programs examine settings where heavy alcohol use is common and encourage the participants to develop ways to reduce the likelihood of alcohol-related problems in those situations. A more direct environmental strategy is suggested in a study of prevention policies (Moore & Gerstein, 1981). The study committee proposed that the environment be modified to reduce potential dangers to drinkers and nondrinkers. One example is the use of air bags or other passive restraint systems to reduce personal injury in alcohol-related traffic accidents. The direct interventions are intriguing because the cooperation of the drinker is not required. The microsetting may not be able to limit the use, but environmental modification may reduce the damage done by careless drug and alcohol users.

In summary, the analysis of the microsetting in treatment and prevention leads to the redirection of environmental influences. Instead of encouraging abuse, the microsetting can be modified to discourage use. Most settings have some features that facilitate use and others that inhibit it. By strengthening the variables that inhibit abuse, alcohol and drug-related problems in the settings may be limited. Studies to design and test prevention and treatment applications are the next step in the development of an appreciation for the microsetting and its influence on substance abuse.

SUMMARY AND CONCLUSIONS

The analysis of the microsetting was based on two important considerations. First, the microsetting is not limited to the built environment. The conceptualization must include the individual who is drinking or using substances, the user's companions and coparticipants and the social influences that result, and the physical setting. The second important point is that the microsetting not only moderates the user's psychological response and interpretation of drug effects but also contributes directly to the development of tolerance and dependence and exerts subtle but consistent influences on the amount and rate of use. A brief review of microsetting effects on the different processes illustrates the extent of the influence.

The setting's contribution to the interpretation of drug effects is relatively clear. Companions in the microsetting help users define the nature and extent of their reponse to drugs and alcohol. Solitary drinkers interpret alcohol intoxication in terms of physical sensations. In contrast, social drinkers are more likely to respond on affective dimensions (Pliner & Cappell, 1974). Similarly, the performance of marijuana smokers on tests of impairment can be altered by companions who act intoxicated or nonintoxicated (Carlin *et al.*, 1972). The influence of nonsocial variables (e.g., music, mood, occasion) on the interpretation of intoxication and the response to drugs remains to be investigated systematically. Phenomenological accounts, however, suggest strong influences.

The microenvironment's contribution to the development of tolerance and dependence is more completely documented. Investigations with laboratory animals consistently demonstrate that tolerance requires repeated pairings of setting stimuli with the physiological effects of the drug (Falk *et al.*, 1982). Tolerance that is evident in one environment may not be apparent in a new setting (Siegel, 1976, 1978). Studies of addicts and alcoholics also find strong evidence of classical conditioning to environmental cues. Dependent users experience craving and withdrawal in response to appropriate setting stimuli (Ludwig *et al.*, 1977; O'Brien *et al.*, 1978). Attention, therefore, to situational factors that strengthen the reinforcing properties of addictive substances may promote the development of effective strategies to prevent dependence.

In addition to moderating the development of tolerance, the microsetting can promote or discourage drug and alcohol use among nondependent users and drinkers. Influences on the level and frequency of use are potentially the most extensive and interesting because they may affect everyone who drinks alcohol, smokes marijuana, or uses other drugs. Microsetting effects on alcohol use are the best documented. For these analyses, the drinking setting is not limited to the physical environment. The drinker and his or her attributes as well as the drinking companions are considered important elements in the microsetting. Studies of alcohol use indicate that young males (Cahalan *et al.*, 1969; Clark & Midanik, 1982) who wish to project an image of a competent drinker (Gusfield *et al.*, 1982) are most likely to drink and to drink heavily. Moreover, much of the drinking occurs in groups (Cutler & Storm, 1975). Group drinkers stay in bars longer and drink more than solitary drinkers (Cutler & Storm, 1975; Sommer, 1965). Groups appear to encourage increased drinking through coercive rituals (buying in rounds) and demands (toasts and requests to "drink up") and by modeling heavy consumption or setting high-consumption norms. Heavy- and light-drinking models reliably facilitate or inhibit the amount drunk (Caudill & Marlatt, 1975). Heavy drinkers respond strongly to heavy-drinking models but appear to be inhibited by models who drink lightly (Lied & Marlatt, 1979). Cold, aloof models may also discourage companions from continuing to drink and prompt them to leave bars more quickly (Reid, 1978). Thus, modeling appears to be an important mechanism in the dynamics of group influences on alcohol use.

Social norms may also encourage heavy consumption. Many observers report the existence of norms that require a minimum amount of drinking, which is usually relatively high (Bruun, 1959). Although no maximum is established informally, norms against gross intoxication are common. Most systematic studies of normative influences, unfortunately, have been limited to adolescent and young adult drinkers. The studies indicate that norms have variable influences and are dependent on the age, sex, and social class of the drinker (Briddle et al., 1980). Although normative influences are expected to alter adult drinking, to depend on the occasion and setting, and to contribute to problem drinking, the lack of normative data from adult drinkers is a serious limitation. Systematic studies are clearly needed to define adult drinking norms and to identify the parameters of their influence.

The physical setting is another important facet in the microsetting. In many cases, this is a bar. Although large open rooms appear to encourage loud socializing and heavy consumption in large groups, darker settings with small tables facilitate intimate conversation between dyads and promote restricted consumption (Storm & Cutler, 1981). The contributions of crowding in these settings are not clear. Studies of the relationships between alcohol use and perceptions of crowding are needed. Although drinking in crowded settings may encourage fights and confrontations, alcohol use may also initially reduce perceptions of crowding and promote casual interactions.

Other facets of the bar may also contribute to alcohol use. An opportunity to systematically vary table prompts and assess the amounts and types of beverage sales would be interesting. Speculation about the impact of advertising on sober and intoxicated drinkers could be addressed directly. A final element in the bar is the bartender. As the dispenser of drinks, his or her influence should be studied thoroughly. Investigations would be especially timely because of growing interest in bartenders' responsibilities to patrons and the public to prevent drinkers from becoming too intoxicated and from driving when they are intoxicated.

These elements of the drinking setting mix and interact on many dimensions and contribute to the pleasure and attractiveness of alcohol use. Misattribution and transfer of excitation appear to contribute to some of the disinhibition and affective responsivity that occurs when drinking (McCarty, 1981; McCarty et al., 1982). Additional systematic studies of these processes are needed to identify and delimit their influence outside controlled laboratory settings.

Eventually, microsetting influences on intoxication, dependence and tolerance, and drug and alcohol use may be applicable in treatment and prevention programs. The examination of current research indicates microsetting variables that discourage as well as encourage use and factors that alter the interpretation of intoxication. The potential, therefore, for effective applications seems strong and should promote continued efforts to include microsetting variables in theories of substance abuse and attempts to understand individual variations in use.

REFERENCES

Argeriou, M. Daily alcohol consumption patterns in Boston; some findings and a partial test of the Tuesday hypothesis. *Journal of Studies on Alcohol*, 1975, *36*, 1578–1583.

Babor, T. F., Greenberg, I., Mendelson, J. H., & Kuehnle, J. C. Experimental analysis of the "happy hour": Effects of purchase price on drinking behavior. *Psychopharmacology*, 1978, *58*, 35–41.

Babor, T. F., Mendelson, J. H., Uhly, B., & Souza, E. Drinking patterns in experimental and barroom settings. *Journal of Studies on Alcohol*, 1980, *41*, 635–651.

Bach, P. J., & Schaffer, J. M. The tempo of country music and the rate of drinking in bars. *Journal of Studies on Alcohol*, 1979, *40*, 1058–1059.

Baum, A., & Valins, S. Architectural mediation of residential density and control: Crowding and the regulation of social contact. In L. Berkowitz (Ed.), *Advances in experimental social psychology* (Vol. 12). New York: Academic Press, 1979.

Becker, H. S. *Outsiders: Studies in the sociology of deviance.* New York: Free Press, 1963.

Blane, H. T., & Hewitt, L. E. *Alcohol and youth. An analysis of the literature, 1960–1975* (NTIS No. PB-268 698). National Institute on Alcohol Abuse and Alcoholism, 1977.

Briddle, B. J., Bank, B. J., & Marlin, M. M. Social determinants of adolescent drinking: What they think, what they do and what I think and do. *Journal of Studies on Alcohol*, 1980, *41*, 215–241.

Bruun, K. *Drinking behavior in small groups.* Helsinki: The Finnish Foundation for Alcohol Studies, 1959.

Bruun, K., Edwards, G., Lumio, M., Makela, K., Pan, L., Popham, R. E., Room, R., Schmidt, W., Skog, O., Sulkunen, P., & Osterberg, E. *Alcohol control policies in public health perspective.* Helsinki: The Finnish Foundation for Alcohol Studies, 1975.

Cahalan, D., Cisin, I. H., & Crossley, H. M. *American drinking practices: A national study of drinking behavior and practices.* New Brunswick, N.J.: Rutgers Center of Alcohol Studies, 1969.

Cappell, H. Tolerance to ethanol and treatment of its abuse: Some fundamental issues. *Addictive Behaviors*, 1981, *6*, 197–204.

Cappell, H., & Pliner, P. Volitional control of marijuana intoxication: A study of the ability to "come down" on command. *Journal of Abnormal Psychology*, 1973, *82*, 428–434.

Carder, B. Environmental influences on marijuana intoxication. In N. A. Krasnegor (Ed.), *Behavioral tolerance: Research and treatment implications* (NIDA Research Monograph

No. 18, DHEW Publication No. ADM 78-551). Washington, D.C.: U.S. Government Printing Office, 1978.

Carlin, A. S., Bakker, C. B., Halpern, L., & Dee Post, R. Social facilitation of marijuana intoxication: Impact of social set and pharmacological activity. *Journal of Abnormal Psychology*, 1972, *80*, 132–140.

Caudill, B. D., & Marlatt, G. A. Modeling influences in social drinking: An experimental analogue. *Journal of Consulting and Clinical Psychology*, 1975, *43*, 405–415.

Cavan, S. *Liquor license: An ethnography of bar behavior*. Chicago: Aldine, 1966.

Clark, W. B. Demographic characteristics of tavern patrons in San Francisco. *Quarterly Journal of Studies on Alcohol*, 1966, *27*, 316–327.

Clark, W. B. Public drinking in bars and taverns. In T. C. Harford & L. S. Gaines (Eds.), *Social drinking contexts* (NIAAA Research Monograph No. 7, DHHS Publication No. ADM 82-1097). Washington, D.C.: U.S. Government Printing Office, 1982.

Clark, W. B., & Midanik, L. Alcohol use and alcohol problems among U.S. adults: Results of the 1979 National Survey. In *Alcohol consumption and related problems* (NIAAA Alcohol and Health Monograph No. 1, DHHS Publication No. ADM 82-1190). Washington, D.C.: U.S. Government Printing Office, 1982.

Collins, R. L., & Marlatt, G. A. Social modeling as a determinant of drinking behavior: Implications for prevention and treatment. *Addictive behaviors*, 1981, *6*, 233–239.

Cook, P. J. The effect of liquor taxes on drinking, cirrhosis, and auto accidents. In M. H. Moore & D. R. Gerstein (Eds.), *Alcohol and public policy: Beyond the shadow of prohibition*. Washington, D.C.: National Academy Press, 1981.

Cooper, A. M., Waterhouse, G. J., & Sobell, M. B. Influence of gender on drinking in a modeling situation. *Journal of Studies on Alcohol*, 1979, *40*, 562–570.

Crawford, G. A. Non-survey observational techniques. In L. G. Richards & L. B. Blevens (Eds.), *The epidemiology of drug abuse* (NIDA Research Monograph No. 10, DHEW publication No. ADM 77-432). Washington, D.C.: U.S. Government Printing Office, 1977.

Cutler, R. E., & Storm, T. Observational study of alcohol consumption in natural settings: The Vancouver beer parlor. *Journal of Studies on Alcohol*, 1975, *36*, 1173–1183.

DeRicco, D. A., & Garlington, W. K. The effects of modeling and disclosure of experimenter's intent on drinking rate in college students. *Addictive Behaviors*, 1977, *2*, 135–139.

Ebin, D. (Ed.). *The drug experience*. New York: Grove Press, 1961.

Falk, J. L., Schuster, C. R., Bigelow, G. E., & Woods, J. H. Progress and need in the experimental analysis of drug and alcohol dependence. *American Psychologist*, 1982, *37*, 1124–1127.

Ferraro, D. P. Behavioral tolerance to marijuana. In N. A. Krasnegor (Ed.), *Behavioral tolerance: Research and treatment implications*. (NIDA Research Monograph No. 18, DHEW publication No. ADM 78-551). Washington, D.C.: U.S. Government Printing Office, 1978.

Fisher, J. C. Psychosocial correlates of tavern use: A national probability sample study. In T. C. Harford & L. S. Gaines (Eds.), *Social drinking contexts* (NIAAA Research Monograph No. 7, DHHS publication No. ADM 82-1097). Washington, D.C.: U.S. Government Printing Office, 1982.

Garlington, W. K., & DeRicco, D. A. The effect of modeling on drinking rate. *Journal of Applied Behavior Analysis*, 1977, *10*, 207–211.

Glad, W., & Adesso, V. J. The relative importance of socially induced tension and behavioral contagion for smoking behavior. *Journal of Abnormal Behavior*, 1976, *85*, 119–121.

Goode, E. *The drug phenomenon: Social aspects of drug taking*. Indianapolis: Bobbs-Merrill, 1973.

Graves, T. D., Graves, N. B., Semu, V. N., & Ah Sam, I. Patterns of public drinking in a multi-ethnic society: A systematic observational study. *Journal of Studies on Alcohol*, 1982, *43*, 990–1009. (a)

Graves, T. D., Graves, N. B., Semu, V. N., & Ah Sam, I. The social context of drinking and violence in New Zealand's multi-ethnic pub settings. In T. C. Harford & L. S. Gaines (Eds.), *Social drinking contexts* (NIAAA Research Monograph No. 7, DHHS publication No. ADM 82-1097). Washington, D. C.: U.S. Government Printing Office, 1982. (b)

Gusfield, J. R., Kotarba, J., & Rasmussen, P. Managing compotence: An ethnographic study of drinking-driving and the context of bars. In T. C. Harford & L. S. Gaines (Eds.), *Social drinking contexts* (NIAAA Research Monograph No. 7, DHHS publication No. ADM 82-1097). Washington, D.C.: U.S. Government Printing Office, 1982.

Harford, T. C. Contextual drinking patterns among men and women. In F. A. Seixas (Ed.) *Currents in alcoholism* (Vol. IV): *Psychiatric, psychological, social and epidemiological Studies.* New York: Grune & Stratton, 1978.

Harford, T. C., & Gerstel, E. K. Age-related patterns of daily alcohol consumption in metropolitan Boston. *Journal of Studies on Alcohol*, 1981, 42, 1062–1066.

Harford, T. C., & Spiegler, D. L. Environmental influences in adolescent drinking. In *Special population issues* (NIAAA Alcohol and Health Monograph No. 4, DHHS publication No. ADM 82-1193). Washington, D.C.: U.S. Government Printing Office, 1982.

Hendricks, R. D., Sobell, M. B., & Cooper, A. M. Social influences on human ethanol consumption in an analogue situation. *Addictive Behaviors*, 1978, 3, 253–259.

Jessor, R., & Jessor, S. L. *Problem behavior and psychosocial development: A longitudinal study of youth.* New York: Academic Press, 1977.

Jessor, R., Chase, J. A., & Donovan, J. E. Psychosocial correlates of marijuana use and problem drinking in a national sample of adolescents. *American Journal of Public Health*, 1980, 70, 604–613.

Jones, R. T. Behavioral tolerance: Lessons learned from cannabis research. In N. A. Krasnegor (Ed.), *Behavioral tolerance: Research and treatment implications* (NIDA Research Monograph No. 18, DHEW publication No. ADM 78-551). Washington, D.C.: U.S. Government Printing Office, 1978.

Kandel, D. B., & Adler, I. Socialization into marijuana use among French adolescents: A cross-cultural comparison with the United States. *Journal of Health and Social Behavior*, 1982, 23, 295–309.

Kraft, D. P. Public drinking practices of college youths: Implications for prevention programs. In T. C. Harford & L. S. Gaines (Eds.), *Social drinking contexts* (NIAAA Research Monograph No. 7, DHHS publication No. ADM 82-1097). Washington, D.C.: U.S. Government Printing Office, 1982.

Krasnegor, N. A. Introduction. In N. A. Krasnegor (Ed.), *Behavioral tolerance: Research and treatment implications* (NIDA Research Monograph No. 18, DHEW publication No. ADM 78-551). Washington, D.C.: U.S. Government Printing Office, 1978.

LeDain, G. (Chairman). *The non-medical use of drugs: Interim report of the Canadian Government Commission of Inquiry.* Baltimore: Penguin Books, 1970.

Leventhal, H. Critique. In J. D. Rittenhouse (Ed.), *Consequences of alcohol & marijuana use: Survey items for perceived assessment* (DHEW publication No. ADM 80-920). Washington, D.C.: U.S. Government Printing Office, 1980.

Lied, E. R., & Marlatt, G. A. Modeling as a determinant of alcohol consumption: Effect of subject sex and prior drinking history. *Addictive Behaviors*, 1979, 4, 47–54.

Ludwig, A. M., Cain, R. B., Wikler, A., Taylor, R. M., & Bendfeldt, F. Physiological and situational determinants of drinking behavior. In M. M. Gross (Ed.), *Alcohol intoxication and withdrawal* (Vol. IIIb) *Studies in alcohol dependence.* New York: Plenum, 1977.

Ludwig, A. F., & Stark, L. H. Alcohol craving: Subjective and situational aspects. *Quarterly Journal of Studies on Alcohol*, 1974, 35, 108–130.

Marlatt, G. A. *Relapse prevention: A self-control program for the treatment of addictive behaviors.* Seattle: University of Washington, 1980.

Marlatt, G. A., & Rohsenow, D. J. Cognitive processes in alcohol use: Expectancy and the balanced placebo design. In N. K. Mello (Ed.), *Advances in substance abuse: Behavioral and biological research.* Greenwich, Conn. JAI Press, 1980.

McCarty, D. Misattribution of ethanol intoxication. *Addictive Behaviors,* 1981, *6,* 369–375.

McCarty, D., Diamond, W., & Kaye, M. Alcohol, sexual arousal, and the transfer of excitation. *Journal of Personality and Social Psychology,* 1982, *42,* 977–988.

McCarty, D., & Ewing, J. A. Alcohol consumption while viewing alcoholic beverage advertising. *International Journal of the Addictions,* 1983, *18,* 1101–1018.

McGlothlin, W. H. Drug use and abuse. In M. R. Rosenzweig & L. W. Porter (Eds.), *Annual review of psychology* (Vol. 26). Palo Alto, Calif. Annual Reviews, 1975.

Mills, K. C., Neal, M. E., & Peed-Neal, I. *Handbook for alcohol education: The community approach.* Cambridge, Mass. Ballinger, 1983.

Moore, M. H., & Gerstein, D. R. (Eds.). *Alcohol and public policy: Beyond the shadow of prohibition.* Washington, D.C.: National Academy Press, 1981.

O'Brien, C. P., Testa, T., Ternes, J., & Greenstein, R. Conditioning effects of narcotics in humans. In N. A. Krasnegor (Ed.), *Behavioral tolerance: Research and treatment implications* (NIDA Research Monograph No. 18, DHEW publicaton No. ADM 78-551). Washington, D.C.: U.S. Government Printing Office, 1978.

Pihl, R. O., & Sigal, H. Motivation levels and the marijuana high. *Journal of Abnormal Psychology,* 1978, *87,* 280, 285.

Pliner, P., & Cappell, H. Modification of affective consequences of alcohol: A comparison of social and solitary drinking. *Journal of Abnormal Psychology,* 1974, *83,* 418–425.

Poulous, C. X., Hinson, R. E., & Siegel, S. The role of Pavlovian processes in drug tolerance and dependence: Implications for treatment. *Addictive Behaviors,* 1981, *6,* 205–211.

Price, R. H. Risky situations. In D. Magnusson (Ed.), *Toward a psychology of situations: An interactional perspective.* Hillsdale, N.J.: Erlbaum, 1981.

Rachal, J. V., Maisto, S. A., Guess, L. L., & Hubbard, R. L. Alcohol use among youth. In *Alcohol consumption and related problems* (NIAAA Alcohol and Health Monograph No. 1, DHHS publication No. ADM 82-1190). Washington, D.C.: U.S. Government Printing Office, 1982.

Reid, J. B. Study of drinking in natural settings. In G. A. Marlatt & P. E. Nathan (Eds.), *Behavorial approaches to alcoholism.* New Brunswick, N.J.: Rutgers Center of Alcohol Studies, 1978.

Reinforcing p-o-p as a sales tool. *Printers' Ink,* October 11, 1963, pp. 62–63.

Rittenhouse, J. D. *Social psychological aspects of drug abuse.* Paper presented at the American Psychological Association Annual Meeting. New York, August 1979.

Rosenbluth, J., Nathan, P. E., & Lawson, D. M. Environmental influences on drinking by college students in a college pub: Behavioral observation in the natural environment. *Addictive Behaviors,* 1978, *3,* 117–121.

Russell, J. A., & Mehrabian, A. Environmental effects on drug use. *Environmental Psychology and Nonverbal Behavior,* 1977, *2,* 109–123.

Schachter, S. The interaction of cognitive and physiological determinants of emotional state. In L. Berkowitz (Ed.), *Advances in experimental social psychology* (Vol. 1). New York: Academic Press, 1964.

Schachter, S., & Singer, J. Cognitive, social and physiological determinants of emotional state. *Psychological Review,* 1962, *69,* 379–399.

Schachter, S., & Wheeler, L. Epinephrine, chlorpromazine, and amusement. *Journal of Abnormal and Social Psychology,* 1962, *65,* 121–128.

Schlegel, R. P., Crawford, C. A., & Sanborn, M. D. Correspondence and mediational properties of the Fishbein model: An application to adolescent alcohol use. *Journal of Experimental Social Psychology,* 1977, *13,* 421–430.

Schuster, C. R. Theoretical basis of behavioral tolerance: Implications of the phenomenon for problems of drug abuse. In N. A. Krasnegor (Ed.), *Behavioral tolerance: Research and treatment implications* (NIDA Research Monograph No. 18, DHEW publication No. ADM 78-551). Washington, D.C.: U.S. Government Printing Office, 1978.

Secord, P. F., & Backman, C. W. *Social psychology.* New York. McGraw-Hill, 1964.

Selzer, M. L., Vinokur, A., & Van Rooijen, L. A self-administered Short Michigan Alcoholism Screening Test (SMAST). *Quarterly Journal of Studies on Alcohol,* 1975, *36,* 117–126.

Siegel, S. Morphine analgesic tolerance: Its situation specificity supports a Pavlovian conditioning model. *Science,* 1976, *193,*323–325.

Siegel, S. A Pavolvian conditioning analysis of morphine. In N. A. Krasnegor (Ed.), *Behavorial tolerance: Research and treatment implications* (NIDA Research Monograph No. 18, DHEW publication No. ADM 78-551). Washington, D.C.: U.S. Government Printing Office, 1978.

Skog, O. Drinking behavior in small groups: The relationship between group size and consumption level. In T. C. Harford & L. S. Gaines (Eds.), *Social drinking contexts* (NIAAA Research Monograph No. 7, DHHS publication No. ADM 82-1097). Washington, D.C.: U.S. Government Printing Office, 1982.

Sommer, R. The isolated drinker in the Edmonton beer parlor. *Quarterly Journal of Studies on Alcohol,* 1965, *26,* 95–110.

Storm, T., & Cutler, R. E. Observations of drinking in natural settings: Vancouver beer parlors and cocktail lounges. *Journal of Studies on Alcohol,* 1981, *42,* 972–997.

Straus, R. The challenge for reconceptualization. *Journal of Studies on Alcohol* (Supplement No. 8), November, 1979.

Strickler, D. P., Dobbs, S. D., & Maxwell, W. A. The influence of setting on drinking behaviors: The laboratory vs. the barroom. *Addictive Behaviors,* 1979, *4,* 339–344.

Thompson, H. S. *Fear and loathing in Las Vegas.* New York: Random House, 1972.

Thompson, H. S. *The great shark hunt: Strange tales from a strange time.* New York: Summit Books, 1979.

Watson, D. B., & Sobell, M. B. Social influences on alcohol consumption by black and white males. *Addictive Behaviors,* 1982, *7,* 87–91.

Weil, A. T. Altered states of consciousness. In P. M. Wald & P. B. Hutt (Chairmen), *Dealing with drug abuse: A Report to the Ford Foundation.* New York: Praeger, 1972. (a)

Weil, A. T. *The natural mind: A new way of looking at drugs and the higher consciousness.* Boston: Houghton Mifflin, 1972 (b)

Weil, A. T., Zinberg, N. E., & Nelson, J. M. Clinical and psychological effects of marijuana in men. *Science,* 1968, *162,* 1234–1242.

Wilkins, J. W. *The influence of presituational decision-making and modeling on the alcohol consumption of light and heavy social drinkers.* Unpublished doctoral dissertation, University of North Carolina at Chapel Hill, 1980.

Woolverton, W. R., & Schuster, C. R. Behavioral tolerance to cocaine. In N. A. Krasnegor (Ed.), *Behavorial tolerance: Research and treatment implications* (NIDA Research Monograph No. 18, DHEW publication No. ADM 78-551). Washington, D.C.: U.S. Government Printing Office, 1978.

Zajonc, R. B. Social facilitation. *Science,* 1965, *149,* 269–274.

Zeichner, A., & Pihl, R. O. Effects of alcohol and behavior contingencies on human aggression. *Journal of Abnormal Behavior,* 1979, *88,* 153–160.

Zillmann, D. Attribution and misattribution of excitatory reactions. In J. H. Harvey, W. Ickes, & R. F. Kidd. *New directions in attribution research* (Vol. 2). Hillsdale, N.J.: Erlbaum, 1978.

CHAPTER 9

Macroenvironmental Factors as Determinants of Substance Use and Abuse

GERARD J. CONNORS and ARTHUR R. TARBOX

INTRODUCTION

There is little doubt that the use and abuse of alcohol and drugs is a process that is multidetermined, and there exists a variety of factors that can significantly affect substance use. The purpose of this chapter is to outline and discuss the role of one class of factors—macroenvironmental variables—on the use of alcohol and drugs.

The term *macroenvironmental* is used to denote those environmental factors that are ubiquitous and thus operate on a broadly based scale. Examples include governmental regulations on the price and availability of alcohol, cultural factors, and urbanization. Macroenvironmental factors stand in contrast to microenvironmental influences, which involve the more immediate drinking or drug-use context. (Microenvironmental factors are discussed in detail by McCarty in Chapter 8 of this volume.)

A second focus of this chapter is to discuss how macroenvironmental factors can affect the individual drinker or drug user. Where appropriate, we will discuss how individual differences may mediate the influence of and response to specific macroenvironmental factors.

GERARD J. CONNORS and ARTHUR R. TARBOX • Department of Psychiatry and Behavioral Sciences, University of Texas Medical School at Houston, Houston, Texas 77030.

The chapter is divided into three sections. The variety of governmental influences that impact on substance use and abuse is discussed in the first section. The second section assesses the predominant macrosocial factors influencing substance use and abuse. Finally, in the third section, the influence of macroenvironmental factors is summarized. In addition, some questions regarding the interplay between macroenvironmental factors and individual differences are discussed.

MACROENVIRONMENTAL INFLUENCES ON SUBSTANCE USE AND ABUSE

GOVERNMENTAL INFLUENCES

Taxation and Price

One of the most basic factors influencing the use of alcohol and drugs is the financial cost involved in their procurement. At least in the case of alcohol, taxes are a major determinant of the overall price paid for the commodity.

Taxes on alcohol in the United States date to the late 1770s (Hu, 1950). Taxes initially were intended to discourage overpricing (not, incidentally, to curb excessive drinking) and to generate revenue for the state (Popham, Schmidt, & de Lint, 1976). It was not until later that taxation was proposed as a mechanism for preventing dypsomania and protecting the social order, an interest that coincided with the rise of the temperance movement (Popham et al., 1976). The only time that taxation has not systematically affected the price of alcohol in recent times was during Prohibition. Since the repeal of Prohibition in 1933, however, federal and state governments have established varying forms of administrative control for the manufacture, distribution, and sale of alcohol. These guidelines were designed, according to McCarthy and Douglass (1959) to

> (a) correspond with the expressed will of the people in each state for the regulated sale of alcoholic beverages; (b) avoid the return of the evils of social irresponsibility which had been attributed to the alcoholic-beverage industry under pre-Prohibition systems and (c) ensure an adequate tax revenue to units of government. (p. 429)

State and federal taxes and fees imposed on alcohol in the United States today account for about half the price paid for spirits and about one-fifth of the price for beer or wine (Cook, 1981). Despite the proportionately large tax, there has been a steady decrease in the past two decades in the price of alcohol, relative to the consumer price index (CPI), at least in the United States. Cook (1981) has calculated that the prices for spirits, beer, and wine have decreased 48%, 27%, and 20%, respectively, from 1960–1980, when compared to the CPI. Researchers have studied these decreases in the real cost of alcohol to determine whether they are associated with concomitant increases in alcohol consumption. Several studies have shown that demand for alcohol, indeed, is responsive to price (e.g., Cook, 1981; Houthakker & Taylor, 1966; Niskanen, 1962; Popham *et al.*, 1978; Simon, 1966a). In fact, Moore and Gerstein (1981) have reported that even relatively small changes in price can affect alcohol consumption rates.

Although alcohol consumption appears to be price elastic (e.g., changes in price are inversely related to demand), the influence of other variables that may influence demand and consumption remains less understood. For example, the role of income level on consumption, in general, and its interaction with price, in particular, are unclear (Parker & Harman, 1978). A second issue is whether different types of beverages are equally price elastic. Although the demand for spirits appears price elastic, Lau (1975) and Ornstein (1980) have found that the demand for beer tends to be price inelastic and that wine may or may not be price elastic. Another issue is the extent to which price changes affect consumption *per se*, as opposed to sales. Sales data provide only an approximate estimate of consumption; the rates of moonshining, bootlegging, and underreported sales are not known. These issues and others have been discussed in more detail by Parker and Harman (1978) and Schmidt and Popham (1978).

A related and perhaps more critical question is whether negative consequences of alcohol consumption abate in response to increases in taxes and the overall price of alcohol. This issue is particularly important when one considers the potential roles of taxation and cost of alcohol as public policy interventions. One variable reflecting negative consequences that has received considerable attention is the liver cirrhosis rate. In 1941, for example, Jolliffe and Jellinek noted that the death rate from liver cirrhosis was closely related to the rate of alcohol consumption, a finding that has been supported in subsequent research (e.g., Cook, 1981; Popham, Schmidt, & de Lint, 1978). In a related way, Cook (1981) has provided data indicating that increases in liquor taxes result in decreased consumption overall as well as decreased heavy-drinking rates. Cook also noted that auto fatality rates decreased as liquor taxes rose. The data reflecting rates of heavy drinking are particularly notable because they suggest that the pricing of alcohol affects a range of drinker types, not just, for example, light drinkers.

In summary, it appears that increases in the price of alcohol generally effect decreases in the demand for alcohol; they affect heavy as well as moderate drinkers and are correlated with decreases in liver cirrhosis and auto fatality rates.

Data on the effects of price on the use and abuse of other drugs are lacking. Supply and demand clearly influence the price of any given substance (as either supply or demand increase or decrease), but the net effect on drug consumption is not clear. Some have argued that drugs are price elastic (i.e., increasing cost will decrease demand and usage), but this hypothesis does not always hold true. Brecher *et al.* (1972) have noted that heroin, for example, is price inelastic, and that demand remains the same when price increases. However, it is not clear whether this price inelasticity applies equally to addicted as well as nonaddicted users of heroin.

It is quite clearly the case that governmental policies affect the price of drugs, usually through their effect on either the supply of, or demand for, drugs. However, it remains unclear as to which approach will be more effective in curtailing use and/or negative social consequences of drug use/abuse. It has been argued that efforts to decrease supply (and thus in many cases increase costs) serve simply to attract more entrepreneurs to the "business" (Brecher *et al.*, 1972). Further, Phares (1973) maintains that supply policies, at least as applied to heroin, only intensify and expand the social costs associated with its use. Efforts to influence demand may be more effective in that they are intended to decrease users' desire for the substance. Such efforts include disseminating educational materials regarding negative effects of drug use and the offering of alternatives to drug abusers (e.g., methadone maintenance strategies). Additional research may shed more light on the relative benefits of supply-versus-demand control policies.

Regulating Legal Drinking Age

Once it was decided that the experiment called Prohibition had failed in its goal to curb alcohol abuse in the United States, the Twenty-first Amendment was signed into effect. Since that time, each state has had the power to determine its own internal alcohol distribution patterns, including regulation of the minimum age required for purchasing alcohol. The minimum age for most states was set at 21 years, and that requirement was constant until the 1970s when many states, under significant pressure from an increasingly vocal youthful population, lowered the drinking age to 18. Notably, this trend appears now to be reversing, and it has been proposed that an older minimum drinking age be established on a nationwide basis.

One argument favoring lowering the drinking age espouses the "forbidden fruit" theory (Wilkinson, 1970). Its proponents hypothesize that young adults will abuse alcohol less when it is legally available than when it has to be obtained illicitly. However, others have feared that increasing the availability of alcohol to young adults would actually serve to increase the rate of alcohol abuse (Cohen, 1981; Popham *et al.*, 1976). In support of the latter hypothesis, there have been several reports demonstrating predicted increases in alcohol-related motor vehicle accidents and fatalities and in juvenile crime among 18–20-year-olds (Cucchiaro, Fereira, & Sicherman, 1974; Douglass, Filkins, & Clark, 1974; Williams, Rich, Zador, & Robertson, 1974; Yoakum, 1979). For example, alcohol-related car accidents increased in Michigan from 15% to 25% following that state's reduction of the minimum drinking age in 1972 (Douglass, 1980a). Partly in response to these statistics, Michigan, in 1978, enacted legislation to return the minimum drinking age to 21. Wagenaar (1982a) performed a comprehensive analysis of crash data before and after this 1978 change in the minimum drinking age and found that car accidents involving 18–20-year-olds were significantly reduced following the change in legislation. Such findings have led officials to reassess the use of drinking age as a public policy tool for minimizing negative effects of alcohol use. In New York, for example, officials have concluded that reducing availability by increasing the minimum age to purchase alcohol is a viable means for reducing alcohol-related automotive accidents among 18–20-year-olds and that such legislation should be part of any comprehensive drunk-driving prevention strategy (Lillis, Williams, Chupka, & Williford, 1982).

Several caveats should be noted in interpreting the preceding data. Nathan (1983) concluded that data on changes in the legal drinking age are difficult to interpret because of correlated increases in overall alcohol availability and consumption between 1972 and 1978, a reduction in driving overall due to the energy crisis, and increases in the price of bottled and canned beer in 1979. Nathan (1983) argues that these events may have interacted with changes in the legal drinking age to obscure any interpretations reflective of causality. In addition, there have been questions about the durability of increased alcohol-related problems in the 18–20-year-old population. Douglass and Freedman (1977) and White-head (1977) have reported that long-term effects may be much less pronounced, at least in terms of auto accidents. Miller, Nirenberg, and McClure (1983) speculate that the effects of changes in drinking age may be similar to apparent short-term effects of other related legislation, and they cite the example of the introduction of the 0.08 (g alcohol/100ml blood) alcohol concentration (BAC) legal limit law in Britain. This legislation was followed by an immediate reduction in the number of "alcohol-related problems." However, the problem rate returned to baseline within several years. Thus, although increasing the legal drinking age may reduce drunk-driving and alcohol-related accidents in the short term, the durability of these effects remains unclear.

A related issue and one that is particularly pertinent is whether the increased availability of alcohol inherent in lowering age restrictions increases youthful consumption of alcohol. Several studies have reported increases in the number of self-identified "drinkers" as well as an increased frequency of self-reported drinking since the reduction in legal age (Smart & Goodstadt, 1977; Smart & Schmidt, 1975). Wagenaar (1982b) reported a significant, but temporary, increase in aggregate draft beer sales in Michigan after the drinking age was lowered in 1972, but there was no such increase in total beer, package beer, or wine consumption. In contrast, there were significant decreases in total beer and package beer distribution and large increases in draft beer distribution in the 1979–1980 period after Michigan's drinking age was raised from 18 to 21. These data offer some support for availability restrictions as a prevention measure. However, there were confounding variables present in that a beverage container deposit law was instituted at the same time as the increase in drinking age, and Michigan also endured a major economic recession during this 1979–1980 period.

In summary, it would appear that lowering the legal drinking age has led to increased consumption and alcohol-related problems among the 18–20-year-old population (Whitehead & Wechsler, 1980). In addition, such legislative actions also seemed to have resulted in an increased rate of alcohol-related traffic accidents (Douglass, 1980b). Long-term effects of reducing availability by manipulating the minimum drinking age remain unclear at this time and certainly are worthy of further investigation.

Regulating Sales through Monopoly versus Private Enterprise Systems

As noted earlier, responsibility for regulating the availability of alcohol in the United States was given to the individual states following the repeal of Prohibition. In this regard, each state's alcohol beverage control (ABC) board has been responsible for the institution of its own guidelines. ABC boards in 32 states and in the District of Columbia license private alcohol-related businesses. In the remaining 18 states, ABC boards have maintained responsibility for the actual sale of alcoholic beverages.

Popham et al. (1976) compared monopoly states within the United States to states with licensed private businesses and reported no significant differences in terms of level of alcohol consumption nor in liver cirrhosis mortality rates. Similar data have been reported by Simon (1966b) and Efron, Keller, and Gurioli (1974) regarding per capita consumption. However, there is evidence that in countries with a government monopoly that emphasizes vigorous control rather than increased revenue a substantial decrease in alcohol consumption and concomitant problems can be realized (Christie, 1965). Governmental controls imposed by ABC agencies in the United States, on the other hand, have been geared primarily to provide tax revenue, maintain an orderly alcoholic beverage sales market, and to control crime in the liquor trade (Room & Mosher, 1979; Medicine in the Public Interest, Inc., 1979). Thus, it would appear that how a monopoly system is administered is critical. However, it remains to be seen whether these same controls that proved effective in decreasing alcohol consumption within certain state monopoly systems will be as effective within licensing systems.

Effects of Limiting Hours and Days of Sale

State and national governments have regulated hours and days of sale of alcoholic beverages for many years in the belief that this is an effective control measure. However, Popham and his colleagues (Popham, 1962; Popham et al., 1976) have reported that such strategies actually have resulted in insignificant changes in overall consumption of alcohol. For example, Popham (1962) reported an apparent correlation between tavern closing hours and arrests for drunkenness exhibited between 8 A.M. Monday and 8 A.M. the following Sunday. However, when arrests were plotted for each hour from 8 A.M. Sunday to 8 A.M. Monday morning—during which time all taverns were closed—an almost identical pattern emerged, suggesting that hours of sale reflect the drinking habits of the community rather than the reverse.

Number and Types of Sales Outlets

It has been argued that the prevalence of drunkenness will be positively correlated with the number of sales outlets for alcohol. However, this may not be so (Blane & Hewitt, 1977; de Lint, 1976; Popham, 1956). In fact, data for Canada have shown that the highest rates of drunkenness occurred in the areas with the fewest numbers of outlets per unit of population (Popham et al., 1978). Other studies also have demonstrated negative correlations between drunkenness rates and outlet rates (e.g., Mass Observation, 1943). In another report, Popham et al. (1978) provided data for both England and the United States, demonstrating no significant relationship between alcohol abuse and the number of sales outlets.

A related issue concerns the availability of alcohol in food establishments. Popham and Schmidt (1958) examined the impact of permitting cocktail lounges in dining establishments in Ontario in 1947 and found no significant differences in alcohol consumption, drunkenness convictions, or reported rates of alcoholism compared to the adjacent province of Manitoba where such lounges were not permitted. Elsewhere, Bryant (1954) reported no support for the hypothesis that introduction of liquor by the drink in the state of Washington would lead to any increases in consumption or alcohol-related arrests.

Limiting off-premises availability of alcoholic beverages appears to have had little, if any, significant effect in reducing alcohol abuse as well. Entine (1963) concluded that limiting the number of package stores in the United States, primarily in New York State and the Northeast region, did not reduce off-premises consumption. However, Simon (1966b) reported a significant correlation between per capita consumption and retail outlet rates, but the author interpreted these findings as evidence that the number of retail outlets increases as a function of increasing alcohol consumption rather than the reverse holding true. Certainly, severely limiting the availability of alcoholic beverages by reducing the number of outlets beyond the point of mere inconvenience might impact on consumption, and it has been reported that opening new outlets in such circumstances did correlate with increased consumption (Kuusi, 1957). However, this increase in alcohol consumption was not accompanied by increases in alcohol-related problems but instead was associated with a decline in "bootleg" production of alcoholic beverages. Overall, it remains unknown as to how large an increase in availability (regardless of the definition) would be required to impact on individual consumption in general and alcohol abuse in particular (Smart, 1977).

Legal Sanctions Regarding On-Premises Sales

There has been considerable interest recently concerning the legal as well as moral or ethical responsibility of serving alcoholic beverages on premises to an already inebriated customer. In one study, Room and Mosher (1979) described a 2-year pilot study on a program designed to identify licensed on-premises sales outlets that had served alcohol to customers subsequently arrested for driving while intoxicated (DWI). Once identified, these licensees were sent a letter by the state ABC board informing them of what had transpired, reminding them of their legal responsibilities, and identifying their potential liability. The board also provided certain educational materials and offered training in identifying and dealing with drunken patrons. The preliminary results provided by Mosher and Wallack (1979) were encouraging, at least in terms of voluntary participation by licensees in such training and increased demand for more education/training programs. The interest in incorporating such programs is a relatively unique example of fusing governmental controls (e.g., ABC sanctions) with specific educational programs (e.g., teaching bartenders behavioral techniques for moderating alcohol consumption) in reducing the incidence of alcohol-related problems.

Restricting Sales of Specific Beverages

Clinicians who deal with alcohol abusers often hear the argument, "I don't have a problem with my drinking; I only drink beer." The viewpoint argued is that beer is the drink of moderation and that more stringent restrictions should be imposed on the sales of "hard liquor," in terms of either its availability or taxation. Similar arguments have been offered in advocating a lessening of restrictions on the availability of so-called "soft drugs" (e.g., marijuana) as opposed to "hard drugs" (e.g., heroin, amphetamines). Research on alcohol, however, has not supported these arguments Kalant, LeBlanc, and Wilson (1974), for example, compared the relative effects of beer, wine, and spirits and found no differences in relative blood alcohol levels achieved. There also were no significant differences found among the various tests of cognitive and physical impairment as a function of beverage type. In addition, increasing the availability of beer relative to spirits may not achieve the desired effects. Borkenstein and his colleagues (Borkenstein, Crowther, Shumate, Ziel, & Zylman, 1964) assessed the blood alcohol levels of a large sample of drivers involved in motor vehicle accidents and of a control sample of drivers randomly given tests to assess blood alcohol levels. Groups did not differ significantly on critical variables such as age and socioeconomic status. All subjects also were asked what type of alcoholic beverage they typically consumed. Not surprisingly, the authors report that a significantly higher proportion of drinking drivers was found in the group involved in accidents and the probability of such involvement increased rapidly as a function of increasing blood alcohol level. They also found a significant difference in beverage preference in that more of the drivers involved in accidents reported beer to be their beverage of choice (64%) compared to the control group (58%). In addition, the proportion of control subjects who preferred beer increased greatly with higher blood alcohol levels. Furthermore, among those not found to be drinking while driving, the ratio of beer drinkers to liquor consumers was 1.4 : 1; among those legally intoxicated (BAC of 0.08% or greater), the ratio was 4 : 1.

Studies in various nations also have not supported the notion that beer is a more benign agent than spirits. Beer was reported to be the beverage of choice of many alcohol abusers in Australia (Wilkinson, Santamaria, Rankin, & Martin, 1969); Czechoslovakia (Skala, 1967); Germany (Lelbach, 1974); and Ontario (Popham *et al.*, 1978). In general, these and other surveys offer little evidence to support the hypothesis that beverage type is a critical variable in alcohol abuse. Rather, total absolute alcohol consumed appears to be the significant variable.

Restriction of Availability of Drugs Other than Alcohol

The attitude internationally toward most drugs other than alcohol has been one of total prohibition regarding availability of the agent. The goal historically in the United States, beginning with the implementation of the 1914 Harrison Narcotic Act, has been, in general, to keep drugs away from potential users. Much has been written and much controversy generated about such prohibition. Some have argued (e.g., Brecher *et al.*, 1972) that prohibitions on psychoactive substances, including alcohol, simply do not work. Further, it has been argued that the prohibition on any given drug simply serves to raise the price of that substance through illicit marketing. This hypothesis has also been used to support the argument that increasing the price of illicit substances through prohibition greatly increases crime statistics, ranging from crimes committed by addicts to finance their purchases to the more systematic involvement of organized crime responsible for much of the international trafficking of illicit drugs. In addition, prohibition has arguably led to the proliferation of adulterated, contaminated, and at times even more potent versions of those drugs. Finally, it has been noted by Brecher *et al.* (1972) that excessive reliance on prohibition can lull a culture into a false confidence that nothing more need be done except to rely on the law and drug enforcement agencies. In the following sections, the governmental influences that affect the use of drugs other than alcohol are discussed.

Restriction of Availability of Marijuana and Hashish

No other area of drug use and abuse has been so widely discussed, apart from alcohol, than the controversy surrounding the decriminalization of marijuana and hashish. One of the most comprehensive reviews of this controversy was developed by the Canadian government in the late 1960s, and this has since been published as the Le Dain commission interim report (1970). Regarding the availability of the agent, they cite a preponderance of data indicating that the use of marijuana was, at that time, increasing among all age groups of the population, especially among youth. The commission concluded that increased usage indicated that attempts to suppress, or even control, the use of marijuana, were failing and would continue to fail. In addition, the report found that the negative effects of drugs among youth, coupled with a growing disrespect for public law enforcement, made the attempt to suppress cannabis far worse than any harm derived from the actual possession of marijuana. Furthermore, it was reported that the use of cannabis as an illicit drug caused users to come into contact with criminal elements they would otherwise have avoided. In summary, the report concluded that marijuana should be made available under government-controlled conditions of quality and availability.

Certainly marijuana has been far more available throughout the United States, and indeed throughout the world, over the past decade. Only 10 years ago, Brotman and Suffet (1973) wrote that "one thing is unmistakably clear; marijuana use is a fact of American life" (p. 1106). Within only 5 years, Akers (1977) described just how available marijuana had become in the United States:

> Marijuana is smoked in an offhand casual way . . . before, during, or after sports events, dates, public gathering, parties, music festivals, class or work will do; there is no special place, time, or occasion for marijuana smoking. The acceptable places and occasions are as varied as those for drinking alcohol. (p. 112)

Despite accurate predictions 10 years ago that a leveling off of marijuana use was to be expected (e.g., National Commission on Marijuana and Drug Abuse, 1973), epidemiological studies clearly indicate that marijuana continues to be the most widely used of all illicit drugs (Jessor, 1979). However, it does appear that use of marijuana has consistently declined, at least among high-school seniors, since 1979 (Johnston, Bachman, & O'Malley, 1982).

The availability of marijuana in terms of supply to the United States from various international sources has been well documented, but perhaps more to the point is the observation that the availability and widespread use of marijuana may be a rather unusual example of very rapid cultural change, a change not coincidentally associated with major cultural shifts and attitudes regarding recreation and pleasure in general. As such, the key role concerning the availability of marijuana may well indeed prove to be that of the social environment in general and friendship patterns in particular. Variations in marijuana use are fairly indistinct when one examines various macroenvironmental factors. If present trends continue, the role of social and demographic variables will be minimal at best. This appears true for urbanicity or population density (Johnston, Bachman, & O'Malley, 1977) as well as for race and socioeconomic status (Miller, Cisin, & Harrell, 1978). Sex differences, as well, seem to be dropping out as significant predictors of marijuana use and have all but disappeared (Akers, Krohn, Lanza-Kaduce, & Radosevich, 1977; Jessor & Jessor, 1977; Wechsler & McFadden, 1976). Kandel (1974) was one of the first to conclude that "marijuana use by one's friends may be the critical variable" (p. 208) in influencing one's decision to use marijuana. In general, then, it appears that marijuana use varies closely with the context of social interaction—that is, with social models, with social reinforcements, and with social controls. Macroenvironmental influences appear to impact only minimally on the use of marijuana. Given the widespread availability of marijuana and the public's degree of enculturation to it, it may be more useful to address the problem of its abuse as opposed to marijuana use *per se* (Jessor, 1979; Ray, 1978).

Restriction of Availability of Opiates

Prior to the passage of the Harrison Narcotic Act in 1914, there had been a period of growth in terms of narcotics-dispensing clinics throughout the United States. Some actually dispensed morphine or heroin or both, and others gave addicted patients prescriptions for their drugs (Terry & Pellens, 1928). Brecher *et al.* (1972) and others have argued that the majority of these clinics "did a remarkably good job" (p. 116), but they were closed by the Treasury Department's narcotics unit in 1920 because of concerns that these clinics might contribute inadvertently to the amount of opiates available on the illicit market.

The experience of Great Britain does not parallel that of drug enforcement agencies in the United States. Prior to the turn of the 20th century, opiate use in Britain was much like that in the United States; that is, opiates were on open sale and were dispensed in large quantities without medical prescription. This changed in 1920 when Parliament, in response to the 1912 Hague Convention for the international control of narcotics, passed the Dangerous Drugs Act that was designed to limit opiate availability solely to medical outlets. The British decided not to prohibit all opiate prescribing, as was done in the United States. This, of course, enabled Great Britain to maintain statistics on the number of physically addicted patients receiving heroin or morphine at any given time. The results of this experiment, as described by Brecher *et al.* (1972), were extremely positive in that, by 1935, Great Britain reported to the League of Nations that there were only 700 opiate addicts left in the entire nation. In 1951 this figure reached a low of 301 patients for the entire country (see Schur, 1968). Statistics began to change, however, in the 1960s, and by 1966 laws were enacted taking the privilege of prescribing opiates away from the medical profession as a whole and limiting such privileges instead to specific clinics working with opiate abusers.

Restriction of Availability of Other Drugs

The relative availability of selected other drugs will be discussed only briefly. Among such drugs we would consider amphetamines, cocaine, barbiturates, inhalants, and hallucinogens (e.g., LSD, PCP). Each of these substances is distinguished from the drugs previously discussed in that their possession and use are more strongly censured. In addition, relatively less pharmacological and psychosocial research has been conducted on the effects of these substances. As with many of the other drugs cited in this chapter, availability of the agent appears to be increasing despite governmental regulations and attempts to decrease such availability. Cocaine, amphetamines, and barbiturates, in particular, have become more available and more utilized in the past decade (National Institute on Drug Abuse, 1982).

The relative availability of heroin is representative of the problems facing clinicians and legislators. Bensinger and Miller (1981) have described the impact of law enforcement efforts nationally and internationally to reduce drug trafficking in general. They reviewed several programs that have met with "limited success" (p. 598). Based on their review, the authors concluded that recent law-enforcement-created decreases in heroin availability in the past several years in the United States have engendered the following: (a) a net decrease in the number of individuals who are actually narcotics addicts; (b) consumption of a lower purity and, therefore, less dangerous and less addictive heroin; (c) a decline in exposure to and familiarity with heroin among the nonaddicted populations; and (d) a marked decrease in heroin-related deaths due to overdosage. The authors summarize these results by stating that "this represents a significant achievement directly attributed to law enforcement efforts" (p. 599). Others have investigated trends in perceived availability, however, and have reported that the availability of heroin has been fairly stable over the last 5 years (Johnston et al., 1982).

Methadone Maintenance Programs

Methadone maintenance programs are an example of a broad-based governmental intervention designed to decrease drug abuse. Methadone maintenance has been proposed as an alternative to heroin, based on the notion that the heroin addict who enters a methadone maintenance program will no longer be seen as a criminal but as medically ill (Dole & Joseph, 1977). In addition, the cost of treating such a patient with methadone is quite low, less than a dollar a day. However, perhaps the major attractions of methadone maintenance for clinicians are that it prevents the acute affects of withdrawal from heroin, does not offer a similar "high" as heroin (and, it is argued, is therefore less "addicting"), can actually block the effect of heroin during stabilization and detoxification, is relatively long acting, and may be taken orally.

Opponents of methadone maintenance programs have argued that such continued drug use is immoral, that it ignores the social conditions believed to spawn drug abuse, and that programs are under a medical aegis rather than more appropriate social agencies or mental health organizations (for a review, see Jaffe, 1979). Some of the most vocal opponents of such maintenance programs have been ex-addicts running drug-free therapeutic communities who believe that the use of methadone is simply substituting one addictive drug for another.

The majority of treatment-evaluation studies concerning the effectiveness of methadone maintenance programs have concluded that such programs have demonstrated worth for narcotic addicts and should be continued. Much data indicate that detoxification is not at all automatic in methadone programs (Cushman, Jr., 1974; Mezritz, Slobetz, Kleber, & Riordan, 1974), but that of those who complete detoxification, as many as 35% were drug free and doing generally well up to 6 years later (Stimmel, Goldberg, Rotkopf, & Cohen, 1977). In addition, most outcome studies report a significant drop in criminal behavior and arrests (Sells, 1979). Furthermore, methadone programs, compared to other narcotic abuse treatment programs, typically report the longest tenure in treatment, with the Drug Abuse Reporting Program noting the median time in treatment to be over 1 year (Sells, 1974). In all narcotic treatment evaluation studies, length of stay and favorableness of termination have been positively correlated with outcome (Sells, 1979).

Other Legislative Actions

Another mechanism through which governmental action may exert widespread influence over the use of alcohol and drugs is legislative action that defines what abuse of licit substances entails. In addition, legislation typically mandates penalties for the violation of such regulations. Two cornerstone laws specifying the parameters of appropriate uses of alcohol, for example, are reflected in statutes regarding public intoxication and driving while under the influence of alcohol. Guidelines outlining acceptable or appropriate uses of other drugs are rare because

use of most nonprescribed psychoactive substances is illegal on an *a priori* basis.

Although it is unlikely that any given drug will be removed from the current register of controlled drugs and illicit drugs, this is not always the case. A case in point is marijuana. In this regard, states have progressively been tempering their restrictions on the possession and use of marijuana. One of the earliest legislative movements toward decriminalization was enacted by Oregon in 1973, and as of 1980 ten additional states had enacted decriminalization measures (Single, 1981). In addition, Goode (1975) has noted that there has been a concomitant reduction in surveillance and enforcement rates in various states that have not enacted specific decriminalization statutes. Assessments of these legislative actions have been reviewed by Single (1981), who concluded that decriminalization has not resulted in significant increases in marijuana use.

A variety of questions arises when legislators address the aforementioned issues. Perhaps the most tangled is determining where to draw the line between one's freedom of choice to use a given substance and the rights of society to be protected from potential negative consequences of that drug's use. Another complicated issue is determining how to classify a given psychoactive substance. The process of classification can involve a variety of considerations. According to Blum (1974), these considerations include classification according to chemical structure, pharmacology, behavioral effect, medicinal use, and resultant subjective states. Such classification processes typically precede any significant efforts to sanction or prohibit the use of a given drug. Frequently, however, it is the case that concerned groups will push for the prohibition of a particular substance on moral grounds, as seen in the development of laws in the United States banning opium and marijuana in 1909 and 1937, respectively (Kalant & Kalant, 1971).

A related question is evaluating the balance between positive and negative outcomes of prohibiting the use of a given substance. The national prohibition against alcohol earlier this century, for example, was effective in reducing liver cirrhosis rates but was said to be quite costly in terms of expenditures for law enforcement, the rise of organized crime, and lowered respect for the law. It is arguable that a similar scenario is developing regarding marijuana and perhaps other substances as well. Further, it has been contended that the popularity of marijuana matured during the prohibition of alcohol (Brecher *et al.*, 1972), suggesting that large-scale controls and sanctions regarding drugs may need to apply simultaneously to other substances as well. The issue of sanctioning drug use in various forms has been addressed more comprehensively elsewhere (Brecher *et al.*, 1972; Carroll, 1981).

Summary

Any government that is concerned with modifying the use of alcohol and drugs is clearly confronted with a complex array of social, economic, psychological, legal, and even philosophical issues. Legal restrictions on the consumption of alcohol and drugs have historically addressed only one aspect of a behavior that has existed throughout recorded history and that involves many aspects of any given culture and society (Brecher *et al.*, 1972). Nevertheless, some conclusions may be reached from the extensive research regarding governmental influences surveyed herein.

The major limiting factor identified thus far in investigating alcohol and drug use has been price. This has been noted mostly in the consumption of alcohol, with consumption and alcohol abuse studied as a function of taxation. Research, especially the work of Cook (1981), indicates that increasing taxes on alcoholic beverages brings about decreases in demand, liver cirrhosis rates, and auto fatalities. These reductions hold across heavy as well as moderate drinker populations. Some have argued that increasing price effects a decrease in consumption of drugs other than alcohol, but valid studies in this area are lacking.

Alcohol is one drug whose licit sale and, therefore, availability has been regulated in various ways. Lowering of the minimum age required to purchase alcoholic beverages has been consistently associated with significant increases in automobile collisions and related fatalities. In addition, some researchers have reported a consistent correlation between minimum-age laws in various states and drinking by high-school students in those states (Maisto & Rachal, 1980). However, the long-term effects of controlling availability of alcohol by manipulating the minimum drinking age still demand further investigation (Whitehead & Wechsler, 1980).

The availability of alcohol has also been regulated governmentally by such measures as limiting sales to certain days of the week or hours of the day, by permitting sales only in government-directed monopoly systems, by restricting the number and type of sales outlets, and by prohibiting the sales of certain specific beverages (e.g., spirits versus wine or beer). In brief, the effects of regulating hours and days when alcohol may be purchased appear to have a relatively insignificant impact on the overall consumption and use of alcohol. Governmental monopoly systems have been able to decrease alcohol-related problems, but this effect has only been realized when the political aim was vigorous control rather than generating revenues. Number of sales outlets would appear to have little, if any, significant impact on alcohol abuse, and the availability of liquor by the drink has not been shown to yield an increase in alcohol consumption, alcohol-related arrests, or reported rates of alcoholism. Restricting sales of specific beverages based on alcohol content, such as spirits, has not been shown to decrease alcohol abuse, and, in fact, some studies have reported data indicating that beer is the beverage of choice of many alcohol abusers. One promising area of research noted herein is the use of legal sanctions against proprietors (licensed outlets) serving alcohol to inebriated customers in an effort to reduce the incidence of alcohol-related problems.

Turning to the issue of availability of drugs other than alcohol, one is confronted with a lack of systematic data, particularly because the general attitude internationally following passage of the Harrison Narcotic Act of 1914 in the United States has been one advocating total prohibition. One remarkable exception was the experience in Great Britain regarding the limited availability of opiates, especially heroin and morphine, through medical outlets. Some have argued that results of such limited availability were very positive, especially in terms of reducing the number of addicted patients. Others have argued that law enforcement efforts to reduce availability have been most effective, particularly in the case of heroin. According to surveys by the National Institute on Drug Abuse, the perceived availability of amphetamines and barbiturates, according to students in the United States, has risen gradually since 1979, but only in the case of amphetamines has there been a concomitant increase in use. Furthermore, the use of cocaine has risen substantially over the past 5 years, although its perceived availability, according to students in the United States, has remained constant since 1980. The use and availability of inhalants also appear to have changed very little in the past 5 years. In general, the relationship between availability and use of the agent is, as yet, unclear.

Marijuana use has been better documented and researched than most drugs and remains an example of the complexities surrounding availability and drug use. The availability of marijuana is widespread, and social/demographic variables no longer reliably predict its use. Many have concluded that governmental influences are minimal concerning use of marijuana and that its use is largely a function of social interaction. For example, it was noted that decriminalization of possession and use of marijuana has not yielded increases in its use.

Despite the existence of a variety of rules and regulations regarding alcohol and drugs, the extent to which drug use and abuse has been affected is not clear. It does appear, however, that such proscriptions have not prevented people from abusing drugs, as is evidenced by the number of persons who have remained addicted to alcohol and drugs. It is possible, of course, that fewer persons have initiated drug use as a result of legal factors, but data are not available to fully support such a position. Further, it is not likely that legislative action will effectively reduce substance abuse. Such an outcome, according to Westermeyer (1982), would require "a nation-wide integration of virtually all social institutions: law enforcement, religion, health, education, ethic enclaves, and special interest groups" (pp. 29–30), and such a coalition is rarely formed on any issue, let alone one as volatile as alcohol and drug abuse.

SOCIAL INFLUENCES

Sociocultural Factors

Cultural factors have long been associated with discussions on the use and abuse of alcohol and drugs, and these influences are hypothesized to impact significantly on drinking and drug-use behaviors. Societies for aeons have used a variety of psychoactive substances, and guidelines for the appropriate or acceptable use of these substances typically became incorporated as part of the normative structure of each society. This process is perhaps now much more in flux than in the past, especially in Western societies, given rapid cultural change, the introduction of numerous new drugs, and the apparent tendency for drug usage to increase across all populations. Nevertheless, societies in large part continue to dictate what and how psychoactive substances are used by their members.

The influences of culture have been studied much more with respect to alcohol than for any other substance. Curiously, though, much of the extant research in the United States at least addresses the use of alcohol among only a relatively few populations. Particularly focused upon are the Irish (e.g., Stivers, 1976); Jews (e.g., Snyder, 1958); and North American Indians (e.g., Leland, 1976; MacAndrew & Edgerton, 1969). It has been noted, for example, that Irish-Americans and Jewish-Americans evince quite different drinking patterns and rates of alcohol abuse (e.g., Bales, 1946; Snyder, 1958; Stivers, 1976). Studies have indicated that a large proportion of Jews drink alcohol but that relatively few experience alcohol-related problems. Drinking among the Irish, on the other hand, is associated with a relatively high rate of alcohol abuse and alcohol-related problems. In this regard, cultural distinctions have been proposed as the source of the distinctive drinking patterns. Specifically, the use of alcohol by Jews has been an inherent component of religious ceremony and ritual, a relationship that Bales (1946) has described in detail. The Irish, on the other hand, are said to view alcohol much more as a social lubricant, a way of demonstrating solidarity and of coping with the stressors within one's life. More recent data have supported the differential uses of alcohol as a function of its role (religious versus social, etc.) (e.g., Cahalan, Cisin, & Crossley, 1969; Cahalan & Room, 1974; Kandel & Sudit, 1982; Snyder, Palgi, Eldar, & Elian, 1982).

Although most reports characterizing the use of alcohol within different cultures are fascinating and informative, they remain for the most part descriptive. Explanations for why such differences occur have been elusive, and few mechanisms have been hypothesized to account for sociocultural variations. Two reports, however, are noteworthy in that they propose specific mechanisms that may account for cultural variations in alcohol use and alcohol effects.

In discussing alcohol use among different cultural groups, Bales (1946) described three sociocultural organizational factors. (It is noteworthy that Bales's general factors are equally applicable to the use of other drugs as well.) The first factor described by Bales is "the degree to which the culture operates to bring about acute needs for adjustment, or inner tensions, in its members" (p. 482) (e.g., anxiety, guilt, suppressed aggression). This function is perhaps the most common among diverse cultures. Horton (1943), in a widely cited survey, studied over 50 societies in terms of their use of alcohol and indexes of anxiety. His finding, in brief, was that "the primary function of alcoholic beverages in all societies is the reduction of anxiety" (p. 223).

The second sociocultural influence described by Bales is the type of attitudes regarding drinking that a society develops for its members (e.g., what roles for alcohol has the culture identified). Cultures, according to Bales, typically prescribe one of four categories of attitudes regarding drinking: Complete abstinence, ritual attitude, convivial attitude, or utilitarian attitude.

The third cultural influence is "the degree to which the culture provides suitable substitute means of satisfaction" because, Bales notes,

if the inner tensions are sufficiently acute certain individuals will become compulsively habituated to alcohol in spite of opposed social attitudes unless substitute ways of satisfaction are provided. (Bales, 1946, p. 482)

Bales notes, incidently, that the use of other drugs is perhaps the most common substitute to alcohol.

A second comprehensive assessment of cultural influences affecting alcohol use has been provided by MacAndrew and Edgerton (1969). These investigators describe (in a highly readable monograph) a sociocultural interpretation of alcohol use and alcohol effects. In this regard, they propose that people learn about drunkenness what their society "knows" about drunkenness; and, accepting and acting upon the understanding thus imparted to them, they become the living confirmation of their society's teachings. (p. 88)

MacAndrew and Edgerton also note that many societies frequently absolve a member's behavior from certain transgressions while intoxicated via a mechanism labeled *time-out.*

It is not unlikely that sociocultural forces influence the use of other drugs in ways that are quite similar to Bales's (1946) and MacAndrew and Edgerton's (1969) analyses of alcohol use. MacAndrew and Edgerton note, for example, that the time-out phenomenon is typically characterized by the creation of an "altered state of consciousness" (p. 168) and that although this altered state is most commonly produced by alcohol, any psychoactive substance could be used (depending on sociocultural guidelines). There are, however, differences in the sociocultural milieus. For example, the legal status of the psychoactive agent used will affect the number of users and the size of the drug-using culture overall. In addition, the places and contexts in which the drug will be present will be quite different than in the case of alcohol. Nevertheless, it should not be assumed that the influence of these drug cultures will be any less powerful than in the case of alcohol. Drug cultures can be just as, if not more, influential as in the use of alcohol (see, for example, Becker, 1963).

In summary, sociocultural factors clearly exert a significant influence over the use of and response to psychoactive substances. It should be noted that the examples of sociocultural drinking patterns described herein pertained to American ethnic populations. Although the variables that have been discussed operated in other cultures as well, the relative influence of each factor can vary considerably. In addition, cultures vary in terms of which drugs are approved for use and to what extent. Several of the Middle Eastern cultures, for example, are a case in point. In these societies, religious influences tend to be much more prominent in determining the use of different substances. For example, the use of opium may be a fairly accepted practice, whereas the use of alcohol typically is associated with quite severe penalties.

Occupational Factors

Another social/environmental influence that may affect substance use and abuse is the occupational environment. This phenomenon has been studied mostly with respect to alcohol use, and it is upon this substance that we will concentrate our attention. An excellent historical perspective on concern about alcohol abuse in the workplace has been provided by Fillmore and Caetano (1982).

More central to the focus of the present chapter is the prevalence of differential alcohol/alcoholism rates in various occupations. Whitehead and Simpkins (1983) have provided a comprehensive review of this literature and identified some of the more high-risk occupations for alcohol abuse difficulties. These occupations include, but are not limited to, entertainers, salespeople, army and navy personnel, executives, and physicians. The standard mortality rates for these groups generally are elevated.

Hitz (1973) has noted that no specific job characteristic is likely to account for workers in certain positions being more prone to alcohol problems. Hitz does, however, note that some positions provide more acceptance of drinking behavior than do others. She also offers several suggestions that may in part account for differential rates of alcohol abuse across occupations. The first is "selective recruitment," whereby heavy drinkers are more likely to take a position where alcohol is available and/or its use sanctioned (e.g., bartending). A second hypothesis is that such drinking will be more probable when the job setting is loosely structured or supervised. A third explanation offered by Hitz is that "certain occupations may for various reasons (geographic isolation, unusual working hours or shifts, particularly esoteric skills required) form subcultural groups or cliques" (p. 504) that are characterized in part by ritualized drinking. And finally, Hitz notes that some jobs may push one to drink because they are boring or alienating in nature.

Other researchers have reported similar findings. Schuckit and Gunderson (1974), for example, studied Navy personnel hospitalized for alcoholism treatment. In studying their job assignments, Schuckit and Gunderson found that those men in nontechnical positions (e.g., deck mate, clerical, construction) had a much higher prevalence of alcoholism relative to those in positions requiring more skill, education, and aptitude (e.g., communications and electronics technicians, engineers). In another report reviewing the correlation between alcoholism rates and various occupations, Plant (1977) identified three major risk factors: the availability of alcohol during working hours, social pressures to drink, and separation from normal social and sexual relations (e.g., a job in which social outlets are restricted).

Although alcohol abuse is clearly associated with some occupations to a greater extent than with others, it is unclear in most studies whether a causal relationship is operating or whether certain individuals are selectively attracted to these high-risk positions. Plant (1979) addressed this issue by comparing recruits to a high-risk industry (alcohol production) with recruits to several low-risk jobs. Plant found that the alcohol production recruits were significantly heavier drinkers prior to their employment in the high-risk positions than were those recruited to the low-risk positions. These data suggest that persons attracted to high-risk occupations may be predisposed to alcohol abuse problems. However, the Plant study is notable in that follow-up interviews for periods of up to 3 years were conducted with these workers. In this regard, Plant found that current occupational status was highly correlated with alcohol consumption and alcohol abuse. This finding in part was based on follow-up interviews with high-risk workers who later were employed in low-risk positions (alcohol consumption and problems tended to decrease) and low-risk workers who later worked in high-risk jobs (increases in consumption and problems were found). Thus, although certain jobs do seem to attract heavier drinkers, the structural characteristics of any given position also influence alcohol consumption and alcohol-related problems.

Geographic Setting

A final macroenvironmental influence affecting substance use and abuse is the geographic environment. Two central themes are discussed when geographic setting is considered. The first is region of the country, and the second is the degree of urbanization.

Differences in drinking problems long have been known to vary as a function of geographic area. Cahalan et al. (1969) noted that the highest proportions of drinkers in general as well as heavy drinkers were found in the New England, Middle Atlantic, East North Central (e.g., Michigan, Wisconsin, Ohio, Indiana, Illinois), and Pacific regions of the country. Lower proportions were reported for the Southern states and for the Mountain region. These differences likely reflect differences in urbanization as well as economics, according to Cahalan et al. (1969). Similar findings have been reported in a more recent survey of national drinking practices (Clark & Midanik, 1982). Clark and Midanik also note that problem-drinking rates do not parallel the proportions of nondrinkers. In another report, Cahalan and Room (1974) studied national drinking data with a particular focus on problem drinking among men. In comparing the geographic regions noted earlier, Cahalan and Room found that "dryer" regions when compared to "wetter" regions had higher rates of abstainers and lower rates of heavy intake without negative consequences. The two types of regions did not differ in terms of the proportion of drinkers who drank without problems. It also was found that there was a higher proportion of drinkers "at risk" for problematic drinking in the "wetter" regions. Despite these differences, the proportions of drinkers experiencing "high consequences" related to their alcohol consumption did not differ in the "dryer" and "wetter" regions (15 and 13%, respectively). Cahalan and Room note that these findings are consistent with the hypothesis "that a given level of intake in the drier regions of the country is associated with a higher level of consequences . . . than is true in the wetter regions" (p. 176).

National survey studies also have examined drinking patterns as a function of urbanization. Cahalan *et al.* (1969) found that there are fewer abstainers and infrequent drinkers in highly urbanized areas than in less urbanized areas and that there are a greater number of heavy drinkers. As in the case of drinking as a function of occupation, current structural characteristics appear to be a critical determinant of consumption. Cahalan *et al.* found that individuals tended to mirror the prevailing drinking customs of their environment, even if they were raised in an area with different drinking customs. In terms of drinkng problems, Cahalan and Room (1974) found that the highest prevalence of problem drinking among American men was in the highly urbanized areas. Differences between rural areas and towns/smaller cities in problem-drinking rates were inconsistent, but generally small. Differences between rural and urban areas in problem-drinking rates were more pronounced in "dryer" regions of the country.

Although the use of other drugs has not been as extensively studied as the use of alcohol, geographic differences have been assessed. A recent report issued by the National Institute on Drug Abuse (1981) indicated that the prevalence of ever using most drugs (excluding heroin) was in rural areas about two-thirds the rate for metropolitan areas. However, it was noted that such differences are declining and may eventually disappear.

The NIDA (1981) report provided other pertinent information regarding geographic variation. In terms of demographics, variables such as age, education, or sex did not differentiate rural and metropolitan drug users. The survey found that the ratio of male to female users in both the rural and metropolitan areas was 3 : 2. There were no differences in age of drug use initiation.

Data collected on geographic region showed that differences in drug use in rural versus metropolitan areas were more pronounced in the South and in the North Central regions. Much smaller differences were found in the Northeastern and Western regions of the country.

Summary

Although they are more difficult to specify than governmental influences, social factors clearly operate to affect alcohol and drug use. In this regard, the influences of sociocultural variables, occupational factors, and geographic setting are clearly identifiable. Sociocultural factors, for example, have been widely cited as important variables that dictate how a given group of individuals will use psychoactive substances. However, the mechanisms through which these sociocultural variables exert their influence are not clearly understood, although efforts have been made to develop models to account for their influence (Bales, 1946; MacAndrew & Edgerton, 1969). Predicting how individuals will differentially respond to these influences, however, is a question that remains unanswered.

Two other social influences have received considerable attention. The first includes occupational factors. In this regard, surveys have demonstrated that alcohol consumption, for example, is higher among workers in certain occupations (e.g., entertainers, sales personnel, armed forces personnel) than in other occupations. Although some occupations do seem to attract heavy drinkers, it is also the case that structural aspects of any given position (including its acceptance of alcohol or drug use) do significantly affect the employee's use of the substance.

The final social factor discussed was geographic setting (including region of the country and degree of urbanization). Several national surveys have shown that drinking patterns vary as a function of geographic region, variations that likely reflect economic factors and differences in urbanization (Cahalan et al., 1969; Clark & Midanik, 1982). Further, as in the case of occupation, structural characteristics of one's environment appear to be a critical determinant of consumption. Cahalan et al. (1969), for example, found that individuals tend to mirror the prevailing drinking customs of their environment. Finally, in terms of drug use, geographic differences (i.e., rural versus urban influences) have been declining in recent years and are likely to disappear soon.

MACROENVIRONMENTAL INFLUENCES AND THE INDIVIDUAL

Although there has been much attention focused on macroenvironmental factors that influence alcohol and drug use, relatively little is known of the interaction between these factors and the individual. For example, it is recognized that pricing policies and legislation regarding drinking age operate pandemically, and statistics demonstrate that on a broad-based scale these macroenvironmental factors influence alcohol consumption and its consequences. However, these effects are studied with populations and not with the individual. It is as if a population homogeneity was assumed, and as a result, individual variation within a given population or subgroup has not been systematically assessed.

The macroenvironmental influence of sociocultural factors is a case in point. Although each sociocultural group develops and applies its own guidelines for the use of alcohol and drugs, these norms clearly will not affect each individual in the same way, and the extent of influence will likely fall on a continuum ranging from little influence to maximum influence on alcohol and drug use. It is known, for example, that some Orthodox Jews abuse alcohol and that some Irish-American males abstain from alcohol. However, little is known about these individuals and in what ways they may differ from the "modal" Orthodox Jew and Irish-American male, respectively. Even less is known about what differentiates individuals at other points on the continuum. It may be that for some individuals, the differentiation can be attributed to biological factors (e.g., tolerance), whereas for others it may reflect cognitive factors (e.g., individual expectancies regarding drug effects). Such a phenomenon has been mentioned by Straus (1982), who noted that there frequently exists

> a conflict between the reality of individual variability in capacities for drinking and a lack of recognition of or respect for the variability in the sociocultural norms that govern the way people perceive they are supposed to drink in social settings. (p. 145)

Thus, although it does appear that macroenvironmental factors do influence substance use, variations within populations studied remain unspecified. Future research is needed to specify the parameters of the impact of macroenvironmental factors as a function of individual characteristics (e.g., personality characteristics, past drug use, family drug use, etc.). It is not until such work is conducted that the interface between macroenvironmental, microenvironmental, and individual variables can be understood.

GENERAL SUMMARY

The purpose of this chapter has been to discuss a variety of macroenvironmental factors that influence the use and abuse of various substances. Most of the research in this regard has focused on alcohol, and for that reason much of the chapter has centered on the use and abuse of alcohol.

Two types of macroenvironmental influences were identified. The first group of broad-based, environmental variables described herein revolved around governmental influences and attempts at control. Although legal restrictions were viewed as having significant drawbacks in their potential utility for reducing alcohol and drug abuse, some tentative and optimistic conclusions were offered. First, the impact of price through taxation on limiting alcohol consumption and abuse was found to be a major factor. Heroin, on the other hand, may be one drug that is "price inelastic," and increasing price may not necessarily reduce demand. Second, data consistently indicate that increased availability of one drug (i.e., alcohol) via lowered minimum drinking age regulations is associated with increases in some measures of alcohol consumption and with automobile accidents/fatalities. On the other hand, other governmental attempts to control availability of alcohol through various measures such as limiting sales of spirits versus beer or restricting the number of sales outlets were found to have little, if any, impact on alcohol abuse and related problems.

Fiscal factors and the regulation of sales primarily have applicability in the area of alcohol use and abuse. Other governmental actions legislating the usage of drugs apply to all drugs, especially in that most governments define the use of psychoactive substances without medical prescription as *illegal*. Thus, the norm for legislation regarding other drug use has been total prohibition. The impact of such a philosophy on drug use and the resulting controversies were reviewed. One set of data gathered in Great Britain up until the 1960s offered some optimism for limited availability of opiates as a means of reducing the number of addicted individuals. Others have pointed with optimism to the results of intensive law enforcement efforts to reduce drug availability through the interruption of drug-trafficking networks. Unfortunately, studies indicate that, in general, the relationship between availability of an illicit drug and its use is far from clear cut. Data regarding the use of marijuana were reviewed as a case in point. The importance of sociocultural and individual characteristics has been thus brought into focus.

The second type of macroenvironmental factors includes sociocultural influences. Three central influences were discussed: sociocultural, occupational, and geographic. A large body of literature exists regarding the variety of sociocultural influences that operate within any given population. In addition, one's occupation also influences whether, and the manner in which, various substances are used. Similarly, different areas of the country and locations with different degrees of urbanization will affect the use of drugs. These forces typically are more diffuse in their influence than are the more explicity outlined governmental factors, but are certainly no less forceful in their impact.

Although macroenvironmental factors clearly do influence drug-taking behavior, they frequently are not considered when studying the drug use of any given individual. One reason is that they are not as immediate to the individual as the drinking context, others in the environment, specific expectancies regarding the drug's effects, and so on.

Nevertheless, significant progress in understanding the multidetermined use of alcohol and drugs is not likely to be better understood until the interface between macroenvironmental, microenvironmental, and individual factors is elucidated.

REFERENCES

Akers, R. L. *Deviant behavior: A social learning approach* (2nd ed.). Belmont, Calif.: Wadsworth, 1977.

Akers, R. L., Krohn, M. D., Lanza-Kaduce, L., & Radosevich, M. *Social learning in adolescent drug and alcohol behavior: A Boys Town Center Research Report.* Boys Town, Nebr.: The Boys Town Center for the Study of Youth Development, 1977.

Bales, R. F. Cultural differences in rates of alcoholism. *Quarterly Journal of Studies on Alcohol*, 1946, *6*, 480–499.

Becker, H. S. *Outsiders.* New York: The Free Press, 1963.

Bensinger, P. B., & Miller, D. E. International narcotic drug trafficking: The impact of law enforcement. In J. H. Lowinson & P. Ruiz (Eds.), *Substance abuse: Clinical problems and perspectives.* Baltimore: Williams & Wilkins, 1981.

Blane, H. T., & Hewitt, L. E. *Mass media, public education, and alcohol: A state of the art review.* Paper prepared for NIAAA, Contract NIA-76-12, 1977.

Blum, R. H. Decisions and data. In R. H. Blum, D. Bovet, J. Moore, & Associates. *Controlling drugs.* San Francisco: Jossey-Bass, 1974.

Borkenstein, R. F., Crowther, E. F., Shumate, R. P., Ziel, W. B., & Zylman, R. *The role of the drinking driver in traffic accidents* (Report of the Department of Police Administration). Bloomington: Indiana University, 1964.

Brecher, E. M. & the Editors of Consumer Reports. *Licit and illicit drugs.* Boston: Little, Brown, 1972.

Brotman, R., & Suffet, F. Marijuana use: Values, behavioral definitions and social control. In National Commission on Marijuana and Drug Abuse, *Drug use in America: Problem in perspective* (Appendix). (Vol. 1): *Patterns and consequences of drug use.* Washington, D.C.: U.S. Government Printing Office, 1973.

Bryant, C. W. Effects of sale of liquor by the drink in the state of Washington. *Quarterly Journal of Studies on Alcohol*, 1954, *15*, 320–324.

Cahalan, D., & Room, R. *Problem drinking among American men.* New Brunswick, N.J.: Rutgers Center of Alcohol Studies, 1974.

Cahalan, D., Cisin, I. H., & Crossley, H. M. *American drinking practices.* New Brunswick, N.J.: Rutgers Center of Alcohol Studies, 1969.

Carroll, J. F. X. Perspectives on marijuana use and abuse and recommendations for preventing abuse. *American Journal of Drug and Alcohol Abuse*, 1981, *8*, 259–282.

Christie, N. Scandinavian experience in legislation and control. In *National conference on legal issues in alcoholism and alcohol usage.* Boston: Boston University Law–Medicine Institute, 1965.

Clark, W. B., & Midanik, L. Alcohol use and alcohol problems among U. S. adults: Results of the 1979 national survey. In *Alcohol consumption and related problems* (Alcohol and Health Monograph No. 1). Rockville, Md.: National Institute on Alcohol Abuse and Alcoholism, 1982.

Cohen, S. *The substance abuse problems.* New York: Haworth Press, 1981.

Cook, P. J. The effect of liquor taxes on drinking, cirrhosis, and auto accidents. In M. H. Moore & C. R. Gerstein (Eds.), *Alcohol and public policy: Beyond the shadow of prohibition*. Washington, D.C.: National Academy Press, 1981.

Cucchiaro, S., Fereira, J., & Sicherman, A. *The effect of the 18-year-old drinking age on auto accidents*. Cambridge: Massachusetts Institute of Technology Operation Research Center, 1974.

Cushman, P., Jr. Detoxification of rehabilitated methadone patients: Frequency and predictors of long-term success. *American Journal of Drug and Alcohol Abuse*, 1974, *1*, 393–408.

de Lint, J. *Alcohol control policies, a strategy for prevention: A critical examination of the evidence*. Paper presented at the International Conference on Alcoholism and Drug Dependence, Liverpool, England, 1976.

Dole, V. P., & Joseph, H. *The long-term outcome of patients treated with methadone maintenance*. Paper presented at the New York Academy of Sciences Conference on Recent Developments in Chemotherapy of Narcotic Addiction, Washington, D.C., November 1977.

Douglass, R. L. Legal drinking age and traffic casualties: A special case of changing alcohol availability in public health context. *Alcohol and Health Research World*, 1980, *4*, 18–25. (a)

Douglass, R. L. The legal drinking age and traffic casualties: A special case of changing alcohol availability in public health context. In H. Wechsler (Ed.), *Minimum-drinking-age laws*. Lexington, Mass.: D. C. Health, 1980. (b)

Douglass, R. L., & Freedman, J. A. *A study of alcohol-related casualties and alcohol beverage availability policies in Michigan*. Ann Arbor: Highway Safety Research Institute, 1977.

Douglass, R. L., Filkins, L. D., & Clark, F. A. *The effect of lower legal drinking age on youth crash involvement: Final report to U.S. Dept. of Transportation, National Highway Traffic Safety Administration*. Ann Arbor: Highway Safety Research Institute, University of Michigan, 1974.

Efron, V., Keller, M., & Gurioli, C. *Statistics on consumption of alcohol and on alcoholism*. New Brunswick, N.J.: Rutgers Center of Alcohol Studies, 1974.

Entine, A. D. *The relationship between the number of sales outlets and the consumption of alcoholic beverages in New York and other states* (Study Paper No. 2). Albany: New York State Moreland Commission of the Alcoholic Beverage Control Law, 1963.

Fillmore, K., & Caetano, R. Epidemiology of alcohol abuse and alcoholism in occupations. In *Occupational alcoholism: A review of research issues* (Research Monograph No. 1). Rockville, Md.: National Institute on Alcohol Abuse and Alcoholism, 1982.

Goode, E. Sociological aspects of marijuana use. *Contemporary Drug Problems*, 1975, *4*, 397–445.

Hitz, D. Drunken sailors and others. *Quarterly Journal of Studies on Alcohol*, 1973, *34*, 496–505.

Horton, D. J. The functions of alcohol in primitive societies: A cross-sectional study. *Quarterly Journal of Studies on Alcohol*, 1943, *4*, 199–320.

Houthakker, H. S., & Taylor, L. D. *Consumer demand in the United States, 1929–1970*. Cambridge: Harvard University Press, 1966.

Hu, T.-Y. *The liquor tax in the United States, 1791–1947*. New York: Columbia University Press, 1950.

Jaffe, J. H. The swinging pendulum: The treatment of drug users in America. In R. L. Dupont, A. Goldstein, & J. O'Donnell (Eds.), *Handbook on drug abuse*. Washington, D.C.: National Institute on Drug Abuse, 1979.

Jessor, R. Marijuana: A review of recent psychosocial research. In R. L. Dupont, A. Goldstein, & J. O'Donnell (Eds.), *Handbook on drug abuse.* Washington, D.C.: National Institute on Drug Abuse, 1979.

Jessor, R., & Jessor, S. L. *Problem behavior and psychosocial development: A longitudinal study of youth.* New York: Academic Press, 1977.

Johnston, L. D., Bachman, J. G., & O'Malley, P. M. *Drug use among American high school students 1975–1977.* Washington, D.C.: National Institute on Drug Abuse, U.S. Government Printing Office, 1977.

Johnston, L. D., Bachman, J., & O'Malley, P. M. *Student drug use, attitudes, and beliefs: National trends 1975–1982.* Rockville, Md.: National Institute on Drug Abuse, U.S. Department of Health and Human Services, 1982.

Jolliffe, N., & Jellinek, E. M. Vitamin deficiences in alcoholism: Part VII, Cirrhosis of the liver. *Quarterly Journal of Studies on Alcohol,* 1941, 2, 544–583.

Kalant, H., & Kalant, O. J. *Drugs, society and personal choice.* Don Mills, Ontairo: General Publishing, 1971.

Kalant, H., LeBlanc, A. E., & Wilson, A. *Sensorimotor and physiological effects of various alcoholic beverages.* Paper presented at the 6th International Conference on Alcohol, Drugs and Traffic Safety, Toronto, 1974.

Kandel, D. B. Interpersonal influences on adolescent illegal drug use. In E. Josephson & E. Carroll (Eds.), *Drug use: Epidemiological and sociological approaches.* Washington, D.C.: Hemisphere (Halsted-Wiley), 1974.

Kandel, D. B., & Sudit, M. Drinking practices among urban adults in Israel: A cross-cultural comparison. *Journal of Studies on Alcohol,* 1982, 43, 1–16.

Kuusi, P. *Alcohol sales experiment in rural Finland.* Helsinki: The Finnish Foundation for Alcohol Studies, 1957.

Lau, H. H. Cost of alcoholic beverages as a determinant of alcohol consumption. In R. J. Gibbins, Y. Israel, H. Kalant, R. E. Popham, W. Schmidt, & R. G. Smart (Eds.), *Research advances in alcohol and drug problems* (Vol. 2). New York: Wiley, 1975.

Le Dain, C. *Interim Report of the Commission of Inquiry into the non-medical use of drugs.* Ottawa: Queen's Printer for Canada, 1970.

Leland, J. *The firewater myth: Alcohol addiction among North American Indians.* New Brunswick, N.J.: Rutgers Center of Alcohol Studies, 1976.

Lelbach, W. K. Organic pathology related to volume and pattern of alcohol use. In R. J. Gibbins, Y. Israel, H. Kalant, R. E. Popham, W. Schmidt, & R. G. Smart (Eds.), *Research advances in alcohol and drug problems* (Vol. 1). New York: Wiley, 1974.

Lillis, R. P., Williams, T. P., Chupka, J. Q., & Williford, W. R. *Highway safety considerations in raising the minimum legal age for purchase of alcoholic beverges to nineteen in New York State.* Albany: New York State Division of Alcoholism and Alcohol Abuse, 1982.

MacAndrew, C., & Edgerton, R. B. *Drunken comportment.* Chicago: Aldine, 1969.

Maisto, S. A., & Rachal, J. V. Indications of the relationship among adolescent drinking practices, related behaviors, and drinking-age laws. In H. Wechsler (Ed.), *Minimum-drinking-age laws.* Lexington, Mass.: D. C. Health, 1980.

Mass Observation. *The pub and the people.* London: Gollancz, 1943.

McCarthy, R. G., & Douglass, E. M. Systems of legal control. In R. G. McCarthy (Ed.), *Drinking and intoxication.* New Haven: College and University Press, 1959.

Medicine in the Public Interest, Inc. *The effects of alcoholic beverage control laws.* Washington, D.C.: MIPI, 1979.

Mezritz, M., Slobetz, F., Kleber, H., & Riordan, C. *A follow-up study of successfully detoxified methadone maintenance patients.* Paper presented at the First National Drug Abuse Conference, Chicago, April 1974.

Miller, J. D., Cisin, I. H., & Harrell, A. V. *Highlights from the National Survey on Drug Abuse: 1977.* Washington, D.C.: Social Research Group, George Washington University, 1978.

Miller, P. M., Nirenberg, T. D., & McClure, G. Prevention of alcohol abuse. In B. Tabakoff, P. B. Sutker, & C. L. Randall (Eds.), *Medical and social aspects of alcohol abuse.* New York: Plenum Press, 1983.

Moore, M. H., & Gerstein, D. R. (Eds.). *Alcohol and public policy: Beyond the shadow of prohibition.* Washington, D.C.: National Academy Press, 1981.

Mosher, J. F., & Wallack, L. M. *The DUI project: Description of an experimental program conducted by the California Department of Alcoholic Beverage Control.* Sacramento: California Department of Alcoholic Beverage Control, June, 1979.

Nathan, P. E. Failures in prevention: Why we can't prevent the devastating effect of alcoholism and drug abuse. *American Psychologist,* 1983, *38,* 459–467.

National Commission on Marihuana and Drug Abuse. *Drug use in America: Problem in perspective.* Washington, D.C.: U.S. Government Printing Office, 1973.

National Institute on Drug Abuse. *Drug abuse in rural America.* Washington, D.C.: Department of Health and Human Services, 1981.

National Institute on Drug Abuse. *Student drug use, attitudes, and beliefs: National trends 1975–1982.* Washington, D.C.: Department of Health and Human Services, 1982.

Niskanen, W. A. *The demand for alcoholic beverages: An experiment in econometric method.* Santa Monica: Rand Corporation, 1962.

Ornstein, S. I. The control of alcohol consumption through price increases. *Journal of Studies on Alcohol,* 1980, *41,* 807–818.

Parker, D. A., & Harman, M. S. The distribution of consumption model of prevention of alcohol problems: A critical assessment. *Journal of Studies on Alcohol,* 1978, *39,* 377–399.

Phares, D. The simple economics of heroin and organizing public policy. *Journal of Drug Issues,* 1973, *3,* 186–200.

Plant, M. A. Alcoholism and occupation: A review. *British Journal of Addiction,* 1977, *72,* 309–316.

Plant, M. A. Occupations, drinking patterns and alcohol-related problems: Conclusions from a follow-up study. *British Journal of Addiction,* 1979, *74,* 267273.

Popham, R. E. *Study of the urban tavern.* Toronto: Addiction Research Foundation, 1956.

Popham, R. E. The urban tavern: Some preliminary remarks. *Additions,* 1962, *9,* 16–28.

Popham, R. E., & Schmidt, W. *Statistics of alcohol use and alcoholism in Canada, 1871–1956.* Toronto: University of Toronto Press, 1958.

Popham, R. E., Schmidt, W., & de Lint, J. The effects of legal restraint on drinking. In B. Kissin & H. Begleiter (Eds.), *The biology of alcoholism* (Vol. 4). *Social aspects of alcoholism.* New York: Plenum Press, 1976.

Popham, R., Schmidt, W., & de Lint, J. Government control measures to prevent hazardous drinking. In J. A. Ewing & B. A. Rouse (Eds.), *Drinking.* Chicago: Nelson-Hall, 1978.

Ray, O. S. *Drugs, society, and human behavior* (2nd ed.). St. Louis: Mosby, 1978.

Room, R., & Mosher, J. F. Out of the shadow of treatment: A role of regulatory agencies in the prevention of alcohol problems. *Alcohol Health and Research World,* 1979, *4,* 11–17.

Schmidt, W., & Popham, R. E. The single distribution theory of alcohol consumption: A rejoinder to the critique of Parker and Harman. *Journal of Studies on Alcohol,* 1978, *39,* 400–419.

Schuckit, M. A., & Gunderson, E. K. K. The association between alcoholism and job type in the U.S. Navy. *Quarterly Journal of Studies on Alcohol,* 1974, *35,* 577–585.

Schur, E. M. *Narcotic addiction in Britain and America.* Bloomington: Indiana University Press, 1968.

Sells, S. B. *The effectiveness of drug abuse treatment: Patient profiles, treatment, and outcomes* (Vol. 2). Cambridge, Mass.: Ballinger, 1974.

Sells, S. B. Treatment effectiveness. In R. L. Dupont, A. Goldstein, & J. O'Donnell (Eds.), *Handbook on drug abuse.* Washington, D.C.: National Institute on Drug Abuse, 1979.

Simon, J. L. The price elasticity of liquor in the U.S. and a simple method of determination. *Econometrics,* 1966, *34,* 193–205. (a)

Simon, J. L. The economic effects of state monopoly of packaged liquor retailing. *Journal of Political Economics,* 1966, *74,* 188–194. (b)

Single, E. W. The impact of marijuana decriminalization. In Y. Israel, F. B. Glaser, H. Kalant, R. E. Popham, W. Schmidt, & R. G. Smart (Eds.), *Research advances in alcohol and drug problems* (Vol. 6). New York: Plenum Press, 1981.

Skala, J. Some characteristic signs of alcoholism in Czechoslovakia. *International Council on Alcohol and Alcoholism,* 1967, *1,* 21–34.

Smart, R. G. The effects of two liquor store strikes on drunkenness, impaired driving and traffic accidents. *Journal of Studies on Alcohol,* 1977, *38,* 1785–1789.

Smart, R. G., & Goodstadt, M. Effects of reucing the legal alcohol-purchasing age on drinking and drinking problems: A review of empirical studies. *Journal of Studies on Alcohol,* 1977, *38,* 1313–1323.

Smart, R. G., & Schmidt, W. Drinking and problems from drinking after a reduction in the minimum drinking age. *British Journal of Addictions,* 1975, *70,* 347–358.

Snyder, C. R. *Alcohol and the Jews: A cultural study of drinking and sobriety.* New Haven: Yale Center of Alcohol Studies, 1958.

Snyder, C. R., Palgi, P., Eldar, P., & Elian, B. Alcoholism among the Jews in Israel: A pilot study. *Journal of Studies on Alcohol,* 1982, *43,* 623–654.

Stimmel, B., Goldberg, J., Rotkopf, E., & Cohen, M. Ability to remain abstinent after methadone detoxification: A six-year study. *Journal of the American Medical Association,* 1977, *237,* 1216–1220.

Stivers, R. *A hair of the dog: Irish drinking and American stereotype.* University Park, Pa.: Pennsylvania State Press, 1976.

Straus, R. The social costs of alcohol in the perspective of change, 1945–1980. In E. L. Gomberg, H. R. White, & J. A. Carpenter (Eds.), *Alcohol, science and society revisited.* Ann Arbor: University of Michigan Press, 1982.

Terry, C. E., & Pellens, M. *The opium problem.* New York: Bureau of Social Hygiene, Inc., 1928.

Wagenaar, A. C. Aggregate beer and wine consumption: Effects of changes in the minimum legal drinking age and a mandatory beverage container deposit law in Michigan. *Journal of Studies on Alcohol,* 1982, *43,* 469–487. (a)

Wagenaar, A. C. Raised legal drinking age and automobile crashes: A review of the literature. *Abstracts and Reviews in Alcohol and Driving,* 1982, *3,* 3–8. (b)

Wechsler, H., & McFadden, M. Sex differences in adolescent alcohol and drug use: A disappearing phenomenon. *Journal of Studies on Alcohol,* 1976, *37,* 1291–1301.

Westermeyer, J. Sociocultural aspects of alcohol and drug use and abuse. In J. Solomon & K. A. Keeley (Eds.), *Perspectives in alcohol and drug abuse.* Boston: John Wright, 1982.

Whitehead, P. C. *Alcohol and young drivers: Impact and implications of lowering the drinking age* (Monograph Series #1). Ottawa: Department of National Health and Welfare, 1977.

Whitehead, P. C., & Simpkins, J. Occupational factors in alcoholism. In B. Kissin & H. Begleiter (Eds.), *The biology of alcoholism* (Vol. 6). *The pathogenesis of alcoholism.* New York: Plenum, 1983.

Whitehead, P. C., & Wechsler, H. Implications for future research and public policy. In H. Wechsler (Ed.), *Minimum-drinking-age laws.* Lexington, Mass.: D. C. Health, 1980.

Wilkinson, R. *The prevention of drinking problems: Alcohol control and cultural influences.* New York: Oxford University Press, 1970.

Wilkinson, P., Santamaria, J. N., Rankin, J. G., & Martin, D. Epidemiology of alcoholism:

Social data and drinking patterns of a sample of Australian alcoholics. *Medical Journal of Australia*, 1969, *1*, 1020–1025.

Williams, A. F., Rich, R. F., Zador, P. L., & Robertson, L. S. *The legal minimum drinking age and fatal motor vehicle crashes.* Washington, D.C.: Insurance Institute for Highway Safety, 1974.

Yoakum, C. Many states reconsidering lowered drinking-age laws. *Traffic Safety*, 1979, *79*, 24–28.

PART IV

Determinants of Recovery from Substance Abuse Problems

CHAPTER 10

Individual Differences in Response to Treatment

GLENN R. CADDY and TRUDY BLOCK

In examining the research literature regarding individual differences in response to treatment for the various addictive behaviors, one finds much evidence in the alcoholism literature and very little information bearing on this issue in the literature on the other addictive behaviors. Moreover, what little research on individual differences in treatment responsiveness does exist in other drug abuse literature tends to parallel the findings in the alcoholism field. Thus, the focus of this chapter will be directed toward individual differences in response to alcoholism treatments only.

Although the alcoholism literature is replete with treatment outcome evaluation studies, it is the exception when the influence of individual differences is addressed directly. Demographic data, for example, frequently are reported to offer a summary description of the sample under investigation and to demonstrate the essential equality of the various treatment groups. Rarely are such data examined as a predictor of treatment success. Similarly, biological, psychological, and social factors are commonly examined in order to facilitate the classification of subjects and/or to offer an etiological perspective. Very infrequently, however, are such factors employed to differentiate alcohol-abusing individuals in terms of their propensity to benefit from various types of treatments.

Classically, alcoholism treatment outcome studies have concerned

GLENN R. CADDY • Department of Psychology, Nova University, Ft. Lauderdale, Florida 33314. TRUDY BLOCK • Clinical Psychology Institute, Ft. Lauderdale, Florida, 33316.

themselves with treatment effectiveness and have ignored or minimized many of those subject-related variables that may effect treatment success. There have been a number of correlational studies that have examined the subject by treatment relationship, but because they employed these very correlational methodologies, they do not definitively establish a causal relationship between specific individual subject variables and responsiveness to treatment. Consequently, individual differences in alcoholism recovery, for the most part, can only be inferred through an examination of the subject-related variables of those alcoholic patients who relapse or who achieve success following a particular intervention.

There can be little question but that the universe of patients that we label *alcoholic* is comprised of distinctly different subgroups vis-à-vis biological, psychological, social, and other factors. Nevertheless, systems of treatment have been applied to elements of a heterogeneous population as if the assumption of homogeneity had been met. Given the evidence supporting the proposition of alcoholism *subgroup* homogeneity, a more fruitful approach to treatment, it would seem, would be to tailor treatment programming specifically to meet the needs of these individual groups as well as individuals within these groups. The serious investigation of individual differences in alcoholics would appear imperative in order both to determine the parameters of these various alcoholic subgroups and to set the stage for evaluating the types of treatments most effectively applied within these subpopulations.

This chapter will examine research addressing the biological differences (including gender and neurological differences), sociocultural differences (encompassing demographics, social, and cultural variables), and psychological differences (unidimensional as well as multidimensional variables) in alcoholic subjects as these differences relate both to success and failure in treatment outcome. Additionally, the interactive effects of the aforementioned factors and various treatment modalities will be discussed. Before addressing the aforementioned variables, however, we will briefly present data related to the matter of spontaneous remission and the extent to which research bearing on the phenomenon implicates individual differences.

SPONTANEOUS REMISSION

Despite the fact that the phenomenon of spontaneous remission in alcoholism has received scant attention in the treatment literature, there can be little question but that the phenomenon exists and requires attention in any comprehensive review of the alcoholism treatment literature (see the review by Smart, 1976; Tuchfeld, 1981). In fact, Edwards, Orford, Egert, Guthrie, Hawker, Hensman, Mitcheson, Oppenheimer, and Taylor's (1977) study of minimum intervention documented the finding that extratreatment effects may contribute to as much change in the behavior of some alcoholics as do traditional treatment procedures. Cahalan's (1970) national study, Knupfer's (1972) intensive analysis of San Francisco adults, and Saunders, Phil, and Kershaw's (1979) community survey in England have all provided evidence confirming that formal treatment need not always represent the basis for recovery. But, as Smart (1976) has concluded,

> Clear statements about spontaneous recovery are difficult. The problem has not been directly approached in many treatment studies or in special surveys. (p. 284)

Of course, to the extent that the concept of spontaneous remission is contradictory to the widely held view that alcoholism is both progressive and irreversible, the relative lack of research on the topic is quite understandable. Doubtless, too, the "problem" of lack of subjects for follow-up in spontaneous remission research is also a factor here.

Saunders and Kershaw (1979) observed that changes in life circumstances such as marriage or new employment may precipitate spontaneous remission and that such changes may be a part of "growing up." Nevertheless, as Knupfer (1972) noted, "Spontaneous or not, the motivation for recovery is . . . to a large extent mysterious" (p. 259). Using standardized life-history-taking procedures, Tuchfeld (1981) found that 51 of 162 persons who responded to solicitations to participate in the study had resolved their alcoholism without the aid of formal treatment. He then studied these 51 individuals (35 males and 16 females). There are several findings of this study that are worthy of comment. First, several variables appear to preclude some people from even considering formal treatment as a source of assistance. Resistance to being labeled *alcoholic* and negative attitudes toward conventional treatment procedures were paramount in such decision making. Certainly, adamant self-attributions of success and vigorous rejection of institutional forms of treatment were highly correlated. There were also numerous factors associated with initiating the commitment to resolution of the problem, the most important being, respectively, personal illness or accident, alcoholism education, religious experience, intervention by family, intervention by friends, drinking-related financial problems, alcohol-related death or illness of another person, alcohol-related legal problems, and finally, extraordinary events such as personal humiliation, pregnancy, and personal identity crises. Tuchfeld also reported that his subjects' initial commitment to change was not sufficient to sustain a resolution of the problem behavior. Changes in social circumstances, reinforcement from family and friends, and the existence of rather stable social and economic support systems were all relevant maintenance factors. What were characterized as "commitment mechanisms" also served to support the termination of drinking. Of particular significance here was the use of religion and of rhetorical justification, this latter being a type of "side betting" (Becker, 1963) that with time provides a cognitive basis for commitment. The assertion here is that as people expand their "vocabulary of motives" (Mills, 1940), they become clearer regarding the nature of their past problem, a phenomenon that sustains commitment over time. In attempting to develop a model to account for spontaneous remission, Tuchfeld proposed a resolution of alcohol problems that is roughly comparable from one drinker to the next. He suggested that internal, psychological commitment typically is activated by social variables in the drinker's environment. Recognition of these phenomena and commitment to change, says Tuchfeld, require reinforcement by socially based maintenance factors if disengagement from problem drinking is to result in a sustained recovery sequence. Clearly, few, if any, cases in this study could be regarded as *spontaneous* remissions, if such a term implies the development of a pattern of recovery (typically abstinence) without external influence.

Obviously, there are numerous factors that could be described as individual differences and that such a study would point to as the essence of spontaneous remission in the individual case. We do not have available, however, either an adequate number of such studies or the capacity to make valid predictions from our present data base vis-à-vis those drinkers who will commit to and succeed in the process that has been termed *spontaneous remission*.

BIOLOGICAL FACTORS

There have been countless attempts in the literature to establish a causative relationship between the appearance of alcoholism and any one of a plethora of biologically based factors. Genetic predisposition involving sex-linked transmission, racial differences, neurological (especially hemispheric) differences, and the like have all been implicated in the emergence of alcoholism in the individual case. With the possible exception of some sex-related treatment differences, however, there is virtually no evidence in the literature demonstrating any clear relationship between a subject's biological state and his or her responsiveness to therapeutic intervention. Such an assertion, of course, does not preclude the possibility of differential treatment responsiveness being associated with biological/genetic considerations. For this reason, we will offer a brief analysis of those biological factors that may be related to the treatment outcome of alcoholism.

GENDER

Although gender is a biologically dependent variable, clearly, social, cultural, and other environmental forces impact on its expression, and this fact must be seen to influence the results of studies relating gender and alcoholism. An interesting linkage has been established between premenstrual tension and female drinking (Beckman, 1979). In this study, investigating sexual feelings and behaviors of female alcoholics, Beckman noted that women tended to increase drinking during premenstruum. The data, however, were insufficient to conclude that premenstrual tension led to excessive drinking, and Beckman posited that perhaps the premenstruum may have been a convenient rationalization for heavy drinking. Although we are aware of no studies in the literature that show a differential responsiveness to treatment to be related to the menstrual cycle, it is not unreasonable to posit that relapse or temporary slips in the commitment to abstinence of some alcoholic females may be associated with the emotional by-products of hormonal changes. But to ascribe alcoholic drinking to hormonal changes is most definitely beyond the scope of the current evidence in this area, particularly given the fact that alcohol acts as a muscle relaxant and that its use may be correlated with tension reduction.

Keil and Busch (1981) view differences in drinking patterns between men and women as being primarily due to differences in access to alcohol and situations that include drinking and to differences in prescribed social roles. Mitigating against such a tendency, however, is the fact that the use of medication (and, therefore perhaps, by generalization, the use of alcohol for purposes of self-medication) tends to be reinforced by physicians more readily with women patients than with men (Collier, 1982). But, in the final analysis, it is clear that even today more men drink alcohol than do women and that of all those in our society who do drink alcohol, it is men who drink greater quantities, and they do so more overtly (Cahalan, 1970; Cahalan & Room, 1974; Cahalan, Cisin, & Crossley, 1969; Gomberg, 1976, 1981; Horn & Wanberg, 1973). To presume that gender *per se* is a contributing factor of any major significance to treatment responsiveness in alcoholics would be folly, and in fact the evidence bearing on these matters is contradictory. Kammeier and Conley (1979) noted that the females they studied at Hazelden exhibited higher recovery rates than did males, particularly those who rated high on indexes of social stability (measured in terms of marital and employment status). Seelye (1979), on the other hand, found that women were less responsive to therapeutic interventions employed in their alcoholism treatment program. Males, by comparison, were overrepresented in treatment success categories that included both abstinence and restricted drinking. Several points regarding these studies are noteworthy. First, in Kammeier and Conley's study women who would appear to experience greater rewards in their life produced the greatest responsiveness to treatment. So, too, it was also true in Seelye's study: the men who proved most therapeutically successful held positions that would seem to contribute to accomplishment and a sense of self-worth. Thus, it may well be that treatment success is far more related to variables that are not gender specific. Rather, it would seem from studies such as those cited before that factors contributing to a generally satisfying life-style may be far more predictive of therapeutic success than the more obvious factor of gender. Support for this position was provided by Pemberton (1967) who noted that women who had been dependent on their husbands for interests and contacts outside the home (widowed, separated, and divorced) responded more poorly to treatment than women who still had satisfying relationships or those who were independently able to lead a satisfying and productive life. As Gomberg (1976) points out, "One of the major keys to prognosis lies in this familial-social environment" (p. 157).

HEMISPHERIC DIFFERENCES

There is also some suggestion and a greater degree of speculation that has implicated hemispheric dominance with treatment progress and relapse probability. Smith and Chyatte (1983) found that among alcoholics who relapsed following treatment, left-handers outnumbered right-handers 6 to 1. Those patients who were successful in treatment were primarily right handed (29 to 4). The authors suggested that left-handed alcoholics are a specifically pathology-prone subgroup. They went on to speculate that these subjects may have a common history of neonatal brain insult that results in a greater propensity to exhibit maladjustment than their left-hemisphere-dominant peers. Furthermore, these investigators showed left-handers to be more anxious than right-handed alcoholics, and they hypothesized that right-hemisphere-dominant alcoholics may use alcohol to relieve anxiety disproportionately, relative to left-hemisphere-dominant alcoholics.

Together with the combination of soft findings and speculation reflected in the study by Smith and Chyatte, we have a research methodology that most surely is weak and that must be questioned. First, the report of the study provides no indication of the nature of the intervention technologies employed, nor does it provide clear treatment outcome indexes. Second, it seems obvious from the report that no matching of left-handed and right-handed subjects was possible, and it would be expected simply by chance that subjects selected on the basis of handedness would constitute groups that would differ in a number of respects. Finally, as is obvious from the preceding comments, the study employed post hoc correlational analyses as the primary statistical procedure. Given the aforestated considerations, it is clear that requirements for both internal and external validity have been violated, and the results, therefore, could be attributed to any number of factors other than hemispheric differences.

RACE

Overall, there is really no consistently presented evidence that supports an assumption that racially related physiognomic factors predispose Indians, Eskimos, Caucasians, and/or other racial groupings to alcoholism. (See for example, Brod, 1975; Brown, 1981; Fenna, Shaefer, & Mix, 1971; MacAndrew & Edgerton, 1969; Price, 1975; Reed, 1978; Sievers, 1968; Westermeyer, 1972; Wolff, 1972, 1973). Given the aforementioned, it would appear unwarranted to tailor treatment packages specifically to racial groups on the basis of racial considerations, even if such a tailoring could be achieved. Rather, in providing treatment to people of a specific racial makeup, we would seem well served to develop the components of the treatments to address social, cultural, and psychological factors that may uniquely characterize individuals of a specific racial identity. Furthermore, the etiological variables and variables related to treatment outcome appear to be ubiquitous and are certainly not specific to particular racial groups. Thus, treatment aimed at the more general attributes, social, cultural, and psychological, of the human condition may be more fruitful than an emphasis on racial variables and differences.

SUMMARY

Few studies have addressed genetic factors as predictor variables in treatment outcome, with the exception of gender and perhaps race. In general, there is no evidence that biological factors appreciably influence recovery rates in alcoholics. With respect to gender and treatment outcome, the evidence shows that women who enter treatment facilities recover at the same or at better rate than their male counterparts (Gomberg, 1976). There is also no credible evidence that genetic factors *per se* influence recovery or relapse rates for women. Similarly, regarding race as a predictor of treatment responsiveness, there again appears no credible support for viewing race in and of itself as relevant to treatment sucess or failure. In fact, the data addressing both etiological and treatment-implicated biological variables in alcoholism, the disease concept notwithstanding, are so weak as to hardly justify further research in this area at this time. Multiple factors involving internal psychological changes and external environmental/interpersonal variables appear to overwhelm the relevance of any biologically related hypotheses in accounting for therapeutic gains or losses.

SOCIOCULTURAL FACTORS

Sociocultural factors that describe the alcoholic and that have been implicated in treatment responsiveness include the demographic variables, social variables, and cultural variables that describe a drinker. Virtually all of the recently published studies, at least, have shown an increased commitment to the reporting of statistics such as subjects' ages, marital status and stability, occupation and employment stability, socioeconomic status, drinking history, and religious affiliation. Although in the decade of the 1960s a number of studies sought to use such data to predict treatment responsiveness, more recent literature has tended to employ these data descriptively rather than as predictive of treatment outcome.

DEMOGRAPHIC VARIABLES

Demographic variables (age, sex, marital status, occupation, education, and socioeconomic status) frequently are reported in isolation. Yet, there may well be an interactive effect of these variables on treatment outcome. Kissin, Rosenblatt, and Machover (1968) have pointed to a consistent pattern of demographic variables that they believe predict favorable treatment outcome. Being 40 to 45 years old or older, being married, having achieved at least some postsecondary education, functioning within a skilled occupation, and doing so with stability are variables, all of which have been implicated in treatment success. According to Kissin, Rosenblatt, and Machover (1968), the more a patient conforms to the aforementioned pattern, the more favorable is his or her prognosis.

Age

There are a substantial number of studies that show older alcohol-abusing individuals to profit more from treatment than their younger peers. Selzer and Holloway (1957), Kissin *et al.* (1968), Bateman and Petersen (1972), Lundquist (1973), Pokorny, Miller, and Cleveland (1968), and Wolff and Holland (1964) have all shown alcoholic patients under 35 years of age to display higher rates of relapse than their older brethren. These findings also have more recently been replicated by Kammeier and Conley (1979). Although Kissin *et al.* (1968) reported their younger patients to do better in inpatient treatment settings, these investigators found that alcoholic subjects 45 years old or older are more successful when involved in outpatient services.

There can be little question but that increasing age is negatively correlated with alcohol consumption in the community at large. It is noteworthy in that regard that despite the widely held view that alcoholism is a progressive condition, in fact alcoholics too have been shown to reduce their levels of consumption with increasing age (MacIntyre, 1979). It may well be the case that for at least some alcohol-abusing patients, higher levels of treatment responsiveness are associated with increasing age. The patterns of alcohol consumption that characterized the early drinking years of such individuals now can no longer be sustained without provoking quite profound and negative physiologically based consequences. These consequences may also integrate with other negatively colored operants involving interpersonal, social, psychological, and other factors. The result, ultimately, may be that the patient recognizes that he or she must finally act to change his or her drinking practices and perhaps also his or her life in general. (This is the process that commonly is referred to in the self-help literature as *hitting bottom*.) Such a position, unfortunately, all too often is not reached early in the career of a person who eventually will be labeled *alcoholic*. Age is most definitely one of the factors contributing to motivation to change that, presumably, is of central relevance to treatment outcome. Finally, beyond the factor of age, both the specific techniques and the orientations of the interventions would seem to be implicated in the age-by-treatment-outcome relationship. It is reasonable to assume, for example, that relatively younger individuals may not be particularly responsive to alcohol-related treatment services, not because of their age or lack of motivation, but because the treatment *per se* is poorly geared to meeting the needs of younger patients. It is one thing for a treatment program to demand abstinence, say, of a 50-year-old alcoholic with serious physiological and other sequelae to his or her drunkeness; it is another matter entirely to impose the commitment to lifelong abstinence on a 22-year-old drunkard who has not yet come to appreciate the posible consequences of his or her drinking over the course of his or her life. Thus, although age clearly is a variable relevant to treatment outcome, it would seem likely that the interaction of age and treatment is the essential variable as far as treatment outcome is concerned.

Marital Status

The research examining a hypothetical relationship between marital status and treatment outcome shows anything but a consistency of findings, despite the large number of attempts to explore this relationship. Hunt and Azrin (1973) in the Community Reinforcement Treatment Program found marital status to be an important index of treatment success. Similarly, Kammeier and Conley (1979) have noted a positive relationship between marital status (married at admission) and inpatient treatment success. Cummings's (1977) data also suggest the possibility of a causal relationship between marital status and remaining in therapy, the latter presumably being a variable relevant to treatment success. Cummings reported that patients who terminated therapy early were more likely to be divorced than were those who completed the treatment program. On the other hand, van Dijk and van Dijk-Koffeman (1973) failed to show any relationship between marital status data and indexes of treatment outcome (see also Kissin *et al.*, 1968; Lundquist, 1973).

Marital status *per se*, of course, may not be the relevant predictor variable as far as treatment outcome is concerned. In fact, marital stability would appear to be a more relevant predictor of therapeutic outcome, if the hypothesized significance of a strong interpersonal bonding is to be considered important in facilitating progress in therapy. Stinson, Smith, Amidjaya, and Kaplan (1979) conducted a study in which marital stability and the general quality of the marital relationship were found to have a greater bearing on treatment outcome than simply the marital status index. Such a finding notwithstanding, Caddy, Addington, and Trenschel (in press) employed marital status and satisfaction as an adjunctive measure predicting aftercare treatment outcome success across a 12-month follow-up period. In their comprehensive aftercare study, these investigators failed to show the marital status/satisfaction constellation to be an adequately powerful predictor of success. Rather, several other treatment and subject-related variables contributed to the primary proposition of the accounted for variance.

Occupation

Whether or not an alcohol-abusing individual is employed at the time of his or her admission for treatment appears an important variable with respect to treatment outcome (Kammeier & Conley, 1979). But, as with marital status, simply being employed is hardly predictive of treatment success. Occupational stability and satisfaction appear to have a far stronger relationship to positive treatment outcome than does merely the existence of employment (Cummings, 1977; Kissin *et al.*, 1968). Moreover, Lundquist (1973) has proposed that alcoholics who are most motivated to succeed in treatment are those who have relatively high-paying positions that they do not wish to lose.

There are also data dealing with occupational status that suggest this index to be somewhat sensitive to the sometimes profound levels of impairment that a number of alcohol-abusing individuals experience. Ashley, Olin, le Riche, Kornaczewski, Schmidt, and Rankin (1981), for example, noted a deterioration in occupational status occurring in their subjects in the year preceding admission to an inpatient treatment program. Although such occupational deterioration is certainly a correlate of a more general deterioration that predicts hospital or other treatment program admission, there is no evidence that clearly implicates such a state of affairs with subsequent posttherapeutic success.

A case can be made that a relationship may exist between the occupational status of an alcohol-abusing individual and the nature of the treatment programming to which he or she is subjected. The logic behind this assertion, of course, is that even in alcoholism, which clearly is a condition contributing to the decline of one's occupational and socioeconomic status, the level of occupational functioning does offer prediction for the type of treatment that may be most appropriate to the individual client. Gallen (1976), for example, reported that subjects in a traditional group psychotherapy program who were married, had some level of occupational skill, and possessed a higher IQ showed the greatest treatment successes. However, subjects with poor work stability, coming from unskilled occupations, and possessing generally limited IQ showed more improvement when provided broad spectrum behavior therapy procedures than those subjects who were seen to be functioning at a higher occupational and intellectual level. It may well be the case that a treatment program that is relatively concrete and addresses specific difficulties (and requires little in the way of introspection) may offer a more appropriate therapeutic outcome for those alcohol-abusing individuals who function intellectually in a rather limited manner and who correspondingly hold positions of lower occupational status.

In addition to employment status *per se*, the type of employment engaged in by an individual appears to influence alcohol consumption and treatment responsiveness. It has been well established that certain occupations (i.e., merchant marines, military service, alcohol-producing professions) place individuals at a higher risk for excessive alcohol consumption. Furthermore, a significant decline in drinking was observed when individuals obtained employment where social pressures to drink were reduced (Plant, 1979). The aforementioned notwithstanding, employment or the type of employment in and of itself appears to be less prognostic of treatment success than are job satisfaction and a supportive work milieu.

Employment Stability and Satisfaction

There are a number of investigations that, similar to the marital status/satisfaction indexes, support the contention that being employed *per se* is not the crucial factor in the prediction of treatment outcome. Rather, stability in the vocational realm has been shown to be related to success in treatment. Kissin *et al.* (1968) noted that occupational stability (defined as having held only one job or having a steady job for an extended period) was highly predictive of treatment success as was a satisfactory work milieu (Hart & Stueland, 1979). But, those alcoholics who exhibited adjustment problems in vocational life aspects were more resistant to rehabilitation gains (Hart & Stueland, 1979). Individuals who had attained moderate drinking following treatment and who subsequently relapsed into heavy drinking were characterized by a work environment that was perceived as high pressure and lacking in support (Finney & Moos, 1981). However, a job change to a more satisfactory work environment fostered spontaneous remission (MacIntyre, 1979).

Socioeconomic Status

Although higher socioeconomic status has been correlated with positive treatment outcome (Blancy, Radford, & MacKenzie, 1975; Pokorny, Miller, & Cleveland, 1968), there is recent evidence that indicates that social stability (as measured by marital status and employment) rather than social status is the real correlate of treatment success (Armor, Polich, & Stambul, 1976). Costello (1980) also has demonstrated that when a high degree of social stability is present at the time of admission to treatment and continues throughout a 2-year follow-up period, the social stability variable may be shown to be related to reduced alcohol consumption.

Positive correlations between higher socioeconomic status and rates of alcoholism recovery and between lower socioeconomic status and unfavorable outcome also have been reported by van Dijk and van Dijk-Koffeman (1973). Similar findings also have been presented by Seelye (1979). Certainly, the educational level of an individual (of which SES is a function) appears to be consistently correlated with treatment success. Lundquist (1973) has suggested that a better education may enable the alcoholic patient to have a greater insight into his or her problems and facilitate help-seeking behavior. Even though Miller and Joyce (1979), for example, reported that lower income and less well-educated subjects in their study proved successful in recovering from alcoholism, in this study the sample consisted primarily of middle-class subjects with at least 14 years of education.

Finally, there is evidence (Blane & Meyers, 1964) that showed that lower-middle-class alcoholics respond more favorably to treatment that addresses concrete and specific issues rather than offers an insight orientation. This finding parallels the data reported by Gallen (1976) regarding occupation and type of treatment (insight oriented vs. behavioral). Given the research evidence provided by the aforementioned authors, Cahn's (1960) recommendation that treatment services for alcoholic patients be instituted on a social class basis so that such services might better meet the needs of those seeking treatment appears highly appropriate and warranted, though it is unlikely to be instituted given the existent sociopolitical realities.

Drinking History

In addition to the demographic variables previously discussed, an alcoholic individual's previous drinking history appears to have some bearing not only on the prognosis but also on the treatment goal most appropriate for that individual. Kissin *et al.* (1968) reported that prior alcohol-related hospitalizations are highly related to a negative prognosis. Furthermore, the consumption of large quantities of alcohol over a long period of time was shown to be unfavorable to recovery as were repeated treatments and relapses (Lundquist, 1973; Skinner & Allen, 1982). With respect to treatment goal, Miller and Joyce (1979) noted that alcohol-abusing patients with less of a history of drinking problems were more successful when controlled drinking was the treatment goal, whereas those individuals who had a more severe drinking history fared better when abstention was the goal of treatment.

Although the evidence for the aforementioned is credible, it is unlikely that history in and of itself is the crucial factor in an alcoholic's continued excessive drinking. In light of the previously discussed demographic factors and the social and psychological factors to be addressed subsequently, it would appear that drinking history may not be as relevant as are the current forces operating in an individual's life. For a thorough discussion of incentive variables that maintain alcoholismic drinking behavior, see Caddy (1978). Such variables include the positive reinforcement effects associated with the psychopharmacological properties of alcohol (e.g., euphoria and relaxation) and with the social aspects of alcohol use (e.g., acceptance into a drinking group), the negative reinforcement associated with aversive environmental events (e.g., relief of boredom), or they are related to aversive physical states (e.g., relief from physical discomfort of withdrawal). There are other explanations such as the power motivation hypothesis presented by McClelland and colleagues (McClelland, Davis, Kalin, & Wanner, 1972).

Summary

Under the heading *demographic variables* we have presented the rather static subject-related descriptors of age, marital status, occupation, and socioeconomic status. Overall, it appears that increasing age, although not relevant to prevention, does correlate to at least some degree with success in the sort of therapeutic procedures commonly employed in the management of alcoholism. Regarding marital status, the research data only marginally support the existence of a positive relationship between marital status and treatment outcome. Marital stability, on the other hand, appears more relevant to outcome success following alcoholism therapy.

Further, addressing the typically correlated variables of occupational and socioeconomic status, both of which are commonly related to educational achievement and intelligence, we see again that occupational and socioeconomic stability is more predictive of positive treatment outcome than simple status indexes. Additionally, there are stong reasons to speculate on the importance of considering these specific variables in the development of any specific therapeutic approaches to individuals.

Finally, there is evidence that an individual's drinking history has implications both for prognosis as well as for the treatment goal best suited to the individual case. However, current life aspects may be more relevant in treatment outcome than drinking history itself.

SOCIAL AND CULTURAL VARIABLES

Success in treatment may not be as much a function of differences inherent in the individual as it is due to differences within the environmental context. Social variables and the amount of aftercare support may well interact with unique attributes of the individual drinker in some differentially weighted manner both in prediction and treatment outcome.

Within the social variables, we will view marital, family, and peer relationships, issues of employment, community involvement, and the social history of the drinker's alcohol use practices; however, it would violate all we know about human behavior if we did not assume an interactive effect for a number of these variables and the broader cultural context as they relate to treatment outcome. A study by Moos and Finney (1983) makes this point very clear. These investigators reported that pre-treatment job satisfaction in their alcoholic patients was positively correlated with treatment outcome. For those of their alcoholic subjects who had supportive families, however, the work situation was not as crucial. If the individual was not living within a supportive family milieu but the work situation was perceived as supportive, Moos and Finney reported a better treatment outcome even after the effects of demographic variables were partialled out.

Marital Relationship

Certainly a substantial number of studies have reported marital status to be an important determinant in treatment outcome. Other research, however, has shown that marital stability and the quality of the marital relationship rather than marital status *per se* is a major factor in treatment success (Cummings, 1977; Stinson, Smith, Amidjayu, and Kaplan, 1979). And there is evidence to support the proposition that marrying a spouse who has the capacity to exert effective social control on the alcoholismic drinking of his or her mate can facilitate the process of recovery even in the absence of therapeutic intervention (see, for example, Bailey & Steward, 1967; Kendall, 1965).

There is, of course, evidence from other sources that has implicated the spouse of the drinker as causative in the relapse process. In this regard, Finney, Moos, and Chan (1981) found that the lack of effective social control on the part of the spouse contributed to heightened relapse rates in individuals who drank moderately following release from their treatment program. There is also the unfortunate evidence of clinical practice that points to the "enabling" qualities of many spouses of alcoholics and even the "enabling" family. Although it is widely considered that alcoholism is a progressive condition, it is the sine qua non of the condition that it follows from heavy-drinking practices. Many people, especially women, become emotionally involved with a person exhibiting what Keller (1976) refers to as *alcoholismic drinking*. Thereafter, a belief system is evolved that reflects either (1) that the drinker can be changed and will change; and/or (2) that what may become pathological drinking can be tolerated if the alternative would provide an unacceptable level of perceived threat to the spouse, the relationship, the family, or all of these. In such enabling situations, the spouse and/or the family more generally may be seen to provide the social/interpersonal context within which both the behavior and the cognitions of the drinker appear to support an ultimately self-destructive series of life events.

Perhaps the most striking clinical implication of the enabling phenomenon is the extent to which it becomes central to so much of the life of the "alcoholic" marriage or family. When the identified patient undergoes alcoholism therapy it may be the exception, not the rule, when the rather covert but rigid enabling patterns are broken down. To the extent that such patterns are sustained, the prognosis in treatment must be guarded. Also related to the enabling pattern is evidence that when a female has a spouse who is a problem drinker, it is far more likely that she, too, will be a heavy drinker, thereby camouflaging what may otherwise be an impassable gulf between them. As Gomberg (1981) has shown, this does not seem to be as consistently the case with males whose wives are heavy drinkers.

Family Relationships

Obviously, family relationship variables are an extension of marital relationship variables and so the issues dealt with under that heading apply, generally, here as well. Alcohol abuse runs in families and sets the stage for a vast array of other specific emotional difficulties throughout the family. Further, in many instances there is evidence that the family context provides a framework for the emergence of psychopathology that co-exists with alcoholism in the individual case. The family-related etiological considerations notwithstanding, the real questions from a treatment point of view are (1) what family dynamics support early intervention in the development of alcoholism and (2) what family dynamics predict treatment outcome?

In their review of recent literature, Moos and Finney (1983) concluded that the more cohesive and supportive the alcohol-abusing individual's family, the better the prognosis. Such cohesiveness would appear equally relevant to the concept of early intervention and sometimes will act against the enabling process. There is also evidence (Finney, Moos & Mewborn, 1980) that families that display an active recreational orientation tend to serve the alcoholic member by reducing depressive symptomatology and by otherwise facilitating improvement. Conversely, family conflict appears related to increases in alcohol consumption and the appearance of depression.

Cummings (1977) has shown that family and community support were related to patients returning for follow-up and aftercare services (see also Hunt & Azrin, 1973). Not surprisingly, family involvement during treatment and in aftercare services (when combined with teaching the patient and his or her family problem-solving skills) has been shown consistently to foster recovery and aid in relapse prevention (Ahles, Schlundt, Prue, & Rychtarik, 1983; Caddy, Addington, & Trenschel, in press). The problem for the clinician, of course, is that our research addressing the relationship between family variables and treatment outcome, as with an analysis of the vast number of treatment-related variables, does not permit us to determine confidently and on an a priori basis the specific family-related variables that predict treatment responsiveness in the individual case.

Peer Influence

The drinking of alcohol is learned and conducted in a social context. For some novitiate drinkers, this context both condones and supports a drinking pattern that is deviant from the outset (see Jessor & Jessor, 1973; Jessor, Collins, & Jessor, 1972). The extent to which social influences impact drinking is difficult to evaluate, however, for it is the individual drinker's unique perception of his or her peer context that, in many cases, provides the effective social stimulus components for the act of drinking. Williams and Brown (1974) investigated the effects of peer interaction on the drinking behavior of alcoholics and nonalcoholics in a structured social drinking experiment and noted that peer influence did not modify the alcohol consumption of alcoholics (perhaps because of a ceiling effect) but that it led "normal" drinkers to increase their consumption. Brown (1974) reported similar results and suggested that drinking does not seem to be correlated with social interaction in the same way for alcoholics and nonalcoholics.

Such findings, of course, do not imply any lack of social support for the act of drinking alcoholismically. Mello (1972), for example, noted that intoxication often permits the taking on of intergroup roles, sexual and otherwise, that are not normally available to a person during sober periods. Further, Marlatt (1978) reports that over 50% of his alcoholic patients who relapsed cited the social pressure exerted by friends and former drinking associates as major factors in their relapse (29% due to criticism and negative evaluation and 23% due to direct or indirect social pressure). Even in the case of the solitary drinker, a lack of social inter-action does not mean that social reinforcement is not maintaining that person's behavior.

Bacon (1973) offered a sociodynamic account of the development of alcoholism that implicates peers and the social context as crucial. Ac-cording to this view, the essential process in the development of alco-holism in males is *dissocialization*. This process involves, first, a reduction in the number and variety of the drinker's social activities and then a movement into social groups more tolerant of his drinking. According to this formulation, alcohol is used repeatedly to ease difficulties so that drinking becomes progressively more individually, rather than socially, motivated. Even on skid row there is the peer influence of the bottle gangs in the life of the urban nomad (Spradley, 1970).

There has been relatively little research specifically addressing the role of peer relationships vis-à-vis treatment outcome. In essence, the findings of the work that has been done in this area simply pro-vide support for the adage that "birds of a feather [tend to] flock to-gether."

It would seem to go without saying, therefore, that disengagement from peers who are heavy drinkers inevitably must facilitate the prospect of recovery from alcoholismic drinking (Bailey & Stewart, 1967; Kendall, 1965). And certainly within the fellowship of Alcoholics Anonymous (A.A.), it is the influence of a sober model, namely the sponsor, and the en-couragement to abstain via peer group pressure that aids the individual in remaining sober.

The increasing appreciation of the relevance of the alcoholics' peer relations and other aspects of his or her social system has led to the development of treatment procedures directed specifically to this system. Thus, for example, the development of social skills training directed to individuals particularly vulnerable to social pressure to drink has shown substantial success in specifically selected subjects (see the review by Miller, 1978). Moreover, specific services directed toward aiding the pa-tient to cope with his or her interpersonal (especially peer) environment have been developed as an important component in the relapse preven-tion approaches of Marlatt (Marlatt, 1978; Marlatt & Gordon, 1980). Within the context of these social-skills-based treatment approaches, as with other approaches, it is crucial that a comprehensive evaluation of the specific therapeutic needs of the individual case be conducted in order to adopt a prescriptive approach to the delivery of these services.

Cultural Variables

Cultural variables provide the setting within which the social processes occur. Ours is a multiracial and multiethnic society that traditionally has permitted a wide range of drinking practices. So great, in fact, has been the range of normative drinking across various subcultural groupings that normative drinking is perhaps best defined in terms of that drinking that is not alcoholism.

Pittman (1967) has identified four cultural types on the basis of their attitudes toward drinking—permissive, overpermissive, ambivalent, and abstinent. The United States, according to this classification, is an ambivalent culture. Room's (1975) criticism of explanation of alcohol problems in terms of ambivalence in drinking norms notwithstanding, the fact remains that cultures do differ widely in their patterns of drinking and alcoholism and in their propensity to provoke alcoholism.

Statistically, clear relationships have been established linking cultural/ethnic background and the epidemiology of alcohol problems. The Irish, for example, have become widely stereotyped as producing a disproportionate number of male drunkards. The Jews, on the other hand, traditionally have been identified as very temperate users of alcohol. The problem, of course, is that such statistical relationships are based on group data and consequently have little bearing on the individual case (Hersen & Barlow, 1976; Sidman, 1960).

There have been a small number of studies that have related cultural/ethnic background and success in alcoholism thereapy. Kissin *et al.* (1968) demonstrated, for example, that ethnic background did not appear prognostic except as this variable related more broadly to the patients' social stability. Irrespective of the quality of the cultural/ethnic context, all problem drinkers developed their drinking prowess within the context of their particular culture and its ethnic and social subgroupings. The fact of the matter is that even when treatment involves a temporary removal of the drinker from his cultural/social setting, inevitably it is to that same setting to which he or she ultimately returns. It is not surprising, therefore, that high rates of relapse are reported with such unfortunate frequency in the alcoholism treatment literature. Thus, even if one accepts the premise that the cultural context either increases or decreases the likelihood of the emergence of problem drinking in the individual case, it is extremely unlikely that this context can be changed "therapeutically." True, the social subgroup that supports a drinker can be modified but not the larger cultural context—at least not in the short term. For these reasons, it would seem that changes in the cultural setting may be relevant only to changes in the epidemiology of alcoholism if contemplated over a protracted historical period. The cultural context is relevant in the modification of the individual drinker only if culturally correlated attitudes can be modified.

Summary

Under the heading of social and cultural variables, the primary focus in understanding alcoholism and its therapeutic responsiveness has been the social/interpersonal dimension, the cultural variables being viewed as an influential, but less powerful, backdrop. Marital relationships, family relationships, and peer influences were all noted to be of substantial relevance to the emergence and maintenance of alcoholism. The interactions between these variables were seen to have relevance to the prognosis of the individual case, but it was also acknowledged that prognostication regarding the individual on the basis of these variables is at best tenuous. Specific social skills training procedures were seen to be important elements in addressing modifications of the social dynamics supporting alcoholism in selected cases.

PSYCHOLOGICAL/PERSONALITY FACTORS

Intraindividual attributes that may be characterized as primarily psychological are sometimes assumed to be the most powerful factors affecting the establishment, maintenance, and recovery of a person engaged in the alcoholic process. The psychological forces accounting for alcoholism may be classified either as *unidimensional* or *multidimensional* variables. Within the unidimensional context, etiologically oriented research has been based largely upon the premise that a single variable may contribute a substantial amount of the variance within the domain of psychological factors that may account for alcoholism. In fact, the very use of the term *alcoholism* implies that the condition exists as a unitary phenomenon.

The multidimensional approach, on the other hand, conceptualizes the construct *alcoholism* as being broad in scope and involving a subtle, yet powerful, interplay of multiple psychological and situational forces, the resultant of which becomes labeled *alcoholism*, not on the basis of the behavior *per se* but of its consequences.

Within this section, we will present some of the research literature bearing on the unidimensional and multidimensional approaches to alcohol abuse and dependence, and we will address individual differences in psychological functioning as these differences relate to treatment outcome.

The unidimensional variables include locus of control, field dependence/independence, the capacity to develop alternative coping skills, and the drinkers' response to environmental stressors. Under this heading, we will address only the alternative coping skills and response to environmental stressors as locus of control and field dependence/independence are extensively discussed elsewhere in this volume.

Alternative Coping Skills

Several studies (Baekeland, 1977; Baekeland & Lundwall, 1975; Brissett, Laundergan, Kammeier, & Biele, 1980) have indicated that individuals who modified their life-styles such that problems associated with alcohol abuse were avoided may have positive outcomes despite a resumption of drinking. More specifically, Brissett et al. (1980) have viewed the process of recovery as a lifelong attempt to cope with alcohol-related difficulties rather than as simply a strict adherence to abstinence. Thus, the acquisition of alternative skills designed to facilitate avoidance of alcohol may be considered particularly important in the reduction of the rates of relapse and in facilitating recovery from alcohol abuse and dependence.

Alternative skills training is usually focused on a specific area of deficit such as lack of assertiveness, marital skills deficits, or inability to self-manage. But as Miller (1978) points out, most drinking by alcoholics is triggered by a variety of circumstances. Therefore, training in a number of skills that may be considered alternative to the use of alcohol may be required. The effectiveness of treatment programs that emphasize alternative skills training in order to reduce relapse rates is quite impressive (Azrin, 1976; Hunt & Azrin, 1973; Miller & Eisler, 1977; Miller, Taylor, & West, 1980; Sobell & Sobell, 1973).

Clearly, the development of alternative coping skills would appear crucial to the best interests of many alcoholic patients. Again, however, improving the coping strategies and interpersonal skills of alcohol-abusing individuals would not seem to be the sine qua non of success and recovery. To the extent, though, that such procedures may be determined to be relevant on an individual case basis, they are useful and justified.

Coping with Stress

In many respects, coping with stress is linked to the previously described development of alternative skills. It has been widely acknowledged in the alcoholism treatment literature that individual perceptions of increased environmental stress are commonly associated with increases in alcohol consumption (Higgins & Marlatt, 1973, 1975; Miller, Hersen, Eisler, & Hilsman, 1974). Moos, Finney, and Chan (1981) demonstrated that negative life events such as death of a family member or friend and economic or legal problems are more prevalent among relapsed alcoholics than among recovered patients or demographically matched nonalcoholic controls. These investigators reported their subjects to be particularly vulnerable during the first 6 months following treatment in that the number of negative events occurring during these first 6 months were found to be highly predictive of treatment outcome at a 2-year follow-up.

Although in the aforementioned research the severity of the stressor appears implicated, less severe stressors have also led to a resumption of drinking. Marlatt and Gordon (1980) categorized the emotional states that immediately preceded relapse. They arrived at a grouping of the following intrapersonal factors attributable to stressful experiences: (1) coping with negative emotional states (frustration, anger, depression); (2) coping with negative physiological/physical states; (3) enhancement of positive emotional states; (4) testing personal control; and (5) giving in to temptation.

Again, the extent to which an individual copes with stress and the manner of this coping is highly predictive of outcome and probablility of relapse in the management of alcohol abuse and dependence. Similarly, some alcoholic patients are either exposed to disproportionately, or experience disproportionately, any number of stressors. Although their capacity to cope with some of these stressors may be considerable, no doubt their capacity to deal with others is somewhat more limited. As previously noted, the unique attributes of the individual case must be taken into account in determining the appropriate elements to be introduced to a therapeutic regimen to facilitate the management of environmental and other stressors that otherwise may set the stage for drinking.

MULTIDIMENSIONAL VARIABLES

In some respects, the legitimacy of the distinction between unidimensional and multidimensional variables should be noted en passant, for even those variables regarded as unidimensional are in fact complex and are articulated through a range of behavioral components. Given the foregoing caveat, nevertheless, variables of greater complexity can be conceptualized as accounting for or supporting human functioning, and it is these variables that we may conceptualize as *multidimensional*. Within this heading we will note some of the general personality features by which alcohol-abusing individuals have been characterized and that appear to play a significant role in treatment responsiveness. We will also address the influence of the degree of psychological adjustment and psychopathology in alcoholic individuals as these factors relate to the recovery process.

PERSONALITY CHARACTERISTICS

Certainly, personality variables have received much attention in the context of the etiology of alcoholism (see for example, Armstrong, 1958; Blane, 1968; Cahalan & Room, 1974; Irwin, 1968, Kilpatrick, Sutker, & Smith, 1976; Lisansky, 1960; Williams, 1976). Their status regarding prognosis during and subsequent to treatment, however, has been substantially less addressed, and certainly it has not been consistently investigated. Moreover, and this may in part account for the foregoing limitations, the evidence that is available relating personality variables with the prediction of treatment outcome is at best inconsistent.

A number of investigators (Blane, 1968; Blane & Myers, 1963; McCord & McCord, 1960; Tarnower & Toole, 1968) have reported a positive relationship between treatment outcome and dependency, for example. According to McCord, McCord, and Gudeman (1960), drinking satisfies dependency needs by facilitating a sense of dependence. Nevertheless, investigators such as Muzekari (1965) and Pokorny et al. (1968) have noted improvement due to the treatment of alcoholics who were passive and/or socially isolated, a finding that would seem contradictory to the proposition that dependency, as a personality attribute, predicts a favorable treatment outcome in alcoholic patients. Such confusion and inconsistency characterizes much of the treatment outcome literature that addresses the prognostic relevance of other multidimensionally measured personality-related attributes of alcoholics (intellectual functioning, affiliative needs, and the like).

Other factors commonly considered within the personality domain and apparently of significance as far as treatment outcome is concerned are the cognitions of the alcoholic individual vis-à-vis his or her conceptualization of the emergence, current status, and future course of the "condition."

Caddy (1978), although arguing against the existence of an "alcoholic" personality or specific "alcoholic" cognitive style, nevertheless has asserted that certain self-perceptions are central to all multivariate behavior disorders. In the case of alcoholism, these variables include the way a drinker sees himself or herself, the way that person sees drinkers and the drinking, and the conceptualizations that he or she and his or her significant others hold regarding alcohol dependence.

Clancy (1960) has articulated that there is considerable procrastination before an alcohol abuser accepts his or her alcoholism, and Caddy (1978) has indicated that there are powerful conceptual changes that occur when a person surrenders to the acceptance of the label. The central factor from a cognitive viewpoint, however, involves the aligning of the drinker's self-concept with his or her conceptualizaton about alcoholism. Surely, the extent to which so much debate and confusion exists regarding the concept of alcoholism (Pattison, Sobell, & Sobell, 1977) gives one pause to recognize the importance that has been placed on the conceptual framework of the disorder. The reason for this emphasis, of course, is that our society holds various and sometimes contradictory views regarding the nature of alcoholism (Linsky, 1972; Marconi, 1967). Siegler, Osmond, and Newell (1968) have described eight separate models for alcoholism, and Caddy, Goldman, and Huebner (1976a, 1976b) have clustered these various models into the *disease* model, the *symptomatic* model, and the *behavioral* model.

Each of the aforementioned views of alcoholism carries with it different treatment implications. Linsky (1972) used survey methodology to explore relationships between beliefs about the etiology of alcoholism and preferred methods of control. He noted that the different models of alcoholism held by different individuals brought with them different treatment implictions (see also Aubert & Messinger, 1958; Glock, 1964). Stoll (1968) has summarized these general findings as follows:

> (1) to the extent that individuals believe non-conformity to be conscious defiance of rules ... they will prefer to restrict and castigate deviants, and
>
> (2) to the extent that individuals believe non-conformity to be the result of external forces ... they will prefer to treat or cure deviations without accompanying opprobrium. (p. 121)

Given the aforementioned, it makes eminently good sense that considerable controversy would exist regarding the nature of alcoholism and that individuals living out this disorder in their own lives may hold perspectives that may be both somewhat confusing and vehemently held. The significance of all this is that just as there may be no alcoholic personality, so too, there may be no such unitary condition as alcoholism (Caddy, 1978; Horn & Wanberg, 1969, 1970; Sobell & Sobell, 1975). Yet, such a possibility does not appear to bear on the nature of treatment services provided for the management of alcoholism. All too often, it can be argued, unitary treatments have rendered services based on the unitary traditional perspective of alcoholism to individuals presumed to suffer from a similar condition that they were expected to view similarly. All this has occurred despite the evidence of a range of conceptualizations of the condition that emanate from the community at large. In fact, for many treatment programs the evidence of success in the earliest parts of treatment involves little more than the breaking down of *denial* (a rather unfortunately chosen term indicating simply that the patient and the treatment system did not conceptualize the patient's condition in an essentially identical fashion). To the extent, therefore, that alcoholics as a class have been seen within treatment circles to be more similar than unique as individuals, and equally, to the extent that alcoholism has been seen as univariate rather than a multivariate disorder, it is not surprising that individual differences in the patients' conceptualizations regarding alcoholism and their condition have not been taken into account, and they certainly have not been studied. It is no less surprising that the procrastination referred to earlier does occur and that the resistance to the traditional perspective that Caddy, Addington, and Trenschel (in press) have noted also does occur, and in substantial proportion. It must seem obvious, therefore, that we view the lack of any substantive effort to take into account the complex interactions that exist between a patient's concept of himself or herself and his or her views regarding alcohol abuse and dependence to be a major topic of concern.

A final multidimensional factor is *motivation* to engage in and succeed in the treatment process. This construct has been variously presented in the literature as a somewhat static personality variable or as an internal cognitive state, constantly responding to external incentives. Just as there are numerous reinforcement contingencies for alcohol use and dependence, so, too, are there numerous reinforcers for recovery. The problem, of course, is that the incentives that influence the behavior of a drinker are mediated by that individual's idiosyncratic cognitions regarding the use of alcohol and its avoidance or regulation.

The view that alcohol serves as a negative reinforcer by enhancing one's psychological state via tension reduction, as noted previously, has been widely cited as an explanation for alcoholismic drinking (see Freed, 1967, 1968; Hughes, Forney, & Gates, 1963; Masserman, Jacques, & Nicholson, 1945; Smart, 1965; Vogel-Sprott, 1967). But such explanations often have little to do with the problems of the individual case. In fact, although some of the most credible research does suggest a modest decrease in anxiety at the beginning of a drinking sequence, subsequent drinking commonly leads to an increase in both anxiety and depression (see for example, McNamee, Mello, & Mendelson, 1968; Mendelson & Mello, 1966; Mendelson, La Dou, & Solomon, 1964; Nathan & O'Brien, 1971; Vanderpool, 1969).

Studies such as these, especially given the tendency of alcoholic subjects to have little recollection of their alcohol-induced unpleasant mood states, suggest that even in those individuals who have experienced extremely negative consequences of their alcoholismic drinking, the expectations of positive effects following the use of alcohol provide a significant part of the initial incentive to drink again. Unfortunately, many alcoholic individuals seeking to maintain or recapture the initial positive effects of alcohol drink themselves into states of consciousness, which, in some instances, prove to be anything but that which they were striving to achieve. Although it may be possible to explain the initiation and continuation of drinking in terms of the operation of either the positive or negative reinforcement paradigms, it is probably more likely, as Keehn (1970) has suggested, that the act of drinking depends on multiple schedules of control by both positive and negative reinforcements. Certainly, however, the combined effects of the immediacy and the potency of the reinforcements that follow the act of drinking are more than adequate on most occasions to enable most alcoholismic drinkers to overcome the disincentives that may derive from the awareness of the possibility of the negative consequences that follow such drinking.

An analysis of the various motivational elements noted before is crucial to an understanding of the dynamics of drinking in the individual case. Such an analysis is equally crucial in understanding the probable causes of relapse, at least in part, and is surely relevant as far as any multivariate treatment planning is concerned. It is to the treatment implications of the concept of *motivation* that we will now turn.

The motivation of the alcoholismic drinker is frequently presented, and we believe appropriately so as being of major significance as a prognostic factor in treatment outcome. In studies surveying the attitudes both of professionals and laypersons alike, alcoholic individuals tend to be viewed as "choosing" to drink, thereby entrapping themselves in their own alcoholism (Linsky, 1970; Pattison, Bishop, & Linsky, 1968; Sterne & Pittman, 1965). Paradoxically, as noted previously, this intention is attributed to alcoholics even though the traditional perspective of alcoholism proposes an inability on the part of the drinker to control his or her drinking. Nonetheless, it may well be as Armor, Polich, and Stambul (1978) have asserted, the attribution that alcoholism is a self-chosen disease may lead to the assumption that unless the drinker deliberately chooses treatment and evidences a high level of motivation to change, he or she will not profit from therapy. In this regard, of course, it is noteworthy to recall that earlier in this chapter we suggested that participation in alcoholism therapy was in no small respect a product of the unique interaction of the drinker's perception of himself or herself, the problem, and the orientation/perspective being offered by the treatment program.

Certainly, there are a number of studies that have reported high levels of motivation to be related to favorable treatment outcome (Baekeland, Lundwall, & Shanahan, 1973; Gerard & Saenger, 1966). Aharen, Oqiluie, and Partington (1967), on the other hand, found that no measure of motivation that they employed predicted treatment outcome. Of course, the very circularity and the ambiguity in usage of the term *motivation* have not gone unnoticed in the alcoholism treatment literature (see for example, Sterne & Pittman, 1965), and surely the importance of the difference between the construct of *extrinsic* versus *intrinsic* motivation also has been considered (Baekeland, Lundwall, & Kissin, 1975).

Finally, the motivation of an alcoholic person often has been considered from the point of view of the therapist and as such has been evaluated in terms that are based on positive and accepting attitudes both to the therapist and to the treatment. Here, too, the problem for the researcher is first to develop an acceptable operational definition of motivation and thereafter to establish the extent to which perhaps various forms of the multidimensional construct termed *motivation* actually predict specific treatment outcome. There can be little question but that our limited technology is incapable of providing either an adequate definition or a suitable measure of the construct we call motivation.

Psychopathology

Although alcohol abuse and alcoholism present major problems of social concern, to view alcoholism as the sole or even primary disturbance of people so labeled really does not present the complexity crucial to an understanding of the intrapsychic forces operating within the individual drinker. Within the context of formal diagnostic classification, such as that presented in the third edition of the *Diagnostic and Statistical Manual of Mental Disorders* (DSM-III) (1980), alcohol abuse and dependence are simply two categories within the overall substance use disorders category. This category, of course, is only one of a number of those that are found within the Axis I schema. Moreover, within the DSM-III multiaxial approach, it is possible to establish a diagnosed personality disorder on a second axis coincident with one or more Axis I diagnoses. Such an approach to comprehensive diagnostic assessment fits particularly well with the multivariate idiographic perspective developed by Caddy (1978) and reflects both the richness and complexity of individuals who experience the alcoholic condition. It is indeed unfortunate that very few treatment programs rendering services to such people view their patients as possessing such complexity. For to fail to appreciate the complexity of the unique interplay of personality and other attributes, both pathological and otherwise, is to fail to understand the unique therapeutic needs of the individual case.

Without engaging in the circularity of the which-came-first argument, it is inconceivable from our perspective that alcoholism as a pure entity can exist without other attendant psychopathology. By this, we do not mean that additional diagnoses *must* necessarily be applied to the alcohol-abusing individual, but if a comprehensive functional analysis of the patient's drinking behavior is undertaken, it will virtually always be determined that the drinking is simply one element, and one that is quite understandable, in a complex of other dysfunctional processes. In fact, even in those instances in which a former drinker establishes his or her abstinence, continued pathological cognitions, behaviors, and interactions all too often prove to be the rule rather than the exception. Within lay circles, such an observation distinguishes the "dry" alcoholic from the "sober" alcoholic. The psychological forces that act on a person and provoke alcoholismic drinking and the dynamics that follow the consequences of a sustained pattern of such drinking cannot be considered innocuous with respect to their impact on the cognitions and style of functioning of the individual. Thus, the compromises, adjustments, and violations that inevitably parallel such drinking will undoubtedly result in the emergence of pathology that extends beyond the actual act of drinking.

Here again, we have the problem of measurement and of recognizing that just as drinking is variable across individuals, so too the pathology that accompanies it is variable across those diagnosed *alcoholic*. Logically, there is no reason to presume that a common pathology should underlie or be coincident with alcoholismic drinking. Yet, many studies exploring psychopathology and alcoholism appear to be based on just such an assumption. The aforestated, though, does not preclude the possibility that certain forms of diagnosable psychopathology may not appear more frequently than others in subjects diagnosed as alcoholic.

Historically, one of the earliest attempts to classify alcoholics within the context of an overall psychopathological state was offered by Knight (1937) when he proposed that two types of alcoholics could be distinguished. The *essential* alcoholic was characterized as emotionally dependent, pleasure seeking, irresponsible, unreliable, insincere, and incapable of establishing long-term goals or intimate relations with others.

Knight described the *reactive* alcoholic quite differently, almost the reverse in fact. In addition to these personality traits, Knight described the reactive alcoholics as being better educated, having a later onset of problem drinking, and generally showing a more favorable prognosis. In subsequent research, Dale and Ebaugh (1951) interpreted essential alcoholism to be an expression of neuroses characterized by excessive dependency, sensitivity, and insecurity, whereas reactive alcoholics were described as showing depressive features (see also Rudie & McGaughran, 1961). Subsequent research, however, has shown the "essential" irrelevance of this categorization of the psychopathology/alcoholism linkage (Blum & Levine, 1975; Levine & Zigler, 1973; Sugerman, Reilly, & Albahary, 1965).

A second early approach to examining the nature of the relationship between alcoholism and other forms of psychopathology emerged from the observations of Pitts & Winokur (1943), who noted a particularly close relationship between alcoholism and affective disorders (see also Skinner & Allen, 1982). Of particular significance was the finding that as many as 50% of the female alcoholics studied by these authors exhibited symptoms of other psycholopathology.

Schuckit, Pitts, Reich, King, and Winokur (1969) interviewed 70 consecutive female admissions to an alcoholism unit and classified each according to a variety of psychiatric diagnoses. Of the total, 39 were classified as primary alcoholics, 19 as having an affective disorder, 6 as sociopathic, and the remainder with a variety of conditions. Despite the conviction by Schuckit *et al.* that there was merit to attempts to differentiate primary from affective alcoholics, the support for a primary/affective typology is in no way strong (see, for example, studies by Winokur, Rimmer, & Reich, 1971; Winokur, Reich, Rimmer, & Pitts, 1970).

A third approach to relating alcoholism and psychopathology has involved attempts to group psychiatric syndromes and/or profiles with alcoholic patients. By far, the bulk of the research exploring the psychopathology attendant to alcoholism has involved use of the Minnesota Multiphasic Personality Inventory (MMPI). In terms of single-scale performance, Hoffman (1976) reports that the psychopathic deviate scale (Pd) of the MMPI is most often the peak score in alcoholic samples. The most frequent combination of MMPI scales is 4-2 and 2-4 where the Pd score is elevated concurrently with depression (D). There also have been factor-analytic studies of MMPI performance by alcoholics. Goldstein & Linden (1969), for example, derived four subtypes: (1) psychopathic and emotional instability; (2) psychoneurotic; (3) mixed psychopathic; and (4) alcoholism with paranoid and drug addiction. Using a basically similar procedure, Hill, Haertzen, and Davis (1962) had obtained three MMPI factors from their alcoholic sample: (1) undifferentiated psychopath; (2) primary psychopath; and (3) neurotic psychopath (see also Partington & Johnson, 1969). From such studies, it appears that psychopathic features very often enter into the description of the alcoholic patient.

There also have been more complicated conclusions from MMPI studies with alcoholics and other individuals. Overall (1973) undertook a discriminant function analysis of the MMPI profiles of alcoholics and illicit drug users and reported that if MMPI Scales 4 (Pd) and 9 (Ma) were elevated relative to Scales 3 (Hy) and 7 (Pt), then the MMPI profile suggested illicit drug use. An elevation of Scales 3 and 7 in addition to 4 and 9 scale elevation suggested alcoholism. We also have Rosen's (1960) interesting finding that the MMPI profiles of general psychiatric outpatients did not differ from those of outpatient alcoholics but that the group-average MMPI profiles obtained from different alcoholism treatment populations did differ significantly. Finally, there are the findings that show MMPI profile scores to vary with demographic characteristics such as age (Hoffman & Nelson, 1971; McGinnis & Ryan, 1965) and race (Hugo, 1970) and with respect to other matters such as the recency of alcohol intoxication or withdrawal (Libb & Taulbee, 1971; see also the review by Clopton, 1978). In summary, the findings from various MMPI studies with alcoholics show an underlying diversity of psychopathology among alcoholic patients.

Despite all of the work that has explored the relationship between alcoholism and concurrent psychopathology, there have been few studies that have addressed the prognostic utility of the various psychopathology typologies that have been observed. The personality profile most consistently associated with negative alcoholism treatment effects has not surprisingly been the sociopathic profile (Muzekari, 1965; Pokorny et al., 1968). More recently, Svanum and Dallas (1981) have explored the relationship between MMPI types and treatment outcome and have reported that the typology they found did provide some prognostic utility. Specifically, their Type I patients (normal limit acting out) had the highest likelihood of sobriety at the end of 12 months of follow-up. Regarding this finding, however, two facts should be taken into consideration. First, type of membership accounted for only a very small percentage of the variance observed. Second, the relatively positive prognosis reported for their Type I subjects probably reflected the lower degree of overall pathology evident in subjects that comprised this type rather than the particular configuration of the scales. Certainly, too, the background characteristics of Type I patients in this study also reflected a relatively positive prognostic picture. It seems, overall again, that the evidence for a direct link between alcoholism-attendant psychopathology and treatment responsiveness is incontrovertible. However, we are still ill equipped to determine whether certain pathological personality profiles or diagnostic categories either facilitate or disrupt the probability of a successful therapeutic outcome.

Summary

The research with respect to most of the variables we have termed *unidimensional* is equivocal at best. The value of investigating such variables may be in matching a given treatment approach to the individual rather than in classification or prognosis. The acquisition of alternative skills to drinking, on the other hand, may be an appropriate treatment approach, provided the alcoholic's drinking behavior can functionally be related to a deficit in his or her behavioral repertoire. Quite likely, training in a number of such skills may be required in order to reduce the risk of relapse. Coping with stress, again, must be highly individualized due to individual differences in the capacity to tolerate stressors of varying severity.

Despite the fact that the aforementioned variables are commonly presented as unitary attributes, they are not isolated parts of an individual's internal or external environments. Rather, they co-exist and interact with other aspects of the individual, and, as such, they may differentially influence his or her potential for successful (or unsuccessful) treatment outcome.

Research examining the hypothesized "alcoholic personality" has not unequivocally substantiated the existence of a constellation of personality traits that differentiates alcoholics from other clinical groups or "normals." Barnes (1979), in an excellent review, addresses various personality factors that may be relevant in the etiology of alcoholism. However, how, or if, any such factors are related to treatment outcome can, at present, only be regarded as speculation. There is also little evidence to show that any such traits are definitively implicated in successful recovery from alcoholismic drinking. Although *motivation* is frequently employed to account for treatment success, there is no adequate operational definition, nor is there a suitable measure of this construct. Until our technology advances in the aforementioned respects, the utility of this variable in research must be seen to be severely limited.

A number of studies cited explored the relationship between alcoholism and concurrent psychopathology, but few addressed the utility in prognosis of such concurrent psychopathology. Thus far, only a sociopathic profile has been consistently linked to a negative treatment outcome, and only a weak relationship between Svanum and Dallas's (1981) Type I patients and sobriety at 12 months follow-up has been demonstrated. Overall, no specific personality factors nor a constellation of personality traits has been isolated that would, reliably, predict treatment outcome in the individual case.

TREATMENT STRATEGIES AND INDIVIDUAL DIFFERENCES

To the extent that there are diverse personality and other patterns among alcoholic patients, two related questions are suggested. First, are alcoholics with certain personality and other characteristics likely to benefit from certain specific treatment programs? Second, can specific attributes of an individual alcoholic patient be used to predict which type of treatment will be beneficial? Pattison (1974a, 1974b) suggested that there may be several alcoholic populations that may be treated by several different methods leading to different patterns of outcome. He asserted:

> It may be possible to match a certain type of patient with a certain type of facility and treatment method to yield the most effective outcome....Treatment programs can maximize effectiveness by clearly specifying what population they propose to serve, what goals are feasible with that population, and what methods can be expected to best achieve those goals. (Pattison, 1974b, p. 59)

Throughout this chapter we have stated that alcoholics are not the same, though to date, outcome studies have rarely attempted to isolate subpopulations that may differentially respond to specific treatments. Thus, present treatment programs appear relatively similar, for there is a common belief within both the professional and paraprofessional treatment community that the progression of the "disease" of alcoholism transforms individuals into a somewhat homogeneous population of alcoholics. Paradoxically, the unitary progression concept has persisted even though some 40 years ago Bowman and Jellinek (1941) had theorized that no one therapeutic modality could be successful for all those who exhibit a drinking problem. In fact, Bowman and Jellinek had proposed the need for studies in which large heterogeneous, randomly assigned samples would be exposed to a variety of therapeutic interventions in order to evaluate possible patient therapy interactions. Jellinek (1960) again addressed the homogeneity issue when he proposed his typology of alcoholics and indicated that individuals assigned to the different subtypes, and even individuals within a subtype, may enter the hypothesized progression at various points.

Pattison, Coe, and Rhodes (1969) suggested several possible models that could be adopted in designing and evaluating alcoholism treatment programs. They proposed a research orientation in which a heterogeneous population of alcoholics could be randomly assigned to various treatment programs and in which outcomes for each subpopulation by treatment combination could be evaluated. Similarly, Kissin, Platz, and Su (1970) proposed that the overall efficacy of alcoholism treatment was related to (1) the degree of match of the patients' characteristics with those of ideal patients who present as intellectually superior, socially stable, psychologically intact, and well motivated; and (2) general treatment modality acceptability. Kissin *et al.* also specified three treatment orientations that they characterized as the *medical model*, the *psychological model*, and the *social model* (see also Caddy *et al.*, 1976a, 1976b).

Kissin and his co-workers (Kissin *et al.*, 1968; Kissin *et al.*, 1970) have attempted one of the most direct examinations of the patient by treatment match to date. By employing a design that combined random assignment to treatment with a variable of permitting or not permitting patients to reassign themselves, these investigators found that treatment acceptors reported more successful outcomes than did treatment rejectors. The range of treatment alternatives made available was also positively related to better outcome. In general, the most socially and psychologically intact clients chose psychotherapy; drug therapy was selected by slightly less well-intact subjects; and alcoholism rehabilitation programming was chosen by most debilitated patients (Kissin *et al.*, 1970). By empirically comparing treatment successes and failures in three treatment groups, Kissin *et al.* (1968) reported the following interactive relationships: alcoholics who were most socially and psychologically competent benefitted most from psychotherapy; alcoholics who were socially effective but less competent psychologically benefitted most from drug therapy; and those who were evaluated to be socially incompetent but particularly psychologically effective benefitted from an inpatient rehabilitation model program.

Much of the context of this chapter has argued for the notion that the extent to which alcoholic patients may improve in various treatment settings may be contingent on the fit between the patient's needs, broadly defined, and the methods, facilities, and goals of the therapeutic program. Gerard and Saenger (1966) have provided data suggesting that outpatient treatment appears best suited to socially stable alcoholics. Intermediate care, as noted earlier, seems particularly suited to the socially deprived alcoholic who requires a social alternative to his or her particular subculture. And certain hospital settings that emphasize a biochemical etiology of alcoholism may provide the appropriate medical rationalization that permits relatively high-status alcoholics to maintain their status and yet, at the same time, receive treatment.

Numerous other psychological variables have been hypothesized as predictive of a differential treatment effect. Therapeutic emphasis on sympathy, support, and permissiveness has been considered particularly important for overly dependent alcoholics, whereas more directive, educationally oriented techniques may be most appropriate with a more independent alcoholic client (Blane, 1968; Blane & Meyers, 1963). Those patients who displayed affiliative needs and extroversion appeared to be particularly well suited to A.A. intervention (Trice, 1957) as were those who exhibited a high level of insecurity and tended to identify with the also recovering peer counselor (Lyons, Welte, Sokolow, Hynes, & Brown, 1981). Aversion therapy has been shown to be most effective with patients who were introverted, solitary drinkers, (Vogel, 1960, 1961) and those who had experienced prolonged heavy social drinking but had adequate resources to derive gratification from sobriety (Thimann, 1949; Voegtlin & Broz, 1949). Those patients who were highly anxious were not likely to benefit from therapy that included self-confrontation or traditional psychotherapy (Schaeffer, Sobell, & Mills, 1971; Wallgren & Barry, 1970). Disulfiram therapy appeared to be most beneficial for patients who were older (Baekeland, Lundwall, Kissin, & Shanahan, 1971; Sereny & Fryatt, 1966), socially stable (Rudfeld, 1958), and highly motivated (Baekeland et al., 1971; Rudfeld, 1958). As discussed earlier, females tended to respond best when treatment was of a medical orientation (Gomberg, 1976; Lyons et al., 1981).

Turning now to several more recent studies, Smart and Kissin both reported results that at first blush appeared directly contradictory. Smart (1978) studied 1,091 alcoholics who were treated in a variety of individual-versus-group programs and followed up 1 year later. He found that treatment characteristics explained only a small part of the variance in treatment outcome. When compared with the explanatory power of patient characteristics, Smart reported that the best outcomes were from patients who showed alcoholic symptomatology but were relatively socially stable. In essence, Smart concluded that treatment outcome is best predicted by what the patient brings to treatment rather than what happens to him or her in treatment. Kissin (1977) studied 458 patients and examined the effect of treatment orientation (rather than procedures) on specific client types. In fact, Kissin was examining a composite variable that reflected the medical, psychological, or social orientation. He concluded that treatment outcome was a function of general patient-related prognostic factors and specific treatment-based prognostic factors.

Finally, regarding the drinking-related goal in alcoholism therapy and the ongoing controversy of abstinence versus restricted drinking, Miller and Caddy (1977), unfortunately without the benefit of data-based support, have proposed criteria to be employed when contemplating the most appropriate drinking goal across the range of people requiring therapeutic attention. Miller and Caddy deduced (1) that controlled drinking is an attainable and maintainable goal for some but not all problem drinkers; and (2) that present diagnostic criteria for alcoholism do not adequately predict differential response to treatment and have failed to discriminate potential controlled drinkers from those for whom abstinence is necessary. The authors further suggested that both abstinence and control-oriented therapies be developed, evaluated, and improved and that new diagnostic criteria be sought to permit more appropriate differential assignment to treatment modalities.

Miller and Caddy's proposed criteria for a controlled drinking goal included (1) the patient's refusal to consider abstinence; (2) strong external demands to drink; (3) younger patient with apparent "early stage" problem drinking; or (4) prior failure to respond to reputable therapy oriented toward abstinence. The criteria for an abstinence goal were as follows: (1) evidence of progressive liver disease such that continued use of alcohol could be life threatening; (2) evidence of other health problems (i.e., cardiac anomalies or psychiatric disorders) that might be exacerbated by moderate alcohol use; (3) request for abstinence; (4) strong external demands for abstention; (5) pathological intoxication (uncontrolled or bizarre behavior following even moderate alcohol use); (6) evidence of recent physiological addiction; (7) use of medications considered dangerous when consumed with alcohol; (8) current successful abstinence followng a history of severe drinking problems; or (9) prior failure to respond to reputable therapy oriented toward moderation.

Also regarding the question of drinking goal, Orford (1973) undertook a comparison of alcoholics who believed that their drinking was "mainly controlled" with others who believed their drinking to be totally uncontrolled. He found that the "totally uncontrolled" drinkers considered themselves alcoholics and preferred abstinence as a treatment goal. The mainly controlled drinkers, on the other hand, did not consider themselves alcoholics even though they were in treatment for alcohol abuse. Further, the "mainly controlled" drinkers were found to be less willing to accept abstinence-oriented treatment even though they were ready to admit the disadvantages of their drinking behavior.

Given the complexity of the foregoing, it is not surprising that the present state of the art in the alcoholism treatment community appears to ignore the possible advantage to be gained by attempts to match either particular alcoholic patients to particular treatment programs or to truly individualize and tailor elements within a treatment system to meet the unique needs of the individual case. Of course, there is another major consideration that must be addressed in contemplating any attempt to match in some scientific manner the attributes of the client and the features and capacities of a treatment program. Even today, unfortunately, we are considerably limited in the technology that would permit such matching in order to produce an optimal outcome. When attempting to match a specific personality profile to a specific treatment procedure, in order to determine its relative appropriateness we must be able to validly measure both the specific personality profile and the elements of the treatment program that may be presumed to be most potent.

For example, in attempting to match a specific personality type to a suitable treatment, we must, within a small margin of error, be able to measure specific personality traits. Psychometrically, for individual decisions, reliability coefficients should exceed .90 (Nunnally, 1967), and as this is rarely the case in test instruments currently in use, treatment matching based upon personality type appears questionable scientifically, if not impossible from the outset. What is required in this regard is the development of more refined measurement instrumentation. Whether such instrumentation will be available in the foreseeable future must be a matter for speculation at this time.

Given such caveats as noted before, what then can be said about our present understanding of the methods by which the patient by treatment interaction may be maximized? Clearly, much more research addressing the patient by treatment interaction is warranted. It would seem reasonable, for example, for those systems engaged in the treatment of alcohol-related difficulties to expand the scope of a number of services that currently they offer, and at the same time, for these systems to encourage their patients to take a more influential role in selecting elements of the treatment that they would consider to be of special relevance to their needs. Certainly, expanding the conceptual framework within which alcoholism is viewed by the patient would appear highly desirable as would expanding the goals of treatment currently available within alcoholism treatment programming. Finally, given the idiosyncratic needs of the individual case, it would seem desirable to further expand and investigate the nature of aftercare services available to alcohol-abusing individuals.

CONCLUSIONS

The traditional unitary view of alcoholism has been successfully challenged in the recent literature by a conceptualization of the *condition* that is multivariate in nature with respect to definition, etiology, treatment approaches, and responsiveness. Given the growth in the recognition of the validity of the multivariate approach to alocholism, it would be folly to continue to assume that any single variable would predict treatment outcome or that treatment outcome could be established based on only one variable change. It is far more likely that biological, sociocultural, and personality variables interact with one another as well as with the treatment strategies employed to produce the complex we define as successful (or unsuccessful) responsiveness to treatment. Annis's (1973) question "What specific interventions produce specific changes in specific patients under what specific condition?" appears particularly appropriate in light of the aforestated. To this question, however, may well be added the following: "What multivariate indexes of treatment outcome should be employed to evaluate the impact of treatment in the individual case?"

To conduct a research experiment to answer all these questions would, however, be an extremely large undertaking and one unlikely to be conducted given the sociopolitical zeitgeist currently existing in the United States. (In fact, at least some research of this quality is being conducted elsewhere.)

Throughout much of this chapter and in reviews of the literature such as that offered by Ogborne (1978) we may glean some answers to the preceding questions. Summarizing Ogborne's review, for example, it may be concluded with respect to demographic and sociocultural factors that high socioeconomic status, a stable marriage or relationship, a steady and supportive employment milieu, higher education (12 years or more), a stable residential setting, and no criminal record (or few convictions) have all been related to a good prognosis irrespective of the type of treatment employed. Further, even minimal practice of religion, achievement of some kind, and less time spent in the military seem positively related to the recovery process as does a periodic drinking pattern, a shorter history of problem drinking, and less impairment due to drinking. Regarding psychological/personality variables, Ogborne found that treatment responsiveness was predicted from an alcoholic's capacity for insight, a desire to change, an optimistic outlook, and positive self-regard and/or the capacity for moderate self-criticism. Psychopathology, in general, was related to failure in treatment, but patients exhibiting mild personality disorders, psychoneuroses, and affective disorders tended to improve with treatment.

Given a commitment to the multivariate approach, inevitably, there must be a commitment to a thorough assessment and functional analysis of the individual and his or her behavioral repertoire. Based upon such an evaluation, an appropriate treatment suited to the individual's needs can then be planned and instituted. Very likely, the selected treatments would involve a broad spectrum approach where reeducation and rehabilitation impacts a number of the patient's life aspects (socioeconomic, employment, marital, peer relationships, and psychological/personality difficulties). Additionally, the treatment modalities employed with a particular individual (group or individual and insight-oriented or more concretely based orientations) equally would be chosen on the basis of the needs of the individual client.

Such an approach is idealistic, however, as it assumes that each and every person presenting for treatment would have the same array of options. As Armor *et al.* (1978) have pointed out, this tends not to be the case. Intermediate care settings, for example, (where treatment is less intensive) receive a disproportionate share of clients of low socioeconomic status and who have unstable social characteristics. Inpatient hospital settings, on the other hand (with more intensive treatments, albeit of briefer duration) receive few of such disadvantaged clients.

The greatest advantage of the multivariate perspective is that it complicates the picture of alcohol-related difficulties and in so doing paints a picture that is credible and relevant to the needs of the individual case. Even in conceptualizing what constitutes effective treatment responsiveness, the multivariate perspective encourages complexity rather than simplicity.

Examining a number of the treatment outcome studies in which a multivariate perspective of alcoholism was assumed, we see a multivariate array of treatment outcome measures being employed to tap a variety of possible changes in the individual following his or her treatment. Thus, for example, Sobell and Sobell (1973, 1976) employed treatment outcome variables that dealt specifically with drinking as well as other adjunctive measures that addressed aspects of the health, vocational, and relational aspects of their patients' lives and gathered these data from multiple sources (the patient, collateral sources, and various official records). The gathering of such a complex of treatment outcome measures is critical if we are to understand the unique responsiveness to treatment of an individual drinker and if we are to design research studies that have both individual clinical relevance and relevance to the economic and sociopolitical context within which alcoholism treatment exists. It is evident that substantial additional research in the area is warranted.

REFERENCES

Aharan, C. H., Oqiluie, R. D., & Partington, J. T. Clinical indicators of motivation in alcoholic patients. *Quarterly Journal of Studies on Alcohol*, 1967, *28*, 486–492.

Ahles, T. A., Schlundt, D. G., Prue, D. M., & Rychtarik, R. G. Impact of aftercare arrangements on the maintenance of treatment success in abusive drinkers. *Addictive Behaviors*, 1983, *8*, 53–58.

Annis, H. M. Treatment research: Past and future directions (Substudy No. 541). Toronto: Addictions Research Foundation, 1973.

Armor, D. J., Polich, J. M., & Stambul, H. B. *Alcoholism and treatment.* Santa Monica: The Rand Corporation, 1976.

Armor, D. J., Polich, J. M., & Stambul, H. B. *Alcoholism and treatment.* New York: Wiley, 1978.

Armstrong, J. D. The search for the alcoholic personality. *Annals of the American Academy of Political and Social Sciences,* 1958, *315,* 40–47.

Ashley, M. J., Olin, J. S., le Riche, W. H., Kornaczewski, A., Schmidt, W., & Rankin, J. G. Morbidity patterns in hazardous drinkers: Relevance of demographic, sociologic, drinking, and drug use characteristics. *The International Journal of the Addictions,* 1981, *16,* 593–625.

Aubert, U., & Messinger, F. The criminal and the sick. *Inquiry,* 1958, *1,* 137–160.

Azrin, N. H. Improvements in the community-reinforcement approach to alcoholism. *Behaviour Research and Therapy,* 1976, *14,* 339–348.

Bacon, S. D. The process of addiction to alcohol: Social aspects. *Quarterly Journal of Studies on Alcohol,* 1973, *34,* 1–27.

Baekeland, F. Evaluation of treatment methods in chronic alcoholics. In B. Kissin & H. Begleiter (Eds.), *The biology of alcoholism* (Vol. 5). *Treatment and rehabilitation of the chronic alcoholic.* New York: Plenum Press, 1977.

Baekeland, F., & Lundwall, L. Dropping out of treatment: A clinical review. *Psychological Bulletin,* 1975, *82,* 738–783.

Baekeland, F., Lundwall, L., Kissin, B., & Shanahan, T. Correlates of outcome in disulfiram treatment of alcoholism. *Journal of Nervous and Mental Disorders,* 1971, *153,* 1–9.

Baekeland, F., Lundwall, L., & Shanahan, T. Correlates of patient attrition in the outpatient treatment of alcoholism. *Journal of Nervous and Mental Disorders,* 1973, *157,* 99–107.

Baekeland, F., Lundwall, L., & Kissin, B. Methods for the treatment of chronic alcoholism: A critical appraisal. In Y. Israel (Ed.), *Research advances in alcohol and drug problems,* Vol. II. New York: Wiley, 1975.

Bailey, M. B., & Steward, J. Normal drinking by persons reporting previous problem drinking. *Quarterly Journal of Studies on Alcohol,* 1967, *28,* 305–315.

Barnes, G. E. The alcoholic personality. *Journal of Studies of Alcohol,* 1979, *40,* 571–634.

Bateman, N. I., & Petersen, D. M. Factors related to outcome of treatment for hospitalized white male and female alcoholics. *Journal of Drug Issues,* 1972, *2,* 66–74.

Becker, H. S. *Outsiders: Studies in the sociology of deviance.* London: Free Press of Glencoe, 1963.

Beckman, L. J. Reported effects of alcohol on the sexual feelings and behavior of women alcoholics and non-alcoholics. *Journal of Studies on Alcohol,* 1979, *40,* 272–282.

Blancy, R., Radford, I. S., & MacKenzie, G. A Belfast study of the prediction of outcome in the treatment of alcoholism. *British Journal of the Addictions,* 1975, *70,* 41–50.

Blane, H. T. *The personality of the alcoholic: Guises of dependency.* New York: Harper & Row, 1968.

Blane, H. T., & Meyers, W. R. Behavioral dependence and length of stay in psychotherapy among alcoholics. *Quarterly Journal of Studies on Alcohol,* 1963, *24,* 503–510.

Blane, H. T., & Meyers, W. R. Social class and establishment of treatment relations by alcoholics. *Journal of Clinical Psychology,* 1964, *20,* 287–290.

Blum, J., & Levine, J. Maturity, depression and life events in middle aged alcoholics. *Addictive Behaviors,* 1975, *1,* 37–45.

Bowman, K. M., & Jellinek, E. M. Alcohol addiction and its treatment. *Quarterly Journal of Studies on Alcohol,* 1941, *2,* 98–176.

Brissett, D., Laundergan, J. C., Kammeier, M. L., & Biele, M. Drinkers and non-drinkers at three and a half years after treatment: Attitudes and growth. *Journal of Studies on Alcohol*, 1980, *41*, 945–952.

Brod, T. M. Alcoholism as a mental health problem of native Americans. *Archives of General Psychiatry*, 1975, *32*, 1385–1391.

Brown, R. A. *A comparison of the control of alcoholic and non-alcoholic drinking.* Unpublished doctoral dissertation, University of Auckland, 1974.

Brown, R. A. Ethnic origin, beverage preference, and group composition in relation to alcohol consumption by problem drinkers. *The International Journal of the Addictions*, 1981, *16*, 1117–1124.

Caddy, G. R. Toward a multivariate analysis of alcohol abuse. In P. E. Nathan, G. A. Marlatt, & T. Loberg (Eds.), *Alcoholism: New directions in behavioral research and treatment.* New York: Plenum Press, 1978.

Caddy, G. R., Goldman, R. D., & Huebner, R. Group differences in attitudes towards alcoholism. *Addictive Behaviors*, 1976, *1*, 281–286. (a)

Caddy, G. R., Goldman, R. D., & Huebner, R. Relationships among different domains of attitudes towards alcoholism: Model, cost, and treatment. *Addictive Behaviors*, 1976, *1*, 159–167. (b)

Caddy, G. R., Addington, Jr., H. J., & Trenschel, W. R. A comparative evaluation of aftercare technologies in the management of alcohol dependence, in press.

Cahalan, D. *Problem drinkers: A national survey.* San Francisco: Jossey-Bass, 1970.

Cahalan, D., & Room, R. *Problem drinking among American men.* New Brunswick, N.J.: Rutgers Center of Alcohol Studies, 1974.

Cahalan, D., Cisin, I. H., & Crossley, M. *American drinking practices: A national study of drinking behavior and attitudes.* New Brunswick, N.J.: Rutgers Center of Alcohol Studies, 1969.

Cahn, S. *The treatment of alcoholics: An evaluative study.* New York: Oxford University Press, 1970.

Clancy, J. A defense against sobriety. *Quarterly Journal of Studies on Alcohol*, 1960, *21*, 269–276.

Clopton, J. R. Alcoholism and the MMPI. *Journal of Studies on Alcohol*, 1978, *39*, 1540–1558.

Collier, H. V. *Counseling women: A guide for therapists.* New York: The Free Press, 1982.

Costello, R. M. Alcoholism aftercare and outcome: Crosslagged panel and path analyses. *British Journal of Addiction*, 1980, *75*, 49–53.

Cummings, R. E. A three-year study of VA inpatient alcoholic treatment using demographic and psychological data. *Rehabilitation Literature*, 1977, *38*, 153–156.

Dale, P. W., & Ebaugh, F. G. Personality structure with relation to tetraethylthiuram disulfide (antabuse) therapy of alcoholism. *Journal of the American Medical Association*, 1951, *146*, 314–319.

Diagnostic and statistical manual of mental disorders (DSM-III). Washington, D.C.: American Psychiatric Association, 1980.

Edwards, G., Orford, J., Egert, S., Guthrie, S., Hawker, A., Hensman, C., Mitcheson, M., Oppenheimer, E., & Taylor, C. Alcoholism: A controlled trial of treatment versus "advice." *Journal of Studies on Alcohol*, 1977, *38*, 1004–1031.

Fenna, D., Shaefer, O., Mix, L. Ethanol metabolism in various racial groups. *Canadian Medical Association Journal*, 1971, *105*, 472–475.

Finney, J. W., & Moos, R. H. Characteristics and prognosis of alcoholics who became moderate drinkers and abstainers after treatment. *Journal of Studies on Alcohol*, 1981, *42*, 94–105.

Finney, J. W., Moos, R. H., & Mewborn, C. R. Post-treatment experiences and treatment outcome of alcoholic patients six months and two years after hospitalization. *Journal of Consulting and Clinical Psychology*, 1980, *48*, 17–29.

Finney, J. W., Moos, R. H., & Chan, D. A. Length of stay and program component effect in the treatment of alcoholism: A comparison of two techniques for process analyses. *Journal of Consulting and Clinical Psychology*, 1981, 49, 120–131.

Freed, E. X. The effect of alcohol upon approach–avoidance conflict in the white rat. *Quarterly Journal of Studies on Alcohol*, 1967, 28, 236–254.

Freed, E. X. Effects of self-intoxication upon approach–avoidance conflict in the rat. *Quarterly Journal of Studies on Alcohol*, 1968, 29, 323–329.

Gallen, M. Prediction of improvement in two contrasting alcoholism treatment programs. *Newsletter for Research in Mental Health and Behavioral Sciences*, 1976, 18, 31–32.

Gerard, D. L., & Saenger, G. *Outpatient treatment of alcoholism: A study of outcome and its determinants.* Toronto: University of Toronto Press, 1966.

Glock, G. Y. Image of man and public opinion. *Public Opinion Quarterly*, 1964, 28, 539–546.

Goldstein, S., & Linden, J. Multivariate classification of alcoholics by means of the MMPI. *Journal of Abnormal Psychology*, 1969, 74, 661–669.

Gomberg, E. S. Alcoholism in women. In Kissin, B. & Begleiter, H. (Eds.), *Social aspects of alcoholism.* New York: Plenum Press, 1976.

Gomberg, E. S. Women, sex roles, and alcohol problems. *Professional Psychology*, 1981, 12, 146–155.

Hart, L. S., & Stueland, D. An application of the multidimensional model of alcoholism to program effectiveness: Rehabilitation status and outcome. *Journal of Studies on Alcohol*, 1979, 40, 645–655.

Hersen, M., & Barlow, D. H. *Single case experimental designs: Strategies for studying behavior change.* New York: Pergamon, 1976.

Higgins, R. L., & Marlatt, G. A. Effects of anxiety arousal on the consumption of alcohol by alcoholics and social drinkers. *Journal of Consulting and Clinical Psychology*, 1973, 41, 426–433.

Higgins, R. L., & Marlatt, G. A. Fear of interpersonal evaluations as a determinant of alcohol consumption in male social drinkers. *Journal of Abnormal Psychology*, 1975, 84, 644–651.

Hill, E., Haertzen, C., & Davis, H. An MMPI factor analytic study of alcoholics, neurotic addicts, and animals. *Quarterly Journal of Studies on Alcohol*, 1962, 23, 411–431.

Hoffman, H. Personality measurement for the evaluation and prediction of alcoholism. In R. Tarter & A. Sugerman (Eds.), *Alcoholism: Interdisciplinary approaches to an enduring problem.* Reading, Mass. Addison-Wesley, 1976.

Hoffman, H., & Nelson, P. C. Personality characteristics of alcoholics in relation to age and intelligence. *Psychological Reports*, 29, 143–146, 1971.

Horn, J. L., & Wanberg, K. W. Symptom patterns related to the excessive use of alcohol. *Quarterly Journal of Studies on Alcohol*, 1969, 30, 35–58.

Horn, J. L., & Wanberg, K. W. Dimensions of perception of background and current situation of alcoholic patients. *Quarterly Journal of Studies on Alcohol*, 1970, 31, 633–658.

Horn, J. L., & Wanberg, K. W. Females are different: On the diagnosis of alcoholism in women. In M. E. Chafetz (Ed.), *Proceedings of the First Annual Alcoholism Conference of the National Institute on Alcohol Abuse and Alcoholism.* Rockville, Md.: U.S. Department of Health, Education and Welfare, 1973.

Hughes, F. W., Forney, R. B., & Gates, P. W. Performance in human subjects under delayed auditory feedback after alcohol, a tranquilizer (Benquinamide) or Benquinamide-alcohol combination. *Journal of Psychology*, 1963, 55, 25–32.

Hugo, J. A. *A comparison of responses of Negro and white outpatient alcoholics on the Minnesota Multiphasic Personality Inventory.* Master's thesis, Alabama University, 1970.

Hunt, G. M., & Azrin, N. H. A community reinforcement approach to alcoholism. *Behaviour Research and Therapy*, 1973, 11, 91–104.

Irwin, T. Attacking alcohol as a disease. *Today's Health*, 1968, 46, 21–23.

Jellinek, E. M. *The disease concept of alcoholism.* New Brunswick, N.J.: Hillhouse Press, 1960.

Jessor, R., & Jessor, S. L. Problem drinking in youth: Personality, social and behavioral antecedents and correlates. *Proceedings of the Second Annual Alcoholism Conference.* Washington, D.C.: NIAAA, 1973.

Jessor, R., Collins, M. T., & Jessor, S. L. On becoming a drinker: Social psychological aspects of an adolescent transition. *Annals of the New York Academy of Sciences,* 1972, *197,* 199–213.

Kammeier, M. L., & Conley, J. J. Toward a system for prediction of post-treatment abstinence and adaptation. *Current Alcohol,* 1979, *6,* 111–119.

Keehn, J. D. Reinforcement of alcoholism: Schedule control of solitary drinking. *Quarterly Journal of Studies on Alcohol,* 1970, *31,* 28–39.

Keil, T. J., & Busch, J. A. Female–male differences in massed drinking: Results from a household survey. *The International Journal of the Addictions,* 1981, *16,* 1491–1503.

Keller, M. The disease concept of alcoholism revisited. *Journal of Studies on Alcohol,* 1976, *37,* 1694–1717.

Kendall, R. E. Normal drinking by former alcoholic addicts. *Quarterly Journal of Studies on Alcohol,* 1965, *26,* 247–257.

Kilpatrick, D. G., Sutker, P. B., & Smith, A. D. Deviant drug and alcohol use: The role of anxiety, sensation seeking, and other personality variables. In M. Zuckerman & C. D. Spielberger (Eds.), *Emotions and anxiety: New concepts, methods, and applications.* New York: Wiley, 1976.

Kissin, B. Patient characteristics and treatment specificity in alcoholism. In *Recent advances in the study of alcoholism.* Amsterdam: Excerpta Medical, 1977.

Kissin, B., Rosenblatt, S. M., & Machover, S. Prognostic factors in alcoholism. *Psychiatric Research Reports,* 1968, *24,* 22–43.

Kissin, B., Platz, A., & Su, W. H. Social and psychological factors in the treatment of alcoholism. *Journal of Psychiatric Research,* 1970, *8,* 13–27.

Knight, R. P. The dynamics and treatment of chronic alcohol addiction. *Bulletin of the Menninger Clinic,* 1937, *1,* 233–250.

Knupfer, G. Ex-problem drinkers. In M. Roff, L. N. Robins, & M. Pollack (Eds.), *Life history research in psychopathology* (Vol. 2). Minneapolis, University of Minnesota Press, 1972.

Levine, J., & Zigler, E. The essential-reactive distinction in alcoholism: A developmental approach. *Journal of Abnormal Psychology,* 1973, *81,* 242–249.

Libb, J. W., & Taulbee, E. S. Psychotic-appearing MMPI profiles among alcoholics. *Journal of Consulting Psychology,* 1971, *27,* 101–102.

Linsky, A. S. The changing public views on alcoholism. *Quarterly Journal of Studies on Alcohol,* 1970, *31,* 692–704.

Linsky, A. S. Theories of behavior and social control of alcoholism. *Social Psychiatry,* 1972, *7,* 47–52.

Lisansky, E. S. The etiology of alcoholism: The role of psychological predisposition. *Quarterly Journal of Studies on Alcohol,* 1960, *21,* 314–343.

Lundquist, G. A. R. Alcohol dependence. *Acta Psychiatrica Scandinavica,* 1973, *49,* 332–340.

Lyons, J. P., Welte, J. W., Sokolow, L., Hynes, G., & Brown, J. *Variation in alcoholism treatment orientation: Differential impact upon specific subpopulations.* New York: Research Institute on Alcoholism, 1981.

MacAndrew, C., & Edgerton, R. B. *Drunken comportment: A social explanation.* Chicago: Aldine, 1969.

MacIntyre, D. Alcohol related problems among male patients admitted to a general medical ward—their identification and follow-up. *Health Bulletin,* 1979, *37,* 213–217.

Marconi, J. Scientific theory and operational definitions in psychotherapy with special references to alcoholism. *Quarterly Journal of Studies on Alcohol*, 1967, *28*, 631–640.

Marlatt, G. A. Craving for alcohol, loss of control, and relapse. In P. E. Nathan, G. A. Marlatt, & T. Loberg (Eds.), *Alcoholism: New directions in behavioral research and treatment*. New York: Plenum Press, 1978.

Marlatt, G. A., & Gordon, R. J. Determinants of relapse: Implications for the maintenance of behavioral change. In P. Davidson & S. Davidson (Eds.), *Behavioral medicine: Changing health lifestyles*. New York: Brunner/Mazel, 1980.

Masserman, J. H., Jacques, M. B., & Nicholson, M. R. Alcohol as preventive of experimental neuroses. *Quarterly Journal of Studies on Alcohol*, 1945, *6*, 281–299.

McClelland, D. C., Davis, W. N., Kalin, R., & Wanner, E. *The drinking man*. New York: The Free Press, 1972.

McCord, W., & McCord, J. *Origins of alcoholism*. Stanford: Stanford University Press, 1960.

McCord, W., McCord, J., & Gudeman, J. *Origins of alcoholism*. Stanford: Stanford University Press, 1960.

McGinnis, C. H., & Ryan, C. W. The influence of age on MMPI scores of chronic alcoholics. *Journal of Clinical Psychology*, 1965, *22*, 271–272.

McNamee, H. B., Mello, N. K., & Mendelson, J. H. Experimental analysis of drinking patterns of alcoholics: Concurrent psychiatric observations. *American Journal of Psychiatry*, 1968, *124*, 1063–1069.

Mello, N. K. Behavioral studies of alcoholism. In B. Kissin & H. Begleiter (Eds.), *The biology of alcoholism* (Vol. 2). *Physiology and Behavior*. New York: Plenum Press, 1972.

Mendelson, J. H., & Mello, N. K. Experimental analysis of drinking behavior of chronic alcoholics. *Annals of the New York Academy of Sciences*, 1966, *133*, 828–845.

Mendelson, J. H., La Dou, J., & Solomon, P. Experimentally induced chronic intoxication and withdrawal in alcoholics: Psychiatric findings. *Quarterly Journal of Studies on Alcohol*, 1964, *Supplement No. 2*, 40–52.

Miller, P. M. Altrnative skills training in alcoholism treatment. In P. E. Nathan, G. A. Marlatt, & T. Loberg (Eds.), *Alcoholism: New directions in behavioral research and treatment*. New York: Plenum Press, 1978.

Miller, P. M., & Eisler, R. M. Assertive behavior of alcoholics: A descriptive analysis. *Behavior Therapy*, 1977, *8*, 146–149.

Miller, P. M., Hersen, M., Eisler, R. M., & Hilsman, G. Effects of social stress on operant drinking of alcoholics and social drinkers. *Behaviour Research and Therapy*, 1974, *12*, 67–72.

Miller, W. R., & Caddy, G. R. Abstinence and controlled drinking in the treatment of problem drinkers. *Journal of Studies on Alcohol*, 1977, *38*, 986–1003.

Miller, W. R., & Joyce, M. A. Prediction of abstinence, controlled drinking, and heavy drinking outcomes following behavioral self-control training. *Journal of Consulting and Clinical Psychology*, 1979, *47*, 773–775.

Miller, W. R., Taylor, C. A., & West, J. C. Focused versus broad spectrum behavior therapy for problem drinkers. *Journal of Consulting and Clinical Psychology*, 1980, *48*, 590–601.

Mills, C. W. Situated actions and vocabulary of motives. *American Sociology Review*, 1940, *5*, 904–913.

Moos, R. H., & Finney, J. W. The expanding scope of alcoholism treatment evaluation. *American Psychologist*, 1983, *38*, 1036–1044.

Moos, R. H., Finney, J. W., & Chan, D. A. The process of recovery from alcoholism: I. Comparing alcoholic patients with matched community controls. *Journal of Studies on Alcohol*, 42, 1981, 383–402.

Muzekari, L. H. The MMPI in predicting treatment outcome in alcoholism. *Journal of Consulting Psychology,* 1965, *29,* 281.

Nathan, P. E., & O'Brien, J. S. An experimental analysis of the behavior of alcoholics and non-alcoholics during prolonged experimental drinking. *Behavior Therapy,* 1971, *2,* 455–476.

Nunnally, J. C. *Psychometric theory.* New York: McGraw-Hill, 1967.

Ogborne, A. C. Patient characteristics as predictors of treatment outcome for alcohol and drug abusers. In Y. Israel (Ed.), *Research advances in alcohol and drug problems* (Vol. 4). New York: Plenum, 1978.

Orford, J. A comparison of alcoholics whose drinking is totally uncontrolled and those whose drinking is mainly controlled. *Behaviour Research and Therapy,* 1973, *11,* 575–576.

Overall, J. E. MMPI personality patterns of alcoholics and narcotics addicts. *Quarterly Journal of Studies on Alcohol,* 1973, *34,* 104–111.

Partington, J., & Johnson, F. Personality types among alcoholics. *Quarterly Journal of Studies on Alcohol,* 1969, *30,* 21–33.

Pattison, E. M. Drinking outcomes of alcoholism treatment: Abstinence, social, modified, controlled, and normal drinking. In N. Kessel, A. Hawker, & H. Chalke (Eds.), *Alcoholism: A medical profile.* London: B. Edsall, 1974. (a)

Pattison, E. M. The rehabilitation of the chronic alcoholic. In B. Kissin & H. Begleiter (Eds.), *The biology of alcoholism* (Vol. 3). New York: Plenum Press, 1974. (b)

Pattison, E. M., Bishop, L. A., & Linsky, A. S. Changes in public attitudes on narcotic addiction. *American Journal of Psychiatry,* 1968, *125,* 160–167.

Pattison, E. M., Coe, R., & Rhodes, R. I. Evaluation of alcoholism treatment: A comparison of three facilities. *Archives of General Psychiatry,* 1969, *20,* 478–488.

Pattison, E. M., Sobell, M. B., & Sobell, L. C. (Eds.), *Emerging concepts of alcohol dependence.* New York: Springer, 1977.

Pemberton, D. A. A comparison of the outcome of treatment in female and male alcoholics. *British Journal of Psychiatry,* 1967, *113,* 367–373.

Pittman, D. J. *Alcoholism.* New York: Harper & Row, 1967.

Pitts, F. N., Jr., & Winokur, G. Affective disorder, VII. Alcoholism and affective disorder. *Journal of Psychiatric Research,* 1943, *4,* 246–251.

Plant, M. A. *Drinking careers: Occupations, drinking habits, drinking problems.* Tavistock, England: Methuen, 1979.

Pokorny, A. D., Miller, B. A., & Cleveland, S. E. Response to treatment of alcoholism. *Quarterly Journal of Studies on Alcohol,* 1968, *29,*364–381.

Price, J. An applied analysis of North American Indian drinking patterns. *Human Organization,* 1975, *34,* 17–26.

Reed, T. E. Racial comparisons of alcohol metabolism: Background, problems, and results. *Alcoholism: Clinical and Experimental Research,* 1978, *2,* 83–87.

Room, R. Normative perspectives on alcohol use and problems. *Journal of Drug Issues,* 1975, *5,* 358–368.

Rosen, A. C. A comparative study of alcoholic and psychiatric patients with the MMPI. *Quarterly Journal of Studies on Alcohol,* 1960, *21,* 253–266.

Rudfeld, K. Recovery from alcoholism by treatment with antabuse combined with social and personal counseling: A statistical calculation of the prognosis in different social groups. *Danish Medical Bulletin,* 1958, *5,* 212–216.

Rudie, R., & McGaughran, L. Differences in developmental experiences, defensiveness, and personality organizations between two classes of problem drinkers. *Journal of Abnormal and Social Psychology,* 1961, *62,* 659–665.

Saunders, W. M., Phil, M., & Kershaw, P. W. Spontaneous remission from alcoholism—a community study. *British Journal of Addiction,* 1979, *74,* 251–265.

Schaefer, H. H., Sobell, M. B., & Mills, K. C. Some sobering data on the use of self confrontation with alcoholics. *Behavior Therapy*, 1971, *2*, 28–39.

Schuckit, M., Pitts, F. N., Jr., Reich, T., King, L. J., & Winokur, B. Alcoholism I: Two types of alcoholism in women. *Archives of General Psychiatry*, 1969, *20*, 301–306.

Seelye, E. E. Relationship of socioeconomic status, psychiatric diagnosis and sex to outcome of alcoholism treatment. *Journal of Studies on Alcohol*, 1979, *40*, 57–62.

Selzer, M. L., & Holloway, W. H. A follow-up study of alcoholics admitted to a state hospital. *Quarterly Journal of Studies on Alcohol*, 1957, *18*, 98–120.

Sereny, G., & Fryatt, M. A follow-up evaluation of the treatment of chronic alcoholics. *Canadian Medical Association Journal*, 1966, *94*, 8–12.

Sidman, M. *Tactics of scientific research: Evaluating experimental data in psychology*. New York: Basic Books, 1960.

Siegler, M., Osmond, H., & Newell, S. Models of alcoholism. *Quarterly Journal of Studies on Alcohol*, 1968, *29*, 571–591.

Sievers, M. L. Cigarette and alcohol usage by Southwestern American Indians. *American Journal of Public Health*, 1968, *58*, 71–81.

Skinner, H. A., & Allen, B. A. Alcohol dependence syndrome: Measurement and validation. *Journal of Abnormal Psychology*, 1982, *91*,199–209.

Smart, R. G. Effects of alcohol on conflict and avoidance behavior. *Quarterly Journal of Studies on Alcohol*, 1965, *26*, 187–205.

Smart, R. G. Spontaneous recovery in alcoholics: A review and analysis of the available research. *Drug and Alcohol Dependence*, 1976, *1*, 277–285.

Smart, R. G. Do some alcoholics do better in some types of treatment than others? *Drug and Alcohol Dependence*, 1978, *3*, 65–75.

Smith, V., & Chyatte, C. Left-handed versus right-handed alcoholics: An examination of relapse patterns. *Journal of Studies on Alcohol*, *44*, 553–555.

Sobell, L. C., & Sobell, M. B. Outpatient alcoholics give valid self-reports. *Journal of Nervous and Mental Disease*, 1975, *161*, 32–42.

Sobell, M. B. & Sobell, L. C. Individualized behavior therapy for alcoholics. *Behaviour Research and Therapy*, 1973, *4*, 49–72.

Sobell, M. B., & Sobell, L. C. Second year treatment outcome of alcoholics treated by individualized behaviour therapy: Results. *Behaviour Research and Therapy*, 1976, *14*, 195–215.

Spradley, J. P. *You owe yourself a drunk: An ethnography of urban nomads*. Boston: Little, Brown, 1970.

Sterne, M. W., & Pittman, D. J. The concept of motivation: A source of institutional and professional blockage in the treatment of alcoholics. *Quarterly Journal of Studies on Alcohol*, 1965, *26*, 41–57.

Stinson, D. J., Smith, W. G., Amidjaya, I., & Kaplan, J. M. Systems of care and treatment outcomes for alcoholic patients. *Archives of General Psychiatry*, 1976, *36*, 535–539.

Stoll, C. S. Images of man and social control. *Social Forces*, 1968, *47*, 119–127.

Sugarman, A. A., Reilly, D., & Albahary, R. Social competence and essential-reactive distinction in alcoholism. *Archives of General Psychiatry*, 1965, *12*, 552–556.

Svanum, S., & Dallas, C. L. Alcoholic MMPI types and their relationship to patient characteristics, polydrug abuse, and abstinence following treatment. *Journal of Personality Assessment*, 1981, *45*, 278–287.

Tarnower, S. M., & Toole, H. M. Evaluation of patients in an alcoholism clinic for more than 10 years. *Diseases of the Nervous System*, 1968, *29*, 28–31.

Thimann, J. Conditioned reflex treatment of alcoholism: II. The risks of its application, its indications, contra-indications and psychotherapeutic aspects. *New England Journal of Medicine*, 1949, *241*, 406–410.

Trice, H. M. A study of the process of affiliation with Alcoholics Anonymous. *Quarterly Journal of Studies on Alcohol,* 1957, *18,* 39–54.

Tuchfeld, B. S. Spontaneous remission in alcoholics: Empirical observations and theoretical implications. *Journal of Studies on Alcohol,* 1981, *42,* 626–641.

Vanderpool, J. A. Alcoholism and the self-concept. *Quarterly Journal of Studies on Alcohol,* 1969, *30,* 59–77.

van Dijk, W. K., & van Dijk-Koffeman, A. A follow-up study of 211 treated male alcoholic addicts. *British Journal of the Addictions,* 1973, *68,* 3–24.

Voegtlin, W. L., & Broz, W. R. The conditioned reflex treatment of chronic alcoholism: X. An analysis of 3,125 admissions over a period of ten and a half years. *Annals of Internal Medicine,* 1949, *30,* 580–597.

Vogel, M. D. The relation of personality factors to GSR conditioning of alcoholics: An exploratory study. *Canadian Journal of Psychology,* 1960, *14,* 275–280.

Vogel, M. D. The relationship of personality factors to drinking patterns of alcoholics: An exploratory study. *Quarterly Journal of Studies on Alcohol,* 1961, *22,* 394–400.

Vogel-Sprott, M. Alcohol effects on human behavior under reward and punishment. *Psychopharmacologia,* 1967, *11,* 337–344.

Wallgren, H., & Barry, H. *Actions of alcohol* (Vol. II). Amsterdam: Elsevier, 1970.

Westermeyer, J. Chippewa and majority alcoholism in the twin cities: A comparison. *Journal of Nervous and Mental Disease,* 1972, *155,* 322–327.

Williams, A. F. The alcoholic personality. In B. Kissin & H. Begleiter (Eds.), *The biology of alcoholism* (Vol. 4). New York: Plenum Press, 1976.

Williams, R. J., & Brown, R. A. Differences in baseline drinking behavior between New Zealand alcoholics and normal drinkers. *Behaviour Research and Therapy,* 1974, *12,* 287–294.

Winokur, G., Rimmer, J., & Reich, T. Alcoholism. IV. Is there more than one type of alcoholism? *British Journal of Psychiatry,* 1971, *118,* 525–531.

Winokur, G., Reich, T., Rimmer, J., & Pitts, F. N., Jr. Alcoholism. III. Diagnosis and familial psychiatric illness in 259 alcoholic probands. *Archives of General Psychiatry,* 1970, *23,* 104–111.

Wolff, P. H. Ethnic differences in alcohol sensitivity. *Science,* 1972, *175,* 449–450.

Wolff, P. H. Vasomotor sensitivity to alcohol in diverse Mongoloid populations. *American Journal of Genetics,* 1973, *25,* 193–199.

Wolff, S., & Holland, L. A. A questionnaire follow-up of alcoholic patients. *Quarterly Journal of Studies on Alcohol,* 1964, *25,* 108–118.

CHAPTER 11

The Significance of Environmental Factors for the Design and the Evaluation of Alcohol Treatment Programs

ALAN C. OGBORNE, MARK B. SOBELL, and LINDA C. SOBELL

INTRODUCTION

An increasing body of evidence suggests that environmental factors can influence the long-term treatment outcome of alcohol abusers.* Certain environmental factors have also been found to be positively associated with the natural recovery (i.e., without treatment) of individuals with alcohol problems. Much of this evidence, however, comes from studies designed to answer other research questions (e.g., the comparative effectiveness of various treatments). In this chapter, the research describing the relationships between environmental factors and outcomes is briefly

---

* Because the populations studied have varied greatly in severity of dependence, the term *alcohol abusers* will be used to describe this conglomerate population except when the matter being discussed requires a more specific definition.

ALAN C. OGBORNE • Addiction Research Foundation and University of Western Ontario, London, Ontario, N6A 5B9, Canada. MARK B. SOBELL and LINDA C. SOBELL • Addiction Research Foundation and University of Toronto, Toronto, Ontario M5S 2S1, Canada. The views expressed in this chapter are those of the authors and do not necessarily reflect those of the Addiction Research Foundation.

reviewed, and the implications of this research for the design and evaluation of treatment are discussed.

ENVIRONMENTAL FACTORS AND OUTCOMES

Although empirical demonstrations of the influence of environmental factors on treatment outcomes are relatively recent, several convergent lines of research and thinking illustrate the potential importance of these factors.

EPIDEMIOLOGICAL STUDIES

The first line of research consists of epidemiological studies that have shown that the prevalence of problem drinking varies with demographic, sociocultural, and economic factors (Cahalan, 1970; de Lint & Schmidt, 1971; Popham, Schmidt, & de Lint, 1976; Suurvali & Shain, 1981; Vaillant & Milofsky, 1982; Whitehead, 1976). In this regard, a person's environment can range from being broadly supportive of, indifferent to, or even antithetical to various treatment goals and strategies. For example, alcohol abusers who have easy access to alcohol and whose peer and cultural groups drink excessively are likely to find it more difficult to abstain or drink moderately than are individuals who associate with moderate drinkers or nondrinkers and for whom alcohol is expensive or otherwise difficult to obtain. Thus, treatments that ignore the cultural and economic climates within which alcohol abusers must function may be less successful than treatments designed to help patients cope with inherent environmental influences.

LABORATORY STUDIES

The second line of evidence derives from laboratory studies that show that alcohol consumption by alcohol abusers can be influenced by many environmental variables, such as (a) role modeling (Caudill & Lipscomb, 1980; Caudill & Marlatt, 1975; Garlington & DeRicco, 1977); (b) social reinforcement of declared intents to abstain (Alterman, Gottheil, Skoloda, & Grasberger, 1974); (c) manipulation of stress in the context of social or isolated drinking (Allman, Taylor, & Nathan, 1972); (d) degree of effort required to obtain alcohol (Funderburk & Allen, 1977a, 1977b; Mello & Mendelson, 1965); and (e) environmental reinforcement contingencies associated with drinking (Bigelow, Liebson, & Griffiths, 1974; Cohen, Liebson, Faillace, & Allen, 1971; Miller, 1975). It has also been postulated that a subclinical withdrawal syndrome conditioned to environmental and/or interoceptive cues might contribute to relapse following periods of abstinence (Ludwig, Wikler, & Stark, 1974).

TREATMENT OUTCOME STUDIES

The third line of evidence linking environmental factors to treatment outcomes concerns the posttreatment environments of treated alcohol abusers. In this work, stable aspects of posttreatment social environments as well as the occurrence of stressful life events have been implicated as factors affecting treatment outcomes, the former usually having a positive effect and the latter a negative effect on outcomes. The examination of environmental factors and their effects on the treatment outcomes of alcohol abusers is a relatively new area of research.

Orford and Edwards (1977) were among the first to study the influence of environmental factors on the outcomes of treated alcohol abusers. One of the strongest conclusions that emerged from their work with married male alcoholics was that

> relatively cohesive couples were more than twice as likely to find themselves in the "good" than in the "bad" outcome group at follow-up, whilst relatively non-cohesive couples were more than three times as likely to find themselves in the "bad" group. (p. 72)

The best known work in this area has been conducted by Moos and his colleagues. Their studies have systematically evaluated the relationships between environmental resources and treatment outcomes for a variety of populations and treatments and found that patients with stable family and/or work environments prior to treatment functioned significantly better after treatment than those patients who lacked such resources (reviewed in Moos, Cronkite, & Finney, 1982). These investigators have also found the quality of the resources (i.e., positive family milieu, positively perceived work environment) to be significantly related to outcome (Bromet & Moos, 1977). A study by Ward, Bendel, and Lange (1982) confirmed the findings of Moos and his colleagues, in that environmental resources of family and work satisfaction were found to be significantly related to the posttreatment functioning of alcohol abusers. Costello (1980), in a metaanalysis of treatment studies with varying degrees of aftercare, has also suggested that posttreatment environmental factors can positively affect treatment outcome.

Although social support and employment seem to be generic environmental factors associated with beneficial treatment outcomes, Marlatt and his colleagues have identified several specific environmental factors associated with a high risk of relapse to drinking (reviewed in Marlatt & Gordon, 1980). Among the most salient environmental features associated with relapse are situations accompanied by negative emotional states (e.g., depression, anxiety), social pressures encouraging drinking, and interpersonal conflicts (e.g., disagreements, confrontations). Ludwig (1972) also found that alcoholics often attribute their resumption of drinking to various environmental factors (the most frequently reported precipitant of drinking being relief from psychological distress). In summary, the aforementioned studies, although primarily correlational, clearly suggest that the environment within which alcohol abusers must function after treatment needs to be carefully assessed and considered in the context of treatment planning.

Another posttreatment factor that may significantly affect outcomes is formal or informal (e.g., A.A.) therapeutic programs or contacts. For example, "posttreatment treatments" are quite common (Polich, Armor, & Braiker, 1981), and unfortunately, this complicates the evaluation of a given treatment under study (i.e., if 6 months after treatment discharge a subject's functioning is marginal and she or he begins using a new therapeutic support and improves, is the improvement related to the earlier treatment, the posttreatment treatment, an interaction of both treatments, or neither treatment?). Also, multiple follow-up contacts (typically evaluated by subjects as expressions of concern, being therapeutically supportive, or stimulating self-review) may also positively affect treatment outcomes (Gallen, 1974; Sobell & Sobell, 1981).

Finally, from a social learning or social psychology perspective (Miller, 1980; Pattison, Sobell, & Sobell, 1978), it is not surprising that posttreatment environmental factors seem to affect the prognosis of treated alcohol abusers. Such models not only assume that environmental contingencies play a prominent role in the induction, maintenance, and generalization of all forms of behavior, but they further demand that attention be paid to the characteristics of the environments to which treated individuals must return (Maisto & Cooper, 1980).

Natural Recovery without Treatment

The fourth line of evidence that suggests the importance of environmental factors in alcohol treatment outcomes is a growing body of evidence showing that many alcohol abusers recover without the aid of any formal treatment (reviewed in Tuchfeld, 1976, 1981). Several years ago, Smart (1975/1976) concluded that the reasons for natural recovery were not well understood. However, he did suggest that certain general factors such as changes in health, jobs, marriage, and living conditions might be related to such recoveries. Several other studies (Sauders & Kershaw, 1979; Stall, 1983; Tuchfeld, 1976, 1981; Valliant, 1981) have supported this line of reasoning by reporting that certain environmental variables are linked *both* to the process of natural recovery and to the maintenance of recovery from drinking problems. The two most salient features of the environment that have been found to be associated with the natural recovery and maintenance of recovery from drinking problems are positive changes in a person's social milieu and positive vocational satisfaction or vocational changes. Other factors implicated as important are changes in health as well as previous success at self-control (e.g., stopping smoking).

The accruing evidence that alcohol abusers do recover without formal treatment and that certain aspects of their environment seem to be strongly associated with their recovery brings to mind the insightful proposal made by Orford and Edwards (1977) several years before most of these studies were conducted. They suggested that

> the way ahead in alcoholism treatment research should increasingly embrace the closer study of "natural" forces which can be captured and exploited by planned intervention. (p. 3)

Research since that time has strengthened the importance of their recommendation.

ENVIRONMENTAL CHANGES AS A FOCUS OF TREATMENT

The fifth and final major line of evidence suggesting that environmental factors can have a major impact on treatment outcome derives from a small number of studies that have specifically used environmental change as a focus of treatment. The most direct emphasis on environmental changes has been in studies reported by Azrin (1976), Hunt & Azrin (1973), and Miller (1975). A major objective of these studies was to provide chronic alcoholics with access to environmental reinforcers (e.g., work, goods, shelter) contingent upon abstinence or reduced drinking. The results of both Azrin's and Miller's studies impressively demonstrated that subjects in the contingent reinforcement groups were quite successful in reducing their drinking in comparison to control groups with noncontingent access to reinforcers. However, the treatments were quite labor intensive and required elaborate resources. Such intensive programs are unlikely to be practical or realistic for most service providers. Questions also exist about whether and how the effectiveness of the intervention (i.e., contingencies) will be sustained after the research phase, as is highlighted by the refusal of the agencies involved in Miller's (1975) study to continue providing a treatment with demonstrated effectiveness after the project's completion.

Despite these practical problems, these studies do provide demonstrations of the impact that environmental factors can have on treatment outcomes. Given that there is very little evidence to date for alcohol treatment effectiveness (e.g., Polich et al., 1981), any method with demonstrated effectiveness is a worthy focus for future research. Manipulation of environmental resources as part of treatment might be easier and have a more enduring effect with a less chronic population and one that, as compared to chronic alcoholics, has more intact resources (e.g., friends, family, work).

EXPERIMENTAL STUDIES

Several other experimental studies lend empirical support to a hypothesis that alcohol abusers, in contrast to nonproblem drinkers, are more responsive to environmental alcohol-related stimuli than to internal alcohol-related stimuli (Brown & Williams, 1975; Buck, 1979; Tucker, Vuchinich, & Sobell, 1979; Williams, 1977). If this hypothesis is valid, then alcohol abusers may be especially vulnerable to environmental drinking cues (e.g., sight of drinks, bars, social pressure, advertising). This vulnerability would presumably persist in posttreatment environments unless moderated by treatment or other means.

STUDIES OF POPULATIONS OTHER THAN ALCOHOL ABUSERS

The recent recognition of the importance of posttreatment environmental factors in the study of alcohol problems has been paralleled by an increasing recognition of the contribution of social and physical environments to the onset and prognosis of other mental health and drug abuse problems (Clum, 1975; Cushman, 1974; Dohrenwend, 1975; Harding, Zinberg, Stelmack, & Barry, 1980; King, 1978; Kiritz & Moos, 1974; La Rocco, House, & French, 1980; Orford & Feldman, 1980; Phillips & Bierman, 1981; Sadava & Forsyth, 1977; Snarr & Ball, 1974; Strauss, 1979). Studies of drug abusers have drawn particular attention to the influence of deviant and nondeviant peer group influences and task demands on the maintenance, control, and cessation of illicit drug use (Becker, 1963; Ogborne & Stimson, 1975; Rubington, 1967; Schasre, 1966) and to the conditioning of drug effects to environmental stimuli (Barbarin, 1979). The work of Marlatt and Gordon (1980) has revealed substantial commonalities across addictive behaviors (i.e., smoking, eating, drug and alcohol use) in terms of factors associated with relapse.

Considered in the context of a larger perspective, the study of the relationships between environmental factors and alcohol problems and their resolution may be viewed as a part of the overall study of the relationships between environmental factors and health and mental health problems.

IMPLICATIONS FOR THE DESIGN AND EVALUATION OF TREATMENT

The preceding review has summarized findings from diverse lines of research that support the hypothesis that environmental factors can have a major influence on the attainment and maintenance of recovery from alcohol problems. This, of course, has implications for the ways in which treatments are designed, delivered, and evaluated. In particular, it will be argued that pretreatment assessment, treatment design, delivery, and outcome evaluation should be viewed as related elements in the treatment process rather than as isolated elements in a linear chain. This and other implications are discussed next.

ASSESSMENT AND TREATMENT STRATEGIES

Based on the available evidence, it would seem that treatment strategies that either ignore or deal minimally with environmental factors are likely to have limited generalizability to the posttreatment environment. Strategies that take account of the posttreatment environment include those that have been geared to help individuals cope with immutable aspects of their environments as well as those that have emphasized the need for environmental change.

Assessment

The evaluation of person–environment interactions should be a major component of the clinical assessment process, regardless of treatment orientation. Such interactions should also be monitored over time, and assessments should be modified to reflect any changes that occur. This is important because the assessment constitutes the basis and justification for any particular treatment. However, assessment is usually viewed as a process that precedes treatment rather than as an ongoing dynamic process concurrent with treatment. This is unfortunate because valuable additional assessment information is often revealed over the course of treatment, especially in outpatient settings. Although most clinicians probably modify their assessments and treatments to reflect changes in patients' life circumstances, such "changes in midstream" are seldom mentioned in the literature (see Case No. 1 in Noel, Sobell, Cellucci, Nirenberg, & Sobell, 1982) or systematically evaluated.

Because treatment strategies are based on a clinical evaluation of the patient, the course of events following the implementation of treatment strategies provides a major data base (e.g., what rate of behavior change can be sustained by the patient?) for clinicians to evaluate the viability of the initial strategies and the accuracy of the initial assessment. In other words, some initial treatment strategies might be considered tentative and likely to require modification depending upon intervening events during treatment. Also some patients might be reluctant to disclose certain information early in treatment, whereas others might only come to recognize previously ignored influences on their drinking late in treatment. Furthermore, because person–environment interactions are reciprocal, changes may occur in setting events for drinking either as a result of treatment or because extratreatment events provide new risk situations or an increased chance of certain risks. In summary, greater emphasis should be given to conceptualizing assessment as a dynamic process that is ongoing throughout the course of treatment (see Sobell, Sobell, & Nirenberg, 1982).

Another aspect of assessment that is vital to the interpretation of person–environment interactions is the evaluation of how individuals encode and react to their environment (Mischel, 1973). In terms of treatment, this is important because at times knowledge of the objective environment may not be as important for understanding person–environment interactions as is knowledge of the subjectively perceived environment. In fact, in some cases a major focus of treatment might be on changing subjective perceptions to be more in line with objective reality. Thus, treatment strategies should be designed to take account of the influence of individual-specific cognitive factors (e.g., locus of control, attribution, perceived self-efficacy) (Bandura, 1977; Phillips & Bierman, 1981).

Treatment Strategies

One treatment strategy that has been used to help individuals cope with immutable aspects of their environments is cue exposure training (Blakey & Baker, 1980; Hodgson & Rankin, 1976). Alcohol-related cues pervade the environment, and although exposure to these cues can be reduced by avoiding drinking-cue-laden environments (e.g., bars, parties), it is unrealistic to imagine avoiding all such cues (e.g., beverage advertisements, portrayals of drinking on television, restaurants serving alcoholic beverages, beverage stores, and a plethora of other stimulus sources). Cue exposure training is based on the hypothesis that individuals with a high tolerance for alcohol will, in the presence of drinking-related stimuli, experience an aversive conditioned response that can, in turn, precipitate drinking (a type of learned escape response). Regardless of whether exposure training is based on a classical conditioning (Blakey & Baker, 1980) or an operant conditioning conceptualization (Hodgson & Rankin, 1976), the cue exposure procedure is likely to better prepare individuals for coping with immutable aspects of their environments. In fact, one would expect the effect of such procedures to be cumulative because some extinction of the drinking response would naturally occur by refraining from drinking in the presence of drinking cues. Relaxation training (e.g., Marlatt & Marques, 1977) and similar methods are further examples of treatment interventions intended to help alcohol abusers deal with immutable aspects of their environments.

Other individual-focused treatment interventions have been designed to provide patients with a means of changing and dealing more effectively with their environments. Some examples include social skills training (Chaney, O'Leary, & Marlatt, 1978) and drink refusal training (Foy, Miller, Eisler, & O'Toole, 1976). An important consideration in using these strategies is the reciprocal nature of person–environment interactions over time. For example, drink refusal training could precipitate a temporary increase in peer pressure to drink or social ostracism. In such cases, treatment should (a) address the possibility that in the short run changing the person's responses to the environment could conceivably lead to additional environmental impetus for drinking; and (b) provide continuity of care so that patients can experience and cope successfully with situations evaluated as potential setting events for excessive drinking. In this regard, it has been suggested (see Sobell & Sobell, 1978) that outpatient treatment be gradually (vs. abruptly) terminated by lengthening the interval between sessions while carefully monitoring the patient's functioning. This shaping procedure may be best characterized as using a performance criterion for determining the appropriateness of treatment termination (see Case No. 3 in Noel et al., 1982). Such a procedure might be particularly appropriate for treatment of alcohol problems because there is a high rate of problem recurrence following treatment (Polich et al., 1981).

Another approach aimed at helping alcohol abusers deal with environmental precipitants of drinking is relapse prevention. Marlatt's research (Marlatt 1978; Cummings, Gordon, & Marlatt, 1980; Marlatt & Gordon, 1980) provides an excellent example of how treatment can be specifically designed to deal with anticipated environmental stressors. A detailed analysis of situations retrospectively reported by substance abusers as having precipitated a relapse showed a strong consistency across studies, with negative emotional states, social pressure, and interpersonal conflict being the three precipitants of relapse most frequently reported by alcohol abusers. Based on these results, relapse prevention strategies were developed to train patients in constructive coping responses to identified high-risk situations. The relapse prevention approach also emphasizes the management of relapses that occur. Basically, patients are trained to rapidly terminate episodes of excessive drinking so as to minimize the consequences of relapse and to help them construe the relapse as a learning experience rather than a personal failing.

Although some of the aforementioned strategies obviously involve some attempts to change the environment, other treatment procedures have directly emphasized environmental change. For example, Azrin (1976; Hunt & Azrin, 1973) has demonstrated the efficacy of a multifaceted community-reinforcement approach in the treatment of chronic alcohol abusers. As noted earlier, a major objective of this treatment was to provide patients with access to "natural reinforcers" (e.g., wife's attention) contingent upon continued abstinence. In light of this research (Azrin, 1976; Hunt & Azrin, 1973) and increasing suggestions that various aspects of the environment (e.g., social support) are subject to experimental manipulations (see Gottlieb, 1983), additional research of this nature is needed. Unfortunately, to date few investigations have emphasized environmental modifications.

Patients, as with all of us, encounter new situations and events almost daily. Thus, outpatient treatment should be the treatment of choice, whenever feasible, because it allows a therapist to evaluate a patient's ongoing functioning in the natural environment. Also changes during treatment should be induced *in vivo* or by idiosyncratic simulations (e.g., role playing) of real-life situations.

Assessing and Interpreting Outcomes

Despite recent advances in assessing and evaluating alcohol treatment effectiveness (reviewed in Sobell & Sobell, 1982), such evaluations remain laborious, multifaceted, and exacting. The reason is simple: a person's life is complex and is affected daily by a host of person–environment interactions. Thus, it should not be surprising that the success of any treatment may be enhanced or thwarted by one or more extratreatment factors.

Obviously, the first criterion of treatment effectiveness is whether the intervention produces any observable behavioral changes. Beyond that, however, the ultimate evaluation of a treatment's overall efficacy is whether the changes observed during treatment are maintained after treatment has ceased. Treatment effects can, in fact, be distinguished from the generalization and maintenance of behavior changes induced by treatment (Bandura, 1977; Mash & Terdal, 1976), and when this is done it becomes apparent that a variety of treatment effects (behavioral changes) have been documented with alcohol abusers (reviewed in Sobell, Sobell, Ersner-Hershfield, & Nirenberg, 1982). However, the maintenance of treatment effects (i.e., evidence of stable functioning beyond 12 to 18 months) has not been well established, perhaps owing to a relative lack of long-term evaluations. It deserves mention, though, that this deficiency (i.e., failure to demonstrate long-term maintenance of treatment effects) is not unique to the alcohol field, as treatment outcome studies of other behavioral disorders have been similarly criticized (reviewed in Agras & Berkowitz, 1980; Kazdin & Wilson, 1978; see also LaDouceur & Auger, 1980).

Interactions of Posttreatment Factors with Treatment Effects

Despite the successful induction and generalization of a variety of behavioral changes with alcohol abusers, the lack of evidence for maintenance of treatment effects might simply be related to the controlled and somewhat artificial nature of the treatment setting (i.e., many "real world" factors are not operating on a person's behavior). Thus, when patients attempt to function in their extratreatment environments, and particularly without treatment supports (i.e., after treatment), a variety of expected as well as unexpected factors may interact with the treatment effects. On the one hand, if significant factors are encountered after treatment that are concordant with treatment, then we might hypothesize a more successful outcome for patients. On the other hand, we might expect significant undesirable (both expected and unexpected) posttreatment factors to detract from or negate treatment effects.

Treatment outcome evaluations can help identify the contributions of posttreatment environmental factors to treatment outcomes. For instance, if certain extratreatment factors or a complex of factors are found to be related to successful outcomes, then this information could be used to design more efficacious treatments. However, a necessary precursor to such treatment advances is the systematic measurement of environmental factors. Unfortunately, such evaluations have been rare, probably owing to the fact that such a task involves comprehensive evaluations of situations that patients encounter.

The major problem that complicates the various research strategies that have been used to investigate the relationships between environmental factors and the course of alcohol problems (treated or untreated) is that most of the studies have been retrospective. Typically, alcohol abusers have been asked to recall environmental factors long after the events have occurred. As noted earlier, although some factors (e.g., marital status, periods of employment) can be objectively verified or corroborated, others (e.g., interpersonal conflicts, job problems) are more susceptible to subjective distortion or selective recall, although they may actually be related to outcome. In this regard, there is some question in the literature about the reliability of subjects' reports of life events, including major life events (e.g., deaths), over extended periods of time (see Casey, Masuda, & Holmes, 1967; Jenkins, Hurst, & Rose, 1979; also reviewed in Monroe, 1982a, 1982b; Rabkin & Struening, 1976).

Obviously, the instruments used to assess life events are in need of refinement and validation if these scales (originally developed to identify major life events associated with the onset of illness) are to be used for investigating the relationships between life events and treatment outcomes. Admittedly, retrospective studies have practical advantages in that cross-sectional data can be rapidly gathered. However, expedience is only of value if the data are relatively complete and reliable. A preferred alternative research strategy, although one that would require a larger investment of time and resources, is the conduct of prospective studies. Because such designs can incorporate frequent assessments of environmental factors and of drinking behavior outcomes, this would allow for better measurement of the temporal relationships between these domains.

In evaluating the contribution of posttreatment factors to subjects' functioning, investigators must consider several issues. First, is the patterning, sequencing, or frequency of life events critical? For example, can peer pressure to drink with friends after work on paydays be resisted if no other problems exist? Although there has been a tendency to examine the impact of singularly characterized life events (e.g., job loss, divorce), it is also likely that life events might have an interactive impact (e.g., multiple financial problems combined with frustration at work, inflated cost of living, and a new baby in the family). Second, what is an adequate interval over which to evaluate the impact of multiple life events and their long-term effect on patients' functioning? For example, although a relative's death or a job loss might affect a persons's functioning in the short run (e.g., 6 months), over a longer interval (e.g., 1 to 2 years) the person might be evaluated as functioning quite well. Further, not all life events will occur for all patients during any specified evaluation interval; also some life events will have a low probability of occurrence (e.g., retirement, death of a spouse). Third, considering the foregoing, we must also recognize the practical limitations on the extent to which outcome studies can establish the permanence of treatment-induced behavior change (i.e., few investigators have the opportunity or resources to conduct large-scale longitudinal studies).

Whether prospective or retrospective in design, the majority of future investigations on this topic are likely to be correlational. To achieve maximal contributions from correlational research, it is suggested that investigators design studies as tests of hypotheses, either through path analysis (Cronkite & Moos, 1978, 1980) or through methods of statistical control and prediction. For example, if pretreatment problem severity and progress in treatment can be relatively well controlled, one might test specific hypotheses about which patients are likely to have the best or worst treatment outcomes given the presence of particular environmental factors.

Another consideration related to correlational methods involves the use of appropriate controls. For example, in studies of natural recovery, it is not sufficient to simply examine the types of life events that are associated with natural recovery, as it is necessary to know that the same types of events did not occur for other individuals who had similar problems but did not recover (Saunders & Kershaw, 1979). Likewise, a study of the relationship of coping styles to outcomes would lack importance if it were to be demonstrated that other persons with equivalent coping styles had negative outcomes. Thus, control or comparison groups are needed even for the interpretation of correlational findings. Lastly, investigators need to measure the relationships between individual differences, cognitive styles (how people interpret their environments), and environmental factors so that inferences can be made about the relative contributions to outcome from each domain.

Considering the dearth of studies examining posttreatment factors with alcohol abusers, the following is suggested as a first approximation to collecting relevant outcome data: (a) environmental events should be assessed both pre- and posttreatment; (b) an extended follow-up period (i.e., 2 years) seems necessary to capture certain types of life events and to establish the effects that those events have on treatment outcome; (c) outcome data should be gathered at least every 12 months, and although a comprehensive checklist should be used to insure that all subjects attend to all possible types of life events, an open-ended interview should also be used to probe for additional information; (d) the valence (desirable, undesirable, neutral) of each life event should be assessed, as well as the time sequence or data of the life event; this latter suggestion is important because events may compound with one another so that the importance of any particular event or situation and its effect on drinking behavior may be determined largely by events and situations preceding or surrounding it; and (e) when asking subjects to rate the impact (i.e., desirability) of the event on their life, it should be clear whether the evaluation relates to when the event occurred or at the time of the interview.

FURTHER RESEARCH IMPLICATIONS

With the exception of the work of Moos and his colleagues (Cronkite & Moos, 1980) and Marlatt and Gordon (1980), most of the studies suggesting that environmental factors may play a critical role in determining treatment outcomes have been presented in the absence of a guiding conceptual framework. Often this occurs because the research was not explicitly designed to investigate environmental factors. If the relationship of environmental factors to treatment outcomes were a primary focus of research, more appropriate research questions could be phrased (Israel, 1980), and several new areas of research could be explored, as noted next.

ENVIRONMENTAL FACTORS AND PERSON–ENVIRONMENT INTERACTIONS

Which environmental factors are important? Presently, research addressing this question must be considered as exploratory. In this regard, large-scale correlative and multivariate studies are likely to have considerable value in identifying relevant environmental events. When possible, variables should be operationally defined and quantitatively scaled. Open-ended probing, however, is also likely to yield meaningful information. For example, in a study of the natural recovery process, Tuchfeld (1976, 1981) conducted open-ended interviews and found that a large proportion of former problem drinkers reported that prior to resolving their drinking problem, they had first successfully achieved control over other behaviors, most notably smoking. This suggests that self-efficacy-enhancing experiences (Bandura, 1977) might prepare an individual for successfully dealing with drinking problems and that treatments might be designed to include a graduated series of self-control exercises.

Another area needing investigation is the identification of factors related to different types of outcomes; such findings might have immediate applicability for differential treatment planning. Also, it seems likely that person–environment interactions will be an increasing focus of research. For example, if we except that differences in coping abilities influence treatment outcomes, then the same environmental factors might be expected to have different effects on outcomes for different individuals. As a start, exploratory research examining how individuals successfully or unsuccessfuly cope with self-identified positive and negative life events is needed. However this type of research proceeds, problems surrounding how to validly assess environmental influences may also develop. For example, when factors are readily amenable to objective assessment (e.g., job loss, divorce, having a child), there are few measurement problems. However, occasions will arise when important variables are largely defined by patients' interpretations, which, of course, are vulnerable to subjective distortions (Skinner & Sheu, 1982). This problem is particularly acute with retrospective studies. Finally, if cognitive variables (e.g., patients' interpretations of environmental influences) are important mediating links in person–environment interactions, then evaluations limited to objectively verifiable events may not be sensitive to these variables.

A final concern relates to the premature termination of treatment. Engaging in treatment involves personal costs for patients (monetary and nonmonetary—time, reactions of significant others, changed social relationships), and these costs must be weighed against patients' perceived long-term benefits of treatment. To this end, Moos and his colleagues (Moos, Finney, & Cronkite, 1980) have suggested that attention to extra-treatment factors affecting decisions to remain in or leave treatment could have distinct clinical benefit. Unfortunately, this also is a neglected area of research.

TARGET POPULATIONS

Investigations of different subject populations might be expected to provide different perspectives on posttreatment factors related to treatment outcome. The most obvious population type consists of clinically treated persons. Here, it would seem fruitful to examine the ways that specific treatment components might interact with environmental factors, both during and after treatment. For example, if patients were given training in problem-solving skills (Sobell & Sobell, 1978) or social skills (Chaney et al., 1978), then one could evaluate the extent to which those skills were used by patients after treatment to cope with potential relapse situations. This problem is particularly suited to multivariate research (see the models used by Cronkite & Moos, 1980, and by Polich *et al.*, 1981).

A second population that merits study is individuals who have recovered from alcohol problems without formal treatment. In fact, several years ago Orford and Edwards (1977) suggested that such studies may be particularly valuable to the development and evaluation of new treatment strategies (i.e., factors associated with the natural recovery process could be specifically evaluated as part of a treatment study). The previously cited example from the Tuchfeld studies (1976, 1981) provides a good example of the potential treatment implications of such research.

The final population deserving investigation involves normal drinkers. As Ewing (1980) has pointed out, very little research has been conducted examining protective factors of alcohol problems for the general drinking population. Although such factors may well be biological in nature (Goodwin, 1980), environmental circumstances and individual differences in response styles must also be considered. Because environmental factors can be expected to affect all populations, it will be important to determine whether subpopulations can be characterized in terms of their being differentially vulnerable to, or having different response patterns to, different types of environmental influences.

SUMMARY AND CONCLUSIONS

Environmental factors have been found to be significantly related to the outcomes of treated alcohol abusers as well as individuals who have recovered without formal treatment. These factors, therefore, should be considered throughout the entire course of treatment, including the design, assessment, delivery, and evaluation of treatment. Unfortunately, most published studies suggesting that environmental factors may play a role in determining outcomes have been retrospective and correlative. Although a variety of viable prospective research strategies exist, to date little empirical work of this nature has been published.

It is clear that the investigation of environmental factors related to alcohol treatment outcomes is a fertile area for research. Further, this type of research is viewed as being able to enhance our understanding of the natural history of alcohol problems, as well as having implications for the conduct of treatment. Social learning approaches to treatment, in particular, can be expected to benefit from knowledge resulting from such research. Finally, it is argued that research in this area would be more valuable if it had a primary rather than an ancillary research focus.

REFERENCES

Agras, W. S., & Berkowitz, R. Clinical research in behavior therapy: Halfway there. *Behavior Therapy*, 1980, *11*, 472–487.

Allman, L. R., Taylor, H. A., & Nathan, P. E. Group drinking during stress: Effects on drinking behavior, affect, and psychopathology. *American Journal of Psychiatry*, 1972, *129*, 669–678.

Alterman, L. R., Gottheil, E., Skoloda, T. E., & Grasberger, J. C. Social modification of drinking in alcoholics. *Quarterly Journal of Studies on Alcohol*, 1974, *35*, 917–924.

Azrin, N. H. Improvements in the community-reinforcement approach to alcoholism. *Behaviour Research and Therapy*, 1976, *14*, 339–348.

Bandura, A. Self-efficacy: Toward a unifying theory of behavior change. *Psychological Review*, 1977, *84*, 191–215.

Barbarin, O. A. Recidivism in drug analysis. *Addictive Behaviors*, 1979, *4*, 121–132.

Becker, H. Becoming a marijuana user. *American Journal of Sociology*, 1963, *59*, 235–242.

Bigelow, G., Liebson, I., & Griffiths, A. Alcoholic drinking: Suppression by a brief time-out procedure. *Behaviour Research and Therapy*, 1974, *12*, 107–115.

Blakey, R., & Baker, R. An exposure approach to alcohol abuse. *Behaviour Research and Therapy*, 1980, *18*, 319–325.

Bromet, E., & Moos, R. H. Environmental resources and the posttreatment functioning of alcohol patients. *Journal of Health and Social Behavior*, 1977, *18*, 326–338.

Brown, R. A., & Williams, R. J. Internal and external cues relating to fluid intake in obese and alcoholic persons. *Journal of Abnormal Psychology*, 1975, *84*, 660–665.

Buck, F. M. A test of heightened external responsiveness in an alcoholic population. *Journal of Abnormal Psychology*, 1979, *88*, 361–368.

Calahan, D. *Problem drinkers.* San Francisco: Jossey-Bass, 1970.

Casey, R. L., Masuda, M., & Holmes, T. H. Quantitative study of recall of life events. *Journal of Psychosomatic Research*, 1967, *11*, 239–247.

Caudill, B. D., & Lipscomb, T. R. Modeling influences on alcoholics' rates of alcohol consumption. *Journal of Applied Behavior Analysis*, 1980, *13*, 355–365.

Caudill, B. D., & Marlatt, G. A. Modeling influences in social drinking: An experimental analogue. *Journal of Consulting and Clinical Psychology*, 1975, *43*, 405–415.

Chaney, E. F., O'Leary, M. R., & Marlatt, G. A. Skill training with alcoholics. *Journal of Consulting and Clinical Psychology*, 1978, *48*, 1092–1104.

Clum, G. A. Intrapsychic variables and the patient's environment as factors in prognosis. *Psychological Bulletin*, 1975, *82*, 413–431.

Cohen, M., Liebson, I. A., Faillace, L. A., & Allen, R. P. Moderate drinking by chronic alcoholics. *Journal of Nervous and Mental Disease*, 1971, *153*, 434–444.

Costello, R. H. Alcoholism aftercare and outcome: Cross-lagged panel and path analyses. *British Journal of Addiction*, 1980, *75*, 49–53.

Cronkite, R. C., & Moos, R. H. Evaluating alcoholism treatment programs: An integrated approach. *Journal of Consulting and Clinical Psychology,*. 1978, *46*, 1105–1119.

Cronkite, R. C., & Moos, R. H. Determinants of the posttreatment functioning of alcoholic patients: A conceptual framework. *Journal of Consulting and Clinical Psychology*, 1980, *48*, 305–316.

Cummings, C., Gordon, J. R., & Marlatt, G. A. Relapse: Prevention and prediction. In W. R. Miller (Ed.), *The addictive behaviors.* New York: Pergamon, 1980.

Cushman, P. Detoxification of rehabilitated methadone patients: Frequency and predictors of long-term success. *American Journal of Drug and Alcohol Abuse*, 1974, *1*, 393–408.

de Lint, J., & Schmidt, W. The epidemiology of alcoholism. In Y. Israel & J. Mardones (Eds.), *Biological basis of alcoholism.* New York: Wiley, 1971.

Dohrenwend, B. P. Sociocultural and socio-psychological factors in the genesis of mental disorders. *Journal of Health and Social Behavior,* 1975, *16,* 365–392.

Ewing, J. A. Biopsychosocial approaches to drinking and alcoholism. In W. E. Fann, I. Karacan, A. D. Pokorny, & R. L. Williams (Eds.), *Phenomenology and treatment of alcoholism.* New York: Spectrum, 1980.

Foy, D. W., Miller, P. M., Eisler, R. M., & O'Toole, D. H. Social-skills training to teach alcoholics to refuse drinks effectively. *Journal of Studies on Alcohol,* 1976, *37,* 1340–1345.

Funderburk, F. R., & Allen, R. P. Alcoholics' disposition to drink: Effects of abstinence and heavy drinking. *Journal of Studies on Alcohol,* 1977, *38,* 410–425. (a)

Funderburk, F. R., & Allen, R. P. Assessing the alcoholic's disposition to drink. In M. Gross (Ed.), *Alcohol intoxication and withdrawal* (Vol. 3). New York: Plenum Press, 1977. (b)

Gallen, M. Toward an understanding of follow-up research with alcoholics. *Psychological Reports,* 1974, *34,* 877–878.

Garlington, W. K., & DeRicco, D. A. The effect of modelling on drinking rate. *Journal of Applied Behavioral Analysis,* 1977, *10,* 207–211.

Goodwin, D. W. The genetics of alcoholism *Substance and Alcohol Actions/Misuse,* 1980, *1,* 101–117.

Gottlieb, B. H. Social support as a focus of integrative research in psychology. *American Psychologist,* 1983, *38,* 278–287.

Harding, W. M., Zinberg, N. E., Stelmack, S. M., & Barry, M. Formerly addicted now controlled opiate users. *International Journal of the Addictions,* 1980, *15,* 47–60.

Hodgson, R., & Rankin, H. Modification of excessive drinking by cue exposure. *Behaviour Research and Therapy,* 1976, *14,* 305–307.

Hunt, G. M., & Azrin, N. H. A community-reinforcement approach to alcoholism. *Behaviour Research and Therapy,* 1973, *11,* 91–104.

Israel, Y. What makes good research, 1. *British Journal of Addictions,* 1980, *75,* 339–341.

Jenkins, C. D., Hurst, M. W., & Rose, R. M. Life changes: Do people really remember? *Archives of General Psychiatry,* 1979, *36,* 379–384.

Kazdin, A. E., & Wilson, G. T. *Evaluation of behavior therapy: Issues, evidence and research strategies.* Cambridge, Mass.: Ballinger, 1978.

King, L. M. Social and cultural influences on psychopathology. *Annual Review of Psychology,* 1978, *29,* 405–433.

Kiritz, S., & Moos, R. H. Physiological effects of social environments. *Psychosomatic Medicine,* 1974, *36,* 96–114.

LaDouceur, R., & Auger, J. Where have all the follow-ups gone? *The Behavior Therapist,* 1980, *3,* 10–11.

La Rocco, J. M., House, J. S., & French, J. R. P. Social support, occupational stress and health. *Journal of Health and Social Behavior,* 1980, *21,* 202–218.

Ludwig, A. M. On and off the wagon: Reasons for drinking and abstaining by alcoholics. *Quarterly Journal of Studies on Alcohol,* 1972, *33,* 91–96.

Ludwig, A. M., Wikler, A., & Stark, L. H. The first drink: Psychobiological aspects of craving. *Archives of General Psychiatry,* 1974, *30,* 539–547.

Maisto, S. A., & Cooper, A. M. A historical perspective on alcohol and drug treatment outcome research. In L. C. Sobell, M. B. Sobell, & E. Ward (Eds.), *Evaluating alcohol and drung abuse treatment effectiveness: Recent advances.* New York: Pergamon, 1980.

Marlatt, G. A. Craving for alcohol, loss of control and relapse: A cognitive-behavioral analysis. In P. E. Nathan, G. A. Marlatt, & T. Løberg (Eds.), *Alcoholism: New directions in behavioral research and treatment.* New York: Plenum Press, 1978.

Marlatt, G. A., & Gordon, J. R. Determinants of relapse: Implications for the maintenance of behavior change. In P. Davidson (Ed.), *Behavioral medicine: Changing health lifestyles.* New York: Brunner/Mazel, 1980.

Marlatt, G. A., & Marques, J. K. Meditation, self-control and alcohol use. In R. B. Stuart (Ed.), *Behavioral self-management: Strategies, techniques and outcomes.* New York: Brunner/Mazel, 1977.

Mash, E. J., & Terdal, L. G. (Eds.), *Behavior therapy assessment, diagnosis, design and evaluation.* New York: Springer, 1976.

Mello, N. K., & Mendelson, J. H. Operant analysis of drinking patterns of chronic alcoholics. *Nature,* 1965, *206,* 43–46.

Miller, P. M. A behavioral intervention program for chronic public drunkenness offenders. *Archives of General Psychiatry,* 1975, *32,* 915–922.

Miller, W. R. (Ed.). *The addictive behaviors.* New York: Pergamon Press, 1980.

Mischel, W. Toward a cognitive social learning reconceptualization of personality. *Psychological Review,* 1973, *80,* 252–283.

Monroe, S. M. Life events assessment: Current practices, emerging trends. *Clinical Psychology Review,* 1982, *2,* 435–453. (a)

Monroe, S. M. The assessment of life events: Retrospective versus concurrent strategies. *Archives of General Psychiatry,* 1982, *39,* 606–610. (b)

Moos, R. H., Finney, J. W., & Cronkite, R. C. The need for a paradigm shift in evaluations of treatment outcome: Extrapolations from the Rand research. *British Journal of Addictions,* 1980, *75,* 347–350.

Moos, R. H., Cronkite, R. C., & Finney, J. W. A conceptual framework for alcoholism treatment evaluation. In E. M. Pattison & E. Kaufman (Eds.), *Encyclopedic handbook of alcoholism.* New York: Gardner, 1982.

Noel, N. E., Sobell, L. C., Cellucci, T., Nirenberg, T., & Sobell, M. B. Behavioral treatment of outpatient problem drinkers: Five clinical case studies. In W. M. Hay & P. E. Nathan (Eds.), *Clinical case studies in the behavioral treatment of alcoholism,* New York: Plenum Press, 1982.

Ogborne, A. C., & Stimson, G. V. Follow-up of a representative sample of heroin addicts. *The International Journal of the Addictions,* 1975, *10,* 1061–1071.

Orford, J., & Edwards, G. *Alcoholism: A comparison of treatment and advice, with a study of the influence of marriage.* England: Oxford University Press, 1977.

Orford, J., & Feldman, P. (Eds.). *Psychological problems: The social context.* New York: Wiley, 1980.

Pattison, E. M., Sobell, M. B., & Sobell, L. C. *Emerging concepts of alcohol dependence.* New York: Springer, 1977.

Phillips, J. S., & Bierman, K. L. Clinical psychology: Individual methods. *Annual Review of Psychology,* 1981, *32,* 405–438.

Polich, J. M., Armor, D. J., & Braiker, H. B. *The course of alcoholism: Four years after treatment.* New York: Wiley, 1981.

Popham, R. E., Schmidt, W., & de Lint, J. The effects of legal restraint on drinking. In B. Kissin & H. Begleiter (Eds.), *The biology of alcoholism,* (Vol. 4). New York: Plenum Press, 1976.

Rabkin, J. G., & Struening, E. L. Life events, stress, and illness. *Science,* 1976, *194,* 1013–1020.

Rubington, E. Drug addiction as a deviant career. *International Journal of the Addictions,* 1967, *2,* 3–20.

Sadava, S. W., & Forsyth, R. Turning on, turning off, and relapse: Social psychological determinants of status change in cannabis use. *International Journal of the Addictions,* 1977, *12,* 509–528.

Saunders, W. M., & Kershaw, P. W. Spontaneous remission from alcoholism—A community study. *British Journal of Addiction,* 1979, *74,* 251–265.

Schasre, E. Cessation patterns among neophyte heroin users. *International Journal of the Addictions,* 1966, *1,* 23–32.

Skinner, H. A., & Sheu, W. Reliability of alcohol use indices: The Lifetime Drinking History and the MAST. *Journal of Studies on Alcohol,* 1982, *43,* 1157–1170.

Smart, R. B. Spontaneous recovery in alcoholics: A review and analysis of the available research. *Drug and Alcohol Dependence,* 1975/1976, *1,* 277–285.

Snarr, R. W., & Ball, J. C. Involvement in a drug subculture and abstinence following treatment among Puerto Rican narcotic addicts. *British Journal of Addiction,* 1974, *69,* 243–249.

Sobell, L. C., & Sobell, M. B. Frequent follow-up with alcohol abusers as data gathering and after care. *International Journal of Addictions,* 1981, *16,* 1077–1086.

Sobell, L. C., & Sobell, M. B. Alcoholism treatment outcome evaluation methodology. In Alcohol and Health Monograph No. 3, *Prevention, intervention and treatment: Concerns and models.* Rockville, Md.: National Institute on Alcohol Abuse and Alcoholism, 1982.

Sobell, L. C., Sobell, M. B., & Nirenberg, T. Differential treatment planning for alcohol abusers. In E. M. Pattison & E. Kaufman (Eds.), *Encyclopedic handbook of alcoholism.* New York: Gardner Press, 1982.

Sobell, M. B. & Sobell, L. C. *Behavioral treatment of alcohol problems: Individualized therapy and controlled drinking.* New York: Plenum Press, 1978.

Sobell, M. B., Sobell, L. C., Ersner-Hershfield, S., & Nirenberg, T. Alcohol and drug problems. In A. S. Bellack, M. Hersen, & A. E. Kazdin (Eds.), *International handbook of behavior modification and therapy.* New York: Plenum Press, 1982.

Stall, R. An examination of spontaneous remission from problem drinking in the bluegrass region of Kentucky. *Journal of Drug Issues,* 1983, *13,* 191–206.

Strauss, J. S. Social and cultural influences on psychopathology. *Annual Review of Psychology,* 1979, *30,* 397–415.

Surrvali, H., & Shain, M. *The relationship between environmental aspects of work, mental health and drinking practices: Evidence and proposals* (Substudy No. 1172). Toronto Addiction Research Foundation, 1981.

Tuchfeld, B. S. *Changes in patterns of alcohol use without the aid of formal treatment: An exploratory study of former problem drinkers* (Final Report, Contract No: ADM 281-75-0023; RTI Project 24U-1158). Research Triangle Park, N.C.: Research Triangle Institute, August 1976.

Tuchfeld, B. S. Spontaneous remission in alcoholics; Empirical observations and theoretical implications. *Journal of Studies on Alcohol,* 1981, *42,* 626–641.

Tucker, J. A., Vuchinich, R. E., & Sobell, M. B. Differential discriminative stimulus control of nonalcoholic beverage consumption in alcoholics and normal drinkers. *Journal of Abnormal Psychology,* 1979, *88,* 145–152.

Vaillant, G. E. Paths out of alcoholism. In National Institute of Alcohol Abuse and Alcoholism Research Monograph No. 5, *Evaluation of the alcoholic: Implications for research, theory and treatment.* Washington, D.C.: National Institute of Alcohol Abuse and Alcoholism, 1981.

Vaillant, G. E., & Milofsky, E. S. The etiology of alcoholism: A prospective viewpoint. *American Psychologist,* 1982, *37,* 494–503.

Ward, D. A., Bendel, R. B., & Lange, D. A reconsideration of environmental resources and the posttreatment functioning of alcoholic patients. *Journal of Health and Social Behavior,* 1982, *23,* 310–317.

Whitehead, P. An epidemiological description of the development of drug dependence: Environmental factors and prevention. *American Journal of Drug and Alcohol Abuse,* 1976, *3,* 323–338.

Williams, R. J. Effects of deprivation and pre-loading on the experimental consumption of tea by alcoholics and social drinkers. *British Journal of Addiction,* 1977, *72,* 31–35.

CHAPTER 12

Determinants of
Substance Abuse Relapse

JALIE A. TUCKER, RUDY E. VUCHINICH, and CAROLE V. HARRIS

Research on the short-term effectiveness of treatments for alcohol, cigarette, and drug abuse suggests that most individuals may expect immediate amelioration of their problem upon entering a formal treatment program (e.g., Dole & Joseph, 1978; Lichtenstein, 1982; Miller & Hester, 1980). The prognosis over the long run, however, is not so optimistic. Approximately two-thirds of individuals who successfully complete treatment programs for various substance abuse disorders relapse within 3 months after treatment. At 12 months, relapse rates often exceed 75% or more (e.g., Hunt, Barrett, & Branch, 1971; Marlatt, 1978; Schachter, 1982). These high relapse rates appear to be relatively independent of the particular addictive disorder, the type of treatment intervention, or its guiding conceptual framework. Such findings force consideration of the determinants of relapse as a core problem in substance abuse research and treatment.

In their seminal work on substance abuse relapse, Marlatt and his colleagues (Cummings, Gordon, & Marlatt, 1980; Marlatt, 1978; Marlatt & Gordon, 1980) distinguished two general strategies for approaching the relapse problem. One assumes that the treatment interventions are in-

JALIE A. TUCKER, RUDY E. VUCHINICH, and CAROLE V. HARRIS • Department of Psychiatry and Center for Alcohol Research, University of Florida, Gainesville, Florida 32610. Preparation of this manuscript was supported in part by Grant No. 1-P50-AA05793 from the National Institute on Alcohol Abuse and Alcoholism.

adequate. Treatment packages are then expanded, often in a "shotgun" fashion, in the hope of more fully eliminating the substance abuse disorder (Marlatt & Gordon, 1980, pp. 410–411). However, because such "broad spectrum" treatments typically fail to effect further reductions in posttreatment relapses, the authors argued convincingly for a second strategy: once behavior change is initiated through professional treatments or other means (e.g., self-help, environmental transitions), what variables, broadly defined, in the individual's natural environment converge to produce either continued behavior maintenance or disruption of the behavior change—that is, relapse? When conceived in this second manner, the development of more comprehensive and presumably more effective therapeutic interventions to reduce relapse rates seems premature without an understanding of the variables that precipitate relapse episodes in the environments in which they occur. For this reason, this chapter reviews the available evidence pertaining to the determinants of substance abuse relapse, including alcohol, smoking, and drug (mainly heroin) relapses.

A number of different kinds of evidence can inform an analysis of the relapse problem, two of which are beyond the scope of this chapter. First, given the parsimonious assumption that variations in substance use behaviors lie on a continuum and that the variables that control substance use also lie on continuua (e.g., Pattison, Sobell, & Sobell, 1977), the question of why individuals relapse is a small part of the larger question of why individuals use such substances at all. Evidence bearing on this larger issue could fill a library, let alone a book chapter. We must therefore exclude from the review the vast majority of studies that address the determinants of substance use in both clinical and normal populations.

Second, strictly speaking, all studies of substance abuse treatment outcome are relevant to addressing the relapse problem. Because of the volume of this literature and the availability of several excellent reviews (Lichtenstein, 1982; Miller & Hester, 1980; Ogborne, 1978), the bulk of these studies are excluded here. Equally important, however, is that most treatment outcome studies are informative only about the incidence, and not the determinants, of relapses following treatment. Moreover, even though certain treatment-related variables may predict short-term outcomes, relapse rates over more extended temporal intervals are generally high regardless of the type of treatment administered. This implies that the determinants of relapse may be relatively unrelated to treatment variables.

Therefore, this chapter is limited to a review of research concerned primarily with the prediction and determinants of relapse following cessation of alcohol, tobacco, and heroin abuse, with or without professional help. The literature included is quite diverse; in all three substance abuse domains a variety of personality, demographic, cognitive, physiological, environmental, and behavioral variables have been investigated, and many different conceptual systems have been employed to impose order on the relapse data. Notwithstanding this diversity, the majority of studies fall within one of two general classes: (1) studies that seek to identify predictors of relapse over time or that assess differences in relevant variables between groups of relapsed and nonrelapsed subjects; and (2) studies that investigate specific events surrounding discrete relapse episodes of (former) substance abusers who have remained abstinent for a period of time. Because the available evidence suggests that studies of the latter type are more likely to yield informative generalizations about the determinants of relapse, within each substance domain the present review is organized according to these two general classes of studies.

After the review, consistencies that exist across substance abuse areas in the variables that influence relapse are summarized; the limited evidence available suggests that specific environmental events and transitions are important determinants of substance abuse relapse. Then, methodological problems in the relevant research are described, followed by a discussion of the more difficult and underresearched issue of which aspects of the substance abuser's natural environment should be measured if the variables controlling relapse occurrences are to be identified for eventual use in developing effective prevention strategies. This final section is guided by recent work on behavioral-economic theories of choice (e.g., Rachlin, Battalio, Kagel, & Green, 1981) as applied to substance abuse and by our own research on alcoholic relapse.

ISSUES REGARDING THE DEFINITION OF RELAPSE

In the most general sense, using the term *relapse* to refer to an individual's status during a posttreatment interval implies that he or she is once again exhibiting the problems for which he or she originally entered treatment. Defining relapse therefore is, in many ways, equivalent to defining substance abuse problems in general. This task, unfortunately, is not as easy as one might suppose (cf. Babor, 1981). When abstinence is considered the only viable goal of treatment, relapse is easily defined as any use of the abused substance after treatment. It is now recognized, however, that substance use behavior may be only one of several dimensions along which populations of substance abusers must be characterized, with functioning in the areas of work, interpersonal relations, and physical health having considerable clinical importance. Moreover, individuals may be considerably improved despite the fact that they continue to use a given substance, and relationships between substance use and functioning in the other areas are not well understood. For these reasons, no universally accepted definition of relapse exists, and studies differ widely in how the term is used. In this chapter, we focus on substance use behaviors as the main characteristic of relapse and describe the various authors' definitions in the review of studies.

As a further consideration, the same definition of relapse probably will not be equally useful for clinical and research purposes. For clinical purposes, an individual's impairment must be judged at least with respect to the substance use, physical dependence, and any adverse consequences of the substance use. Although an individual's location in this array will be the result of the convergence of numerous variables operating at different levels and in different time frames, the practical clinician often must override this complexity and make a dichotomous judgment. In a research context, however, attending to the nuances and continuous nature of these relationships and inquiring into variables related to nonproblem substance use are important because they may be the same as those that control the manifestation of behavior at the problem end of the continuum.

A final definitional consideration is whether it may be overly restrictive to limit the notion of relapse to changes in substance use in treatment populations. As two authors have noted (e.g., Schachter, 1982; Tuchfield, 1981), receipt of formal treatment may be only one of many variables that affect substance use. Although the majority of studies reviewed involve treatment populations, studies of relapse in substance abusers who quit without professional help are also included.

ALCOHOLIC RELAPSE

The disease model of alcoholism (e.g., Jellinek, 1960) exerts considerable influence in the literature on alcoholic relapse, if not as a directive conceptual framework, then at least as an orientation against which virtually all the evidence is compared. The model's concepts of craving for alcohol and loss of control over drinking have suffered cogent criticism as explanations of relapse (e.g., Marlatt, 1978), and most would agree that these notions are without empirical or clinical utility. Ludwig and Wikler (1974), on the other hand, argued that craving is a viable concept and proposed a revised version that interprets the phenomenon in terms of classical conditioning and cognitive labeling of physiological arousal. In his critique, however, Marlatt (1978) maintained that this revised notion of craving suffers the same conceptual problems as the original version and that the relevant evidence does not support Ludwig and Wikler's (1974) reformulation.

Regardless of the explanatory mechanisms, the empirical implications of Ludwig and Wikler's hypothesis are useful in that they suggest a search for correlations between environmental events and drinking behavior. The discovery of such correlations would be helpful even though they may be more usefully interpreted with concepts other than classical conditioning and cognitive labeling. Much the same may be said of the notion of *loss of control* over drinking. Evidence of nonabstinent but successful treatment outcomes (e.g., Heather & Robertson, 1981; Sobell, 1978) has esentially disproved the classical formulation of loss of control. Nevertheless, the general relationship proposed in the loss-of-control notion between alcohol consumption at one point in time and the likelihood of continued or increased consumption at later times remains a legitimate empirical question.

An increasingly popular, cognitive/social learning formulation of relapse (Marlatt, 1978) has a two-sequence structure that at an empirical level is not unlike the two-stage disease model of relapse. The first stage, or the variables leading to the first drinking episode, involves the individual entering a "high-risk" situation for which alcohol consumption is his or her most effective coping response. The second stage, or the variables leading to continued or later consumption, involves a sequence of the cognitive states of cognitive dissonance and internal attributions for failure, which promote further drinking.

These are the dominant themes in current conceptualizations of the process of alcoholic relapse. Other, less dominant, approaches have been proposed, but they are best discussed later with the appropriate data.

PREDICTIVE AND CORRELATIONAL STUDIES OF ALCOHOLIC RELAPSE

Multiple Follow-Up Treatment Outcome Studies

Five studies involved multiple follow-up assessments of alcoholic patients over extended time periods after treatment. Armor, Polich, and Stambul (1978) assessed 220 patients at 6 and 18 months following treatment; Polich, Armor, and Braiker (1981) assessed 475 patients, some of whom were the same patients in the Armor *et al.* (1978) report, at 18 and 48 months; Paredes, Gregory, Rundell, and Williams (1979) assessed 279 patients at 6 and 18 months; Finney and Moos (1981) assessed 120 patients at 6 and 24 months; and Moberg, Krause, and Klein (1982) assessed 569 patients at 3 months and a subset of 213 patients at 9 months. In each study, the patients were interviewed at both follow-up points and placed in one of several outcome status categories on the basis of their drinking behavior. Although the studies differed somewhat in the criteria used to define the categories, all had abstinent, controlled or moderate drinking, and relapsed or nonremission categories. The relevant data from these studies are percentages of patients in each outcome status at the later follow-up in relation to their status at the earlier follow-up, which address the relationship between drinking behavior at different points in time.

With the exception of the data reported by Armor *et al.* (1978), in each study a higher percentage of patients were categorized as relapsed at the second follow-up if they had also been drinking at the time of the first follow-up. The patients most likely to have relapsed at the second follow-up were those who were categorized as relapsed at the first follow-up, whereas the patients least likely to have relapsed at the second follow-up were those who had been abstinent for 6 months or more at the first follow-up.

Overall, these studies suggest that drinking during the early periods of the posttreatment interval is related to increased risk of problem drinking and relapse during later periods. For two reasons, however, this generalization should be considered extremely weak, especially as it may apply to the drinking behavior of any particular individual. First, substantial proportions of individual subjects showed variable drinking patterns over the follow-up periods and thus fluctuated between outcome status categories; most transitions occurred in the direction of decreased improvement, but increased improvement was not uncommon. Second, Polich *et al.* (1981) found that certain life circumstances during the follow-up intervals (e.g., marriage) may dramatically modify the relationship between drinking behavior at different points during the interval. For example, for subjects over 40 years of age with medium dependence symptoms at intake and for subjects under 40 with severe dependence, those who were married had lower relapse rates at 4 years if they abstained at 18 months, whereas those who were not married had lower relapse rates at 4 years if they engaged in nonproblem drinking at 18 months.

These considerations suggest that the relationship between drinking behavior at different points in time is at best indirect and that drinking at any time may be more directly related to individuals' current life circumstances than to earlier or later alcohol consumption. This possibility has important implications for approaching the relapse problem.

First, the empirical relationship indicated by the loss-of-control notion and the proposed explanatory mechanisms are questioned, in that alcohol consumption by an individual early in the posttreatment interval does not always predate a protracted relapse. Second, the structural requirement that relapse models contain two conceptually distinct stages also is questioned. Rather than positing stages that connect drinking behavior at different points in time to each other, perhaps we need a model that connects drinking behavior episodes of various durations and intensities to the environmental circumstances that exist at the time the episode occurs.

Social-Learning Approaches to Relapse

Applications of social learning theory to alcoholic relapse have emphasized coping skills and cognitive expectations as determinants of relapse episodes. Three studies (Litman, Eiser, Rawson, & Oppenheim, 1977, 1979; Rosenberg, 1983) used cross-sectional designs to investigate differences along these dimensions between groups of relapsed and abstinent alcoholics, and two studies (Eastman & Norris, 1983, Study 3; Rist & Watzl, 1983) used prospective methods to assess their value in predicting relapses after treatment.

Litman *et al.* (1977, 1979) developed a questionnaire regarding relapse-related issues, which was administered to 120 inpatient and outpatient alcoholics and an unspecified number of "former" alcoholic patients. Of the total sample, 49 subjects had relapsed (no definition of relapse was given) within 2 weeks prior to completing the questionnaire, and 29 subjects had not relapsed for 6 months or more. A discriminant function analysis performed on the data from these 78 subjects found five variables that best distinguished between the two subject groups. "Cognitive control," physical dependence, age, and "positive thinking" were higher in the group that had not relapsed, whereas those who had relapsed reported more situations as dangerous for relapse.

Rosenberg (1983) assessed differences in coping skills, life events, and social suports between 22 relapsed and 20 nonrelapsed veterans who had completed an inpatient tratment program. The nonrelapsed patients had been abstinent or controlled drinkers (i.e., less than 3 oz of ethanol per day) for at least 6 months, and the relapsed patients had returned to the hospital for detoxification. No differences were found between the groups on the social support measures. Although the total number of life events was the same for the two groups, nonrelapsed subjects reported more positive changes and less negative changes than did relapsed subjects. On the coping skills measures, nonrelapsers were less compliant in drinking situations requiring assertiveness and were more likely to report that they would not drink in the situations.

Eastman and Norris (1982, Study 3) investigated the relationship between expectations of alcohol's effects and relapse in 62 males and 27 females in outpatient treatment for alcohol problems. Fifty-two subjects had at least some positive expectations about alcohol, and 37 subjects had completely negative expectations. Within 2 months after the assessment, 71% of the subjects with positive expectations relapsed (i.e., drank any alcohol), whereas only 7% of the subjects with negative expectations relapsed during this period. In addition, 44 of the subjects had rated the likelihood that they would relapse on a 7-point scale, and 77% of these subjects who gave ratings of 5 or more relapsed.

Rist and Watzl (1983) assessed the assertiveness skills of 145 females in an inpatient alcohol treatment program. At 3 and 18 months following their discharge, the subjects were interviewed regarding their drinking behavior. Two outcome categories were used for the 3-month follow-up data, abstinent ($n = 82$) and relapsed ($n = 63$), with relapse defined as any drinking during the 3 months; three categories were used at 18 months, abstinent ($n = 47$), improved ($n = 26$), and unimproved or worse ($n = 72$). For the 3-month outcomes, subjects who relapsed had reported lower assertiveness while in treatment, but for the 18-month outcomes no differences were found in any of the ratings that the subjects had made during treatment.

These studies suggest that some of the variables made salient in a social learning approach may be worth investigating. A relationship seems to exist between certain aspects of coping skills in social situations and relapse, but this relationship is relatively weak and dissipates over time. Also, at least over the short run, subjects seem fairly accurate in being able to predict the occurrence of their relapses, and those who view the effects of alcohol positively seem more likely to relapse than those who view them negatively.

STUDIES OF EVENTS SURROUNDING ALCOHOLIC RELAPSE EPISODES

Several studies have investigated possible relationships between stressful life events and drinking episodes in alcoholics during the posttreatment interval. At a general level, Moos, Bromet, Tsu, and Moos (1979) and Finney, Moos, and Mewborn (1980) have reported small but statistically significant correlations between negative life events and patients' functioning during posttreatment intervals. Of perhaps greater interest are several studies that investigated this relationship at a more detailed level. In a prospective study of relapse determinants, Hore (1971) had 14 outpatient alcoholics report weekly on any alcohol consumption and the occurrence of significant life events; they reported daily on levels of anxiety and depression for up to 6 months. Relapse was defined as any drinking behavior. Although there was no overall correlation between the number of events and number of relapses, Hore noted a temporal relationship between events and relapse for 7 of the 14 subjects. The subjects' reported levels of anxiety and depression were not related to relapse episodes.

Other investigators have retrospectively assessed the role of life events in relapse episodes by asking groups of relapsed alcoholics about the reasons for their drinking episodes. Ludwig (1972) interviewed 161 alcoholics who had relapsed (defined as any drinking) within 1 year after treatment and asked them the reasons for drinking. These stated reasons were categorized by Ludwig as follows: (1) psychological distress, 25%; (2) no specified reason, 19%; (3) family problems, 13%; (4) the effects of alcohol or pleasure, 11%; (5) sociability, 10%; (6) curiosity, 7%; (7) employment problems, 5%; (8) craving, 1%; and (9) other, 9%.

In a similar series of retrospective studies, Marlatt and his colleagues asked alcoholics about the types of situations in which they took their first drink after discharge from treatment. Marlatt (1978) interviewed 48 subjects who had had at least one drink within 90 days after discharge and found that the circumstances surrounding the drinking episodes could be categorized as follows: (1) frustration and/or anger, 29%; (2) social pressure to drink, 23%; (3) intrapersonal temptation, 21%; (4) negative emotional states, 10%; and (5) other (e.g., celebration drinking), 10%. Chaney, O'Leary, and Marlatt (1978) repeated this procedure with 25 other alcoholics and found the following percentages in the same categories: (1)15.5%; (2) 17%; (3) 15.5%; (4) 43%; and (5) 9%. Marlatt and Gordon (1980) contacted 70 alcoholics within 90 days after discharge and conducted similar interviews but used a slightly expanded categorization system. According to this new system, 61% of the initial drinking episodes were due to intrapersonal determinants (negative emotional states, 38%; negative physical states, 3%; testing personal control over drinking, 9%; urges and temptations, 11%), and 39% of the episodes were due to interpersonal determinants (interpersonal conflict, 18%; social pressure, 18%; positive emotional states, 3%). In addition, 90% of the subjects had more than one drink during this initial episode, and 69% of the subjects had at least one other drinking episode prior to the interview.

These studies do not support any confident generalizations, but some tentative consistencies seem apparent. Approximately one-half of the subjects reported that their drinking episodes were related to either stressful events or a negative affective state. A smaller proportion of the subjects implicated social pressure as being related to their drinking, and a still smaller number reported that their drinking was related to positive events or feelings.

Two final studies (Hull & Young, 1983; Vuchinich & Tucker, 1984) have investigated life events as determinants of relapse from novel but quite different perspectives. Hull and Young approached the relapse problem from the perspective of Hull's self-awareness model of alcohol consumption (1981), which holds that the primary motive for drinking is that alcohol reduces self-awareness and thus precludes negative self-reactions. Thirty-five alcoholics in a detoxification program completed a self-consciousness inventory and a survey regarding life events over the past 12 months. Hull and Young predicted that life events should have no relationship to relapse in subjects who were low in self-consciousness; but, for those who were high in self-consciousness, predominantly negative events should lead to relapse, and positive events should lead to recovery. The subjects were contacted at 3 and 6 months after discharge, and relapse was defined as drinking at a level similar to that reported in the pretreatment interval. Consistent with predictions, of the high self-conscious subjects, 70% of those who had experienced predominantly negative events had relapsed at 3 months, whereas only 14% of those who had experienced positive events had relapsed. For the low self-consciousness subjects, no differences were found between those who had experienced predominantly negative or positive events. These findings are interesting, but two ambiguities in the relationship between these data and the model cloud the implications of this work for a general approach to relapse. First, it is unclear, according to the model, why individuals who are low in self-consciousness would ever have become alcoholics at all because they would not seem to have needed to drink to reduce something that was already low. Second, it is unclear why individuals who were high in self-consciousness but had experienced predominantly positive events prior to treatment would have been drinking to an extent that required treatment.

The second study was guided by the conceptual framework provided by behavioral theories of choice (cf. Vuchinich, 1982; Vuchinich & Tucker, 1983). In general, this approach suggests that alcohol consumption will vary as a function of two classes of variables: (1) the constraints that exist on access to alcohol; and (2) what other activities are also available and the constraints that exist on access to them. Because constraints on access to alcohol probably are fairly constant, variables in the second class probably are the more important determinants of alcohol consumption. As applied to an analysis of relapse, drinking episodes should be more likely after events that predict a decreased availability of activities in other life areas that are rewarding. Furthermore, such events should be more likely to produce a drinking episode if they are relevant to life–health areas that have been disrupted by the individual's alcohol consumption in the past. The framework also suggests that drinking episodes should be more likely to occur when the individual enters a situation in which alcohol is immediately available, but these episodes should be less severe than those that are related to events that signal changes in access to valued activities.

While in an inpatient treatment program, 26 alcoholics were interviewed regarding their past drinking behavior and the degree to which it had disrupted their functioning in the areas of (1) intimate relations; (2) family relations; (3) social relations; (4) vocational functioning; (5) financial status; and (6) physical health. For 6 months after discharge, subjects recorded, on a daily basis, the amount of any alcohol consumption, the situation in which the drinking occurred, and the occurrence of any life events. An event was considered to be related to a drinking episode if it occurred not more than 3 days prior to the drinking episode.

The 26 subjects reported 271 events and 133 drinking episodes during the 6-month period. Independent raters categorized the events as positive or negative and as being most relevant to one of the six life–health areas described before. The drinking episodes were categorized as *event-related* and *nonevent-related.*

Overall, the total number of negative events reported was significantly correlated with the total number of drinking episodes ($r = .63, p < .05$), but the total number of positive events was not ($r = .37$, n.s.). To evaluate the hypothesis that events relevant to life areas that had been disrupted by past alcohol use would be more likely to precipitate a drinking episode, subjects' disruption scores in the six life–health areas were individually correlated with the proportion of events that occurred in that life area that were related to a relapse episode. Significant relationships were found between disruption scores in a given life-health area and the occurrence of relevant events (1) between Intimate Relations Scores and negative events ($r = .74, n = 11, p < .05$); (2) between Family Relations Scores and total events ($r = .48, n = 13, p < .10$); (3) between Vocational Functioning Scores and total events ($r = .48, n = 16, p < .10$); (4) between Financial Status Scores and negative events ($r = -.85, n = 6, p < .05$); and (5) between Physical Health Scores and positive events ($r = -.88, n = 5, p < .05$). It had also been predicted that event-related drinking episodes would be more severe than nonevent-related relapses. Correlated groups *t*-tests for the 15 subjects who had both kinds of drinking episodes compared the number of days per episode, number of drinks per episode, and number of drinks per day during the episode. On all three measures, the event-related relapses were more severe than the nonevent-related relapses. Overall, these data are consistent with hypotheses derived from theories of choice as applied to alcoholic relapse and implicate specific life-event occurrences as important relapse determinants.

SMOKING RELAPSE

Unlike the disease model of alcoholism in research on alcoholic relapse, no single conceptual approach has been the standard against which research on smoking relapse has been evaluated. In part due to the national focus on the health hazards of smoking, such as the Surgeon General's report in 1964, research on smoking behavior and relapse has not been directly tied to changes during posttreatment intervals. Moreover, approaches to smoking recidivism based on clinical models of psychopathology are generally lacking, especially in the early research (e.g., Eisinger, 1971; Graham & Gibson, 1971). Nevertheless, as addictive behaviors have emerged in recent years as a unified area of scientific inquiry, concepts from the mainstream of psychological research and theorizing have been increasingly applied to the problem of smoking recidivism. As discussed later, among the more popular applications are studies of the role of self-efficacy expectations in smoking relapses and applications of a model of therapeutic change to the smoking cessation process. Isolated studies also have examined the relationship between smoking relapses and demographic and treatment-related variables, life events, mood states, and additional variables relevant to Marlatt's cognitive-behavioral model of relapse.

Predictive and Correlational Studies of Smoking Relapse

Self-Efficacy Studies

Three studies (Condiotte & Lichtenstein, 1981; DiClemente, 1981; McIntyre, Lichtenstein, & Mermelstein, 1983) investigated smokers' self-efficacy expectations as predictors of smoking relapses, and a fourth study (Schlegel & Kunetsky, 1977) assessed the predictive value of smokers' pretreatment treatment-outcome expectancies, which appear to be similar to the self-efficacy construct. Postulated by Bandura (1977) as a cognitive mechanism underlying behavior change, self-efficacy expectations are hypothesized to determine the initiation and maintenance of behaviors required to alter maladaptive response patterns, such as those required in smoking cessation.

In a 12-week follow-up study (Condiotte & Lichtenstein, 1981), 78 participants were assessed prior to treatment regarding their self-efficacy expectations of quitting smoking following treatment. These same variables were assessed at weekly intervals for the first 5 weeks posttreatment and then at 8 and 12 weeks posttreatment. A multiple regression analysis revealed that the higher the subjects' self-efficacy scores at treatment termination, the greater the probability that they would remain abstinent and the longer the duration of time that elapsed prior to relapse. Further analyses showed excellent correspondence between the clusters of specific situations included on the self-efficacy questionnaire in which subjects reported experiencing low self-efficacy at treatment termination and the clusters of situations in which their posttreatment relapses occurred.

McIntyre *et al.* (1983) administered the Condiotte and Lichtenstein (1981) self-efficacy scale before and after treatment to 74 smokers in a 7-week behavioral group program. Subjects' scores were examined as predictors of their smoking status at 1, 3, 6, and 12-month follow-up intervals. Subjects were dichotomized into smoking or abstinent groups, apparently based on their reported smoking behavior during the week preceding each follow-up interview; carbon monoxide measures were said to corroborate their self-reports. Abstinence rates at the end of treatment and at 3, 6, and 12 months posttreatment were 60.5%, 35.4%, 33.8%, and 20.7%, respectively. Subjects' pretreatment self-efficacy scores were unrelated to any measure of their smoking behavior, but their posttreatment scores were significantly correlated with their smoking status at all follow-up points except 1 year.

In a 5-month follow-up study (DiClemente, 1981), subjects from two commercial smoking cessation programs (combined $n = 34$) and ex-smokers who quit without professional help ($n = 29$) were administered a 12-item self-efficacy scale 4 weeks after they quit smoking. Follow-up interviews conducted 5 months later showed that 42 subjects had remained abstinent and 21 had relapsed. Abstinent subjects had significantly higher self-efficacy scores than did relapsed subjects, and relapsed subjects' self-reports regarding the precipitants of their actual relapses also showed moderate correspondence with the specific environmental situations included on the self-efficacy scale.

Schlegel and Kunetsky (1977) collected pretreatment measures of the treatment-outcome expectancies of 28 smokers in a commercial cessation program and compared their responses with those obtained from 56 untreated, matched control subjects. Immediately and 6 weeks after the

5-day program, 67.9% and 46.4% of the treatment participants had remained abstinent. Control subjects sustained their baseline smoking rates across both assessment intervals. Subjects' pretreatment expectations of achieving their treatment goals related significantly to their posttreatment smoking status. When subjects were blocked into high and low-expectancy groups, treated subjects with high expectations maintained their reductions in smoking across both posttreatment assessments, whereas treated subjects with low expectations showed a significant increase in recidivism from the immediate assessment to the 6-week posttreatment assessment, which approached the smoking levels of untreated control subjects.

Taken together, these studies support the predictive validity of the construct of self-efficacy with respect to smoking relapses over relatively short time periods (i.e., less than 1 year) following smoking cessation in both treated and untreated ex-smokers.

Transtheoretical Model of Change Studies

Three studies investigated Prochaska's (1979) "transtheoretical model" of therapeutic change as applied to smoking cessation and relapse (DiClemente & Prochaska, 1982; Prochaska & DiClemente, 1983; Prochaska, Crimi, Lapsanski, Martel, & Reid, 1982). The model posits 5 stages of change (precontemplation, contemplation, action, maintenance, and relapse) and 10 change processes that are hypothesized to be utilized differentially during the 5 change stages (consciousness raising, self-liberation, social liberation, self-reevaluation, environmental reevaluation, counterconditioning, stimulus control, reinforcement management, dramatic relief, and helping relationships).

DiClemente and Prochaska (1982) reported follow-up data pertinent to Prochaska's model that apparently were obtained from the same subjects using the same procedures employed in DiClemente's (1981) self-efficacy study. In the 1982 research, the variables of interest were subjects' scores on a "Change-Process" questionnaire developed by DiClemente (1978) to assess the 10 change processes hypothesized by the model. Subjects completed the questionnaire within 4 weeks after they quit smoking, and their change-process scores were used to predict smoking status at 5 months. Although the follow-up data showed that abstainers gained more weight and reported less difficulty in remaining abstinent than relapsers, the two groups did not differ significantly on any of the 10 change-process variables.

The two remaining studies (Prochaska et al., 1982; Prochaska & DiClemente, 1983) used cross-sectional methodologies to compare change processes reported by groups of abstinent and relapsed smokers; thus, at best, they can establish only correlational, not predictive, relationships between smoking behavior and change-process variables. In the Prochaska *et al.* study, 38 ex-smokers who had abstained for 6 months or more and 24 active smokers who had quit for a minimum of 24 hours before relapsing were administered the Change-Process questionnaire described by DiClemente and Prochaska (1982) and the self-efficacy scale developed and used by DiClemente (1981). Across all stages of change, subjects who relapsed indicated that they relied relatively more on "environmental" change processes (e.g., social liberation, social management contingencies), whereas successful abstainers reported that they relied more on "personal experiential" processes (e.g., self-liberation). Relapsers also had significantly lower self-efficacy scores, which is consistent with the studies reviewed earlier. Subjects reported the greatest relapse risks being associated with drinking coffee or tea and with experiences of both positive and negative emotional states.

In a larger, cross-sectional study involving 872 untreated subjects, Prochaska and DiClemente (1983) divided subjects into one of five groups based on their smoking behavior at the time the study was conducted: (1) long-term quitters who had remained abstinent for 6 months or more; (2) recent quitters who had been abstinent less than 6 months; (3) "contemplators" who anticipated quitting within the next year; (4) "immotives" who expressed no plans to quit; and (5) relapsers (n = 196) who had quit and then returned to smoking within the year prior to the study. All subjects completed a version of the Change-Process questionnaire used in the two earlier studies, the results of which failed to differentiate the relapsed subjects from all other groups, except from those subjects who expressed no plans to quit smoking; these "immotive" subjects reported using 8 of the 10 hypothesized change processes significantly less than any other group. Thus, the proposed model of change appears to have little value in differentiating relapsers from individuals who have either successfully quit or who are contemplating quitting. Overall, the results of these three studies provide little support for the transtheoretical model of change as applied to smoking behavior and relapse.

Demographic, Personality, and Treatment-Related Predictors of Smoking Relapse

Four longitudinal studies (Eisinger, 1971; Heinold, Garvey, Goldie, & Bossé, 1982; Pomerleau, Adkins, & Pertschuk, 1978; Prochaska & Lapsanski, 1982) examined various demographic, personality, and treatment-related predictors or relapse. Three additonal studies (Graham & Gibson,

1971; Perri, Richards, & Schultheis, 1977; Schacter, 1982) used cross-sectional designs with groups of active and former smokers to examine correlational relationships between these variables and subjects' smoking behavior.

In the study by Eisinger (1971), 570 subjects who had reported having stopped smoking in an earlier study conducted in 1964 were interviewed again in 1966 and reclassified as (continued) former smokers ($n = 497$) or as recidivists ($n = 73$). Self-report data pertinent to smoking behavior and attitudes, demographic, health, and social environmental variables were collected during both interviews and were examined as predictors of relapse in a stepwise multiple discriminant analysis. Relapsed subjects were more likely to be female, over 50 years of age, to have no small children in the home, to have relatively fewer friends who had quit smoking, and to have quit smoking shortly after the 1964 Surgeon General's report on smoking was issued. In addition, recidivists reported greater expectations of eventually experiencing smoking-related health problems and of continuing to smoke 5 years hence; they also cited the expense of smoking as a reason for having stopped smoking initially.

Prochaska and Lapsanski (1982) examined life-event occurrences during the 6 months preceding treatment in predicting the smoking status at 4-months posttreatment of 35 subjects who participated in a smoking cessation clinic. At the end of treatment, subjects who had quit ($n = 20$) had significantly lower positive and total life-event questionnaire scores that did subjects who were still smoking. At four months posttreatment, data from subjects who had relapsed ($n = 12$) were combined with those of subjects who had never quit ($n = 15$) and were compared with the responses of subjects who had remained abstinent during the follow-up interval ($n = 8$). This comparison showed only that successful abstainers had significantly lower positive (pretreatment) life-event scores.

In the prospective study by Pomerleau et al. (1978), 100 smokers who completed an 8-week behavioral program were contacted for 1- and 2-year follow-up assessments. At the end of the program, 61% of the subjects had stopped smoking, 32% were abstinent after 1 year, and 29% of the subset of subjects ($n = 56$) who were contacted after 2 years had remained abstinent. Successful outcomes at the end of treatment were predicted by (1) relatively lower pretreatment rates and duration of smoking; (2) lower body weight; and (3) compliance with the self-monitoring requirements of the program. These variables were unrelated, however, to subsequent recidivism. Instead, subjects who had reported during pretreatment assessments of smoking while experiencing dysphoric moods relapsed more than did subjects who had reported smoking while experiencing positive or neutral mood states. In addition to implicating negative mood states in relapse episodes, the results suggest that predictors of short-term treatment outcome may be relatively independent of the variables that predict relapse over more extended temporal intervals.

In the final longitudinal study of predictors of smoking relapse (Heinold *et al.*, 1982), 32 ex-smokers who had been abstinent for at least 1 year and 32 relapsed smokers were administered a smoking motives questionnaire that they had also completed 8 years earlier (in 1973) when all subjects were smoking. Responses of the two groups were similar in 1973, and those of recidivists did not change substantially across the two administrations. In contrast, ex-smokers obtained significantly higher scores from the first to the second administration on four of six smoking motives (habit, reduction of negative affect, stimulation, and sensorimotor manipulation). Although these data reveal little about motivational determinants of relapse, they make an important methodological point. As the authors noted, many cross-sectional studies that compare both active and former smokers are eliciting information that is current for smokers and that is retrospective for ex-smokers. The data obtained are thus qualitatively different and may be differentially susceptible to documented biases in recall processes (e.g., Nisbett & Wilson, 1977). For this reason, the authors argued convincingly for the use of longitudinal designs in smoking research on relapse.

In the first of three cross-sectional studies of demographic and treatment-related variables associated with smoking relapse, Graham and Gibson (1971) interviewed a large sample of subjects, who were divided into four groups based on their self-reported smoking behavior: (1) ex-smokers who had quit for a minimumn of 1 year ($n = 116$); (2) smokers who had quit for a minimum of 1 week and then relapsed ($n = 269$); (3) smokers who had never tried to quit ($n = 399$); and (4) individuals who had never smoked ($n = 205$). The results of primary interest concern those interview questions that differentiated ex-smokers from relapsed smokers. Successful quitters were more likely to have quit the first time they attempted to stop smoking (89% quit on their intitial try), whereas 42% of the relapsed smokers had stopped and then relapsed two or more times. Both subject groups reported experiencing some smoking-related withdrawal symptoms, and although the authors noted that relatively more recidivists reported such symptoms, no statistical tests were reported for this variable. Relapsed subjects also reported that they had fewer smoking-related health problems than did successful ex-smokers, but overall knowledge of the health hazards of smoking did not differentiate the groups. Finally, the smoking behavior of the subjects' immediate family related significantly with their own, particularly that of their fathers and wives; relapsed subjects were more likely to have family members who had relapsed, and successful quitters were more likely to have family members who had quit.

Perri, Richards, and Schultheis (1977) assessed self-reported differ-ences in the behavioral strategies used by ex-smokers who had quit without professional help ($n = 24$) and those used by smokers who had relapsed after quitting on their own ($n = 24$). Successful abstainers were said to have relied relatively more on self-reinforcement techniques and to have generally employed a greater number and variety of techniques (e.g., behavioral problem solving, stimulus control techniques). Relapsed subjects, in contrast, reported that smoking typically occurred in con-junction with other habitual behaviors, such as after meals. These data suggest the potential utility of self-control procedures in maintaining smoking abstinence, but the retrospective, cross-sectional nature of the data base limits inferences that might be made about smoking relapse precipitants.

In the final cross-sectional study, Schachter (1982) interviewed two samples of subjects who had never received professional help to either stop smoking or lose weight. Ninety-four of the 161 total subjects reported a history of cigarette smoking, and 63.6% of these subjects had quit at the time the interview was conducted. Schacter contrasted this self-cure rate with the commonly observed 10%–25% abstinence rate at 1 year after professional treatment and argued that relapse rates obtained from single treatment intervention studies exaggerate the recalcitrance of addictive problems (i.e., "people who cure themselves do not go to therapists" p. 437). Moreover, Schachter emphasized that such single intervention studies also fail to assess the potentially cumulative outcomes of multiple attempts to stop or reduce an addictive behavior. Although the study's retrospective method and the nonrandom subject population limit its generality, it raises important concerns about the self-selected nature of subjects included in treatment-related relapse studies and poses ques-tions about differential variables that may affect addictive behaviors inside and outside the context provided by professional treatment.

As a whole, few specific conclusions can be drawn from the available studies of demographic, personality, and treatment-related variables as-sociated with smoking relapses. However, these studies raise several im-portant conceptual and methodological points regarding the relative su-periority of longitudinal (vs. cross-sectional) designs in research on relapse and the value of studying relapse rates and determinants in both treated and untreated subject populations.

STUDIES OF EVENTS SURROUNDING SMOKING RELAPSE EPISODES

Only two studies (Marlatt & Gordon, 1980; Schiffman, 1982) investi-gated events surrounding discrete relapse episodes in smokers who had remained abstinent for a period of time. As part of their larger retrospective study of the determinants of relapse in alcoholics, heroin addicts, and smokers, Marlatt and Gordon (1980) reported data on the smoking relapses of 35 subjects who completed a smoking cessation program. All subjects were contacted by mail within 90 days of treatment termination and asked for information concerning the circumstances surrounding their first use, if any, of cigarettes after treatment. Subjects' questionnaire responses were categorized by raters according to the relapse determinant system developed by the authors, which was described earlier. Similar results were obtained across all three substance abuse behaviors. For smoking specifically, 57% and 43% of the relapses were classified as intra- and interpersonally determined, respectively; the three most frequently cited subclasses were negative emotional states (43%), social pressure (25%), and interpersonal conflict (12%). Negative physical states bore no relationship to smoking relapses, which suggests that physiological withdrawal symptoms are not important determinants of relapse. Smoking relapses also tended to occur most frequently during the evening hours (61%).

Schiffman (1982) conducted interviews with 183 ex-smokers who telephoned a relapse-counseling hotline regarding situational, affective, and physiological variables associated with actual or anticipated relapses. During the telephone interview, 39% of the subjects reported that they had already relapsed, whereas 61% had not yet relapsed and were considered to be having a "relapse crisis." No procedures were included to verify the subjects' self-reports, and no follow-up measures were collected after the telephone interviews. Relapse crises, as defined previously, were most likely to occur in the subjects' home (56%); with other people present (61%), approximately half of whom were smoking; in conjunction with eating or drinking (59%), including alcoholic beverages; and following experiences of negative affect or stress (52%). Also, 54.3% of the subjects reported that their relapse crises were not related to physical symptoms associated with smoking cessation. This pattern of results for relapse crises generally held for actual relapse episodes. The presence of another smoker and the subjects' consumption of alcohol were especially likely to be associated with an actual relapse. Also, subjects who reported engaging in some type of coping response (cognitive or behavioral) were less likely to relapse.

Taken together, both studies suggest the importance of environmental and affective determinants of smoking relapses, and neither study strongly implicated physiological withdrawal symptoms as determinants of relapse episodes. However, the Marlatt and Gordon (1980) study relied on retrospective self-reports that may be susceptible to recall biases, and the Schiffman (1982) study employed a nonrandom subject population. Neither study sought to corroborate the subjects' self-reports.

NARCOTIC RELAPSE

The primary focus of this section is on heroin relapse, as few studies have investigated relapse to other classes of drugs. The issue of relapse for heroin addicts differs somewhat from other substance abusers because methadone maintenance is the predominant treatment. Introduced in 1964 by Dole and Nyswander, methadone is a synthetic narcotic analgesic that blocks the action of heroin and other opiates. Methadone had been used both short term to detoxify an addict from heroin and long term for maintenance, often for periods lasting 5 years or more (e.g., Dole & Joseph, 1978). Although eventual detoxification from methadone is usually a treatment goal even when it is used for long-term maintenance, this practice of lengthy maintenance means that two general types of relapse can occur with ex-addicts: (1) ex-addicts who have been detoxified from either heroin or methadone may relapse; and (2) ex-heroin addicts who are on methadone maintenance may relapse to heroin use. Whenever possible in the literature review, the status of subjects along this dimension is specified. Furthermore, because of the almost universal use of methadone in the treatment of heroin addiction, the majority of studies relevant to heroin relapse have investigated treatment-related predictors of relapse (e.g., patient status at treatment termination) or demographic variables assessed at treatment intake. The illegality of heroin has further reduced research opportunities for investigating heroin use among nontreatment populations.

PREDICTIVE AND CORRELATIONAL STUDIES OF HEROIN RELAPSE

Demographic, Personality, and Treatment-Related Predictors of Heroin Relapse

Two long-term follow-up studies (Harrington & Cox, 1979; Vaillant, 1973) selected cohorts of identified narcotic addicts and then assessed their status after a substantial period of time. These studies followed between 50 and 100 addicts and reported that, after 20 years, approximately 25% had died, between 25% and 45% were actively addicted, a maximum of 35% had achieved stable abstinence, and 11% to 17% could not be located. In addition, Vaillant (1973) reported that 40% of his sample had been addicted for 15 years or more and that three variables were predictive of relapse: (1) less than 4 years of employment prior to hospitalization; (2) being raised in a culture different from that in which their parents had been raised; and (3) never marrying. Several variables (i.e., education and parental loss) that had been predictive of relapse at a 12-year follow-up (Vaillant, 1966) no longer held. These studies attest to the longevity of heroin addiction and to the instability of demographic variables as predictors of relapse over time.

Bess, Janus, and Rifkin (1972) assessed personality correlates of heroin relapse by comparing the MMPI profiles of 17 ex-addicts with those of a matched group of recidivists. Relapsed subjects had significantly higher scores on the MMPI validity scale of frequency (F) and on the clinical scales of depression, paranoia, psychasthenia, and schizophrenia. Relapsed addicts also had higher scores on the experimental scales of dependency and prejudice and lower scores on ego strength and dominance. Replications of these findings do not appear to exist.

One retrospective interview study (Judson & Goldstein, 1982) investigated pretreatment and treatment variables as relapse predictors in a large sample (n = 171) of addicts who had received short-term methadone treatment (minimum 6 months). Of the 19 variables studied 5 years posttreatment, 4 differentiated between subjects (17%) who had remained abstinent since receipt of methadone treatment and subjects (72%) who had used heroin or had an arrest in the year prior to the interview. The pretreatment variables predictive of relapse were higher criminal activity, higher alcohol use, and having a Spanish surname; the only variable identified during treatment that was predictive of relapse was greater daily heroin use. Although this study identified correlates of relapse, the authors noted that the highest correlation was r = .26, and they concluded that none of the variables was a strong predictor of long-term outcome.

In a similar evaluation of demographic and treatment-related predictors of relapse, Riordan, Mezritz, Slobetz, and Kleber (1976) interviewed 38 ex-addicts an average of 19.5 months after methadone treatment and detoxification. Their relapsed subjects (32% of the sample) were more likely to be Caucasian, better educated, to have had fewer arrests prior to methadone detoxification, and to have had a longer course of addiction than nonrelapsed subjects. Variables not predictive of posttreatment drug use were current employment, length of detoxification, average maintained methadone dosage, and age at admission.

Several studies (Cushman, 1978; Des Jarlais, Joseph, & Dole, 1981; Dole & Joseph, 1978; Millman, Khuri, & Nyswander, 1978; Pugliese, Maselli, Hess, & Leone, 1976–1977) examined patients' discharge status at termination of methadone treatment as a predictor of subsequent relapse.

The majority of these studies assessed drug use in large samples of narcotics users (e.g., Dole & Joseph, 1978, selected 1544 subjects) at follow-up intervals ranging from 51 days to 34 months posttreatment. In general, these studies divided the subjects into groups based on the nature of their discharge from treatment. Typical discharge categories were (1) "good standing," or with staff approval; (2) "premature," or without staff approval; and (3) "administratively discharged," or program rule violators. These groups were then assessed regarding posttreatment drug abuse, deaths, and incarcerations. All studies reported a lower incidence of relapse to drug use (from 15% to 61% lower) for those patients who were categorized as discharged in good standing, as well as lower rates for death and incarceration. Other isolated predictors of relapse that were reported included employment status (Cushman, 1978) and length of addiction (Millman et al., 1978). Des Jarlais et al. (1981) and Dole and Joseph (1978) also noted substantially lower relapse rates (17% and 3%, respectively) for those subjects who remained on methadone.

These studies of discharge status consistently demonstrate the importance of status at treatment termination as a powerful predictor of relapse to narcotic use, and they further emphasize the usefulness of methadone maintenance in deterring the illicit use of narcotics.

Life Events

One study (Rhoads, 1983) investigated stressful life events in predicting heroin use after treatment. Forty-nine clients who were discharged from a heroin detoxification program were interviewed at monthly intervals for 3 months to assess the availability of social supports and the occurrence of positive and negative stressful life events. For female subjects (n = 21), negative life events in combination with few social supports were reported to lead to drug use over a 1 month period. This relationship, however, did not hold for male subjects (n = 28).

Studies with Vietnam Veterans

In contrast to the preceding studies that generally reported high relapse rates following treatment interventions, two investigations of heroin relapse (O'Brien, Nace, Mintz, Myers, & Ream, 1980; Robins, Helzer, Hesselbrock, & Wish, 1980) reported surprisingly low relapse rates for servicemen who had used drugs while in Vietnam following their return to the United States. Robins et al. interviewed a random sample of approximately 600 Army enlisted men, 281 of whom reported an addiction to heroin while in Vietnam. Although 43% of those addicted reported occasional use after their return to the United States, only 12% relapsed to addiction levels. Receipt of treatment, in either Vietnam or the U.S., was not related to relapse.

In a similar but smaller sample study of drug use by Vietnam veterans, O'Brien *et al.* (1980) interviewed 125 men who received drug treatment while in the service and 77 controls who received medical treatment in the U.S. for nondrug-related health problems. Of the total sample (*n* = 202), 76% reported either experimental drug use or addiction while in the service. After discharge from the service, only 9% reported using narcotics, and 8% felt they were addicted. For the subset of subjects who had been treated for drugs, the relapse rates were 29% and 18%, respectively, for those servicemen who considered themselves narcotics users or addicts upon their return to the U.S. These rates, like those reported by Robins *et al.* (1980), are well below the rates obtained in heroin studies that employed nonveteran populations and point to the seemingly powerful effects of environmental changes on drug relapses.

The preceding studies indicate the wide variety of variables that have been investigated with respect to heroin relapse. Overall, status at treatment termination appears to be a good predictor of subsequent heroin use, but none of the demographic or other subject characteristics investigated have been found to be reliably related to heroin relapse. The studies involving veteran addicts further suggest the role of environmental changes in heroin relapse.

Studies Relevant to Theories of Drug Relapse

Some investigations have sought to assess the validity of several prominent theories of drug relapse. Waldorf and Biernacki (1979) reviewed nine studies on "spontaneous remission" among heroin abusers, which they considered analogous to the maturation hypothesis advanced by Winick (1962); this hypothesis simply proposes that most addicts tend to mature out of addiction by age 35, presumably because the problems that originally led to an individual's heroin use "became less salient and less urgent" (p. 5) over time. Waldorf and Biernacki found evidence for natural recovery over time in all nine studies reviewed. However, seven of the studies relied on uncorroborated self-reports, one used arrest records, and only one utilized urine samples. In addition, only three studies provided length of abstinence criteria, and none was lengthy enough to rule out the natural cyclicity of heroin use. The Harrington and Cox (1979) 20-year follow-up study, described earlier, was also considered to be a reasonable test of Winick's theory. Noting that all but one of their 51 subjects had passed the age of 40 at the 20-year follow-up mark, and that only one was drug free, the authors concluded that the theory did not hold. Because of the methodological problems noted previously, however, as a whole these studies cannot be considered as providing conclusive data on the spontaneous remission or maturation issue.

Several studies (McAuliffe, 1982; O'Brien & Ternes, 1979; Sideroff & Jarvik, 1980) evaluated Wikler's (1965) conditioned withdrawal hypothesis. Presumably, whenever an ex-addict encounters environments previously associated with actual drug withdrawal, the individual experiences a conditioned withdrawal syndrome and responds to the elicited symptoms by taking drugs and ultimately becoming readdicted. McAuliffe (1982) interviewed 40 street addicts who had at least one period of abstinence from heroin outside of an institution concerning their experience of conditioned drug withdrawal symptoms (i.e., sleeplessness, diarrhea, chills) and heroin use. Only 11 (27.5%) reported having experienced such symptoms, only 2 took opiates to alleviate the symptoms, and none of the addicts linked the occurrence of symptoms to previous situations associated with drug withdrawal. Instead, they either could not account for the symptoms, or they attributed them to boredom, drug craving, or being anxious.

O'Brien and Ternes (1979) and Sideroff and Jarvick (1980) evaluated Wikler's model with narcotics addicts in laboratory settings. O'Brien and Ternes used a classical conditioning procedure with eight volunteers from a methadone treatment program. Injections of naloxone, a short-acting narcotic antagonist that precipitates withdrawal symptoms in persons physically dependent on narcotics, were used as the unconditioned stimulus and were paired with a tone and a peppermint odor (conditioned stimulus). After several conditioning trials, test trials were administered, and the conditioned response most frequently observed was tearing of the eyes, a general feeling of sickness, and running of the nose. Six patients reported persistence of the effects in their natural environments and began to feel withdrawal symptoms whenever anyone around them ate peppermint candy. In addition to the laboratory procedures, a questionnaire regarding stimuli associated with withdrawal sickness or drug craving was administered to 100 patients on methadone maintenance. The majority reported sickness feelings (62%) and craving (58%) to the questionnaire stimuli. These findings lend support for Wikler's model, but the relationship of conditioned withdrawal to heroin relapses in the subjects' natural environments is unknown.

In the Sideroff and Jarvick (1980) study, heroin-addicted and normal subjects were shown a videotape of heroin-related stimuli, during which time their heart rate and galvanic skin response were monitored. The drug-addicted subjects exhibited significant increases on both measures as compared to controls, and they evidenced self-reported increases in levels of craving, anxiety, and depression. A replication of the physiological responses to the videotaped stimuli has also been reported (Sideroff, 1980). Although these findings suggest that heroin addicts show differential physiological and subjective responses to heroin-related stimuli compared to nonaddicts, it is again unclear what relation this difference bears to their drug-taking behavior in the natural environment. Overall, these studies provide only limited support for the conditioned withdrawal hypothesis.

STUDIES OF EVENTS SURROUNDING HEROIN RELAPSE EPISODES

Only three studies of relapse to narcotic use have directly investigated events surrounding actual relapse episodes (Chaney, Roszell, & Cummings, 1982; Marlatt & Gordon, 1980; Stephens & Cottrell, 1972).

Using a sample of 236 addicts who had received 6 months of inpatient (methadone) treatment, Stephens and Cottrell (1972) mailed questionnaires assessing drug use, employment, and educational status to the patients and their counselors approximately 6 months after their discharge. Return rates were 85% for the counselors ($n = 200$) and 42% for the addicts ($n = 100$). Of the 200 patients, only 13% had remained abstinent for a minimum of 6 months, leading to a relapse rate of 87%, with 64.5% of these subjects considered to be readdicted. The counselors reported problems with family or girlfriends (31%), craving for narcotics (29%), and inadequate personality (27%) as causes of the patients' relapses. The addicts, however, listed craving for heroin and a desire to get high (49%) as primary causes, with only 25% citing heroin use as an attempt to alleviate stress or to combat personal faults or depression. Regarding reasons for nonrelapse, the counselors and patients agreed that a desire to stay clean, followed by the effectiveness of treatment, and support from the subjects' families were most important.

The two final investigations of heroin relapse (Chaney et al., 1982; Marlatt & Gordon, 1980) were guided by Marlatt's cognitive-behavioral model of relapse. As part of their larger study of substance abuse relapse, Marlatt and Gordon obtained descriptions of relapse situations from 32 heroin addicts who were contacted 90 days following their termination from either methadone maintenance therapy or from an abstinence-oriented therapeutic community. The information obtained concerned the addicts' first use of heroin or other illegal opiates following treatment. Using the categorization system developed by the authors (described earlier), the relapses were classified as due to (1) negative emotional states (28%); (2) negative physical states (9%); (3) positive emotional states (16%);

(4) interpersonal conflict (13%); and (5) social pressure (34%). Overall, 53% and 47% of relapse episodes were characterized as due to intrapersonal and interpersonal determinants, respectively.

Chaney *et al.* (1982) selected male veterans on methadone maintenance who had evidenced a minimum of a 1-month abstinence from unauthorized drugs prior to relapse (30%), which occurred an average of 3.9 months after the start of the abstinence period. Drug taking was monitored by random weekly urinalyses. Subjects who relapsed were administered a questionnaire subsequent to their relapse, but the time of administration in relation to the relapse was not specified. The questionnaire included demographic and historical information as well as information about the relapse (e.g., time, place, others present, thoughts, mood). Relapses were categorized according to Marlatt's system. Of the 38 relapses, 32% were categorized as due to coping with negative physiological states not associated with prior substance abuse; 16% involved coping with physiological states that were associated with prior substance abuse; 16% followed social pressure; 8% were due to coping with interpersonal frustration or anger; and 24% were due to coping with negative emotional states other than frustration or anger. There were no occurrences in Marlatt's remaining categories. In addition, extended (rather than single event) relapses were associated with greater pretreatment levels of steady drug use. Subjects who had extended relapses also were more likely to report that they had been thinking about using drugs prior to the relapse, and they were less likely to report that the relapse was due to external pressure.

Consistent with the similar smoking and alcohol relapse studies, these studies generally point to the importance of environmental and emotional factors in determining heroin relapse episodes.

DISCUSSION

VARIABLES RELATED TO SUBSTANCE ABUSE RELAPSE

Despite the diversity of theory, method, and findings in the literature, some tentative generalizations are suggested. First, consistent demographic or personality predictors of substance abuse relapse are lacking (e.g., Bess, Janus, & Rifkin, 1972; Eisinger, 1971; Polich *et al.*, 1981). Likewise, across all three substance abuse areas, relevant studies suggested that physiological withdrawal symptoms have a relatively minor influence on the occurrence of relapse episodes (e.g., Marlatt & Gordon, 1980; McAuliffe, 1982; Schiffman, 1982).

Second, with respect to treatment-related variables, heroin relapse rates are considerably lower for ex-addicts who are receiving methadone maintenance than for those who are not (e.g., Cushman, 1978; Des Jarlais et al., 1981; Dole & Joseph, 1978). However, because methadone administration is the only specific component of most heroin treatment programs, such maintained ex-addicts were, in effect, never discharged from treatment. Similarly, although studies of smoking (e.g., McIntyre et al., 1983) and alcoholic (e.g., Polich et al., 1981) relapse suggest that overall drug use status at treatment termination (e.g., abstinent or not) is correlated with relapse, other more specific variables related directly to treatment appear to be poor predictors of posttreatment relapse. The study of smoking teatment outcome and relapse by Pomerleau et al. (1978), in particular, suggests that predictors of short-term treatment outcome may be relatively independent of those that predict relapse, and vice versa. These data thus suggest that the important questions raised by the relapse problem pertain to what variables influence drug use and nonuse transitions over time at the individual subject level, with treatment being only one such potential influence.

Third, positive but inconsistent relationships have been observed between measures of mood states and life-event occurrences and relapse episodes in all three substance abuse areas. Although these variables may occasionally correlate with relapse occurrences, it seems doubtful that aggregated measures of life-event occurrences or measures of transitory mood states will eventually yield a consistent enough data base upon which to develop a comprehensive approach to relapse, including strategies for relapse prevention.

Fourth, direct assessments of the effects of specific environmental events on relapse episodes are much more limited, but the results obtained are encouraging, particularly in light of the inconsistent relationships observed between other types of variables and relapse episodes. Our prospective study of alcoholic relapse (Vuchinich & Tucker, 1983) found that specific environmental events were related to some relapse episodes and that relapse episodes that were related to environmental events were more severe than those that were not. Similar conclusions were reached by Tuchfield (1981), who interviewed individuals who had not entered treatment but who had had periods of problem and nonproblem drinking and who implicated specific environmental events as being the main determinants over time of their periods of abusive drinking and apparent "spontaneous remission."

Within the smoking relapse literature, studies that used self-efficacy ratings (e.g., Condiotte & Lichtenstein, 1981; DiClemente, 1981; McIntyre et al., 1983; Prochaska et al., 1982) also provide evidence for the importance of situational determinants of smoking relapse. Most self-efficacy scales employed in these studies described environmental situations that ex-smokers had identified as being likely to cause them to relapse. Thus, in essence, the positive relationships observed between subjects' self-efficacy scores and their relapse episodes reflected the subjects' ability to predict accurately those situations in which they would relapse (see, especially, Condiotte & Lichtenstein's 1981 data). Although this relationship may be a self-fulfilling prophecy, it may instead reflect subjects' inherently greater access to information about the circumstances surrounding their substance abuse behavior patterns. To the extent that the subjects' responses on the situationally based self-efficacy scales reflect the effects of those circumstances, these findings suggest that specific environmental events may be important determinants of smoking relapses. This is consistent with other studies that found smoking relapses to be associated with the presence of other smokers (e.g., Graham & Gibson, 1971; Schiffman, 1982) and with the consumption of alcoholic and nonalcoholic beverages (e.g., Prochaska *et al.*, 1982; Schiffman, 1982).

The two studies within the heroin relapse literature that employed veteran populations (O'Brien *et al.*, 1980; Robins *et al.*, 1980) also provide indirect support for the influence of environmental variables on heroin relapse. The relatively low relapse rates observed in servicemen addicts upon their return to the U.S. contrast sharply with the 70% to 90% rates observed in studies in which ex-addicts returned after treatment to the same environments where their original heroin use had occurred. Although the specific environmental changes leading to this dramatic reduction are unknown (e.g, decreased heroin availability in the U.S., absence of combat-related stress), it nevertheless speaks to the potentially powerful effect of environmental changes on drug-taking behavior.

STATUS OF THEORETICAL FORMULATIONS OF RELAPSE

A second general issue concerns the status of the various conceptual formulations of relapse in relation to the available data. No single formulation emerges as superior. Marlatt's (1978) cognitive-behavioral model had generated much needed interest in the relapse problem and has provided a preliminary, heuristically useful classification system of relapse situations. However, its dependence on internal cognitive processes and its lack of operational criteria for specifying *a priori* the high-risk situations that may lead to relapse in individual substance abusers render its empirical status uncertain at this point.

Within the heroin relapse literature, Wikler's conditioned withdrawal hypothesis received indirect support from two laboratory analog studies (O'Brien & Ternes, 1979; Sideroff & Jarvik, 1980), but the one relevant study that used a clinical population of heroin addicts (McAuliffe, 1982) did not support Wikler's formulation. The data relevant to Winick's (1962) maturation hypothesis are equivocal.

Finally, within the smoking relapse literature, Prochaska's transtheoretical model of change as applied to smoking behavior has not been well supported (e.g., DiClemente & Prochaska, 1982; Prochaska et al., 1982; Prochaska & DiClemente, 1983). Thus, no single theoretical formulation of the relapse process seems generally satisfactory. In light of the recency of much of the relevant empirical work, more descriptive research seems needed before well substantiated conceptual analyses of substance abuse relapse can be advanced.

THE PROBLEM OF AGGREGATED RELAPSE RATES

A third general issue concerns the practice of reporting aggregated or mean relapse rates that are collapsed across multiple substance abusers. This practice may obscure the temporal patterning and controlling variables of the substance use behaviors of individuals, which is the level at which treatments for substance abuse problems usually are targeted. Within the alcohol literature, for example, although overall rates of relapse were relatively stable in studies that included multiple follow-up assessments (e.g., Armor et al., 1978; Moberg et al., 1982; Paredes et al., 1979; Polich et al., 1981), the alcohol consumption levels of different individuals varied considerably from one follow-up assessment to the next. Similar data from narcotics studies that included lengthy follow-up periods (e.g., Cushman, 1978; Des Jarlais et al., 1981) likewise suggest that individuals evince variability, and perhaps cyclicity, over time in their drug use patterns that may be masked by aggregated relapse rates. Although comparable studies with multiple, lengthy follow-up intervals are generally lacking in the smoking literature reviewed here, Schachter's (1982) and Graham and Gibson's (1971) studies with untreated ex-smokers also imply that individuals may stop smoking and relapse multiple times, regardless of whether or not they eventually quit smoking permanently.

The important point is that because aggregated relapse rates may not adequately represent the controlling variables and substance abuse behaviors of individuals, studies of substance abuse relapse should collect and report data obtained at the individual subject level, even if aggregated, summary statistics are also calculated. Such a within-subject approach would yield information that is directly useful for the development of treatment interventions for use with individual substance abuse clients, and it would also directly assess the temporal sequencing of drug use and nonuse transitions in individuals over time.

The Issue of Generalization Across Addictions Regarding Relapse Determinants

A final, general issue concerns the as yet unanswerable question about whether similar or different types of variables determine relapses to alcohol, tobacco, and narcotic use. Although these addictive behaviors certainly have the occurrence of relapse as a common feature, so do many other behavioral, psychological, and medical problems, so that aspect alone is inadequate to support an assumption of common controlling variables of relapse episodes. The risk of oversimplification involved in positing common determinants of relapse is obvious, and, based on the available research, it is not yet clear how similar or different the determinants of alcohol, cigarette, and narcotic relapse will eventually prove to be.

Part of the reason this issue of common determinants is largely unresolved at present is due to the disparate methodologies that characterize the entire relapse literature, along with the lack of a guiding conceptual framework or empirical focus. These related issues are discussed in the remaining section of this chapter.

Future Directions in Research on Relapse

Methodological Considerations

Although methodological diversity often characterizes a relatively new research area, such as research on substance abuse relapse, greater rigor and the use of a more consistent methodological approach seem indicated. Self-reports of substance use by individual subjects as the major measurement methodology is unlikely to change. Therefore, the primary methodological issues are two fold: (1) How best can we get individual substance users to give valid and reliable reports on variables considered important to relapse because they, rather than the investigator, have direct access to this information? (2) What conceptual and empirical issues should guide research decisions about what variables to assess in research on relapse, in light of the available data? The main concern here is with characterizing and measuring determinants of relapse in individual substance abusers in their natural environments because this type of data base seems best suited for eventually developing treatment and relapse prevention strategies for use by clinicians with individual clients. The first question about measurement practices is discussed here, and the more difficult issues pertaining to what variables to measure are discussed in the next and final section of the chapter.

The issues and procedures involved in obtaining valid self-reports of substance use have been well articulated in the alcohol literature (e.g., Maisto, Sobell, & Sobell, 1979; Maisto, Sobell, Cooper, & Sobell, 1979; Sobell & Sobell, 1975) and need not be reiterated here. By comparison, the smoking and narcotics literatures have paid much less attention to this important issue. The following research practices seem to be minimal procedural requirements for use in self-report studies of relapse.

Whenever possible, self-report data on substance use and relevant precipitating variables should be obtained prospectively rather than retrospectively, with as much specificity as possible regarding the quantities of substances consumed on a continuous (e.g., daily) basis. The superiority of prospective, longitudinal designs that frequently assess and independently corroborate the substance use reports of individual subjects seems obvious, but the vast majority of existing relapse studies have used retrospective methodologies that often involve cross-sectional comparisons between groups of ex-abusers and relapsed abusers. As Heinold *et al.* (1982) have cogently argued, this latter research practice creates additional interpretational problems because ex-abusers are being asked for historical information, whereas relapsed abusers are being asked for contemporary information. Moreover, even among the lengthy prospective studies, these data were often collected infrequently (e.g., at 6-month or longer follow-up intervals), which forces a reliance on retrospective reports pertaining to the preceding follow-up interval. At present, the most useful frequency at which to collect these data remains an empirical question, but a prudent approach would appear to indicate data collection as frequently as possible, ideally daily.

The common practice of using infrequent assessments of substance use behaviors also has contributed to the lack of operational consistency in the criteria used to define a relapse episode. For example, some studies (e.g., Judson & Goldstein, 1982; Pugliese *et al.*, 1976–1977) consider subjects to have relapsed if they report any use of the abused substance during a given period of time; in other studies (e.g., Condiotte & Lichtenstein, 1981; Vaillant, 1973), substance use at the time of, or shortly before, data collection was used to classify subjects as relapsed or abstinent, and any prior use during the remaining time between follow-up assessments apparently was ignored. This practice of classifying subjects into relapsed or abstinent groups based on their reported substance use over variable and often dysynchronous periods of time avoids addressing the important issue of relapse severity and duration. Instead, in keeping with the notion that drug use and nonuse transitions are the important aspects incorporated into the relapse concept, the use of continuous measures of both the quantity and duration of substance use and nonuse over time seems most appropriate. Moreover, as Schachter (1982) has emphasized, there is no *a priori* reason to restrict research on substance use transition to treatment populations. Indeed, it is unlikely that an adequate account of the variables controlling such drug use transitions will emerge from studies that only collect data from treatment populations and that dichotomize subjects into relapsed versus abstinent categories. As Pattison *et al.* (1977) have argued, substance use behaviors lie on a continuum and should be represented as such in the data.

Conceptual Considerations: Theories of Choice as Applied to Relapse

Pre-supposing the development of adequate self-report measures of substance use behaviors, what sorts of other variables should subjects be asked to record? The available research directs attention away from demographic, physiological, and treatment-related variables, but it is less informative about what variables might be fruitfully investigated. As summarized earlier, some preliminary evidence suggests that relapse episodes and drug use transitions may be related to the occurrence of specific environmental events. Given the diversity of environmental events that might be measured, however, some sort of guiding conceptual framework is essential in initially selecting sets of environmental events for study in relation to relapse and other drug use transitions.

In our work on alcoholic relapse and the determinants of alcohol consumption (Vuchinich, 1982; Vuchinich & Tucker, 1983), we have found the general analytic framework provided by behavioral-economic theories of choice (e.g., Ainslie, 1975; Rachlin *et al.* 1981) to be useful. Whether or not relevant research will eventually bear out the empirical utility of this approach is largely unknown, particularly as it may apply to substance abuse problems other than alcohol. Nevertheless, the general behavioral approach is well established in the basic research literature on substance use behaviors in both animal (e.g., Falk & Tang, 1977) and human (e.g., Bigelow, Griffiths, & Liebson, 1975) subjects.

Theories of choice seek a molar account of the variables that control how an individual's behavior is distributed among the set of available activities. Our interest is in the variables that control the individual's preference for substance use. Such preferences may shift abruptly and dramatically as with an abstinent individual who relapses and whose ensuing drug taking captures increasing amounts of his or her behavior. Basic research has identified three sets of variables that influence such preferences (e.g., Rachlin *et al.*, 1981): (1) direct constraints on access to the reinforcer of interest; (2) other reinforcers that are available; and (3) constraints on access to the latter.

A consideration of substance abuse relapse in this vein raises the general question of under what set of environmental conditions, or contexts, does substance use emerge from the totality of available activities as the most preferred activity? Perhaps this issue can be addressed by investigating how substance use varies as a function of two general classes of variables: (1) constraints that are imposed directly on access to the substance; and (2) other reinforcers that are available and constraints imposed directly on access to them.

Variables in the first class have been shown to influence alcohol consumption. When the requirements to obtain alcohol have been increased, consumption has been found to decrease in both normal and alcoholic subjects (e.g., Babor, Mendelson, Greenberg, & Kuehnle, 1978; Bigelow & Liebson, 1972; Mello, McNamee & Mendelson, 1968; Strickler, Dobbs, & Maxwell, 1979). Similar relationships may or may not hold for other substances. In most natural environments, the constraints that exist on access to alcohol or cigarettes are probably minor and invariant, whereas access to narcotics is probably more limited. To the extent that this is the case, the first class of variables may be relatively less important determinants of smoking and alcohol relapses compared to narcotics relapses.

Notwithstanding this potential difference, however, the second class of variables—the availability of other reinforcers and constraints on their access—probably are the more critical determinants of forms of substance abuse. The common question remains under what environmental contexts will an individual seek out and use a given substance? Based on behavioral-economic theories of choice and our work on alcoholic relapse, some tentative hypotheses may be advanced about the nature of these environmental contexts. First, if an environmental event is correlated with decreased availability of valued nondrug commodities or activities, preference for alcohol or other substances may increase after the event. Conversely, if the availability of valued nondrug rewards remains constant, the individual should continue engaging in activities that lead to their receipt (e.g., continue to work) and remain abstinent or use a given substance in a nonproblem manner.

Second, preference for substance use should increase when the individual encounters a situation in which the substance is immediately available. Substance use episodes precipitated by these events, however, should be less severe than those precipitated by the class of events that signal losses of anticipated rewards because preferences for substance use should decrease as soon as the individual leaves the immediate environment in which the substance is available. This predicted relationship is derived fairly directly from Ainslie's (1975) theory of impulse control and was supported by our data on alcoholic relapse.

A third implication concerns the prediction of which sets of potential environmental events from among those that signal losses of future rewards are most likely to precipitate substance use episodes in any given individual. Such predictions may be made on the basis of the individual's past substance use behavior patterns: to the extent that past substance use disrupted functioning in a given life-health area (e.g., job, marriage), events signalling future losses of rewards in those areas will be the events most likely to precipitate a serious substance abuse relapse. Thus, for example, for an alcoholic individual whose past drinking had disrupted his or her marriage but not his or her vocational stability, a negative event related to the marriage should be more likely to precipitate a relapse than a negative event related to the individual's job. This type of relationship between drinking and events that either were or were not associated with past disruptions due to alcohol consumption was generally found in our relapse study.

Further speculation about this approach would be premature without more data. The important methodological point is that techniques must be developed for charcterizing and assessing the allocation of behavior to activities other than substance use because these would comprise more than one-half of the analysis. It may seem paradoxical that this approach to the determinants of substance use, including relapse, directs attention to behaviors and valued commodities other than the abused substance. However, abused substances are generally readily available to anyone at almost any time. Despite this ready availability, the vast majority of individuals do not use them at abusive or addictive levels, so we must ask what other aspects of these individual's environments render their preferences for engaging in nondrug-related activities higher than their preferences for drugs.

Posing the question of drug use and abuse in this way may prove useful in addressing the problem of substance abuse relapse, and it may facilitate work in at least two related areas. First, it may promote a better interchange between the human and animal literatures on the determinants of substance use. In the case of schedule-induced polydipsia (cf. Falk & Tang, 1977), for example, alcohol is established as a reinforcer by manipulating access to reinforcers other than alcohol. Such phenomena may be important in establishing and maintaining alcohol and other substances as reinforcers in humans, but this could not be decided until methods and measures are developed that would allow empirical investigations with humans.

Second, in the alcohol abuse treatment outcome literature (e.g., Maisto & McCollum 1978), there currently is an emphasis on measuring changes in areas of life health such as marital and job stability. These are precisely the types of variables to which our attention is directed in applying behavior-economic theories of choice to substance abuse relapse. Methods developed in basic research from this perspective may prove useful in studies of both treatment outcome and substance abuse relapse, and the conceptual framework may provide a means of better understanding the relationship between substance use and changes in other important life areas.

REFERENCES

Ainslie, G. A. Specious reward: A behavioral theory of impulsiveness and impulse control. *Psychological Bulletin*, 1975, *82*, 463–496.

Armor, D. J., Polich, J. M, & Stambul, H. B. *Alcoholism and treatment*. New York: Wiley, 1978.

Babor, T. F. (Ed.). *Evaluation of the alcoholic: Implications for research, theory, and treatment* (NIAAA Research Monograph No. 5). Washington, D.C.: U.S. Government Printing Office, 1981.

Babor, T. F., Mendelson, J., Greenberg, I., & Kuehnle, J. Experimental analysis of the "happy hour": Effects of purchase price on alcohol consumption: *Psychopharmacology*, 1978, *58*, 35–41.

Bandura, A. Self-efficacy: Toward a unifying theory of behavioral change. *Psychological Review*, 1977, *84*, 191–215.

Bess, B., Janus, S., & Rifkin, A. Factors in successful narcotics renunciation. *American Journal of Psychiatry*, 1972, *128*, 861–865.

Bigelow, G., Griffiths, R., & Liebson, I. Experimental models for the modification of human drug self-administration: Methodological developments in the study of ethanol self-administration by alcoholics. *Federation Proceedings*, 1975, *34*, 1785–1792.

Bigelow, G., & Liebson, I. Cost factors controlling alcoholic drinking. *The Psychological Record*, 1972, *22*, 121–132.

Chaney, E. F., O'Leary, M. R., & Marlatt, G. A. Skill training with alcoholics. *Journal of Consulting and Clinical Psychology*, 1978, *46*, 1092–1104.

Chaney, E., Roszell, D., & Cummings, C. Relapse in opiate addicts: A behavioral analysis. *Addictive Behaviors*, 1982, *7*, 291–297.

Condiotte, M. M. & Lichtenstein, E. Self-efficacy and relapse in smoking cessation programs. *Journal of Consulting and Clinical Psychology*, 1981, *49*, 648–658.

Cummings, C., Gordon, J. R., & Marlatt, G. A. Relapse: Prevention and prediction. In W. R. Miller (Ed.), *The addictive behaviors*. Elmsford, N.Y.: Pergamon, 1980.

Cushman, P. Methadone maintenance: Long-term follow-up of detoxified patients. *Annals of the New York Academy of Sciences*, 1978, *311*, 165–172.

Des Jarlais, D., Joseph, H., & Dole, V. Long-term outcomes after termination from methadone maintenance treatment. *Annals of the New York Academy of Sciences*, 1981, *362*, 231–238.

DiClemente, C. C. *Perceived change processes in the successful cessation of smoking behavior and the maintenance of this change*. Unpublished doctoral dissertation, University of Rhode Island, 1978.

DiClemente, C. C. Self-efficacy and smoking cessation maintenance: A preliminary report. *Cognitive Therapy and Research*, 1981, *5*, 175–187.

DiClemente, C. C., & Prochaska, J. O. Self-change and therapy change of smoking behavior: A comparison of processes of change in cessation and maintenance. *Addictive Behaviors*, 1982, *7*, 133–142.

Dole, V., & Joseph, H. Long-term outcome of patients treated with methadone maintenance. *Annals of the New York Academy of Sciences*, 1978, *311*, 181–190.

Eastman, C., & Norris, H. Alcohol dependence, relapse, and self-identity. *Journal of Studies on Alcohol*, 1982, *43*, 1214–1231.

Eisinger, R. A. Psychosocial predictors of smoking recidivism. *Journal of Health and Social Behavior*, 1971, *12*, 355–362.

Falk, J. L., & Tang, M. Animal model of alcoholism: Critique and progress. *Alcohol Intoxication and Withdrawal*, 1977, *3*, 465–493.

Finney, J. W., & Moos, R. H. Charcteristics and prognoses of alcoholics who become moderate drinkers and abstainers after treatment. *Journal of Studies on Alcohol*, 1981, *42*, 94–105.

Finney, J. W., Moos, R. H., & Mewborn, C. R. Posttreatment experiences and treatment outcome of alcoholic patients six months and two years after hospitalization. *Journal of Consulting and Clinical Psychology*, 1980, *48*, 17–29.

Graham, S., & Gibson, R. W. Cessation of patterned behavior: Withdrawal from smoking. *Social Science and Medicine*, 1971, *5*, 319–337.

Harrington, P., & Cox, T. A twenty-year follow-up of narcotics addicts in Tucson, Arizona, *American Journal of Drug and Alcohol Abuse*, 1979, *6*, 25–37.

Heather, N., & Robertson, I. *Controlled drinking*. London: Metheun, 1981.

Heinold, J. W., Garvey, A. J., Goldie, C., & Bossé, R. Retrospective analysis in smoking cessation research. *Addictive Behaviors*, 1982, *7*, 347–353.

Hore, B. D. Life events and alcoholic relapse. *British Journal of the Addictions*, 1971, *66*, 83–88.

Hull, J. G. A self-awareness model of the causes and effects of alcohol consumption. *Journal of Abnormal Psychology*, 1981, *90*, 586–600.

Hull, J. G., & Young, R. D. The self-awareness reducing effects of alcohol consumption: Evidence and implications. In J. Suls & A. G. Greenwald (Eds.), *Social psychological perspectives on the self* (Vol. 2). Hillsdale, N.J.: Erlbaum, 1983.

Hunt, W. A., Barrett, L. W., & Branch, L. G. Relapse rates in addiction program. *Journal of Clinical Psychology*, 1971, *90*, 586–600.

Jellinek, E. M. *The disease concept of alcoholism*. New Brunswick, N.J.: Hillhouse Press, 1960.

Judson, B., & Goldstein, A. Prediction of long-term outcome for heroin addicts admitted to a methadone maintenance program. *Drug and Alcohol Dependence*, 1982, *10*, 383–391.

Lichtenstein, E. The smoking problem: A behavioral perspective. *Journal of Consulting and Clinical Psychology*, 1982, *6*, 804–819.

Litman, G. L., Eiser, J. R., Rawson, N. S. B., & Oppenheim, A. N. Towards a typology of relapse: A preliminary report. *Drug and Alcohol Dependence*, 1977, *2*, 157–162.

Litman, G. L., Eiser, J. R., Rawson, N. S. B., & Oppenheim, A. N. Differences in relapse precipitants and coping behaviour between alcohol relapses and survivors. *Behaviour Research and Therapy*, 1979, *17*, 89–94.

Ludwig, A. M. On and off the wagon: Reasons for drinking and abstaining by alcoholics. *Quarterly Journal of Studies on Alcohol*, 1972, *33*, 91–96.

Ludwig, A. M., & Wikler, A. "Craving" and relapse to drink. *Quarterly Journal of Studies on Alcohol*, 1974, *35*, 108–130.

Maisto, S. A., & McCollum, J. B. The use of multiple measures of life-health to assess alcohol treatment outcome: A review and critique. In L. C. Sobell, M. B. Sobell, & E. Ward (Eds.),

Evaluating alcohol and drug abuse treatment effectiveness: Recent advances. New York: Pergamon, 1978.

Maisto, S. A., Sobell, M. B., Cooper, A. M., & Sobell, L. C. Test-retest reliability of retrospective self-reports in three populations of alcohol abusers. *Journal of Behavioral Assessment,* 1979, *1,* 315–326.

Maisto, S. A., Sobell, L. C. & Sobell, M. B. Comparison of alcoholics' self-reports of drinking behavior with reports of collateral informants. *Journal of Consulting and Clinical Psychology,* 1979, *47,* 106–112.

Marlatt, G. A. Craving for alcohol, loss of control, and relapse: A cognitive-behavioral analysis. In P. E. Nathan, G. A. Marlatt, & T. Løberg (Eds.), *Alcoholism: New directions in behavioral research and treatment.* New York: Plenum Press, 1978.

Marlatt, G. A., & Gordon, J. R. Determinants of relapse: Implications for the maintenance of behavioral change. In P. Davidson & S. Davidson (Eds.), *Behavioral medicine: Changing health lifestyles.* New York: Brunner/Mazel, 1980.

McAuliffe, W. A test of Wikler's theory of relapse: The frequency of relapse due to conditioned withdrawal sickness. *The International Journal of the Addictions,* 1982, *17,* 19–33.

McIntyre, K. O., Lichtenstein, E., & Mermelstein, R. J. Self-efficacy and relapse in smoking cessation: A replication and extension. *Journal of Consulting and Clinical Psychology,* 1983, *51,* 632–633.

Mello, N. K., McNamee, H. B., & Mendelson, J. H. Drinking patterns in chronic alcoholics: Gambling and motivation for alcohol. *Psychiatric Research Reports,* 1968, *24,* 83–118.

Miller, W. R., & Hester, R. K. Treating the problem drinker: Modern approaches. In W. R. Miller (Ed.), *The addictive behaviors.* Elmsford, N.Y.: Pergamon, 1980.

Millman, R., Khuri, E., & Nyswander, M. Therapeutic detoxification of adolescent heroin addicts. *Annals of the New York Academy of Sciences,* 1978, *311,* 153–164.

Moberg, D. P., Krause, W. K., & Klein, P. E. Posttreatment drinking behavior among inpatients from an industrial alcoholism program. *The International Journal of the Addictions,* 1982, *17,* 549–567.

Moos, R. H., Bromet, E., Tsu, V., & Moos, B. Family characteristics and the outcome of treatment for alcoholism. *Journal of Studies on Alcohol,* 1979, *40,*78–88.

Nisbett, R. E., & Wilson, T. D. Telling more than we can know: Verbal reports on mental processes. *Psychological Review,* 1977, *84,* 231–259.

O'Brien, C., Nace, E., Mintz, J., Meyers, A., & Ream, N. Follow-up of Vietnam veterans: Relapse to drug use after Vietnam Service. *Drug and Alcohol Dependence,* 1980, *5,* 333–340.

O'Brien, C. P, & Ternes, J. W. Conditioning as a cause of relapse in narcotic addiction. In E. L. Gottheil, A. T. McLellan, K. A. Dudley, & A. I. Alterman (Eds.), *Addiction research and treatment: Converging trends.* New York: Permagon, 1979.

Ogborne, A. C. Patient characteristics as predictors of treatment outcomes for alcohol and drug abusers. In Y. Israel, R. B. Glaser, H. Kalant, R. E. Popham, W. Schmidt, & R. G. Smart (Eds.), *Recent advances in alcohol and drug problems* (Vol. 4). New York: Plenum Press, 1978.

Paredes, A., Gregory, D., Rundell, O. H., & Williams, H. L. Drinking behavior, remission, and relapse: The Rand report revisited. *Alcoholism: Clinical and Experimental Research,* 1979, *3,* 3–10.

Pattison, E. M., Sobell, M. B., & Sobell, L. C. *Emerging concepts of alcohol dependence.* New York: Springer, 1977.

Perri, M. G., Richards, C. S., & Schultheis, K. R. Behavioral self-control and smoking reduction: A study of self-initiated attempts to reduce smoking. *Behavior Therapy,* 1977, *8,* 360–365.

Polich, J. M., Armor, D. J., & Braiker, H. B. *The course of alcoholism: Four years after treatment.* New York: Wiley, 1981.

Pomerleau, O., Adkins, D., & Pertschuk, M., Predictors of outcome and recidivism in smoking cessation treatment. *Addictive Behaviors*, 1978, *3*, 65–70.

Prochaska, J. O. *Systems of psychotherapy: A transtheoretical analysis*. Homewood, Il.: Dorsey, 1979.

Prochaska, J. O., & DiClemente, C. C. Stages and processes of self-change of smoking: Toward an integrative model of change. *Journal of Consulting and Clinical Psychology*, 1983, *51*, 390–395.

Prochaska, J. O., & Lapsanski, D. V. Life changes, cessation and maintenance of smoking: A preliminary report. *Psychological Reports*, 1982, *50*, 609–610.

Prochaska, J. O., Crimi, P., Lapsanski, D., Martel, L., & Reid, P. Self-change processes, self-efficacy and self-concept in relapse and maintenance of cessation of smoking. *Psychological Reports*, 1982, *51*, 983–990.

Pugliese, A., Maselli, A., Hess, D. & Leone, A. Detoxification of methadone maintenance patients: A follow-up study. *Drug Forum*, 1976–77, *5*, 359–368.

Rachlin, H., Battalio, R., Kagel, J., & Green, L. Maximization theory in behavioral psychology. *The Behavioral and Brain Sciences*, 1981, *4*, 371–417.

Rhoads, D. A longitudinal study of life stress and social support among drug abusers. *The International Journal of the Addictions*, 1983, *18*, 195–222.

Riordan, C., Mezritz, M., Slobetz, F., & Kleber, H. Successful detoxification from methadone maintenance. *Journal of the American Medical Association*, 1976, *235*, 2604–2607.

Rist, F., & Watzl, H. Self assessment of relapse risk and assertiveness in relation to treatment outcome of female alcoholics. *Addictive Behaviors*, 1983, *8*, 121–127.

Robins, L., Helzer, J., Hesselbrock, M., & Wish, E. Vietnam veterans three years after Vietnam: How our study changed our view of heroin. In L. Brill & C. Winick (Eds.), *The yearbook of substance use and abuse* (Vol.2). New York: Human Sciences Press, 1980.

Rosenberg, H. Relapsed versus non-relapsed alcohol abusers: Coping skills, life events, and social support. *Addictive Behaviors*, 1983, *8*, 183–186.

Schachter, S. Recidivism and self-cure of smoking and obesity. *American Psychologist*, 1982, *37*, 436–444.

Schiffman, S. Relapse following smoking cessation: A situational analysis. *Journal of Consulting and Clinical Psychology*, 1982, *50*, 71–86.

Schlegel, R. P., & Kunetsky, M. Immediate and delayed effects of the "Five-Day Plan to Stop Smoking" including factors affecting recidivism. *Preventive Medicine*, 1977, *6*, 454–461.

Sideroff, S. Readdiction liability testing: A proposal. *British Journal of Addiction*, 1980, *75*, 405–412.

Sideroff, S., & Jarvik, M. Conditioned responses to a videotape showing heroin related stimuli. *International Journal of the Addictions*, 1980, *15*, 529–536.

Sobell, M. B. Alternatives to abstinence: Evidence, issues, and some proposals. In P. E. Nathan, G. A. Marlatt, & T. Løberg (Eds.), *Alcoholism: New directions in behavioral research and treatment*. New York: Plenum Press, 1978.

Sobell, L. C., & Sobell, M. B. Outpatient alcoholics give valid self-reports. *The Journal of Nervous and Mental Disease*, 1975, *161*, 32–42.

Stephens, R., & Cottrell, E. A follow-up study of 200 narcotic addicts committed for treatment under the Narcotic Addict Rehabilitation Act (NARA). *British Journal of Addiction*, 1972, *67*, 45–53.

Strickler, D. P., Dobbs, S. D., & Maxwell, W. A. The influence of setting on drinking behaviors: The laboratory vs. the barroom. *Addictive Behaviors*, 1979, *4*, 339–344.

Tuchfield, B. S. Spontaneous remission in alcoholics: Empirical observations and theoretical implications. *Journal of Studies on Alcohol*, 1981, *42*, 626–641.

Vaillant, G. A 12-year follow-up of New York narcotic addicts: IV. Some determinants and characteristics of abstinence. *American Journal of Psychiatry,* 1966, *123,* 573–584.

Vaillant, G. A 20-year follow-up of New York narcotic addicts. *Archives of General Psychiatry,* 1973, *29,* 237–241.

Vuchinich, R. E. Have behavioral theories of alcohol abuse focused too much on alcohol consumption? *Bulletin of the Society of Psychologists in Substance Abuse,* 1982, *1,* 151–154.

Vuchinich, R. E., & Tucker, J. A. Behavioral theories of choice as a framework for studying drinking behavior. *Journal of Abnormal Psychology,* 1983, *92,* 408–416.

Vuchinich, R. W., & Tucker, J. A. *Identifying the determinants of alcoholic relapse.* Manuscript in preparation, 1984.

Waldorf, D., & Biernacki, P. Natural recovery from heroin addiction: A review of the incidence literature. *Journal of Drug Issues,* 1979, *426,* 281–289.

Wikler, A. Conditioning factors in opiate addiction and relapse. In E. Wilner & G. Kassebaum (Eds.), *Narcotics.* New York: McGraw-Hill, 1965.

Winick, C. Maturing out of narcotic addiction. *Bulletin on Narcotics,* 1962, *14,* 1–7.

PART V

Summary

CHAPTER 13

Toward a Biopsychosocial Theory of Substance Abuse

MARK GALIZIO and STEPHEN A. MAISTO

Theoretical integration of the fast-accumulating literature in the substance abuse field has been sadly lacking. Most theories have been developed from a single perspective or level of analysis, and in many cases they were inconsistent with data from other approaches on the day the theory was published. For example, Peele (1981) reviewed several theoretical approaches that emphasized that a complete "answer" to substance abuse problems was to be found by analysis of genetic or biochemical factors alone. As Peele showed, these analyses completely ignored other data that clearly indicated the importance of environmental and psychosocial factors. Yet in the same paper, Peele proposed a theoretical approach that denied the importance of any biological factors! To illustrate the current lack of integration in the field, consider again the recent edited collection on drug abuse theory (Lettieri, Sayers, & Pearson, 1980) that included over 40 completely distinct theories. Particularly noteworthy in the Lettieri *et al.* collection was that most of the theories tended to incorporate only a narrow band of data, and their generalizability beyond a highly limited domain appeared poor. Clearly, there is a need for theoretical integration in the substance abuse field, and a careful

MARK GALIZIO • Department of Psychology, University of North Carolina at Wilmington, Wilmington, North Carolina 28406.   STEPHEN A. MAISTO • Department of Psychology, Vanderbilt University, Nashville, Tennessee 37240.

inspection of the preceding chapters should convince the reader that such integration will require a model that incorporates factors from several disciplines: in short, a "biopsychosocial" model.

Biopsychosocial approaches have been basic to the development of behavioral medicine in general (Schwartz, 1982) and have been recently proposed in the analysis of alcoholism (Ewing, 1980; Moos & Finney, 1983). For example, in Ewing's model the probability of a given individual's developing a substance abuse problem is given by the conjoint risk/protective values of each of four factors: availability (such as cost of the substance, etc.), social factors, psychological factors, and constitutional factors (including genetic and biochemical variables). Some factors are viewed as protective (such as strong antialcohol religious beliefs or high cost of a substance), whereas others are thought to place the individual at risk (such as psychological distress or family history of alcoholism). We believe that the chapters in this volume indicate that such a multifactor model is necessary for the prediction and control of substance abuse in general, although as the chapters reveal, we would argue for more than four levels of analysis.

As an example of the application of this approach, consider a cultural subgroup that may be considered at extraordinarily high risk for alcoholism and other substance abuse problems: the Eskimo and Indian peoples of arctic Alaska. Although it is difficult to make precise estimates of the extent of substance abuse risk in this group, it is generally agreed to be substantially higher than is typical in other states (Peterson, Segal, & Heasley, 1979). Some early explanations for the problem emphasized the genetic uniqueness of these people and proposed the existence of some genetically determined differences in alcohol metabolization or sensitivity to account for the high risk. However, the results of studies designed to test the genetic susceptibility hypothesis have been mixed at best (see Schaefer, 1981, for a review). Segal (1983) has recently reviewed some alternative explanations. One interesting possibility derives from the early history of the Eskimo people. Until white settlers and gold seekers arrived in the Arctic, the Eskimo had no exposure to psychoactive substances. Because there was no cultural heritage to help integrate psychoactive substance use safely into the Eskimo social structure, the introduction of alcohol (and later, other drugs) to them may illustrate the importance of cultural factors as protective factors in societies that have dealt with such substances for centuries. However, another factor that may, in part, account for the high risk of this group is its experience in the past century of massive sociocultural change. Old ways are rapidly changing as kayaks and bone weapons are replaced by high-powered cruisers, exploding harpoons, and, for some, life in urban environments like Anchorage. In the villages, Eskimoes are faced with a disintegrating culture, and in the cities a lack of education and social assimilation leads to generally low socioeconomic status. These problems apparently lead to a high overall level of psychological distress (as suggested by a very high suicide rate; Segal, 1983). Further, as Segal points out, many of the Eskimo leaders have well-known alcohol problems and thus serve as dubious role models. Clearly, a variety of psychosocial factors may contribute to a high risk for substance abuse in the Eskimo. Finally, the extremes of the arctic environment (6 months of darkness and subzero temperatures and isolation) may be viewed as exacerbating factors in the sense that they increase the likelihood of boredom, loneliness, and depression. In summary, nearly every variable that the contributors to this volume have indicated as risk factors are present in an extreme in the Eskimo, and the factors identified as protective tend to be lacking.

The high rate of substance abuse problems of these people can thus be viewed as consistent with a biopsychosocial model but also illustrates a fundamental problem for the approach. At the present time such models can only identify factors or variables that can be demonstrated to be protective or to increase risk, but the relative variance accounted for by these various factors is largely unknown. Thus, in the case of the Eskimo, it is clear that a host of factors place the group at risk, but it is not at all clear which variables account for the greatest amount of variance and which may be trivial in the particular case. Until more specificity can be provided, the biopsychosocial approach will only be a framework. Still, the framework suggests some research approaches that may ultimately allow for greater specificity. In general, we would argue, the most useful research will be multivariate and interdisciplinary in nature. We suspect that it will become increasingly common to include blood assays, urinalysis, and indexes of brain function along with personality tests, demographic data, and experimental analysis of response to drugs. In animal research, we hope to see measures of behavior under various types of environmental controls along with radioactive binding and metabolization assays. An integration of the numerous research strategies discussed in this volume will ultimately be necessary to make the biopsychosocial framework a workable and testable theory.

Another point that emerges from the chapters in this volume is that the relative contribution of the multiple factors may vary from drug to drug and along the continuum of substance abuse patterns or stages. Differences in the neuropharmacological actions of the different drugs of abuse as well as in culturally defined attitudes and cognitions may change the relationship between the variance accounted for by the various factors with regard to a specific substance. Further, it is clear from analysis of the chapters of this book that different factors may assume greater or lesser significance depending on the stage in development of substance abuse patterns. For example, it may be that cultural factors exert their greatest influence on the initial decision to experiment with a particular substance. Biological factors may be seen to account for relatively more variance in determining continuation of use and in the transition from use to abuse. Here is where genetic differences in drug sensitivity and metabolism, the development of tolerance, conditioned or otherwise, abstinence phenomena, and the reinforcing properties of the drug may play a critical role. Finally, psychosocial and environmental factors may be most critical in the determination of cessation and relapse (see Lettieri *et al.*, 1980, for a review of these stages). Although these general conclusions seem warranted from our review of the chapters presented here, it should be apparent that more detailed analysis of all factors by drug and by stage will be required before the type of model we describe can attain theoretical status.

This book is the product of our attempt to show the utility in viewing individual differences in substance abuse as the result of biological, psychological, and social factors. As such, the contributing authors together have written summaries of the most recent, empirically guided thinking about how variables comprising each of these three domains affect the use of a variety of substances. They have shown that there is ample evidence that each of the levels of analysis—biological, psychological, and social—separately can help to explain substance use. They also accentuate the point that what the field needs now, and what we hope this book helps to initiate, is research designed to create more significant, multiple-level theories. We believe that such work will greatly enhance our understanding of, and our ability to, modify the widespread problems of substance abuse.

REFERENCES

Ewing, J. A. Biopsychosocial approaches to drinking and alcoholism. In W. E. Fann, I. Karacan, A. D. Pokorny, & R. L. Williams (Eds.), *Phenomenology and Treatment of Alcoholism.* New York: Spectrum, 1980.

Lettieri, D. J., Sayers, M., & Pearson, H. W. (Eds.). *Theories on Drug Abuse: Selected Contemporary Perspectives* (NIDA Research Monograph 30). Rockville, Md.: National Institute of Drug Abuse.

Moos, R. H., & Finney, J. W. The expanding scope of alcoholism treatment evaluation. *American Psychologist*, 1983, *38*, 1036–1044.

Peele, S. Reductionism in the psychology of the eighties: Can biochemistry eliminate addiction, mental illness, and pain? *American Psychologist*, 1981, *36*, 807–818.

Peterson, J., Segal, B., & Heasley, R. Perception of alcohol and alcoholism among Alaskan communities. *Journal of Alcohol and Drug Education*, 1979, *25*, 31–35.

Schwartz, G. E. Testing the biopsychosocial model: The ultimate challenge facing behavioral medicine. *Journal of Consulting and Clinical Psychology*, 1982, *50*, 1040–1053.

Schaefer, J. M. Firewater myths revisited: Review of findings and some new directions. *Journal of Studies on Alcohol*, 1981, *Supplement #9*, 99–117.

Segal, B. Alcohol and alcoholism in Alaska: Research in a multicultural and transitional society. *The International Journal of Addictions*, 1983, *18*, 379–392.

Index